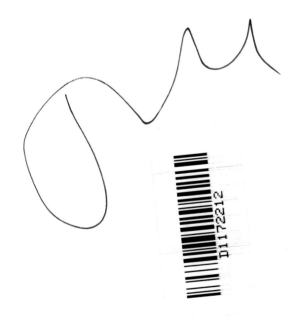

Criminal Law

Criminal Law

Concepts, Crimes, and Defenses

GEOFFREY S. CORN

George R. Killam Jr. Chair of Criminal Law and
Director of the Center for Military Law & Policy
Texas Tech University School of Law

CHRIS JENKS

Professor of Law
SMU Dedman School of Law

KENNETH WILLIAMS

Professor of Law
South Texas College of Law Houston

CAROLINA ACADEMIC PRESS

Durham, North Carolina

ISBN: 978-1-5310-2219-8
eISBN: 978-1-5310-2220-4
LCCN: 2022938695

Carolina Academic Press
700 Kent Street
Durham, NC 27701
(919) 489-7486
www.cap-press.com

Printed in the United States of America

Contents

PART TWO | CRIMES

PART THREE | DEFENSES

Table of Cases

Online Materials

Additional content for *Criminal Law: Concepts, Crimes, and Defenses* is available on Carolina Academic Press's *Core Knowledge for Lawyers* (CKL) website.

Core Knowledge for Lawyers is an online teaching and testing platform that hosts practice questions and additional content for both instructors and students.

To learn more, please visit:

coreknowledgeforlawyers.com

Instructors may request complimentary access through the "Faculty & Instructors" link.

PART ONE
General Principles

Chapter 1

Criminal Sanction and Why We Punish

I. Why Punish?

Why do we punish people who violate criminal laws? In beginning the study of law, this is an important question to consider, especially as many of you are taking the first steps on career paths that will lead to *you* making decisions that impact if, when, and how criminal law is applied. Penal sanction, meaning punishment adjudged pursuant to a criminal conviction (whether as the result of a finding of guilt after a contested trial or an admission of guilt pursuant to a plea of guilty), may result in the deprivation of liberty, the imposition of fines, the obligation to pay restitution, or in some cases even the forfeiture of the right to life itself. These potential punishments, coupled with the stigmatization that results from being adjudged guilty of violating societal penal norms, should not be arbitrarily imposed. Instead, there must be some rational relationship between society's interests and the imposition of penal sanction.

Criminal laws are similar to a code of conduct. They are enacted by legislative bodies with two primary goals: first, deter individuals from engaging in certain behavior that harms society; second, punish those individuals who violate the law. Criminal law is unique in that it is the only body of law in which an individual can be subjected to penal sanction, meaning punishment on behalf of the state. Indeed, the very title of the cases you will read, *State v. White, People v. Brown, United States v. Black*, reflect the fact that criminal cases are brought by and on behalf of the people through the agent of the state responsible for prosecuting violations of the law.

In contrast, tort law may provide a remedy for an aggrieved plaintiff, but the action is between two individual members of society and cannot result in a penal sanction or consequence. Thus, criminal law is enforced by and on behalf of the state; only the government may seek punishment for transgressions. When an individual violates the criminal law, the social harm is inflicted on the entire community, not just a specific individual; while a victim will often file a complaint and have a substantial influence on whether the case proceeds to trial, it is the prosecuting attorney that ultimately makes the decision to charge, prosecute, dismiss, or accept a plea offer for the offense, even if the victim objects to the disposition. In short, the decision of if, when, and how to implement the penal law is vested exclusively in the executive of the government; for states, this is normally a district attorney or attorney general; for the federal government, this is the Attorney General acting through district United States Attorneys.

Another unique aspect of criminal law is that violations might also impact an individual's life beyond the immediate punishment imposed following conviction. For instance, a criminal conviction will often result in a long-term (if not permanent) impediment to the convict obtaining a job, voting, owning a firearm, receiving public assistance, renting an apartment, or obtaining student loans. This is a manifestation of the reality that a criminal conviction carries a much more significant stigma than a finding of civil liability for a tort or a breach of some civil obligation.

By enacting and enforcing criminal laws, the government seeks to serve several purposes. The first purpose is deterrence, which may be both individual and general. Individual deterrence seeks to deter the defendant from engaging in criminal misconduct in the future; general deterrence seeks to demonstrate to others who might violate the law the negative ramifications of doing so. Another way of thinking of general deterrence is that an offender is punished for the purpose of sending a message to others who might contemplate committing the same crime. The deterrent purpose is most effective when offenders are caught and punished. Thus, increasing the visibility of police by hiring more officers and locating existing officers in ways that materially heighten the perceived risk of apprehension can deter crime. At the same time, there's little evidence that increasing the severity of punishment has a deterrent impact.

Punishment provides the second criminal law purpose—retribution. "The distinctive aspect of retributivism is that the moral desert of an offender is a sufficient reason to punish him or her."[1] An offender is punished because he or she deserves it. The retributive purpose is not served when an individual is wrongly convicted, because that individual did not deserve to be punished. Retribution also requires that an offender be punished in proportion to the harm that he or she has caused. Thus, an offender who steals a television deserves to be punished but does not deserve to be sentenced to death for doing so. Retribution is a controversial theory of punishment, because some believe it to be barbaric and inappropriate in an advanced society.

The third purpose criminal law serves is to protect society through incapacitation. An offender's ability to commit crimes in the outside world is severely restricted by imprisoning him or her. Incapacitation is justified by the need to protect society. This is the rationale relied on by states to enact habitual offender statutes that impose life sentences for defendants convicted multiple times; the recidivism is treated as evidence that the defendant cannot be rehabilitated and therefore represents a permanent threat to society. Incapacitation should, of course, only be justified to the extent

---

1. Michael S. Moore, *The Moral Worth of Retribution* in RESPONSIBILITY, CHARACTER, AND THE EMOTIONS: NEW ESSAYS IN MORAL PSYCHOLOGY, 179-182 (Ferdinand Schoeman ed. 1987).

that the individual poses a risk to society. Ideally, this is a judgment that should be vested in the court (judge or jury) imposing the sentence. However, many criminal laws impose mandatory sentences, a reflection of the legislative assumption that punishment should "fit the crime." This results in certain conclusive presumptions that certain convictions demand specified terms of confinement. Ultimately, these mandatory sentence provisions may result in incapacitation that is not justified by the actual facts and circumstances of the offense. Consider a defendant convicted of first-degree murder for a mercy killing of his father who was suffering a painful terminal illness who begged the son to end the suffering. Now imagine that the defendant pled guilty and was subjected to a mandatory sentence of life in prison without the possibility of parole. If you were the prosecuting attorney in that case, would you feel that justice was served?

The final purpose served by the criminal law is rehabilitation. Punishment is used as a means of changing the offender's mental outlook and behavior. For instance, in some jurisdictions, in lieu of imprisonment, non-violent offenders may be required to seek treatment and are only imprisoned for failing to do so. Rehabilitation may also be an aspect of punishment through incarceration, although the effectiveness of such efforts has often been criticized and the extent to which inmates are offered opportunities that contribute to rehabilitation varies from state to state.

II. Capital Punishment

Deterrence and retribution have been most debated in the context of capital punishment. Because of the long delays in carrying out the death penalty, are the deterrent and retributive value of the punishment undermined? Consider the following excerpts from concurring and dissenting opinions of Justices Scalia and Breyer about whether the purposes of deterrence and retribution are served by capital punishment. However, it's not just capital punishment that triggers debates over the penal logic and value of certain punishments. To that end, consider the situation faced by the defendants in *Queen v. Dudley and Stephens* and whether punishing them serves any of the purposes of the criminal law.

In 1791, the Eighth Amendment to the U.S. Constitution became part of the U.S. Bill of Rights. The Amendment specifically prohibits "cruel and unusual punishment." Although the government has the right to punish offenders who violate the criminal law, the Eighth Amendment requires that "this power be exercised within the limits of civilized standards."[2] Therefore, pursuant to the Eighth Amendment, the Supreme Court has placed specific limits on the government's power to punish offenders. First, the Amendment prohibits torture and particularly barbarous punishments such as disemboweling.[3] Second, the Amendment requires proportionality

2. *Trop v. Dulles*, 356 U.S. 86, 100 (1958).
3. *See Weems v. United States*, 217 U.S. 349 (1910).

in sentencing. This means that the punishment for a crime must not exceed the enormity of the crime.[4] For instance, even though rape is a serious crime, taking the life of an offender who rapes but does not kill his victim is excessive.[5] Third, the imposition of punishment must serve some purpose, such as deterrence, retribution or rehabilitation, and "cannot be so totally without penological justification that it results in the gratuitous infliction of suffering."[6] Finally, a punishment that might be acceptable at one moment may be deemed unacceptable later. Thus, the Court has recognized that "the words of the Amendment are not precise, and that their scope is not static" and that "[t]he Amendment must draw its meaning from the evolving standards of decency that mark the progress of a maturing society."[7]

Glossip v. Gross
576 U.S. 863 (2015)
U.S Supreme Court

[Richard E. Glossip was an Oklahoma death row inmate with a pending execution date. Oklahoma employed a three-drug cocktail to carry out its executions. However, it became increasingly difficult for the state to obtain the three drugs due to pressure placed on drug companies by anti-capital punishment advocates. In response, Oklahoma changed its execution protocol, including the drugs to be administered during an execution. The inmate would initially be injected with a sedative, midazolam, which had never been previously used in Oklahoma executions. After a prior execution during which the inmate had not died instantly, Glossip sued state officials, maintaining that midazlolam would not render him unable to feel pain associated with with the administration of the other drugs. Glossip's claim was based on previous U.S. Supreme Court rulings that an execution method violates the Eighth Amendment prohibition on cruel and unusual punishment if it produces severe pain and suffering. The Supreme Court rejected Glossip's claim, holding that there was insufficient evidence that midazlolam entailed a risk of severe pain. Justices Scalia and Breyer filed separate opinions which addressed whether capital punishment continued to serve the purposes, primarily deterrence and retribution, upon which the Court had previously based its ruling that it was constitutional.]

SCALIA, J. (Concurring)

And finally, Justice Breyer speculates that it does not "seem likely" that the death penalty has a "significant" deterrent effect. It seems very likely to me, and there are statistical studies that say so. See, *e.g.*, Zimmerman, State Executions, Deterrence, and the Incidence of Murder, 7 J. Applied Econ. 163, 166 (2004) ("[I]t is estimated that each state execution deters approximately fourteen murders per year on average");

---

4. *Id.* at 366-367.
5. *Coker v. Georgia*, 433 U.S. 584 (1977).
6. *Gregg v. Georgia*, 428 U.S. 153, 183 (1976).
7. *Dulles, supra note* 2 at 100-101.

Dezhbakhsh, Rubin, & Shepherd, Does Capital Punishment Have a Deterrent Effect? New Evidence from Postmoratorium Panel Data, 5 Am. L. & Econ. Rev. 344 (2003) ("[E]ach execution results, on average, in eighteen fewer murders" per year); Sunstein & Vermeule, Is Capital Punishment Morally Required? Acts, Omissions, and Life-Life Tradeoffs, 58 Stan. L. Rev. 703, 713 (2005) ("All in all, the recent evidence of a deterrent effect from capital punishment seems impressive, especially in light of its 'apparent power and unanimity'"). But we federal judges live in a world apart from the vast majority of Americans. After work, we retire to homes in placid suburbia or to high-rise co-ops with guards at the door. We are not confronted with the threat of violence that is ever present in many Americans' everyday lives. The suggestion that the incremental deterrent effect of capital punishment does not seem "significant" reflects, it seems to me, a let-them-eat-cake obliviousness to the needs of others. Let the People decide how much incremental deterrence is appropriate.

BREYER, J. (Dissenting)

The second constitutional difficulty resulting from lengthy delays is that those delays undermine the death penalty's penological rationale, perhaps irreparably so. The rationale for capital punishment, as for any punishment, classically rests upon society's need to secure deterrence, incapacitation, retribution, or rehabilitation. Capital punishment by definition does not rehabilitate. It does, of course, incapacitate the offender. But the major alternative to capital punishment—namely, life in prison without possibility of parole—also incapacitates.

Thus, as the Court has recognized, the death penalty's penological rationale in fact rests almost exclusively upon a belief in its tendency to deter and upon its ability to satisfy a community's interest in retribution. Many studies have examined the death penalty's deterrent effect; some have found such an effect, whereas others have found a lack of evidence that it deters crime. Compare (Scalia, J., concurring) (collecting studies finding deterrent effect), with, e.g., Sorensen, Wrinkle, Brewer, & Marquart, Capital Punishment and Deterrence: Examining the Effect of Executions on Murder in Texas, 45 Crime & Delinquency 481 (1999) (no evidence of a deterrent effect); Bonner & Fessenden, Absence of Executions: A Special Report, States With No Death Penalty Share Lower Homicide Rates, N.Y. Times, Sept. 22, 2000, p. A1 (from 1980–2000, homicide rate in death penalty States was 48% to 101% higher than in non-death-penalty States); Radelet & Akers, Deterrence and the Death Penalty: The Views of the Experts, 87 J. Crim. L. & C. 1, 8 (1996) (over 80% of criminologists believe existing research fails to support deterrence justification); Donohue & Wolfers, Uses and Abuses of Empirical Evidence in the Death Penalty Debate, 58 Stan. L. Rev. 791, 794 (2005) (evaluating existing statistical evidence and concluding that there is "profound uncertainty" about the existence of a deterrent effect).

Recently, the National Research Council (whose members are drawn from the councils of the National Academy of Sciences, the National Academy of Engineering, and the Institute of Medicine) reviewed 30 years of empirical evidence and concluded that it was insufficient to establish a deterrent effect and thus should "not be used to inform" discussion about the deterrent value of the death penalty. National

Research Council, Deterrence and the Death Penalty 2 (D. Nagin & J. Pepper eds. 2012); accord, *Baze v. Rees*, 553 U.S. 35, 79, 128 S. Ct. 1520, 170 L. Ed. 2d 420 (2008) (Stevens, J., concurring in judgment) ("Despite 30 years of empirical research in the area, there remains no reliable statistical evidence that capital punishment in fact deters potential offenders").

I recognize that a "lack of evidence" for a proposition does not prove the contrary. But suppose that we add to these studies the fact that, today, very few of those sentenced to death are actually executed, and that even those executions occur, on average, after nearly two decades on death row. DPIC, Execution List 2014. Then, does it still seem likely that the death penalty has a significant deterrent effect?

Consider, for example, what actually happened to the 183 inmates sentenced to death in 1978. As of 2013 (35 years later), 38 (or 21% of them) had been executed; 132 (or 72%) had had their convictions or sentences overturned or commuted; and 7 (or 4%) had died of other (likely natural) causes. Six (or 3%) remained on death row. BJS 2013 Stats, at 19 (Table 16).

The example illustrates a general trend. Of the 8,466 inmates under a death sentence at some point between 1973 and 2013, 16% were executed, 42% had their convictions or sentences overturned or commuted, and 6% died by other causes; the remainder (35%) are still on death row. *Id.*, at 20 (Table 17); see also Baumgartner & Dietrich, Most Death Penalty Sentences Are Overturned: Here's Why That Matters, Washington Post Blog, Monkey Cage, Mar. 17, 2015 (similar).

Thus an offender who is sentenced to death is two or three times more likely to find his sentence overturned or commuted than to be executed; and he has a good chance of dying from natural causes before any execution (or exoneration) can take place. In a word, executions are *rare*. And an individual contemplating a crime but evaluating the potential punishment would know that, in any event, he faces a potential sentence of life without parole.

These facts, when recurring, must have some offsetting effect on a potential perpetrator's fear of a death penalty. And, even if that effect is no more than slight, it makes it difficult to believe (given the studies of deterrence cited earlier) that such a rare event significantly deters horrendous crimes. See *Furman*, 408 U.S., at 311-312, 92 S. Ct. 2726, 33 L. Ed. 2d 346 (White, J., concurring) (It cannot "be said with confidence that society's need for specific deterrence justifies death for so few when for so many in like circumstances life imprisonment or shorter prison terms are judged sufficient").

But what about retribution? Retribution is a valid penological goal. I recognize that surviving relatives of victims of a horrendous crime, or perhaps the community itself, may find vindication in an execution. And a community that favors the death penalty has an understandable interest in representing their voices. But see A. Sarat, Mercy on Trial: What It Means To Stop an Execution 130 (2005) (Illinois Governor George Ryan explained his decision to commute all death sentences on the ground that it was "cruel and unusual" for "family members to go through this . . . legal limbo for [20] years").

The relevant question here, however, is whether a "community's sense of retribution" can often find vindication in "a death that comes," if at all, "only several decades after the crime was committed." *Valle v. Florida*, 564 U.S. 1067, 1068, 132 S. Ct. 1, 180 L. Ed. 2d 940, 941 (2011) (Breyer, J., dissenting from denial of stay). By then the community is a different group of people. The offenders and the victims' families have grown far older. Feelings of outrage may have subsided. The offender may have found himself a changed human being. And sometimes repentance and even forgiveness can restore meaning to lives once ruined. At the same time, the community and victims' families will know that, even without a further death, the offender will serve decades in prison under a sentence of life without parole.

I recognize, of course, that this may not always be the case, and that sometimes the community believes that an execution could provide closure. Nevertheless, the delays and low probability of execution must play some role in any calculation that leads a community to insist on death as retribution. As I have already suggested, they may well attenuate the community's interest in retribution to the point where it cannot by itself amount to a significant justification for the death penalty. In any event, I believe that whatever interest in retribution might be served by the death penalty as currently administered, that interest can be served almost as well by a sentence of life in prison without parole (a sentence that every State now permits, see ACLU, A Living Death: Life Without Parole for Nonviolent Offenses 11, and n. 10 (2013)).

Finally, the fact of lengthy delays undermines any effort to justify the death penalty in terms of its prevalence when the Founders wrote the Eighth Amendment. When the Founders wrote the Constitution, there were no 20- or 30-year delays. Execution took place soon after sentencing. See P. Mackey, Hanging in the Balance: The Anti-Capital Punishment Movement in New York State, 1776–1861, p. 17 (1982); T. Jefferson, A Bill for Proportioning Crimes and Punishments (1779), reprinted in The Complete Jefferson 90, 95 (S. Padover ed. 1943); 2 Papers of John Marshall 207-209 (C. Cullen & H. Johnson eds. 1977) (describing petition for commutation based in part on 5-month delay); *Pratt v. Attorney Gen. of Jamaica*, [1994] 2 A.C., at 7 (same in United Kingdom) (collecting cases). And . . . we cannot return to the quick executions in the founding era.

Notes and Questions

1. Do the lengthy delays in carrying out a death sentence undermine its deterrent and retributive purposes? Do you think most people who watch the news and see a story about an execution being carried out really know much about the crime? Or the victim? Or the time it took to reach the execution date? Justice Scalia cites studies indicating that as many as eighteen lives might be saved by a single execution. If this is accurate, would the death penalty be morally *required*?

2. Would the deterrent and retributive values of capital punishment increase significantly by eliminating delays? Or would eliminating the delays exacerbate other

problems, for instance, more wrongful convictions, racial discrimination, etc., while contributing little to goals of deterrence and retribution?

3. If the people through their lawmaking representatives include death as a permissible penalty for the most heinous murders, does it suggest that for some cases, a prosecutor bears an ethical obligation to allow a jury to decide whether a convicted murderer should be sentenced to death? Consider the case of Major Nidal Hasan, an Army psychiatrist who murdered 13 victims, injured 30 more, and attempted to kill more than 100 others packed into a building on November 5, 2009. Hasan showed absolutely no remorse during his military trial, even though he was offered the opportunity to present mitigating and extenuating evidence. In fact, he offered no evidence after deciding to represent himself. Military law reserves the death penalty for only the most heinous and aggravated murders. If prosecutors chose not to pursue to the death penalty for Major Hasan, would it functionally negate that authorized penalty for all future cases? Is it even possible to deter such murders?

4. What if a defendant sentenced to death never meets that fate? Does this negate the penal value or logic in imposing a death sentence? There are currently four inmates on death row in military prison, Hasan among them. Yet no military prisoner has been executed in more than 60 years. What value is there in pursuing the death penalty under such circumstances?

III. Punishment Principles

The debate over the deterrent and retributive values of capital punishment goes to the heart of whether the death penalty should even exist. Some criminal laws clearly serve a deterrent and retributive purpose. No reasonable person would argue that laws against murder do not have some deterrent and retributive impact and are therefore necessary. However, there are specific contexts in which the application of an otherwise valid law can be questioned.

The Queen v. Dudley and Stephens
14 Q.B.D. 273 (1884)
Queen's Bench Division

LORD COLERIDGE, C J.

The two prisoners, Thomas Dudley and Edwin Stephens, were indicted for the murder of Richard Parker on the high seas on the 25th of July in the present year. They were tried before my Brother Huddleston at Exeter on the 6th of November, and, under the direction of my learned Brother, the jury returned a special verdict, the legal effect of which has been argued before us, and on which we are now to pronounce judgment. The special verdict . . . is as follows.

That on July 5, 1884, the prisoners, Thomas Dudley and Edward [sic] Stephens, with one Brooks, all able-bodied English seamen, and the deceased also an English boy, between seventeen and eighteen years of age, the crew of an English yacht, a registered English vessel, were cast away in a storm on the high seas 1,600 miles from the Cape of Good Hope, and were compelled to put into an open boat belonging to the said yacht. That in this boat they had no supply of water and no supply of food, except two 1 lb. tins of turnips, and for three days they had nothing else to subsist upon. That on the fourth day they caught a small turtle, upon which they subsisted for a few days, and this was the only food they had up to the twentieth day when the act now in question was committed. That on the twelfth day the remains of the turtle were entirely consumed, and for the next eight days they had nothing to eat. That they had no fresh water, except such rain as they from time to time caught in their oilskin capes. That the boat was drifting on the ocean, and was probably more than 1000 miles away from land. That on the eighteenth day, when they had been seven days without food and five without water, the prisoners spoke to Brooks as to what should be done if no succour came, and suggested that some one should be sacrificed to save the rest, but Brooks dissented, and the boy, to whom they were understood to refer, was not consulted. That on the 24th of July, the day before the act. now in question., the prisoner Dudley proposed to Stephens and Brooks that lots should be cast who should be put to death to save the rest, but Brooks refused to consent, and it was not put to the boy, and in point of fact there was no drawing of lots. That on the day the prisoners spoke of their families, and suggested it would be better to kill the boy that their lives should be saved, and Dudley proposed that if there was no vessel in sight by the morrow morning the boy should be killed. That next day, the 25th of July, no vessel appearing, Dudley told Brooks that he had better go and have a sleep, and made signs to Stephens and Brooks that the boy had better be killed. The prisoner Stephens agreed to the act, but Brooks dissented from it. That the boy was then lying at the bottom of the boat quite helpless and extremely weakened by famine and by drinking sea water, and unable to make any resistance, nor did he ever assent to his being killed. The prisoner Dudley offered a prayer asking forgiveness for them all if either of them should be tempted to commit a rash act, and that their souls might be saved. That Dudley, with the assent of Stephens, went to the boy, and telling him that his time was come, put a knife into his throat and killed him then and there; that the three men fed upon the body and blood of the boy for four days; that on the fourth day after the act had been committed the boat was picked up by a passing vessel, and the prisoners were rescued, still alive, but in the lowest state of prostration. That they were carried to the port of Falmouth, and committed for trial at Exeter. That if the men had not fed upon the body of the boy they would probably not have survived to be so picked up and rescued, but would within four days have died of famine. That the boy, being in a much weaker condition, was likely to have died before them. That at the time of the act in question there was no sail in sight, nor any reasonable prospect of relief. That under these circumstances there appeared to the prisoners every probability that unless they then fed or very soon fed upon the boy or one of themselves they would die of starvation. That there was no appreciable chance of saving life except by killing some one for the others to eat. That assuming any necessity to kill anybody, there was no greater necessity for killing the boy than any of the other three men. But whether upon the whole matter by the jurors found the killing of Richard Parker by Dudley and Stephens be felony and murder the jurors are ignorant, and pray the advice of the Court thereupon, and if upon the whole matter the Court shall be of opinion that the killing of Richard Parker be felony and murder, then the jurors say that Dudley and Stephens were each guilty of felony and murder as alleged in the indictment. . . .

From these facts, stated with the cold precision of a special verdict, it appears sufficiency that the prisoners were subject to terrible temptation, to sufferings which might break down the bodily power of the strongest man, and try the conscience of the best. Other details yet more harrowing, facts still more loathsome and appalling, were presented to the jury, and are to be found recorded in my learned Brother's notes. But nevertheless this is clear, that the prisoners put to death a weak and unoffending boy upon the chance of preserving their own lives by feeding upon his flesh and blood after he was killed, and with the certainty of depriving him of any possible chance of survival. The verdict finds in terms that "if the men had not fed upon the body of the boy they would probably not have survived," and that "the boy being in a much weaker condition was likely to have died before them." They might possibly have been picked up next day by a passing ship; they might possibly not have been picked up at all; in either case it is obvious that the killing of the boy would have been an unnecessary and profitless act. It is found by the verdict that the boy was incapable of resistance, and, in fact, made none; and it is not even suggested that his death was due to any violence on his part attempted against, or even so much as feared by, those who killed him. Under these circumstances the jury say that they are ignorant whether those who killed him were guilty of murder, and have referred it to this Court to determine what is the legal consequence which follows from the facts which they have found. . . .

[T]he real question in the case [is] whether killing under the circumstances set forth in the verdict be or not be murder. The contention that it could be anything else was, to the minds of us all, both new and strange, and we stopped the Attorney General in his negative argument in order that we might hear what could be said in support of a proposition which appeared to us to be at once dangerous, immoral, and opposed to all legal principle and analogy. . . . First it is said that it follows from various definitions of murder in books of authority, which definitions imply, if they do not state, the doctrine, that in order to save your own life you may lawfully take away the life of another, when that other is neither attempting nor threatening yours, nor is guilty of any illegal act whatever towards you or any one else. But if these definitions be looked at they will not be found to sustain this contention. . . .

It is . . . clear . . . that the doctrine contended for receives no support from the great authority of Lord Hale. It is plain that in his view the necessity which justified homicide is that only which has always been and is now considered a justification. . . . Lord Hale regarded the private necessity which justified, and alone justified, the taking the life of another for the safeguard of one's own to be what is commonly called "self defence." (Hale's Pleas of the Crown, i. 478.)

But if this could be even doubtful upon Lord Hale's words, Lord Hale himself has made it clear. For in the chapter in which he deals with the exemption created by compulsion or necessity he thus expresses himself—"If a man be desperately assaulted and in peril of death, and cannot otherwise escape unless, to satisfy his assailant's fury, he will kill an innocent person then present, the fear and actual force will not acquit him of the crime and punishment of murder, if he commit the fact [sic], for he ought rather to die himself than kill an innocent; but if he cannot otherwise save his own life the law permits him in his own defence to kill the assailant, for by the violence of the assault, and the offence committed upon him by the assailant himself, the law of nature, and necessity, hath made him his own protector. . . ." (Hale's Pleas of the Crown, vol. i. 51.)

But, further still, Lord Hale in the following chapter deals with the position asserted by the casuists, and sanctioned, as he says, by Grotius and Puffendorf, that in a case of extreme necessity, either of hunger or clothing; "theft is no theft, or at least not punishable as theft, as some even of our own lawyers have asserted the same." "But," says Lord Hale, "I take it that here in England, that rule, at least by the laws of England, is false; and therefore, if a person, being under necessity for want of victuals or clothes, shall upon that account clandestinely and animo furandi steal another man's goods, it is felony, and a crime by the laws of England punishable with death." (Hale, Pleas of the Crown, i. 54.) If, therefore, Lord Hale is clear—as he is—that extreme necessity of hunger does not justify larceny, what would he have said to the doctrine that it justified murder? [The opinion then reviewed other early text writers and found that none of them supported the defendants' contentions.]

Is there, then, any authority for the proposition which has been presented to us? Decided cases there are none. . . . The American case cited by my Brother Stephen in his Digest [*United States v. Holmes*, 26 F. Cas. 360, 1 Wall. Jr. 1 (C.C.E.D. Pa. 1842)], from Wharton on Homicide, in which it was decided, correctly indeed, that sailors had no right to throw passengers overboard to save themselves, but on the somewhat strange ground that the proper mode of determining who was to be sacrificed was to vote upon the subject by ballot, can hardly, as my Brother Stephen says, be an authority satisfactory to a court in this country. . . .

The one real authority of former time is Lord Bacon, who . . . lays down the law as follows: "Necessity carrieth a privilege in itself. Necessity is of three sorts—necessity of conservation of life, necessity of obedience, and necessity of the act of God or of a stranger. First of conservation of life; if a man steals viands to satisfy his present hunger, this is no felony nor larceny. So if divers be in danger of drowning by the casting away of some boat or barge, and one of them get to some plank, or on the boat's side to keep himself above water, and another to save his life thrust him from it, whereby he is drowned, this is neither se defendendo nor by misadventure, but justifiable." . . . Lord Bacon was great even as a lawyer; but it is permissible to much smaller men, relying upon principle and on the authority of others, the equals and even the superiors of Lord Bacon as lawyers, to question the soundness of his dictum. There are many conceivable states of things in which it might possibly be true, but if Lord Bacon meant to lay down the broad proposition that man may save his life by killing, if necessary, an innocent and unoffending neighbour, it certainly is not law at the present day. . . .

Now it is admitted that the deliberate killing of this unoffending and unresisting boy was clearly murder, unless the killing can be justified by some well recognised excuse admitted by the law. It is further admitted that there was in this case no such excuse, unless the killing was justified by what has been called "necessity." But the temptation to the act which existed here was not what the law has ever called necessity. Nor is this to be regretted. Though law and morality are not the same, and many things may be immoral which are not necessarily illegal, yet the absolute divorce of law from morality would be of fatal consequence; and such divorce would follow if the temptation to murder in this case were to be held by law an absolute defence of it. It is not so. To preserve one's life is generally speaking a duty, but it may be the plainest and the highest duty to sacrifice it. War is full of instances in which it is a man's duty not to live, but to die. The duty, in case of shipwreck, of a captain to his crew, of the crew to the passengers, of soldiers to women and children, as in the noble case of the Birkenhead; these duties impose on men the moral necessity, not of the preservation, but of the sacrifice of their lives for others, from which in no country, least of all, it is to be hoped, in England, will men ever shrink, as indeed, they have not shrunk. It is not correct, therefore, to say that there is any absolute or unqualified necessity to preserve one's life. *Necesse est ut eam, non ut vivam*, is a saying of a Roman officer quoted by Lord Bacon himself with high eulogy in the very chapter on necessity to which so much reference has been made. It would be a very easy and cheap display of commonplace learning to quote from Greek and Latin authors, from Horace, from Juvenal, from Cicero, from Euripides, passage after passage, in which the duty of dying for others has been laid down in glowing and emphatic language as resulting from the principles of heathen ethics; it is enough in a Christian country to remind ourselves of the Great Example whom we profess to follow. It is not needful to point out the awful danger of admitting the principle which has been contended for. Who is to be the judge of this sort of necessity? By what measure is the comparative value of lives to be measured? Is it to be strength, or intellect, or what? It is plain that the principle leaves to him who is to profit by it to determine the necessity which will justify him in deliberately taking another's life to save his own. In this case the weakest, the youngest, the most unresisting, was chosen. Was it more necessary to kill him than one of the grown men? The answer must be "No"—

> So spake the Fiend, and with necessity,
> The tyrant's plea, excused his devilish deeds.

It is not suggested that in this particular case the deeds were "devilish," but it is quite plain that such a principle once admitted might be made the legal cloak for unbridled passion and atrocious crime. There is no safe path for judges to tread but to ascertain the law to the best of their ability and to declare it according to their judgment; and if in any case the law appears to be too severe on individuals, to leave it to the Sovereign to exercise that prerogative of mercy which the Constitution has intrusted to the hands fittest to dispense it.

It must not be supposed that in refusing to admit temptation to be an excuse for crime it is forgotten how terrible the temptation was; how awful the suffering; how hard in such trials to keep the judgment straight and the conduct pure. We are often compelled to set up standards we cannot reach ourselves, and to lay down rules which we could not ourselves satisfy. But a man has no right to declare temptation to be an excuse, though he might himself have yielded to it, nor allow compassion for the criminal to change or weaken in any manner the legal definition of the crime. It is therefore our duty to declare that the prisoners' act in this case was willful murder, that the facts as stated in the verdict are no legal justification of the homicide; and to say that in our unanimous opinion the prisoners are upon this special verdict guilty of murder.

Notes and Questions

1. Are any of the purposes of the criminal law served by punishing these individuals? If so, which ones? If not, why not?

2. Captain Rogelio Maynulet was tried for assault with intent to commit murder for shooting a mortally wounded and completely incapacitated enemy insurgent in the head following an engagement in Iraq. Maynulet had an exemplary record as a commander and had on more than one occasion placed himself in mortal danger to protect Iraqi civilians. Maynulet candidly admitted his action and said he made the decision to end the insurgent's suffering only after he was told by his medic that there was nothing to be done to help him and that he would die within 10 minutes. Would you have recommended a criminal trial for Maynulet had you been the prosecutor? If you were on the jury responsible for selecting a sentence and you were instructed you could sentence Maynulet to anything from no punishment to the maximum permissible sentence of 20 years confinement, what would you vote for?

3. Consider the case of Roswell Gilbert, a 75-year-old Florida man who was convicted of premeditated and deliberate murder for killing his 73-year-old wife. Gilbert's motive was to end his wife's suffering from an incurable illness; what Gilbert called an act of love. Gilbert was convicted and sentenced to 25 years confinement with no chance of parole as mandated by Florida law. As you will learn, a defendant need not have an evil motive to be guilty of first-degree murder; so long as the murder was intended and calculated, guilt is established (absent a defense like self-defense). Does the mandatory sentence align with the actual culpability for Gilbert?

Some courts have imposed on a defendant in lieu of or in addition to imprisonment public shaming. Public shaming involves a court-imposed sanction in which an individual is forced to publicly disgrace or humiliate themselves. Public shaming was common at one time in American history. Convicted individuals would be required to walk around in public wearing a "scarlett letter" or some other display of wrongdoing to cast scorn on them. Public shaming waned over time but is making a comeback. Judges are imposing public shaming as part of a defendant's sentencing. They claim it serves a rehabilitative purpose.

In most jurisdictions, it is the judge who decides the defendant's sentence, following conviction, within the range authorized by the legislature through the statute. However, there are some jurisdictions that allow for the jury that convicted the defendant to also impose his sentence. In Texas, for instance, a defendant may elect to be sentenced by the jury that convicted him.[8] When either the judge or jury sentences the defendant, the sentence is imposed at least partially in order to achieve the goals of punishment. This jury instruction is an example of how the goals of punishment are translated into guidance to jurors:

> In adjudging a sentence, you are restricted to the kinds of punishment which I will now describe ((IF NO MANDATORY MINIMUM SENTENCE) or you may adjudge no punishment). There are several matters which you should consider in determining an appropriate sentence. You should bear in mind that our society recognizes five principal reasons for the sentence of those who violate the law. They are rehabilitation of the wrongdoer, punishment of the wrongdoer, protection of society from the wrongdoer, and deterrence of the wrongdoer and those who know of (his) (her) crime(s) and (his) (her) sentence from committing the same or similar offenses. The weight to be given any or all of these reasons, along with all other sentencing matters in this case, rests solely within your discretion.

United States v. Gementera

379 F.3d 596 (2004)
Ninth Circuit Court of Appeals

O'SCANNLAIN, J

We must decide the legality of a supervised release condition that requires a convicted mail thief to spend a day standing outside a post office wearing a signboard stating, "I stole mail. This is my punishment."

Shawn Gementera pilfered letters from several mailboxes along San Francisco's Fulton Street on May 21, 2001. A police officer who observed the episode immediately detained Gementera and his partner in crime, Andrew Choi, who had been stuffing the stolen letters into his jacket as Gementera anxiously kept watch. After indictment, Gementera entered a plea agreement pursuant to which he pled guilty to mail theft, see 18 U.S.C. § 1708, and the government dismissed a second count of receiving a stolen U.S. Treasury check.

The offense was not Gementera's first encounter with the law. Though only twenty-four years old at the time, Gementera's criminal history was lengthy for a man of his relative youth, and it was growing steadily more serious. At age nineteen, he was convicted of misdemeanor criminal mischief. He was twice convicted at age twenty of

---

8. *See* Tex. Code Crim. Proc. Art. 37.07 § 2(b).

driving with a suspended license. At age twenty-two, a domestic dispute led to convictions for driving with a suspended license and for failing to provide proof of financial responsibility. By twenty-four, the conviction was misdemeanor battery. Other arrests and citations listed in the Presentence Investigation Report included possession of drug paraphernalia, additional driving offenses (most of which involved driving on a license suspended for his failure to take chemical tests), and, soon after his twenty-fifth birthday, taking a vehicle without the owner's consent.

On February 25, 2003, Judge Vaughn Walker of the United States District Court for the Northern District of California sentenced Gementera. The U.S. Sentencing Guidelines range was two to eight months incarceration; Judge Walker sentenced Gementera to the lower bound of the range, imposing two months incarceration and three years supervised release. He also imposed conditions of supervised release. One such condition required Gementera to "perform 100 hours of community service," to consist of "standing in front of a postal facility in the city and county of San Francisco with a sandwich board which in large letters declares: 'I stole mail. This is my punishment.'" Gementera later filed a motion to correct the sentence by removing the sandwich board condition.

Judge Walker modified the sentence after inviting both parties to present "an alternative form or forms of public service that would better comport with the aims of the court." In lieu of the 100-hour signboard requirement, the district court imposed a four-part special condition in its stead. Three new terms, proposed jointly by counsel, mandated that the defendant observe postal patrons visiting the "lost or missing mail" window, write letters of apology to any identifiable victims of his crime, and deliver several lectures at a local school. It also included a scaled-down version of the signboard requirement:

> The defendant shall perform 1 day of 8 total hours of community service during which time he shall either (i) wear a two-sided sandwich board-style sign or (ii) carry a large two-sided sign stating, "I stole mail; this is my punishment," in front of a San Francisco postal facility identified by the probation officer. For the safety of defendant and general public, the postal facility designated shall be one that employs one or more security guards. Upon showing by defendant that this condition would likely impose upon defendant psychological harm or effect or result in unwarranted risk of harm to defendant, the public or postal employees, the probation officer may withdraw or modify this condition or apply to the court to withdraw or modify this condition.

On March 4, 2003, the court denied the Rule 35 motion and amended the sentence as described above. Gementera timely appealed. . . .

Gementera asserts, . . . that humiliation or so-called "shaming" conditions are not "reasonably related" to rehabilitation. . . . [In this case] the defendant pled guilty. His plea decision is unremarkable, though, given that he had been apprehended red-handed. Reflecting upon the defendant's criminal history, the court expressed concern that he did not fully understand the consequences of his continued criminality, and had not truly accepted responsibility. The court explained:

> This is a young man who needs to be brought face-to-face with the consequences of his conduct. He's going down the wrong path in life. At age 24, committing this kind of an offense, he's already in a criminal history category 4, two-thirds of the way up the criminal history scale. He needs a wake-up call.

The court also determined that Gementera needed to be educated about the seriousness of mail crimes in particular, given that they might appear to be victimless:

> One of the features of Mr. Gementera's offense is that he, unlike some offenders did not, by the very nature of this offense, come face-to-face with his victims.

> He needs to be shown that stealing mail has victims; that there are people who depend upon the integrity and security of the mail in very important ways and that a crime of the kind that he committed abuses that trust which people place in the mail. He needs to see that there are people who count on the mails and integrity of the mails. How else can he be made to realize that than by coming face-to-face with people who use the postal service? That's the idea.

... [T]he district court concluded that public acknowledgment of one's offense—beyond the formal yet sterile plea in a cloistered courtroom—was necessary to his rehabilitation.

It is true, of course, that much uncertainty exists as to how rehabilitation is best accomplished. Were that picture clearer, our criminal justice system would be vastly different, and substantially improved. By one estimate, two-thirds of the 640,000 state and federal inmates who will be released in 2004 will return to prison within a few years. *The Price of Prisons*, N.Y. Times, June 26, 2004, at A26. *See* Bureau of Justice Statistics, Dep't of Justice, *Recidivism of Prisoners Released in 1994* (2002) (finding 67.5% recidivism rate among study population of 300,000 prisoners released in 1994). The cost to humanity of our ignorance in these matters is staggering.

Gementera and amicus contend that shaming conditions cannot be rehabilitative because such conditions necessarily cause the offender to withdraw from society or otherwise inflict psychological damage, and they would erect a per se bar against such conditions. *See* Toni Massaro, *Shame, Culture, and American Criminal Law*, 89 Mich. L. Rev. 1880, 1920–21 (1991) ("When it works, it redefines a person in a negative, often irreversible way" and the "psychological core" it affects cannot thereafter be rebuilt.); *see generally* June Price Tagney et al., *Relation of Shame and Guilt to Constructive Versus Destructive Responses to Anger Across the Lifespan*, 70 J. Psych. & Soc. Psych. 797–98 (1996); June Price Tagney et al., *Shamed into Anger? The Relation of Shame and Guilt to Anger and Self-Reported Aggression*, 62 J. Psych & Soc.

Psych. 669–675 (1992). Though the district court had no scientific evidence before it, as Gementera complains, we do not insist upon such evidence in our deferential review. Moreover, the fact is that a vigorous, multifaceted, scholarly debate on shaming sanctions' efficacy, desirability, and underlying rationales continues within the academy. *See, e.g.*, Dan M. Kahan & Eric A. Posner, *Shaming White-Collar Criminals: A Proposal for Reform of the Federal Sentencing Guidelines*, 42 J.L. & Econ. 365, 371 (1999) (urging use of stigmatic punishments for white-collar criminals); Stephen P. Garvey, *Can Shaming Punishments Educate?*, 65 U. Chi. L. Rev. 733, 738–39 (1998); Dan M. Kahan, *What Do Alternative Sanctions Mean?*, 63 U. Chi. L. Rev. 591 (1996) (arguing that shaming sanctions reinforce public norms against criminality). By no means is this conversation one-sided.

Criminal offenses, and the penalties that accompany them, nearly always cause shame and embarrassment. *United States v. Koon*, 34 F.3d 1416, 1454 (9th Cir. 1994) ("Virtually all individuals who are convicted of serious crimes suffer humiliation and shame, and many may be ostracized by their communities."). Indeed, the mere fact of conviction, without which state-sponsored rehabilitation efforts do not commence, is stigmatic. The fact that a condition causes shame or embarrassment does not automatically render a condition objectionable; rather, such feelings generally signal the defendant's acknowledgment of his wrongdoing. *See Webster's Ninth New Collegiate Dictionary* 1081 (1986) (defining shame as "a painful emotion caused by consciousness of guilt, shortcoming, or impropriety"); *see also Gollaher* [*v. United States*], 419 F.2d at 530. We have recognized that "the societal consequences that flow from a criminal conviction are virtually unlimited," and the tendency to cause shame is insufficient to extinguish a condition's rehabilitative promise, at least insofar as required for our flexible reasonable relation test.

While the district court's sandwich board condition was somewhat crude, and by itself could entail risk of social withdrawal and stigmatization, it was coupled with more socially useful provisions, including lecturing at a high school and writing apologies, that might loosely be understood to promote the offender's social reintegration. *See* Note, *Shame, Stigma, and Crime: Evaluating the Efficacy of Shaming Sanctions in Criminal Law*, 116 Harv. L. Rev. 2186 (2003) (proposing how shaming sanctions may be structured to promote social reintegration most effectively); John Braithwaite, *Crime, Shame and Reintegration* 55 (1989) ("The crucial distinction is between shaming that is reintegrative and shaming that is disintegrative (stigmatization). Reintegrative shaming means that expressions of community disapproval, which may range from mild rebuke to degradation ceremonies, are followed by gestures of reacceptance into the community of law-abiding citizens."). We see this factor as highly significant. In short, here we consider not a stand-alone condition intended solely to humiliate, but rather a comprehensive set of provisions that expose the defendant to social disapprobation, but that also then provide an opportunity for Gementera to repair his relationship with society—first by seeking its forgiveness and then by making, as a member of the community, an independent contribution to the moral formation of its youth. These provisions, tailored to the specific needs of the offender, counsel in favor of concluding that the condition passes the threshold of being reasonably related to rehabilitation.

Accordingly, we hold that the condition imposed upon Gementera reasonably related to the legitimate statutory objective of rehabilitation. . . .

Notes and Questions

1. Do you agree that the public shaming furthered Gementera's rehabilitation or was it likely to cause psychological harm and social withdrawal?

2. The Court rejected Gementera's claim that the public shaming violated the Eighth Amendment prohibition on cruel and unusual punishment. According to the court, there was no evidence that the punishment exceeded the bounds of "civilized society" or other evolving standards of decency that mark the progress of a maturing society.

Formative Assessments

1. You are the prosecutor assigned to the misdemeanor division of the District Attorney's office. You receive a police report that three teenagers shoplifted a six-pack of beer from a convenience store. All three admitted the crime. All three come from a very poor part of the city and attended a low-performing high school. Two of the teens are graduating in a month with no higher education prospects; one has defied the odds and earned an appointment to the United States Military Academy at West Point. His father meets with you and tells you that unless the charge is dropped, he will forfeit his appointment. The other two teens have agreed to accept deferred adjudication whereby they will conduct 50 hours of community service and pay a fine in exchange for the charges being dismissed 6 months from now. How would you respond to the father's request?

2. Bernard Madoff was sentenced to 150 years in prison after pleading guilty to 11 federal felony charges resulting from the massive ponzi scheme he ran for decades. What is the logic of such a lengthy sentence for someone who is 71 at the time of sentencing? What penal interests are served by such a sentence?

3. While in prison, Madoff was diagnosed with terminal kidney disease. His attorney petitioned the court to grant him early compassionate release. The court denied the request. Did the denial serve the interests of justice? Would your answer be the same if his case was obscure and few people would even notice his release?

Chapter 2
An Introduction to Criminal Accountability

I. Due Process and Fair Notice

Imagine your state or city had just one criminal law: *Anything a police officer decides is bad for the community is a crime.* As absurd as this is, it highlights how fundamentally unfair it would be if the government could subject us to criminal condemnation without first putting us on fair notice what the law prohibited. The source of that unfairness would be manifold. First, we would constantly have to wonder whether our conduct ran afoul of the criminal law. Second, it would allow the government to decide *after* we did something that they didn't like what we did and therefore subject us to criminal sanction. Third, it would invite arbitrary and discriminatory enforcement of criminal law by empowering individual officers to decide what is criminal and who should be arrested and punished.

The prohibition against fundamentally unfair state action is at the core of substantive due process protected by the Fifth and Fourteenth Amendments of the U.S. Constitution. While you will learn much more about the concept of substantive due process in your Constitutional Law course, for our purposes, any law that is assessed by a court as "fundamentally unfair" violates this protection. In the context of criminal law, this issue arises when a defendant asserts that a law he has been charged with violating was so vague that it failed to provide the average person with fair notice of what it prohibited, implicating all of the problems highlighted by the hypothetical "one law" above.

In the case that follows, the Supreme Court considered the constitutionality of a local loitering statute. As you read it, consider how the Court emphasizes the relationship between fair notice and fundamental fairness.

City of Chicago v. Morales

527 U.S. 41 (1999)

U.S. Supreme Court

JUSTICE STEVENS announced the judgment of the Court and delivered the opinion of the Court with respect to Parts I, II, and V, and an opinion with respect to Parts III, IV, and VI, in which JUSTICE SOUTER and JUSTICE GINSBURG join.

In 1992, the Chicago City Council enacted the Gang Congregation Ordinance, which prohibits "criminal street gang members" from "loitering" with one another or with other persons in any public place. The question presented is whether the Supreme Court of Illinois correctly held that the ordinance violates the Due Process Clause of the Fourteenth Amendment to the Federal Constitution.

I

Before the ordinance was adopted, the city council's Committee on Police and Fire conducted hearings to explore the problems created by the city's street gangs, and more particularly, the consequences of public loitering by gang members. Witnesses included residents of the neighborhoods where gang members are most active, as well as some of the aldermen who represent those areas. Based on that evidence, the council made a series of findings that are included in the text of the ordinance and explain the reasons for its enactment.

The council found that a continuing increase in criminal street gang activity was largely responsible for the city's rising murder rate, as well as an escalation of violent and drug related crimes. It noted that in many neighborhoods throughout the city, "the burgeoning presence of street gang members in public places has intimidated many law abiding citizens." 177 Ill. 2d 440, 445, 687 N.E.2d 53, 58 (1997). Furthermore, the council stated that gang members "establish control over identifiable areas . . . by loitering in those areas and intimidating others from entering those areas; and . . . [m]embers of criminal street gangs avoid arrest by committing no offense punishable under existing laws when they know the police are present. . . ." *Ibid*. It further found that "loitering in public places by criminal street gang members creates a justifiable fear for the safety of persons and property in the area" and that "[a]ggressive action is necessary to preserve the city's streets and other public places so that the public may use such places without fear." Moreover, the council concluded that the city "has an interest in discouraging all persons from loitering in public places with criminal gang members." *Ibid*.

The ordinance creates a criminal offense punishable by a fine of up to $500, imprisonment for not more than six months, and a requirement to perform up to 120 hours of community service. Commission of the offense involves four predicates. First, the police officer must reasonably believe that at least one of the two or more persons present in a "public place" is a "criminal street gang membe[r]." Second, the persons must be "loitering," which the ordinance defines as "remain[ing] in any one place with no apparent purpose." Third, the officer must then order "all" of the persons to disperse and remove themselves "from the area." Fourth, a person must disobey the officer's order. If any person, whether a gang member or not, disobeys the officer's order, that person is guilty of violating the ordinance. *Ibid.*

Two months after the ordinance was adopted, the Chicago Police Department promulgated General Order 92-4 to provide guidelines to govern its enforcement. That order purported to establish limitations on the enforcement discretion of police officers "to ensure that the anti-gang loitering ordinance is not enforced in an arbitrary or discriminatory way." Chicago Police Department, General Order 92-4, reprinted in App. to Pet. for Cert. 65a. The limitations confine the authority to arrest gang members who violate the ordinance to sworn "members of the Gang Crime Section" and certain other designated officers, and establish detailed criteria for defining street gangs and membership in such gangs. *Id.,* at 66a–67a. In addition, the order directs district commanders to "designate areas in which the presence of gang members has a demonstrable effect on the activities of law abiding persons in the surrounding community," and provides that the ordinance "will be enforced only within the designated areas." *Id.,* at 68a–69a. The city, however, does not release the locations of these "designated areas" to the public.

II

During the three years of its enforcement,[6] the police issued over 89,000 dispersal orders and arrested over 42,000 people for violating the ordinance. In the ensuing enforcement proceedings, two trial judges upheld the constitutionality of the ordinance, but eleven others ruled that it was invalid. In respondent Youkhana's case, the trial judge held that the "ordinance fails to notify individuals what conduct is prohibited, and it encourages arbitrary and capricious enforcement by police."

The Illinois Appellate Court affirmed the trial court's ruling in the *Youkhana* case, consolidated and affirmed other pending appeals in accordance with *Youkhana,* and reversed the convictions of respondents Gutierrez, Morales, and others. . . .

The Illinois Supreme Court affirmed. It held "that the gang loitering ordinance violates due process of law in that it is impermissibly vague on its face and an arbitrary restriction on personal liberties." . . .

In support of its vagueness holding, the court pointed out that the definition of "loitering" in the ordinance drew no distinction between innocent conduct and conduct calculated to cause harm. "Moreover, the definition of 'loiter' provided by the ordinance does not assist in clearly articulating the proscriptions of the ordinance." *Id.,* at 451–452, 687 N.E.2d, at 60–61. Furthermore, it concluded that the ordinance was "not reasonably susceptible to a limiting construction which would affirm its validity."

---

6. The city began enforcing the ordinance on the effective date of the general order in August 1992 and stopped enforcing it in December 1995, when it was held invalid in *Chicago v. Youkhana,* 277 Ill. App. 3d 101, 660 N.E.2d 34 (1995). Tr. of Oral Arg. 43.

We granted certiorari, 523 U.S. ___ (1998), and now affirm. Like the Illinois Supreme Court, we conclude that the ordinance enacted by the city of Chicago is unconstitutionally vague.

III

The basic factual predicate for the city's ordinance is not in dispute. As the city argues in its brief, "the very presence of a large collection of obviously brazen, insistent, and lawless gang members and hangers-on on the public ways intimidates residents, who become afraid even to leave their homes and go about their business. That, in turn, imperils community residents' sense of safety and security, detracts from property values, and can ultimately destabilize entire neighborhoods." The findings in the ordinance explain that it was motivated by these concerns. We have no doubt that a law that directly prohibited such intimidating conduct would be constitutional, but this ordinance broadly covers a significant amount of additional activity. Uncertainty about the scope of that additional coverage provides the basis for respondents' claim that the ordinance is too vague.

Vagueness may invalidate a criminal law for either of two independent reasons. First, it may fail to provide the kind of notice that will enable ordinary people to understand what conduct it prohibits; second, it may authorize and even encourage arbitrary and discriminatory enforcement. See *Kolender v. Lawson,* 461 U.S., at 357. Accordingly, we first consider whether the ordinance provides fair notice to the citizen and then discuss its potential for arbitrary enforcement.

IV

"It is established that a law fails to meet the requirements of the Due Process Clause if it is so vague and standardless that it leaves the public uncertain as to the conduct it prohibits. . . ." *Giaccio v. Pennsylvania,* 382 U.S. 399, 402–403 (1966). The Illinois Supreme Court recognized that the term "loiter" may have a common and accepted meaning, 177 Ill. 2d, at 451, 687 N.E.2d, at 61, but the definition of that term in this ordinance—"to remain in any one place with no apparent purpose"—does not. It is difficult to imagine how any citizen of the city of Chicago standing in a public place with a group of people would know if he or she had an "apparent purpose." If she were talking to another person, would she have an apparent purpose? If she were frequently checking her watch and looking expectantly down the street, would she have an apparent purpose?

Since the city cannot conceivably have meant to criminalize each instance a citizen stands in public with a gang member, the vagueness that dooms this ordinance is not the product of uncertainty about the normal meaning of "loitering," but rather about what loitering is covered by the ordinance and what is not. The Illinois Supreme Court emphasized the law's failure to distinguish between innocent conduct and conduct threatening harm. Its decision followed the precedent set by a number of state courts that have upheld ordinances that criminalize loitering combined with some other overt act or evidence of criminal intent. However, state courts have uniformly invalidated laws that do not join the term "loitering" with a second specific element of the crime.

The city's principal response to this concern about adequate notice is that loiterers are not subject to sanction until after they have failed to comply with an officer's order to disperse. "[W]hatever problem is created by a law that criminalizes conduct people normally believe to be innocent is solved when persons receive actual notice from a police order of what they are expected to do." We find this response unpersuasive for at least two reasons.

First, the purpose of the fair notice requirement is to enable the ordinary citizen to conform his or her conduct to the law. "No one may be required at peril of life, liberty or property to speculate as to the meaning of penal statutes." *Lanzetta v. New Jersey*, 306 U.S. 451, 453 (1939). Although it is true that a loiterer is not subject to criminal sanctions unless he or she disobeys a dispersal order, the loitering is the conduct that the ordinance is designed to prohibit. If the loitering is in fact harmless and innocent, the dispersal order itself is an unjustified impairment of liberty. If the police are able to decide arbitrarily which members of the public they will order to disperse, then the Chicago ordinance becomes indistinguishable from the law we held invalid in *Shuttlesworth v. Birmingham*, 382 U.S. 87, 90 (1965).[29] Because an officer may issue an order only after prohibited conduct has already occurred, it cannot provide the kind of advance notice that will protect the putative loiterer from being ordered to disperse. Such an order cannot retroactively give adequate warning of the boundary between the permissible and the impermissible applications of the law.

Second, the terms of the dispersal order compound the inadequacy of the notice afforded by the ordinance. It provides that the officer "shall order all such persons to disperse and remove themselves from the area." App. to Pet. for Cert. 61a. This vague phrasing raises a host of questions. After such an order issues, how long must the loiterers remain apart? How far must they move? If each loiterer walks around the block and they meet again at the same location, are they subject to arrest or merely to being ordered to disperse again? As we do here, we have found vagueness in a criminal statute exacerbated by the use of the standards of "neighborhood" and "locality." *Connally v. General Constr. Co.*, 269 U.S. 385 (1926). We remarked in *Connally* that "[b]oth terms are elastic and, dependent upon circumstances, may be equally satisfied by areas measured by rods or by miles." *Id.*, at 395.

Lack of clarity in the description of the loiterer's duty to obey a dispersal order might not render the ordinance unconstitutionally vague if the definition of the forbidden conduct were clear, but it does buttress our conclusion that the entire

---

29. "Literally read . . . this ordinance says that a person may stand on a public sidewalk in Birmingham only at the whim of any police officer of that city. The constitutional vice of so broad a provision needs no demonstration." 381 U.S., at 90.

ordinance fails to give the ordinary citizen adequate notice of what is forbidden and what is permitted. The Constitution does not permit a legislature to "set a net large enough to catch all possible offenders, and leave it to the courts to step inside and say who could be rightfully detained, and who should be set at large." *United States v. Reese,* 92 U.S. 214, 221 (1876). This ordinance is therefore vague "not in the sense that it requires a person to conform his conduct to an imprecise but comprehensible normative standard, but rather in the sense that no standard of conduct is specified at all." *Coates v. Cincinnati,* 402 U.S. 611, 614 (1971).

V

The broad sweep of the ordinance also violates "'the requirement that a legislature establish minimal guidelines to govern law enforcement.'" *Kolender v. Lawson,* 461 U.S., at 358. There are no such guidelines in the ordinance. In any public place in the city of Chicago, persons who stand or sit in the company of a gang member may be ordered to disperse unless their purpose is apparent. The mandatory language in the enactment directs the police to issue an order without first making any inquiry about their possible purposes. It matters not whether the reason that a gang member and his father, for example, might loiter near Wrigley Field is to rob an unsuspecting fan or just to get a glimpse of Sammy Sosa leaving the ballpark; in either event, if their purpose is not apparent to a nearby police officer, she may—indeed, she "shall"—order them to disperse.

Recognizing that the ordinance does reach a substantial amount of innocent conduct, we turn, then, to its language to determine if it "necessarily entrusts lawmaking to the moment-to-moment judgment of the policeman on his beat." *Kolender v. Lawson,* 461 U.S., at 359 (internal quotation marks omitted). As we discussed in the context of fair notice, see *supra,* the principal source of the vast discretion conferred on the police in this case is the definition of loitering as "to remain in any one place with no apparent purpose."

As the Illinois Supreme Court interprets that definition, it "provides absolute discretion to police officers to determine what activities constitute loitering." . . .

Nevertheless, the city disputes the Illinois Supreme Court's interpretation, arguing that the text of the ordinance limits the officer's discretion in three ways. First, it does not permit the officer to issue a dispersal order to anyone who is moving along or who has an apparent purpose. Second, it does not permit an arrest if individuals obey a dispersal order. Third, no order can issue unless the officer reasonably believes that one of the loiterers is a member of a criminal street gang.

Even putting to one side our duty to defer to a state court's construction of the scope of a local enactment, we find each of these limitations insufficient. That the ordinance does not apply to people who are moving—that is, to activity that would not constitute loitering under any possible definition of the term—does not even address the question of how much discretion the police enjoy in deciding which stationary persons to disperse under the ordinance. Similarly, that the ordinance does not permit an arrest until after a dispersal order has been disobeyed does not provide any guidance to the officer deciding whether such an order should issue. The "no apparent purpose" standard for making that decision is inherently subjective because its application depends on whether some purpose is "apparent" to the officer on the scene.

Presumably an officer would have discretion to treat some purposes—perhaps a purpose to engage in idle conversation or simply to enjoy a cool breeze on a warm evening—as too frivolous to be apparent if he suspected a different ulterior motive. Moreover, an officer conscious of the city council's reasons for enacting the ordinance might well ignore its text and issue a dispersal order, even though an illicit purpose is actually apparent.

It is true, as the city argues, that the requirement that the officer reasonably believe that a group of loiterers contains a gang member does place a limit on the authority to order dispersal. That limitation would no doubt be sufficient if the ordinance only applied to loitering that had an apparently harmful purpose or effect, or possibly if it only applied to loitering by persons reasonably believed to be criminal gang members. But this ordinance, for reasons that are not explained in the findings of the city council, requires no harmful purpose and applies to non-gang members as well as suspected gang members. It applies to everyone in the city who may remain in one place with one suspected gang member as long as their purpose is not apparent to an officer observing them. Friends, relatives, teachers, counselors, or even total strangers might unwittingly engage in forbidden loitering if they happen to engage in idle conversation with a gang member.

Ironically, the definition of loitering in the Chicago ordinance not only extends its scope to encompass harmless conduct, but also has the perverse consequence of excluding from its coverage much of the intimidating conduct that motivated its enactment. As the city council's findings demonstrate, the most harmful gang loitering is motivated either by an apparent purpose to publicize the gang's dominance of certain territory, thereby intimidating nonmembers, or by an equally apparent purpose to conceal ongoing commerce in illegal drugs. As the Illinois Supreme Court has not placed any limiting construction on the language in the ordinance, we must assume that the ordinance means what it says and that it has no application to loiterers whose purpose is apparent. The relative importance of its application to harmless loitering is magnified by its inapplicability to loitering that has an obviously threatening or illicit purpose.

Finally, in its opinion striking down the ordinance, the Illinois Supreme Court refused to accept the general order issued by the police department as a sufficient limitation on the "vast amount of discretion" granted to the police in its enforcement. We agree. See *Smith v. Goguen*, 415 U.S. 566, 575 (1974). That the police have adopted internal rules limiting their enforcement to certain designated areas in the city would not provide a defense to a loiterer who might be arrested elsewhere. Nor could a person who knowingly loitered with a well-known gang member anywhere in the city safely assume that they would not be ordered to disperse no matter how innocent and harmless their loitering might be.

VI

In our judgment, the Illinois Supreme Court correctly concluded that the ordinance does not provide sufficiently specific limits on the enforcement discretion of the police "to meet constitutional standards for definiteness and clarity."[35] 177 Ill. 2d, at 459, 687 N.E.2d, at 64. We recognize the serious and difficult problems testified to by the citizens of Chicago that led to the enactment of this ordinance. "We are mindful that the preservation of liberty depends in part on the maintenance of social order." *Houston v. Hill,* 482 U.S. 451, 471–472 (1987). However, in this instance the city has enacted an ordinance that affords too much discretion to the police and too little notice to citizens who wish to use the public streets.

Accordingly, the judgment of the Supreme Court of Illinois is

Affirmed.

Notes and Questions

1. Why did the responding party (in this case the City of Chicago) assert the Court should reject the complaint? How did the Court resolve the dispute, and most importantly what rule or principle of law provided the legal foundation for the resolution? *Also be sure to read the footnotes; if they are included in the reprint, it means they must be important.*

2. The opinion indicated that, "The Constitution does not permit a legislature to 'set a net large enough to catch all possible offenders, and leave it to the courts to step inside and say who could be rightfully detained, and who should be set at large.' *United States v. Reese,* 92 U.S. 214, 221 (1876)." Consider how this sentence indicates the invalidity of the hypothetical "one crime" presented at the beginning of this section. Why not let a judge "step in" and clarify whether what the police officer felt was criminal conduct was or was not? Imagine how this might impact two citizens brought before two different judges by two different police officers?

> Loitering and vagrancy statutes have a sordid history and were often linked to racial oppression. It might surprise you that the Thirteenth Amendment to the Constitution did not completely prohibit involuntary servitude, but instead included this qualification: "except as a punishment for crime whereof the party shall have been duly convicted." In his Pulitzer Prize winning book titled, *Slavery by Another Name: The Re-Enslavement of Black Americans from the Civil War to World War II,* Douglas A. Blackmon detailed how the concept

---

35. This conclusion makes it unnecessary to reach the question whether the Illinois Supreme Court correctly decided that ordinance is invalid as a deprivation of substantive due process. For this reason, Justice Thomas, and Justice Scalia [dissents omitted], are mistaken when they assert that our decision must be analyzed under the framework for substantive due process set out in *Washington v. Glucksberg,* 521 U.S. 702 (1997).

of convict leased labor and peonage—involuntary servitude imposed as punishment for a criminal offense—was used pervasively throughout the southern United States as a tool of oppression and as a mechanism to functionally enslave black (and to a lesser extent poor white) citizens for decades. The unfortunate reality was that loitering and vagrancy laws were central to this practice. When some local industry or farm would need laborers, the local sheriff would simply round up poor men and charge them with one of these vague offenses. Quickly convicted, they would often be subjected to a criminal fine that they obviously could not pay. At that point, some person who wanted their servitude would pay the fine, and the prisoner would be indentured to that person for whatever period of time the judge decided would be necessary to work off the debt. Blackmon's book details the terror this inflicted on African American communities, including the reality that many of the victims of this practice were dispatched to penal servitude with no notice to families, for indefinite periods of time, with no judicial oversight to ensure they were ever released. Nor was there any oversight of working or living conditions, which were routinely brutal.

The relationship between this ugly history of leased labor peonage and vagrancy and loitering statutes reinforces the central premise of the *Morales* decision: that criminal laws must places some limit on the discretion of those entrusted with enforcement to protect the public from arbitrary and abusive government action that can result in profoundly negative consequences.

3. There are other rare situations when a criminal statute will run afoul of a right protected by the Constitution. A statute may be unconstitutionally overbroad, meaning that it impermissibly infringes on a protected First Amendment right. For example, if the statute penalizes protected speech or expression, even if highly offensive, it will be considered unconstitutionally overbroad. For example, in *R.A.V. v. City of St. Paul*, 505 U.S. 377 (1992), the Supreme Court struck down the city's Bias Motivated Crime ordinance in a case involving a teenager convicted for burning a cross on the lawn of an African-American family. The ordinance at issue provided that:

Whoever places on public or private property, a symbol, object, appellation, characterization or graffiti, including, but not limited to, a burning cross or Nazi swastika, which one knows or has reasonable grounds to know arouses anger, alarm or resentment in others on the basis of race, color, creed, religion or gender commits disorderly conduct and shall be guilty of a misdemeanor.

The Supreme Court noted that,

When the basis for the content discrimination consists entirely of the very reason the entire class of speech at issue is proscribable, no significant danger of idea or viewpoint discrimination exists. Such a reason, having been adjudged neutral enough to support exclusion of the entire class of speech from First Amendment protection, is also neutral enough to form the basis of distinction within the class. To illustrate: a State might choose to prohibit only that obscenity which is the most patently offensive *in its prurience*—*i.e.*, that which involves the most lascivious displays of sexual activity. But it may not prohibit, for example, only that obscenity which includes offensive *political* messages. See *Kucharek v. Hanaway*, 902 F.2d 513, 517 (CA7 1990), cert. denied, 498 U.S. 1041 (1991).

The Court then concluded that,

> Applying these principles to the St. Paul ordinance, we conclude that, even as narrowly construed by the Minnesota Supreme Court, the ordinance is facially unconstitutional. Although the phrase in the ordinance, "arouses anger, alarm or resentment in others," has been limited by the Minnesota Supreme Court's construction to reach only those symbols or displays that amount to "fighting words," the remaining, unmodified terms make clear that the ordinance applies only to "fighting words" that insult, or provoke violence, "on the basis of race, color, creed, religion or gender." Displays containing abusive invective, no matter how vicious or severe, are permissible unless they are addressed to one of the specified disfavored topics. Those who wish to use "fighting words" in connection with other ideas—to express hostility, for example, on the basis of political affiliation, union membership, or homosexuality—are not covered. The First Amendment does not permit St. Paul to impose special prohibitions on those speakers who express views on disfavored subjects.

A statute might unconstitutionally prohibit private conduct protected by due process. For example, in *Lawrence v. Texas*, 539 U.S. 558 (2003), the Supreme Court struck down a law that criminalized consensual sodomy because it unconstitutionally intruded upon the right to privacy protected by due process.

4. Your client is charged with the following offense:

> Vagrancy: Any person found within the city limits without the ability to show on demand of a law enforcement officer an adequate means of income shall be guilty of a misdemeanor.

What would be the most effective constitutional argument to make in support of a motion to dismiss this charge?

II. Crime, Statutes, and the Common Law Origins

It is quite rare that a criminal statute will violate constitutional limitations. In almost all cases, this means that the assessment of criminal responsibility—whether an individual is guilty of committing a crime—will begin with the text of the statutory provision the prosecution alleges was violated. This statutory provision will be identified in the criminal charge. Understanding the origins of these provisions and how they are interpreted is therefore an important pillar in the foundation of criminal law.

Every jurisdiction in the United States, including territories and the armed forces, defines crimes in the form of criminal statutes. The content of these statutes obviously varies from jurisdiction to jurisdiction, but there are many commonalities, especially in terms of crimes and defenses proscribed by these statutes. This commonality is the result of two primary influences. First, almost all criminal statutes were originally enacted to codify what was known as the common law—the law established by judicial opinions over the centuries. As Chief Justice Chase noted in 1821,

> The common law of England is derived from immemorial usage and custom, originating from Acts of Parliament not recorded, or which are lost, or have been destroyed. It is a system of jurisprudence founded on the immutable principles of justice, and denominated by the great luminary of the law of England, the perfection of reason. The evidences of it are treatises of the sages of the law, the judicial records and adjudications of the Courts of justice of England.

Chief Justice Chase, *State v. Buchanan*, 5 Harris & J. 317, 365 (Md. 1821).

The colonists brought the English Common Law with them and continued to develop American Common Law until the era of codification took hold. This means that certain common law principles or concepts permeate many contemporary statutory crimes. It also means that when a court is called upon to interpret the meaning of a statute, it may look to the common law predecessor to the statute to aid in that interpretation. This is why many of the cases included in this text, while interpreting statutory provisions, will reference the common law.

Second, in an effort to better align criminal statutes throughout the United States and aid legislatures in reforming their criminal laws, following a ten-year study, the American Law Institute published a Model Penal Code (MPC) in 1962. This is not a statute in itself, but instead a comprehensive penal statute proposed for states to adopt. Many jurisdictions since that time have amended their criminal statutes, or penal codes, to adopt this proposal. However, it was also common for these states to retain certain pre-MPC provisions in their revised penal codes, or to otherwise reject or modify provisions of the MPC. Indeed, only one state adopted the MPC as published, but almost immediately revisited the decision and modified the statute. But even in jurisdictions that have adopted the bulk of the MPC, because many of the crimes and defenses in the Code are themselves derived from the common law. Accordingly, common law principles remain relevant even when interpreting the MPC.

What does this mean for you as a student of criminal law? First, throughout the course, you will be learning "common law" principles and rules, not because there is any jurisdiction that today follows the "common law" exclusively, but because those rules and principles are widely reflected in many contemporary penal codes. Second, you will also be learning about certain widely adopted MPC provisions, especially those that substantially deviate from the common law. Again, this is not because there are any penal codes that reflect a verbatim adoption of the MPC, but because in those states that have generally adopted the MPC these differences are important to be familiar with. Third, the law that will always dictate the outcome of a particular case is the penal provision that has actually been enacted by that jurisdiction's legislature. *Accordingly, when your case references the penal code provision at issue, it is that provision that must be analyzed and understood.* Finally, and perhaps most importantly, you are neither required or expected to memorize multiple penal codes. Instead, because the crimes and defenses we study (and those commonly tested on the multistate portion of the bar examination) are generally derived from the common law, you will be learning general common law definitions. Where the professor believes you must also learn a MPC variant or perhaps a federal or state law variant, you can consider these as exceptions to the general rule.

The next case illustrates how the common law origin of statutory crimes may have a profound influence on judicial interpretation of a criminal statute, and the limits of the courts in determining the meaning of a particular penal provision.

Keeler v. Superior Court of Amador County

2 Cal. 3d 619 (1970)

Supreme Court of California En Banc

MOSK, J.

In this proceeding for writ of prohibition we are called upon to decide whether an unborn but viable fetus is a "human being" within the meaning of the California statute defining murder (Pen. Code, § 187). We conclude that the Legislature did not intend such a meaning, and that for us to construe the statute to the contrary and apply it to this petitioner would exceed our judicial power and deny petitioner due process of law.

The evidence received at the preliminary examination may be summarized as follows: Petitioner and Teresa Keeler obtained an interlocutory decree of divorce on September 27, 1968. They had been married for 16 years. Unknown to petitioner, Mrs. Keeler was then pregnant by one Ernest Vogt, whom she had met earlier that summer. She subsequently began living with Vogt in Stockton, but concealed the fact from petitioner. Petitioner was given custody of their two daughters, aged 12 and 13 years, and under the decree Mrs. Keeler had the right to take the girls on alternate weekends.

On February 23, 1969, Mrs. Keeler was driving on a narrow mountain road in Amador County after delivering the girls to their home. She met petitioner driving in the opposite direction; he blocked the road with his car, and she pulled over to the side. He walked to her vehicle and began speaking to her. He seemed calm, and she rolled down her window to hear him. He said, "I hear you're pregnant. If you are you had better stay away from the girls and from here." She did not reply, and he opened the car door; as she later testified, "He assisted me out of the car. . . . [I]t wasn't roughly at this time." Petitioner then looked at her abdomen and became "extremely upset." He said, "You sure are. I'm going to stomp it out of you." He pushed her against the car, shoved his knee into her abdomen, and struck her in the face with several blows. She fainted, and when she regained consciousness petitioner had departed.

Mrs. Keeler drove back to Stockton, and the police and medical assistance were summoned. She had suffered substantial facial injuries, as well as extensive bruising of the abdominal wall. A Caesarian section was performed and the fetus was examined *in utero*. Its head was found to be severely fractured, and it was delivered stillborn. The pathologist gave as his opinion that the cause of death was skull fracture with consequent cerebral hemorrhaging, that death would have been immediate, and that the injury could have been the result of force applied to the mother's abdomen. There was no air in the fetus' lungs, and the umbilical cord was intact.

Upon delivery the fetus weighed five pounds and was 18 inches in length. Both Mrs. Keeler and her obstetrician testified that fetal movements had been observed prior to February 23, 1969. The evidence was in conflict as to the estimated age of the fetus; the expert testimony on the point, however, concluded "with reasonable medical certainty" that the fetus had developed to the stage of viability, i.e., that in the event of premature birth on the date in question it would have had a 75 percent to 96 percent chance of survival.

An information was filed charging petitioner, in count I, with committing the crime of murder (Pen. Code, § 187) in that he did "unlawfully kill a human being, to wit Baby Girl VOGT, with malice aforethought." In count II petitioner was charged with wilful infliction of traumatic injury upon his wife (Pen. Code, § 273d), and in count III, with assault on Mrs. Keeler by means of force likely to produce great bodily injury (Pen. Code, § 245). His motion to set aside the information for lack of probable cause (Pen. Code, § 995) was denied, and he now seeks a writ of prohibition; as will appear, only the murder count is actually in issue. . . .

I

Penal Code section 187 provides: "Murder is the unlawful killing of a human being, with malice aforethought." The dispositive question is whether the fetus which petitioner is accused of killing was, on February 23, 1969, a "human being" within the meaning of the statute. If it was not, petitioner cannot be charged with its "murder" and prohibition will lie.

Section 187 was enacted as part of the Penal Code of 1872. Inasmuch as the provision has not been amended since that date, we must determine the intent of the Legislature at the time of its enactment. But section 187 was, in turn, taken verbatim from the first California statute defining murder, part of the Crimes and Punishments Act of 1850. (Stats. 1850, ch. 99, § 19, p. 231.) Penal Code section 5 (also enacted in 1872) declares: "The provisions of this code, so far as they are substantially the same as existing statutes, must be construed as continuations thereof, and not as new enactments." We begin, accordingly, by inquiring into the intent of the Legislature in 1850 when it first defined murder as the unlawful and malicious killing of a "human being."

It will be presumed, of course, that in enacting a statute the Legislature was famil-iar with the relevant rules of the common law, and, when it couches its enactment in common law language, that its intent was to continue those rules in statutory form. (*Baker v. Baker* (1859) 13 Cal. 87, 95-96; *Morris v. Oney* (1963) 217 Cal. App.2d 864, 870 [32 Cal. Rptr. 88].) This is particularly appropriate in considering the work of the first session of our Legislature: its precedents were necessarily drawn from the common law, as modified in certain respects by the Constitution and by legislation of our sister states.

We therefore undertake a brief review of the origins and development of the com-mon law of abortional homicide. . . . From that inquiry it appears that by the year 1850—the date with which we are concerned—an infant could not be the subject of homicide at common law *unless it had been born alive.*

Against this background, a series of infanticide prosecutions were brought in the English courts in mid-19th century. In each, a woman or her accomplice was charged with murdering a newborn child, and it was uniformly declared to be the law that a verdict of murder could not be returned unless it was proved the infant had been born alive.

By the year 1850 this rule of the common law had long been accepted in the United States. As early as 1797 it was held that proof the child was born alive is necessary to support an indictment for murder (*State v. McKee* (Pa.) Addison 1), and the same rule was reiterated on the eve of the first session of our Legislature (*State v. Cooper* (1849) 22 N.J.L. 52).

While it was thus "well settled" in American case law that the killing of an unborn child was not homicide, a number of state legislatures in the first half of the 19th century undertook to modify the common law in this respect. The movement began when New York abandoned the common law of abortion in 1830 . . .

In the years between 1830 and 1850 at least five other states followed New York. In California, however, the pattern was not repeated. Much of the Crimes and Punish-ments Act of 1850 was based on existing New York statute law; but although a section proscribing abortion was included in the new Act (§ 45), the Legislature declined to adopt any provision defining and punishing a special crime of feticide.

We conclude that in declaring murder to be the unlawful and malicious killing of a "human being" the Legislature of 1850 intended that term to have the settled common law meaning of a person who had been born alive, and did not intend the act of feticide—as distinguished from abortion—to be an offense under the laws of California.

Nothing occurred between the years 1850 and 1872 to suggest that in adopting the new Penal Code on the latter date the Legislature entertained any different intent.

Any lingering doubt on this subject must be laid to rest by a consideration of the legislative history of the Penal Code of 1872. The Act establishing the California Code

Commission (Stats. 1870, ch. 516, § 2, p. 774) required the commissioners to revise all statutes then in force, correct errors and omissions, and "recommend all such enactments as shall, in the judgment of the Commission, be necessary to supply the defects of and give completeness to the existing legislation of the State. . . ." In discharging this duty the statutory schemes of our sister states were carefully examined, and we must assume the commissioners had knowledge of the feticide laws noted hereinabove. Yet the commissioners proposed no such law for California, and none has been adopted to this day.

That such an omission was not an oversight clearly appears, moreover, from the commissioners' explanatory notes to Penal Code section 187. After quoting the definitions of murder given by Coke, Blackstone, and Hawkins, the commissioners conclude: "A child within its mother's womb is not a 'human being' within the meaning of that term as used in defining murder."

When there is persuasive evidence of a legislative intent contrary to the views expressed in code commissioners' notes, those views will not be followed in construing the statute. Here, however, the views of the commissioners are in full accord with the history of section 187; and as we have seen, the Legislature made no significant change in that statute when it was codified into the Penal Code.

It is the policy of this state to construe a penal statute as favorably to the defendant as its language and the circumstances of its application may reasonably permit; just as in the case of a question of fact, the defendant is entitled to the benefit of every reasonable doubt as to the true interpretation of words or the construction of language used in a statute. (*Walsh v. Department of Alcoholic Bev. Control* (1963) 59 Cal.2d 757, 764-765 [31 Cal. Rptr. 297, 382 P.2d 337], and cases cited.) We hold that in adopting the definition of murder in Penal Code section 187 the Legislature intended to exclude from its reach the act of killing an unborn fetus.

II

The People urge, however, that the sciences of obstetrics and pediatrics have greatly progressed since 1872, to the point where with proper medical care a normally developed fetus prematurely born at 28 weeks or more has an excellent chance of survival, i.e., is "viable"; that the common law requirement of live birth to prove the fetus had become a "human being" who may be the victim of murder is no longer in accord with scientific fact, since an unborn but viable fetus is now fully capable of independent life; and that one who unlawfully and maliciously terminates such a life should therefore be liable to prosecution for murder under section 187. We may grant the premises of this argument; indeed, we neither deny nor denigrate the vast progress of medicine in the century since the enactment of the Penal Code. But we cannot join in the conclusion sought to be deduced: we cannot hold this petitioner to answer for murder by reason of his alleged act of killing an unborn—even though viable—fetus. To such a charge there are two insuperable obstacles, one "jurisdictional" and the other constitutional.

Penal Code section 6 declares in relevant part that "No act or omission" accomplished after the code has taken effect "is criminal or punishable, except as prescribed or authorized by this code, or by some of the statutes which it specifies as continuing in force and as not affected by its provisions, or by some ordinance, municipal, county, or township regulation. . . ." This section embodies a fundamental principle of our tripartite form of government, i.e., that subject to the constitutional prohibition against cruel and unusual punishment, the power to define crimes and fix penalties is vested exclusively in the legislative branch. . . . In order that a public offense be committed, some statute, ordinance or regulation prior in time to the commission of the act, must denounce it; likewise with excuses or justifications—if no statutory excuse or justification apply as to the commission of the particular offense, neither the common law nor the so-called 'unwritten law' may legally supply it." (*People v. Whipple* (1929) 100 Cal. App. 261, 262 [279 P. 1008].)

Settled rules of construction implement this principle. Although the Penal Code commands us to construe its provisions "according to the fair import of their terms, with a view to effect its objects and to promote justice" (Pen. Code, § 4), it is clear the courts cannot go so far as to create an offense by enlarging a statute, by inserting or deleting words, or by giving the terms used false or unusual meanings. . . .

Applying these rules to the case at bar, we would undoubtedly act in excess of the judicial power if we were to adopt the People's proposed construction of section 187. As we have shown, the Legislature has defined the crime of murder in California to apply only to the unlawful and malicious killing of one who has been born alive. We recognize that the killing of an unborn but viable fetus may be deemed by some to be an offense of similar nature and gravity; but as Chief Justice Marshall warned long ago, "It would be dangerous, indeed, to carry the principle, that a case which is within the reason or mischief of a statute, is within its provisions, so far as to punish a crime not enumerated in the statute, because it is of equal atrocity, or of kindred character, with those which are enumerated." (*United States v. Wiltberger* (1820) 18 U.S. (5 Wheat.) 76, 96 [5 L.Ed. 37, 42].) Whether to thus extend liability for murder in California is a determination solely within the province of the Legislature. For a court to simply declare, by judicial fiat, that the time has now come to prosecute under section 187 one who kills an unborn but viable fetus would indeed be to rewrite the statute under the guise of construing it. Nor does a need to fill an asserted "gap" in the law between abortion and homicide—as will appear, no such gap in fact exists—justify judicial legislation of this nature: to make it "a judicial function 'to explore such new fields of crime as they may appear from time to time' is wholly foreign to the American concept of criminal justice" and "raises very serious questions concerning the principle of separation of powers." (*In re Davis* (1966) 242 Cal. App.2d 645, 655-656 & fn. 12 [51 Cal. Rptr. 702].)

The second obstacle to the proposed judicial enlargement of section 187 is the guarantee of due process of law. Assuming *arguendo* that we have the power to adopt the new construction of this statute as the law of California, such a ruling, by constitutional command, could operate only prospectively, and thus could not in any event reach the conduct of petitioner on February 23, 1969.

The first essential of due process is fair warning of the act which is made punishable as a crime.

This requirement of fair warning is reflected in the constitutional prohibition against the enactment of ex post facto laws (U.S. Const., art. I, §§ 9, 10; Cal. Const., art. I, § 16). When a new penal statute is applied retrospectively to make punishable an act which was not criminal at the time it was performed, the defendant has been given no advance notice consistent with due process. And precisely the same effect occurs when such an act is made punishable under a preexisting statute but by means of an unforeseeable *judicial* enlargement thereof. (*Bouie v. City of Columbia* (1964) 378 U.S. 347 [12 L.Ed.2d 894, 84 S.Ct. 1697].)

We conclude that the judicial enlargement of section 187 now urged upon us by the People would not have been forseeable to this petitioner, and hence that its adoption at this time would deny him due process of law.

Let a peremptory writ of prohibition issue restraining respondent court from taking any further proceedings on Count I of the information, charging petitioner with the crime of murder.

Notes and Questions

1. What is a Writ of Prohibition? During your readings, you will encounter many new legal terms. It is essential practice to take a moment to determine the meaning of such terms in order to better understand the decision and to develop your professional vocabulary.

2. Notice how the court identified another important benefit of the fair notice requirement: protection against *ex post facto* punishment. Unless an offense is fairly defined *prior to* the act or omission that results in the allegation of criminal violation, a defendant could be subjected to criminal conviction and sanction for something that was not a crime when committed. This would be considered fundamentally unfair in violation of due process and also qualify as invalid *ex post facto* punishment.

3. Notice also how the court turned to the common law meaning of murder to aid interpreting the statutory meaning of the crime. But why did the court reject the state's request to simply adopt an updated interpretation of human being based on medical knowledge that was alien to those who established the common law crime of murder?

4. It is likely you will be troubled by this decision. After all, why should Keeler get away with the viscous killing of the unborn but viable child? The answer lies in the limits of judicial interpretation. Unlike common law predecessors, courts no longer make up, or derive from the natural order, what should and should not be a

crime. Instead, the answer to that question is vested exclusively in We the People, as reflected in the statutory enactments of the representatives we elect. But that also means that the legislature has unquestioned authority to amend or supplement the law at any time, a point emphasized by the court. Indeed, not long after this decision, the California legislature amended the definition of murder to provide, "Murder is the unlawful killing of a human being, or a fetus, with malice aforethought."

III. What Is a Presumption and Why Does It Matter?

"Presumed innocent unless proven guilty." Most Americans have heard this phrase, but few really understand what it means. Contrary to common misconception, it really has nothing to do with whether or not an individual actually committed a crime; whether or not she is *in fact* guilty. Indeed, it would be an odd system of criminal justice if prosecutors were required to *believe* the person they were charging and prosecuting was actually innocent. Instead, the presumption of innocence is a legal starting point in any criminal trial: the person who is accused of a crime by the government must be treated by the court as if she or he is innocent unless the prosecution proves guilt beyond a reasonable doubt. Hence, the tag line at the end of the television show *Cops* most of us have heard, "all suspects are innocent until proven guilty," is actually a bit misleading. To be accurate, it should say, "all suspects are *legally presumed* innocent until proven guilty."

This is the procedural and evidentiary foundation of criminal law, and there is much to unpack inside this simple concept. First, the presumption of innocence is derived from a defendant's right to due process, applicable in federal courts pursuant to the Fifth Amendment of the Constitution or in state courts pursuant to the Fourteenth Amendment. In essence, the *process a defendant is due* before the government may lawfully condemn him for committing a crime is that the prosecution must rebut the presumption of innocence.

> It might surprise you to learn that what most Americans assume is the legal requirement to prove a defendant guilty—proof beyond a reasonable doubt—was not required as a matter of constitutional due process in state criminal trials until 1970. In that year, the United States Supreme Court decided the case of *In re Winship*, 397 U.S. 358 (1970), in which it considered, "the single, narrow question whether proof beyond a reasonable doubt is among the 'essentials of due process and fair treatment' required during the adjudicatory stage when a juvenile is charged with an act which would constitute a crime if committed by an adult." The Court noted that,
>
> > The requirement that guilt of a criminal charge be established by proof beyond a reasonable doubt dates at least from our early years

as a Nation. The "demand for a higher degree of persuasion in criminal cases was recurrently expressed from ancient times, [though] its crystallization into the formula 'beyond a reasonable doubt' seems to have occurred as late as 1798. It is now accepted in common law jurisdictions as the measure of persuasion by which the prosecution must convince the trier of all the essential elements of guilt."

And that,

The reasonable doubt standard plays a vital role in the American scheme of criminal procedure. It is a prime instrument for reducing the risk of convictions resting on factual error. The standard provides concrete substance for the presumption of innocence—that bedrock "axiomatic and elementary" principle whose "enforcement lies at the foundation of the administration of our criminal law." *Coffin v. United States, supra,* at 156 U.S. 453. As the dissenters in the New York Court of Appeals observed, and we agree, "a person accused of a crime . . . would be at a severe disadvantage, a disadvantage amounting to a lack of fundamental fairness, if he could be adjudged guilty and imprisoned for years on the strength of the same evidence as would suffice in a civil case."

The Court then held that, "Lest there remain any doubt about the constitutional stature of the reasonable doubt standard, we explicitly hold that the Due Process Clause protects the accused against conviction except upon proof beyond a reasonable doubt of every fact necessary to constitute the crime with which he is charged."

Second, as reflected in *In re Winship*, the presumption of innocence is directly linked to the prosecution's burden of proof. If a presumption is a starting conclusion, it means that whenever a criminal case begins, the *finder of fact*—either a jury or when tried without a jury the judge fulfilling that function—must consider the defendant not guilty.

In practical terms, this means a criminal defendant may always "put the prosecution to its proof." Because it is the government that is accusing the individual, it is the government's burden to rebut the legal presumption of innocence. Consider how this this allocation of burden imposed on the prosecution is reflected when a judge advises a defendant who indicates a desire to plead guilty that, even if she knows she is guilty, she may still plead not guilty, "Do you understand that even though you believe you are guilty, you have the legal right to plead not guilty and to place upon the government the burden of proving your guilt beyond a reasonable doubt?" No matter how obviously guilty he may be, or even if he believes he is guilty, a defendant has an absolute right to plead not guilty and require the prosecution to prove guilt beyond a reasonable doubt.

But what exactly must the prosecution prove? The obvious answer is the crime the defendant is charged with. But there is more complexity involved. As you will learn through your study of criminal law, crimes are defined by component "elements," and it is these elements that must be proven beyond a reasonable doubt. Consider this admonition provided to a defendant who chooses to plead guilty:

> I am going to explain the elements of the offense(s) to which you have pled guilty. By "elements," I mean those facts which the prosecution would have to prove beyond a reasonable doubt before you could be found guilty if you had pled not guilty.

Much of your study of criminal law will be focused on learning the material elements of various offenses, which often fall into four broad categories: The *act* element (the physical act or omission that is alleged to have been criminal); the *causation* element (proof the criminal act "caused" the criminal harm or result); the *mens rea* element (the defined criminal state of mind that actuated or set in motion the criminal act that caused the criminal harm); and the attendant circumstance (some other fact that must be established beyond a reasonable doubt in order to convict the defendant). So, imagine a defendant is charged with murder, and that the law defines murder as the "unlawful intentional killing of a human being." In order to convict, the prosecution must prove the following elements beyond a reasonable doubt:

1. The Act Element: That the defendant engaged in an act or omission (as defined by law);

2. The Causation Element: That legally caused a death;

3. The Mens Rea/Culpable Mental State Element: As the result of an intent to kill (as legally defined); and

4. The Attendant Circumstance Element: That the victim was a human being.

If after deliberation, the finder of fact has reasonable doubt as to even one of these elements, the prosecution has failed to rebut the presumption of innocence and the verdict must be not guilty.

Practice Pointer

It is useful to think of the material elements of an offense as the pillars to a foundation of structure. Unless all pillars are solid, the foundation crumbles. In this sense, unless the prosecution can *produce* evidence of each element or "pillar," and then *persuade* a jury or judge that these pillars are solid enough to support the foundation/prove the offense, the foundation crumbles. In a very real sense, prosecutors are in the business of constructing the crime, and defense lawyers are in the demolition business: the prosecution bears the burden of laying the foundation by providing evidence of all material elements; the defense lawyer's strategy will often be to demonstrate to the court or to the jury that one of those pillars is missing or perhaps so weak that it cannot sustain the edifice of crime.

It is therefore useful to always ask what those pillars are for any given crime. This is another way of identifying the material elements of the offense. In some jurisdictions, there are pattern jury instructions that explain this, although this is rarely an aspect of the penal statute itself. So, for example, consider the crime burglary defined by one statute as:

> BURGLARY—Any person subject to this chapter who, with intent to commit an offense under this chapter, breaks and enters the building or structure of another shall be punished as a court may direct.

This statutory definition is broken down into material elements as follows:

ELEMENTS:

(1) That (state the time and place alleged), the accused unlawfully broke and entered the dwelling house of another, namely: (state the name of the person alleged);

(2) That both the breaking and entering were done in the nighttime; and

(3) That the breaking and entering were done with the intent to commit therein the offense of (state the offense allegedly intended).

Accordingly, in this jurisdiction if a defendant is charged with burglary, these three elements are the pillars that support the foundation to prove the crime, and it is the prosecution that must produce evidence on each element and then persuade the fact finder that this evidence rebuts the presumption of innocence beyond a reasonable doubt. The defense, however, need not prove anything to prevail. Instead, the foundation will crumble if the defense is able to demonstrate the absence or insufficiency of one of these pillars.

Third, because the prosecution bears the burden of proof to rebut the presumption of innocence, that burden must be defined in evidentiary terms. And because due process demands that the prosecution's evidentiary burden be sufficiently demanding to protect against erroneous convictions, guilt must be established beyond a reasonable doubt. While most Americans are equally familiar with that term, very few genuinely understand what it means. Your understanding begins by recognizing this burden of proof really refers to two burdens: the burden of production and the burden of persuasion.

The burden of production refers to the prosecution's obligation to introduce, or "produce," evidence on each material element of the offense so that guilt is at least *a rational* result. This is done by offering evidence, which is information that meets the requirements of the law of evidence. While this is not a class on evidence, it is important that you understand from the outset of your study that information is not the same as evidence. Evidence is information that qualifies as worthy for use in the trial. Evidence generally falls into three broad categories: direct evidence, circumstantial evidence, and opinion evidence. It is another myth of most people that direct evidence is the best type of evidence. In fact, there is no rule of priority, and it is the finder of fact that is responsible for assigning weight, what the law calls probative value (tendency to prove something), to *all* types of evidence. Consider someone buying a used car. Direct evidence would include the condition of the car observed by that person. Circumstantial evidence would be some fact or circumstance that would support an inference, such as observing an oil stain on the ground under the car and drawing from that fact the inference that the car has an oil leak. The buyer might also take the car for a mechanic's inspection and rely on that expert's opinion as to the quality of the car. None of these sources of "evidence" is *per se* better than the other; the buyer will decide how to allocate weight to each source. This is the same process used by juries and judges when they consider evidence.

Practice Pointer

Because *mens rea,* or the defined criminal mental state, is almost always an element of a crime that the prosecution must prove beyond a reasonable doubt, it is important that you begin to understand the relationship between evidence and *mens rea*. There are times when a prosecution will offer direct evidence of the defendant's criminal state of mind, for example, a statement of intent heard by another witness or perhaps recorded by law enforcement officers. Thus, to prove the requisite "intent to commit a felony therein" in a burglary case, a prosecutor might be able to offer evidence that the defendant told someone of his intent to commit that felony; that this is why he decided to break and enter into the victim's dwelling house. However, in many cases, such direct evidence of *mens rea* will be unavailable. Accordingly, it is common practice for the prosecution to offer *circumstantial* evidence to prove the defendant's *mens rea* by inference drawn from that evidence. In this sense, the prosecutor will rely on objectively established facts and circumstances to persuade the finder of fact that the defendant acted with the requisite criminal state of mind. For example, if a defendant is apprehended near the scene of a suspected burglary with property belonging to the homeowner, it would be reasonable to infer from that circumstantial evidence that: 1. The defendant broke and entered into the home, and 2. He did so with the intent to commit a larceny therein. Or when proving the defendant acted with the intent to kill, the finder of fact may rely on the circumstantial evidence related to the nature of the weapon used and the nature of the wound inflicted to infer what the defendant intended.

In this regard, it is important that you distinguish between *motive* and *intent*. Motive is not intent. Motive is *why* someone does something; intent is the mental decision to do it. For example, a defendant may kill a victim based on the motive of putting the victim out of the misery of a terminal illness, but that motive is circumstantial evidence that supports the inference that the defendant intended to kill the victim. Accordingly, motive is often powerful circumstantial evidence offered to prove intent.

Your instinct to identify evidence that proves or negates requisite elements of a crime will develop over time. But at this stage of your development, you should practice identifying what you believe is the critical evidence in the cases you read and what elements of a crime of defense the evidence tends to prove or disprove.

The prosecutor must satisfy this burden of production in what is known as the case-in-chief; the part of the criminal trial that begins when the prosecution begins offering evidence and ends when the prosecution rests its case. It is during this phase of the trial that the prosecutor offers *prima facie* proof of guilt: evidence that "on its face" proves each element of the offense. When the prosecution rests, indicating satisfaction of this burden of production, a defendant will often make a motion for acquittal or for a finding of not guilty.

When this happens, the judge must consider all of the evidence introduced to that point, along with any rational inferences supported by that evidence, and assess whether based on that evidence it would be rational for a jury to find the defendant guilty. This is known as the "rational result" test, and simply means that if the judge considers the evidence so lacking on a material element that guilt could not even be a rational result, she must find the defendant not guilty without ever submitting the charge to the jury. Why? Because unless the prosecution "produced" sufficient evidence to support a rational conclusion that the defendant is guilty, allowing a jury to convict would produce an "irrational" result. This does not mean the judge must be convinced guilt is the *only* rational result; that is the ultimate question for the jury when it decides whether the prosecution has met the burden of *persuasion*. Instead, so long as guilt is *a* rational result—even if a finding of not guilty is also *a* rational result, the prosecution has satisfied the initial burden of production.

In the case that follows, consider how the Supreme Court distinguishes between the burden of production and the burden of persuasion as it establishes the standard for deciding when a conviction must be reversed based on insufficiency of evidence. To fully understand this opinion, you have to understand a bit about a federal habeas corpus proceeding. Pursuant to the federal habeas corpus statute, federal courts have authority to overturn state convictions when those convictions deprive a citizen of a federal constitutional right. After Jackson's conviction in a Virginia court became final by being upheld on appeal, he challenged the legality of his continued incarceration by invoking this habeas corpus statute in a petition to a federal court and alleging that Virginia had upheld his conviction in violation of his federal constitutional right to due process. In short, he argued that the evidence presented at his trial was insufficient to justify his conviction based on the proof beyond a reasonable doubt standard.

Jackson v. Virginia
443 U.S. 307 (1979)
U.S. Supreme Court

STEWART, J., delivered the opinion of the Court, in which BRENNAN, WHITE, MARSHALL, and BLACKMUN, JJ., joined. STEVENS, J., filed an opinion concurring in the judgment, in which BURGER, C.J., and REHNQUIST, J., joined, *post* 443 U.S. 326. POWELL, J., took no part in the consideration or decision of the case.

MR. JUSTICE STEWART delivered the opinion of the Court.

The Constitution prohibits the criminal conviction of any person except upon proof of guilt beyond a reasonable doubt. *In re Winship,* 397 U.S. 358. The question in this case is what standard is to be applied in a federal habeas corpus proceeding when the claim is made that a person has been convicted in a state court upon insufficient evidence.

I

The petitioner was convicted after a bench trial [a trial without a jury] in the Circuit Court of Chesterfield County, Va., of the first-degree murder of a woman named Mary Houston Cole. Under Virginia law, murder is defined as "the unlawful killing of another with malice aforethought." Premeditation, or specific intent to kill, distinguishes murder in the first from murder in the second degree; proof of this element is essential to conviction of the former offense, and the burden of proving it clearly rests with the prosecution.

That the petitioner had shot and killed Mrs. Cole was not in dispute at the trial. . . . The State's evidence established that she had been a member of the staff at the local county jail, that she had befriended him while he was imprisoned there on a disorderly conduct charge, and that, when he was released, she had arranged for him to live in the home of her son and daughter-in-law. Testimony by her relatives indicated that, on the day of the killing, the petitioner had been drinking and had spent a great deal of time shooting at targets with his revolver. Late in the afternoon, according to their testimony, he had unsuccessfully attempted to talk the victim into driving him to North Carolina. She did drive the petitioner to a local diner. There the two were observed by several police officers, who testified that both the petitioner and the victim had been drinking. The two were observed by a deputy sheriff as they were preparing to leave the diner in her car. The petitioner was then in possession of his revolver, and the sheriff also observed a kitchen knife in the automobile. The sheriff testified that he had offered to keep the revolver until the petitioner sobered up, but that the latter had indicated that this would be unnecessary, since he and the victim were about to engage in sexual activity.

Her body was found in a secluded church parking lot a day and a half later, naked from the waist down, her slacks beneath her body. Uncontradicted medical and expert evidence established that she had been shot twice at close range with the petitioner's gun. She appeared not to have been sexually molested. Six cartridge cases identified as having been fired from the petitioner's gun were found near the body.

After shooting Mrs. Cole, the petitioner drove her car to North Carolina, where, after a short trip to Florida, he was arrested several days later. In a post-arrest statement, introduced in evidence by the prosecution, the petitioner admitted that he had shot the victim. He contended, however, that the shooting had been accidental. When asked to describe his condition at the time of the shooting, he indicated that he had not been drunk, but had been "pretty high." His story was that the victim had attacked him with a knife when he resisted her sexual advances. He said that he had defended himself by firing a number of warning shots into the ground, and had then reloaded his revolver. The victim, he said, then attempted to take the gun from him, and the gun "went off" in the ensuing struggle. He said that he fled without seeking help for the victim because he was afraid. At the trial, his position was that he had acted in self-defense. Alternatively, he claimed that, in any event, the State's own evidence showed that he had been too intoxicated to form the specific intent necessary under Virginia law to sustain a conviction of murder in the first degree.

The trial judge, declaring himself convinced beyond a reasonable doubt that the petitioner had committed first-degree murder, found him guilty of that offense. . . . A petition for writ of error to the Virginia Supreme Court on the ground that the evidence was insufficient to support the conviction was denied. The petitioner then commenced this habeas corpus proceeding in the United States District Court for the Eastern District of Virginia, raising the same basic claim . . . the District Court found the record devoid of evidence of premeditation, and granted the writ. The Court of Appeals for the Fourth Circuit reversed the judgment. . . . The court was of the view that some evidence that the petitioner had intended to kill the victim could be found in the facts that the petitioner had reloaded his gun after firing warning shots, that he had had time to do so, and that the victim was then shot not once, but twice. The court also concluded that the state trial judge could have found that the petitioner was not so intoxicated as to be incapable of premeditation.

We granted certiorari to consider the petitioner's claim that, under *In re Winship, supra*, a federal habeas corpus court must consider not whether there was any evidence to support a state court conviction, but whether there was sufficient evidence to justify a rational trier of the facts to find guilt beyond a reasonable doubt.

II

Our inquiry in this case is narrow. The petitioner has not seriously questioned any aspect of Virginia law governing the allocation of the burden of production or persuasion in a murder trial. As the record demonstrates, the judge, sitting as factfinder in the petitioner's trial, was aware that the State bore the burden of establishing the element of premeditation, and stated that he was applying the reasonable doubt standard in his appraisal of the State's evidence. . . . His sole constitutional claim, based squarely upon *Winship,* is that the District Court and the Court of Appeals were in error in not recognizing that the question to be decided in this case is whether any rational factfinder could have concluded beyond a reasonable doubt that the killing for which the petitioner was convicted was premeditated. The question thus raised goes to the basic nature of the constitutional right recognized in the *Winship* opinion.

III

A

This is the first of our cases to expressly consider the question whether the due process standard recognized in *Winship* constitutionally protects an accused against conviction except upon evidence that is sufficient fairly to support a conclusion that every element of the crime has been established beyond a reasonable doubt. . . . [T]he answer to that question, we think, is clear.

In *Winship,* the Court held for the first time that the Due Process Clause of the Fourteenth Amendment protects a defendant in a criminal case against conviction "except upon proof beyond a reasonable doubt of every fact necessary to constitute the crime with which he is charged." In so holding, the Court emphasized that proof beyond a reasonable doubt has traditionally been regarded as the decisive difference between criminal culpability and civil liability. The standard of proof beyond a reasonable doubt, said the Court, "plays a vital role in the American scheme of criminal procedure," because it operates to give "concrete substance" to the presumption of innocence, to ensure against unjust convictions, and to reduce the risk of factual error in a criminal proceeding. At the same time, by impressing upon the factfinder the need to reach a subjective state of near certitude of the guilt of the accused, the standard symbolizes the significance that our society attaches to the criminal sanction, and thus to liberty itself.

The constitutional standard recognized in the *Winship* case was expressly phrased as one that protects an accused against a conviction except on "proof beyond a reasonable doubt." In short, *Winship* presupposes as an essential of the due process guaranteed by the Fourteenth Amendment that no person shall be made to suffer the onus of a criminal conviction except upon sufficient proof—defined as evidence necessary to convince a trier of fact beyond a reasonable doubt of the existence of every element of the offense.

B

. . . The *Winship* doctrine requires more than simply a trial ritual. A doctrine establishing so fundamental a substantive constitutional standard must also require that the factfinder will rationally apply that standard to the facts in evidence. A "reasonable doubt," at a minimum, is one based upon "reason." Yet a properly instructed jury may occasionally convict even when it can be said that no rational trier of fact could find guilt beyond a reasonable doubt, and the same may be said of a trial judge sitting as a jury . . . . Under *Winship,* which established proof beyond a reasonable doubt as an essential of Fourteenth Amendment due process, it follows that, when such a conviction occurs in a state trial, it cannot constitutionally stand.

After *Winship*, the critical inquiry on review of the sufficiency of the evidence to support a criminal conviction must be not simply to determine whether the jury was properly instructed, but to determine whether the record evidence could reasonably support a finding of guilt beyond a reasonable doubt. But this inquiry does not require a court to "ask itself whether it believes that the evidence at the trial established guilt beyond a reasonable doubt." Instead, the relevant question is whether, after viewing the evidence in the light most favorable to the prosecution, any rational trier of fact could have found the essential elements of the crime beyond a reasonable doubt. This familiar standard gives full play to the responsibility of the trier of fact fairly to resolve conflicts in the testimony, to weigh the evidence, and to draw reasonable inferences from basic facts to ultimate facts. Once a defendant has been found guilty of the crime charged, the factfinder's role as weigher of the evidence is preserved through a legal conclusion that, upon judicial review, *all of the evidence* is to be considered in the light most favorable to the prosecution. The criterion thus impinges upon "jury" discretion only to the extent necessary to guarantee the fundamental protection of due process of law.

IV

Turning finally to the specific facts of this case, we reject the petitioner's claim that, under the constitutional standard dictated by *Winship*, his conviction of first-degree murder cannot stand. A review of the record in the light most favorable to the prosecution convinces us that a rational factfinder could readily have found the petitioner guilty beyond a reasonable doubt of first-degree murder under Virginia law.

There was no question at the trial that the petitioner had fatally shot Mary Cole. The crucial factual dispute went to the sufficiency of the evidence to support a finding that he had specifically intended to kill her. This question, as the Court of Appeals recognized, must be gauged in the light of applicable Virginia law defining the element of premeditation. Under that law, it is well settled that premeditation need not exist for any particular length of time, and that an intent to kill may be formed at the moment of the commission of the unlawful act. *Commonwealth v. Brown*, 90 Va. 671, 19 S.E. 447. From the circumstantial evidence in the record, it is clear that the trial judge could reasonably have found beyond a reasonable doubt that the petitioner did possess the necessary intent at or before the time of the killing.

The prosecution's uncontradicted evidence established that the petitioner shot the victim not once, but twice. The petitioner himself admitted that the fatal shooting had occurred only after he had first fired several shots into the ground and then reloaded his gun. The evidence was clear that the two shots that killed the victim were fired at close, and thus predictably fatal, range by a person who was experienced in the use of the murder weapon. Immediately after the shooting, the petitioner drove without mishap from Virginia to North Carolina, a fact quite at odds with his story of extreme intoxication. Shortly before the fatal episode, he had publicly expressed an intention to have sexual relations with the victim. Her body was found partially unclothed. From these uncontradicted circumstances, a rational factfinder readily could have inferred beyond a reasonable doubt that the petitioner, notwithstanding evidence that he had been drinking on the day of the killing, did have the capacity to form and had in fact formed an intent to kill the victim.

The petitioner's calculated behavior both before and after the killing demonstrated that he was fully capable of committing premeditated murder.

For these reasons, the judgment of the Court of Appeals is affirmed.

It is so ordered.

Notes and Questions

1. *Jackson v. Virginia* involved review of a habeas corpus petition, but the holding provides the standard for a trial judge to assess whether a prosecutor satisfies the burden of production. As the Court notes, the question is not whether the judge believes the prosecutor has introduced evidence that indicates guilt is the *only* rational finding in the case, but instead whether that evidence indicates guilt could be *a* rational finding. At that point, the case should continue. At the close of the case, the question will be whether the evidence is sufficient to persuade the jury (or the judge acting as the trier of fact) that guilt is the *only* rational result.

2. When a prosecutor stands before a court and announces, "the prosecution rests," she must be confident that sufficient evidence has been admitted into the record to support the *prima facie* burden of production and withstand a motion for acquittal. Two simple checklists will provide confidence this burden has indeed been met. First, the prosecutor must ensure all the evidence she intended to introduce has in fact been *admitted* into evidence. Testimony is admitted when it is offered without objection, or when any defense objection is denied; exhibits are admitted when the judge accepts them into evidence on request of the party offering the exhibit. If a prosecutor offers an exhibit but forgets to ask the judge to admit the exhibit, the court will not consider it evidence when deciding a motion to acquit. Second, an "elements" checklist, which is a list of all the material elements the prosecutor must prove that cross-references the evidence that has been admitted to satisfy that element. Using such a checklist will mitigate the risk that the prosecution rests without realizing it overlooked introduction of evidence necessary to satisfy the *prima facia* burden of production.

3. Notice that Jackson asserted *two* defense theories. The first was that his intoxication "negated" premeditation. When courts refer to "negating" a material element, it really means some evidence or inference *blocks* the prosecution from satisfying its burden of proving that element beyond a reasonable doubt. This is what is best understood as a *failure of proof* defense theory: the prosecution failed to prove a requisite element beyond a reasonable doubt. But be careful not to assume the defense has a burden to prove the *absence* of that element. Because it is a material element

of the charged offense, all the defense has to do is offer or highlight some evidence that erects that obstacle to block the prosecution from proving it. At that point, it is the prosecution's burden to *persuade* the jury (or, as in *Jackson*, the trial judge acting as the fact finder) that the obstacle either doesn't exist, or if it does, it is not strong enough to prevent proving the element beyond a reasonable doubt. So, while the defense may have a functional burden to produce some evidence to demonstrate a failure to prove a material element, the ultimate burden of persuasion never shifts from the prosecution to prove that element. We can assume that the trial judge in *Jackson* considered the evidence Jackson was intoxicated (the obstacle to premeditation), and either didn't believe it (so there was no obstacle), or was persuaded by the prosecution that, even if intoxicated, he was still able to premeditate the killing.

Jackson also asserted that he acted in self-defense. This is a different type of defense called an *affirmative* defense. An affirmative defense does not contest the proof of a material element, but instead operates to negate the *unlawful* nature of the act because, pursuant to a legally recognized defense theory, the unique circumstances of the incident indicate that what is normally unlawful was in this particular case not unlawful. Affirmative defenses fall into two broad categories: justifications and excuses. Justifications are all about necessity: it was absolutely necessary for the defendant to take the law into his own hands to prevent a greater harm. Self-defense is the classic justification defense: a killing that would normally be unlawful was not because the defendant's action was necessary to prevent an imminent unlawful threat of death or great bodily harm. Note that when a defendant like Jackson asserts self-defense, he is not asserting he did not intend to kill, but instead that there is "more to the story" that shows what is normally unlawful is, in his case, justified and lawful.

Excuses focus on the lack of genuine mental culpability: because the defendant's reasoning process was so overwhelmed, it is not fair to hold her criminally responsible for the act. Hence, the criminal conduct is "excused." Lack of mental responsibility (insanity) is the classic excuse defense: if she is so severely mentally ill she believes her neighbor is a tree and kills the neighbor with an axe believing she is chopping down a tree, she will likely be not guilty based on the insanity defense because it serves no credible purpose to punish her. Because justification and excuse defenses do not challenge proof of a material element, it is legally permissible to put the burden on the defendant to prove the defense. For this reason, it is common in the U.S. that the defense bears the burden of proving an affirmative defense by a preponderance of the evidence (more likely than not), although some jurisdictions require the prosecution to disprove the defense beyond a reasonable doubt. Justification and excuse defenses will be covered in detail later in your course.

4. Lesser Included Offenses. What would have happened in *Jackson* if the judge had not been persuaded beyond a reasonable doubt that Jackson acted with premeditation? Would the result have been a complete acquittal? The answer requires you to understand the concept of a "lesser included offense." When a charged offense includes all of the elements of a lesser offense *plus* some additional element, the lesser offense is considered *necessarily included* in the greater offense, and therefore a lesser

included offense. In other words, by proving the greater offense, the prosecution has automatically proved the lesser offense. However, where the prosecution fails to prove the additional material element for the charged greater offense, conviction for the lesser included offense should be the result if the prosecution proved all of the necessarily included elements. For example, where the only difference between first-degree murder and second-degree murder is proof beyond a reasonable doubt the defendant acted with premeditation, a failure to prove *only* that element would result in conviction for the lesser included offense of unpremeditated second-degree murder. And the step down to a lesser offense might continue. Assume the difference between second-degree murder and manslaughter is proof beyond a reasonable doubt the defendant acted with malice. If there is reasonable doubt as to *that* element only, the defendant should be convicted of manslaughter. Consider this note from a standard jury instruction for premeditated murder:

> NOTE 2: Lesser included offenses otherwise raised. When the accused denies premeditated design to kill, or other evidence in the case tends to negate such design, an instruction on unpremeditated murder will ordinarily be necessary. If the denial extends to any intent to kill or inflict great bodily harm, or other evidence tends to negate such intent, an instruction on involuntary manslaughter must ordinarily be given.

5. Persuading a jury (or judge) that guilt is the only fair and rational finding based on the evidence is the prosecution's ultimate burden. But because it must be based on evidence and the rational inferences drawn from that evidence, the burden of production can be understood as the laying of an evidentiary foundation for the burden of persuasion. But remember that the burden of production means there is sufficient evidence to make guilt *a* rational option, not the *only* rational option. In other words, just because a prosecutor satisfies the burden of production does not mean the jury will be persuaded that guilt is the only rational option. So, try and remember this: *a prosecutor does not get to persuade unless she first produces; but just because she produces does not mean she will be able to persuade.*

6. Defendant is a member of a violent gang. One night he witnesses a shootout between a fellow gang member and members of an opposition gang. He sees Victim, an opposition gang member, get shot and fall to the ground. Once the shooting dies down, he walks over to Victim with a friend, tells the friend, "I'm going to do him," and shoots him twice in the head from point-blank range. Defendant is brought to trial for murder. The prosecution calls an expert witness who testifies that in his medical opinion the Victim, although on the verge of death from the original shots, was still alive when Defendant shot him. A second prosecution witness offers a similar opinion, but on cross-examination, concedes the evidence is not conclusive that the Victim was alive and he may have already been dead when Defendant shot him. At the close of the prosecution case-in-chief, Defendant moves for a finding of not guilty/acquittal on the murder charge based on the testimony of the second expert witness. You are the judge. Will you grant the motion and find the Defendant not guilty of murder?

The Charging Process

All criminal cases begin with a charge. In almost all cases, the charge will either take the form of a *criminal information*—a formal charge sworn by a prosecutor and filed with a court of appropriate jurisdiction, or a *true bill of indictment*—a charge alleged by a grand jury after reviewing evidence presented by a prosecutor in a non-adversarial proceeding. Indictment by grand jury is required for federal felony offenses and in some states, but not all. Whether by information or indictment, the charging instrument will identify the article of the criminal statute allegedly violated (the charge) and then provide a statement of the factual allegation (the specification). For example:

18 U.S.C. § 2119

The grand jury charges that on or about *(date)* at *[Tampa, Florida]* , in the *[Middle]* District of *[Florida]* [JOHN DOE] defendant herein, with the intent to cause death or serious bodily harm, did take from the person or presence of another, to wit, *(victim)* , by force and violence and intimidation, a motor vehicle that had been transported, shipped, or received in interstate commerce, that is, a 1996 Chevrolet Camaro, all in violation of Title 18, United States Code, Section 2119.

No matter what charging mechanism is used, the charge must satisfy two requirements. First, it must properly allege an offense. Second, it must be supported by probable cause, defined as facts and circumstances that indicate a fair probability that the defendant committed the crime.

A defendant may seek to have the charge dismissed by the court before the trial process ever begins. This is done by filling a motion to dismiss (or to quash the indictment). These motions are rarely successful, because the standard of probable cause is quite low and normally easily satisfied by the prosecution. But if the court concludes that the evidence is so completely lacking that it does not even warrant allowing the charge to go to trial, the motion will be granted. For example, if a defendant is charged with murder and the defense offers proof that the alleged victim is actually still alive, the charge must be dismissed. Or if the court determines that the charging document fails to properly allege an offense, meaning that even assuming the truth of the factual allegations, the conduct does not amount to the alleged crime, the charge will be dismissed. For example, if a defendant is charged with burglary but the specification alleges he broke into his own home, the charge would be dismissed because burglary requires a breaking and entering of the dwelling house of *another*; thus, even if the allegation is true, it is not the alleged crime.

If the burden of production is satisfied, meaning the judge denies a motion for acquittal, the next phase in the case is completely at the discretion of the defense. Because the defense has no burden to prove innocence—remember innocence is presumed as the starting point of the trial—the defense may simply forego offering any evidence and challenge the sufficiency of the prosecutor's evidence to prove guilt beyond a reasonable doubt. In most cases, however, the defense will offer evidence for one of two purposes. First, as noted above, the defense may argue the prosecution failed to prove a material element beyond a reasonable doubt by offering evidence that creates doubt on that material element. For example, if the prosecution seeks to prove a defendant acted with intent to kill and is relying on an inference of such intent from the fact that the defendant shot the victim, the defense might offer evidence showing the firearm was defective to suggest it fired accidentally; or that he was not trying to hit the victim but only scare him; or that he intended to shoot to wound.

The defense may also, as noted above, offer evidence of an affirmative defense. This is a defense theory, recognized by the law in the jurisdiction, that arises *after* the prosecution has met the burden of proving all the elements of the charged offense. In the hypothetical above, imagine the defendant testified he shot the victim intending only to wound him but also to defend himself. If intent to kill was a required element to prove the charged offense, the jury would be instructed to *first* decide whether the evidence proved that intent beyond a reasonable doubt. They will also be instructed to that *if* they find the defendant acted with intent to kill, they should *then* consider whether the defendant acted in self-defense. Thus, as noted above, an affirmative defense doesn't challenge the sufficiency of proof on any element of the offense, but is really like offering evidence that explains there "is more to the story."

Once the defense rests, the prosecution may offer more evidence to rebut the defense evidence. For example, if the defendant calls an expert to offer an opinion the gun was defective in a murder case, the prosecution may rebut that testimony with a different expert. Once all the evidence is presented, both parties will normally make a summation or closing argument to the jury. It is at that point that the jury must decide whether the totality of the evidence proves each element of the alleged offense beyond a reasonable doubt. This is the burden of persuasion, and with the exception of an affirmative defense, this burden is *always* on the prosecution. What exactly does beyond a reasonable doubt mean? At its simplest, it means that based on all the evidence, guilt is the *only* rational, or "reasonable," conclusion. In contrast, a reasonable doubt exists when guilt is not the only rational conclusion. Thus, the burden of persuasion means the prosecution must persuade the finder of fact that based on the evidence, there is only *one* fair and rational conclusion: guilt. In the example above, if a jury is not sure whether the defect in the firearm was why the victim was shot or whether it was an intentional act by the defendant, and that an accident is one of two rational explanations for the shooting, the prosecution has failed to meet its burden of persuasion on the intent element, and the jury should vote to acquit.

Satisfying the burden of persuasion by proving every element of the offense beyond a reasonable doubt does not mean the finder of fact must be convinced there is no doubt the defendant is guilty. In this sense, proof beyond a reasonable doubt tolerates the possibility that an innocent defendant will be convicted. But this burden of proof is the most demanding in our law, and is intended to mitigate the risk of a false conviction. Consider this definition of proof beyond a reasonable doubt:

> A reasonable doubt is an honest, conscientious doubt suggested by the material evidence or lack of it in the case. It is an honest misgiving generated by insufficiency of proof of guilt. "Proof beyond a reasonable doubt" means proof to an evidentiary certainty, although not necessarily to an absolute or mathematical certainty. The proof must exclude every fair and reasonable hypothesis of the evidence except that of guilt.

Quite simply, our criminal justice system is far more willing to accept the acquittal of an actually guilty defendant than the conviction of an actually innocent defendant. Indeed, during this course, you will encounter cases where a defendant seems to have been guilty but because of a failure of proof must be acquitted. Unfortunately, however, even with this demanding burden, it is an unfortunate reality that "cautious" does not always equate to "correct."

Visualizing the Criminal Trial Process

Criminal Case Stages

Stage	Charge	Trial	Deliberation
Description	Seriousness of charge (misdemeanor or felony) & State practice dictate the form of a criminal charge	PRO offers evidence for each element of offense	PRO & DEF make closing arguments regarding ultimate question of guilt
Evidence Required	Fair probability of offense (probable cause)	Sufficient evidence that provides enough proof of each element (could reasonable juror convict) ***Burden of production**	Totality of evidence (including inferences) persuades finder of fact that all elements proven beyond a reasonable doubt ***Burden of persuasion**
Motions/ Outcome	DEF Motion to Dismiss	DEF Motion for not guilty finding (Acquittal)	Guilty/Not Guilty
Standard	Must properly allege violation of statute and charge must be supported by probable cause	Judge assesses whether guilt is at least *A Reasonable Option* based on the evidence All inferences & credibility assessments favor PRO	Finder of fact (judge or jury) determines whether guilt is the ***Only Reasonable Conclusion*** Finder of fact determines evidence weight & credibility

© 2012 Geoffrey S. Corn

PRO = Prosecution
DEF = Defense

How Does a Court Decide Whether to Grant a Motion to Dismiss for Insufficient Proof?

As the image above indicates, the process of a criminal trial involves three important "gates" a prosecutor must pass through based on the available proof: first, overcoming a defense motion to dismiss for lack of probable cause; second, overcoming a defense motion for acquittal for failing to satisfy the burden of production; and finally, rebutting the presumption of innocence by satisfying the burden of persuasion.

Many students (and practitioners) struggle to understand the difference between a motion to dismiss and a motion for acquittal. The impact of defense success in each of these is very different. As you know from reading *Jackson v. Virginia* and the notes that followed, a motion for acquittal is made after the prosecution rests its case, and challenges the sufficiency of the prosecution's *prima facia* evidence by asserting that it is insufficient to support even a rational finding of guilt. If the court agrees, it means the prosecution has failed to satisfy the burden of production and, as a result, the court must enter a finding of not guilty on that charge. This means the defendant has been acquitted, and it would violate double jeopardy to retry the defendant on that charge.

A motion to dismiss asks the court to terminate the charge against the defendant because the prosecution cannot establish probable cause to support the allegation. If granted, the charge is dismissed; if denied, the charge is "bound over" for trial. In most jurisdictions, this motion will normally be adjudicated at a preliminary hearing or preliminary examination, and will be decided by the presiding judge.

The ultimate question the judge must resolve is whether there is probable cause to support the charge. Probable cause is a very low standard, normally defined as a fair probability based on a common sense, non-technical consideration of all the evidence presented. In most jurisdictions, the rules of evidence are relaxed at a preliminary hearing, so the court may be considering information that will not be admissible in evidence at a trial. As noted in *State v. Dunn*, 121 Wis. 2d 389 (1984), 359 N.W.2d 151:

> A defendant may be bound over for trial when the evidence at the preliminary hearing is sufficient to establish probable cause that a felony has been committed and that the defendant probably committed it ...

> "At common law it was customary, if not obligatory, for an arrested person to be brought before a justice of the peace shortly after arrest. ... The justice of the peace would 'examine' the prisoner and the witnesses to determine whether there was reason to believe the prisoner had committed a crime. If there was, the suspect would be committed to jail or bailed pending trial. If not, he would be discharged from

custody." *Gerstein v. Pugh*, 420 U.S. 103, 114–15 (1975) (citations and footnote omitted).

The *Dunn* decision offers insight into what is really meant by probable cause for a judge deciding a motion to dismiss:

> The focus of the judge at a preliminary hearing is to ascertain whether the facts and the reasonable inferences drawn therefrom support the conclusion that the defendant probably committed a felony. If inferences must be drawn from undisputed facts, as in this case, only reasonable inferences can be drawn. We stress that a preliminary hearing is not a proper forum to choose between conflicting facts or inferences, or to weigh the state's evidence against evidence favorable to the defendant. *State ex rel. Evanow*, 40 Wis. 2d at 228. That is the role of the trier of fact at trial. If the hearing judge determines after hearing the evidence that a reasonable inference supports the probable cause determination, the judge should bind the defendant over for trial. ***Simply stated, probable cause at a preliminary hearing is satisfied when there exists a believable or plausible account of the defendant's commission of a felony.***
>
> Requiring an examining judge to bind a defendant over for trial when there exists a set of facts that supports a reasonable inference that the defendant probably committed a felony sufficiently satisfies the purpose for preliminary hearings, i.e., that the accused is not being prosecuted too hastily, improvidently, or maliciously and that there exists a substantial basis for bringing the prosecution. . . .

State v. Dunn, 121 Wis. 2d 389, 397–398 (1984) (emphasis added).

Finally, unlike granting a motion for acquittal, granting a motion to dismiss at this preliminary stage of a case does not implicate double jeopardy. This means the prosecution can re-charge the defendant if it acquires additional sufficient evidence. This is because the protection of double jeopardy requires that the defendant had been in *prior* jeopardy for the same offense, and jeopardy attaches only when the trial jury is empaneled or, if a bench trial, when the prosecution calls the first witness.

Understanding—and being able to distinguish—the burden of production and the burden of persuasion is important and not just for criminal law.

Formative Assessments

1. You are the judge in the court-martial of a service-member accused of deserting his post during the hostilities in Afghanistan. Desertion "in time of war" is a capital offense, and the prosecution is seeking the death penalty. The defense files a motion

to dismiss the capital charge based on the text of the Manual for Courts-Martial, the regulation that implements the Uniform Code of Military Justice (UCMJ). That text provides that for purposes of offenses defined in the UCMJ, "time of war" means, "periods of war declared by Congress or the factual determination by the President that the existence of hostilities warrants a finding that a time of war exists for purposes of [all UCMJ offenses]." There is no such presidential finding, but the prosecution argues that because the operation is being conducted pursuant to a Joint Resolution enacted by Congress authorizing the use of military force (AUMF), and because Congress no longer formally declares war (last formal declaration was 1942), the court should treat the AUMF as the equivalent of a declaration of war. Will you grant or deny the motion?

2. On July 15, 2011, Casey Anthony was acquitted for, *inter alia,* first degree murder of her daughter. The prosecution was unable to produce any direct evidence Anthony killed the victim. Instead, it relied on circumstantial evidence suggesting Anthony had both motive and opportunity to kill the child, including the discovery of duct tape in her residence, evidence of Anthony providing false information to police during the investigation, and witness testimony about the strong odor of decomposition from the trunk of her car. Should the trial judge have allowed the murder charge to go to the jury? If not, why not?

Chapter 3

Actus Reus

I. Introduction

Actus reus—or "guilty act"—is considered to be the "cornerstone of discussion on the nature of criminal liability."[1]

In explaining actus reus, this chapter also introduces you to some of the challenges in learning American criminal law. Sometimes criminal law concepts and terms are comprised of one element and its meaning is self-evident. But for many concepts, including actus reus, there are several elements, some of which will not be intuitive or obvious. For example, there are three different elements of actus reus, one of which involves committing an act or taking action (which you might expect from the word "actus"), while the other two involve not doing something and possessing an item (which you probably wouldn't expect).

Actus reus typically refers to the conduct constituting an offense—the first element. But not all offenses require conduct. "In the absence of an act, liability may be based upon an omission to perform a legal duty of which the person is physically capable [second element], or upon a person's knowing possession of contraband for a period of time sufficient to terminate the possession [third element]."[2]

Similarly, elements will differ between common law and the MPC. Sometimes the differences are substantive and significant. Other times, as with actus reus, the common law and the MPC use different approaches or words to reach a substantially similar outcome.

Before this chapter provides an overview of the different elements of actus reus, consider why criminal law needs an act requirement. Professor Paul Robinson, a noted criminal law commentator, explains that there are several rationales for the act requirement, with some being stronger than others.

> By requiring an act, the law excludes from liability those persons who only fantasize about committing an offence and those persons who may

---

1. Paul H. Robinson, *Should the Criminal Law Abandon the Actus Reus/Mens Rea Distinction?*, 187, *in* ACTION AND VALUE IN CRIMINAL LAW (Stephen Shute et al eds. 1993).
2. Paul H. Robinson, *Mens Rea*, *in* ENCYCLOPEDIA OF CRIME & JUSTICE 997–998 (2002).

indeed form an intention to commit an offence but whose intention is not sufficiently firm that it will mature into action. . . .

[T]he act requirement provides some minimal objective confirmation that the defendant's intention does exist. Upon observing an action consistent with the intention, we feel more sure of the defendant's intention and her willingness to act upon it. . . .

The act requirement is [also] useful in providing a time and place of occurrence of an offence. While one's intention may range over a long period of time and many places, the conduct constituting the offence can [normally] be identified with a particular time and place.

Recall from Chapter 2 that in order to obtain a criminal conviction, a prosecutor must prove each material element of the crime or offense beyond a reasonable doubt. While the material elements for a given crime vary, the one constant is that *all crimes require a criminal act or actus reus.* While most crimes also normally require proof of other elements, most notably a criminal mens rea (the mental state), proof beyond a reasonable doubt the defendant committed the proscribed criminal act is a requirement for any conviction, even for the small category of crimes requiring no mens rea. Quite simply, a prosecutor's failure to prove the alleged actus reus is an absolute bar to conviction.

II. Overview

A. Actus Reus Element One—Voluntary Act

"[T]he criminal law's act requirement [mandates] that there be a simple bodily movement that is caused by a volition before criminal liability attaches."[3] The MPC states that "[a] person is not guilty of an offense unless his liability is based on conduct which includes a voluntary act . . . ,"[4] a codification of the common law concept of actus reus.

Importantly, *actus reus is not just bodily movement but bodily movement that is willed or volitional.* What are bodily movements which are not willed or not volitional? Consider a physical examination where a doctor taps a seated patient's knee with a rubber hammer. For patients with a healthy neurological system, what happens? The patient's knee jerks and the lower leg partially extends. The leg moved not because the patient wanted it to but as an example of a reflex or involuntary muscular response.

---

3. MICHAEL MOORE, ACT AND CRIME: THE PHILOSOPHY OF ACTION AND ITS IMPLICATIONS FOR CRIMINAL LAW, 45 (1993).
4. MPC § 2.01(1).

Examples of bodily movements which are not willed or volitional include: a reflex or convulsion; a bodily movement during unconsciousness or sleep; conduct during hypnosis or resulting from hypnotic suggestion; and a bodily movement that otherwise is not a product of the effort or determination of the actor, either conscious or habitual.[5] You should consider these as "red flags" that there may be a barrier to proving the actus reus element, but absent any indication of such involuntary physical action, it is normal and logical to infer that physical action was the product of will or volition. In other words, a prosecutor need not offer evidence of volition in every case; proof of the physical action infers volition absent some evidence suggesting otherwise.

B. Actus Reus Element Two—Culpable Omission

As the Supreme Court of Montana explained, "[f]or criminal liability to be based upon a failure to act, there must be a duty to act, and the person must be physically capable of performing the act."[6]

The second element of actus reus is a culpable omission. Omission refers to the failure to take action or commit a voluntary act. Culpable refers to blame, and to be more clear, legal blame. With a culpable omission, not doing something you were physically capable of doing may constitute the actus reus. It's easy to identify when someone doesn't do something, and generally, the physical capacity to perform the act isn't in question. The key to understanding what renders an omission culpable is to recognize when that failure to act is culpable, when it is legally blame worthy. The answer is that omissions or failures to act are legally blame worthy *only* when the person was a under a legal duty to act, was physically capable of taking the action, and failed to do so. The failure to act *absent* proof of legal duty, no matter how morally reprehensible, does not qualify as a culpable omission.

Being under a legal duty to act such that your failure to do so may constitute the actus reus of a criminal offense is very much an exception.[7] Normally, society does not criminalize inaction. This is referred to as "the American bystander rule." The rule recognizes that there is not, as a general matter, a legal duty for a person to render aid or rescue or call for help when someone else is at risk or in danger. Additionally, it doesn't matter if the aid or assistance could be provided without risk or even inconvenience to the rescuer. Society may recognize a moral duty to help each other, but failing to perform a moral duty cannot constitute the actus reus of a criminal offense.

---

5. *See* MPC § 2.01(2).

6. *State v. Kuntz*, 298 Mont. 146, 150 (2000).

7. One commentator argues that under conventional omission analysis, "legal duty" is an "imperfect proxy" for what the focus should be—"an appropriate causal relationship between the omission and the harm before liability is imposed." Arthur Leavens, *A Causation Approach to Criminal Omissions*, 76 Cal. L. Rev. 547 (1988). Consider making a note to return to Professor Leaven's contention after you have learned about criminal law causation.

In terms of culpable omissions, only where there is a legal duty to act may the failure to do so constitute the actus reus. "Thus, an Olympic swimmer may be deemed by the community as a shameful coward, or worse, for not rescuing a drowning child in the neighbor's pool, but she is no criminal."[8]

At common law, there are a number of exceptions to the bystander rule. The exceptions refer to situations where there is a legal duty to act based on:

(1) A personal relationship

(2) Statute

(3) Contract

(4) Voluntary assumption of care

(5) Creation of the peril

The cases and discussions that follow elaborate on the exceptions. Minor variations of the facts of a case may significantly change the assessment of legal duty and whether any of the exceptions apply. Returning to the Olympic swimmer from above, if the person drowning was her minor child or her spouse, who she could have but chose not to rescue, that failure to act would be a culpable omission constituting the actus reus. Similarly, if the swimmer was hired as a lifeguard, her not acting would be culpable. Where there is no personal relationship or contract, there wouldn't be a duty to act. But if the swimmer voluntarily elects to rescue the person and then abandons the effort, they may have voluntarily assumed a duty of care such that the abandonment constitutes a culpable omission. Finally, if the Olympic swimmer, knowing the person was not a strong swimmer, had talked them into swimming, the swimmer may be under a duty to act due to having created the peril, the risk of drowning.

> An example of a morally reprehensible omission that was insufficient to support criminal liability involved a U.S. Army solider whose girlfriend beat her 18-month-old son to death over a weekend. The soldier was present the entire time and had countless opportunities to save the child from the reign of terror that ultimately led to his death. However, the soldier had no legal *duty* to intervene on his behalf and did absolutely nothing to save or protect the child. When the death was discovered and the soldier confessed to his presence and inaction, military prosecutors tried to find some theory of legal duty to support a charge of murder by omission. They ultimately charged the soldier alleging a "quasi-familial" duty. However, the military judge dismissed the charge for failing to allege a valid offense. Like the common law and almost all U.S. jurisdictions, military law did not recognize any such legal duty. As a result, there was no basis to impose criminal responsibility for the soldier's unquestionably immoral conduct.

---

8. *Kuntz, supra* note 6, at 150 (quoting LeFave & Scott, Substantive Criminal Law § 3.3(a) (1986)).

The MPC, like the common law, provides that, "[l]iability for the commission of an offense may not be based on an omission unaccompanied by action unless: the omission is expressly made sufficient by the law defining the offense; or a duty to perform the omitted act is otherwise imposed by law."[9]

C. Actus Reus Element Three—Possession as an Act

The last type of actus reus is possession. Although not further discussed, this element is highlighted here for those criminal law classes which include either diagraming the material elements of various crimes and/or substantive discussion of status offenses.

The majority of offences are defined in terms of acting (element one) or omitting/failing to act (element two). But there are many crimes, notably involving possession of prohibited items or substances, which are considered status offenses.[10]

To provide a brief illustration of how possession as an act may arise, assume that police stop Mary and search the purse she was carrying, finding a small baggie of methamphetamine, which Mary claims to never have seen before. Was Mary in possession of the methamphetamine? The common law did not consider possession as part of the actus reus, but the MPC does. Under the MPC, "[p]ossession is an act . . . if the possessor knowingly procured or received the thing possessed or was aware of his control thereof for a sufficient period to have been able to terminate his possession."[11]

III. Voluntary Act

As you read the *Lara* case, pay particular attention to the role and importance of jury instructions.

State v. Lara
183 Ariz. 233 (1995)
Supreme Court of Arizona, En Banc

MARTONE, Justice.

Miguel Lara was convicted of aggravated assault. The court of appeals reversed, concluding that Lara was entitled to a "voluntary act" instruction and a lesser included offense instruction on disorderly conduct. *State v. Lara*, 179 Ariz. 578, 880 P.2d 1124 (App. 1994). Disagreeing with these conclusions, and believing that the "voluntary act" instruction raised an issue of importance, we granted review.

---

9. MPC § 2.01(3).

10. *See* J. Paul McCutcheon, *Knowledge and the Actus Reus of Possession Offences*, 32 IRISH JURIST 119 (!997).

11. MPC § 2.01(4).

After having been stalked and assaulted by Lara, Al Bartlett called the Tucson police and complained that Lara would not leave his house. Tucson police officer Kucsmas answered the call and was told by Bartlett that Lara was inside. Kucsmas walked in, saw Lara lying down on a couch and asked him to stand up. Lara got up and pointed a knife at Kucsmas. Kucsmas backed off and called for help. He retreated down a corridor, drew his pistol and told Lara to stop or he would shoot. Instead, Lara continued to walk towards him, called him names and slashed at him with the knife. Lara backed Kucsmas out of the house, swung the knife at him and said he was going to kill him. Finally, with Kucsmas backed into a fence, Lara raised his knife and lunged at him. Kucsmas then shot Lara.

Lara was charged with attempted murder and aggravated assault. A defense psychologist testified that Lara was suffering from some organic brain impairment and personality disorder. In such a person, he would expect to see a reduced ability to use good judgment in social situations, increased agitation, and an increased tendency to fly off into a tantrum or rage as if by reflex. Based on this sort of testimony, Lara asked for a voluntary act instruction under A.R.S. §13-201 and §13-105(34).[1] The trial court rejected the instruction. . . . The jury found Lara guilty of aggravated assault but acquitted him of attempted first degree murder.

A.R.S. §13-201 provides as follows:

> The minimum requirement for criminal liability is the performance by a person of conduct which includes a voluntary act or the omission to perform a duty imposed by law which the person is physically capable of performing.

A.R.S. §13-105(34)[2] defines "voluntary act" as "a bodily movement performed consciously and as a result of effort and determination." The court of appeals held that Lara was entitled to an instruction on these statutes because it believed that the expert testimony would have supported a finding that his behavior was "reflexive rather than voluntary." 179 Ariz. at 582, 880 P.2d at 1128. We disagree.

A.R.S. §13-201 is a codification of the common law requirement of actus reus that a crime requires an act. A guilty mind (mens rea) is not enough. And, under §13-105(34), an act means a conscious bodily movement caused by effort and determination. This is consistent with the common law. See Salmond on Jurisprudence 380-84 (8th ed. 1930); Sanford H. Kadish & Monrad G. Paulsen, Criminal Law and Its Processes 201–08 (1969); IV Roscoe Pound, Jurisprudence 410 (1959). Stating the obverse, then, a bodily movement while unconscious, asleep, under hypnosis,

---

1. Defendant's Requested Instruction No. 4 was:
   The State must prove that the defendant did a voluntary act forbidden by law. 'Voluntary act' means a bodily movement performed consciously and as a result of effort and determination.
2. Now §13-105(37).

or during an epileptic fit, is not a voluntary act. 1 Rudolph J. Gerber, Criminal Law of Arizona 201-1 (1993). The autonomic nervous system controls involuntary bodily functions. The heart muscle pumps without our intervention. Our lungs can ingest air without thought. Our eyes shut reflexively when the ophthalmologist tests us for glaucoma. These are the sorts of bodily movements that would not be "performed consciously and as a result of effort and determination" within the meaning of our statute.

Lara's expert testimony falls far short of this. He was not unconscious. He was relentless in his effort and determination. He was thus not entitled to a voluntary act instruction under A.R.S. § 13-201.

Recommended Arizona Jury Instruction Criminal Standard 17 (1989) . . . provides: "The State must prove that the defendant did a voluntary act forbidden by law." . . .

. . . [T]his instruction is . . . appropriate only if there is evidence to support a finding of a bodily movement performed unconsciously and without effort and determination. . . . As we have held, this is not such a case.

We affirm the judgment of the trial court. We vacate those parts of the opinion of the court of appeals that address the voluntary act. . . .

Notes and Questions

1. The *Lara* case is an "en banc" decision. En banc is French for "on the bench" and refers to when all the judges of a particular court hear a case. At trial, there is a single judge. On appeal, normally a group of the judges who serve on or at that court will sit as a panel. On occasion, all the judges of a particular appellate court will hear a case, which is reflected in the opinion by the words en banc.

2. In the United States, we know if there is an appeal that the defendant was found guilty of something at trial. While there are any number of bases of appeal, many of the criminal law cases you will read involve jury instructions. Often, an appellate defense attorney will argue that the trial judge failed to properly instruct the jury. But what is a jury instruction? As the Legal Information Institute explains,

> Jury instructions are instructions for jury deliberation that are written by the judge and given to the jury. At trial, jury deliberation occurs after evidence is presented and closing arguments are made. Jury instructions are the only guidance the jury should receive when deliberating and are meant to keep the jury on track regarding the basic procedure of the deliberation and the substance of the law on which their decision is based. Attorneys will propose instructions to the judge at the end of trial, often seeking specific phrasing that is advantageous to their client. However, the judge makes the final decision about content and phrasing. Jury instructions

should ideally be brief, concise, nonrepetitive, relevant to the case's details, understandable to the average juror, and should correctly state the law without misleading the jury or inviting unnecessary speculation.

3. The court in *Lara* noted that a bodily movement "while unconscious, asleep, under hypnosis, or during an epileptic fit, is not a voluntary act." What is the legal significance of a bodily movement not qualifying as a voluntary act?

a. Unconscious/asleep. "An 'act' committed while one is unconscious is in reality no act at all. It is merely a physical event or occurrence for which there can be no criminal liability." *State v. Utter*, 4 Wash. App. 137, 479 P.2d 946 (1971). In another case, an individual, Newman, was arrested and prosecuted for driving under the influence of intoxicants and claimed to suffer from a sleep walking disorder and that when the police pulled him over that he was sleep-driving. Newman acknowledged being intoxicated but not to being conscious while he was driving. As a result, according to Newman, his driving of his car was not a voluntary action and could not serve as the actus reus for the DUI charge. Newman claimed to have suffered from previous sleepwalking incidents, which was corroborated by a friend, though Newman had never previously sleep-walked outside his apartment. The trial court refused to allow Newman to present sleep-driving evidence. The Oregon Supreme Court reversed and held that Newman should be allowed to present evidence about whether he was conscious at the time he was allegedly committing the DUI. However, the court added that

> the state was entitled to present evidence that [Newman's] drinking or other volitional act resulted in [his] driving that evening. . . . [T]he state may also show a voluntary act with evidence that [Newman] had engaged in "sleep-driving" prior to this incident and failed to take adequate precautions to remove access to his car keys.

Oregon v. Newman, 353 Or. 632, 646 (2013).

One way a prosecutor may rebut evidence of lack of volition is to prove that there was a predicate volitional act (becoming intoxicated) that resulted in the involuntary act. Remember that the key when considering whether bodily movements were voluntary or willed/volitional is control. Could the person control their movements or not? Recognize, though, that defense attorneys and prosecutors bring different perspectives on where to ask the control question. Consider a nurse who has diabetes but fails to take prescribed insulin. During a hypoglycaemic episode, the nurse assaults a patient for which the nurse is criminally charged. Defense attorneys argued that the nurse's bodily movements in striking the patient were involuntary and caused by the drop in blood sugar. The prosecution did not dispute the potential byproducts of a hypoglycaemic episode but instead argued that the nurse, in not taking insulin as he knew he should, was the cause of the episode. In essence, the defense was arguing that there could not be criminal liability for uncontrollable bodily movements while the prosecution contended that the nurse did have control over taking—or not—the prescribed insulin. Thus, the defense was arguing involuntary act and the prosecution for culpable omission, which is discussed in the next section. The court agreed that "a self-induced incapacity will not excuse . . . nor will one which could have been reasonably foreseen as a result of either doing or omitting to do something, for example, taking alcohol against medical advice after using certain prescribed drugs or failing to have regular meals while taking insulin." *R. v. Quick* [1973] Q.B. 910.

Similarly, a host of defendants have claimed to have "sleep [insert name of action]" as the result of having taken prescription sleeping aids like "ambien." *See* Jamie Ducharme, *Roseanne Barr Just Used the 'Ambien Defense.' So Have Accused Murderers and Drunk Drivers*, TIME, May 30, 2018, https://time.com/5295281/ambien-defense-history/. This claim is more appropriately discussed as voluntary intoxication in Chapter 18.

b. Hypnosis. As discussed above, the MPC lists "conduct during hypnosis or due to hypnotic suggestion" as an example of involuntary behavior. It's unclear how often—if at all—criminal acts are allegedly being performed by individuals under hypnosis. One British commentator claimed that not one criminal defendant in the United Kingdom had successfully asserted that hypnosis precluded their committing voluntary acts. *See* James Mason, *The Willed Trance: Volition, Voluntariness and Hypnotised Defendants*, 85 J. CRIM. L. 26 (2020).

c. Epileptic fit. Epilepsy is a common but serious neurological condition, the main symptom of which is seizures, sudden spikes in the brain's electrical activity which briefly affect how the brain functions. There are different types of epileptic seizures, one of which involves involuntary muscle spasms. The word involuntary reflects that these spasms do not constitute voluntary acts. Imagine a person driving a car near a pedestrian mall/walkway has an epileptic seizure. As a result of the seizure, both the person's arms straighten causing the car to swerve onto the pedestrian mall/walkway, running over and killing three people. Should the driver be charged with the deaths? Does your answer depend on whether the driver knew he suffered from epilepsy? *See* Paul Walsh, *Charges: Man with History of Epileptic Seizures Kept Driving, Killed 3 in Crash Near MSP*, STAR TRIBUNE, Aug. 30, 2017, https://www.startribune.com/charges-man-with-history-of-epileptic-seizures-kept-driving-killed-3-in-crash-near-msp/442240593/. What if the driver knew he suffered from epilepsy and that he was supposed to take prescribed daily medication but failed to do so the day of the crash? Assume you are the district attorney, with what actus reus would you charge Mr. Haynes (the subject of the *Star Tribune* story above) with? What if you were Mr. Haynes' defense attorney; what is your actus reus argument?

Google your state's driver's license application form, which likely contains a section similar to that used by Texas:

REQUIRED INFORMATION FROM DRIVER LICENSE APPLICANTS ONLY (FOR CONFIDENTIAL USE OF THE DEPARTMENT ONLY)
MEDICAL HISTORY QUESTIONS

YES NO

1. ☐ ☐ Do you currently have or have you ever been diagnosed with or treated for any medical condition that may affect your ability to safely operate a motor vehicle?
   Examples, including but not limited to: Diagnosis or treatment for heart trouble, stroke, hemorrhage or clots, high blood pressure, emphysema (within the past two years) • progressive eye disorder or injury (i.e., glaucoma, macular degeneration, etc.) • loss of normal use of hand, arm, foot or leg • blackouts, seizures, loss of consciousness or body control (within the past two years) • difficulty turning head from side to side • loss of muscular control • stiff joints or neck • inadequate hand/eye coordination • medical condition that affects your judgment • dizziness or balance problems • missing limbs

   Please explain and identify your medical condition: _____

2. ☐ ☐ Do you have a mental condition that may affect your ability to safely operate a motor vehicle? If yes, how? Please explain:

3. ☐ ☐ Have you ever had an epileptic seizure, convulsion, loss of consciousness, or other seizure?

4. ☐ ☐ Do you have diabetes requiring treatment by insulin?

5. ☐ ☐ Do you have any alcohol or drug dependencies that may affect your ability to safely operate a motor vehicle or have you had any episodes of alcohol or drug abuse within the past two years?

6. ☐ ☐ Within the past two years have you been treated for any other serious medical conditions? Please explain:

7. ☐ ☐ Have you **EVER** been referred to the Texas Medical Advisory Board for Driver Licensing?

Notice how the questions are much broader than epilepsy. What do the conditions asked about have in common in terms of actus reus?

4. As mentioned above, the MPC also lists "bodily movement that otherwise is not a product of the effort or determination of the actor, either conscious or habitual" as not constituting a voluntary act. This provision allows for the potential of a defendant establishing that they didn't try to perform the bodily movement, that the movement was not their goal and that the movement was caused by something outside the defendant's control. In practice, defendants often struggle with introducing sufficient evidence to generate such an "automatism" jury instruction. *See State v. Utter*, 4 Wash. App. 137, 479 P.2d 946 (1971) (discussing a World War II veteran's attempts to characterize stabbing his son in the chest as a conditioned response from military training. Utter killed his son in 1970, had received military training in 1942 and could only testify to two instances, both in the 1950s, where he reacted violently towards people approaching him from the rear). Additionally, Utter claimed no memory of stabbing his son or the circumstances leading up to it. A conditioned response, "an act or a pattern of activity occurring so rapidly, so uniformly as to be automatic in response to a certain stimulus" could fall under the MPC provision. The court did not believe Utter introduced "substantial evidence" to support his conditioned response claim. Do you agree?

5. A 2011 law review article contended that automatistic behavior or dissociative state in veterans with post-traumatic stress disorder (PTSD) could negate the actus reus element "such that the veteran is not engaged in a voluntary act and therefore not criminally culpable." Melissa Hamilton, *Reinvigorating Actus Reus: The Case for Involuntary Actions by Veterans with Post Traumatic Stress Disorder*, 16 Berk. J. Crim. L. 340, 342 (2011). The law review article referenced a *New York Times* investigation of 121 cases "in which Iraq and Afghanistan veterans were allegedly involved in a homicide after returning to the United States." *Id.* Purportedly, combat trauma and other deployment stresses were factors that "appear[ed] to set the stage for" the homicides. Hamilton warns that "[t]he relationship between PTSD and criminal offending is

considered to be so significant that the president of the National Veterans Federation, who has authored a book on PTSD, warns that the criminal justice system is facing an epidemic of veterans with PTSD being charged with crimes." *Id.*

6. Volition is normally inferred from physical action. This means that a defendant challenging the voluntariness of a physical action bears an implied burden of production: the defense must offer (or point to) some evidence that supports a finding the act was involuntary. As the court in *Lara* explained, a jury instruction on proving the actus reus element is appropriate "only if there is evidence to support a finding of a bodily movement performed unconsciously and without effort and determination." Without this rule, the prosecution would be required to present evidence of volition in every case involving an alleged criminal act.

IV. Culpable Omission

Recall from the introduction that the key to the second type of actus, culpable omission, is the existence of legal duty to act. Only where there is a duty to act can the failure to do so constitute a culpable omission and the actus reus of a criminal offense. As you read *Pestinikas*, there is a clear focus on the underlying contract. Before reading the case, briefly review the other exceptions to the bystander rule discussed above. Would any other exceptions potentially apply in *Pestinikas*?

Commonwealth v. Pestinikas
421 Pa. Super. 371 (1992)
Pennsylvania Superior Court

WIEAND, Judge:

The principal issue in this appeal is whether a person can be prosecuted criminally for murder when his or her failure to perform a contract to provide food and medical care for another has caused the death of such other person. The trial court answered this question in the affirmative and instructed the jury accordingly. The jury thereafter found Walter and Helen Pestinikas guilty of murder of the third degree in connection with the starvation and dehydration death of ninety-two (92) year old Joseph Kly. [1] On direct appeal from the judgment of sentence,[2] the defendants contend that the trial court misapplied the law and gave the jury incorrect instructions. They argue, therefore, that they are entitled to an arrest of judgment because of the insufficiency of the evidence against them or at least a new trial because of the trial court's erroneous instructions to the jury.

---

1. The jury acquitted both defendants of criminal conspiracy, and Walter Pestinikas was also acquitted of intimidating witnesses.

2. Each appellant was sentenced to serve a term of imprisonment for not less than five (5) years nor more than ten (10) years. Separate convictions for recklessly endangering another person were deemed to merge for sentencing purposes in the convictions for murder of the third degree.

Joseph Kly met Walter and Helen Pestinikas in the latter part of 1981 when Kly consulted them about pre-arranging his funeral. In March, 1982, Kly, who had been living with a stepson, was hospitalized and diagnosed as suffering from Zenker's diverticulum, a weakness in the walls of the esophagus, which caused him to have trouble swallowing food. In the hospital, Kly was given food which he was able to swallow and, as a result, regained some of the weight which he had lost. When he was about to be discharged, he expressed a desire not to return to his stepson's home and sent word to appellants that he wanted to speak with them. As a consequence, arrangements were made for appellants to care for Kly in their home on Main Street in Scranton, Lackawanna County.

Kly was discharged from the hospital on April 12, 1982. When appellants came for him on that day they were instructed by medical personnel regarding the care which was required for Kly and were given a prescription to have filled for him. Arrangements were also made for a visiting nurse to come to appellants' home to administer vitamin B-12 supplements to Kly. Appellants agreed orally to follow the medical instructions and to supply Kly with food, shelter, care and the medicine which he required.

According to the evidence, the prescription was never filled, and the visiting nurse was told by appellants that Kly did not want the vitamin supplement shots and that her services, therefore, were not required. Instead of giving Kly a room in their home, appellants removed him to a rural part of Lackawanna County, where they placed him in the enclosed porch of a building, which they owned, known as the Stage Coach Inn. This porch was approximately nine feet by thirty feet, with no insulation, no refrigeration, no bathroom, no sink and no telephone. The walls contained cracks which exposed the room to outside weather conditions. Kly's predicament was compounded by appellants' affirmative efforts to conceal his whereabouts. Thus, they gave misleading information in response to inquiries, telling members of Kly's family that they did not know where he had gone and others that he was living in their home.

After Kly was discharged from the hospital, appellants took Kly to the bank and had their names added to his savings account. Later, Kly's money was transferred into an account in the names of Kly or Helen Pestinikas, pursuant to which moneys could be withdrawn without Kly's signature. Bank records reveal that from May, 1982, to July, 1983, appellants withdrew amounts roughly consistent with the three hundred ($300) dollars per month which Kly had agreed to pay for his care. Beginning in August, 1983 and continuing until Kly's death in November, 1984, however, appellants withdrew much larger sums so that when Kly died, a balance of only fifty-five ($55) dollars remained. In the interim, appellants had withdrawn in excess of thirty thousand ($30,000) dollars.

On the afternoon of November 15, 1984, when police and an ambulance crew arrived in response to a call by appellants, Kly's dead body appeared emaciated, with his ribs and sternum greatly pronounced. Mrs. Pestinikas told police that she and her husband had taken care of Kly for three hundred ($300) dollars per month and that she had given him cookies and orange juice at 11:30 a.m. on the morning of his death. A subsequent autopsy, however, revealed that Kly had been dead at that time and may have been dead for as many as thirty-nine (39) hours before his body was found. The cause of death was determined to be starvation and dehydration. Expert testimony opined that Kly would have experienced pain and suffering over a long period of time before he died.

At trial, the Commonwealth contended that after contracting orally to provide food, shelter, care and necessary medicine for Kly, appellants engaged in a course of conduct calculated to deprive Kly of those things necessary to maintain life and thereby cause his death. The trial court instructed the jury that appellants could not be found guilty of a malicious killing for failing to provide food, shelter and necessary medicines to Kly unless a duty to do so had been imposed upon them by contract. The court instructed the jury, inter alia, as follows:

> In order for you to convict the defendants on any of the homicide charges or the criminal conspiracy or recklessly endangering charges, you must first find beyond a reasonable doubt that the defendants had a legal duty of care to Joseph Kly. There are but two situations in which Pennsylvania law imposes criminal liability for the failure to perform an act. One of these is where the express language of the law defining the offense provides for criminal [liability] based upon such a failure. The other is where the law otherwise imposes a duty to act. Unless you find beyond a reasonable doubt that an oral contract imposed a duty to act upon Walter and Helen Pestinikas, you must acquit the defendants.

Appellants contend that this was error.

The applicable law appears at 18 Pa.C.S. § 301(a) and (b) as follows:

> (a) General rule. A person is not guilty of an offense unless his liability is based on conduct which includes a voluntary act or the omission to perform an act of which he is physically capable. (b) Omission as basis of liability. Liability for the commission of an offense may not be based on an omission unaccompanied by action unless: (1) the omission is expressly made sufficient by the law defining the offense; or (2) a duty to perform the omitted act is otherwise imposed by law.

With respect to subsection (b), Toll, in his invaluable work on the Pennsylvania Crimes Code, has commented

> ... [Subsection (b)] states the conventional position with respect to omissions unaccompanied by action as a basis of liability. Unless the omission is expressly made sufficient by the law defining the offense, a duty to perform the omitted act must have been otherwise imposed by law for the omission to have the same standing as a voluntary act for purposes of liability. *It should, of course, suffice, as the courts now hold, that the duty arises under some branch of the civil law. If it does, this minimal requirement is satisfied, though whether the omission constitutes an offense depends as well on many other factors.*

Toll, Pennsylvania Crimes Code Annotated, § 301, at p. 60, quoting Comment, Model Penal Code § 2.01 (emphasis added).

In *State v. Brown*, 129 Ariz. 347, 631 P.2d 129 (1981), the Court of Appeals for Arizona affirmed a manslaughter conviction of the operator of a boarding home in connection with the starvation death of a ninety-eight-year-old resident. The Arizona Court interpreted a statutory provision which is similar to Section 301 of the Pennsylvania Crimes Code in the following manner:

> As stated in A.R.S. Sec. 13-201 and demonstrated by the case law, the failure to perform a duty imposed by law may create criminal liability. In the case of negligent homicide or manslaughter, the duty must be found outside the definition of the crime itself, perhaps in another statute, or in the common law, or in a contract. The most commonly cited statement of the rule is found in *People v. Beardsley*, 150 Mich. 206, 113 N.W. 1128 (1907): "The law recognizes that under some circumstances the omission of a duty owed by one individual to another, where such omission results in the death of the one to whom the duty is owing, will make the other chargeable with manslaughter. ... This rule of law is always based upon the proposition that the duty neglected must be a legal duty, and not a mere moral obligation. It must be a duty imposed by law or by contract, and the omission to perform the duty must be the immediate and direct cause of death. (citations omitted)" 113 N.W. at 1129.
>
> In *Jones v. United States*, 308 F.2d 307 (C.A.D.C.1962), the court stated:
>
> "There are at least four situations in which the failure to act may constitute breach of a legal duty. One can be held criminally liable: first, where a statute imposes a duty to care for another; second, where one stands in a certain status relationship to another; third, where one has assumed a contractual duty to care for another; and fourth, where one has voluntarily assumed the care of another and so secluded the helpless person as to prevent others from rendering aid." 308 F.2d at 310.

State v. Brown, supra, 129 Ariz. at 349-350, 631 P.2d at 131-132 (footnote omitted).

A similar rationale was employed by the Supreme Court of Virginia in *Davis v. Commonwealth*, 230 Va. 201, 335 S.E.2d 375 (1985), which upheld the conviction of a woman for involuntary manslaughter in the death by starvation and exposure of her elderly mother. The *Davis* Court held that the evidence had established the breach of an implied contract to care for her mother, in return for which the defendant had been permitted to live in her mother's home and share her mother's social security benefits. The legal principles upon which this holding was based were explained by the Supreme Court of Virginia as follows:

> A legal duty is one either "imposed by law, or by contract." *Pierce v. Commonwealth*, 135 Va. 635, 651, 115 S.E. 686, 691 (1923). When a death results from an omission to perform a legal duty, the person obligated to perform the duty may be guilty of culpable homicide. *Biddle v. Commonwealth*, 206

Va. 14, 20, 141 S.E.2d 710, 714 (1965); Pierce, 135 Va. at 651, 115 S.E. at 691. If the death results from a malicious omission of the performance of a duty, the offense is murder. On the other hand, although no malice is shown, if a person is criminally negligent in omitting to perform a duty, he is guilty of involuntary manslaughter. *Biddle*, 206 Va. at 20, 141 S.E.2d at 714.

Davis v. Commonwealth, supra, 230 Va. at 205, 335 S.E.2d at 378.

"The omission or neglect to perform a legal duty resulting in death may constitute murder where the omission was willful and there was deliberate intent to cause death. So also, willfully allowing one to be exposed to conditions which will probably result in death, where there is a duty to protect such person, constitutes murder." 40 C.J.S., Homicide, § 41, at p. 402 (citations omitted).

As a general rule, where one person owes to another either a legal or a contractual duty, an omission to perform that duty resulting in the death of persons to whom the duty was owing renders the person charged with the performance of such duty guilty of a culpable homicide. If several enter into a joint undertaking imposing upon all alike a personal duty in respect of its performance, the death of a third party by reason of the neglect or omission of such duty renders them all jointly liable. The duty imposed, however, must be a plain duty. It must be one on which different minds must agree, or generally agree, and which does not admit of any discussion as to its obligatory force. Where doubt exists as to what conduct should be pursued in a particular case, and intelligent men differ as to the proper action to be taken, the law does not impute guilt to anyone, where, from the omission to adopt one course instead of another, fatal consequences follow to others. The law does not enter into the reasons governing the conduct of men in such cases to determine whether they are culpable. Again, the duty must be one which the party is bound to perform by law or by contract, and not one the performance of which depends simply upon his humanity, or his sense of justice or propriety. It has been said that a legal duty to assist another does not arise out of a mere moral duty. Furthermore, where a legal duty is shown to have existed, it must also appear as a condition to culpability that the death was the direct and immediate consequence of the omission.

Consistently with this legal thinking we hold that when, in 18 Pa.C.S. § 301(b)(2), the statute provides that an omission to do an act can be the basis for criminal liability if a duty to perform the omitted act has been imposed by law, the legislature intended to distinguish between a legal duty to act and merely a moral duty to act. A duty to act imposed by contract is legally enforceable and, therefore, creates a legal duty. It follows that a failure to perform a duty imposed by contract may be the basis for a charge of criminal homicide if such failure causes the death of another person and all other elements of the offense are present. Because there was evidence in the instant case that Kly's death had been caused by appellants' failure to provide the food and medical care which they had agreed by oral contract to provide for him, their omission to act was sufficient to support a conviction for criminal homicide, and the trial court was correct when it instructed the jury accordingly.

Our holding is not that every breach of contract can become the basis for a find-ing of homicide resulting from an omission to act. A criminal act involves both a physical and mental aspect. An omission to act can satisfy the physical aspect of criminal conduct only if there is a duty to act imposed by law. A failure to provide food and medicine, in this case, could not have been made the basis for prosecuting a stranger who learned of Kly's condition and failed to act. Even where there is a duty imposed by contract, moreover, the omission to act will not support a prosecu-tion for homicide in the absence of the necessary mens rea. For murder, there must be malice. Without a malicious intent, an omission to perform duties having their foundation in contract cannot support a conviction for murder. In the instant case, therefore, the jury was required to find that appellants, by virtue of contract, had undertaken responsibility for providing necessary care for Kly to the exclusion of the members of Kly's family. This would impose upon them a legal duty to act to pre-serve Kly's life. If they maliciously set upon a course of withholding food and medi-cine and thereby caused Kly's death, appellants could be found guilty of murder.

Appellants' reliance upon *Commonwealth v. Konz*, 498 Pa. 639, 450 A.2d 638 (1982), is misplaced. In that case, the Court did not consider criminal respon-sibility for an omission to perform a duty imposed by contract, but considered only the nature of the duties arising from the marital relationship. The Court held that where a husband was aware of his condition, i.e., diabetes, and competently made a voluntary decision to forego further treatment, i.e., insulin, his wife was not criminally liable for failing to summon medical help. Because Konz was care-fully limited by the Court to its own facts, it provides little, if any, guidance in the instant case.

With respect to the alleged insufficiency of the evidence, it may also be observed that appellants' culpable conduct, according to the evidence, was not limited merely to an omission to act. It consisted, rather, of an affirmative course of conduct calcu-lated to deprive Kly of the food and medical care which was otherwise available to him and which was essential to continued life. It included efforts to place Kly beyond the ability of others to provide such needs. Such a course of conduct, the jury could find, as it did, had been pursued by appellants willfully and maliciously, who thereby caused Kly's death.

Appellants argue that, in any event, the Commonwealth failed to prove an enforce-able contract requiring them to provide Kly with food and medical attention. It is their position that their contract with Kly required them to provide only a place for Kly to live and a funeral upon his death. This obligation, they contend, was fulfilled. Although we have not been provided with a full and complete record of the trial, it seems readily apparent from the partial record before us, that the evidence was suf-ficient to create an issue of fact for the jury to resolve. The issue was submitted to the jury on careful instructions by the learned trial judge and does not present a basis entitling appellants to post-trial relief.

AFFIRMED.

Notes and Questions

1. If not for the contract, do you think the court in *Pestinakis* would still have found a duty to act existed? If so, on what basis?

2. Returning to the common law list of exceptions to the bystander rule previewed in the introduction:

a. A personal relationship. A duty to act clearly exists between parent-child and between spouses. Beyond that, courts are reluctant to recognize a duty. What do you think? The night before Jack and Jill marry, Jill has no legal duty to help Jack but then does have a duty 24 hours later? How strictly should the parent-child relationship be defined? What if the biological parents are deceased and the child's grandparents have raised him since birth? Should the grandparents have a legal duty to act under the parent-child personal relationship?

b. Statute. Statutory duty means just that, that there is a statute which imposes a legal duty to act. For example, most public-school teachers and medical providers are subject to a statutory obligation to report suspected child abuse; failing to do so could be alleged as a basis for criminal liability for subsequent injury to the child.

c. Contract. This is largely *Pestinikas*. In terms of finding a legal duty to act such that the failure to do so could constitute a culpable omission, courts seem to prefer contract-based duties involving money over the often ambiguous alternatives.

d. Voluntary assumption of care. Where someone voluntarily begins to render assistance or provide care, but then ceases to do so and a criminal harm results, the inaction may constitute a culpable omission. Courts generally limit volunteers having a legal duty to act to situations where, having assumed care, the volunteer acts in a way that deters others from providing assistance and/or the volunteer has secluded the individual from other potential assistance.

e. Creation of the peril. This exception to the bystander rule arises when culpable action imperils another. For example, a hunter who negligently shots another hunter would be under a duty to seek medical aid for the victim.

3. In 2019, Michele Carter was convicted of killing her primarily online boyfriend Conrad Ray, who committed suicide. *See Commonwealth v. Carter*, 481 Mass. 352, 115 N.E.3d 559 (2019). The case is the rare example of criminal liability for the death of someone who killed themselves. Carter and Conrad exchanged thousands of text messages and talked on the phone but rarely met in person. By way of example, Carter sent Conrad more than 1,000 text messages in the week prior to his death. Conrad had a history of mental illness and a previous failed suicide attempt, all of which Carter knew. At trial, both the prosecution and defense focused on the text messages, but that focus appears to have been misplaced. Carter elected to be tried by a judge and not a jury. In his ruling, the judge focused on the morning Conrad killed himself and how Carter, over the phone, convinced him to drive to a Kmart parking lot early in the morning where and when his efforts to kill himself were less

likely to be interrupted than if he had tried at home, where he lived with his parents. Conrad funneled car exhaust into the truck and re-entered the truck. After sitting in the truck filling with toxic exhaust fumes (carbon-monoxide), he got out, at which time Carter cajoled and manipulated him to return. Conrad returned to his truck and subsequently died from breathing in the fumes. After Conrad's death Carter sent friends text messages acknowledging that she could have saved Conrad. Starting with the baseline, the bystander rule that individuals generally don't have a legal duty to help someone, which exception(s) do you think the judge relied on to find that Carter had a legal duty to act such that her failure to do so constituted a culpable omission and the actus reus of a criminal offense? Do you agree with the result that Carter was criminally responsible for Conrad's suicide?

4. Fraternity hazing deaths. There have been a number of incidents during fraternity initiations where aspiring or new members of the fraternity are forced to drink large amounts of alcohol. In several tragic cases, serious injury and even death have resulted. In 2017, a 19-year-old sophomore, Tim Piazza, was undergoing hazing at the Beta Theta Pi fraternity at Penn State University. The hazing consisted of drinking large amounts of alcohol as part of an obstacle course referred to as "The Gauntlett." At some point, Piazza fell on the stairs and was knocked unconscious. Fraternity members carried him to a couch but prohibited anyone from calling 911 as the fraternity was not supposed to be serving alcohol at all, let alone to underage individuals like Piazza. Throughout the night, Piazza partially regained consciousness and would roll off the couch or fall trying to climb the stairs. By the time fraternity members called for medical aid, Piazza's blood alcohol level was .40, he had a ruptured spleen, and his brain had so swollen that surgeons removed half his skull in an unsuccessful effort to relieve the pressure. Piazza was pronounced dead the day after the party. Did the fraternity members have a *legal* duty to act? Do you distinguish between those who saw Piazza fall and did nothing from those who may have just seen him passed out and did nothing? What of the members who prohibited an earlier call for medical assistance? Would your answers change if the Fraternity had a code by which all members pledged to look out for or always help a brother member? *See* Sheryl Gay Stolberg, *18 Penn State Students Charged in Fraternity Death*, N.Y. TIMES, May 5, 2017, https://www.nytimes.com/2017/05/05/us/penn-state-fraternity -death-timothy-piazza.html.

5. Bystanders Beware? It's important to remember that culpable omissions as actus reus are the exception to the norm—the bystander rule. The bystander rule recognizes that we do not have a legal duty to help each other. There are any number of unfortunate examples of the bystander rule applied. In Ohio, a man took video of teens dying in a car crash rather than call for help. The only criminal charge he faced was trespass as he reached into the teens' car to record the video. *See Ohio man who recorded aftermath of fatal crash gets 30 days in jail*, REUTERS, Jan. 13, 2016, https:// www.reuters.com/article/us-ohio-video/ohio-man-who-recorded-aftermath-of-fatal -crash-gets-30-days-in-jail-idUSKCN0US0B120160114. In Long Island, as many as 70 people witnessed an 18-year-old stabbing a 16-year-old outside a strip mall. *See*

Madeleine Thompson, *A New York student was fatally stabbed while onlookers took a video of his suffering*, CNN, Sept. 20, 2019, https://www.cnn.com/2019/09/18/us/new-york-teen-fatally-stabbed-video/index.html According to police, the onlookers "videoed his death, instead of helping him." *Id.* In that case, the onlookers faced no criminal liability at all. While you may find the application of the bystander rule disheartening, consider returning to this note after you read Chapter 15 Liability for the Conduct of Another. While bystanders are not subject to criminal liability for failing to help, very little is required for a bystander to become an accomplice. As will be discussed in Chapter 15, even verbal encouragement, if offered with the intent of facilitating the crime, is enough to transition a bystander into an accomplice. As you will learn, accomplices face the same liability as principals. In the Long Island example, if one of the onlookers had done nothing more than yelled encouragement to the 18-year-old attacker, if that encouragement was offered with the intent of facilitating the crime, then the onlooker could be charged with the same crime as the attacker—in that case, second degree murder.

6. The state may, of course, change this bystander equation by imposing a statutory obligation to act when feasible to prevent harm, or, more commonly, a statutory obligation to report criminal misconduct. Consider the following Florida statute:

Duty to report sexual battery; penalties.—A person who observes the commission of the crime of sexual battery and who:

(1) Has reasonable grounds to believe that he or she has observed the commission of a sexual battery;

(2) Has the present ability to seek assistance for the victim or victims by immediately reporting such offense to a law enforcement officer;

(3) Fails to seek such assistance;

(4) Would not be exposed to any threat of physical violence for seeking such assistance;

(5) Is not the husband, wife, parent, grandparent, child, grandchild, brother, or sister of the offender or victim, by consanguinity or affinity; and

(6) Is not the victim of such sexual battery is guilty of a misdemeanor of the first degree.

Why do you think Florida would enact such a specific duty to report provision? Would a person who observes a robbery, aggravated (non-sexual) assault, or murder have any obligation to report the offense? Why not enact a broader provision applicable to all felonies? To all violent crimes?

Formative Assessments

1. All criminal offenses require which of the following:

A. Actus reus

B. Mens rea

C. Attendant circumstances

D. Actus reus and mens rea

E. Actus reus, mens rea and attendant circumstances

2. Barney and Fred have been neighbors for years but have never gotten along. Many of their arguments end with one—or both—wishing out loud that the other would die. One day, Barney observes Fred trying to operate a new piece of yard equipment. In the process, Fred badly cuts himself. The cut is so deep that Fred needs both hands to apply pressure. Fred sees Barney next door sitting on his porch and talking on his phone. Fred yells to Barney to call 911. Barney hears Fred, ends his call and begins filming Fred and posting video segments to the website "Am I the Dummy?" Barney remains on his porch the entire time. He does not call for help, and Fred bleeds to death in Fred's front yard. Barney's actions—and inaction—cause an uproar in the community and there are calls for police to arrest Barney. Which of the following most accurately reflects Barney's legal liability, if any?

A. Criminal liability requires a culpable act. Barney's recording Fred and posting the video to a website constituted one or more culpable acts.

B. Barney did not owe a legal duty of care to Fred as his neighbor. Because of that, Barney's subsequent inaction was not a culpable omission.

C. Barney owed a legal duty of care to Fred as his neighbor. Barney's subsequent failure to call 911 constitutes a culpable omission.

D. Criminal liability requires a culpable act. There is no way for someone who does nothing/takes no action (like Barney) can commit a culpable act.

3. Bodily movement is the key component of the criminal law act requirement.

A. True

B. False

4. Howard was arrested for his role in a fight at local bar. Howard was sitting at the bar drinking a beer when Eddie, someone Howard didn't know, placed his hand on Howard's right shoulder in an effort to move closer to the bar to order a drink. Howard, using his right arm/hand immediately struck Eddie, knocking him unconscious. What is Howard's strongest argument that he did not commit a criminal act?

A. That he struck Eddie as the result of having consumed multiple energy drinks.

B. That he struck Eddie as the result of having consumed multiple alcoholic drinks.

C. That he struck Eddie as the result of having ingested methamphetamine.

D. That he struck Eddie as the result of a neurologic condition involving his right shoulder/arm/hand.

Chapter 4

The Criminal Mental State

I. Introduction

Mens rea is a term that is used to denote the requisite mental state for criminal culpability. Literally translated, mens rea means "the guilty mind." In practical terms, mens rea refers to the criminal mental state that actuates or sets in motion the criminal act, omission, or possession that produces the prohibited social harm. The requisite criminal mental state is established by the definition of the crime, and serves two functions. First, it establishes the mental state the prosecution must prove beyond a reasonable doubt in order to secure conviction for the offense. Second, it will often dictate the *degree* of culpability for a particular offense. For example, in the many jurisdictions that define crimes such as murder in degrees, mens rea will be required to prove murder, but may also distinguish different degrees of murder.

While there are many minor or regulatory offenses that require no mens rea, such as traffic offenses, outside this category, almost all crimes require proof of a criminal mental state, or mens rea. The exception to this rule is a small group of serious offenses called strict liability crimes, such as statutory rape, bigamy, and in some jurisdictions, adultery. These crimes are established by proving the criminal act and the social harm (the *reus*) with no requirement to prove *any* criminal mental state to establish culpability. Such crimes are disfavored by courts based on a core axiom of criminal law: criminal culpability requires a criminal mind that moves the criminal hand. One without the other is simply unworthy of penal punishment.

A. The Evolution of Mens Rea

Perhaps the most frustrating aspect of learning about mens rea is the variety of terminology used throughout statutes and jurisprudence. There is simply no uniform "list" of mens rea terms, and in many cases, a term will mean different things in different jurisdictions. For example, a common sense understanding of the mens rea term *intent* would suggest a purpose to achieve a certain outcome. However, as you will learn, intent is often satisfied by proof the defendant acted with the mental state of purpose *or* knowledge of substantial certainty.

To facilitate your understanding of criminal law, our coverage of mens rea will focus on the most widely utilized terms and definitions. This will require learning terminology in two broad categories: terms used in jurisdictions that continue to follow traditional common law definitions of crimes, and those that have adopted the MPC. The common law is the logical starting point as the terms and definitions are woven into MPC terminology.

B. Common Law Mens Rea Terms

The following mens rea terms, developed through common law jurisprudence, are widely integrated into criminal statutes today.

1. Malice

Malice is a key term in common law jurisprudence and remains important in relation to the crimes of murder and arson in common law jurisdictions. The precise meaning of malice, however, has vexed courts through the centuries. Today, where malice is defined as the requisite mens rea element of a crime, it is generally established by proof that the defendant intended a result (such as an intent to kill), or that the defendant acted recklessly in a manner that manifested an extreme unjustifiable risk to others. As you can see, the term malice does not mean what it instinctively suggests: evil motive. Instead, it is really a term that has become superfluous, as what matters is *how* to prove malice, and that *how* is by proof of intent or extreme recklessness.

2. Intent

Intent, in turn, is established by proof that the defendant acted with purpose, meaning conscious objective; or that the defendant acted with knowledge, meaning she was substantially certain her act or omission would cause the prohibited result or that the item possessed was as alleged.

3. Willful

Willful, which will often be used in the definition of first-degree murder, means the defendant acted with purpose. So, for example, when first-degree murder is defined as a "willful" killing, it means the defendant must have acted with the purpose, or conscious objective, to kill the victim. In this sense, willful is a more restrictive term than intent, as it is not established by *either* purpose or knowledge, but only purpose. This is reflected in the following discussion from a case requiring proof of willful conduct where the defendant requested the following instruction: "willfully means something more than intention to commit the offense. It implies committing the offense purposely and designed in violation of the law." The trial court rejected the requested instruction, and as the appellate court noted with approval, "the trial court declined to give defendant's proffered instruction, and, instead instructed the jury that [t]he term willfully means that the act is done purposely and without justification or excuse." *State v. Breathette*, 202 N.C. App. 697, 690 S.E.2d 1 (N.C. Ct. App. 2010).

4. Reckless

Reckless is a term used for many crimes that are defined in terms of a criminal result (such as involuntary manslaughter, the unintentional reckless killing of a human being); or in terms of criminal conduct that does not need to cause a result (such as reckless driving or reckless endangerment). A defendant is reckless when he is consciously aware that his conduct creates an unjustified and substantial risk to others. Whether the risk is unjustifiable is determined by the finder of fact by asking whether it was a risk a reasonable person would not have created.

Notice that both knowledge and recklessness require proof that the defendant was consciously aware that his conduct created an unjustifiable risk. The difference is that to prove knowledge (and in common law jurisdictions, in so doing, prove intent), the finder of fact must be convinced beyond a reasonable doubt that the defendant acted with a conscious certainty the risk would manifest in an outcome. In contrast, while recklessness requires proof the defendant knew he was creating an unjustifiable risk, he need not expect the risk to manifest in an outcome. Thus, the classic reckless defendant knows he is creating an unjustifiable risk but believes he will get away with it.

5. Criminal Negligence

Criminal negligence is established by proving a defendant created an unjustified risk *without* being consciously aware he was doing so, where a reasonable person *would not* have created the risk. Thus, the difference between reckless and negligent conduct is whether the defendant was aware of the risk creation and ignored it (recklessness); or whether the defendant was ignorant of the risk but should have been aware of it and avoided it (negligence). In most jurisdictions, ordinary or "civil" negligence is insufficient to establish criminal culpability. Instead, the prosecution must prove *gross* deviation from the reasonable standard of care. Like the determination that the risk created was unreasonable, the determination of whether it exceeded ordinary negligence and was a gross deviation is a question of fact.

6. Model Penal Code

The MPC drew from the common law but endeavored to eliminate superfluous or confusing mens rea terminology. As a result, the MPC defines four categories of mens rea: purpose (meaning conscious objective), knowledge (meaning a subjective substantial certainty), recklessness (meaning conscious disregard of an unjustified and substantial risk), and criminal negligence (meaning the creation of an unjustified and substantial risk without conscious awareness). Note that each of these mens rea terms is derived from the common law. However, the MPC dispenses with terms like malice, willfulness, and the conflation of purpose *and* knowledge into the term intent.

This chart provides a visual depiction of different levels of mens rea. Notice how each ascending level essentially includes the lower level. More importantly, notice what must be added to ascend this mens rea pyramid.

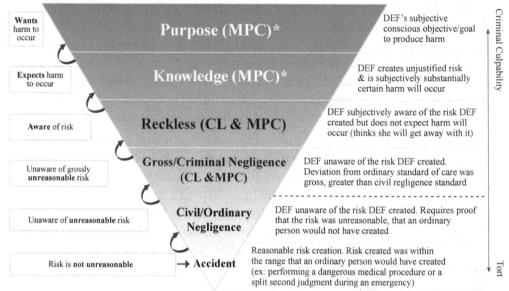

Additional Mens Rea Terms

Malice: Common law term established by proof of intent to kill, or intent to inflict grievous bodily harm, or unintended killing resulting from unreasonable risk creation that is objectively extreme.

*Intent: Common law term established by proof of Purpose OR Knowledge. The term "intent" at common law is normally defined as purpose or knowledge.

Willful: Normally a synonym for Purpose

II. Now What?

A. Mens Rea and Guilt

How do these various mens rea terms relate to criminal responsibility? The answer lies in the definition of each offense a defendant is charged with. That definition will almost always include the requisite mens rea, or criminal mental state, necessary to establish guilt. So, step one in assessing guilt is understanding what mens rea is required to prove the alleged offense; step two is to ensure a proper understanding of what that mens rea term means; step three is to determine whether the evidence is sufficient to prove that mental state beyond a reasonable doubt.

B. Mens Rea and Lesser or "Necessarily" Included Offenses

As depicted in the diagram above, proof of one mens rea element will often implicitly include proof of mens rea elements that support a lesser level of culpability. For example, if a prosecutor proves murder by proving a defendant killed with malice because the reckless risk he created was objectively extreme, that necessarily also proves the defendant acted with the ordinary recklessness required to prove involuntary manslaughter.

Accordingly, it is important to understand that when reasonable doubt exists in relation to the mens rea required to prove the alleged offense, it may result in a finding that the defendant acted with the requisite mens rea to prove a lesser or necessarily included offense. Thus, in the example, if a jury concludes the defendant caused the victim's death as the result of a reckless state of mind, but is not persuaded beyond a reasonable doubt that the risk created was sufficiently extreme to prove malice, they should acquit the defendant of the alleged murder but convict the defendant of the lesser included offense of involuntary manslaughter.

It is therefore useful to visualize the proof requirements for moving up the "mens rea pyramid" from the lowest to the highest level of criminal culpability. What this pyramid illustrates is that, in most cases, each increasing level of mental culpability builds on a lower level. This conception will ideally contribute to: 1. Understanding the differences between the various mens rea requirements, and 2. Assessing when failure to prove the mens rea required for an alleged crime will result in conviction for a lesser included offense.

C. General and Specific Mens Rea

In jurisdictions with criminal statutes that reflect common law principles, many crimes are characterized as "general" or "specific" intent crimes. This characterization is intended to indicate the nature of the requisite mens rea required for conviction, and as is explored in the next chapter, becomes extremely important when assessing the impact of mistakes of fact and, to a lesser extent, mistakes of law.

Understanding general versus specific intent is complicated. First, the very characterization is confusing because it applies to mens rea elements other than intent. For example, recklessness or gross negligence are almost always considered general "intent" elements, even though it is obvious they *are not* based on proof of intent. As a result, it is useful to think in terms of general versus specific *mens rea*. Second, all crimes that require proof of a specific mens rea element will also include an underlying general mens rea element. Thus, it is also misleading to speak in terms of general or specific intent crimes. The much more effective approach is to consider the alleged crime and then analyze the nature of the mens rea element or elements needed to prove guilt. For example, burglary, defined in the common law as *the unlawful breaking and entering of the dwelling house of another at night with intent to commit a felony therein* really requires proof of *two* mens rea elements: the intent to break and enter, *and* the intent to commit a felony therein.

When a crime such as burglary requires proof of two mens rea elements, the first is normally considered a general mens rea element and the second the specific mens rea element. Another way to distinguish these two types of elements is to ask which of them actuates or sets in motion the criminal act—which will be the general mens rea element; and which is an *additional* mental state—which will be the specific mens rea element? Thus, for burglary, the intent to break and enter is the intent to do the act of the crime: break and enter, thus a general mens rea element. However, guilt requires proof of an additional mens rea element: the intent to commit a felony therein, which is therefore the specific mens rea element.

The easiest way to identify a specific mens rea element is that it is defined as *with intent to*. While this is not always included in the definition of a crime, it is often the "flag" that will indicate such an element.

D. Objective vs. Subjective States of Mind

To effectively analyze proof of the various criminal mental states falling under the term mens rea, it is necessary to understand the difference between a subjective and objective state of mind. Subjective simply refers to the mind of the defendant: what did the defendant actually know, believe, or intend? Criminal mental states such as willfulness, purpose, and knowledge are purely subjective in nature. In other words, to prove such a mental state the prosecution must convince the fact-finder what was actually in the defendant's mind. In contrast, an objective state of mind is one that is judged from the perspective of a reasonable person. This "reasonable person" standard is central to proving both recklessness and negligence: did the defendant create a risk that a reasonable person would have avoided? As will be illustrated below, when making this assessment, most jurisdictions require the fact-finder to consider the *context* the defendant found herself in; thus, it is useful to think of the objective standard as one of *contextual* reasonableness. Also, as will be illustrated later, recklessness has *both* a subjective and objective component.

E. Proving Mens Rea

While this is not a text on evidence or trial practice, it is important to begin to understand just how prosecutors prove the mens rea element or elements required to satisfy the criminal burden of proof. Evidence offered to meet this burden normally falls within two categories, direct and circumstantial. In some cases, a prosecutor may also offer opinion evidence to contribute to proving mens rea. When necessary to prove a subjective mens rea element, direct evidence would include statements by the defendant indicating his subjective state of mind as it relates to the criminal act or omission. In most contested cases (where the defendant pleads not guilty), such evidence may be lacking. As a result, prosecutors rely on circumstantial evidence from which the fact-finder will be permitted to draw logical inferences. For example, if a prosecutor seeks to prove intent to kill, the nature of the weapon used and location and extent of the victim's wounds will often support an inference of intent. Motive is also important circumstantial evidence from which a fact-finder may infer a subjective state of mind, as with proof of intent to kill where the defendant reaps a financial windfall from the victim's death. Note that motive *is not* a mens rea element, but instead is circumstantial evidence of mens rea: a fact-finder may properly infer that a defendant intends the outcome he is motivated to produce.

Practice Pointer

Prosecutors routinely rely on rational inferences to prove mens rea, especially subjective criminal mental states. It is unsurprising that when prosecutors have compelling direct evidence of this element, a defendant will be far more likely to negotiate a plea of guilty. For example, if police elicit a confession that a defendant not only killed a victim, but intended to do so, the probability of conviction may lead the defendant to conclude a negotiated plea bargain is his best option. Without such direct evidence, proving the criminal mental state will turn on the ability of the prosecutor to persuade the fact-finder that the totality of the circumstantial evidence supports only one rational inference: that the alleged crime was actuated by the requisite mens rea. And remember, so long as that inference is rational, the trial judge should allow the jury to decide whether, after all evidence is introduced, it is the *only* rational inference. If the jury is so persuaded, the mens rea element is proved; if the jury believes the alleged mental state is only one of several rational inferences—for example that shooting a victim in the leg was intended either to kill *or* to seriously injure—the mens rea is not established beyond a reasonable doubt.

III. Application

A. Malice

Malice is the essential mental element for the crime of murder at common law as well as a limited number of other crimes, the most relevant today is arson. But malice is also a misleading term because it logically suggests ill-will or an evil motive. In fact, malice has specific meaning in criminal law distinct from those considerations and is normally established by proof defendant acted with intent to cause the prohibited result (for murder, death of a human being) or, if acting without intent, created an unjustified extreme risk that result would occur. Many jurisdictions have abandoned the term for this very reason: what function does the term serve *if* it is established by more specific mens rea requirements? For those jurisdictions that retain malice as a criminal mental element, the answer lies in the continuing influence of the traditional common law. For example, consider the following definition of malice in Section 188 of the California Penal Code as it relates to the crime of murder:

(a) For purposes of Section 187, malice may be express or implied.

(1) Malice is express when there is manifested a deliberate intention to unlawfully take away the life of a fellow creature.

Accordingly, intent to kill, even if motivated for a good reason (for example a mercy killing), proves malice. But what is meant by "implied" malice? As you read the following case, notice how malice is the essential mens rea element the defendant argues was not supported by the evidence. What is the essence of that argement? And why does the court conclude that the evidence was indeed sufficient even conceding the defendant never acted with the intent to kill his victim?

United States v. Fleming
739 F.2d 945 (4th Cir. 1984)
Fourth Circuit Court of Appeals

HARRISON L. WINTER, Chief Judge:

This case requires us to decide whether a non-purposeful vehicular homicide can ever amount to murder. We conclude that it can.

Defendant David Earl Fleming was convicted of second-degree murder, in violation of 18 U.S.C. § 1111, in the death of Margaret Jacobsen Haley.

[18 U.S.C. § 1111 provides, Murder is the unlawful killing of a human being with malice aforethought. Every murder perpetrated by poison, lying in wait, or any other kind of willful, deliberate, malicious, and premeditated killing; or committed in the perpetration of, or attempt to perpetrate, any arson, escape, murder, kidnapping, treason, espionage, sabotage, aggravated sexual abuse or sexual abuse, child abuse, burglary, or robbery; or perpetrated as part of a pattern or practice of assault or torture against a child or children; or perpetrated from a premeditated design unlawfully and maliciously to effect the death of any human being other than him who is killed, is murder in the first degree. Any other murder is murder in the second degree.]

Mrs. Haley was the driver of an automobile with which an automobile operated by the defendant collided when defendant lost control while traveling at a high rate of speed.

Fleming's car was observed at about 3:00 p.m. on June 15, 1983, traveling southbound on the George Washington Memorial Parkway in northern Virginia at speeds variously estimated by witnesses as between 70 and 100 miles per hour. The speed limit on the Parkway is, at most points, 45 miles per hour. Fleming several times directed his southbound car into the northbound lanes of the Parkway in order to avoid traffic congestion in the southbound lanes. Northbound traffic had to move out of his way in order to avoid a head-on collision. At one point, a pursuing police officer observed Fleming steer his car into the northbound lanes, which were separated from the southbound lanes at that point and for a distance of three-tenths of a mile by a raised concrete median, and drive in the northbound lanes, still at a high rate of speed, for the entire length of the median. At two other points, Fleming traveled in northbound lanes that were separated from the southbound lanes by medians.

Approximately six miles from where his car was first observed traveling at excessive speed, Fleming lost control of it on a sharp curve. The car slid across the northbound lanes, striking the curb on the opposite side of the highway. After striking the curb, Fleming's car straightened out and at that moment struck the car driven by Mrs. Haley that was coming in the opposite direction. Fleming's car at the moment of impact was estimated by witnesses to have been traveling 70 to 80 miles per hour; the speed limit at that point on the Parkway was 30 miles per hour. Mrs. Haley received multiple severe injuries and died before she could be extricated from her car.

Fleming was pulled from the wreckage of his car and transported to a Washington hospital for treatment. His blood alcohol level was there tested at .315 percent.

Fleming was indicted by a grand jury on a charge of second-degree murder and a number of other charges which are not relevant to this appeal. He was tried before a jury on the murder charge and convicted.

Defendant maintains that the facts of the case cannot support a verdict of murder. Particularly, defendant contends that the facts are inadequate to establish the existence of malice aforethought, and thus that he should have been convicted of manslaughter at most.

Malice aforethought, as provided in 18 U.S.C. § 1111(a), is the distinguishing characteristic which, when present, makes a homicide murder rather than manslaughter. See *Stevenson v. United States*, 162 U.S. 313, 320, 16 S. Ct. 839, 841, 40 L. Ed. 980 (1896).[2] Whether malice is present or absent must be inferred by the jury from the whole facts and circumstances surrounding the killing. *Brown v. United States*, 159 U.S. 100, 103, 16 S. Ct. 29, 30, 40 L. Ed. 90 (1894).

Proof of the existence of malice does not require a showing that the accused harbored hatred or ill will against the victim or others. See *United States v. Celestine*, 510 F.2d 457, 459 (9 Cir. 1975). Neither does it require proof of an intent to kill or injure. See, e.g., *United States v. Shaw*, 701 F.2d 367, 392 n.20 (5 Cir. 1983); *United States v. Black Elk*, 579 F.2d 49, 51 (8 Cir. 1978); LaFave & Scott, Criminal Law 541 (1972). Malice may be established by evidence of conduct which is "reckless and wanton and a gross deviation from a reasonable standard of care, of such a nature that a jury is warranted in inferring that defendant was aware of a serious risk of death or serious bodily harm." *Black Elk, supra,* 579 F.2d at 51, quoting, in the context of a criminal action under Sec. 1111(a), *United States v. Cox*, 509 F.2d 390, 392 (D.C. Cir. 1974). To support a conviction for murder, the government need only have proved that defendant intended to operate his car in the manner in which he did with a heart that was without regard for

---

2. Malice aforethought is a concept that originated with the common law and is used in 18 U.S.C. § 1111(a) in its common law sense. See *Stevenson, supra,* 162 U.S. at 320, 16 S. Ct. at 841. The statute's terms, since known to and derived from the common law, are referable to it for interpretation. *United States v. Pardee,* 368 F.2d 368, 374 (4 Cir. 1966). Accordingly, we do not confine our consideration of the precedents to decisions of federal courts interpreting the federal statute, but rather consider other sources which may shed light on the issues of this case.

the life and safety of others. *Shaw, supra,* 701 F.2d at 392 n. 20 (dicta). See also *United States v. Hinkle,* 487 F.2d 1205, 1207 (D.C. Cir. 1973).[3]

We conclude that the evidence regarding defendant's conduct was adequate to sustain a finding by the jury that defendant acted with malice aforethought. It is urged upon us, however, that a verdict of murder in this case should be precluded by the existence of a statute defining and proscribing involuntary manslaughter, 18 U.S.C. § 1112(a). Defendant maintains that vehicular homicide where no purpose on the part of the accused to have caused death or injury has been shown should result only in conviction of involuntary manslaughter. Otherwise, defendant argues, all drunk driving homicides and many reckless driving ones will be prosecutable as murder. We are not persuaded by the argument.

The difference between malice, which will support conviction for murder, and [recklessness], which will permit of conviction only for manslaughter, is one of degree rather than kind. See, e.g., *United States v. Dixon,* 419 F.2d 288, 292-293 (D.C. Cir. 1969) (Leventhal, J., concurring) (difference between murder and manslaughter lies in the quality of the accused's awareness of the risk). See also Holmes, The Common Law 59 (1881) (The difference between murder and manslaughter lies "in the degree of danger attaching to the act in the given state of facts.") In the vast majority of vehicular homicides, the accused has not exhibited such wanton and reckless disregard for human life as to indicate the presence of malice on his part. In the present case, however, the facts show a deviation from established standards of regard for life and the safety of others that is markedly different in degree from that found in most vehicular homicides. In the average drunk driving homicide, there is no proof that the driver has acted while intoxicated with the purpose of wantonly and intentionally putting the lives of others in danger. Rather, his driving abilities were so impaired that he recklessly put others in danger simply by being on the road and attempting to do the things that any driver would do. In the present case, however, danger did not arise only by defendant's determining to drive while drunk. Rather, in addition to being intoxicated while driving, defendant drove in a manner that could be taken to indicate depraved disregard of human life, particularly in light of the fact that because he was drunk his reckless behavior was all the more dangerous.

. . . .

AFFIRMED.

---

3. We note that, even assuming that subjective awareness of the risk is required to establish murder where the killing resulted from reckless conduct, an exception to the requirement of subjective awareness of risk is made where lack of such awareness is attributable solely to voluntary drunkenness. See, e.g., *State v. Trott,* 190 N.C. 674, 130 S.E. 627 (1925); Model Penal Code Sec. 2.08(2) (Tent. Draft No. 9, 1959) ("When recklessness establishes an element of the offense, if the actor, due to self-induced intoxication, is unaware of a risk of which he would have been aware had he been sober, such unawareness is immaterial.") Defendant's state of voluntary intoxication thus would not have been relevant to whether the jury could have inferred from the circumstances of the crime that he was aware of the risk created by his conduct.

Notes and Questions

1. Notice how the court relies on the common law meaning of malice to resolve the appeal. Why? Does footnote 2 of the opinion provide the answer?

2. The defendant argued the evidence did not establish he intended to kill his victim. Did the appellate court disagree? If not, why did the court uphold the conviction?

3. Defining crimes against persons or property as requiring malice remains common in the United States, especially in those states that have not adopted the MPC. As reflected in the California Penal Code and the *Fleming* opinion, malice is established by proof the defendant intended the criminal result, or acted with extreme recklessness (creating a high probability of causing the result and therefore demonstrating an "abandoned and malignant" heart).

B. Intent

As you read the next case, consider how the prosecutor proved the requisite intent to convict the defendant.

People v. Conley
543 N.E.2d 138 (1989)
Illinois Court of Appeals

JUSTICE CERDA delivered the opinion of the court:

The defendant, William J. Conley, was charged with two counts of aggravated battery based on permanent disability and great bodily harm. (Ill. Rev. Stat. 1983, ch. 38, par. 12-4(a).) He was found guilty after a jury trial of aggravated battery based solely on permanent disability on July 17, 1986. The defendant's motions for judgment notwithstanding the verdict or a new trial were denied, and the defendant was sentenced to 30 months' probation including 40 days of periodic imprisonment. On appeal, it is contended that: (1) the State failed to prove beyond a reasonable doubt that the victim incurred a permanent disability and that the defendant intended to inflict a permanent disability. . . . For the following reasons, we affirm.

The defendant was charged with aggravated battery in connection with a fight which occurred at a party on September 28, 1985, in unincorporated Orland Township. Approximately 200 high school students attended the party and paid admission to drink unlimited beer. One of those students, Sean O'Connell, attended the party with several friends. At some point during the party, Sean's group was approached by a group of 20 boys who apparently thought that someone in Sean's group had said something derogatory. Sean's group denied making a statement and said they did not want any trouble. Shortly thereafter, Sean and his friends decided to leave and began walking toward their car which was parked a half block south of the party.

A group of people were walking toward the party from across the street when someone from that group shouted "There's those guys from the party." Someone emerged from that group and approached Sean, who had been walking with his friend Marty Carroll 10 to 15 steps behind two other friends, Glen Mazurowski and Dan Scurio. That individual demanded that Marty give him a can of beer from his six-pack. Marty refused, and the individual struck Sean in the face with a wine bottle, causing Sean to fall to the ground. The offender attempted to hit Marty, but missed as Marty was able to duck. Sean sustained broken upper and lower jaws and four broken bones in the area between the bridge of his nose and the lower left cheek. Sean lost one tooth and had root canal surgery to reposition 10 teeth that had been damaged. Expert testimony revealed that Sean has a permanent condition called mucosal mouth and permanent partial numbness in one lip. The expert also testified that the life expectancy of the damaged teeth might be diminished by a third or a half.

At trial, the State presented Officer Houlihan, Doctor Arnold S. Morof, and five occurrence witnesses. Of the five occurrence witnesses, only Marty Carroll identified Conley as the offender. The only other witness connecting Conley to the crime was another student, Demetrius Kereakas, who testified that he saw Conley throw a bottle at Dan Scurio's car as the four boys left after the incident. The defense recalled State witness Marty Carroll and presented seven witnesses in addition to the defendant. Four of the defense witnesses testified that the defendant was not the offender, but rather that Sean was hit by a Robert Frazer, who is known in school as "Crazy Bob" or "Terminator." The party was held at a residence surrounded by open fields. There were no streetlights and most of the witnesses had been drinking before the incident.

. . . The jury returned a guilty verdict for aggravated battery based on permanent disability. . . .

The defendant initially contends on appeal that the State failed to prove beyond a reasonable doubt that Sean O'Connell incurred a permanent disability. Section 12-4(a) of the Criminal Code of 1961 provides that: "[a] person who, in committing a battery, intentionally or knowingly causes great bodily harm, or permanent disability or disfigurement commits aggravated battery." (Ill. Rev. Stat. 1983, ch. 38, par. 12-4(a).) The defendant contends there must be some disabling effect for an aggravated battery conviction based on permanent disability. [On this issue, the court concluded that "for an injury to be deemed disabling, all that must be shown is that the victim is no longer whole such that the injured bodily portion or part no longer serves the body in the same manner as it did before the injury. Applying this standard to the case at hand, the injuries Sean O'Connell suffered are sufficient to constitute a permanent disability."]

The defendant further argues that the State failed to prove beyond a reasonable doubt that he intended to inflict any permanent disability. The thrust of defendant's argument is that under section 12-4(a), a person must intend to bring about the particular harm defined in the statute. The defendant asserts that while it may be inferred from his conduct that he intended to cause harm, it does not follow that he intended to cause permanent disability. The State contends it is not necessary that the defendant intended to bring about the particular injuries that resulted. The State maintains it met its burden by showing that the defendant intentionally struck Sean.

. . . .

For proper resolution of this issue, it is best to return to the statutory language. Section 12-4(a) employs the terms "intentionally or knowingly" to describe the required mental state. The relevant statutes state:

> "4-4. Intent. A person intends, or acts intentionally or with intent, to accomplish a result or engage in conduct described by the statute defining the offense, when his conscious objective or purpose is to accomplish that result or engage in that conduct." (Ill. Rev. Stat. 1987, ch. 38, par. 4-4.)

> "4-5. Knowledge. A person knows or acts knowingly or with knowledge of:

> "(b) The result of his conduct, described by the statute defining the offense, when he is consciously aware that such result is practically certain to be caused by his conduct." (Ill. Rev. Stat. 1987, ch. 38, par. 4-5.)

Section 12-4(a) defines aggravated battery as the commission of a battery where the offender intentionally or knowingly causes great bodily harm, or permanent disability or disfigurement. Because the offense is defined in terms of result, the State has the burden of proving beyond a reasonable doubt that the defendant either had a "conscious objective" to achieve the harm defined, or that the defendant was "consciously aware" that the harm defined was "practically certain to be caused by his conduct." . . .

Although the State must establish the specific intent to bring about great bodily harm, or permanent disability or disfigurement under section 12-4(a), problems of proof are alleviated to the extent that the ordinary presumption that one intends the natural and probable consequences of his actions shifts the burden of production, though not persuasion, to the defendant. If the defendant presents evidence contrary to the presumption, then the presumption ceases to have effect, and the trier of fact considers all the evidence and the natural inferences drawn therefrom. Intent can be inferred from the surrounding circumstances, the offender's words, the weapon used, and the force of the blow. As the defendant's theory of the case was mistaken identity, there was no evidence introduced negating the presumption of intent. However, even if Conley had denied any intention to inflict permanent disability, the surrounding circumstances, the use of a bottle, the absence of warning and the force of the blow are facts from which the jury could reasonably infer the intent to cause permanent disability. Therefore, we find the evidence sufficient to support a finding of intent to cause permanent disability beyond a reasonable doubt.

. . . .

Judgment affirmed.

Notes and Questions

1. Why did the *Conley* court conclude that the intent required for the alleged offense could be satisfied by proving the defendant acted with either purpose or knowledge? Based on the statutory definition of these terms, what distinguished each?

2. In this jurisdiction, intent and knowledge are defined as distinct mens rea elements. This tracks generally with the MPC, although note that Illinois retained the term "intent" for what the MPC defines as "purpose." In the common law, the term "intent" was understood to be established by *either* purpose or knowledge. Of course, to act with purpose would require the defendant know with substantial certainty that his conduct will produce the criminal result. But might a defendant like Conley act with knowledge without having the purpose to produce that result?

3. What was the proof of intent the court indicated satisfied the prosecution burden?

4. Note that the court indicated how proof of subjective intent may be based on circumstantial evidence, specifically, "that the ordinary presumption that one intends the natural and probable consequences of his actions shifts the burden of production, though not persuasion, to the defendant." Why was reliance on this "ordinary presumption" necessary in this case? Was there any direct evidence of the defendant's intent? And why did the court qualify the effect of this presumption by indicating that the burden of persuasion is not impacted? Was it consistent with due process to characterize this "natural and probably" consequences rule as a presumption?

5. Why was it irrelevant that the defendant may have intended to inflict injury on a different victim? This is often called the doctrine of transferred intent: when a defendant intends to inflict a prohibited result on one victim but inflicts it on a different victim, it is said the intent "transfers" from the intended to the unintended victim. Consider how the jury was likely instructed on this issue:

> When a person with intent to kill or inflict great bodily harm attempts unlawfully to kill or inflict great bodily harm upon a certain person, but, by mistake or inadvertence, kills another person, the individual is still criminally responsible for a killing with intent to kill or inflict great bodily harm because the intent to kill or inflict great bodily harm is transferred from the intended victim of (his) (her) action to the actual victim.

Importantly, however, intent to commit one crime does not "transfer" to support guilt for a different crime. For example, a defendant who intends to steal is not guilty of intent to kill murder if, during the theft, a victim is accidentally killed.

6. Note that Conley's intent to batter (hit) his victim was insufficient to support a conviction for aggravated battery. Why? Because the alleged offense required proof that Conley also intended or knew his conduct would cause great bodily harm or permanent physical disfigurement. Is this "additional" mental element general or specific intent/mens rea? What should the outcome have been had the jury concluded

Conley intended to strike a victim but had reasonable doubt as to the nature of the injury he intended to inflict?

C. Distinguishing Purpose from Knowledge

Like *Conley*, the next case also involves an aggravated battery. However, note how the offense *as alleged* by the prosecutor in the charging instrument leads to a very different result.

Vermont v. Trombly

174 Vt. 459 (2002)
Vermont Supreme Court

Defendant Matthew Trombley appeals his aggravated assault conviction, claiming several errors in the court's jury instructions. Defendant contends that (1) the court improperly instructed the jury to consider whether defendant acted either "purposely" or "knowingly" when defendant was charged with only "purposely" inflicting serious bodily harm. . . . We affirm.

The incident occurred the evening of February 18, 2000, when George Demarais and Matthew Trombley, the defendant, were involved in a fight. Various details of the fight are in dispute.

The two men were at a bar in St. Albans. Both had been drinking. Demarais testified that he had been sitting at the bar with some friends when defendant, whom he did not know, approached him from behind, put him in a headlock, pushed him forward, and punched him several times in the face. Bystanders pulled defendant off Demarais, and shortly thereafter, Demarais left the bar. Defendant testified that he had approached Demarias at the bar because Demarais had been staring at him and he wanted to find out why. He contends a brief struggle then ensued. According to defendant, after Demarais left the bar, defendant noticed that his hand had been cut and he decided to go after Demarais to "talk to him" about what Demarais had done.

The testimony differs as to what happened outside of the bar on Main Street once defendant and Demarais had left the bar. According to Demarais, who was walking away from the bar, defendant grabbed him from behind and punched him at least twelve times before Demarais fell to the ground and started to lose consciousness. Demarais testified that in an effort to defend himself he pulled out a small knife and blindly slashed at defendant over his shoulder. After delivering a few more punches, defendant stopped punching Demarais. According to defendant, he saw Demarais walking down the street, hollered at him to stop, ran towards him, and tackled him. They fell to the ground. After some struggle, defendant felt a pain in his side and became scared and angry. He testified he repeatedly punched Demarais in an effort to get Demarais to stop stabbing him.

Both individuals suffered injuries. Demarais suffered a bruised face. His eyes were swollen shut and he experienced a partial loss of vision. One tooth had been knocked out, and another was hanging by a thread. Defendant suffered multiple stab wounds to his face, the back of his scalp, his neck, hand and chest. The stab wounds were all superficial.

Defendant was charged with aggravated assault under 13 V.S.A. §1024(a)(1). The charge read: "[defendant] was then and there a person who purposely caused serious bodily injury to another, to wit: George Demarais, by knocking some teeth out by repeatedly punching Mr. Demarais in violation of 13 V.S.A. §1024(a)(1)." The jury convicted defendant of aggravated assault. Defendant appeals the jury verdict of guilty, claiming that the court's instructions to the jury were erroneous. . . .

Defendant first argues that the jury charge was improper because it instructed the jury to consider whether defendant acted either "purposely" or "knowingly" when defendant was charged with only "purposely" inflicting serious bodily harm. The trial court judge instructed the jury as follows: "To commit the offense purposely means that [defendant] acted with the conscious purpose of causing serious bodily injury or that he acted under circumstances where he was practically certain that his conduct would cause serious bodily injury." Defendant argues that because the information charged defendant with only "purposely" causing serious bodily injury, the additional charge regarding whether he acted knowingly allowed the jury to improperly consider and weigh evidence going to whether the defendant acted under circumstances where he was practically certain his conduct would cause serious bodily injury.   Defendant argues that a proper jury instruction would have told the jury that to convict defendant it had to find that it was defendant's conscious objective to inflict serious bodily injury on Demarais; if defendant only acted under circumstances where he was practically certain his conduct would result in serious bodily injury to Demarais, the jury could not convict him.

Criminal liability is normally based upon the concurrence of two factors: "an evil-meaning mind" and "an evil-doing hand." *Morissette v. United States*, 342 U.S. 246, 251, 72 S.Ct. 240, 96 L.Ed. 288 (1952). We recognize that one of criminal law's most basic principles is that "a person is not criminally liable for causing a bad result if he or she did not have some culpable mental state with respect to that result." *State v. Doucette*, 143 Vt. 573, 580, 470 A.2d 676, 681 (1983). In the instant case, we must examine the mental element, or mens rea, required for conviction under §1024(a)(1). If the jury instructions failed to charge the proper mental state required for a conviction under aggravated assault, we would find error.

At common law, crimes generally were classified as requiring either "general intent" or "specific intent." This distinction, however, has been the source of much confusion, and in the 1970's a reform movement of sorts began to replace this traditional dichotomy with an alternative analysis of mens rea. The American Law Institute's Model Penal Code exemplifies this new approach. The Code delineates four kinds of culpability: purposely, knowingly, recklessly, and negligently. Model Penal

Code § 2.02(2)(a)-(d) (1985).[1] In doing so, it abandoned the "specific intent"/"general intent" terminology prevalent in traditional criminal law. W. LaFave, Criminal Law § 3.5(e) (2000).[2]

In Act No. 222 of the 1971 Adjourned Session, the Vermont General Assembly enacted 13 V.S.A. § 1024(a)(1), which states that a person is guilty of aggravated assault if he attempts to cause serious bodily injury to another, or causes such injury purposely, knowingly or recklessly under circumstances manifesting extreme indifference to the value of human life. This language is borrowed from the Model Penal Code. . . .

Defendant argues that since the Legislature adopted the Model Penal Code language, which makes a distinction between "purposely" and "knowingly," and because he was charged with only "purposely" causing serious bodily injury, it was erroneous to instruct the jury on the mens rea of "knowingly." We agree.

The modern approach under the Code defines separately the mental states of "purpose" and "knowledge," because there are several areas of the law where it may be critical to distinguish between one's objective and one's knowledge. W. LaFave, supra, § 3.5(b). For example, when a defendant is charged with treason, the government must demonstrate that the defendant acted with a purpose or objective to aid the enemy. *United States v. Bailey*, 444 U.S. 394, 405, 100 S.Ct. 624, 62 L.Ed.2d 575 (1980). In addition, a heightened mental state in the inchoate offenses of attempt and conspiracy "separates criminality itself from otherwise innocuous behavior." *Id.* (citing Model Penal Code § 2.02, Comments, p. 125 (Tent. Draft No. 4, 1955)). Finally, "the statutory and common law of homicide often distinguishes, either in setting the 'degree' of the crime or in imposing punishment, between a person who knows that

---

1. The two kinds of culpability pertinent to this case are "purposely" and "knowingly." The Model Penal Code, § 2.02(2)(a) states that a person acts purposely with respect to a material element of an offense when:

> (i) if the element involves the nature of his conduct or a result thereof, it is his conscious object to engage in conduct of that nature or to cause such a result; and (ii) if the element involves the attendant circumstances, he is aware of the existence of such circumstances or he believes or hopes that they exist.

Model Penal Code § 2.02(2)(b) states that a person acts knowingly with respect to a material element of an offense when:

> (i) if the element involves the nature of his conduct or the attendant circumstances, he is aware that his conduct is of that nature or that such circumstances exist; and (ii) if the element involves a result of his conduct, he is aware that it is practically certain that his conduct will cause such a result.

2. Although the MPC abandoned the "specific intent" and "general intent" terminology, we still find the terms useful, and not without importance in our criminal law. W. LaFave, Criminal Law § 3.5(e) (2000) (explaining that the traditional view is that rules on when mistake of fact or mistake of law will constitute a defense differ depending on what kind of intent is involved); see also *State v. Kinney*, 171 Vt. 239, 243, 762 A.2d 833, 837 (2000) (holding that "[w]hen specific intent is an element of a crime, evidence of either voluntary or involuntary intoxication may be introduced to show that the defendant could not have formed the necessary intent").

another person will be killed as a result of his conduct and a person who acts with the specific purpose of taking another's life." *Bailey*, 444 U.S. at 405, 100 S.Ct. 624. We too conclude that it is important to distinguish between a person who knows another may be seriously injured because of his conduct and a person who acts with the specific purpose of seriously injuring another.

Because the defendant was charged with only "purposely" causing serious bodily injury, the trial court's instruction on the mens rea of "knowingly" was erroneous. . . . [The court then concluded that the erroneous instruction was harmless error, which means there is no reasonable probability that but for that error the outcome would have been different. This was because the defendant asserted he punched the victim to defend himself, but, as the court noted, this means he must have had the *purpose* to batter his victim. As the court noted, "the trial court's inclusion of 'knowingly' in the jury instructions was harmless error in the instant case because defendant's own assertion of self-defense established that he acted with the purpose of inflicting serious bodily injury on Demarais." Whether the battery was legally justified by self-defense was a distinct question and in no way negated his purpose to batter. Thus, had the jury been properly instructed, the outcome would have been the same: guilty.]

Affirmed.

Notes and Questions

1. Could the prosecutor who charged Trombley have alleged he acted with purpose *or* knowledge? Yes, as either criminal mental state falls within the definition of the crime. If charged in such a manner, the jury would be instructed that a finding of either one of those states of mind satisfies the requisite mens rea. But, as the court notes, the prosecution must prove what it alleges.

2. What is harmless error? This is a doctrine that allows an appellate court to uphold a conviction *after* it determines a legal error influenced the outcome. The defendant/appellant bears the burden to establish that error. However, doing so does not result in automatic reversal unless the error is what the Supreme Court has labelled "structural," meaning it impacts the entire structure of the trial (like a biased judge or improperly composed jury). For any other error, the state/prosecution is offered the opportunity to prove there is no reasonable probability the outcome would have been different even without the error. In other words, the court must be persuaded that guilt would have been established beyond a reasonable doubt even without the error.

3. In footnote 2, the court points out that although Vermont adopted, in large measure, the MPC, it may still be useful to think of mental elements in the common law specific/general intent framework. Why?

4. Defendant is charged with violating the federal Material Support to Terrorism statute. Section B of the statute provides:

(1) Unlawful Conduct—

> Whoever knowingly provides material support or resources to a foreign ter-
> rorist organization, or attempts or conspires to do so, shall be fined under
> this title or imprisoned not more than 20 years, or both, and, if the death
> of any person results, shall be imprisoned for any term of years or for life.

Section A of the same statute provides :

> Whoever provides material support or resources or conceals or disguises
> the nature, location, source, or ownership of material support or resources,
> knowing or intending that they are to be used in preparation for, or in
> carrying out, [an act of terrorism] or in preparation for, or in carrying out,
> the concealment of an escape from the commission of any such violation,
> or attempts or conspires to do such an act, shall be fined under this title,
> imprisoned not more than 15 years, or both, and, if the death of any per-
> son results, shall be imprisoned for any term of years or for life.

What must the prosecution prove defendant "knows" to convict for violation of Section B? Is it clear from the text of Section B? Does consideration of Section A help
resolve this question? In fact, in response to uncertainty as to the knowledge element
of Section B, Congress amended Section B to provide:

> To violate this paragraph, a person must have knowledge that the organ-
> ization is a designated terrorist organization (as defined in subsection (g)
> (6)), that the organization has engaged or engages in terrorist activity (as
> defined in section 212(a)(3)(B) of the Immigration and Nationality Act), or
> that the organization has engaged or engages in terrorism (as defined in sec-
> tion 140(d)(2) of the Foreign Relations Authorization Act, Fiscal Years 1988
> and 1989).

In *Holder v. Humanitarian Law Project*, 561 U.S. 1 (2010), the Supreme Court held
that Section B requires proof the defendant *knew* the material support was being
provided to a group that is designated as a Foreign Terrorist Organization or that the
group engages in terrorism, *not* that the defendant *knew* the resources would be used
to support terrorism. The Court contrasted the mens rea requirement for Section A
with Section B to bolster this conclusion.

D. Knowledge and Willful Blindness

Many crimes require proof of knowledge that the criminal result will be inflicted
or of an attendant circumstance. A defendant prosecuted for such an offense may
assert ignorance of the requisite fact. There are two tactics a prosecutor may use to
overcome such an obstacle. First, reliance on the totality of the evidence to persuade
the fact-finder that the defendant is dishonest and did in fact possess the requisite
knowledge; second, evidence of what is known as willful blindness or deliberate
ignorance. Consider this instruction:

"Willful Blindness" as a Way of Satisfying "Knowingly"

In deciding whether [defendant] acted knowingly, you may infer that [defendant] had knowledge of a fact if you find that [he/she] deliberately closed [his/her] eyes to a fact that otherwise would have been obvious to [him/her]. In order to infer knowledge, you must find that two things have been established. First, that [defendant] was aware of a high probability of [the fact in question]. Second, that [defendant] consciously and deliberately avoided learning of that fact. That is to say, [defendant] willfully made [himself/herself] blind to that fact. It is entirely up to you to determine whether [he/she] deliberately closed [his/her] eyes to the fact and, if so, what inference, if any, should be drawn. However, it is important to bear in mind that mere negligence, recklessness or mistake in failing to learn the fact is not sufficient. There must be a deliberate effort to remain ignorant of the fact.

Notice that the instruction opens the door for the jury to draw an inference of knowledge on the part of a defendant. In fact, a jury is always authorized to rely on inference of mens rea. But this type of willful blindness instruction is useful because it provides the jury with clear guidance on precisely what they must be convinced of in order to impute knowledge to the defendant who denies such knowledge. In the next case, consider how such an instruction might have impacted the outcome had the appellate court recognized the applicability of willful blindness as a permissible substitute for actual knowledge?

State v. Nations

676 S.W.2d 282 (1984)
Missouri Court of Appeals

Defendant, Sandra Nations, owns and operates the Main Street Disco, in which police officers found a scantily clad sixteen-year-old girl "dancing" for "tips". Consequently, defendant was charged with endangering the welfare of a child "less than seventeen years old," § 568.050 RSMo 1978. Defendant was convicted and fined $1,000.00. Defendant appeals. We reverse.

. . . .

Specifically, defendant argues the state failed to show she knew the child was under seventeen and, therefore, failed to show she had the requisite intent to endanger the welfare of a child "less than seventeen years old." We agree.

The pertinent part of § 568.050 provides:

"1. A person commits the crime of endangering the welfare of a child if: . . . . (2) He knowingly encourages, aids or causes a child less than seventeen years old to engage in any conduct which causes or tends to cause the child to come within the provisions of subdivision (1)(c) . . . of section 211.031, RSMo. . . ."

... § 568.050 requires the state to prove the defendant "knowingly" encouraged a child "less than seventeen years old" to engage in conduct tending to injure the child's welfare, and "knowing" the child to be less than seventeen is a material element of the crime. See § 562.021.

"Knowingly" is a term of art, whose meaning is limited to the definition given to it by our present Criminal Code. Literally read, the Code defines "knowingly" as actual knowledge—"A person *'acts knowingly'*, or with knowledge, (1) with respect . . . to attendant circumstances when he is aware . . . that those circumstances exist. . . ." (Emphasis original). § 562.016.3. So read, this definition of "knowingly" or "knowledge" excludes those cases in which "the fact [in issue] would have been known had not the person wilfully 'shut his eyes' in order to avoid knowing." Perkins, Criminal Law 942 (2d ed. 1969). The Model Penal Code, the source of our Criminal Code, does not exclude these cases from its definition of "knowingly". Instead, the Model Penal Code proposes that "[w]hen knowledge of the existence of a particular fact is an element of an offense, such knowledge is established if a person is aware of a high probability of its existence. . . ." Model Penal Code § 2.02(7) (Proposed Official Draft 1962). This definition sounds more like a restatement of the definition of "recklessly" than "knowingly". The similarity is intentional. The Model Penal Code simply proposes that wilful blindness to a fact "be viewed as one of acting knowingly when what is involved is a matter of existing fact, but not when what is involved is the result of the defendant's conduct, necessarily a matter of the future at the time of acting."[6] . . .

Our legislature, however, did not enact this proposed definition of "knowingly". Although the definitions of "knowingly" and "recklessly" in our Criminal Code are almost identical to the primary definitions of these terms as proposed in the Model Penal Code . . . the Model Penal Code's proposed expanded definition of "knowingly", encompassing wilful blindness of a fact, is absent from our Criminal Code. The sensible, if not compelling, inference is that our legislature rejected the

---

6. The additional or expanded definition of "knowingly" proposed in § 2.02(7) of the MPC "deals with the situation British commentators have denominated 'wilful blindness' or 'connivance,' the case of the actor who is aware of the probable existence of a material fact but does not satisfy himself that it does not in fact exist. . . . Whether such cases should be viewed as instances of acting recklessly or knowingly presents a subtle but important question.

"The draft proposes that the case be viewed as one of acting knowingly when what is involved is a matter of existing fact, but not when what is involved is the result of the defendant's conduct, necessarily a matter of the future at the time of acting. The position reflects what we believe to be the normal policy of criminal enactments which rest liability on acting 'knowingly,' as is so commonly done. The inference of 'knowledge' of an existing fact is usually drawn from proof of notice of substantial probability of its existence, unless the defendant establishes an honest, contrary belief. The draft solidifies this usual result and clarifies the terms in which the issue is submitted to the jury." Model Penal Code § 2.02(7) commentary at 129-30 (Tent. Draft No. 4, 1953).

expansion of the definition of "knowingly" to include wilful blindness of a fact and chose to limit the definition of "knowingly" to actual knowledge of the fact. Thus, in the instant case, the state's burden was to show defendant actually was aware the child was under seventeen, a heavier burden than showing there was a "high probability" that defendant was aware the child was under seventeen. In short, the state's burden was to prove defendant acted "knowingly", not just "recklessly". The state proved, however, that defendant acted "recklessly", not "knowingly". This we conclude from our review of the record.

. . . .

The record shows that, at the time of the incident, the child was sixteen years old. When the police arrived, the child was "dancing" on stage for "tips" with another female. The police watched her dance for some five to seven minutes before approaching defendant in the service area of the bar. Believing that one of the girls appeared to be "young," the police questioned defendant about the child's age. Defendant told them that both girls were of legal age and that she had checked the girls' identification when she hired them. When the police questioned the child, she initially stated that she was eighteen but later admitted that she was only sixteen. She had no identification.

Aside from the child's age, these facts were established by the testimony of a police officer. The state also called the child as a witness. Her testimony was no help to the state. She testified the defendant asked her for identification just prior to the police arriving, and she was merely crossing the stage to get her identification when the police took her into custody. Nor can the state secure help from the defendant's testimony. She simply corroborated the child's testimony; i.e., she asked the child for her identification; the child replied she would "show it to [her] in a minute"; the police then took the child into custody.

These facts simply show defendant was untruthful. Defendant could not have checked the child's identification, because the child had no identification with her that day, the first day defendant "hired" the child. This does not prove that defendant knew the child was less than seventeen years old. At best, it proves defendant did not know or refused to learn the child's age. The latter is the best case for the state. But defendant's refusal to learn the age of this "young" child who was "dancing" "scantily clad" in her disco bar simply proves that defendant was "aware of a high probability" that the child was under seventeen, or, stated otherwise, in the definitional language of our Criminal Code, proves that defendant was conscious of "a substantial and unjustifiable risk" that the child was under seventeen and that defendant's disregard of the risk was a "gross deviation" from the norm. This, however, is not "knowledge" under our Criminal Code. It is "recklessness", nothing more. Having failed to prove defendant knew the child's age was less than seventeen, the state failed to make a submissible case.

Judgment reversed.

Notes and Questions

1. Do you think the defendant suspected the child was underage? Why do you think she lied to the police?

2. Does willful blindness actually permit a finding of knowledge based on recklessness? Or must the fact-finder conclude that the defendant believed the probability of the true fact was higher than would be required to prove recklessness? Consider this excerpt from the concurring judge in *United States v. Jewell*, 532 F.2d 697 (9th Cir. 1976), a case involving a conviction for knowing importation of narcotics into the United States by a defendant who admitted he suspected the trunk of the car he was borrowing might have contained narcotics but chose not to check:

> Finally, the wilful blindness doctrine is uncertain in scope. There is disagreement as to whether reckless disregard for the existence of a fact constitutes wilful blindness or some lesser degree of culpability. Some cases have held that a statute's scienter requirement is satisfied by the constructive knowledge imputed to one who simply fails to discharge a duty to inform himself. There is also the question of whether to use an "objective" test based on the reasonable man, or to consider the defendant's subjective belief as dispositive.

3. What if the finder of fact concludes that defendant was in fact ignorant of the true fact? In other words, what if the defendant in this case testified that she honestly believed the child was of legal age and the jury believes that testimony? Consider the following excerpt from the concurring opinion in *United States v. Jewell*:

> The second defect in the instruction as given is that it did not alert the jury that Jewell could not be convicted if he "actually believed" there was no controlled substance in the car. The failure to emphasize, as does the Model Penal Code, that subjective belief is the determinative factor, may allow a jury to convict on an objective theory of knowledge that a reasonable man should have inspected the car and would have discovered what was hidden inside. One recent decision reversed a jury instruction for this very deficiency, failure to balance a conscious purpose instruction with a warning that the defendant could not be convicted if he actually believed to the contrary.

E. Recklessness and Gross Negligence

The next case turns on the distinction between recklessness and negligence. Recall that both criminal mental states involve an objective assessment of whether the defendant created an unjustified or unreasonable risk; a risk a reasonable person would not have created under the circumstances. As you read the case, consider: 1. What distinguishes recklessness from negligence, and 2. How is the substantial and unjustified risk properly assessed?

Colorado v. Hall

999 P.2d 207 (2000)

Supreme Court of Colorado, En Banc

Justice BENDER delivered the Opinion of the Court.

I. Introduction

We hold that Nathan Hall must stand trial for the crime of reckless manslaughter. While skiing on Vail mountain, Hall flew off of a knoll and collided with Allen Cobb, who was traversing the slope below Hall. Cobb sustained traumatic brain injuries and died as a result of the collision. The People charged Hall with felony reckless manslaughter.

At a preliminary hearing to determine whether there was probable cause for the felony count, the county court found that Hall's conduct "did not rise to the level of dangerousness" required under Colorado law to uphold a conviction for manslaughter, and the court dismissed the charges. On appeal, the district court affirmed the county court's decision. The district court determined that in order for Hall's conduct to have been reckless, it must have been "at least more likely than not" that death would result. Because the court found that "skiing too fast for the conditions" is not "likely" to cause another person's death, the court concluded that Hall's conduct did not constitute a "substantial and unjustifiable" risk of death. Thus, the district court affirmed the finding of no probable cause.

The charge of reckless manslaughter requires that a person "recklessly cause[] the death of another person." § 18-3-104(1)(a), 6 C.R.S. (1999). For his conduct to be reckless, the actor must have consciously disregarded a substantial and unjustifiable risk that death could result from his actions. See § 18-1-501(8). We hold that, for the purpose of determining whether a person acted recklessly, a particular result does not have to be more likely than not to occur for the risk to be substantial and unjustifiable. A risk must be assessed by reviewing the particular facts of the individual case and weighing the likelihood of harm and the degree of harm that would result if it occurs. Whether an actor consciously disregarded such a risk may be inferred from circumstances such as the actor's knowledge and experience, or from what a similarly situated reasonable person would have understood about the risk under the particular circumstances.

We hold that under the particular circumstances of this case, whether Hall committed the crime of reckless manslaughter must be determined by the trier of fact. Viewed in the light most favorable to the prosecution, Hall's conduct of skiing straight down a steep and bumpy slope, back on his skis, arms out to his sides, off-balance, being thrown from mogul to mogul, out of control for a considerable distance and period of time, and at such a high speed that the force of the impact between his ski and the victim's head fractured the thickest part of the victim's skull created a substantial and unjustifiable risk of death to another person. A reasonable person could infer that the defendant, a former ski racer trained in skier safety, consciously disregarded that risk. For the limited purposes of a preliminary hearing, the prosecution provided sufficient evidence to show probable cause that the defendant recklessly caused the victim's death. Thus, we reverse the district court's finding of no probable cause and we remand the case to that court for trial.

II. Facts and Procedural History

On April 20, 1997, the last day of the ski season, Hall worked as a ski lift operator on Vail mountain. When he finished his shift and after the lifts closed, Hall skied down toward the base of the mountain. The slopes were not crowded.

On the lower part of a run called "Riva Ridge," just below where the trail intersects with another called "North Face Catwalk," Hall was skiing very fast, ski tips in the air, his weight back on his skis, with his arms out to his sides to maintain balance. He flew off of a knoll and saw people below him, but he was unable to stop or gain control because of the moguls.

Hall then collided with Cobb, who had been traversing the slope below Hall. The collision caused major head and brain injuries to Cobb, killing him. Cobb was taken to Vail Valley Medical Center, where efforts to resuscitate him failed. Hall's blood alcohol level was .009, which is less than the limit for driving while ability impaired. A test of Hall's blood for illegal drugs was negative.

The People charged Hall with manslaughter (a class 4 felony) and misdemeanor charges that are not relevant to this appeal. At the close of the prosecution's case at the preliminary hearing, the People requested that, with respect to the manslaughter count, the court consider the lesser-included charge of criminally negligent homicide (a class 5 felony).

The county court held a preliminary hearing to determine whether there was probable cause to support the felony charges against Hall. At the preliminary hearing, the People presented testimony from an eyewitness, the coroner who conducted the autopsy on Cobb's body, an investigator from the District Attorney's office, and the detective who investigated the accident for the Eagle County Sheriff's department.

Judge Buck Allen, who serves as a judge for several mountain towns and lives in Vail, testified that he is an expert skier and familiar with Vail's slopes. He was making a final run for the day when he first noticed Hall on the slope. Allen was on part of the run called "Lower Riva," which is just below the "North Face Catwalk." From that part of the slope, Allen had a direct line of sight to the bottom of the run. Allen said that he could see other skiers traversing the slope below him at least from their waists up and that there were no blind spots on that part of the run.

Hall passed Allen skiing "at a fairly high rate of speed." Allen estimated that Hall was skiing about three times as fast as he was. Allen stated that Hall was "sitting back" on his skis, tips in the air, with his arms out to his sides in an effort to maintain his balance. Hall was skiing straight down the fall line; that is, he was skiing straight down the slope of the mountain without turning from side-to-side or traversing the slope. Hall "bounded off the bumps as he went," and "[t]he terrain was controlling

[Hall]" rather than the other way around. In Allen's opinion, Hall was skiing too fast for the skill level he demonstrated, and Hall was out of control "if you define 'out of control' as [not] being able to stop or avoid someone." Although he watched Hall long enough to note Hall's unsafe skiing approximately two or three seconds Allen did not see the collision.

Detective McWilliam investigated the collision for the Eagle County Sheriff's office. McWilliam testified that Deputy Mossness said that while Hall could not remember the collision, Hall admitted that as he flew off a knoll and looked down, he saw people below him but could not stop because of the bumps:

> Mr. Hall told [the deputy] that he had been skiing that day, he was an employee of Vail Associates. That he was coming down the mountain and that he said he flew off of a knoll, looked down and saw some people below him down the slope, tried to slow down, and that because of the bumps, he wasn't able to stop. And he doesn't remember beyond that point. But he was told that somebody that he had collided with someone.

McWilliam testified that he interviewed Jonathan Cherin, an eyewitness to the collision between Hall and Cobb. Cherin stated that he saw Hall skiing straight down the slope at a high speed and out of control. He said that Cobb, who appeared to be an inexperienced skier, traversed the slope below Hall when Hall hit some bumps, became airborne, and struck Cobb.

McWilliam testified that Deputy Bishop, an officer on the scene, told McWilliam about the observations of other witnesses to the collision. Bruce Yim said that Hall was skiing too fast, that he was out of control, and that Hall collided with Cobb as Cobb traversed the slope. Loic Lemaner, who was skiing below Cobb at the time of the collision, saw Hall after the collision. Lemaner said that after the collision, Hall struck Lemaner's skis and poles, breaking one of Lemaner's poles in half. . . .

Sandberg, an investigator for the District Attorney's office, testified that he spoke with Mark Haynes, who had been Hall's high school ski coach. Haynes told Sandberg that in the years he coached Hall, Hall was one of the top two or three skiers on the team and that Hall was "talented and aggressive." . . .

Dr. Ben Galloway, the coroner who performed the autopsy on Cobb's body, testified that Cobb died from a single and traumatic blow to his head that fractured his skull and caused severe brain injuries. . . .

Galloway testified that Hall struck Cobb just below his right ear, in an area of the skull where the bones are thickest and "it takes more force to fracture those areas" than other areas of the skull. Galloway described the injury as an "extensive basal skull fracture" with "components" or smaller fractures that extended from the major fracture. . . . Galloway opined that Hall must have been travelling at a very high rate of speed to generate the force necessary to cause Cobb's skull fracture and brain injuries. . . .

Following the presentation of these witnesses, the county court considered whether there was sufficient evidence to find probable cause that Hall recklessly caused Cobb's death. The county court reviewed other Colorado manslaughter cases where courts found substantial and unjustified risks of death resulting from conduct such as firing a gun at a person or kicking an unconscious person in the head. The court found that Hall's conduct which the court characterized as skiing "too fast for the conditions" did not involve a substantial and unjustifiable risk of death and "does not rise to the level of dangerousness required under the current case law" to sustain a count of manslaughter. . . . The county court therefore dismissed the manslaughter count.

The prosecution appealed the county court's decision to the district court pursuant to Crim. P. 5(a)(4)(IV). The district court agreed with the county court that the prosecution failed to establish probable cause. The court held that Hall's conduct did not involve a substantial risk of death because any risk created by Hall had a less than fifty percent chance of causing another's death. . . .

The People petitioned this court pursuant to C.A.R. 49, and we granted certiorari to consider the following:

(1) Whether the district court erred by establishing "more likely than not" as the level of substantial risk of death that a defendant must disregard for a finding of probable cause that he caused the death of another recklessly; and

(2) Whether the district court reviewed the wrong criteria and neglected the evidence relating specifically to this case in affirming the county court's dismissal of a manslaughter charge at preliminary hearing.

III. Discussion

. . .

B. Manslaughter and Recklessness

. . . To provide background for our explanation of recklessness, we review the history of culpable mental states under our criminal code. We then examine the separate elements of recklessness, which require that an actor consciously disregard a substantial and unjustifiable risk that a result will occur or that a circumstance exists. See § 18-1-501(8). Based on this review, we hold that to determine whether a risk is substantial and unjustified, a trier of fact must weigh the likelihood and potential magnitude of harm presented by the conduct and consider whether the conduct constitutes a gross deviation from the reasonable standard of care. Whether a person consciously disregards such a risk may be inferred from either the actor's subjective knowledge of the risk or from what a reasonable person with the actor's knowledge and experience would have been aware of in the particular situation.

. . . .

In the past, courts and legislatures developed a variety of definitions for different mental states, creating confusion about what the prosecution had to prove in a criminal case. See Model Penal Code § 2.02, cmt. at 230 (1985) [hereinafter MPC]. Depending on the specific crime charged and the jurisdiction, juries might be instructed to determine whether the defendant acted with "'felonious intent,' 'criminal intent,' 'malice aforethought,' 'guilty knowledge,' 'fraudulent intent,' 'wilfulness,' 'scienter,' . . . or 'mens rea,' to signify an evil purpose or mental culpability." *Morissette v. United States*, 342 U.S. 246, 252, 72 S. Ct. 240, 96 L. Ed. 288 (1952).

. . . In order to eliminate the confusion created by this variety of ill-defined mental states, the Model Penal Code suggested that criminal codes articulate and define the specific culpable mental states that will suffice for criminal liability. See MPC § 2.02, cmt. at 229.

As part of a complete revision of Colorado's criminal code in 1971, the General Assembly followed the Model Penal Code's suggestion and adopted a provision specifically defining four culpable mental states: "intentionally," "knowingly," "recklessly," and "criminal negligence" . . . to define clearly the different levels of culpability that could be required for the commission of various offenses. . . .

To be convicted of any crime other than a strict liability crime, a defendant must act with one of these four culpable mental states, depending on the statutory definition of each particular crime. If the elements for the required mental state are not satisfied, the defendant cannot be convicted of the crime charged.

To demonstrate that Hall committed the crime of manslaughter, the prosecution must provide sufficient evidence to show that the defendant's conduct was reckless. § 18-3-104(1)(a). Thus, we focus on describing the mental state of recklessness and determining whether Hall's conduct meets that definition.

As Colorado's criminal code defines recklessness, "A person acts recklessly when he consciously disregards a substantial and unjustifiable risk that a result will occur or a that circumstance exists." § 18-1-501(8). Thus, in the case of manslaughter, the prosecution must show that the defendant's conduct caused the death of another and that the defendant:

1) consciously disregarded

2) a substantial and

3) unjustifiable risk that he would

4) cause the death of another.

We examine these elements in detail.

Substantial and Unjustifiable Risk

To show that a person acted recklessly, the prosecution must establish that the person's conduct created a "substantial and unjustifiable" risk. The district court construed some of our earlier cases as requiring that the risk of death be "at least more likely than not" to constitute a substantial and unjustifiable risk of death. In interpreting our cases, the court relied on an erroneous definition of a "substantial and unjustifiable" risk. Whether a risk is substantial must be determined by assessing both the likelihood that harm will occur and the magnitude of the harm should it occur. We hold that whether a risk is unjustifiable must be determined by assessing the nature and purpose of the actor's conduct relative to how substantial the risk is.

Finally, in order for conduct to be reckless, the risk must be of such a nature that its disregard constitutes a gross deviation from the standard of care that a reasonable person would exercise.

A risk does not have to be "more likely than not to occur" or "probable" in order to be substantial. A risk may be substantial even if the chance that the harm will occur is well below fifty percent. See *People v. Deskins*, 927 P.2d 368, 373 (Colo.1996) (finding reckless conduct where defendant disregarded risk that "any of the cars on the road" on a particular night might contain children) (emphasis omitted); see also Wayne R. LaFave & Austin W. Scott, Jr., Substantive Criminal Law § 3.7(f) at 336 (1986). Some risks may be substantial even if they carry a low degree of probability because the magnitude of the harm is potentially great. For example, if a person holds a revolver with a single bullet in one of the chambers, points the gun at another's head and pulls the trigger, then the risk of death is substantial even though the odds that death will result are no better than one in six. As one court remarked,

> If the potential of a risk is death, that risk is always serious. Therefore, only some likelihood that death will occur might create for most people a "substantial and unjustifiable" risk. . . .

Whether a risk is substantial is a matter of fact that will depend on the specific circumstances of each case. Some conduct almost always carries a substantial risk of death, such as engaging another person in a fight with a deadly weapon or firing a gun at another. . . . In such instances, the substantiality of the risk may be evident from the nature of the defendant's conduct and the court will not have to examine the specific facts in detail.

Other conduct requires a greater inquiry into the facts of the case to determine whether it creates a substantial risk of death. In *Moore v. People*, we affirmed a manslaughter conviction where the defendant kicked the victim to death. 925 P.2d 264, 269 (Colo. 1996). While "kicking another" may not necessarily involve a substantial risk of death, a trier of fact can find that repeatedly kicking the head and torso of someone already beaten unconscious can create a substantial risk of death. See id. Similarly, driving a car is not conduct that by its nature necessarily involves a substantial risk of death to others, but after viewing the facts of a particular case closely a court may determine that the defendant created a substantial risk of death. See, e.g., *People v. Clary*, 950 P.2d 654, 658-59 (Colo.App.1997) (finding that driving a truck without adequate brakes constituted reckless conduct for vehicular homicide count).

A court cannot generically characterize the actor's conduct (e.g., "driving a truck") in a manner that ignores the specific elements of the conduct that create a risk (e.g., driving a truck with failing brakes on a highway). For example, "installing a heater" carries little risk under normal circumstances. However, the Connecticut Supreme Court held that improperly wiring a 120-volt heater to a 240-volt circuit, failing to use a lock nut to connect the heater to the circuit breaker, and using other faulty installation techniques creates a substantial risk of "catastrophic fire" and death. See *State v.*

Salz, 226 Conn. 20, 627 A.2d 862, 865, 869–71 (1993). Thus, to determine whether the conduct created a substantial risk of death, a court must inquire beyond the general nature of the defendant's conduct and consider the specific conduct in which the defendant engaged.

As well as being substantial, a risk must be unjustifiable in order for a person's conduct to be reckless. Whether a risk is justifiable is determined by weighing the nature and purpose of the actor's conduct against the risk created by that conduct. . . . If a person consciously disregards a substantial risk of death but does so in order to advance an interest that justifies such a risk, the conduct is not reckless. For example, if a surgeon performs an operation on a patient that has a seventy-five percent chance of killing the patient, but the patient will certainly die without the operation, then the conduct is justified and thus not reckless even though the risk is substantial. . . .

In addition to the separate analyses that are applied to determine whether a risk is both "substantial" and "unjustified," the concept of a "substantial and unjustifiable risk" implies a risk that constitutes a gross deviation from the standard of care that a reasonable law-abiding person would exercise under the circumstances. . . . A substantial and unjustifiable risk must constitute a "gross deviation" from the reasonable standard of care in order to justify the criminal sanctions imposed for criminal negligence or reckless conduct, as opposed to the kind of deviation from the reasonable standard of care that results in civil liability for ordinary negligence.

Whether a risk is substantial and unjustified is a question of fact. . . . In the limited context of a preliminary hearing, the court must determine whether a risk was substantial and unjustified by considering the evidence presented *in the light most favorable to the prosecution*, and the court must ask whether a reasonable person could "entertain" the belief though not necessarily conclude beyond a reasonable doubt that the defendant's conduct was reckless based on that evidence.

Conscious Disregard

In addition to showing that a person created a substantial and unjustifiable risk, the prosecution must demonstrate that the actor "consciously disregarded" the risk in order to prove that she acted recklessly. A person acts with a conscious disregard of the risk created by her conduct when she is aware of the risk and chooses to act despite that risk . . . In contrast to acting "intentionally" or "knowingly," the actor does not have to intend the result or be "practically certain" that the result will occur, he only needs to be "aware" that the risk exists. . . .

Although recklessness is a less culpable mental state than intentionally or knowingly, it involves a higher level of culpability than criminal negligence. Criminal negligence requires that, "through a gross deviation from the standard of care that a reasonable person would exercise," the actor fails to perceive a substantial and unjustifiable risk that a result will occur or a circumstance exists. . . . An actor is criminally negligent when he should have been aware of the risk but was not, while recklessness requires that the defendant actually be aware of the risk but disregard it. See [*People v.*] *Shaw*, 646 P.2d at 380. Thus, even if she should be, a person who is not actually aware that her conduct creates a substantial and unjustifiable risk is not acting recklessly.

A court or trier of fact may infer a person's subjective awareness of a risk from the particular facts of a case, including the person's particular knowledge or expertise. . . .

Hence, in a reckless manslaughter case, the prosecution must prove that the defendant acted despite his subjective awareness of a substantial and unjustifiable risk of death from his conduct. Because absent an admission by the defendant such awareness cannot be proven directly, the court or trier of fact may infer the defendant's awareness of the risk from circumstances such as the defendant's training, knowledge, and prior experiences, or from what a reasonable person would have understood under the circumstances.

Risk of Death

The final element of recklessness requires that the actor consciously disregard a substantial and unjustifiable risk of a particular result, and in the case of manslaughter the actor must risk causing death to another person. The risk can be a risk of death to another generally; the actor does not have to risk death to a specific individual. . . . Because the element of a "substantial and unjustifiable risk" measures the likelihood and magnitude of the risk disregarded by the actor, any risk of death will meet the requirement that the actor, by his conduct, risks death to another. That is, only a slight risk of death to another person is necessary to meet this element.

[The court then concluded that the evidence presented at the preliminary hearing was sufficient to establish probable cause of a reckless killing and therefore reinstated the charge].

V. Conclusion

The prosecution provided sufficient evidence at the preliminary hearing to induce a person of reasonable prudence and caution to entertain the belief that Hall consciously disregarded a substantial and unjustifiable risk that he might collide with and kill another skier. A court must inquire into the specific facts of each case to determine whether a risk was substantial and unjustified based on the likelihood of the risk, the potential magnitude of the harm, and the nature and purpose of the actor's conduct. In most instances, "skiing too fast for the conditions" does not create a substantial and unjustifiable risk of death, but the facts in this case are sufficient to lead a reasonable person to determine that Hall consciously disregarded such a risk. Although a reasonable person would not necessarily conclude that the evidence proves beyond a reasonable doubt that Hall committed reckless manslaughter, the evidence is sufficient to meet the limited purpose and low threshold at a preliminary hearing to establish probable cause. Thus, we remand this case to the district court for trial.

Notes and Questions

1. Don't fall into the trap of asking whether the evidence was sufficient to convict Hall. Note that what is at issue here is whether the judge presiding over the *preliminary hearing* and the district court that upheld his ruling properly applied the probable cause standard. Note also that the Supreme Court emphasizes that the judge at that hearing is obligated to view the evidence "in a light most favorable to the prosecution." Why? Because it is the defendant who is moving to dismiss the charge, and that means all credibility assessments and inferences must be considered to favor the "non-moving" party, i.e., the prosecution. In other words, all the Supreme Court was deciding was whether the evidence presented by the prosecution at the preliminary hearing was sufficient to allow the state to proceed to trial. It is only at that point that the burden of proving guilt beyond a reasonable doubt becomes applicable. Hall's case was in fact tried to a jury, and Hall was convicted of the lesser included offense of criminally negligent homicide. *See Skier Found Guilty in Man's Death*, CBS.com, November 14, 2000.

2. Why would a jury convict for that offense instead of reckless manslaughter?

3. What is the nature of the "risk" a defendant must be subjectively aware of to support a reckless homicide conviction? Is a finding that a driver is texting and driving, and therefore subjectively aware of the risk of causing an accident, sufficient to satisfy this burden?

4. If the assessment of the substantial and unjustified nature of the risk is an inherently fact-based judgment made on a case-by-case basis, isn't there some risk that two different juries might reach different conclusions on very similar evidence?

5. What type of evidence do you think is normally relied on to satisfy the subjective awareness component of recklessness?

6. Defendant is charged with reckless manslaughter as the result of killing the victim when he discharged of his pistol in a crowded room. The evidence conclusively establishes that the defendant brought his newly purchased pistol to a frat party to show it off to his frat brothers. While in the living room with at least 15 other guests and residents in the room, he was twirling the pistol and tossing it between both hands. When he dropped the pistol, it fired, and the round instantly killed another member of the fraternity. At that moment, the defendant said, "How? I thought the pistol was unloaded" and showed his friends the ammunition clip that was in his pocket. Other witnesses testified that defendant had no experience with firearms; that this was the first time he had owned or handled a pistol; and that he was not required to undergo any training before he bought the pistol. Based on these facts, if you were a juror, would you be convinced beyond a reasonable doubt defendant is guilty?

F. Strict Liability Offenses

Historically there have been a small number of crimes requiring no criminal mental state for guilt. These crimes are known as strict liability offenses, with guilt based on proof of the criminal act or omission and result. Two traditional examples are bigamy and statutory rape. However, because mens rea is considered so fundamental to criminal culpability, strict liability offenses are normally limited to regulatory type offenses; code violations that normally result in minor penalties such as fines. In that context, strict liability is a logical compromise between the needs of society and protection from injustice. Just imagine how complicated it would be if guilt for a traffic offense such as a stop sign violation required proof of mens rea.

The traffic context highlights one of the most significant aspects of a strict liability offense: as there is no requirement to prove *any* mens rea, a mistake, no matter how reasonable, is simply irrelevant to establishing guilt. Thus, it is irrelevant whether the driver cited for failing to stop at a stop sign saw the sign because, even if she did not, her mistake in no way impacts guilt. So long as there was a stop sign and she didn't stop, she is guilty.

Beyond the realm of regulatory offenses, however, strict liability crimes are generally disfavored. This is because imposition of serious punishment and the stigma for being convicted of more than a minor regulatory offense is generally considered unjust absent proof of a criminal mental state. Because of this, the MPC establishes a rule that the absence of an express mens rea requirement in a crime triggers a presumption that guilt requires proof of at least a reckless state of mind. Nonetheless, if the legislative intent to omit a mens rea element in a crime is clear, either by the plain text of the statute or other interpretive indications, the crime will be treated as strict liability. For example, in *Garnett v. Maryland,* 332 Md. 571, 632 A.2d 797 (1993), a defendant appealed his conviction for statutory rape. The court noted:

> To be sure, legislative bodies since the mid-19th century have created strict liability criminal offenses requiring no *mens rea*. Almost all such statutes responded to the demands of public health and welfare arising from the complexities of society after the Industrial Revolution. Typically misdemeanors involving only fines or other light penalties, these strict liability laws regulated food, milk, liquor, medicines and drugs, securities, motor vehicles and traffic, the labeling of goods for sale, and the like. . . . Statutory rape, carrying the stigma of felony as well as a potential sentence of 20 years in prison, contrasts markedly with the other strict liability regulatory offenses and their light penalties.

The court framed the issue as follows:

> Section 463(a)(3) does not expressly set forth a requirement that the accused have acted with a criminal state of mind, or *mens rea.* The State insists

that the statute, by design, defines a strict liability offense, and that its essential elements were met in the instant case when Raymond, age 20, engaged in vaginal intercourse with Erica, a girl under 14 and more than 4 years his junior. Raymond replies that the criminal law exists to assess and punish morally culpable behavior. He says such culpability was absent here. He asks us either to engraft onto subsection (a)(3) an implicit *mens rea* requirement, or to recognize an affirmative defense of reasonable mistake as to the complainant's age. Raymond argues that it is unjust, under the circumstances of this case which led him to think his conduct lawful, to brand him a felon and rapist.

The court rejected Garnett's contention, concluding that,

> We think it sufficiently clear, however, that Maryland's second degree rape statute defines a strict liability offense that does not require the State to prove *mens rea;* it makes no allowance for a mistake-of-age defense. The plain language of § 463, viewed in its entirety, and the legislative history of its creation lead to this conclusion.

The next case illustrates the effect of the presumption that absent clear indication to the contrary, all offenses require proof of some mens rea. The case arose out of a military General Court-Martial. This is a federal criminal trial conducted pursuant to the authority provided by the Uniform Code of Military Justice (UCMJ). The UCMJ was enacted by Congress in 1950 pursuant to the authority provided by Article I of the Constitution to make rules for the land and naval forces. It includes an enumeration of crimes within the scope of military jurisdiction, known as the Punitive Articles. Members of the armed forces (and a small category of others, such as prisoners of war) are subject to this jurisdiction at all times and at all places. One of the most commonly violated provision is Article 92, which makes it a crime to violate a lawful general order. But what indicates a violation? The answer is the order itself. This means that a commanding officer authorized to issue such a general order is in effect filling in the blanks of the statute; she publishes the order indicating what is prohibited, and if violated, it falls within the scope of Article 92. The central issue in this case is whether the general order allegedly violated implicitly required proof of a criminal mental state/mens rea. That question was first resolved by the military judge presiding over the court-martial; then addressed by the Army Court of Criminal Appeals (an appellate court composed of senior Army attorneys); and in the opinion below, by the Court of Appeals for the Armed Forces (an appellate court composed of civilian judges with jurisdiction over all the armed forces).

United States v. Gifford

75 M.J. 140 (2016)
United States Court of Appeals for the Armed Forces

Appellant was charged, inter alia, with three specifications of violating a lawful general order under Article 92, UCMJ, 10 U.S.C. § 892 (2012). The general order prohibited servicemembers twenty-one years of age and older from providing alcohol to individuals under twenty-one years of age for the purpose of consumption. Contrary to his pleas, a general court-martial . . . found Appellant guilty of these three specifications. The panel [jury] reached its verdict after being instructed that the general order required the Government to prove both that (a) Appellant provided alcohol with the intent that it be consumed and (b) Appellant knew that the individuals to whom he was providing the alcohol were under twenty-one years of age. On appeal, however, the United States Army Court of Criminal Appeals (CCA) concluded that the general order "did not include a knowledge of age requirement" . . . . We granted Appellant's petition to determine whether the CCA erred, and if so, to identify the proper legal standard the CCA should have applied in this case.

. . . [C]onsistent with Supreme Court precedent, we conclude that the general order at issue required the Government to prove Appellant's mens rea with respect to the age of the recipients of the alcohol. We further hold that the Government was required to prove, at a minimum, that Appellant acted recklessly in this regard. We therefore reverse the CCA and remand for further proceedings consistent with this opinion.

Background

In December 2011, Appellant, a twenty-nine-year-old infantry specialist, hosted a social event in his barracks room at Camp Humphreys, Republic of Korea. At this party, Appellant provided alcohol to fellow soldiers who were under twenty-one years of age. At the time that he did so, a Second Infantry Division policy letter was in effect which stated, in pertinent part: "Service members who are 21 years of age and over may not distribute or give alcohol to anyone under 21 years of age for the purpose of consumption." There is no dispute that this policy letter constituted a lawful general order within the ambit of Article 92, UCMJ [meaning that violating the order qualified as a crime in violation of the UCMJ].

At trial, the military judge discussed with counsel the wording of the policy letter. He specifically addressed the issue of mens rea, stating:

> The other state of mind issue that's raised by the policy letter is it seems fairly implicitly clear, I guess is one way to put it, that the accused, as an element of the offense, has to have known—it's not only that the person receiving the alcohol was under the age of 21 but he has to have known that. Do both sides agree?

Both trial counsel and trial defense counsel agreed with the military judge's characterization of the burden of proof placed on the Government in this case.

Accordingly, the military judge instructed the [jury] that the Government was required to prove that "the accused actually knew at the time of the alleged offense that the person named in [the] specification [i.e., the recipient of the alcohol] was under 21 years [of age]."

Upon deliberation, the panel found Appellant guilty of each of the three specifications. . . . On direct appeal . . . the CCA opined that the mens rea standard afforded to Appellant at trial was not required by law.

Appellant petitioned this Court and we granted review of the following issue:

> Whether the Army Court of Criminal Appeals erred in holding that Second Infantry Division Policy Letter number 8 (11 January 2010), which prohibits service members who are 21 years of age and older from distributing alcohol to persons under 21 for the purposes of consumption, did not contain an element that Appellant knew that the person to whom distribution was made was under 21 years of age, and therefore imposed strict liability *for* such actions.

II. Analysis

A. Mens Rea Requirement

In the instant case, our first task is to determine whether a mens rea requirement applies to the general order at issue. . . .

1. Proof of Mens Rea is the Rule Rather Than the Exception

As the Supreme Court recognized in *United States v. United States Gypsum Co.*, 438 U.S. 422, 98 S.Ct. 2864, 57 L.Ed.2d 854 (1978), "[the] existence of a *mens rea* is the rule, rather than the exception to, the principles of Anglo-American criminal jurisprudence." *Id.* at 436, 98 S.Ct. 2864 (alteration in original) (citation omitted) (internal quotation marks omitted). The Court further noted in *Morissette v. United States*, 342 U.S. 246, 250, 72 S.Ct. 240, 96 L.Ed. 288 (1952), that "[t]he contention that an injury can amount to a crime only when inflicted by intention is no provincial or transient notion" but is instead "universal and persistent in mature systems of law." If, at trial, the Government is not required to prove that an accused had knowledge of the facts that make his or her actions criminal in order to secure a conviction, then the underlying crime is properly deemed a strict liability offense. *Liparota v. United States*, 471 U.S. 419, 443 n. 7, 105 S.Ct. 2084, 85 L.Ed.2d 434 (1985) (White, J., joined by Burger, C.J., dissenting) ("Under a strict-liability statute, a defendant can be convicted even though he was unaware of the circumstances of his conduct that made it illegal."); *see also Staples v. United States*, 511 U.S. 600, 607 n. 3, 114 S.Ct. 1793, 128 L.Ed.2d 608 (1994) (noting that knowledge "[of] the facts that make [an individual's] conduct fit the definition of [an] offense. . . . is necessary to establish *mens rea*"). However, the Supreme Court has cast a jaundiced eye on such offenses: "While strict-liability offenses are not unknown to the criminal law . . . the limited circumstances in which Congress has created and this Court has recognized such offenses attest to their generally disfavored status." *United States Gypsum Co.,* 438 U.S. at 437-38, 98 S.Ct. 2864 (citations omitted).

On the basis of this general disfavor for strict liability offenses, silence in a criminal statute—or, as in this case, a general order—does not prevent mens rea from being inferred. The Supreme Court has routinely held that while courts should "ordinarily resist reading words or elements into a statute that do not appear on its face," *Dean v. United States,* 556 U.S. 568, 572, 129 S.Ct. 1849, 173 L.Ed.2d 785 (2009) (internal quotation marks omitted) (quoting *Bates v. United States,* 522 U.S. 23, 29, 118 S.Ct. 285, 139 L.Ed.2d 215 (1997)), the "'mere omission from a criminal enactment of any mention of criminal intent' should not be read 'as dispensing with it,'" *Elonis v. United States,* —U.S.—, 135 S.Ct. 2001, 2009, 192 L.Ed.2d 1 (2015) (quoting *Morissette,* 342 U.S. at 250, 72 S.Ct. 240). Rather, an "indication of congressional intent . . . is required to dispense with *mens rea.*" *Staples,* 511 U.S. at 606, 114 S.Ct. 1793 . . .

2. Public Welfare Offenses are an Exception to this General Rule

The general rule that the Government must prove an accused's mens rea in order to secure a criminal conviction is not without exception. The Supreme Court has acknowledged that, in limited circumstances, Congress may purposefully omit from a statute the need to prove an accused's criminal intent, and courts are then obligated to recognize this congressional intent and conform their rulings accordingly. *See, e.g., United States v. Balint,* 258 U.S. 250, 252-53, 42 S.Ct. 301, 66 L.Ed. 604 (1922); *see also Staples,* 511 U.S. at 606, 114 S.Ct. 1793 ("[S]ome indication of congressional intent, express or implied, is required to dispense with *mens rea* as an element of a crime."). In certain instances, this class of legislation produces what is known as a "public welfare offense," *Staples,* 511 U.S. at 606-07, 114 S.Ct. 1793, which uniquely focuses on "social betterment" or "proper care" rather than punishment, *Balint,* 258 U.S. at 251-53, 42 S.Ct. 301 . . .

3. The Underlying Offense Contained in the General Order Was Not a Public Welfare Offense

The Supreme Court has somewhat hesitantly contoured the boundaries of those instances where mens rea may be dispensed with as a prerequisite for conviction. For example, in *Morissette,* Justice Jackson wrote:

> Neither this Court nor, so far as we are aware, any other has undertaken to delineate a precise line or set forth comprehensive criteria for distinguishing between crimes that require a mental element and crimes that do not. We attempt no closed definition, for the law on the subject is neither settled nor static.

342 U.S. at 260, 72 S.Ct. 240; *accord Staples,* 511 U.S. at 620, 114 S.Ct. 1793 (same). This hesitancy notwithstanding, the Supreme Court's core inquiry has remained relatively simple and direct: did Congress *purposefully* omit intent from the statute at issue? *See, e.g., Staples,* 511 U.S. at 620, 114 S.Ct. 1793 ("[O]ur holding depends

critically on our view that if Congress had intended to make outlaws of gun owners who were wholly ignorant of the offending characteristics of their weapons . . . it would have spoken more clearly to that effect."); *United States v. Freed,* 401 U.S. 601, 616, 91 S.Ct. 1112, 28 L.Ed.2d 356 (1971) (Brennan, J., concurring in the judgment) ("[T]he question is solely one of congressional intent."). Thus, as the Supreme Court held in *Balint,* "[whether mens rea is a necessary facet of the crime] is a question of legislative intent to be construed by the court," 258 U.S. at 252, 42 S.Ct. 301. If such an intent can be identified, courts must construe the relevant statute accordingly. . . . This makes clear that the question before us in the instant case is whether the commander—acting pursuant to his congressionally delegated authority—intended to create a public welfare offense through his general order. We cannot divine such an intent and therefore decline to treat the general order as having created a public welfare offense.

If Congress is expected to speak with a clear voice in this context, the same should be expected of a commander. We find no justification for holding commanders to a lower standard than a legislature as they exercise their power to issue a general order with punitive consequence, and we take particular note in the instant case that the commander did not explicitly indicate his intention to create a public welfare offense. Moreover, for the reasons outlined below, we do not find any other basis to conclude that this general order, which stands mute on the subject, was intended to override the traditional call of criminal law that "wrongdoing must be conscious to be criminal." *Morissette,* 342 U.S. at 252, 72 S.Ct. 240.

a. The history of alcohol offenses does not support a conclusion that the commander intended to create a public welfare offense

In *Morissette,* the Supreme Court emphasized the need to examine the historical treatment of a crime in order to determine if Congress purposefully intended to omit scienter from the text of a statute. The Supreme Court noted:

> Congressional silence as to mental elements in an Act merely adopting into federal statutory law a concept of crime already so well defined in common law and statutory interpretation by the states may warrant quite contrary inferences than the same silence in creating an offense new to general law, or for whose definition the courts have no guidance except the Act.

Morissette, 342 U.S. at 262, 72 S.Ct. 240. The Supreme Court also explained the need to explore "legal tradition[s] and [the] meaning of centuries of practice" in discerning the intent of Congress. *Id.* at 263, 72 S.Ct. 240.

In the instant case, history, context, and legal traditions do not provide us with an answer favorable to the Government. True, the foundation of public welfare offenses can be traced back to alcohol related offenses. *Id.* at 256, 72 S.Ct. 240 ("The pilot of the [public welfare] movement in this country appears to be a holding that a tavern-keeper could be convicted for selling liquor to a[] habitual drunkard even if he did not know the buyer to be such." (citing *Barnes v. State,* 19 Conn. 398, 398 (1849))). But it is important to note that laws that apply to businesses that sell liquor are distinguishable from those that regulate the conduct of private citizens. Businesses selling alcohol are far more likely to be viewed as "standing in responsible relation to a public danger" than are mere individuals who provide alcohol to friends and acquaintances for free. *See id.* at 260, 72 S.Ct. 240.

Moreover, there is no modern consensus that offenses involving alcohol necessarily constitute public welfare offenses. . . .

c. The gravity of punishment weighs against finding that the commander intended to create a public welfare offense

The Supreme Court has long recognized that "penalties [for public welfare offenses] commonly are relatively small, and conviction does not [do] grave damage to an offender's reputation." *Morissette,* 342 U.S. at 256, 72 S.Ct. 240. Therefore, the Supreme Court has held that "a severe penalty is a further factor tending to suggest that Congress did not intend to eliminate a *mens rea* requirement." *Staples,* 511 U.S. at 618, 114 S.Ct. 1793; *accord United States Gypsum Co.,* 438 U.S. at 442 n. 18, 98 S.Ct. 2864 (same).

Relevant to the instant case, a violation of Article 92, UCMJ, can be punished with a dishonorable discharge, forfeiture of all pay and allowances, and confinement for up to two years. MCM pt. IV, para. 16.e.(1). It is self-evident that such a punishment is not "relatively small" and instead represents a "severe penalty" that can do "grave damage" to an accused's reputation.

4. Conclusion

Ultimately, we hold that the CCA erred [when it concluded] the general order at issue did not include a mens rea requirement with respect to age. We base our conclusion on (a) the fact that a mens rea requirement is the rule rather than the exception in criminal offenses, even in those instances when a statute is silent on that point; (b) the lack of any overt evidence that the commander intended to create a public welfare offense; and (c) our refusal to intuit such an intent on the commander's behalf, given the historical context of alcohol offenses, the underlying character of the offense, and the gravity of the punishment.

[The court then held that, consistent with the approach reflected in the Model Penal Code, recklessness should be the implicit mens rea requirement when the crime fails to define the requisite mens rea absent clear indication that no mens rea is required.]

Notes and Questions

1. Imagine the defendant honestly and reasonably believed the soldiers he gave the alcohol to were older than 21. If, as the court held, his alleged criminal act (providing the alcohol) had to be reckless to amount to a violation of the order, would his mistake bar conviction? What if his mistake was honest but the military jury concluded it was unreasonable under the circumstances?

2. What language should the order have included if the commander actually wanted the offense to be strict liability?

3. Why might a legislature choose to define a serious crime such as statutory rape as strict liability?

Formative Assessments

1. A state statute requires any person licensed to sell prescription drugs to file with the State Board of Health a report listing the types and amounts of such drugs sold if his sales of such drugs exceed $50,000 during a calendar year. The statutory penalty for failing to file a required report is a maximum fine of $5,000.00 and suspension of the pharmaceutical license for 6 months. Defendant is licensed to sell prescription drugs. During the reporting period, he sold $63,000 worth of prescription drugs but did not file the report. Charged with committing the misdemeanor, Nelson testifies that he did a very poor job of keeping records and did not realize that his sales of prescription drugs had exceeded $50,000. If the jury believes Nelson, he should be found:

A. Guilty, because this is a public welfare offense.

B. Not guilty, because he did not intend to violate the statute.

C. Not guilty, because the statute punishes omissions, and he was not given fair warning of duty to act.

D. Not guilty, because he was not aware of the value of the drugs he had sold.

2. The State Statute defines Murder as follows: "The knowing or intentional and premeditated unlawful killing of a human being. All other murder is murder in the second-degree."

Under which set of facts would a defendant be *least likely* to be convicted of first-degree murder for causing the death of a victim?

A. Defendant, believing he would only cause customers to get sick for a few days, sprinkles a small amount of a toxic substance on a restaurant food bar to protest animal food products.

B. Defendant, angry at his neighbor, sets the neighbor's house on fire. When questioned by police, Defendant says he saw the victim in the home but intended only to destroy the home and believed the victim could easily get out of the house.

C. Defendant suddenly snaps and shoots another customer in a bar. Defendant admits he intended to kill the victim, but the jury concludes he did not have sufficient time to premeditate.

Chapter 5

Mistake and Mens Rea

I. Introduction

Mistake is a factual proposition raised by a defendant in order to prevent — or negate — the requisite mens rea for an alleged offense. Terminology related to mistakes can be somewhat confusing. Mistake is most commonly referred to as a defense theory. This is logical, as it is raised to prevent the prosecution from proving guilt beyond a reasonable doubt. But this also suggests that the defendant bears a burden to prove the alleged mistake. This is wrong. Why? Because mistake is raised as an obstacle to block the prosecution from proving mens rea, a requisite element. This means that once a mistake is raised, the prosecution bears the burden of *disproving* the mistake beyond a reasonable doubt, because disproving the mistake is required to prove the mens rea it purports to negate.

It will be useful for you to picture mens rea and mistake as they operate together. Imagine that when the trial begins, the prosecution is at the "starting line" on the path to reach the mens rea checkered flag at the finish line. Remember, the presumption of innocence means the prosecution bears both the burden of production and burden of persuasion for this mens rea element. Now imagine at some point during the trial, the defendant produces some evidence of a relevant mistake (this might be through cross-examining a prosecution witness or offering evidence in the defense case). Once some evidence of a relevant mistake is produced, it is like the defense has erected an obstacle along the path to the mens rea flag. Because the prosecution bears the burden of persuasion, the prosecution must breach this obstacle in order to reach the mens rea flag. In other words, in order to prove the requisite mens rea, the prosecution must persuade the jury beyond a reasonable doubt that the alleged mistake is insufficient to block proving the requisite mens rea.

While it is common to associate mistakes with "negating" mens rea, the explanation above illustrates why "blocking" mens rea is a better characterization than "negating." Why? Because the term "negate" suggests the mens rea is already established, but in fact, the mistake is an obstacle *to* establishing the mens rea. Remember, mistake is not an *affirmative* defense like self-defense or insanity; it is a *failure of proof* defense used by the defense to raise reasonable doubt as to the requisite mens rea element.

Mistakes fall into two categories: mistakes of fact and mistakes of law. It is important to distinguish between these two types of alleged mistakes because both their relevance and the proof required to overcome them are different. Mistakes of fact are far more common than mistakes of law. This is because, in most cases, mistake of law is simply not raised by the evidence as it is a far more restrictive theory.

A. Mistake of Fact

In common law jurisdictions that continue to classify mens rea as specific or general intent, mistake of fact is always relevant if the alleged mistake would be inconsistent with the requisite mens rea. For example, because burglary requires proof of the specific intent to "commit a felony" in the dwelling of another, if a defendant alleged she thought the home she broke and entered was her own, her state of mind would be incompatible with the requisite mens rea. But what it takes to overcome the mistake obstacle will turn on whether it is erected in the path of a specific intent element or a general intent element.

Recall that specific intent (or mens rea) denotes a purely subjective mental state. Accordingly, so long as the defendant's mistake was subjectively honest, it is a complete defense to the specific intent element, even if the mistake was unreasonable under the circumstances. Thus, in the burglary example, the prosecution would have to persuade the fact finder that the defendant did not in fact harbor a mistake as to the dwelling; if the fact finder had reasonable doubt as to what the defendant actually believed, it means the prosecution failed to prove the requisite specific intent beyond a reasonable doubt. Thus, in common sense terms, when a mistake is raised to block proof of a specific intent element, the prosecution must persuade the jury there was no mistake (in other words, not to believe the defendant). Consider this pattern instruction to illustrate:

IGNORANCE OR MISTAKE — WHERE SPECIFIC INTENT OR ACTUAL KNOWLEDGE IS IN ISSUE:

The evidence has raised the issue of (ignorance) (mistake) on the part of the accused concerning (state the asserted ignorance or mistake) in relation to the offense(s) of (state the alleged offense(s)).

I advised you earlier that to find the accused guilty of the offense(s) of (state the alleged offense(s)), you must find beyond a reasonable doubt that the accused (had the specific intent to _____) (knew that _____) (_____). If the accused at the time of the offense was (ignorant of the fact) (under the mistaken belief) that (state the asserted ignorance or mistake) then (he) (she) cannot be found guilty of the offense(s) of (state the alleged offense(s)).

The (ignorance) (mistake), *no matter how unreasonable it might have been*, is a defense. In deciding whether the accused was (ignorant of the fact) (under the mistaken belief) that (state the asserted ignorance or mistake), you should consider the probability or improbability of the evidence presented on the matter. You should consider the accused's (age) (education) (experience) (_____) along with the other evidence on this issue (including, but not limited to, (here the judge may specify significant evidentiary factors bearing on the issue and indicate the respective contentions of counsel for both sides)).

The burden is on the prosecution to establish the guilt of the accused. If you are convinced beyond a reasonable doubt that at the time of the alleged offense(s) the accused was not (ignorant of the fact) (under the mistaken belief) that (state the asserted ignorance or mistake), then the defense of (ignorance) (mistake) does not exist.

In contrast, when a defendant raises a mistake to prevent proof of a general intent (mens rea) element, the mistake must be both honest and reasonable. In other words, the defendant must have *subjectively* harbored the mistake and it must also be one that a *reasonable* person in the same or similar situation would have made. This means the prosecution may overcome the mistake obstacle in one of two ways: first, the prosecution can convince the fact finder that the defendant did not harbor the mistake (there was no mistake); second, even assuming the defendant harbored the mistake it was not reasonable under the circumstances. Thus, it is easier to *disprove* a mistake related to a general mens rea element than a specific mens rea element because the finder of fact may reject the mistake defense if it was unreasonable. Imagine in the example above the defendant was charged with trespass instead of burglary, and that trespass is defined as the unlawful *reckless or negligent* entry onto the property of another. For such an offense, the defendant is guilty even if she honestly believed she was entering her own home so long as the prosecution persuades the fact finder that the belief was objectively unreasonable under the circumstances. Notice how this alternative means of overcoming the mistake obstacle is reflected in this instruction:

IGNORANCE OR MISTAKE—WHEN ONLY GENERAL INTENT IS IN ISSUE

The evidence has raised the issue of (ignorance) (mistake) on the part of the accused concerning (state the asserted ignorance or mistake) in relation to the offense(s) of (state the alleged offense(s)).

The accused is not guilty of the offense of (_____) if: (1) (he) (she) ((did not know) (mistakenly believed)) that (state the asserted ignorance or mistake) and (2) if such (ignorance) (belief) on (his) (her) part was reasonable. To be reasonable the (ignorance) (belief) must have been based on information, or lack of it, which would indicate to a reasonable person that _____. (Additionally, the (ignorance) (mistake) cannot be based on a negligent failure to discover the true facts.) (Negligence is the absence of due care. Due care is what a reasonably careful person would do under the same or similar circumstances.)

You should consider the accused's (age) (education) (experience) (_____) along with the other evidence on this issue, (including, but not limited to (here the military judge may specify significant evidentiary factors bearing on the issue and indicate the respective contentions of counsel for both sides)). The burden is on the prosecution to establish the accused's guilt. If you are convinced beyond a reasonable doubt that, at the time of the charged offense(s), the accused was not (ignorant of the fact) (under the mistaken belief) that (state the asserted ignorance or mistake), the defense of (ignorance) (mistake) does not exist. Even if you conclude that the accused was (ignorant of the fact) (under the mistaken belief) that (state the asserted ignorance or mistake), if you are convinced beyond a reasonable doubt that, at the time of the charged offense(s), the accused's (ignorance) (mistake) was unreasonable, the defense of (ignorance) (mistake) does not exist.

Recall that the MPC dispensed with the specific/general intent labels. So how does mistake of fact function in an MPC jurisdiction? Essentially the same. According to the MPC, a mistake of fact is relevant if it "negates" the requisite mens rea for an alleged offense. Accordingly, if the offense requires proof of a purely subjective mental state — purpose or knowledge — the mistake need only be honest to negate the mens rea. However, if the offense requires proof of "unreasonable" judgment to prove the mental state — recklessness or negligence — the mistake must be both honest and reasonable.

B. Mistake of Law

Mistake of law is a much more restricted defense theory. Historically, mistake of law was not a recognized defense. However, over time, jurisdictions softened this rule and allowed a defendant to raise a mistake of law in two situations. First, the rare case where knowledge of the law was a requisite mens rea element of the alleged offense. For example, in an omission case where the prosecution must prove as an element of the offense that the defendant *knew* he had a legal obligation to act, an honest mistake or ignorance as to that law would be a complete defense. This is extremely rare, as very few crimes require proof that the defendant knew the law he was violating. Second, where a defendant detrimentally relies on an official statement of the law and engages in illegal conduct, proof of reliance on this mistaken statement is a complete defense. This second theory is also very rare, but is in reality an *estoppel* concept: it is unjust to allow the state to convict a citizen for engaging in conduct that the defendant mistakenly believed was lawful due to an official statement of the law later established as erroneous. However, as the MPC notes, it is essential that the defendant's detrimental reliance was on an authority responsible for interpreting the relevant law: the erroneous interpretation must be in a judicial order or decision, a formal administrative order, or an official interpretation of the law provided by an individual "with responsibility for the interpretation, administration or enforcement" of the law at issue.

> ## Practice Pointer
>
> Mistake law illustrates why it is so important to identify the nature of the mens rea element a defendant is seeking to "block" with evidence of an alleged mistake. Remember that just because a defendant alleges a mistake doesn't automatically mean it is an effective obstacle. But also remember that once alleged, the prosecution bears the burden of proving the mistake is ineffective to block proof of the requisite mens rea. It is also not uncommon for an offense requiring proof of a specific intent element (or in the MPC, purpose or knowledge) to be a "greater" offense to a necessarily included lesser offense that requires proof of only general mens rea (or in the MPC, recklessness or gross negligence). In such a case, an honest mistake may be effective at blocking proof of the specific intent element resulting in acquittal for the greater charged offense, but unreasonable and therefore insufficient to block proof of general mens rea, thereby resulting in a conviction for the lesser included offense. So always ask: 1. What mens rea element is the defendant seeking to block with the alleged mistake? 2. What is required for the mistake to be effective in blocking the requisite mens rea? 3. Has the prosecution persuaded the fact finder that the mistake is ineffective? 4. If not, what impact (if any) does the mistake have on the requisite mens rea for any lesser included offense?

II. Application

A. Is Mistake Relevant?

Whether an alleged mistake is relevant depends on whether there is a mens rea element the mistake obstructs or negates. The following case illustrates the importance of this determination.

State v. Breathette

202 N.C. App. 697 (2010)
North Carolina Court of Appeals

ROBERT C. HUNTER, Judge.

Defendant Yasmin Pecolia Breathette appeals her convictions for taking indecent liberties with a minor. Defendant argues on appeal that the trial court erred by not giving the jury her requested instruction that mistake of age is a valid defense to the offense of indecent liberties. We conclude that mistake of age is not a defense applicable to the charge, and, therefore, the trial court properly refused to instruct the jury on the defense. Consequently, we find no error.

Facts

The State presented evidence at trial tending to establish the following facts: B.W. ("Beth") was born in March 1995 and lived in Taylors, South Carolina with her mother. When Beth was 13 years old she met defendant, who was 19 at the time, on the social networking website MySpace and the two began messaging. Beth's MySpace page indicated that she was 99 years old because she did not "want people to know [her] real age." When defendant asked how old Beth was, Beth told her that she was 17. The two discussed "chilling" together at defendant's apartment, exchanged cell phone numbers, and began texting and calling each other on a daily basis. Defendant, whose MySpace page indicated that she was a lesbian, asked Beth whether she was a lesbian, and Beth told her that she was gay. When texting or talking, they would sometimes discuss "sexual stuff." Sometimes Beth would initiate the sexual conversations and sometimes it was defendant.

Defendant and Beth decided that they wanted to meet in person, so defendant drove from her apartment in Winston-Salem, North Carolina on 4 June 2008, picked up Beth at a designated spot, and drove back to Winston-Salem for the weekend. When defendant and Beth got back to defendant's apartment, they watched TV together and "[t]ongue kiss[ed]."

The next day, 5 June 2008, defendant took Beth over to her friend Francesca's house, where they stayed most of the day. While watching TV, defendant and Beth "made out" on the couch and kissed. Later that night, defendant and Beth went back to defendant's apartment, where they ordered pizza and watched TV and movies. Defendant and Beth later got into defendant's bed, where Beth gave defendant a "hickey" on her neck. Defendant kissed Beth's breast, digitally penetrated her vagina, and performed oral sex on her. After about 10 minutes, they went to sleep.

Defendant and Beth got into an argument on Friday, 6 June 2008 . . . . Defendant left for work on Saturday morning before Beth woke up and Beth texted and called defendant several times during the day, asking for a ride home. Defendant did not want to drive Beth home and the two fought over the phone while defendant was at work. When defendant's supervisor overheard her yelling loudly on the phone at work, she was fired from her job. Defendant came home, yelling at Beth that she made her lose her job. Defendant collected Beth's things, threw them out into the front yard, and locked her out of the apartment. Beth contacted Amanda, one of defendant's friends that she had met during the weekend, and Amanda let Beth spend Saturday night at her house.

The next day, 8 June 2008, Amanda dropped Beth off at Francesca's house, where Beth told Francesca's mother about her fight with defendant and that they had done "sexual stuff." Francesca's mother called the police, who came to get Beth. While there, the police interviewed Beth and she told them that she was 17. Officers took Beth to the police station, where she told them that nothing had happened. Beth's mother arrived in Winston-Salem that evening and drove her home.

Officer J.A. Sheets interviewed defendant on 9 June 2008, at her apartment. Defendant told him that she met Beth on MySpace and that they had met in person because they were interested in dating each other. Defendant also told Officer Sheets that Beth's MySpace page had been changed to indicate that she was 18, although it had originally indicated that she was 21. Defendant told Officer Sheets that they had "fingered" each other, but that only she had performed oral sex. Defendant later texted Beth, asking her why she did not tell defendant her "real age." When Beth responded that she did not know why, defendant texted back that "[Beth] was wrong."

Defendant was charged with two counts of taking indecent liberties with a minor. . . . Defendant then testified that she first came into contact with Beth through MySpace in May 2008. Defendant also found Beth on "downylink.com," a "straight, gay, lesbian, and bisexual Website for people over the age of eighteen." Defendant explained that when she saw Beth on downylink.com, she believed that Beth was over 18 because the website requires all users to verify that they are 18 years old or over. The jury convicted defendant of both charges and the trial court sentenced defendant to two consecutive presumptive-range sentences of 14 to 17 months imprisonment, but suspended the second sentence and imposed 36 months of supervised probation. Defendant timely appealed to this Court.

I. Jury Instructions

A. Mistake of Age Defense

In a written request, defendant asked the trial court to instruct the jury that

> [i]f you do find that the defendant was both acting under a belief that the alleged victim was older than 15 years old and that such belief was reasonable, albeit mistaken, then it would be your duty to render a verdict of not guilty to the charges of taking indecent liberties with a child as the defendant lacked the requisite guilty mind to formulate the specific intent to commit the crime.

Defendant argues that the trial court committed reversible error by not instructing the jury that mistake of age is a defense to the charge of taking indecent liberties with a minor.

If a request is made for an instruction that is a correct statement of the law and is supported by the evidence, the trial court must give the instruction. . . .

The State argues that the trial court properly refused to instruct the jury on the mistake of age defense as the defense is inapplicable to the crime of taking indecent liberties with a minor. . . .

Defendant is correct that "[t]his is a case of first impression," as North Carolina's courts have not specifically addressed whether mistake of age is a recognized defense to a charge of taking indecent liberties with a minor. Generally, "[i]gnorance or mistake as to a matter of fact . . . is a defense if it negatives a mental state required to establish a material element of the crime. . . ." Wayne R. LeFave, *Substantive*

Criminal Law § 5.6, at 394 (2d ed. 2003). In turn, "[w]hether a criminal intent is a necessary element of a statutory offense is a matter of construction to be determined from the language of the statute in view of its manifest purpose and design." *State v. Hales,* 256 N.C. 27, 30, 122 S.E.2d 768, 771 (1961).

N.C. Gen.Stat. § 14-202.1 defines the offense of taking indecent liberties with a minor:

> A person is guilty of taking indecent liberties with children if, being 16 years of age or more and at least five years older than the child in question, he either:
>
> (1) Willfully takes or attempts to take any immoral, improper, or indecent liberties with any child of either sex under the age of 16 years for the purpose of arousing or gratifying sexual desire; or
>
> (2) Willfully commits or attempts to commit any lewd or lascivious act upon or with the body or any part or member of the body of any child of either sex under the age of 16 years.

The statute is unambiguous as to the elements of the crime: the State must prove that (1) the defendant was at least 16; (2) the defendant was five years older than the complainant; (3) the defendant willfully took or attempted to take an indecent liberty with the complainant; (4) the complainant was under 16 at the time the alleged act or attempted act occurred; and (5) the defendant's conduct was for the purpose of arousing or gratifying sexual desire.

Defendant argues that a defendant's knowledge of the complainant's age is an element of taking indecent liberties with a minor, making mistake of age a valid defense to the crime. The plain language of N.C. Gen.Stat. § 14-202.1, however, does not support defendant's contention. The statute only requires that the complainant be "under the age of 16 years" at the time of defendant's conduct constituting the offense. N.C. Gen.Stat. § 14-202.1(a), (b). There is no explicit *mens rea* requirement in N.C. Gen. Stat. § 14-202.1 as to the complainant's age. . . .

"When conduct is made criminal because the victim is under a certain age, it is no defense that the defendant was ignorant of or mistaken as to the victim's age; and it matters not that the defendant's mistaken belief was reasonable." 1 Charles E. Torcia, *Wharton's Criminal Law* § 78, at 563-64 (15th ed. 1996); *accord* Rollin M. Perkins & Ronald N. Boyce, *Criminal Law* § 7, at 919 (3rd ed. 1982) (explaining that "'[c]rimes such as . . . carnal knowledge, seduction, and the like, where the offense depends upon the [victim]'s being below a designated age . . . do require a *mens rea,*' although a reasonable mistake of fact as to [the victim's] age is no defense" (quoting Francis B. Sayre, *Public Welfare Offenses,* 33 Colum. L.Rev. 55, 73–74 (1933))). *See also Morissette v. United States,* 342 U.S. 246, 251 n. 8, 72 S. Ct. 240, 96 L. Ed. 288, 294 n. 8 (1952) (noting "[e]xceptions [to *mens rea* requirement] . . . include sex offenses, such as rape, in which the victim's actual age was determinative despite defendant's reasonable belief that the girl had reached age of consent").

In *People v. Olsen,* 36 Cal. 3d 638, 685 P.2d 52, 205 Cal. Rptr. 492 (1984), the California Supreme Court confronted a virtually identical issue of legislative intent to the one presented in this case, holding that a good faith, reasonable mistake of age was not a defense to a charge of "willfully" committing "lewd or lascivious acts involving children." The California statute at issue in *Olsen,* similar to our indecent liberties statute, provides:

> Any person who *willfully* and lewdly commits any lewd or lascivious act . . . upon or with the body, or any part or member thereof, of a *child who is under the age of 14 years,* with the intent of arousing, appealing to, or gratifying the lust, passions, or sexual desires of that person or the child, is guilty of a felony. . . .

Cal. Penal Code § 288(a) (2009) (emphasis added). Recognizing the "exist[ence] [of] a strong public policy to protect children of tender years[,]" the *Olsen* Court concluded that a mistake of age defense was "untenable," 36 Cal. 3d at 645, 685 P.2d at 56, 205 Cal. Rptr. at 496, and that "one who commits lewd or lascivious acts with a child, even with a good faith belief that the child is [over the designated age], does so at his or her peril[,]" . . .

This Court has similarly noted "the legislative policy, inherent in [N.C. Gen.Stat. § 14-202.1], to provide broad protection to children from the sexual conduct of older persons, especially adults." *State v. Hicks,* 79 N.C.App. 599, 603, 339 S.E.2d 806, 809 (1986). Our Supreme Court has also recognized "the great breadth of protection against sexual contact the statute seeks to afford children and the reasons for it":

> Undoubtedly [N.C. Gen.Stat. § 14-202.1's] breadth is in recognition of the significantly greater risk of psychological damage to an impressionable child from overt sexual acts. We also bear in mind the enhanced power and control that adults, even strangers, may exercise over children who are outside the protection of home or school.

State v. Banks, 322 N.C. 753, 766, 370 S.E.2d 398, 407 (1988) (citation and quotation marks omitted); *accord State v. Harward,* 264 N.C. 746, 749, 142 S.E.2d 691, 694 (1965) (observing that legislative purpose of § 14-202.1 was to "supplement [existing law] and to give even broader protection to children"). We conclude, therefore, that a defendant's mistake as to the complainant's age is not a valid defense to a charge of taking indecent liberties with a minor under N.C. Gen.Stat. § 14-202.1. As the defense is inapplicable, the trial court properly refused to give defendant's proffered instruction on the defense. *See also Darden v. State,* 798 So. 2d 632, 634 (Miss.Ct.App.2001) (holding trial court did not err in refusing to give mistake of age instruction to jury in sexual battery case because mistake of age defense is not valid defense to sex crimes designed to protect children).

Notes and Questions

1. Notice that the defendant's requested instruction would have required an honest *and* reasonable mistake. Based on the facts provided, do you think she reasonably believed the child was of legal age? If so, was it fair to deny her requested instruction?

2. The alleged offense required proof that the defendant engaged in "willful" conduct. If willful is a synonym for "purpose," what did the law require to be willful?

3. If you wanted to allow for a reasonable mistake of fact defense for a defendant charged with this offense, how would you modify the statutory definition?

B. Mistake of Fact

The following case provides several examples of the type of mistake of fact that prevents proof of specific intent.

People v. Navarro

99 Cal. App. 3d Supp. 1 (1979)
California Court of Appeals

NORMAN R. DOWDS, Judge.

Defendant, charged with a violation of Penal Code section 487, subdivision 1, grand theft, appeals his conviction after a jury trial of petty theft, a lesser but necessarily included offense. His contention on appeal is that the jury was improperly instructed. The only facts set forth in the record on appeal are that defendant was charged with stealing four wooden beams from a construction site and that the state of the evidence was such that the jury could have found that the defendant believed either (1) that the beams had been abandoned as worthless and the owner had no objection to his taking them or (2) that they had substantial value, had not been abandoned and he had no right to take them.

The court refused two jury instructions proposed by defendant reading as follows:

Defendant's A

"If one takes personal property with the good faith belief that the property has been abandoned or discarded by the true owner, he is not guilty of theft. This is the case even if such good faith belief is unreasonable. The prosecutor must prove beyond a reasonable doubt that the defendant did not so believe for you to convict a defendant of theft."

Defendant's B

"If one takes personal property with the good faith belief that he has permission to take the property, he is not guilty of theft. This is the case even if such good faith belief is unreasonable.

"The prosecutor must prove beyond a reasonable doubt that the defendant did not so believe for you to convict a defendant of theft."

Instead, the court instructed the jury in the words of the following modified instructions:

Modified — Defendant's A

"If one takes personal property in the reasonable and good faith belief that the property has been abandoned or discarded by the true owner, he is not guilty of theft."

Modified — Defendant's B

"If one takes personal property in the reasonable and good faith belief that he has the consent or permission of the owner to take the property, he is not guilty of theft.

"If you have a reasonable doubt that the defendant had the required criminal intent as specified in these instructions, the defendant is entitled to an acquittal."

Accordingly, the question for determination on appeal is whether the defendant should be acquitted if there is a reasonable doubt that he had a good faith belief that the property had been abandoned or that he had the permission of the owner to take the property or whether that belief must be a reasonable one as well as being held in good faith.

A recent decision by the California Supreme Court throws light on this question. In *People v. Wetmore* (1978) 22 Cal.3d 318 [149 Cal. Rptr. 265, 583 P.2d 1308], defendant was charged with burglary, like theft a specific intent crime. The Supreme Court held that the trial court had erroneously refused to consider at the guilt phase of the trial evidence that, because of mental illness, defendant was incapable of forming the specific intent required for conviction of the crime, instead of receiving such evidence only in respect of his plea of not guilty by reason of insanity. . . .

The court concluded, at page 327: "We therefore hold that evidence of diminished capacity is admissible at the guilt phase whether or not that evidence may also be probative of insanity. The trial court erred when, relying on the *Wells* dictum, it refused to consider evidence of diminished capacity in determining defendant's guilt."

The instant case, does not, of course, involve evidence of mental illness. Evidence was presented, however, from which the jury could have concluded that defendant believed that the wooden beams had been abandoned and that the owner had no objection to his taking them, i.e., that he lacked the specific criminal intent required to commit the crime of theft (intent permanently to deprive an owner of his property). . . .

Earlier California cases are to the same effect. In *People v. Devine* (1892) 95 Cal. 227 [30 P. 378], defendant's conviction of larceny was reversed. He had driven away in a wagon, without any attempt at secrecy, a number of hogs, his own and three bearing another's mark or brand. The Supreme Court pointed out: "There are cases in which all the knowledge which a person might have acquired by due diligence is to be imputed to him. But where a felonious intent must be proven, it can be done only by proving what the accused knew. One cannot intend to steal property which he believes to be his own. He may be careless, and omit to make an effort to ascertain that the property which he thinks his own belongs to another; but so long as he believes it to be his own, he cannot feloniously steal it. . . ." (*Id.* at pp. 230–231.)

Cases in other jurisdictions also hold that where the law requires a specific criminal intent, it is not enough merely to prove that a reasonable man would have had that intent, without meeting the burden of proof that the defendant himself also entertained it. For example, in *State v. Ebbeller* (1920) 283 Mo. 57. [222 S.W. 396], a conviction of knowingly receiving a stolen automobile was reversed because the court gave the following erroneous jury instruction: "'By the term "knowing" that the property was stolen is not meant absolute personal and certain knowledge on the part of the defendant that the property mentioned in the indictment had been stolen, but such knowledge and information in his possession at the time he received the same, if you believe he did receive it, as would put a reasonably prudent man, exercising ordinary caution, on his guard, and would cause such a man exercising such caution, and under circumstances which you believe defendant received the property, to believe and he satisfied that the property had been stolen.'" (222 S.W. at p. 397.)

In reversing, the court pointed out the error in the instruction as follows:

> "It will be noticed that the instruction does permit a conviction if the facts were such as (in the opinion of the jury) would have caused a reasonably prudent person, exercising ordinary caution, to have believed that the property had been stolen at the time received.

> "We are inclined to the view . . . that the learned attorney representing the appellant is correct in stating that—"'The question is not what some other person would have believed and known from the circumstances attending the receipt of the property, but what did this defendant believe and know.'" (*Id.*)

Similarly, in *Kasle v. United States* (6th Cir.1916) 233 Fed. 878 a conviction of receiving stolen goods was reversed because of error in jury instructions which the appellate court read as informing the jury that the defendant could be convicted if a reasonable and honest man of average intelligence would have known the goods were stolen under the facts existing at the time, the court stating: "The effect of such tests was to charge the accused with guilty knowledge or not upon what the jury might find would have induced belief in the mind of a man such as they were told to consider, rather than the belief that was actually created in the mind of the accused; or, at last, the accused might be condemned even if his only fault consisted in being less cautious or suspicious than honest men of average intelligence are of the acts of others. The result of the rule of the charge would be to convict a man, not because guilty, but because stupid. The issue was whether the accused had knowledge — not whether some other person would have obtained knowledge — that the goods had been stolen." (*Id.* at p. 887) . . .

La Fave and Scott, Handbook on Criminal Law (1972) sets forth at page 357 what the authors call the "... rather simple rule that an honest mistake of fact or law is a defense when it negates a required mental element of the crime...." As an example they refer to the crime of receiving stolen property, stating "... if the defendant by a mistake of either fact or law did not know the goods were stolen, even though the circumstances would have led a prudent man to believe they were stolen, he does not have the required mental state and thus may not be convicted of the crime."

In the instant case the trial court in effect instructed the jury that even though defendant in good faith believed he had the right to take the beams, and thus lacked the specific intent required for the crime of theft, he should be convicted unless such belief was reasonable. In doing so it erred. It is true that if the jury thought the defendant's belief to be unreasonable, it might infer that he did not in good faith hold such belief. If, however, it concluded that defendant in good faith believed that he had the right to take the beams, even though such belief was unreasonable as measured by the objective standard of a hypothetical reasonable man, defendant was entitled to an acquittal since the specific intent required to be proved as an element of the offense had not been established.

The People's reliance on *People v. Mayberry* (1975) 15 Cal.3d 143 [125 Cal. Rptr. 745, 542 P.2d 1337] is misplaced. The discussion in that case involved the propriety of an instruction on mistake of fact in respect of charges of rape and kidnaping, general intent crimes, a different question from that here presented.

The judgment is reversed.

Notes and Questions

1. What is the specific intent element required to prove larceny in this case?

2. Did the court conclude Navarro was not guilty? If not, what should happen as the result of his successful appeal?

3. Notice the opinion uses the term "good faith" when referring to the defendant's subjective belief. Good faith in this context is a synonym for "honest," meaning what the defendant actually believed.

4. Do you see the thread that ties together this case with all the cited cases? What did all of the offenses at issue have in common? What was the mistake (no pun intended) made by the trial court in each case?

5. Towards the end of the opinion, the court notes that, "[I]t is true that if the jury thought the defendant's belief to be unreasonable, it might infer that he did not in good faith hold such a belief." What did the court mean? Was the court contradicting itself and suggesting that an unreasonable mistaken belief is *not* a defense to larceny? Try and write an instruction for a jury that incorporates this aspect of the opinion.

C. Mistake and General Intent/Mens Rea

The following opinion illustrates the more demanding standard for mistake when raised to prevent proof of general intent/mens rea.

Commonwealth v. Sherry
(and eight companion cases)
386 Mass. 682 (1982)
Massachusetts Supreme Court

PAUL J. LIACOS, Judge.

Each defendant was indicted on three charges of aggravated rape (G.L. c. 265, Section 22) and one charge of kidnapping (G.L. c. 265, Section 26). A jury acquitted the defendants of kidnapping and convicted them of so much of each of the remaining three indictments as charged the lesser included offense of rape without aggravation. . . . We now affirm each of the defendants' convictions on one charge of rape and vacate each defendant's convictions on the other two charges of rape.

The defendants contend that the trial judge erred [by] refusing to instruct the jury according to the defendants' requests. . . .

There was evidence of the following facts. The victim, a registered nurse, and the defendants, all doctors, were employed at the same hospital in Boston. The defendant Sherry, whom the victim knew professionally, with another doctor was a host at a party in Boston for some of the hospital staff on the evening of September 5, 1980. The victim was not acquainted with the defendants Hussain and Lefkowitz prior to this evening.

According to the victim's testimony, she had a conversation with Hussain at the party, during which he made sexual advances toward her. Later in the evening, Hussain and Sherry pushed her and Lefkowitz into a bathroom together, shut the door, and turned off the light. They did not open the door until Lefkowitz asked them to leave her in peace. At various times, the victim had danced with both Hussain and Sherry.

Some time later, as the victim was walking from one room to the next, Hussain and Sherry grabbed her by the arms and pulled her out of the apartment as Lefkowitz said, "We're going to go up to Rockport." The victim verbally protested but did not physically resist the men because she said she thought that they were just "horsing around" and that they would eventually leave her alone. She further testified that, once outside, Hussain carried her over his shoulder to Sherry's car and held her in the front seat as the four drove to Rockport. En route, she engaged in superficial conversation with the defendants. She testified that she was not in fear at this time. When they arrived at Lefkowitz's home in Rockport, she asked to be taken home. Instead, Hussain carried her into the house.

Once in the house, the victim and two of the men smoked some marihuana, and all of them toured the house. Lefkowitz invited them into a bedroom to view an antique bureau, and, once inside, the three men began to disrobe. The victim was frightened. She verbally protested, but the three men proceeded to undress her and maneuver her onto the bed. One of the defendants attempted to have the victim perform fellatio while another attempted intercourse. She told them to stop. At the suggestion of one of the defendants, two of the defendants left the room temporarily. Each defendant separately had intercourse with the victim in the bedroom. The victim testified that she felt physically numbed and could not fight; she felt humiliated and disgusted. After this sequence of events, the victim claimed that she was further sexually harassed and forced to take a bath.

Some time later, Lefkowitz told the victim that they were returning to Boston because Hussain was on call at the hospital. On their way back, the group stopped to view a beach, to eat breakfast, and to get gasoline. The victim was taken back to where she had left her car the prior evening, and she then drove herself to an apartment that she was sharing with another woman.

The defendants testified to a similar sequence of events, although the details of the episode varied significantly. According to their testimony, Lefkowitz invited Sherry to accompany him from the party to a home that his parents owned in Rockport. The victim was present when this invitation was extended and inquired as to whether she could go along. As the three were leaving, Sherry extended an invitation to Hussain. At no time on the way out of the apartment, in the elevator, lobby, or parking lot did the victim indicate her unwillingness to accompany the defendants.

Upon arrival in Rockport, the victim wandered into the bedroom where she inquired about the antique bureau. She sat down on the bed and kicked off her shoes, whereupon Sherry entered the room, dressed only in his underwear. Sherry helped the victim get undressed, and she proceeded to have intercourse with all three men separately and in turn. Each defendant testified that the victim consented to the acts of intercourse.

. . . .

The essence of the crime of rape, whether aggravated or unaggravated, is sexual intercourse with another compelled by force and against the victim's will or compelled by threat of bodily injury. See G.L. c. 265, Sections 22(a) & (b). At the close of the Commonwealth's case, the evidence viewed in the light most favorable to the Commonwealth established the following. The victim was forcibly taken from a party by the three defendants and told that she would accompany them to Rockport. Despite her verbal protestations, the victim was carried into an automobile and restrained from leaving until the automobile was well on its way. Notwithstanding her requests to be allowed to go home, the victim was carried again and taken into a house. The three defendants undressed and began to undress the victim and to sexually attack her in unison over her verbal protestations. Once they had overpowered her, each in turn had intercourse with her while the others waited nearby in another room.

The evidence was sufficient to permit the jury to find that the defendants had sexual intercourse with the victim by force and against her will . . .

Instructions to the jury. The defendants next contend that because the judge failed to give two instructions exactly as requested, the judge's jury charge, considered as a whole, was inadequate and the cause of prejudicial error. The requested instructions in their entirety are set out in the margin.[1]

The defendants were not entitled to any particular instruction as long as the charge as a whole was adequate. . . .

To the extent the defendants, at least as to the first requested instruction, appear to have been seeking to raise a defense of good faith mistake on the issue of consent, the defendants' requested instruction would have required the jury to "find beyond a reasonable doubt that the accused had *actual knowledge* of [the victim's] lack of consent" (emphasis added). The defendants, on appeal, argue that mistake of fact negating criminal intent is a defense to the crime of rape. The defense of mistake of fact, however, requires that the accused act in good faith and with reasonableness. See *Commonwealth v. Presby*, 14 Gray 65, 69 (1860); *Commonwealth v. Power*, 7 Met. 596, 602 (1844); R. Perkins, Criminal Law 939-940 (2d ed. 1969). Whether a reasonable good faith mistake of fact as to the fact of consent is a defense to the crime of rape has never, to our knowledge, been decided in this Commonwealth. We need not reach the issue whether a reasonable and honest mistake to the fact of consent would be a defense, for even if we assume it to be so, the defendants did not request a jury instruction based on a reasonable good faith mistake of fact. We are aware of no American court of last resort that recognizes mistake of fact, without consideration of its reasonableness, as a defense; nor do the defendants cite such authority. There was no error.

Notes and Questions

1. Rape is almost universally characterized as a "general intent" offense. But what is the mens rea for rape? In most jurisdictions that have addressed this question, the answer is that the state must prove the defendant knew or reasonably should have known the victim did not consent to the sexual intercourse.

2. Notice that this court never reached the question of whether mistake should be recognized as a defense to rape in Massachusetts. Nonetheless, implicitly recognizing

---

1. "Unless you find beyond a reasonable doubt that [the victim] clearly expressed her lack of consent, or was so overcome by force or threats of bodily injury that she was incapable of consenting, and unless you find beyond a reasonable doubt that the accused had actual knowledge of [the victim's] lack of consent, then you must find them not guilty."

"If you find that [the victim] had a reasonable opportunity to resist being taken to Rockport, Massachusetts, from the apartment . . . , and had a reasonable opportunity to avoid or resist the circumstances that took place in the bedroom at Rockport, but chose not to avail herself of those opportunities, then you must weigh her failure to take such reasonable opportunities on the credibility of her claim that she was kidnapped and raped."

rape requires no proof of specific intent, the court concluded that *if* mistake is a defense, the mistake must not only be subjectively honest, but objectively reasonable.

3. Based on the testimony provided by the defendants, do you think a jury may have concluded that the defendants reasonably believed the victim consented to their advances? If so, is the court suggesting the defendants may have had a valid defense to the rape allegation? If a jury concludes a defendant's mistaken assumption that a victim consents to sexual intercourse is reasonable under the circumstances — meaning a mistake a reasonable person would have made — does this mean the victim was not raped? Doesn't the assertion of such a mistake indicate that the victim *in fact* had not consented?

D. Distinguish Mistake from Disagreement

In many cases, a defendant will offer a different interpretation of facts from the interpretation offered by the prosecution. In other words, the defendant will disagree with the inference proposed by the prosecution. As the following opinion notes, a defendant may argue such disagreement to challenge proof of mens rea, but this is not the same as raising a mistake.

Hopson v. State
Unpublished [No. 14-08-00735-CR] (2009)
Texas Court of Appeal

KENT C. SULLIVAN, Judge.

Appellant, Karissa Lou Hopson, was arrested at a house in Lufkin on July 7, 2007 and was charged with two offenses: (1) burglary, by entering a habitation without the owners' consent and with the intent to commit theft; and (2) criminal mischief, by intentionally or knowingly damaging or destroying tangible property without the owners' consent. A jury convicted appellant of both offenses. On appeal of her burglary conviction, appellant insists that the evidence raised a fact issue as to whether she mistakenly believed she was *preventing*, not *committing*, a theft. She contends that this evidence required the trial court to submit a mistake-of-fact instruction to the jury, and that she was harmed by the trial court's refusal to do so. Because we hold that the requested instruction was not necessary, the trial court's judgment is affirmed.

Appellant has not appealed her conviction for criminal mischief.

Background

On July 7, 2007, police officers were summoned to a residence to investigate a suspected burglary in progress. Upon arrival, the officers saw appellant standing on the front porch of the house, holding a large television. Appellant set the television on the porch and approached the officers, claiming that she knew the house owners and that she had their permission to be on the property. However, the officers noticed that several of the house windows had been broken and that appellant had blood on her shirt and hand. The officers also saw that portions of the interior of the house, including furniture, had been damaged. Appellant was arrested at the scene. The owners of the house arrived at the scene roughly thirty minutes later. Both owners indicated that they did not know appellant, and they denied giving her permission to enter the premises or to remove their television from the house.

The State charged appellant with burglary and criminal mischief. Appellant pleaded "not guilty" to both offenses, and a jury trial ensued. Appellant testified on her own behalf and, although she acknowledged that she had entered the residence and that she was carrying the owners' television when the police arrived, she offered a different interpretation of these undisputed facts. That is, she contended that she believed that, through her actions, she was actually thwarting a burglary that was being committed by another man, Cayetano Padierna. In support of this contention, appellant testified that she had stopped at the house to visit the owners, who were her friends. When she arrived, both owners were gone. In their place was Padierna, whom she did not know, who was removing items from the house. Thinking that Padierna was stealing from the owners, appellant confronted him and he left. Appellant then walked to the side of the porch, where she found the television. She picked the television up, claiming that she meant to return it to the house, when the police — who had been summoned by Padierna — arrived and arrested her.

Based on her testimony, appellant contended that she reasonably, but mistakenly, believed Padierna was stealing from the owners and that, by picking up the owners' television, she was acting with the intent to *prevent*, not *commit*, a theft. Appellant asked the trial court to submit the following mistake-of-fact instruction to the jury:

> A defendant who thought she was performing activity may lack the necessary criminal intent where she reasonably believes she acted to prevent a crime. If you believe that at the time of the offense charged, [appellant] reasonably believed that she acted to prevent a [t]heft, then you must find her not guilty.

The trial judge refused the requested instruction. The jury found appellant guilty of burglary and Class A misdemeanor criminal mischief. . . . Appellant timely brought this appeal, in which she contends that the trial court erred by refusing to submit her requested mistake-of-fact instruction, and that a reversal and remand for a new trial is required.

Analysis

Generally, a defendant is entitled to submission of an affirmative defensive instruction on every issue raised by the evidence even if the trial court thinks that the testimony could not be believed. *See Chavers v. State*, 991 S.W.2d 457, 459 (Tex. App. Houston [1st Dist.] 1999, pet. ref'd). In this case, appellant contends that she raised a fact issue as to the mistake-of-fact defense, which is set forth by section 8.02 of the Texas Penal Code: "It is a defense to prosecution that the actor through mistake formed a reasonable belief about a matter of fact if his mistaken belief negated the kind of culpability required for commission of the offense." Tex. Penal Code Ann. § 8.02(a) (Vernon 2003).

Appellant contends her testimony, if believed, would negate a finding that she acted with the intent to commit theft, that is, the degree of culpability required to convict her of burglary. Therefore, she argues that the trial court erred by refusing to submit a mistake-of-fact instruction. However, we hold that the requested instruction was not necessary because appellant's defense — that she lacked the requisite intent to commit theft because of a mistaken belief — was adequately covered by the charge submitted to the jury. Therefore, we conclude the trial court did not err by refusing to submit a defensive issue that merely denied the existence of an essential element of the State's case.

To support her argument, appellant directs us to *Bang v. State*, in which the Thirteenth Court of Appeals held that a mistake-of-fact instruction should be submitted whenever raised by the evidence. 815 S.W.2d 838, 841 (Tex.App. Corpus Christi 1991, no pet.). However, *Bang* was closely followed by *Bruno v. State*, in which the Texas Court of Criminal Appeals indicated that a trial court is not always required to submit an unnecessary mistake-of-fact instruction if the defense is adequately covered by the charge as given. 845 S.W.2d 910, 913 (Tex.Crim.App. 1993). In *Bruno*, the defendant was accused of unauthorized use of a motor vehicle but testified that he believed he had the owner's permission to drive the car. *See id.* at 911. The Court of Criminal Appeals noted that, in some unauthorized-use cases, the defendant alleges that he was given permission to operate the vehicle by a third party he mistakenly believed to be the vehicle's owner. *See id.* at 912 (citing *Gardner v. State*, 780 S.W.2d 259, 263 (Tex.Crim.App. 1989)). Under those facts, a mistake-of-fact instruction becomes necessary because the jury could find that (1) the defendant believed he had the consent of the third party to use the vehicle, and (2) the *true owner* of the vehicle had not given him permission. *Bruno*, 845 S.W.2d at 912. However, in the absence of such a third party, the Court of Criminal Appeals determined that a mistake-of-fact instruction was unnecessary:

> In the absence of this third party, the jury could not believe both the testimony of [the] true owner of the vehicle and the testimony of appellant as it could in *Gardner*. Only one of the incompatible stories could be believed. . . .

The jury heard both stories. As they would have necessarily been required to disbelieve appellant's story before they could find sufficient evidence to convict, the instruction need not have been given in the instant case. Simply because appellant testified that he had the consent of the owner of the vehicle does not entitle him to a mistake of fact instruction. . . .

Here, the jury heard appellant's story. The effect of her testimony, and the thrust of her requested instruction, amounted to an attempt to convince the jury that her intent was something other than the criminal intent — that is, the intent to commit theft — that was necessary for the commission of a burglary. However, to convict her of that offense, the State was already required to prove beyond a reasonable doubt that appellant entered the house, without the effective consent of the owners, *with the intent to commit theft. See* Tex. Penal Code Ann. §30.02(a)(1); *Coleman v. State*, 832 S.W.2d 409, 413 (Tex.App.-Houston [1st Dist.] 1992, pet. ref'd) ("Intent, as an essential element of the offense of burglary, must be proved by the State beyond a reasonable doubt; it may not be left simply to speculation and surmise."). To that end, the jury received the following instruction:

> [I]f you believe from the evidence beyond a reasonable doubt, that the defendant, . . . on or about the 7th day of July, 2007, in the County of Angelina, and State of Texas, as alleged in the indictment, did then and there, *with intent to commit theft*, enter a habitation, without the effective consent of Gregorio Cartagena or Cayetano Ramirez, the owner thereof, you will find the defendant guilty of the offense of Burglary of a Habitation and so say by your verdict, but if you do not so believe, or if you have a reasonable doubt thereof, you will acquit the defendant and say by your verdict "Not Guilty."

The jury was also specifically instructed that it had to acquit the appellant if the State failed to prove, beyond a reasonable doubt, each and every element of the charged offense. Thus, unless the jury found that appellant intended to commit theft, it was required to acquit her of burglary. Therefore, under these facts, the trial court was not required to submit a defensive issue that, in the context of this case, did no more than recast the required element of criminal intent as a defensive issue. . . . As in *Bruno* and *Traylor*, appellant could not have been convicted under the charge given had the jury believed her story that she lacked the intent to commit theft. Apparently, they did not.

The facts of this case may be contrasted with *Bang*, in which the defendant acted on a mistaken belief that his friend, Jesse Mouton, the principal actor in the burglary, actually owned the property in question. *See Bang*, 815 S.W.2d at 840. In that case, Jerry Bang agreed to drive Mouton, a minor, to a particular location and pick him up later. *See id.* When Bang returned, Mouton had an amplifier, a guitar case, and other items which Mouton claimed he owned. *See id.* The items were placed in the trunk of Bang's vehicle and driven to another location. *See id.* Ultimately, it was determined that the property had been stolen from a church, and Bang was charged with burglary. *See id.* at 839. Bang admitted that he intentionally performed certain acts that *resulted in* a burglary and theft of property. However, he claimed not to know that, through his conduct, he was participating in a burglary and theft. *See id.* at 842. Specifically, not knowing that the church was the *true owner* of the stolen items, Jerry Bang intended to appropriate property in a manner that deprived the actual owner — the church — of its property, and such appropriation was unlawful because it was done without the owner's consent. . . .

Under those facts, as in the unauthorized-use cases highlighted in *Bruno*, a mistake-of-fact instruction was necessary in *Bang* because the jury could have convicted him of the elements of the crime, while still believing that he lacked the requisite culpable mental state. Here, by contrast, the jury was squarely required to decide whether appellant acted with either the intent to commit theft or, under her version of the facts, with the intent to *prevent* a theft. As in *Sands* [*v. State*], the absence of a mistake-of-fact instruction did not deprive appellant of the right to have the jury consider her defense. *See Sands*, 64 S.W.3d at 496. Therefore, we hold that the trial court was not required to submit a separate mistake-of-fact instruction to the jury. We overrule appellant's only issue on appeal. . . .

Judgment affirmed.

Notes and Questions

1. What is the requisite mens rea/criminal mental state at issue in relation to the burglary charge?

2. What was the defendant really arguing? The court notes that the defendant requested the following instruction:

> A defendant who thought she was performing activity may lack the necessary criminal intent where she reasonably believes she acted to prevent a crime. If you believe that at the time of the offense charged, [appellant] reasonably believed that she acted to prevent a [t]heft, then you must find her not guilty.

Was this really a mistake of fact instruction? If a defendant honestly believes that committing what is normally a crime is necessary to avert a greater harm, *and* the jury concludes that under the circumstances that belief was reasonable, was the act unlawful? Arguably no, because as you will see in Chapter 16, such an honest and reasonable belief of necessity to break the law is the essence of the justification defense of necessity. For example, what if instead of being found on the porch with the television, the defendant was found with a cellular phone she took from the home without permission and was at that moment calling 911 for an ambulance to respond to a seriously injured child in the street who had just been struck by a hit and run?

3. The court cites the Texas Penal Code provision on mistake, noting it indicates that, "It is a defense to prosecution that the actor through mistake formed a reasonable belief about a matter of fact if his mistaken belief negated the kind of culpability required for commission of the offense." Tex. Penal Code Ann. § 8.02(a) (Vernon 2003). Is this provision logical? Can you see the inconsitency? The provision indicates that a mistake is a defense only if it is reasonable, but then uses the MPC approach indicating that a mistake is a defense if the "mistaken belief negated the kind of culpability required for commission of the offense." If the culpability required for theft is purpose to steal, wouldn't an honest mistake that the property was abandoned or that the defendant had the owner's permission to take it, even if not reasonable, negate the culpability required for commission of the offense? Wouldn't the same analysis apply to knowing possession of stolen property?

4. Notice that the facts were not in dispute, only the inference of the defendant's mens rea derived from those facts. What was the inference the prosecution asked the jury to draw? What about the inference the defendant asked the jury to draw?

5. If the jury were to believe the defendant's testimony in this case, would it indicate the defendant harbored a mistake that negated the requisite mens rea? Or that defendant never formed the requisite mens rea?

6. Why was the instruction on the material elements of the offense sufficient to ensure the jury considered the issue the defendant sought to raise with a mistake instruction?

7. Defendant is charged with larceny for allegedly stealing a power tool from a garage in his neighborhood. The offense requires proof the defendant unlawfully took the personal property of another without consent and with the intent to permanently deprive. Defendant testifies and admits he took the power tool and that he sold it to a pawn shop. However, he also testifies that he knew the owner and that the owner let him have it in payment of an old debt. The owner testifies in rebuttal that he barely knows the defendant and that he neither owed him a debt nor gave him permission to take and sell the power tool. You are the judge. Will you grant a mistake of fact instruction at the request of the defendant?

III. Mistake of Law

As noted earlier, mistake of law is normally not considered a relevant defense. This is based on the long-standing maxim that ignorance of the law does not excuse criminal misconduct (*ignorantia legis neminem excusat*). In the case that follows, the Court of Appeals for the Armed Forces considers whether a Captain who unlawfully killed a wounded and incapacitated enemy in Iraq was improperly denied a mistake of law instruction.

United States v. Maynulet
68 M.J. 374 (2010)
United States Court of Appeals for the Armed Forces

A general court-martial composed of members [a military jury] convicted Appellant, contrary to his pleas, of assault with intent to commit voluntary manslaughter in violation of Article 134, Uniform Code of Military Justice (UCMJ), 10 U.S.C. § 934 (2000). . . .

On Appellant's petition, we granted review of the following issue:

I. Whether the Military Judge Erred When He Refused to Instruct the Members on the Defense of Mistake of Law

For the reasons set forth below, we conclude that the military judge did not err.

Background

Appellant commanded an armor company in Iraq during Operation Iraqi Freedom. On May 21, 2004, Appellant and his company were instructed to set up a traffic control point to support an operation to capture or kill a high-value target (HVT). A vehicle transporting the HVT sped past the check point. After a high-speed chase the vehicle carrying the HVT crashed into a wall and then into a nearby house. Appellant and several soldiers approached the crash site. Several doors of the vehicle were open, indicating the passengers may have fled inside the house.

Appellant sent part of his team into the house to search for the target, ordered the medic to evaluate the wounded driver, who was still in the vehicle, and ordered another soldier to search the vehicle for weapons. The medic pulled the driver from the vehicle. At trial, the medic testified "He was inside the vehicle. . . . I opened the door and pulled him out. . . . I told Captain Maynulet he wasn't going to make it."

Appellant received a radio communication that a detainee inside the house required medical attention and sent the medic inside the house. The medic was then asked at trial about his plan for the injured driver, "To bring [the other detainee] back; . . . and see what I could do for the driver. I'm not sure there was much I could do."

Appellant saw that the driver had a head wound, was making a gurgling sound, and was flapping his arm. The driver was laying inert on the ground and had no weapon nearby. Appellant made no attempt to aid the driver, nor did he attempt to contact his command. Several minutes passed. Appellant radioed his unit to stand by for friendly fire. He discharged two rounds at the driver's head. The first shot missed. Appellant then stepped back to take a second shot, which killed the driver.

At trial Appellant testified that he shot the driver "to put him out of [his] misery." The following exchange took place:

Q. So, did you fire again?

A. Yes, I did.

Q. Why did you do that?

A. He was in a state that I didn't think was dignified. I had to put him out of [his] misery.

Q. Were you authorized to do that?

A. I think I was.

Q. Why?

A. It was the right thing to do. I think it was the honorable thing to do. I don't think allowing him to continue in that state was proper.

Prior to deployment, Appellant received training on the Law of War (LOW) and the Rules of Engagement (ROE). This training consisted of a slide show presentation and a question and answer session presided over by operational law attorneys, brigade trial counsel, and other judge advocates [military lawyers]. Throughout his deployment, Appellant carried a CFLCC (Coalition Forces Land Component Command) ROE Card that stated: "Do not engage anyone who has surrendered or is out of battle due to sickness or wounds."[2] A line at the bottom of the card specified the durational element of the ROE: "These ROE will remain in effect until your commander orders you to transition to post-hostilities ROE."

At trial the military judge denied a defense request that the members be instructed on the defense of mistake of law. Specifically, defense counsel argued that Appellant believed, albeit mistakenly, that he was acting in a manner consistent with the legal training he had received prior to deployment. During a colloquy with the military judge, he explained that "mistake of law may be a defense when the mistake results in the reliance on the decision or announcement of authorized public official or agency." Later during the same colloquy he stated:

> [W]hen Captain Maynulet was told that this guy was going to die and there was nothing that could be done, right, he was guided not by care of the wounded, not to shoot somebody who was out of the battle due to sickness or wounds, but he's guided by preventing unnecessary suffering, and that's what was taught at the briefings, and that's what's in the law.

In justifying his decision to reject Appellant's request for a mistake of law instruction, the military judge responded:

> I can find no authority that would permit a mistake of law defense to apply in this case, based on what I have. . . . [Since it's not a recognized defense under these circumstances, although there is evidence raised of why he did it, that goes to mitigations and motive, but it does not go to a defense. So, at this point in time, I do not believe a mistake of law defense would apply to this case and as such, I will not instruct on it. . . .

Analysis

. . . [A] military judge has a sua sponte duty to instruct on an affirmative defense if reasonably raised. . . . "The test whether an affirmative defense is reasonably raised is whether the record contains some evidence to which the court members may attach credit if they so desire." [*United States v.*] *Davis*, 53 M.J. at 205 (citation omitted).

Appellant claims he was entitled to a mistake of law instruction because he was taught to "eas[e] suffering" during his pre-deployment briefing on the LOW [law

---

2. Appellant received an ROE card from CFLCC during this pre-deployment briefing, which he later carried in his uniform. After Appellant deployed, whenever there was a change to the ROE card a new card was issued.

of war]. Specifically, Appellant argues that the briefing's instruction to ease suffering, simply stating "Humanity — unnecessary suffering," was confusing and induced him to put the driver out of his misery by shooting him in the head. Accordingly, Appellant asserts the military judge erred by refusing to allow the members to determine whether mistake of law was a defense in his case.

It is well settled in civil and military law that mistake of law is generally not a defense to criminal conduct. R.C.M. [Rule for Courts-Martial] 916(i)(1) states the following: "Ignorance or mistake of law, including general orders or regulations, ordinarily is not a defense." *See also Lambert v. California*, 355 U.S. 225, 228, 78 S.Ct. 240, 2 L.Ed.2d 228 (1957). There are a few narrow exceptions to the general rule. One such exception exists when "the mistake results from reliance on the decision or pronouncement of an authorized public official or agency." R.C.M. 916(i)(1) Discussion. However, "reli[ance] on the advice of counsel that a certain course of conduct is legal is not, of itself, a defense." *Id.* In civilian practice, this defense is more generally stated as a "reasonable] reli[ance] upon an erroneous official statement of the law." 1 Wayne R. Lafave, *Substantive Criminal Law* § 5.6(e)(3), at 415 (2d ed.2003); *see also* Joshua Dressier, *Understanding Criminal Law* § 13.02[B][2], at 182 (4th ed.2006).

While the concept alluded to in the discussion to R.C.M. 916(l)(1) is well established in the law, *see, e.g., Cox v. Louisiana*, 379 U.S. 559, 568-71, 85 S.Ct. 476, 13 L. Ed.2d 487 (1965), this Court has yet to hear a case directly relying on this exception.

The problem with Appellant's argument is that the record is devoid of any erroneous pronouncement or interpretation of military law or the law of armed conflict upon which he could have reasonably relied to justify his killing of the injured driver. The best Appellant can argue is that he had a subjective mistaken belief as to what the law allowed. However, this is the very kind of mistake rejected by the general rule regarding mistake of law.

Specifically, Appellant claims Slide 18 of the LOW presentation justifies his action. Slide 18 reads: "Humanity — unnecessary suffering." The next line on the same slide states "Effective," referring to the LOW, because it "motivates enemy to observe same rules." Also, the instructor notes for Slide 18 state: "[Make sure they understand that an enemy breach does not allow us to breach." However, Slide 18 was presented in the context of a longer presentation, including Slide 24 stating, "(4) Soldiers collect and care for the wounded, whether friend or foe." Thus, read with Slide 24, Slide 18 appears to stand for a proposition inapposite to what Appellant argues.

The ROE card, which Appellant carried in his pocket during combat, is even clearer. It states: "Do not engage anyone who has surrendered or is out of battle due to sickness or wounds." This ROE card, unambiguous as it is, would appear to supersede anything Appellant argues he might have learned as part of general training.

Appellant argues that the slides he claims to have relied upon were confusing. This argument is equally unavailing. The slides include clear and comprehensible phrases such as "Violations are Punishable," "Soldiers collect and care for the wounded, whether friend or foe," and "'The Armed Forces of the United States will comply with the law of war during the conduct of all military operations and related activities in armed conflict.'" Appellant was a Captain in the Army, a commissioned officer, and a college graduate. There was no testimony that any other members of the unit, who were Appellant's enlisted subordinates, were confused by the slides or the ROE card.

Also notably absent from the record is any evidence that Appellant received affirmative assurances from briefers or anyone in his chain-of-command that "mercy killing" was lawful. To the contrary, the ROE card specifically instructed him *not* to engage enemy combatants who were out of battle due to wounds. Moreover, Appellant had time to consult with both his command and with medical authorities if he felt that additional legal, medical, or command guidance was needed before deciding how to proceed.

For the reasons stated above, we hold that the military judge did not err in refusing to instruct in accordance with Appellant's request at trial.[3]

Conclusion

The decision of the United States Army Court of Criminal Appeals is affirmed.

Notes and Questions

1. Based on the opinion, was Maynulet asserting a mistake of law or a misunderstanding of law? If the latter, how is that different from a mistake of law?

2. Why do you think the law is so reluctant to allow a criminal defendant to allege a misunderstanding of the law as a defense?

3. Notice that the court indicates there are exceptions to the general rule that mistake of law is no defense. What is the exception Maynulet asserted applied to his case?

---

3. Appellant also argues his reliance on a government official's pronouncements provided him with the defense of entrapment by estoppel. In an estoppel situation, the government is rightly barred from obtaining a conviction because the government — through its representatives acting in an official capacity — is responsible for the defendant's inability to know that his conduct was proscribed. Lafave, *supra*, § 5.6(e), at 412; *see also Cox*, 379 U.S. at 571, 85 S.Ct. 476. Whether entrapment by estoppel and the military defense of "mistake of law" are the same or distinct concepts in total is an issue we need not address in this case. This case is governed by military law and in any event the concepts are parallel in reach as raised in this case. As we have concluded, there is no evidence in the record to support the claim that there was an official decision, pronouncement or interpretation, later determined to be erroneous, upon which he could have reasonably relied or that could have formed the basis of a claim of estoppel.

4. What if the evidence indicated that, when explaining the law of war rule that prohibits infliction of unnecessary suffering, the military lawyer providing the pre-deployment briefing said, "this just means always do the right thing." Would that have necessitated a mistake of law instruction?

5. Imagine the trial judge had granted Maynulet's request and instructed the military jury that, if Maynulet's act of killing the wounded enemy was the result of his mistaken understanding of the law as explained to him by Army lawyers, he should be acquitted. What would the prosecution have to prove to overcome this obstacle?

There are some crimes that by definition require a defendant to *know* his conduct violates the law. In these rare situations, that requisite specific intent — the subjective knowledge of the law — makes a mistaken belief that the conduct *was not* in violation of the law, or ignorance of the law, a relevant defense. In such cases, once the mistake or ignorance is raised by the defense, the prosecution must prove that the defendant actually knew the law or the legal obligation. For example, in *People v. Weiss,* 276 N.Y. 384 (1938), the New York State Court of Appeals reversed a conviction for kidnapping because the trial judge refused to instruct the jury on mistake of law. This was because kidnapping required that "proof beyond a reasonable doubt must be produced that the defendant *willfully intended, without authority of law,* to confine or imprison another." The defendant testified that he had been told by another individual claiming to be a law enforcement officer that he was authorized to assist in the apprehension and detention of the victim. As the appellate court noted, were a jury to believe the defendant's testimony, they could not find that he intended, *without authority of law,* to confine or imprison the victim. Another example of this theory of mistake of law involved a defendant convicted of *willfully* failing to file federal income tax. In *Cheek v. United States,* 498 U.S. 192 (1991), the Supreme Court interpreted the term "willfully" as used in the federal income tax evasion crime to require proof beyond a reasonable doubt the defendant *knew* of his legal obligation to pay income tax. Thus, knowledge of the law was a requisite element of the offense. As a result, the defendant was entitled to an "honest" mistake of law instruction based on his testimony he didn't know he was obligated to pay income tax. In these type cases, mistake of law functions the same as mistake of fact: an honest mistake, even if unreasonable, negates proof defendant actually knew the law. However, as with mistake of fact, a jury may consider the implausibility of the alleged mistake in deciding whether to credit the defendant's testimony or to conclude the prosecution met its burden of proving defendant actually knew the law.

IV. Mistake and the Model Penal Code

The MPC enumerates the rule for mistake of fact and mistake of law. While, as noted above, the MPC abandoned the common law concepts of specific and general intent, the basic concept of mistake of fact functions quite similarly, to include the relationship between a mistake and culpability for a lesser included offense. Specifically, MPC § 2.04 provides:

> (1) Ignorance or mistake as to a matter of fact or law is a defense if:
>
>> (a) the ignorance or mistake negatives the purpose, knowledge, belief, recklessness or negligence required to establish a material element of the offense; or
>>
>> (b) the law provides that the state of mind established by such ignorance or mistake constitutes a defense.
>
> (2) Although ignorance or mistake would otherwise afford a defense to the offense charged, the defense is not available if the defendant would be guilty of another offense had the situation been as he supposed. In such case, however, the ignorance or mistake of the defendant shall reduce the grade and degree of the offense of which he may be convicted to those of the offense of which he would be guilty had the situation been as he supposed.

This formulation of mistake of fact functions almost identically to the common law specific/general intent equation. Because purpose or knowledge are purely subjective states of mind, an honest mistake, no matter how unreasonable, would negate either of those mental elements. In contrast, because recklessness or gross negligence involve an objective assessment of risk creation, an honest mistake would be insufficient to negate either of these elements unless the mistake was also objectively reasonable.

There is, however, one situation where the MPC could produce a different outcome than the common law equation. Recall that recklessness includes *both* a subjective and objective component; the prosecution must prove the defendant was subjectively aware that the act or omission created a risk to others. In the common law, recklessness is treated as a general intent/mens rea element, meaning that only an honest and reasonable mistake functions as a defense. However, the language of the MPC indicates that a defendant could raise an honest mistake to negate the subjective awareness component of recklessness. Even if objectively unreasonable, such mistake or ignorance would negate recklessness and result in a finding of gross negligence and any lesser included offense established by that finding.

This more nuanced application of mistake of fact was addressed by the Supreme Court of New Jersey in *State v. Sexton*, 733 A.2d 1125 (1999). In that case, the defendant, convicted of involuntary manslaughter based on the reckless discharge of a firearm, argued on appeal that he was entitled to a mistake of fact instruction based on evidence indicating he was unaware the pistol was loaded. The state responded that the defendant's subjective state of mind was not relevant to a finding of recklessness. The court noted in response:

... The Sixth Amendment allows a defendant to assert any fact that will negate a material element of a crime. The material elements of manslaughter are the killing of another human being with a reckless state of mind. The culpable mental state is recklessness — the conscious disregard of a substantial and unjustified risk that death will result from the conduct. What mistaken belief will negate this state of mind?

[T]he translation is uncertain at its most critical point: in determining the kind of mistake that provides a defense when recklessness, the most common culpability level, as to a circumstance is required. Recall that a negligent or faultless mistake negates . . . recklessness. While a "negligent mistake" may be said to be an "unreasonable mistake," all "unreasonable mistakes" are not "negligent mistakes." A mistake may also be unreasonable because it is reckless. Reckless mistakes, although unreasonable, will not negate recklessness. Thus, when offense definitions require recklessness as to circumstance elements, as they commonly do, the reasonable-unreasonable mistake language inadequately describes the mistakes that will provide a defense because of the imprecision of the term "unreasonable mistake." Reckless-negligent-faultless mistake language is necessary for a full and accurate description.

Thus, to disprove a reasonable mistake by proving that it is unreasonable, will turn out to be a mixed blessing for defendant. If the State may disprove a reasonable mistake by proving that the mistake was unreasonable, defendant may be convicted because he was negligent, as opposed to reckless, in forming the belief that the gun was unloaded. If recklessness is required as an element of the offense, "a merely negligent or faultless mistake as to that circumstance provides a defense."

Notice how the court distinguished a mistake as to the nature of the risk created (which, if reasonable, negates the objective component of recklessness *and* negligence because both of these mental states require a finding that the risk created was objectively unreasonable) from a mistake as to whether the firearm was even loaded (which would negate recklessness so long as it was subjectively honest but would not necessarily negate negligence). The court emphasized that the key to applying this equation was to emphasize to the jury what exactly must be established to prove the requisite mens rea, and then allow the jury to assess how the alleged mistake relates to that element:

Correctly understood, there is no difference between a positive and negative statement on the issue — what is required for liability versus what will provide a defense to liability. What is required in order to establish liability for manslaughter is recklessness (as defined by the Code) about whether death will result from the conduct. A faultless or merely careless mistake may negate that reckless state of mind and provide a defense.

How can we explain these concepts to a jury? We believe that the better way to explain the concepts is to explain what is required for liability to be established. The charge should be tailored to the factual circumstances of the case. The court should explain precisely how the offered defense plays into the element of recklessness.

As for mistake of law, the MPC includes the "official statement" theory addressed in *Maynulet*. However, the MPC also provides a mistake of law defense in situations where a defendant can establish that ignorance of the law is the result of the government's failure to make the law reasonably available to the public. In either situation, the MPC specifically places the burden of proof on the defendant, thereby treating mistake of law as a genuine affirmative defense. MPC § 2.04 provides:

> (3) A belief that conduct does not legally constitute an offense is a defense to a prosecution for that offense based upon such conduct when:
>
> > (a) the statute or other enactment defining the offense is not known to the actor and has not been published or otherwise reasonably made available prior to the conduct alleged; or
> >
> > (b) he acts in reasonable reliance upon an official statement of the law, afterward determined to be invalid or erroneous, contained in (i) a statute or other enactment; (ii) a judicial decision, opinion or judgment; (iii) an administrative order or grant of permission; or (iv) an official interpretation of the public officer or body charged by law with responsibility for the interpretation, administration or enforcement of the law defining the offense.
>
> (4) The defendant must prove a defense arising under Subsection (3) of this Section by a preponderance of evidence.

Notes & Questions

1. Defendant is charged with reckless destruction of property in a MPC jurisdiction. The allegation is that the defendant was setting off fireworks on July 4th from his driveway. One of his neighbors testifies that she warned the defendant that there was a burn ban in place and that it was too dangerous to set them off, but the defendant responded he was not worried. Some of the fireworks ignited a fire in the woods that ended up burning and destroying a different neighbor's barn. Defendant testifies that he has no recollection of the conversation with the neighbor and that he was not aware of the burn ban. Defendant requests a mistake of fact instruction. Should the judge grant or deny the request?

2. Now assume there is no evidence that anyone warned Defendant about the risk and that Defendant testifies he was not aware of the burn ban. He also testifies he saw fireworks that must have been set off by others in the neighborhood; that he never expected his fireworks would start a fire; and that he feels terrible about what happened. Defendant requests a mistake of fact instruction. Should the judge grant or deny the request? If you were the judge and decided to grant the request, how would you instruct the jury?

When Does a Defendant's Mistake Claim "Block" Proof of the Requisite Mens Rea?

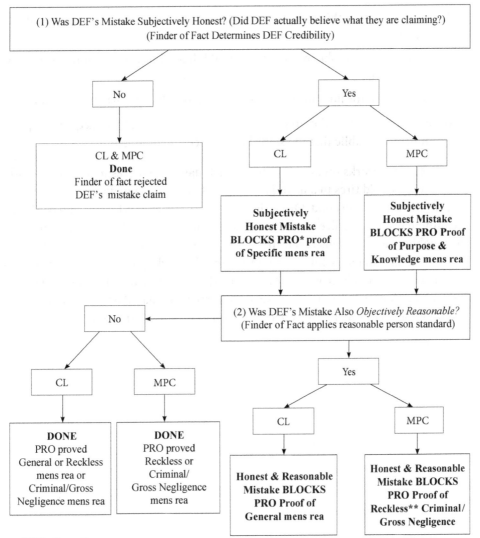

(1) Was DEF's Mistake Subjectively Honest? (Did DEF actually believe what they are claiming?)
(Finder of Fact Determines DEF Credibility)

No

Yes

CL & MPC
Done
Finder of fact rejected
DEF's mistake claim

CL

MPC

Subjectively
Honest Mistake
BLOCKS PRO* proof
of Specific mens rea

Subjectively
Honest Mistake
BLOCKS PRO Proof
of Purpose &
Knowledge mens rea

No

(2) Was DEF's Mistake Also *Objectively Reasonable?*
(Finder of Fact applies reasonable person standard)

CL

MPC

Yes

DONE
PRO proved
General or Reckless
mens rea or
Criminal/Gross
Negligence mens rea

DONE
PRO proved
Reckless or
Criminal/
Gross Negligence
mens rea

CL

MPC

Honest & Reasonable
Mistake BLOCKS
PRO Proof of
General mens rea

Honest & Reasonable
Mistake BLOCKS
PRO Proof of
Reckless** Criminal/
Gross Negligence

* PRO = Prosecution

** When DEF challenges proof of recklessness by claiming that she had no subjective awareness of the risk creation, PRO must prove actual awareness. If the PRO cannot, then the DEF has blocked proof of recklessness but may still have committed an offense with a mens rea of Criminal/Gross Negligence

© 2012 Geoffrey S. Corn

Formative Assessments

1. During a camping trip in a state park, Rose discovered metal signs near a rubbish heap stating, "Natural Wildlife Area — No Hunting." She took two of the signs and used them to decorate her room at home. She is charged with violation of a state statute which provides, "Any person who appropriates, with intent to permanently deprive, property owned by the state shall be guilty of a crime and shall be punished by a fine of not more than $1,000, or by imprisonment for not more than five years, or by both such fine and imprisonment." At trial, Rose admits taking the signs but says

she believed they had been thrown away. In fact, the signs had not been abandoned. Based on this evidence, Rose should be found:

A. Guilty, because this is a public welfare offense and therefore her mistake is irrelevant.

B. Guilty, because she reasonably should have known the signs were not abandoned.

C. Not guilty if the jury finds she honestly believed the signs had been abandoned.

D. Not guilty unless the jury finds that the state had taken adequate steps to inform the public that the signs had not been abandoned.

2. Defendant works on an Army base. Each day as he drives to and from work, he sees a pile of old tires in a field. He wants to take some to make some tire swings for kids in his neighborhood. One of his neighbors is a labor attorney who works for the human resources office on the base. He asks him if it is OK to take the tires, and the neighbor says, "I've also seen them, and it seems to me they are abandoned, so go for it." That Sunday, while loading tires into his pickup truck, he is approached by a federal police officer who cites him for theft of government property. During his trial, he plans to request a mistake of law instruction based on his reliance on his neighbor's advice. You are the judge. Will you grant this instruction?

A. Yes.

B. No.

Chapter 6

Causation

I. Introduction

Causation is the link between the actus reus and the prohibited outcome of crime. Thus, properly understood, while the actus reus refers to the criminal act or omission (or in some cases possession) of crime, causation is the requirement of proving the alleged criminal act or omission (or possession) *legally caused* the result or conduct prohibited by the statute. For most crimes, this link between the actus reus and the prohibited outcome is inherent in proving the act element. For example, when proving burglary, proof that the defendant "broke and entered" the dwelling of another proves *ipso facto* that the defendant's act *caused* the home to be broken into. Or consider reckless driving: this crime, unlike burglary or murder, criminalizes prohibited *conduct* instead of defining a prohibited *result*. But proof of the conduct of driving recklessly *ipso facto* proves they caused the reckless risk.

Causation is especially relevant and at times more challenging for homicide offenses. These offenses prohibit *causing* a result: the death of a human being. As a result, the prosecution must prove that the defendant's act or omission was the *legal cause* of the victim's death. This is the legal meaning of the word "killing" in a homicide crime: the unlawful *killing* of a human being—the common requirement for any criminal homicide—means the evidence must prove beyond a reasonable doubt that the defendant's criminal act or omission (or the criminal act or omission of another whom the defendant is accountable for as an accomplice or a co-conspirator) was the legal cause of the victim's death. This is a material element of every homicide charge, which means reasonable doubt as to the legal cause of death requires acquittal.

It is common in criminal law discourse to define causation as requiring proof of both actual cause (sometimes called cause in fact) and proximate cause. It is, therefore, useful to think of a causation equation: actual cause + proximate cause = legal cause. It is also important to remember that a defendant cannot be a proximate (and therefore legal) cause unless she is first an actual cause, but just because a defendant is an actual cause does not always prove the defendant is the proximate cause. Accordingly, it is logical to analyze homicide causation by first assessing whether the evidence proves the defendant was the actual cause of death. If the answer is no, the defendant cannot be the proximate and legal cause of death. If the answer is yes, then assess whether the defendant is also the proximate cause of the victim's death. If so, the defendant is the legal cause of the death: the "killing" is attributable to the defendant. If not, the defendant is not the legal cause of the victim's death and the defendant would be not guilty of *any* homicide offense.

Practice Pointer

If a victim dies after a defendant unlawfully inflicts an injury on him but the evidence is insufficient to prove the defendant is the legal cause of death, it is highly likely the defendant will nonetheless be guilty of a lesser and necessarily included offense against the person. For example, imagine a defendant gets in a fight with a victim and unlawfully cuts the victim's arm with a broken bottle, causing a cut that normally would not be life-threatening. Imagine also that when the victim is transported to the emergency room, he is unfortunately treated by a physician who is intoxicated while on duty and, as a result, administers a medication that the victim's chart indicated he is severely allergic to. As a result, the victim died. Now imagine the defendant is charged with reckless manslaughter: the unlawful unintentional killing of a human being as the result of reckless conduct, with the infliction of the cut with the broken bottle alleged as the reckless act that resulted in death. As you will see, this is a good example of a fact pattern where the evidence establishes the defendant is an actual cause of death (because, but for the cut, the victim would still be alive), but not the proximate cause (because the intoxicated and grossly negligent doctor is an intervening event that contributed to the death that was objectively unforeseeable and therefore superseding). As a result, the defendant would likely be acquitted of manslaughter. However, the lesser included offense of aggravated battery would not require proof the defendant caused death; only proof the defendant intentionally or recklessly battered the victim with a means likely to cause death or great bodily harm. Thus, although the defendant may not be the legal cause of the victim's death, he should nonetheless be convicted of the lesser included offense of aggravated battery.

A. Cause in Fact

The first step in proving legal causation for a homicide offense is proving the defendant's act or omission was the cause in fact, or actual cause, of the victim's death. There are three distinct legal theories for satisfying this causation requirement.

1. But For

The most common way of satisfying this burden is by proving the defendant was the *but-for* cause of death, meaning but for the defendant's act or omission, the victim would still be alive. Imagine a defendant who shoots a victim in the head at point-blank range with an immediate resulting death. But for that act of shooting, the victim would still be alive. Accordingly, the defendant is the cause in fact, or actual cause, of death.

2. Acceleration

In some situations, a defendant's act or omission speeds up an inevitable death. In a sense, this is always the case, as all humans will die at some point. But where the victim's death would have occurred as the result of some other cause—illness, injury inflicted by another person, self-inflicted injury, etc.—and the defendant speeds up the death, the law treats the defendant's act or omission as an *accelerating* cause. Acceleration of an inevitable death does not satisfy the *but-for* test because the victim would have died anyway. Nonetheless, proof a defendant accelerated an inevitable death establishes that the defendant is the cause in fact, or actual cause, of death.

3. Substantial Factor

Imagine a firing squad: 6 soldiers, each armed with a deadly rifle, and each one fires in unison at the chest of the condemned soldier. A medical examiner concludes that the cause of death is a bullet to the heart and that any one of the six bullets was sufficient to cause death. In this hypothetical, none of the soldiers who fired are "but for" causes of death, because the death would have occurred absent any one of the shots. But each of them did an act that, standing alone, was sufficient to cause death. Each is therefore considered a *substantial factor* in causing the death. In a criminal homicide case, this means that where there is more than one actor who all engage in an act (or criminal omission) that is sufficient to cause death, each of them may be considered the cause in fact of the death. According to one pattern jury instruction,

> If you find that two or more causes have combined to bring about an injury and any one of them operating alone would have been sufficient to cause the injury, each cause is considered to be a proximate cause of the injury if it is a substantial factor in bringing it about, even though the result would have occurred without it. A substantial factor is an important or material factor and not one that is insignificant.

B. Proximate Cause

Proof of legal causation also requires the jury to be convinced beyond a reasonable doubt that the *actual cause* is also the *proximate cause* of the victim's death. In a very real sense, this proximate causation requirement provides the jury with the opportunity to reject responsibility for causing a victim's death when the death is too remote or removed from the defendant's actual cause. This is a necessary limitation, because having actual cause alone be sufficient to prove a defendant caused a death could lead to absurd results, like holding the mother of a murderer responsible for the killing, because "but for" her giving birth to the murderer, the victim would still be alive.

When assessing proximate cause, the jury is granted substantial discretion; discretion that is guided by several key principles. The ultimate question the jury must answer is whether the criminal result—in a criminal homicide case, the death of the victim—was an objectively foreseeable consequence of the defendant's actual cause. Some courts will also use the concept of a "natural and probable" consequence of the actual cause. So how is a jury to decide this question?

First, remember that the burden is on the prosecution to prove causation beyond a reasonable doubt. Accordingly, if the issue of proximate cause is raised by the evidence, the prosecution must persuade the jury beyond a reasonable doubt that the death *was* a foreseeable consequence of the defendant's criminal act or omission; the defendant does not have to prove it *was not*. Second, as a practical matter, the issue of proximate cause will not arise if the death was the direct and immediate result of the cause in fact. So, for example, if a defendant shoots a victim in the head at point-blank range and the victim dies almost immediately, there is nothing to raise a proximate cause question; the actual cause is *ipso facto* the proximate cause.

As a practical matter, this means that proximate cause analysis will be required only where the evidence indicates there was an intervening cause or event that contributed to the victim's death. You may have learned in torts to consider whether there was a superseding intervening cause. But it is useful to inverse these words: first identify the intervening cause (or causes), and only then proceed to the assessment of whether that cause supersedes the defendant's responsibility for the death of the victim. An intervening cause is, as noted, some act or event that comes between the defendant's actual cause and the death. An intervening cause may be the action of a third party (like the intoxicated physician), an act of nature (like a flood, or hurricane, or fire), or the action of the victim (like a victim who refuses easily accessible medical attention that would have saved his life).

Once such an intervening cause is established by the evidence, the ultimate question is whether the jury will treat it as superseding. A superseding cause is one that the jury concludes was objectively unforeseeable. Thus, if the prosecution convinces the jury that the intervening cause was objectively foreseeable, the actual cause is the proximate/legal cause. However, if the jury has reasonable doubt on that point (i.e., if they are not convinced the intervening cause was foreseeable), then they may treat that intervening cause as unforeseeable. An unforeseeable intervention supersedes, or "takes over," responsibility for the death, meaning the defendant is not the proximate/legal cause of death.

How does a jury decide whether an intervening cause is foreseeable or unforeseeable? A typical instruction simply requires them to apply their common sense to decide. Consider this example:

> The (act) (failure to act) must be a proximate cause of death. "Proximate cause" means that the death must have been the natural and probable result of the accused's (act) (failure to act). The proximate cause does not have to be the only cause, but it must be a contributory cause which plays an important

part in bringing about the death. (It is possible for the conduct of two or more persons to contribute each as a proximate cause to the death of another. If the accused's conduct was the proximate cause of the victim's death, the accused will not be relieved of criminal responsibility just because some other person's conduct was also a proximate cause of the death.) (If the death occurred only because of some unforeseeable, independent, intervening cause which did not involve the accused, then the accused may not be convicted of any homicide offense.) The burden is on the prosecution to prove beyond a reasonable doubt (that there was no independent, intervening cause) (and) (that the accused's cause in fact was a proximate cause of the victim's death).

In determining this issue, you must consider all relevant facts and circumstances, (including, but not limited to, (here the judge may specify significant evidentiary factors bearing on the issues and indicate the respective contentions of counsel for both sides)). It is possible for the acts or omissions of two or more persons to contribute, each as a contributing cause, to the death or injury of another. If the accused's conduct was a proximate cause of the victim's death or injury, the accused will not be relieved of criminal responsibility because some other person's acts or omissions also contributed to the same.

(The burden is on the prosecution to establish beyond a reasonable doubt that there was no intervening superseding cause.) Unless you are satisfied beyond a reasonable doubt that the accused's conduct was the proximate cause of the death, you may not find the accused guilty of the offense alleged. However, if you are satisfied beyond a reasonable doubt any intervening event was foreseeable, then the accused is the proximate cause of death.

In practical terms, the ultimate question for the jury is whether there was an intervening act or event, and if so, whether that intervention was *abnormal* under the circumstances. Focusing on this second question—whether in common sense terms the intervening event seems abnormal—will aid substantially in assessing what is or is not a superseding intervention. For example, the death resulting from the gross negligence of an intoxicated physician is certainly something that in common sense terms would appear abnormal. Therefore, it will be very difficult for a prosecutor to prove that such an intervention *should not* supersede responsibility for the victim's death. In contrast, if the physician was unaware that the drug would produce an allergic reaction because the victim was unconscious when brought to the emergency room, it is far less likely a jury would consider providing that drug abnormal under the circumstances.

Or imagine an intoxicated defendant who hits a bicyclist while driving, causing serious bleeding. EMTs arrive and do their best to stabilize the wound while transporting the victim to the hospital. But it is rush hour in a major city, and as a result of the bumper-to-bumper traffic and several cars disabled on the shoulder, the ambulance is unable to get the victim to the emergency room in time to save his life. Here, the traffic is certainly an intervening event, but under the circumstances, it is far from abnormal, which means it should be treated as foreseeable, and the defendant is the actual and proximate cause of death. Had the EMTs stopped for lunch resulting in delay and death of the victim, it would be an abnormal and therefore unforeseeable intervention, superseding responsibility for the death.

C. Special Considerations

When assessing proximate cause, there are three important special considerations. First, as in tort law, the maxim "we take our victim as we find her" applies to proximate cause analysis. This means that a physical vulnerability that is unknown to the defendant is considered objectively foreseeable and will not qualify as a superseding cause. The eggshell skull, or weak heart, or hemophilia are all examples. A defendant cannot avoid responsibility for a homicide by arguing he was unaware of such a vulnerability. Second, a victim who avoids an intervening harm by failing to avail himself of apparent safety or abandoning a place of safety may qualify as a superseding intervention. However, like other intervening causes, the ultimate question will be whether the victim's decision was abnormal under the circumstances. For example, it would be normal and foreseeable that a parent who escaped a burning home would run back into the danger to save a child; it would be abnormal for the same parent to do so to save a PS2 or Xbox.

Finally, it is important to understand that proximate cause assessments are inherently fact-based judgments, meaning that so long as the jury is properly instructed, their causation finding will almost never be reversed on appeal. In practical terms, this means that a proximate cause defense is far more likely to be successful for unintentional killings than for intentional killings. Why? Because when a jury determines that the defendant's actual cause was the result of an intent to kill or an intent to inflict grievous bodily harm, they are unlikely to exonerate the defendant for the homicide based on an intervening cause, even if that cause seems abnormal. Consider the example of the EMTs who stop for lunch while the victim of the defendant's cause in fact is in need of immediate transport to the emergency room. If the defendant was a hitman hired to kill the victim, a jury would be far less inclined to treat the intervening event as superseding than in a case involving an unintentional infliction of injury, like the intoxicated driver.

II. Application

A. Cause in Fact

The following case illustrates the requirement that the prosecution produce evidence that the defendant is the cause in fact in a criminal homicide case, and the three methods of satisfying this burden. As you read the decision, consider what the outcome would have been if the prosecutor had offered Dr. Hofman's opinion in its case-in-chief.

Oxendine v. State

528 A.2d 870 (1987)
Delaware Supreme Court

Defendant, Jeffrey Oxendine, Sr., appeals his conviction in trial by jury in Superior Court of manslaughter in the beating death of his six-year-old son, Jeffrey Oxendine, Jr. [11 Del. C. § 632(1) states: "A person is guilty of manslaughter when: (1) He recklessly causes the death of another person." (Codefendant, Leotha Tyree, was also convicted in the same trial of manslaughter in the death of Jeffrey Oxendine, Jr. and was sentenced to nine years' imprisonment.)] Oxendine was sentenced to twelve years' imprisonment. On appeal, Oxendine's principal argument is that the Trial Court committed reversible error by denying his motion for a judgment of acquittal on the issue of causation. Specifically, he argues that the State's medical testimony, relating to which of the codefendants' admittedly repeated beatings of the child was the cause of death, was so vague and uncertain as to preclude his conviction of any criminal offense.

We conclude that the evidence upon causation was insufficient to sustain Oxendine's conviction of manslaughter, but that the evidence was sufficient to sustain his conviction of the lesser included offense of assault in the second degree. [11 Del. C. § 612(1) states: "A person is guilty of assault in the second degree when: (1) He intentionally causes serious physical injury to another person."] Therefore, we affirm the Trial Court's denial of Oxendine's motion for a judgment of acquittal [for all offenses], direct that he be convicted of assault in the second degree, and remand for entry of judgment of conviction and resentencing for that offense. . . .

The facts may be summarized as follows: On the morning of January 18, 1984, Leotha Tyree, Oxendine's girlfriend, who lived with him, pushed Jeffrey into the bathtub causing microscopic tears in his intestines which led to peritonitis. During a break at work that evening, Oxendine telephoned home and talked to Jeffrey, who complained of stomach pains. When Oxendine returned home from work, he saw bruises on Jeffrey and knew that Tyree had beaten the child during the day. Although Jeffrey continued to complain of a stomachache, he apparently did not tell his father how or when he received the bruises.

The next morning at approximately 7:30 a.m., Oxendine went into Jeffrey's bedroom and began screaming at him to get up. A neighbor in the same apartment building testified to hearing sounds coming from the room of blows being struck, obscenities uttered by a male voice, and cries from a child saying, "Please stop, Daddy, it hurts." After hearing these sounds continue for what seemed like five to ten minutes, the witness heard a final noise consisting of a loud thump, as if someone had been kicked or punched "with a great blow."

Later that day, Jeffrey's abdomen became swollen. When Oxendine arrived home from work at about 5:00 p.m., Tyree told him of Jeffrey's condition and urged him to take Jeffrey to the hospital. Oxendine, apparently believing that Jeffrey was exaggerating his discomfort, went out, bought a newspaper, and returned home to read it. Upon his return, Tyree had prepared to take Jeffrey to the hospital. En route, Jeffrey stopped breathing; and was pronounced dead shortly after his arrival at the hospital.

I

In order to convict Oxendine of manslaughter, the State had to show that his conduct caused Jeffrey's death. 11 Del. C. §261 defines causation as the "antecedent but for which the result in question would not have occurred." 11 Del. C. §261. At trial, the State's original theories of causation were, alternatively, (1) a "combined direct effect," [substantial factor] or (2) an "aggravation" theory.

During its case-in-chief, the State called medical examiners Dr. Inguito and Dr. Hameli, who both testified that Jeffrey's death was caused by intra-abdominal hemorrhage and acute peritonitis, occurring as a result of blunt force trauma to the front of the abdomen. Similarly, each pathologist identified two distinct injuries, one caused more than twenty-four hours before death, and one inflicted less than twenty-four hours before death.

Dr. Inguito could not separate the effects of the two injuries. In his view, it was possible that both the older and more recent hemorrhage could have contributed to the death of the child, but he was unable to tell which of the hemorrhages caused the death of the child. Dr. Inguito could not place any quantitative value on either of the hemorrhages nor could he state whether the fresh hemorrhage or the older hemorrhage caused the death. The prosecutor never asked, nor did Dr. Inguito give, an opinion on whether the second hemorrhage accelerated Jeffrey's death.

Dr. Hameli, on the other hand, was of the opinion that the earlier injury was the underlying cause of death. According to him, the later injury, i.e., the second hemorrhage, "was an aggravating, and probably some factors [sic] contributing," but it was the earlier injury that was the plain underlying cause of death.

The prosecutor, however, did explicitly ask Dr. Hameli if the second injury accelerated Jeffrey's death. The relevant portion of the testimony is as follows:

> Prosecutor: Dr. Hameli, within a reasonable degree of medical certainty and in your expert opinion, did the second hemorrhage accelerate this child's death?
>
> Hameli: I do not know. If you are talking about timewise I assume that's what you are talking about, exploration.
>
> Prosecutor: You cannot give an opinion of that area; is that correct?
>
> Hameli: No.

Oxendine moved for judgment of acquittal at the end of the State's case-in-chief. The Trial Court, however, denied his motion.

As part of her case, codefendant Tyree called Dr. Hofman, a medical examiner, who disagreed about the number of injuries. He perceived only one injury inflicted about twelve hours before death. Subsequently, the prosecutor asked Hofman the following hypothetical question that assumed two blows when Hofman only testified as to one blow:

> *Prosecutor: In your expert medical opinion within a reasonable degree of medical certainty, if this child, given his weakened state as a result of the significant trauma to his abdominal cavity, suffered subsequently another blunt force trauma to the same area, would it accelerate this child's death? . . .*
>
> *Hofman: My opinion, as in a general statement, not knowing this child, it certainly would have an impact on shortening this child's life.*
>
> *Prosecutor: Is then, therefore, your answer yes?*
>
> *Hofman: Yes.*

At the end of trial, Oxendine again moved for judgment of acquittal. The Trial Court denied the motion and instructed the jury on the elements of recklessness, causation and on various lesser included offenses. The ultimate and only theory of causation on which the jury was charged was based on "acceleration." The Trial Court instructed the jury that "[a] defendant who causes the death of another . . . is not relieved of responsibility for causing the death if another later injury accelerates, that is, hastens the death of the other person. Contribution without acceleration is not sufficient." As previously noted, the jury returned verdicts of manslaughter against Oxendine and Tyree.

II

In this case, the evidence established that Oxendine inflicted a nonlethal injury upon Jeffrey after his son had, twenty-four hours earlier, sustained a lethal injury from a previous beating inflicted by Tyree. Thus, for Oxendine to be convicted of manslaughter in this factual context, the State was required to show for purposes of causation under 11 Del.C. § 261 that Oxendine's conduct hastened or accelerated the child's death. The Superior Court correctly instructed the jury that "[c]ontribution [or aggravation] without acceleration is insufficient to establish causation." We do not equate aggravation with acceleration. It is possible to make the victim's pain more intense, i.e., aggravate the injury, without accelerating the time of the victim's death. Thus, in terms of section 261, and as applied to defendant, the relevant inquiry is: but for his infliction of the second injury, would the victim have died when he died? If the second injury caused his son to die any sooner, then defendant, who inflicted the second injury, would be deemed to have caused his son's death within the definition of section 261.

A finding of medical causation may not be based on speculation or conjecture. . . . A doctor's testimony that a certain thing is possible is no evidence at all. *Palace Bar, Inc. v. Fearnot,* Ind. Supr., 269 Ind. 405, 381 N.E.2d 858, 864 (1978). His opinion as to what is possible is no more valid than the jury's own speculation as to what is or is not possible. *Id.* Almost anything is possible, and it is improper to allow a jury to consider and base a verdict upon a "possible" cause of death. *Id.* Therefore, a doctor's testimony can only be considered evidence when his conclusions are based on reasonable medical certainty that a fact is true or untrue. *Id.*

The State's expert medical testimony, even when viewed in the light most favorable to the State, was (1) insufficient to sustain the State's original theories of causation (a "combined direct effect" or an "aggravation" theory); and (2) insufficient to sustain the State's ultimate theory of causation ("acceleration") on which the court instructed the jury. Both of the State's expert witnesses, Dr. Inguito and Dr. Hameli, were unable to state with any degree of medical certainty that the second injury contributed to the death of the child. Dr. Inguito could only testify that it was possible that both the older and more recent hemorrhage could have contributed to the death of the child. As for Dr. Hameli, he testified that the second injury independent of the first injury could have caused death but probably would not cause death. Furthermore, Dr. Hameli explicitly stated that he could not give an opinion as to whether the second injury accelerated Jeffrey's death. Similarly, Dr. Inguito was neither asked nor did he offer an opinion about acceleration.

The record establishes that the only theory of causation under which the State submitted the case to the jury was the acceleration theory. The State apparently abandoned its initial theories of causation and adopted the acceleration theory as the cause of death, based on the testimony of Dr. Hofman, a witness for codefendant Tyree, recalled by the State on rebuttal. That was too late to sustain the State's case-in-chief for manslaughter.

The State concedes that when it closed its case-in-chief it did not have a prima facie case to support acceleration. Therefore, even though the State could, based on Dr. Hofman's testimony, establish a prima facie case of acceleration at the end of the trial, Oxendine's conviction of manslaughter must be set aside for insufficiency of the evidence to establish that his conduct accelerated Jeffrey's death.

Furthermore, even if the State's evidence was sufficient to sustain its original theories of causation, we could not affirm Oxendine's conviction because the jury was not instructed on either of these theories. Although the State may submit alternate theories of causation to the jury, if supported by the evidence, it must establish in its case-in-chief a prima facie basis for each theory that goes to the jury. In this case, the State did not maintain alternate theories throughout the trial. The State abandoned and completely changed its section 261 theories of causation after it closed its case-in-chief. The ultimate and only theory ("acceleration") on which the court instructed the jury was different and not compatible with the State's original theories of causation that it attempted to establish during its case-in-chief. As previously noted, acceleration is not synonymous with either aggravation or the combined effects of two injuries. Thus, when the State was unable to establish at the end of its case-in-chief a prima facie case for acceleration, its case for manslaughter failed.

It is extremely "difficult to be objective about the death of a child. . . . Those responsible ought to be punished. Nevertheless, there must be proof as to who, if anyone, inflicted the injuries that resulted in death." *State v. Lynn*, Wash.Supr., 73

Wash. 2d 117, 436 P.2d 463, 466 (1968) (en banc). "Reprehensible and repulsive as the conduct of the defendant is, nevertheless it is not proof of manslaughter." *State v. Guiles*, Wash.Supr., 53 Wash. 2d 386, 333 P.2d 923, 924 (1959).

The Trial Court, however, properly denied Oxendine's motion for judgment of acquittal at the close of the State's case because its medical testimony was sufficient for a rational trier of fact to conclude beyond a reasonable doubt that Oxendine was guilty of the lesser included offense of assault in the second degree, 11 Del.C. § 612(1). Therefore, we reverse Oxendine's conviction of manslaughter and remand the case to Superior Court for entry of a judgment of conviction and resentence of defendant for the lesser included offense of assault in the second degree.

. . . .

REVERSED AND REMANDED.

Notes and Questions

1. Notice the case involved three potential theories of proving Oxendine was the actual cause, or cause in fact, of Jeffrey's death: but for causation, substantial factor (what the court calls combined direct effect), and acceleration. What opinion would Dr. Inguito or Dr. Hameli have to have given to support each of these theories?

2. Some states recognize a modified form of substantial factor: independent combined contribution. This allows for a finding of actual cause of death when two or more independent actors inflict non-deadly injury that combines to cause death. This may have been the theory the prosecution originally sought to rely on in *Oxendine*. However, once Dr. Hameli testified that he considered the earlier injury inflicted by Tyree to be the cause of Jeffrey's death, the only theory of causation that would support treating Oxendine as the actual cause was acceleration, and there was no evidence offered in the prosecution case in chief to support that theory. Nor does it seem a combined contribution theory was recognized in the jurisdiction because, had it been, Dr. Inguito's testimony should have been sufficient to satisfy the prosecution burden of production on the actual cause question. Recall that the court indicated Inguito opined that, "it was possible that *both* the older and more recent hemorrhage could have *contributed* to the death of the child, but he was unable to tell which of the hemorrhages caused the death of the child."

Accordingly, *if* combined non-deadly contribution was a theory of causation recognized by the court, the conflicting opinions of Inguito and Hameli would require the court to assume the jury would credit Inguito over Hameli when deciding the motion for acquittal. But the appeals court concluded that, when the prosecution rested, the evidence was insufficient to satisfy the burden of production, meaning the trial judge should have entered an acquittal on the homicide charge against Oxendine (although the court's decision may have been based on Inguito's testimony that it was *possible* both injuries contributed to the death).

3. What did the court mean when it noted that aggravation is not the same as acceleration? Do you think the evidence established Oxendine aggravated the injury inflicted by Tyree? If so, why was that insufficient to satisfy the prosecution's burden of production on causation?

4. Didn't the jury have evidence that Oxendine accelerated Jeffrey's death when they deliberated? Wasn't it their prerogative to accord probative value to Dr. Hofman's opinion and disregard the opinions of Dr. Inguito and Dr. Hameli? If so, did *the jury* improperly convict Oxendine of reckless manslaughter?

5. How would you describe the prosecution's causation evidentiary failure: a failure to satisfy the burden of production or a failure to satisfy the burden of persuasion? If not the latter, why was the manslaughter conviction reversed?

6. Do you agree with the court's opinion that the trial court "properly denied Oxendine's motion for judgment of acquittal at the close of the State's case ..."? Should the motion for judgment of acquittal have been denied, or perhaps partially granted? If you had been the trial judge, what would your ruling have been?

7. This is your first exposure to expert opinion evidence. Notice how the court defines what such an opinion must indicate for it to qualify as probative. Why wasn't the *possibility* of acceleration insufficient to satisfy that requirement?

8. You should be bothered by the outcome in *Oxendine*, and it should serve as a powerful reminder that justice requires more than understanding of the law; it requires the lawyers entrusted with the power of the law to leverage that power with due diligence. Why would the prosecution ask causation questions of their only experts without knowing ahead of time how they would answer? Why would the prosecution rest its case *before* speaking with Dr. Hoffman to determine if he could offer an opinion to satisfy their burden of production? Answering these questions is of course somewhat speculative, but it certainly seems to suggest a lack of due diligence. What we know for certain is that there was a witness who, had he been called in the prosecution case-in-chief, would have provided an expert opinion to satisfy the burden of production. We also know that the jury credited that opinion when they improperly considered it. Thus, a lack of due diligence may very well have resulted in Oxendine's acquittal for killing his son.

9. Was there an alternate theory the prosecution should have alleged against Oxendine? What about omission? If so, what medical opinion would have been required to prove Oxendine's reckless omission was the cause in fact of Jeffrey's death?

B. Proximate Cause

As you read the next case, carefully assess how many intervening causes contributed to the victim's death, and then consider whether each was objectively foreseeable.

State v. Smith

2007-Ohio-1884

Ohio Court of Appeals

John Smith appeals his convictions for felonious assault and involuntary man-slaughter stemming from his assault of Bryan Biser, who died after being hit by a single punch to the head. Biser was diabetic and quit taking his medication after the incident. Prior to death, his blood sugar levels were extremely elevated and his bowels had become necrotic. Thus, Smith contends unforeseeable intervening events caused Biser's death. However, based on the testimony from the State's two expert witnesses, a reasonable juror could conclude that Smith's punch and Biser's resulting fall damaged the frontal lobes of Biser's brain. As a normal result of these injuries, Biser became apathetic and disinterested, which in turn, led to his failure to take required medication, and ultimately his death. Biser's lapse in attending to his own care was a response to Smith's assault. Because it was neither unforeseeable nor abnormal, it cannot be an intervening cause that broke the chain of legal causation stemming from the assault. [The court addressed two other assignments of error that are not relevant to the causation issue.]

Facts

A grand jury indicted John Smith with one count of felonious assault and one count of involuntary manslaughter for allegedly causing the death of Bryan Biser by a closed-fist punch to the head. The case proceeded to a jury trial, which produced the following facts. . . .

On April 15, 2005, Bryan Biser spent the afternoon socializing with neighbors at the Hokolesqua Apartments just outside Frankfort, Ohio. Biser sat outside with his neighbor, Shanna Knapp, and split a six-pack beer with her while watching the children playing in a playground just across the parking lot. As they watched the children, two of the kids around the age of five got into a fight. One of the children was a distant relative of Smith's.

When Smith learned that his nephew's child had been in a fight, he walked over to the playground and screamed obscenities at the children. Smith encouraged his five-year-old relative to beat up the other child. Ms. Knapp overheard Smith and approached him near the playground. Ms. Knapp told Smith to stop yelling obsceni-ties and encouraging the children to fight. Ms. Knapp then got into an argument with Smith's nephew, John Rawlings.

Biser approached Ms. Knapp and Rawlings in the parking lot and attempted to stop the arguing by asking everyone to calm down. Smith then walked around a car towards Biser, yelled an obscenity at him, and hit him with a closed fist on the left side of his head while Biser stood with one hand to his side and one hand holding a beverage cup. Biser never raised his arms, squared to fight, or said a threatening word.

As Biser crumpled to the ground, the right side of his face hit a parked car, and then his head hit the pavement. Smith "danced" over Biser, as he lay unconscious, taunting him to get up and fight and challenging everyone else to fight him. Biser remained on the ground while a neighbor, Twila Jones, called 911. One of the children alerted Amy Preston, the apartment complex manager, who was also a nursing assistant, to attend to Biser.

Approximately fifteen minutes after receiving the call, emergency medical technicians (EMTs) Todd Smith and Sharon Flannery arrived on the scene, along with EMT trainee Marilyn Chaffin. Biser regained consciousness, and the EMT's began treating his wounds and transported him to Adena hospital. Biser stated to the EMT's that he was diabetic and had taken his insulin that day. However, the EMT's were not able to take his blood-glucose level because the Accu-check machine malfunctioned. Chaffin testified that she noticed one of Biser's pupils was bigger than the other, but she failed to note this in her report.

Dr. Kashubeck examined Biser at the emergency room of Adena Hospital. In his report, he noted that Biser's pupils were round and equal in size, and that Biser denied any pain anywhere. The report also noted that Biser complained of a laceration to his right eye and a bump to the back of the head, and that he answered questions and followed commands appropriately. Biser refused emergency room treatment for his head injuries and his diabetes, despite an elevated blood-glucose level of 465. Biser stated that he had insulin to treat the diabetes at home and did not want to purchase more at the hospital. He also refused a CAT Scan, which the doctor had recommended. The doctor discharged Biser from the hospital, but ordered him to return immediately if he experienced any vomiting, confusion or vision problems.

Ms. Preston and Ms. Jones went to check on Biser following his return from the hospital that same day, April 15, 2005. Ms. Preston testified that Biser seemed confused and did not remember being involved in a fight, but, instead, told her he had been singing karaoke that night. He acknowledged being at the emergency room and gave Ms. Preston his paperwork from that visit. The next day, April 16, 2005, Ms. Preston and Ms. Jones went again to check on Biser. Ms. Jones testified that Biser did not invite them in, but cracked the door and told them he felt sick to his stomach and asked them to leave him alone.

Biser's cousin, Beth Spangler testified that she visited Biser on three separate occasions on April 16, 2005. She first stopped by in the morning and gave him Advil for his headache. She stopped by again at 1:00 PM, and he continued to complain that his head hurt, and he wanted everyone to go away. Finally, she returned at 5:00 PM and brought him food. She testified that Biser told her he had taken his insulin that day. She also testified that there were two bottles of insulin in the refrigerator.

Ms. Preston testified that on Tuesday, April 19, 2005, she received a voicemail from one of Biser's family members, who had been unable to contact him. Ms. Preston knocked on Biser's door, but received no response. She opened his door with her master key and found Biser lying on the floor, unconscious. She testified that

Biser struggled to breathe, and his feet and left arm had turned black. Ms. Preston instructed a neighbor to call 911, and an ambulance arrived within seven to eight minutes to transport Biser to the hospital.

At the emergency room, Biser underwent a CAT scan of his head, which indicated that he had a possible skull fracture, a small subdural hematoma, and subarachnoid hemorrhage. Additionally, Biser's blood-glucose level was 1,169, and he was in severe diabetic ketoacidosis, a lethal condition resulting from a diabetic's failure to take prescribed insulin. Doctors transported Biser to Grant Medical Center in Columbus, Ohio, where he underwent exploratory surgery in his abdomen. The surgeons discovered that his right bowel and a portion of his right colon were necrotic, a condition from which no one could survive. Biser died several hours later. After performing an autopsy, Deputy Coroner Trent ruled the cause of death to be homicide due to blunt force craniocerebral injuries.

Dr. Glenn Roush, a radiologist, testified that he reviewed Biser's CAT Scan from Biser's emergency room visit on April 19, 2005. He testified that Biser's CAT Scan indicated he had a skull fracture and brain injury that had occurred recently. Dr. Roush also testified that he has "never seen anyone with this sort of injury be able to function."

Dr. William Cox, a forensic neuropathologist serving for the Franklin County Coroner, testified that he reviewed Biser's autopsy protocol, toxicology report, and medical records and determined that the cause of death listed by Dr. Trent on the death certificate was incorrect. Dr. Cox opined that Biser's death resulted from diabetic ketoacidosis. He testified that the punch Biser received and subsequent fall to the ground caused him to suffer contusions to his brain that damaged his frontal lobes. Dr. Cox testified that the damage to Biser's frontal lobes affected his cognitive ability and caused him to become apathetic, uninhibited and disinterested. He further testified that Biser's head injury substantially contributed to his death, and the damage to his frontal lobes "clearly would have adversely affected [Biser's] ability to look after himself."

A jury found Smith guilty on both counts of felonious assault and involuntary manslaughter. After merging the two counts, the trial court sentenced Smith to eight years in prison and ordered him to pay $49,018.33 in restitution, plus court costs on the charge of involuntary manslaughter.

Smith asserts the following assignments of error on appeal:

I. The State Failed to Produce Sufficient Evidence to
Prove that Mr. Smith was Gulty of Involuntary Manslaughter
as Alleged in the Indictment

In his first assignment of error, Smith contends there is insufficient evidence to sustain his conviction of involuntary manslaughter. Smith concedes his felonious assault conviction and focuses his argument solely on his conviction for involuntary manslaughter. A claim of insufficient evidence invokes a due process concern and raises the question of whether the evidence is legally sufficient to support the jury verdict as a matter of law. In analyzing the sufficiency of evidence to sustain a criminal conviction, an appellate court must construe the evidence in a light most favorable to the prosecution. . . . After construing the evidence in this manner, the test for determining sufficiency is whether any rational trier of fact considering the evidence could have found all essential elements of the charged offenses proven beyond a reasonable doubt. . . .

Under R.C. 2903.04(A), a person is guilty of involuntary manslaughter when he causes the death of another "as a proximate result" of the commission of an underlying felony offense. The underlying felony in this case is felonious assault. . . .

Under the common law, a person could not be convicted of the offense of involuntary manslaughter unless the commission of the underlying offense was the "proximate cause" of the death of the victim. . . . In interpreting this new element, the courts of this state have held that the element merely resurrects the prior requirement of proximate cause: "The term 'proximate result' was used by the General Assembly to refine and limit the verb 'cause.' Thus, it is conceivable that [a] defendant's conduct may have caused [the victim's] death in the sense that he set in motion events which culminated in her death, which therefore would not have occurred in the absence of that conduct, but, nevertheless, that the death was not the proximate result of his conduct if it were not the natural, logical, and foreseeable result of his conduct. . . . In this sense, then, 'proximate result' bears a resemblance to the concept of 'proximate cause' in that [a] defendant will be held responsible for those foreseeable consequences which are known to be, or should be known to be, within the scope of the risk created by his conduct. . . . Here, that means that death reasonably could be anticipated by an ordinarily prudent person as likely to result under these or similar circumstances."

Here, Smith concedes that his felonious assault may have been the "but-for" cause of Biser's death. But he contends it did not proximately cause his death because multiple, unforeseeable events interfered with the natural and logical result of Smith's conduct. Smith argues that it was unforeseeable for Biser to refuse a recommended CAT scan and X-ray at the emergency room. Furthermore, it was unforeseeable for Smith to know that Biser was a diabetic and would refuse insulin at the emergency room. Smith claims that Biser's death resulted from his failure to take his insulin for several days, which caused his diabetic ketoacidosis. In light of these intervening circumstances, he contends the ultimate result is too remote from his conduct for the state to hold him accountable for Biser's death.

Courts generally treat the issue of legal causation in the criminal context similarly to that in tort cases because the situations are closely analogous. See, generally, LaFave Substantive Criminal Law (2003), 2nd Ed., Section 6.4(c). When dealing with claims of intervening causation, the proper analysis starts with a determination of whether the intervening act was a mere coincidence or alternatively, a response to the accused's prior conduct. . . . An intervening cause is a coincidence when the defendant's act merely places the victim at a certain place at a certain time, thus subjecting the victim to the vagaries of the intervening cause. LaFave gives the example of "A" shoots at "B" but misses. "B" then varies from his intended route, is struck by lightening [*sic*], and dies. Had "B" continued on his anticipated route, he would not have been injured. The lightening [*sic*] is a coincidence.

An intervening act is a response to the prior acts of the defendant where it involves reaction to the condition created by the defendant. Again from LaFave, "A" shoots "B" who is standing near the edge of a cliff. "B" impulsively jumps off the cliff rather than being the target of a second shot. This impulse may fairly be characterized as a normal response.

This distinction is important because the law will impose a less exacting standard of legal causation where the intervening cause is a response rather than a coincidence. A coincidence will break the chain of legal causation if it was unforeseeable. Thus, in the first example "A" is not criminally liable for "B's" death, notwithstanding he may be charged with an "attempt." However, for a response to break the chain, it must be both abnormal and unforeseeable. The distinction is premised upon a notion of fairness that finds less reason to hold a defendant liable for bad results where the defendant has merely caused the victim to "be at the wrong place at the wrong time." A defendant who has brought the intervening agency into play in response to the danger he has caused is subjected to a more stringent test if he is to break the chain of causation. Thus, in the second example, "A" will face potential criminal liability for "B's" death.

Here the primary intervening events that Smith relies upon to break the chain of causation are Biser's diabetes and failure to take his insulin. Initially, Smith contends it was unforeseeable that Biser would be a diabetic. But courts have routinely held both the tortfeasor and the accused take the victim as they find him. Thus, Biser's preexisting condition does not break the chain of causation.

We must now decide whether Biser's failure to medicate and take care of himself was a coincidence or a response. We conclude it can only be deemed a response. Biser's apathetic conduct occurred as a reaction to the head injuries that Smith caused. Biser's apathy did not happen because he was in the wrong place at the wrong time. This is not a case of "A" hits "B" in the head causing minor injuries; "B" goes to the hospital where he contracts a rare disease from his treating doctor. That sequence would present a coincidence.

Because we are dealing with a response, we must next decide whether Biser's failure to medicate and care for himself was both abnormal and unforeseeable. All the medical testimony in the record indicates the victim's conduct was neither. Dr. Roush testified a person suffering a skull fracture and brain injuries Biser received would not function normally. Dr. Cox testified Smith's punch and the resulting fall caused contusions to Biser's brain and damaged the frontal lobes. Dr. Cox indicated these injuries caused Biser's apathy and adversely affected his ability to care for himself. We believe that it is clearly foreseeable that someone with a fractured skull, a subdural hematoma and a subarachnoid hemorrhage might lose the ability to act rationally.

In doing so, we rely on the proposition that an accused need not foresee the precise consequences of his conduct. To be actionable it is only necessary that the result is within the natural and logical scope of risk created by the conduct. Self-inflicted harm attributable to a victim's weakened conditions are quite normal and do not break the causal chain. Thus, we conclude Biser's failure to medicate and seek proper treatment is neither abnormal nor unforeseeable. In light of this conclusion, Biser's conduct is not an intervening cause that breaks the chain of legal causation set in motion by Smith.

[The court then addressed the other unrelated assignments of error and upheld the conviction and the sentence].

Notes and Questions

1. Notice how the court assessed the foreseeability of Biser's medical condition. Even though Smith was not aware his victim suffered from diabetes, the court rejected the argument that the medical condition was an intervening superseding cause. As the court noted, a defendant "takes the victim as he finds him," meaning unknown physical vulnerabilities are treated as objectively foreseeable.

2. The opinion explains the difference between a responsive versus coincidental intervention. But go back and read that portion of the opinion again. Isn't the ultimate question the same: whether the intervening event was abnormal? It may, as the court notes, be more likely that a coincidental intervention is abnormal, but there are certainly many coincidences that are normal and foreseeable. Consider the example above of the ambulance that gets stuck in traffic. The traffic is an intervening event, and certainly coincidental (the traffic was not a response to the defendant's action that the death in motion). But heavy traffic at rush hour(s) in a major city is certainly not abnormal. Or consider a victim who refuses urgent medical care not because, like Biser, the defendant's act compromised the victim's cognitive reasoning, but instead because the victim "doesn't like doctors." In that situation, the intervening event of foregoing medical care is certainly responsive to the initial injury, but would likely be considered an abnormal response by a jury. Accordingly, when assessing proximate causation, focusing on the relative abnormality of the intervening event will aid substantially.

3. Try using this step-by-step methodology to work through the proximate cause issues raised in the case:

   a. Must have a cause in fact to have proximate (legal) cause

      (1) Cause in fact need not be the exclusive cause:

         (a) Acceleration (hastens result)

         (b) Substantial Factor (more than one cause, each of which is sufficient to bring about death)

BUT

b. Cause in fact is not automatically proximate (legal) cause

c. To be a legal cause, the cause in fact must also be the proximate cause. Accordingly, you must determine:

(1) Is there another *intervening* act or event that contributes to the result;

(2) If so, does it break the causal connection because it is *superseding*?

d. What qualifies as a superseding intervention is a question of fact. The key question that must be resolved is whether the intervention was objectively foreseeable.

(1) Only an unforeseeable intervention supersedes.

e. How does a jury assess foreseeability?

(1) An *abnormal* intervention is most likely to be considered unforseeable and supersedes.

(2) A *normal* intervention is most likely to be considered unforseeable and does not supersede.

f. Remember, foreseeability is an objection question: what would a "reasonable person" foresee as the ultimate result from the defendant's cause in fact?

Formative Assessments

1. Tom had a heart ailment so serious that his doctors had concluded that only a heart transplant could save his life. They therefore arranged to have him flown to another city to have the operation performed. Dan, Tom's nephew, who stood to inherit from him, poisoned him. The poison produced a reaction which required postponing the journey and keeping Tom in the hospital. The plane on which Tom was to have flown crashed, and all aboard were killed. Tom passed away the day after the plane crash. The autopsy concluded the poison killed Tom, but that his heart was so weak he would have died within several days even had he not been poisoned. If charged with criminal homicide, Dan should be found

A. Guilty.

B. Not guilty, because his act did not hasten the deceased's death, but instead prolonged it by one day.

C. Not guilty, because the deceased was already suffering from a fatal illness.

D. Not guilty, because the poison was not the sole cause of death.

2. Now assume that the victim refused to take the flight for the transplant because he was afraid of flying. As a result, the hospital had to arrange for land transport which delayed the treatment for a week. During that week, the victim died. The autopsy discovered the poison in the victim's body and concluded the victim's heart

was too weak to withstand the poison, but that had he received the transplant as originally scheduled, he would have survived. What is Dan's best defense theory:

A. It is speculation that the defendant would have survived had he received the transplant as originally scheduled.

B. The evidence is insufficient to prove Dan was the legal cause of the victim's death.

C. The evidence is insufficient to prove Dan was the actual cause of the victim's death.

3. The defendant is charged with involuntary manslaughter for the death of the victim. The evidence presented by the prosecution establishes that the victim was thrown from the passenger seat of a car being driven by the defendant when the defendant lost control of the car; that the loss of control was the result of the defendant falling asleep at the wheel; that the defendant had been up 24 hours without rest and was rushing back home from a night of partying in order to get to work on time early in the morning; and that the defendant had been drinking some alcohol, although he was slightly within the legal limit. On cross examination, the responding police officer admitted that the victim had not been wearing a seatbelt at the time of the accident. How would you use this evidence to argue for reasonable doubt on behalf of the defendant?

PART TWO

Crimes

Introduction to
Homicide Offenses

I. Introduction

Criminal homicide offenses run a spectrum from negligent killings all the way to planned and calculated killings. Understanding this spectrum of offenses will be facilitated by thinking of homicide crimes in terms of "ingredients" and "erasers": what are the ingredients for each offense, and what erases or "blocks" proof of a requisite ingredient, and what crime, if any, results. In this regard, it is useful to think of homicide offenses as "cocktails": learning the "recipe" for each cocktail will lead you to an accurate assessment of what offense is established by the evidence.

It is also important to recognize that while there are significant variants in homicide statutes throughout the nation, there are some common aspects that serve as foundations for these statutes. In fact, the differences between jurisdictions are often more semantic than substantively significant. For example, in all jurisdictions, murder may be established for both intentional and unintentional killings, although the degree of murder for such killings will vary. Accordingly, it is logical to first consider the foundation for all criminal homicide offenses that applies in any jurisdiction; second, to consider the common law homicide crimes; third, consider some of the most common and important statutory variants.

II. Unlawful Killing of a Human Being: The Universally Required Foundation for All Criminal Homicide

Homicide is the killing of one human being by another. Suicide is not homicide. As indicated in the *Keeler* case in Chapter 2, the meaning of human being at common law required that the victim had been "born alive." California modified that common law rule by statute following that decision, and most jurisdictions today treat a viable fetus as a human being for purposes of homicide crimes.

The world *killing* is the causation requirement for any homicide offense: the evidence must prove beyond a reasonable doubt that the defendant's act, omission, or complicity (if the act or omission is committed by an accomplice or a co-conspirator) is the legal cause of the victim's death. This is an important foundational requirement, because it means the evidence must prove more than that someone died; the evidence must also establish that the defendant was the *actual* and *proximate* cause of the victim's death. If there is reasonable doubt on the causation element, there is no homicide.

Because of the limits of medical forensics, the common law originally imposed an arbitrary causation rule: if the victim died more than a "year and a day" after the alleged criminal act or omission, the death was not proximately caused by the defendant. All states have eliminated or relaxed this rule. For example, California treats a death more than three years after the alleged criminal act or omission as presumptively too remote to prove causation, but the prosecution may rebut that presumption.

Not all homicides are criminal. To be criminal, the evidence must establish an *unlawful* killing of a human being. What proves unlawful? First, the evidence must prove the requisite mens rea for the alleged criminal homicide offense. Second, there must be no legal justification or excuse, such as self-defense or lack of mental responsibility (insanity). Such an affirmative defense is a complete defense and negates or "erases" the word "unlawful." If there is no *unlawful* killing of a human being, there is no *criminal* homicide. As the defense lawyer Paul Bigler in *Anatomy of a Murder* advised his client accused of murder during one of their first meetings: "There are four ways I can defend murder: you didn't do it [no causation]; it was an accident [no mens rea]; it was justified, like self-defense; or it was excused."

Once an unlawful killing of a human being is established, the challenge will be determining *what* homicide crime is supported by the evidence. To that end, it will be useful to think of these offenses as falling into two broad categories: subjectively *expected* or *unexpected*. An expected killing is one where the defendant acted with the purpose to kill, knew with substantial certainty he would kill, or while not intending to kill, did intend to inflict grievous bodily harm (because it would support a finding the defendant knew his conduct was likely to cause death even if it was not his purpose). An unexpected killing is one where the defendant did not expect to kill but created a substantial and unjustified risk of causing death by engaging in reckless or grossly negligent conduct, or by committing an inherently dangerous felony. It is critically important to understand that a criminal homicide in *both* of these categories may qualify as murder or manslaughter. But assessing whether the killing was expected or unexpected will focus analysis on the critical evidence to distinguish between these offenses.

III. Jurisdictional Variants

A. The Common Law

The original common law recognized only two categories of criminal homicide: murder and manslaughter. The unlawful killing of a human being was the common foundation for either offense. What distinguished them was proof of malice: any unlawful killing with malice was murder; any unlawful killing without malice was manslaughter. For expected/intentional killings, malice was established by the intent to kill, unless that intent was formed during a sudden heat of passion triggered by an adequate provocation. Thus, sudden heat of passion blocks or "erases" proof of malice even if the defendant intends to kill or inflict grievous bodily harm. This results in what is commonly called *voluntary* manslaughter: an unlawful *intentional* killing without malice. Unexpected/unintentional killings resulting from substantial and unjustified risk creation—reckless or grossly negligent conduct—normally proved what is commonly called *involuntary* manslaughter: the unlawful *unintentional* killing resulting from reckless or grossly negligent conduct. Where, however, the risk creation manifested a *wanton disregard for the value of human life* or a *depraved indifference to human life,* which essentially meant the jury makes a finding that the risk created was objectively extreme, malice would be implied and the *unintentional* killing would qualify as murder. Many students find this line between unintentional manslaughter and unintentional murder especially confusing. The law, however, vests juries with the responsibility to draw this distinction. In the most general terms, ask this question: if you saw the defendant creating the risk, would you think, "Hey, that seems dangerous," or would you think, "That idiot is going to end up killing someone." If the former, it is most likely manslaughter; if the latter, it is most likely murder.

The common law also included the felony murder doctrine, which treated any killing proximately caused by the attempt, commission, or immediate flight from an inherently dangerous felony as murder. For this offense, the requisite malice for murder was imputed to the defendant as the result of engaging in the felony; the prosecutor's mens rea burden is the mens rea for the alleged predicate felony.

B. Degree Jurisdictions

Because common law murder was always subject to capital punishment, many U.S. jurisdictions have modified murder law to segregate murder by degrees. In these jurisdictions, first-degree or capital murder is considered the most aggravated type of murder; lesser degrees less so. In some jurisdictions, murder is segregated into two degrees: first and second. Others create a third degree of murder, normally reserved for unintentional "depraved indifference" murder.

Whether the jurisdiction defines the base mental element for murder as malice, or uses a more specific term such as intent, purpose, knowledge, or recklessness manifesting an extreme indifference to human life, *if* the jurisdiction segregates murder into degrees it is necessary to identify the additional "ingredient(s)" that elevate murder to the most aggravated level. In other words, all murders will require the base mens rea element; distinguishing between degrees of murder will require proof of some additional element.

At common law, the original "distinguishing" elements were *premeditation* and *deliberation* (sometimes conflated into the singular element of premeditation). As will be explained in the following chapter, these were additional mens rea elements in addition to the base mens rea of malice. In other words, malice *plus* premeditation and deliberation qualified as first-degree murder; malice *without* both premeditation *and* deliberation qualified as second-degree murder. Defining these terms is therefore essential to assess degrees of murder, and will be addressed in the next chapter.

States that segregate murder by degrees have added to the list of additional "ingredients" that aggravate murder to first-degree or capital murder. Accordingly, for each jurisdiction, it is necessary to review this list of aggravating ingredients. Common examples of aggravating elements include a child or law enforcement victim; use of a particularly heinous weapon such as poison or armor-piercing ammunition; use of explosive devices; lying in wait; multiple victims in one criminal incident; or a killing during the attempt, commission, or flight from a specifically identified felony. Importantly, where premeditation and deliberation are included on this aggravating list, other aggravating elements are distinct, meaning proof of murder plus any one of these aggravating elements elevates murder to first degree.

The two wire diagrams on the following pages provide a generalized visual depiction of the assessment of criminal homicide for expected and unexpected killings.

Common Law Criminal Homicide

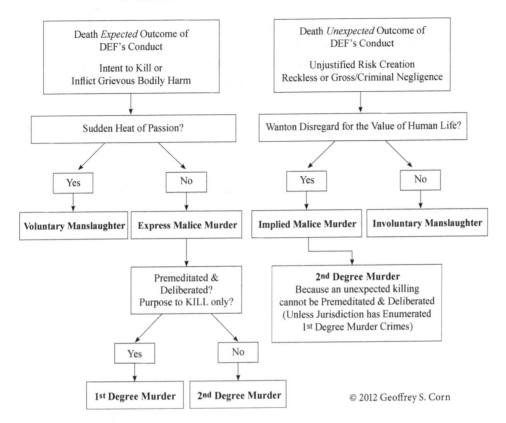

© 2012 Geoffrey S. Corn

C. Model Penal Code

As noted earlier, the MPC dispensed with malice as a mens rea element. Like the common law, the MPC provides that intentional and unintentional killings may qualify as either murder or manslaughter. The MPC also adds a "lower" level of homicide that aligns with grossly negligent killings: negligent homicide.

Murder under the MPC is any unlawful killing as the result of purpose, knowledge, or recklessness manifesting an extreme indifference to the value of human life (the MPC variant of wanton disregard to the value of human life). However, if the defendant forms the purpose or knowledge to kill during an extreme emotional disturbance resulting from a reasonable explanation or excuse, that mental disturbance mitigates murder to manslaughter: the MPC *voluntary* manslaughter variant. A killing resulting from recklessness that *does not* manifest an extreme indifference to the value of human life is manslaughter: the MPC *involuntary* manslaughter variant. If the killing is the result of gross negligence, the crime is negligent homicide.

The MPC does not "grade" murders by degrees. Instead, it proposes that the severity of punishment—to include the possibility of capital punishment—is a matter determined during a distinct sentencing phase of the trial. During that phase, a jury would consider whether the aggravating evidence substantially outweighs the extenuation and mitigation evidence. This approach rejects the view that some murders are *per se* more aggravated than others in favor of the view that the aggravated nature of any murder should be assessed on a case-by-case basis. It is, however, important to note that many states that have adopted the MPC have retained degrees of murder based on defined aggravating elements.

This wire diagram illustrates the assessment of criminal homicide in an MPC jurisdiction:

Model Penal Code Criminal Homicide

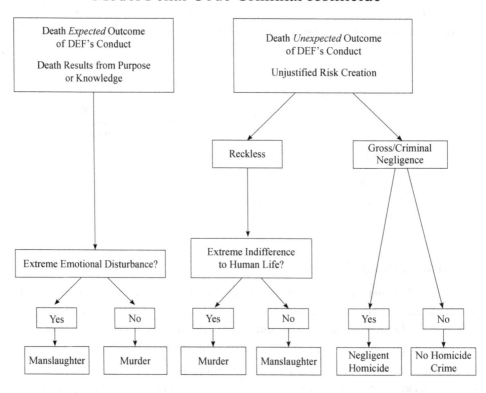

© 2012 Geoffrey S. Corn

Chapter 7

Intentional Criminal Homicide

I. Introduction

Intentional killings run the spectrum from legally justified (for example, when acting in lawful homicidal self-defense) to first-degree murder. At common law, proving an intent to kill was normally sufficient to prove malice, which in turn satisfied the mens rea for murder. However, if the intent to kill was formed during a sudden heat of passion triggered by an adequate provocation, there was no malice and therefore no murder. Instead, the killing was defined as voluntary manslaughter. Over time, most jurisdictions amended their laws to "grade" murder based on proof of an element in addition to malice. This led to defining murder by degree: first-degree murder (sometimes designated as "capital murder") being the most aggravated form; second-degree murder being less aggravated. Some jurisdictions have an additional designation of third-degree murder.

While there are many variations across jurisdictions today as to the degrees of murder and what elevates an offense to the most aggravated category of murder, the original common-law approach was to treat any murder with premeditation and deliberation as first-degree murder, with all other murders falling into the second-degree category. But, as will be explained in more detail below, premeditation and deliberation presuppose proof beyond a reasonable doubt that the defendant acted with the *purpose* to kill: premeditation means that the defendant had at least a brief moment to reflect on the *decision to kill*; deliberation means that the *decision to kill* was "rational." Accordingly, the most common definition of first-degree murder is a *willful* (meaning purpose to kill), *premeditated*, and *deliberate* killing of another human being.

Over time, jurisdictions added to the list of additional elements that would aggravate second-degree murder to first-degree murder. For example, Section 187 of the California Penal Code defines murder as "the unlawful killing of a human being, or fetus, with malice aforethought." Section 189 then provides:

> All murder that is perpetrated by means of a destructive device or explosive, a weapon of mass destruction, knowing use of ammunition designed primarily to penetrate metal or armor, poison, lying in wait, torture, or by any other kind of willful, deliberate, and premeditated killing, or that is committed in the perpetration of, or attempt to perpetrate, arson, rape, carjacking,

robbery, burglary, mayhem, kidnapping, train wrecking, or any act punishable under Section 206, 286, 287, 288, or 289, or former Section 288a, or murder that is perpetrated by means of discharging a firearm from a motor vehicle, intentionally at another person outside of the vehicle with the intent to inflict death, is murder of the first degree.

Note the extensive menu of additional elements or ingredients that elevate second-degree murder to first-degree. Note also that each one of these is distinct, meaning that proof of a malicious killing plus *any* of these additional elements will prove first-degree murder.

The MPC dispensed with both the term malice and with degrees of murder. Pursuant to the MPC, proof that a killing was the result of a purpose to kill or knowledge to a substantial certainty that death would result establishes murder unless the purpose or knowledge was formed during an extreme emotional disturbance. Thus, in theory, the basic common-law equation of intentional killings is reflected in the MPC: if an unlawful killing is the result of an intent to kill (purpose or knowledge), it is murder, unless the mental state arose during an extreme emotional disturbance—the MPC variant of common-law sudden heat of passion—in which case the killing is defined as manslaughter.

Instead of grading murders by degree, the MPC leaves the assessment of aggravating evidence to the sentencing phase of the trial, allowing the imposition of capital punishment for any murder so long as the evidence of aggravation substantially outweighs evidence of mitigation and extenuation. However, most states that have adopted the MPC have modified this approach and retained a distinction between degrees of murder. For example, the Texas Penal Code, which is based on the MPC, provides that:

> (b) A person commits an offense if he:
>
> (1) intentionally or knowingly causes the death of an individual;
>
> (2) intends to cause serious bodily injury and commits an act clearly dangerous to human life that causes the death of an individual; or
>
> (3) commits or attempts to commit a felony, other than manslaughter, and in the course of and in furtherance of the commission or attempt, or in immediate flight from the commission or attempt, he commits or attempts to commit an act clearly dangerous to human life that causes the death of an individual.

Tex. Penal Code § 19.02.

The Code then defines capital murder as follows:

> (a) A person commits an offense if the person commits murder as defined under Section 19.02(b)(1) and:
>
> (1) the person murders a peace officer or fireman who is acting in the lawful discharge of an official duty and who the person knows is a peace officer or fireman;

(2) the person intentionally commits the murder in the course of committing or attempting to commit kidnapping, burglary, robbery, aggravated sexual assault, arson, obstruction or retaliation, or terroristic threat under Section 22.07(a)(1), (3), (4), (5), or (6);

(3) the person commits the murder for remuneration or the promise of remuneration or employs another to commit the murder for remuneration or the promise of remuneration;

(4) the person commits the murder while escaping or attempting to escape from a penal institution;

(5) the person, while incarcerated in a penal institution, murders another:

    (A) who is employed in the operation of the penal institution; or

    (B) with the intent to establish, maintain, or participate in a combination or in the profits of a combination;

(6) the person:

    (A) while incarcerated for an offense under this section or Section 19.02, murders another; or

    (B) while serving a sentence of life imprisonment or a term of 99 years for an offense under Section 20.04, 22.021, or 29.03, murders another;

(7) the person murders more than one person:

    (A) during the same criminal transaction; or

    (B) during different criminal transactions but the murders are committed pursuant to the same scheme or course of conduct;

(8) the person murders an individual under 10 years of age;

(9) the person murders an individual 10 years of age or older but younger than 15 years of age; or

(10) the person murders another person in retaliation for or on account of the service or status of the other person as a judge or justice of the supreme court, the court of criminal appeals, a court of appeals, a district court, a criminal district court, a constitutional county court, a statutory county court, a justice court, or a municipal court.

(b) An offense under this section is a capital felony.

(c) If the jury or, when authorized by law, the judge does not find beyond a reasonable doubt that the defendant is guilty of an offense under this section, he may be convicted of murder or of any other lesser included offense.

Tex. Penal Code § 19.03.

Accordingly, you should think of intent to kill as *normally* (but not always) sufficient to establish the requisite mens rea for murder. You must then assess whether the jurisdiction defines murder by degree, and then assess whether the evidence establishes a defined aggravating element (or elements) beyond a reasonable doubt.

But remember, there are circumstances where intent to kill—even when premeditated and deliberate—does not prove murder. In a common-law jurisdiction where intent is formed during a sudden heat of passion triggered by an adequate provocation, in an MPC jurisdiction where the purpose or knowledge is formed during an extreme emotional disturbance, or if there is some other impediment to proving the requisite mental state for murder (such as imperfect self-defense—an honest but unreasonable judgment of homicidal necessity), the killing will qualify as what is commonly called voluntary manslaughter.

II. Application

A. First-Degree Murder Based on Premeditation and Deliberation

In most jurisdictions, a willful, malicious, premeditated, and deliberate killing constitutes first-degree (or capital) murder. While there are various ways a prosecutor may prove malice (intent to kill (purpose or knowledge), intent to inflict grievous bodily harm without the purpose to kill, extreme recklessness manifesting a wanton disregard to the value of human life), in a degree jurisdiction that requires premeditation and deliberation for first-degree murder, more than proof of malice will be required to prove guilt. Furthermore, only malice established by a purpose to kill will provide a strong enough foundation upon which to "stack" on the additional elements of premeditation and deliberation. So think of building a first-degree murder case like laying a brick foundation: first lay the willful brick (purpose to kill), then stack on top of that brick malice (because there is no sudden heat of passion), then stack on top of that brick premeditation and deliberation.

The following case traces the evolution of premeditated and deliberate murder from its common-law origins to the modern approach. As you read the decision, make a list of all of the required mental elements a prosecutor must prove beyond a reasonable doubt to secure a first-degree murder conviction.

State v. Guthrie
461 S.E.2d 163 (W. Va. 1995)
West Virginia Supreme Court

The defendant, Dale Edward Guthrie, appeals the January 1994, jury verdict of the Circuit Court of Kanawha County finding him guilty of first-degree murder.

. . . .

I. Facts and Procedural Background

It is undisputed that on the evening of February 12, 1993, the defendant removed a knife from his pocket and stabbed his co-worker, Steven Todd Farley, in the neck and killed him. The two men worked together as dishwashers at Danny's Rib House in Nitro and got along well together before this incident. On the night of the killing, the victim, his brother, Tracy Farley, and James Gibson were joking around while working in the kitchen of the restaurant. The victim was poking fun at the defendant who appeared to be in a bad mood. He told the defendant to "lighten up" and snapped him with a dishtowel several times. Apparently, the victim had no idea he was upsetting the defendant very much. The dishtowel flipped the defendant on the nose and he became enraged.

The defendant removed his gloves and started toward the victim. Mr. Farley, still teasing, said: "Ooo, he's taking his gloves off." The defendant then pulled a knife from his pocket and stabbed the victim in the neck. He also stabbed Mr. Farley in the arm as he fell to the floor. Mr. Farley looked up and cried: "Man, I was just kidding around." The defendant responded: "Well, man, you should have never hit me in my face." The police arrived at the restaurant and arrested the defendant. He was given his *Miranda* rights. The defendant made a statement at the police station and confessed to the killing. The police officers described him as calm and willing to cooperate. The confession, which was read to the jury, stated, in part:

> "I arrived at work, at 4:00 o'clock, and was looking forward to another evening of work, I was looking forward to it, because I do enjoy working at Danny's Rib House. Upon my arrival at work I immediately observed the verbal and physical aggression of Mr. Farley. During the evening of work I heard him calling certain employee's 'Boy' and during the evening he referred to me as 'Boy' many times, I did and said nothing, continuing my work, letting it pass. He was really loud, and obnoxious, as I'm sure many employees noticed. As the evening was coming to a close Mr. Farley walked very close by me and said 'that I had an "attitude problem."' It was verbal, I let it pass, continuing my work. After bringing some dishes to the cook, I walked back to the dishwasher to begin drying off some dishes, Mr. Farley approached me and made a sarcastic comment about me being a quiet person, he walked ever closer, to me until he was in my face, as I was trying to carry out my responsibilities. After all these things were said, and even though he was exhibiting physical aggression by coming up to my face, and putting forth what I interpreted to be a challenge, again I did nothing, continuing to carry out my responsibilities. Standing a few inches from my face he took his wet dishrag and hit me once, on the forearm, I did nothing continuing my work. Standing in the same area, he hit me again on the forearm, obviously wanting a confrontation, I gave him none, continuing my work. Standing in the same place he hit me, hard, two times in the face, it really hurt, it was soaking wet, and it stung, as he brought it to bear upon my face, at that moment I thought he was going to go further and hit me, so I reached in my right pants pocket, and retrieved my lock blade knife, that I use for skinning rabbits and squirrells [*sic*] during hunting season. I swung at Mr. Farley with my right hand in which was my knife, he backed up, so I didn't swing twice, he slowly sunk to [the] floor, I ran to the front of the restaurant and yelled out, call the ambulance. All I came to

work for, was to work, and carry out my obligations, having ill will toward no one, and I still have none, but I feel I had the right to respond, finally, to this act of aggression that was perpetrated against me, I do not exhibit aggressive, violent behavior but I felt I had no alternative, or recourse."

It is also undisputed that the defendant suffers from a host of psychiatric problems. He experiences up to two panic attacks daily and had received treatment for them at the Veterans Administration Hospital in Huntington for more than a year preceding the killing. He suffers from chronic depression (dysthymic disorder), an obsession with his nose (body dysmorphic disorder), and borderline personality disorder. The defendant's father shed some light on his nose fixation. He stated that dozens of times a day the defendant stared in the mirror and turned his head back and forth to look at his nose. His father estimated that 50 percent of the time he observed his son he was looking at his nose. The defendant repeatedly asked for assurances that his nose was not too big. This obsession began when he was approximately seventeen years old. The defendant was twenty-nine years old at the time of trial.

The defendant testified he suffered a panic attack immediately preceding the stabbing. He described the attack as "intense"; he felt a lot of pressure and his heart beat rapidly. In contrast to the boisterous atmosphere in the kitchen that evening, the defendant was quiet and kept to himself. He stated that Mr. Farley kept irritating him that night. The defendant could not understand why Mr. Farley was picking on him because he had never done that before. Even at trial, the defendant did not comprehend his utter overreaction to the situation. In hindsight, the defendant believed the better decision would have been to punch out on his timecard and quit over the incident. However, all the witnesses related that the defendant was in no way attacked, as he perceived it, but that Mr. Farley was playing around. The defendant could not bring himself to tell the other workers to leave him alone or inform them about his panic attacks.

In contrast to his written statement, the defendant testified he was unable to recall stabbing the victim. After he was struck in the nose, he stated that he "lost it" and, when he came to himself, he was holding the knife in his hand and Mr. Farley was sinking to the floor.

A psychiatrist, Dr. Sidney Lerfald, testified on behalf of the defendant. He diagnosed the various disorders discussed above. Dr. Lerfald felt the defendant's diagnoses "may have affected his perception somewhat." Nevertheless, it was his opinion the defendant was sane at the time of the offense because he was able to distinguish between right and wrong and could have conformed his actions accordingly.

It was the State's position that the facts supported a first-degree murder conviction. At the close of the State's case-in-chief, the defense moved for a directed verdict contending the State failed to present evidence of malice and premeditation. This motion was denied. The defense argued the facts of the case supported voluntary manslaughter or, at worse, second-degree murder. The jury returned a verdict finding the defendant guilty of first-degree murder with a recommendation of mercy.

II. Discussion

. . . .

A. Sufficiency of the Evidence

First, the defendant strives to persuade us that the record in this case does not support the verdict of guilty of first-degree murder beyond a reasonable doubt. Because this exhortation challenges the sufficiency of evidence to support a jury's verdict, our authority to review is limited.

. . . .

In summary, a criminal defendant challenging the sufficiency of the evidence to support a conviction takes on a heavy burden. An appellate court must review all the evidence, whether direct or circumstantial, in the light most favorable to the prosecution and must credit all inferences and credibility assessments that the jury might have drawn in favor of the prosecution. The evidence need not be inconsistent with every conclusion save that of guilt so long as the jury can find guilt beyond a reasonable doubt. As we have cautioned before, appellate review is not a device for this Court to replace a jury's finding with our own conclusion. On review, we will not weigh evidence or determine credibility. Credibility determinations are for a jury and not an appellate court. On appeal, we will not disturb a verdict in a criminal case unless we find that reasonable minds could not have reached the same conclusion.

. . . .

There is no doubt what inferences and findings of fact the jury had to draw in order to convict the defendant of first-degree murder. The jury must have believed that: (1) The "horseplay" provocation was not sufficient to justify a deadly attack; (2) the defendant was under no real fear of his own from being attacked; (3) the stabbing was intentional; and (4) the time it took the defendant to open his knife and inflict the mortal wound was sufficient to establish premeditation.

The difficult factual question must have been the mental state of the defendant at the time of the stabbing. The evidence was somewhat conflicting on this point. While the evidence offered by the defendant is not impossible to believe, some of his explanations seem unlikely. Guilt beyond a reasonable doubt cannot be premised on pure conjecture. However, a conjecture consistent with the evidence becomes less and less conjecture and moves gradually toward proof, as alternative innocent explanations are discarded or made less likely. The beyond a reasonable doubt standard does not require the exclusion of every other hypothesis or, for that matter, every other *reasonable* hypothesis. It is enough if, after considering all the evidence, direct and circumstantial, a reasonable trier of fact could find the evidence established guilt beyond a reasonable doubt.

After reviewing the record, this Court has some doubt as to whether this is a first-degree murder case; but, at this point, *Jackson*'s own objective standard turns against the defendant. [*Jackson v. Virginia*, 443 U.S. 307 (1979).] It makes absolutely no difference whether we on the appellate bench as jurors would have voted to convict the defendant of a lesser-included offense or whether we would have thought there was some reasonable doubt. To the contrary, the question posed by *Jackson* is whether any rational jury could on the evidence presented think the defendant premeditated and intentionally killed the victim. We do not find the evidence so weak as to render the verdict irrational. A rational jury may well have found the defendant guilty of some lesser-included crime without violating its oath; but, drawing all favorable inferences in favor of the prosecution, a rational jury could also convict. We end by suggesting that variations in human experience suggest it is not unexpected to see a considerable range of reasonable verdicts or estimates about what is likely or unlikely. Thus, we find the evidence sufficient under either the *Jackson* or the [*State v. Starkey*, 161 W. Va. 517 (1978),] standard.

B. Jury Instructions

The principal question before us under this assignment of error is whether our instructions on murder when given together deprive a criminal defendant of due process or are otherwise wrong and confusing.

. . . .

2. Adequacy of Jury Instructions as to the Elements of First-Degree Murder

The purpose of instructing the jury is to focus its attention on the essential issues of the case and inform it of the permissible ways in which these issues may be resolved. If instructions are properly delivered, they succinctly and clearly will inform the jury of the vital role it plays and the decisions it must make. As we said in note 20 of *State v. Miller*, 459 S.E.2d at 127 (1995) "Without [adequate] instructions as to the law, the jury becomes mired in a factual morass, unable to draw the appropriate legal conclusions based on the facts." This is, in essence, what the defendant argues in this case, *i.e.*, the instructions were inadequate and failed to inform the jury of the difference between first- and second-degree murder.

. . . .

The jury was instructed that in order to find the defendant guilty of murder it had to find five elements beyond a reasonable doubt: "The Court further instructs the jury that murder in the first degree is when one person kills another person unlawfully, willfully, maliciously, deliberately and premeditatedly[.]" In its effort to define these terms, the trial court gave three instructions. State's Instruction No. 8,[1] commonly referred to as the *Clifford* instruction, stated:

---

1. As to the other offenses, the jury instruction stated:
   "[M]urder in the second degree is when one person kills another person unlawfully and maliciously, but not deliberately or premeditatedly; that voluntary manslaughter is the intentional, unlawful and felonious but not deliberate or malicious taking of human life under sudden excitement and heat of passion; that involuntary manslaughter is where one person while engaged in an unlawful act, unintentionally causes the death of another person, or when engaged in a lawful act unlawfully causes the death of another person."

"The Court instructs the jury that to constitute a willful, deliberate and pre-meditated killing, it is not necessary that the intention to kill should exist for any particular length of time prior to the actual killing; it is only necessary that such intention should have come into existence for the first time at the time of such killing, or at any time previously."

See State v. Clifford, 52 S.E. 981 (1906). State's Instruction No. 10 stated: "The Court instructs the jury that in order to constitute a 'premeditated' murder an intent to kill need exist only for an instant." State's Instruction No. 12 stated: "The Court instructs the jury that what is meant by the language willful, deliberate and premeditated is that the killing be intentional." State's Instruction Nos. 10 and 12 are commonly referred to as *Schrader* instructions. *See State v. Schrader*, 302 S.E.2d 70 (1982).

The linchpin of the problems that flow from these instructions is the failure ade-quately to inform the jury of the difference between first- and second-degree mur-der. Of particular concern is the lack of guidance to the jury as to what constitutes premeditation and the manner in which the instructions infuse premeditation with the intent to kill.

At common law, murder was defined as the unlawful killing of another human being with "malice aforethought." Because the common law definition of "malice aforethought" was extremely flexible, "it became over time an 'arbitrary symbol' used by trial judges to signify any of the number of mental states deemed sufficient to support liability for murder." John S. Baker, Jr., et al., *Hall's Criminal Law* 268-69 (5th ed. 1993). Nevertheless, most American jurisdictions maintained a law of murder built around common law classifications. Pertinent to this case, the most significant departure from the common law came on April 22, 1794, when the Penn-sylvania Legislature enacted a statute dividing murder into degrees.[2] It decreed that the death penalty would be inflicted only for first degree murder. West Virginia, like most other states, followed the Pennsylvania practice. Indeed, the 1794 Pennsylvania statute is nearly identical to W. Va. Code, 61-2-1 (1991), our murder statute.

The West Virginia Legislature chose not to define the term "premeditated" in W. Va. Code, 61-2-1. As a result, this Court consistently has resorted to the common law.

---

2. The 1794 Pennsylvania statute provided that:

"[A]ll murder, which shall be perpetrated by means of poison, or by lying in wait, or by any other kind of willful, deliberate and premeditated killing, or which shall be committed in the perpetration or attempt to perpetrate any arson, rape, robbery, or burglary, shall be deemed murder of the first degree; and all other kinds of murder shall be deemed murder in the second degree[.]" 1794 Pa. Laws, Ch. 1766, § 2.

W. Va. Code, 61-2-1, states, in part:

"Murder by poison, lying in wait, imprisonment, starving, or by any willful, deliberate and premeditated killing, or in the commission of, or attempt to commit, arson, kidnapping, sexual assault, robbery, burglary, breaking and entering, escape from lawful custody . . . is murder of the first degree. All other murder is murder of the second degree."

In addition to *Clifford*, there are several cases that have made specific attempts to further define premeditation. In *State v. Dodds*, 46 S.E. 228, 231 (1903), we said:

> "'The next ingredient of the crime is that it must be deliberate. To deliberate is to reflect, with a view to make a choice. If a person reflects, though but for a moment before he acts, it is unquestionably a sufficient *deliberation* within the meaning of the statute. The last requisite is that the killing must be *premeditated. To premeditate is to think of a matter before it is executed. The word, premeditated, would seem to imply something more than deliberate, and may mean that the party not only deliberated, but had formed in his mind the plan of destruction.*'"

In *State v. Hatfield*, 286 S.E.2d 402 (1982), we made an effort to distinguish the degrees of murder by indicating that the elements that separate first-degree murder and second-degree murder are deliberation and premeditation in addition to the formation of the specific intent to kill. Deliberation and premeditation mean to reflect upon the intent to kill and make a deliberate choice to carry it out. Although no particular amount of time is required, there must be at least a sufficient period to permit the accused to actually consider in his or her mind the plan to kill. In this sense, murder in the first degree is a calculated killing as opposed to a spontaneous event. After noting the above language in *Dodds*, Justice Miller stated in *Hatfield*:

"The terms 'deliberate' and 'premeditated' have not often been defined in our cases but do carry a certain degree of definitional overlap. This point is made in LaFave Scott, *Criminal Law* § 73, at 563 (1972 ed.):

> "To be guilty of this form of first degree murder the defendant must not only intend to kill but in addition he must premeditate the killing and deliberate about it. It is not easy to give a meaningful definition of the words "premeditate" and "deliberate" as they are used in connection with first degree murder. Perhaps the best that can be said of "deliberation" is that it requires a cool mind that is capable of reflection, and of "premeditation" that it requires that the one with the cool mind did in fact reflect, at least for a short period of time before his act of killing."

. . . .

The source of the problem in the present case stems from language in *State v. Schrader*, 302 S.E.2d 70 (1982). While this Court elaborated on the meaning of premeditation, we gave it a different definition than that approved in *Hatfield* and *Dodds*. In *Schrader*, we stated:

> "Hence, when the West Virginia Legislature adopted the Virginia murder statute in 1868, the meaning of 'premeditated' as used in the statute was essentially 'knowing' and 'intentional.; Since then, courts have consistently recognized that the mental process necessary to constitute 'willful, deliberate and premeditated' murder can be accomplished very quickly or even in the proverbial 'twinkling of an eye.' . . . *The achievement of a mental state*

contemplated in a statute such as ours can immediately precede the act of killing. Hence, what is really meant by the language 'willful, deliberate and premeditated' in W. Va. Code, 61-2-1 [1923] is that the killing be intentional." 302 S.E.2d at 75.

The language emphasized above supplied the legal authority and basis for State's Instruction Nos. 10 and 12.

While many jurisdictions do not favor the distinction between first- and second-degree murder,[3] given the doctrine of separation of powers, we do not have the judicial prerogative to abolish the distinction between first- and second-degree murder and rewrite the law of homicide for West Virginia; unless, of course, we were to declare this classification a violation of due process and force the Legislature to rewrite the law—a bold stroke that we refuse to do. On the other hand, we believe within the parameters of our current homicide statutes the *Schrader* definition of premeditation and deliberation is confusing, if not meaningless. To allow the State to prove premeditation and deliberation by only showing that the intention came "into existence for the first time at the time of such killing" completely eliminates the distinction between the two degrees of murder. Hence, we feel compelled in this case to attempt to make the dichotomy meaningful by making some modifications to our homicide common law.

Premeditation and deliberation should be defined in a more careful, but still general way to give juries both guidance and reasonable discretion. Although premeditation and deliberation are not measured by any particular period of time, there must be some period between the formation of the intent to kill and the actual killing, which indicates the killing is by prior calculation and design. As suggested by the dissenting opinion in *Green v. State*, 450 S.W.2d 27, 34 (1970): "True, it is not necessary to prove premeditation existed for any definite period of time. But it is necessary to prove that it did exist." This means there must be an opportunity for some reflection on the intention to kill after it is formed. The accused must kill purposely after contemplating the intent to kill. Although an elaborate plan or scheme to take life is not required, our *Schrader*'s notion of instantaneous premeditation and momentary deliberation is not satisfactory for proof of first-degree murder. In *Bullock v. United States*, 122 F.2d 213, 214 (1941), the court discussed the need to have some appreciable time elapse between the intent to kill and the killing:

3. The MPC and many of the modern state criminal codes abolish the first- and second-degree murder distinction in favor of classifications based on more meaningful criteria. Interestingly, defining premeditation in such a way that the formation of the intent to kill and the killing can result from successive impulses, *see Schrader, supra* (intent equals premeditation formula), grants the jury complete discretion to find more ruthless killers guilty of first-degree murder regardless of actual premeditation. History teaches that such unbridled discretion is not always carefully and thoughtfully employed, and this case may be an example. In 1994, the Legislature raised the penalty for second degree murder to ten-to-forty years (from five-to-eighteen years), making it less important to give juries the unguided discretion to find the aggravated form of murder in the case of more ruthless killings, irrespective of actual premeditation. The penalties are now comparable.

"To speak of premeditation and deliberation which are instantaneous, or which take no appreciable time, is a contradiction in terms. It deprives the statutory requirement of all meaning and destroys the statutory distinction between first- and second-degree murder. At common law there were no degrees of murder. If the accused had no overwhelming provocation to kill, he was equally guilty whether he carried out his murderous intent at once or after mature reflection. Statutes like ours, which distinguish deliberate and premeditated murder from other murder, reflect a belief that one who meditates an intent to kill and then deliberately executes it is more dangerous, more culpable or less capable of reformation than one who kills on sudden impulse; or that the prospect of the death penalty is more likely to deter men from deliberate than from impulsive murder. The deliberate killer is guilty of first-degree murder; the impulsive killer is not. The quoted part of the charge was therefore erroneous."

Thus, there must be some evidence that the defendant considered and weighed his decision to kill in order for the State to establish premeditation and deliberation under our first-degree murder statute. This is what is meant by a ruthless, cold-blooded, calculating killing. Any other intentional killing, by its spontaneous and nonreflective nature, is second degree murder.

We are asked to overrule the language appearing in *Schrader*, as reflected in State's Instruction No. 8 and, particularly, the language of State's Instruction Nos. 10 and 12, so that there might be some clarity and coherence to the law of homicide. We naturally are reluctant to overrule prior decisions of this Court. . . . Nevertheless, the circumstances of this case are different, and we agree with the defendant that the language in our opinion in *Schrader* virtually eliminates the distinction in this State between first- and second-degree murder, equating as it does premeditation with the formation of the intent to kill. . . .

Finally, we feel obligated to discuss what instruction defining premeditation is now acceptable. What came about as a mere suggestion in *Hatfield*, we now approve as a proper instruction under today's decision. Note 7 of *Hatfield*, 286 S.E.2d at 410, states:

"A more appropriate instruction for first degree murder, paraphrased from 2 Devitt and Blackmar, *Federal Jury Practice and Instructions* § 41.03, at 214, is:

"'The jury is instructed that murder in the first degree consists of an intentional, deliberate and premeditated killing which means that the killing is done after a period of time for prior consideration. The duration of that period cannot be arbitrarily fixed. The time in which to form a deliberate and premeditated design varies as the minds and temperaments of people differ, and according to the circumstances in which they may be placed. Any interval of time between the forming of the intent to kill and the execution of that intent, which is of sufficient duration for the accused to be fully

conscious of what he intended, is sufficient to support a conviction for first
degree murder.'"

. . . .

Based on the foregoing, the judgment of the Circuit Court of Kanawha County is
reversed, and this case is remanded for a new trial.

WORKMAN, Justice, concurring:

I concur with the holding of the majority, but write this separate opinion to reiterate that the duration of the time period required for premeditation cannot be arbitrarily fixed.

. . . .

I agree with the majority in its conclusion that our decision in *State v.
Schrader*, 302 S.E.2d 70 (1982), incorrectly equated premeditation with intent to kill.
However, I must point out that the majority's suggested basis for defining premeditation and deliberation in terms of requiring some "appreciable time elapse between
the intent to kill and the killing" and "some period between the formation of the
intent to kill and the actual killing which indicates that the killing is by prior calculation and design" may create confusion in suggesting that premeditation must be
the deeply thoughtful enterprise typically associated with the words reflection and
contemplation.

. . . .

Accordingly, it is necessary to make abundantly clear that premeditation is sufficiently demonstrated as long as "[a]ny interval of time[, no matter how short that
interval is, lapses] between the forming of the intent to kill and the execution of that
intent[.]" *See Hatfield*, 286 S.E.2d at 410.

Notes & Questions

1. The *Guthrie* court traces the evolution of murder in the common law. What
exactly was the problem with the instruction the trial court gave the jury and how
did it deprive Guthrie of a fair trial?

2. You should have identified the following as what is required to prove first-degree
murder based on premeditation and deliberation:

a. Unlawful: meaning there is no affirmative defense such as self-defense or
insanity;

b. Malicious: meaning the intent to kill did not arise during a sudden heat of passion triggered by an adequate provocation;

c. Willful: meaning the defendant acted with the purpose/objective to kill;

d. Premeditated: meaning the defendant had a brief moment of reflection on his
decision to kill;

e. Deliberate: meaning the defendant made a rational decision to kill.

The first requirement—that the killing was unlawful—will be explained in greater detail in subsequent chapters. Importantly, because this is not a material element of the offense but a question of affirmative defense, in many jurisdictions, the burden of proving a justification or excuse to negate the unlawful nature of the killing would be imposed on the defendant. The four other elements, however, must be established beyond a reasonable doubt, meaning a failure to prove even one of them would result in acquittal for first-degree murder.

3. Based on *Guthrie*, consider the following hypothetical:

> Defendant wanted to be on the travel team for his high school football team. He was a senior who had lettered all three previous years, but a change in the coaching staff and a knee injury meant that he might not make the travel team, and he feared that this would hurt his chances of obtaining a college scholarship. He decided to injure one of the sophomore players, because they had two more years to play, and their future opportunities would not be as seriously impacted by an injury. He carefully thought out his plan. After practice, he waited in the locker room until most of the other players had left. He knew his victim usually took very long showers. When his victim was in the shower, he took out a straight razor that he had brought to the locker room the day before in his gym bag. He put on a ski mask and then rushed into the shower to attack the victim. The victim saw him rushing towards him and tried to run. The victim slipped on the floor and fell, hitting his head on a bench, which rendered him unconscious. Defendant suddenly had a change of heart and ran away. Another player found the victim a few minutes later and called 911. Emergency medical services transported the victim to the hospital, but he was still unconscious. A doctor ordered several medications while treating the victim. One of those medications caused a serious negative reaction which led the victim to go into shock, and he died later that day. The medical examiner determined that the immediate cause of death was the allergic reaction to the medication.

First-degree murder is defined as any unlawful killing that is willful, malicious, premeditated, and deliberate. Second-degree murder is all other murder. Is Defendant guilty of first-or second-degree murder?

4. Based on the court's opinion, do you think the evidence is sufficient to convict Guthrie of first-degree murder on retrial using the revised instruction?

5. What should the verdict be if the jury is convinced beyond a reasonable doubt that Guthrie intended to kill his victim but that he either did not have sufficient time to reflect on the decision to kill *or* he was unable to make a rational decision to kill?

6. What type of evidence should a jury consider when deciding whether the prosecution has met its burden of proving premeditation and deliberation? Might it be the same evidence relied on to prove intent to kill? In a footnote, the *Guthrie* court provided some insight:

In the absence of statements by the accused which indicate the killing was by prior calculation and design, a jury must consider the circumstances in which the killing occurred to determine whether it fits into the first-degree category. Relevant factors include the relationship of the accused and the victim and its condition at the time of the homicide; whether plan or preparation existed either in terms of the type of weapon utilized or the place where the killing occurred; and the presence of a reason or motive to deliberately take life. No one factor is controlling. Any one or all taken together may indicate actual reflection on the decision to kill. This is what our statute means by "willful, deliberate and premeditated killing."

As examples of what type of evidence supports a finding of first degree murder, we identify three categories: (1) "planning" activity—facts regarding the defendant's behavior prior to the killing which might indicate a design to take life; (2) facts about the defendant's prior relationship or behavior with the victim which might indicate a motive to kill; and (3) evidence regarding the nature or manner of the killing which indicate a deliberate intention to kill according to a preconceived design. The California courts evidently require evidence of all three categories or at least extremely strong evidence of planning activity or evidence of category (2) in conjunction with either (1) or (3). *See People v. Anderson*, 447 P.2d 942 (1968). These examples are illustrative only and are not intended to be exhaustive.

And in a subsequent opinion in *State v. Browning*, 485 S.E.2d 1, 5 (W. Va. 1997), the same court noted that:

[a] jury must consider the circumstances in which the killing occurred to determine whether it fits into the first-degree category. Relevant factors include the relationship of the accused and the victim and its condition at the time of the homicide; whether plan or preparation existed either in terms of the type of weapon utilized or the place where the killing occurred; and the presence of a reason or motive to deliberately take life. No factor is controlling. Any one or all taken together may indicate actual reflection on the decision to kill. This is what our statute means by "willful, deliberate and premeditated killing."

7. United States Army Major Nidal Hasan shot and killed 13 victims at Fort Hood, Texas on November 5, 2009. He used a high-power pistol with extended magazines and both a red and green laser sight. During the subsequent investigation, police searched his car, in which they found a bag containing small batteries of the type used for car keys. Police thought these batteries insignificant; not the prosecutor. Why do you think the prosecutor disagreed with police?

8. The obvious rationale for treating a willful, premeditated, and deliberate killing as first-degree murder is that the "cool reflection" on the decision to kill warrants the most severe criminal sanction. But is this always true? Are the instances where

such a killing may be less aggravated than an unintentional killing? Consider the following to cases:

> In *Midgett v. State*, 292 Ark. 278 (Ark. 1987), the evidence established the defendant brutally beat his son over a substantial period of time resulting in the son's death. Midgett's conviction for first-degree murder was overturned on appeal based on insufficient evidence to prove the killing was willful, premeditated, and deliberate. Instead, the appellate court concluded at best the evidence established intent to inflict grievous bodily harm, justifying a conviction for second-degree murder.

> In *State v. Forrest*, 321 N.C. 186 (N.C. 1987), the defendant shot and killed his terminally ill father in his hospital bed. When the nurse and orderly ran into the room the defendant, sobbing, handed them the pistol and told them he had to do it because he promised his father he would not let him suffer. Forrest was convicted of first-degree murder based on the overwhelming evidence that the killing was willful, premeditated and deliberate.

Which of these killings do you feel was more aggravated? Which defendant do you feel deserved more severe punishment? This comparison highlights the potential overbreadth and under-inclusiveness of statutory distinctions between categories of murder. It also reveals one reason why the drafters of the Model Penal Code rejected such distinctions and chose instead to rely on the sentencing phase of the murder trial to adjudge the appropriate penalty. Using such an approach would almost certainly lead to Midgett being punished more severely than Forrest.

B. Intent without Sufficient Evidence of Premeditation

As you read the next case, remember the standard of review for evidentiary sufficiency of a jury verdict. Did the Washington Supreme Court apply that standard? Or did the majority act as a proverbial thirteenth juror and retry the case?

State v. Bingham
719 P.2d 109 (Wash. 1986)
Washington Supreme Court

In his case, we review the sufficiency of the evidence of the premeditation element in an aggravated first-degree murder conviction. The Court of Appeals found the evidence insufficient and reversed and remanded for resentencing for second degree murder. We affirm the Court of Appeals decision.

On February 18, 1982, the raped and strangled body of Leslie Cook, a [mentally challenged] adult, was found in a pasture in Sequim. Cook was last seen alive on February 15, 1982, with respondent Charles Dean Bingham. The Clallam County

Prosecutor, by amended information, charged Bingham with aggravated first degree (premeditated) murder, rape being the aggravating circumstance. The prosecutor also notified Bingham that the State would seek the death penalty.

The evidence presented at trial showed that on February 15, Cook and Bingham got off a bus together in Sequim about 6 p.m. There was no evidence that they knew each other before this time. They visited a grocery store and two residences. Cook was last seen at the residence of Wayne Humphrey and Enid Pratt where Bingham asked for a ride back to Port Angeles. When he was told no, Bingham said they would hitchhike. They left together heading toward the infrequently traveled Old Olympic Highway. None of the witnesses who saw the two heard any argument or observed any physical contact between them. Three days later, Cook's body was found in a field about a quarter mile from the Humphrey-Pratt residence.

At trial, King County Medical Examiner Reay described the results of the autopsy he performed on Cook's body. The cause of death was "asphyxiation through manual strangulation," accomplished by applying continuous pressure to the windpipe for approximately 3 to 5 minutes. Cook had a bruise on her upper lip, more likely caused by a hand being pressed over her mouth than by a violent blow. Tears were found in Cook's vaginal wall and anal ring. Spermatozoa were present. These injuries were inflicted antemortem. Also, there was a bite mark on each of Cook's breasts. Reay testified that these occurred perimortem or postmortem.

Two forensic odontologists testified that the bite mark on one breast matched Bingham's teeth. No conclusive determination could be made with respect to the other bite mark.

The prosecutor's theory, as revealed in both his opening statement and closing argument, was that Bingham wanted to have sex with Cook and that he had to kill her in order to do so. The prosecutor hypothesized that Bingham had started the act while Cook was alive, and that he put his hand over her mouth and then strangled her in order to complete the act. The prosecutor also told the jury that the murder would be premeditated if Bingham had formed the intent to kill when he began to strangle Cook, and thought about that intent for the 3 to 5 minutes it took her to die.

The court instructed the jury on aggravated first-degree murder and on the lesser included offenses of first- and second-degree murder and first degree manslaughter. The court also gave Bingham's proposed instruction on voluntary intoxication.

The jury found Bingham guilty of aggravated first-degree murder. The jury also found, in the penalty phase, that the State had failed to prove that there were insufficient mitigating circumstances to warrant leniency. The trial court therefore sentenced Bingham to life imprisonment without the possibility of release or parole.

. . . .

The Court of Appeals reversed Bingham's conviction in a split decision and remanded for resentencing for second degree murder. . . . The State sought and was granted discretionary review.

We must determine whether evidence of premeditation was sufficiently demonstrated in order for the issue to go to the jury and in order to sustain a finding of premeditated killing.

. . .

Bingham was charged with first degree murder pursuant to RCW 9A.32.030(1)(a), which requires for conviction "a premeditated intent to cause the death of another". The element of premeditation distinguishes first- and second-degree murder. Section (1)(a) of the second-degree murder statute, RCW 9 A. 32.050, requires for conviction "intent to cause the death of another person but without premeditation."

The only statutory elaboration on the meaning of premeditation is found in RCW 9A.32.020(1), which states that premeditation "must involve more than a moment in point of time." Washington case law further defines premeditation as "the mental process of thinking beforehand, deliberation, reflection, weighing or reasoning for a period of time, however short." We recently approved an instruction which defined premeditation as "the deliberate formation of and reflection upon the intent to take a human life." *State v. Robtoy*, 653 P.2d 284 (1982).

Premeditation may be shown by direct or circumstantial evidence. . . . In this case, the State presented no direct evidence. The issue thus becomes whether sufficient circumstantial evidence of premeditation was presented.

. . . .

To show premeditation, the State relied on the pathologist's testimony that manual strangulation takes 3 to 5 minutes. The State argues this time is an appreciable amount of time in which Bingham could have deliberated. Bingham argues that time alone is not enough and that other indicators of premeditation must be shown.

One case, *State v. Smith*, 531 P.2d 843 (1975), was relied heavily upon by the parties, the trial court and the Court of Appeals. In *Smith*, the defendant was convicted of the premeditated first-degree murder of his son. The facts showed that the defendant took his son for a midnight walk by a creek near his house. The next morning he returned home alone and disoriented. The boy's body was found in the river. He had been drowned.

The entire *Smith* discussion on premeditation is as follows:

> Premeditation. Although no definite motive was proven, the jury was presented with substantial evidence of the existence of premeditation. The Smiths had discussed separation, though at the time of the incident had decided not to do so. They had concluded, however, that if they separated, Kathy Smith would receive custody of the children. For premeditation to be inferable by the jury, there must have been a period of time during which the intent to kill is deliberated. This time may be very short provided it is an "appreciable period of time." Looking at the circumstances surrounding the child's death, it is clear that an appreciable period of time did elapse. As recognized by our State Supreme Court, choking takes an appreciable time.

The Court of Appeals majority overruled *Smith* to the extent that it held premeditation can be shown by only evidence of choking because choking takes an appreciable amount of time. The *Smith* facts could also be found to reflect a deliberated decision to kill the child by holding the child's head under water.

A review of the two cases cited in Smith for the proposition that choking takes an appreciable amount of time also shows that more than choking was involved in those cases. In both *State v. Harris*, 385 P.2d 18 (1963) and *State v. Gaines*, 258 P. 508 (1927), the facts show that the injuries were inflicted by various means over some period of time. In *Harris*, the victim

> had been struck on the head several times with a blunt instrument with such force that in one place her skull had been fractured into her brain. Also, additional blows had severely damaged one ear and cheek and fractured her jaw, breaking two teeth. After this terrific beating, her assailant, while she was still alive, tied the vacuum cleaner cord around her neck and strangled her, which was the immediate cause of her death. . . .

In *Gaines*,

> the deceased was first choked into insensibility to an extent which could have produced death. A choking, to have this effect, takes some appreciable time. After the deceased was choked into insensibility, her assailant went to a garbage dump nearby, got a rock, returned and inflicted the wounds upon the head. It cannot be held, under the facts and circumstances of this case, that there was no evidence from which the jury had a right to find deliberation or premeditation.

We find all of these cases, while helpful in understanding the premeditation element, are not determinative of whether manual strangulation alone is sufficient. We agree with the Court of Appeals majority that to allow a finding of premeditation only because the act takes an appreciable amount of time obliterates the distinction between first- and second-degree murder. Having the opportunity to deliberate is not evidence the defendant did deliberate, which is necessary for a finding of premeditation. Otherwise, any form of killing which took more than a moment could result in a finding of premeditation, without some additional evidence showing reflection. Holding a hand over someone's mouth or windpipe does not necessarily reflect a decision to kill the person, but possibly only to quiet her or him. Furthermore, here a question of the ability to deliberate or reflect while engaged in sexual activity exists.

The position of the State and the Court of Appeals dissent appears to be that, if the defendant has the opportunity to deliberate and chooses not to cease his actions, then it is proper to allow the jury to infer deliberation. They offer three cases for the proposition that premeditation may properly be inferred from evidence of the lapse of time to death. While *Harris*, [*State v. Griffith*, 589 P.2d 799 (1979)], and [*State v. Luoma*, 558 P.2d 756 (1977),] do use language regarding reliance on circumstances of the crime to show premeditation, the circumstances showed more action or thought than mere infliction of the fatal act.

In *Harris*, the assailant, after inflicting a terrific head beating, tied a vacuum cleaner cord around the victim's neck and strangled her. The interim time period between the beating and the strangulation, as well as the presence and use of a vacuum cleaner cord in effectuating the victim's death distinguish this case from the manual strangulation situation with which we are presented.

In *Griffith*, some children were hitting a basketball against the house where defendant lived with his mother. The defendant took the ball from the children. He went to his car, got a gun, and placed it on a table next to the front door. Within 5 minutes, two adults went to the house to retrieve the ball. The defendant, while talking to the adults at the front door, reached for the gun, pointed it at the adults, and shot one of them. The court said:

> Although the period of time in which these events transpired was approximately 5 minutes, there was sufficient evidence from which the jury could have found that the defendant formulated an intent and deliberated upon it prior to the shooting.

The planned presence of a weapon necessary to facilitate a killing has been held to be adequate evidence to allow the issue of premeditation to go to the jury.

In *Luoma*, the defendant transported the victim to the crime scene, took her down a bank, positioned her and then crushed her head with a large rock. From the facts in *Luoma*, "[t]he jury could properly conclude that the death was not the result of an impulsive, spontaneous act." We note that the language in *Luoma* focuses on intent, not premeditation. As is clear from the statutory requirements and *State v. Brooks*, 651 P.2d 217 (1982), premeditation is a separate and additional element to the intent requirement for first degree murder.

Here, no evidence was presented of deliberation or reflection before or during the strangulation, only the strangulation. The opportunity to deliberate is not sufficient.

As was recognized in *Austin v. United States*, 382 F.2d 129, 138-39 (D.C. Cir. 1967):

> The facts of a savage murder generate a powerful drive, almost a juggernaut for jurors, and indeed for judges, to crush the crime with the utmost condemnation available, to seize whatever words or terms reflect maximum denunciation, to cry out murder "in the first degree." But it is the task and conscience of a judge to transcend emotional momentum with reflective analysis. The judge is aware that many murders most brutish and bestial are committed in a consuming frenzy or heat of passion, and that these are in law only murder in the second degree. The [State's] evidence suffice[s] to establish an intentional and horrible murder the kind that could be committed in a frenzy or heat of passion. However the core responsibility of the court requires it to reflect on the sufficiency of the [State's] case.

Exercising our responsibility, we find manual strangulation alone is insufficient evidence to support a finding of premeditation. We affirm the Court of Appeals decision.

CALLOW, J. (dissenting)

I would reinstate the aggravated first-degree murder conviction of defendant. Sufficient evidence was presented on premeditation for that issue to be submitted to the jury. The decision on that issue is the function of the jury; not to be taken away.

The standard for reviewing the sufficiency of evidence in a criminal case is "whether, after viewing the evidence in the light most favorable to the prosecution, any rational trier of fact could have found the essential elements . . . beyond a reasonable doubt." The evidence is to be viewed in the light most favorable to the State. The issue of premeditation should only have been taken from the jury if there was no evidence or reasonable inferences therefrom which would sustain the jury's conclusion that the defendant acted with premeditation.

State v. Griffith, 589 P.2d 799 (1979) stated:

> A defendant is entitled to have his theory of the case submitted to the jury under appropriate instructions when the theory is supported by substantial evidence in the record. If any one of the theories argued by defendant was supported by substantial evidence, it should have been submitted to the jury.

. . . Instruction 8 on premeditation given by the trial court is as follows:

> Premeditated means thought over beforehand and describes the mental operation of thinking upon an act before doing it. Premeditation necessarily implies that some time exist between the thought process and commission of the act itself. By this is meant that premeditation cannot occur simultaneously with the act but must precede the act. When a person, after any deliberation, forms an intent to take human life, the killing may follow immediately after the formation of the settled purpose and it will still be premeditated. Premeditation must involve more than a moment in point of time. The law requires some time, however long or short, in which a design to kill is deliberately formed.

. . . .

The majority states "no evidence was presented of deliberation or reflection before or during the strangulation, only the strangulation. The opportunity to deliberate is not sufficient." "[W]e find manual strangulation alone is insufficient evidence to support a finding of premeditation." These statements ignore numerous items of evidence which corroborate the presence of premeditation. I believe a review of the record compels the conclusion that there was sufficient evidence for the jury to conclude that the defendant acted with premeditation. The evidence meets the required standard since it could lead a rational trier of fact to find the essential elements of first-degree murder beyond a reasonable doubt. The rule announced by the majority seems to be that premeditation must take place before the commencement of the act that results in death. Take the farmer's son who begins to fill the bin with wheat as a joke on his brother sleeping at its bottom. Then, realizing that he will inherit the whole farm if he persists, he does so and causes his brother's death. He had time to premeditate and did so in the middle of the act. He has committed aggravated first-degree murder. That a murderer originally commenced an act without intending death does not grant him a carte blanche to persist when he realizes that to do so will kill his victim.

The Washington cases concerning premeditation include *State v. Smith*, 531 P.2d 843 (1975)); *State v. Harris*, 385 P.2d 18 (1963); and *State v. Gaines*, 258 P. 508 (1928). In *Smith* the defendant was found guilty of the first degree murder of his young son. A finding of premeditation was justified because of the circumstances surrounding the young boy's death by drowning. The Court of Appeals opinion stated:

> For premeditation to be inferable by the jury, there must have been a period of time during which the intent to kill is deliberated. This time may be very short provided it is an "appreciable period of time." Looking at the circumstances surrounding the child's death, it is clear that an appreciable period of time did elapse. As recognized by our State Supreme Court, choking takes an appreciable time.

The majority argues that "[t]he *Smith* facts could also be found to reflect a deliberated decision to kill the child by holding the child's head under water." Likewise, the facts in this case could be found to reflect a deliberated decision to kill Leslie Cook by applying between 3 and 5 minutes of continuous and steady pressure to her neck. The act of strangulation inflicted by the defendant upon the deceased is considerably more than just the "[h]olding [of] a hand over someone's mouth or windpipe. . . ."

Here it can be inferred that the defendant thought about the consequences as he choked his victim. The period of premeditation might not have been during the initial squeeze, but the evidence of premeditation certainly was present in the continued application of force, knowing it would bring about death.

. . . .

The State presented substantial circumstantial evidence on the issue of premeditation. The trial court properly left that issue to the jury. The jury found that the defendant did premeditate. I would reinstate the first-degree murder conviction of the defendant.

Notes & Questions

1. Who has the better of the argument, the majority or dissent? Is the dissent arguing that a finding of second-degree murder would have been irrational, or that the evidence supported a rational finding of guilt of *either* first or second-degree murder?

2. Is it possible that the defendant never intended to kill the victim? That the killing was an accidental consequence of his effort to keep her silent or force her to submit to the sexual assault? If the jury followed the instruction on first-degree murder, doesn't this mean they must have rejected that explanation for the strangulation?

3. Notice how the court conflates premeditation and deliberation, taking premeditation to mean *both* premeditation and deliberation. Although not as clear as the

law considered in *Guthrie*, this is not uncommon. For example, consider how the following instruction advises a jury to consider how the inability to think rationally negates premeditation:

> An issue has been raised by the evidence as to whether the accused acted in the heat of sudden "passion." "Passion" means a degree of rage, pain, or fear which prevents cool reflection. If sufficient cooling off time passes between the provocation and the time of the killing which would allow a reasonable person to regain self-control and refrain from killing, the provocation will not reduce murder to the lesser offense of voluntary manslaughter. However, you may consider evidence of the accused's passion in determining whether (he) (she) possessed sufficient mental capacity to have "the premeditated design to kill." An accused cannot be found guilty of premeditated murder if, at the time of the killing, (his) (her) mind was so confused by (anger) (rage) (pain) (sudden resentment) (fear) (or) (_____) that (he) (she) could not or did not premeditate. On the other hand, the fact that the accused's passion may have continued at the time of the killing does not necessarily demonstrate that (he) (she) was deprived of the ability to premeditate or that (he) (she) did not premeditate. Thus, (if you are convinced beyond a reasonable doubt that sufficient cooling off time had passed between the provocation and the time of the killing which would allow a reasonable person to regain (his/her) self-control and refrain from killing), you must decide whether the accused in fact had the premeditated design to kill. If you are not convinced beyond a reasonable doubt that the accused killed with premeditation, you may still find (him) (her) guilty of unpremeditated murder, if you are convinced beyond a reasonable doubt that the death of (state the name of the alleged victim) was caused, without justification or excuse, by an (act) (failure to act) of the accused and (the accused intended to kill or inflict great bodily harm on the victim) (the act of the accused was inherently dangerous to others and showed a wanton disregard for human life).

Does this instruction seem to be focused on the opportunity to reflect on the decision to kill (premeditation) or the ability to do so rationally (deliberation)?

4. Why do you think the trial judge instructed the jury to consider evidence that the defendant was voluntarily intoxicated?

5. Whether defined as an aspect of premeditation or as the distinct element of deliberation, which element do you believe is more likely to be susceptible to reasonable doubt for a willful killing? Consider the following hypothetical:

> Defendant is a Holocaust survivor who lost his wife, three children, and both parents in a death camp. Having been the victim of several muggings, the defendant always carries a small pistol for self-defense when he is out at night. One night, after leaving his synagogue, Defendant is confronted by a group of neo-Nazis. The five young men surround him and pepper him with despicable anti-Semitic slurs. In response. he pleads with them to leave him

alone. They then start telling him the Holocaust was nothing more than a fabrication by the worldwide Jewish conspiracy. At that point. he reveals the tattoo on his arm and says, "Don't tell me it was fake; I lived through it." The neo-Nazis become even more belligerent with their assertions of fabrication. Defendant yells at them to leave him alone but they just keep harassing him. Finally, having reached his limits, Defendant pulls out his pistol and shoots one of his harassers point-blank in the head, killing him instantly. When questioned by police, the defendant was asked why he shot the victim. He responded, "I just lost it. I didn't think any of them were about to hurt me physically, but their taunting just made me snap."

If the defendant were charged with first-degree murder and you were appointed to represent him, how would you challenge the sufficiency of this evidence to support conviction?

C. Voluntary (Intentional) Manslaughter

An unlawful intentional killing will not always support a murder conviction. Where the intent to kill (or inflict grievous bodily harm that results in death) is formed during a sudden heat of passion triggered by an adequate provocation, proof of malice is blocked, resulting in a conviction for manslaughter (often called "voluntary manslaughter"). Accordingly, voluntary manslaughter is an unlawful *intentional* killing *without* malice. It is therefore useful to think of "voluntary" in "voluntary manslaughter" as a synonym for "intentional."

Voluntary manslaughter is based on a simple premise: when a defendant is triggered into a sudden homicidal rage by a provocation that would produce the same reaction in an ordinary person, the killing, while unlawful, is not the result of malice and therefore deserving of partial forgiveness. Hence the lesser crime of manslaughter. Evidence of sudden heat of passion is offered by a defendant charged with murder to prevent or "block" proof of malice. However, homicidal rage alone is not sufficient to mitigate murder to manslaughter; only when the rage is triggered by an *adequate* provocation will the prosecution bear the burden of disproving a sudden heat of passion. Consider the following California instruction:

> A killing that would otherwise be murder is reduced to voluntary manslaughter if the defendant killed someone because of a sudden quarrel or in the heat of passion.
>
> The defendant killed someone because of a sudden quarrel or in the heat of passion if:
>
> 1. The defendant was provoked;
>
> 2. As a result of the provocation, the defendant acted rashly and under the influence of intense emotion that obscured (his/her) reasoning or judgment;

AND

> 3. The provocation would have caused a person of average disposition to act rashly and without due deliberation, that is, from passion rather than from judgment.

Heat of passion does not require anger, rage, or any specific emotion. It can be any violent or intense emotion that causes a person to act without due deliberation and reflection.

In order for heat of passion to reduce a murder to voluntary manslaughter, the defendant must have acted under the direct and immediate influence of provocation as I have defined it. While no specific type of provocation is required, slight or remote provocation is not sufficient. Sufficient provocation may occur over a short or long period of time.

It is not enough that the defendant simply was provoked. The defendant is not allowed to set up (his/her) own standard of conduct. You must decide whether the defendant was provoked and whether the provocation was sufficient. In deciding whether the provocation was sufficient, consider whether a person of average disposition, in the same situation and knowing the same facts, would have reacted from passion rather than from judgment. [If enough time passed between the provocation and the killing for a person of average disposition to "cool off" and regain his or her clear reasoning and judgment, then the killing is not reduced to voluntary manslaughter on this basis.]

The People have the burden of proving beyond a reasonable doubt that the defendant did not kill as the result of a sudden quarrel or in the heat of passion. If the People have not met this burden, you must find the defendant not guilty of murder.

As you read the next case, consider why the defendant was not entitled to a sudden heat of passion instruction.

Girouard v. State

583 A.2d 718 (Md. 1991)
Maryland Court of Appeals

In this case, we are asked to reconsider whether the types of provocation sufficient to mitigate the crime of murder to manslaughter should be limited to the categories we have heretofore recognized, or whether the sufficiency of the provocation should be decided by the factfinder on a case-by-case basis. Specifically, we must determine whether words alone are provocation adequate to justify a conviction of manslaughter rather than one of second-degree murder.

The Petitioner, Steven S. Girouard, and the deceased, Joyce M. Girouard, had been married for about two months on October 28, 1987, the night of Joyce's death. Both parties, who met while working in the same building, were in the army. They married after having known each other for approximately three months. The evidence at trial indicated that the marriage was often tense and strained, and there was some evidence that after marrying Steven, Joyce had resumed a relationship with her old boyfriend, Wayne.

On the night of Joyce's death, Steven overheard her talking on the telephone to her friend, whereupon she told the friend that she had asked her first sergeant for a hardship discharge because her husband did not love her anymore. Steven went into the living room where Joyce was on the phone and asked her what she meant by her comments; she responded, "nothing." Angered by her lack of response, Steven kicked away the plate of food Joyce had in front of her. He then went to lie down in the bedroom.

Joyce followed him into the bedroom, stepped up onto the bed and onto Steven's back, pulled his hair and said, "What are you going to do, hit me?" She continued to taunt him by saying, "I never did want to marry you and you are a lousy fuck and you remind me of my dad." The barrage of insults continued with her telling Steven that she wanted a divorce, that the marriage had been a mistake and that she had never wanted to marry him. She also told him she had seen his commanding officer and filed charges against him for abuse. She then asked Steven, "What are you going to do?" Receiving no response, she continued her verbal attack. She added that she had filed charges against him in the Judge Advocate General's Office (JAG) and that he would probably be court martialed.

When she was through, Steven asked her if she had really done all those things, and she responded in the affirmative. He left the bedroom with his pillow in his arms and proceeded to the kitchen where he procured a long-handled kitchen knife. He returned to Joyce in the bedroom with the knife behind the pillow. He testified that he was enraged and that he kept waiting for Joyce to say she was kidding, but Joyce continued talking. She said she had learned a lot from the marriage and that it had been a mistake. She also told him she would remain in their apartment after he moved out. When he questioned how she would afford it, she told him she would claim her brain-damaged sister as a dependent and have the sister move in. Joyce reiterated that the marriage was a big mistake, that she did not love him and that the divorce would be better for her.

After pausing for a moment, Joyce asked what Steven was going to do. What he did was lunge at her with the kitchen knife he had hidden behind the pillow and stab her 19 times. Realizing what he had done, he dropped the knife and went to the bathroom to shower off Joyce's blood. Feeling like he wanted to die, Steven went back to the kitchen and found two steak knives with which he slit his own wrists. He lay down on the bed waiting to die, but when he realized that he would not die from his self-inflicted wounds, he got up and called the police, telling the dispatcher that he had just murdered his wife.

When the police arrived they found Steven wandering around outside his apartment building. Steven was despondent and tearful and seemed detached, according to police officers who had been at the scene. He was unconcerned about his own wounds, talking only about how much he loved his wife and how he could not believe what he had done. Joyce Girouard was pronounced dead at the scene.

At trial, defense witness, psychologist, Dr. William Stejskal, testified that Steven was out of touch with his own capacity to experience anger or express hostility. He stated that the events of October 28, 1987, were entirely consistent with Steven's personality, that Steven had "basically reach[ed] the limit of his ability to swallow his anger, to rationalize his wife's behavior, to tolerate, or actually to remain in a passive mode with that. He essentially went over the limit of his ability to bottle up those strong emotions. What ensued was a very extreme explosion of rage that was intermingled with a great deal of panic." Another defense witness, psychiatrist, Thomas Goldman, testified that Joyce had a "compulsive need to provoke jealousy so that she's always asking for love and at the same time destroying and undermining any chance that she really might have to establish any kind of mature love with anybody."

Steven Girouard was convicted, at a court trial in the Circuit Court for Montgomery County, of second-degree murder and was sentenced to 22 years' incarceration, 10 of which were suspended. . . .

Petitioner relies primarily on out of state cases to provide support for his argument that the provocation to mitigate murder to manslaughter should not be limited only to the traditional circumstances of: extreme assault or battery upon the defendant; mutual combat; defendant's illegal arrest; injury or serious abuse of a close relative of the defendant's; or the sudden discovery of a spouse's adultery. Petitioner argues that manslaughter is a catchall for homicides which are criminal but that lack the malice essential for a conviction of murder. Steven argues that the trial judge did find provocation (although he held it inadequate to mitigate murder) and that the categories of provocation adequate to mitigate should be broadened to include factual situations such as this one.

The State counters by stating that although there is no finite list of legally adequate provocations, the common law has developed to a point at which it may be said there are some concededly provocative acts that society is not prepared to recognize as reasonable. Words spoken by the victim, no matter how abusive or taunting, fall into a category society should not accept as adequate provocation. According to the State, if abusive words alone could mitigate murder to manslaughter, nearly every domestic argument ending in the death of one party could be mitigated to manslaughter. This, the State avers, is not an acceptable outcome. Thus, the State argues that the courts below were correct in holding that the taunting words by Joyce Girouard were not provocation adequate to reduce Steven's second-degree murder charge to voluntary manslaughter.

Initially, we note that the difference between murder and manslaughter is the presence or absence of malice. Voluntary manslaughter has been defined as "an *intentional* homicide, done in a sudden heat of passion, caused by adequate provocation, before there has been a reasonable opportunity for the passion to cool." *Cox v. State,* 534 A.2d 1333 (1988).

There are certain facts that may mitigate what would normally be murder to manslaughter. For example, we have recognized as falling into that group: (1) discovering one's spouse in the act of sexual intercourse with another; (2) mutual combat; (3) assault and battery. There is also authority recognizing injury to one of the defendant's relatives or to a third party, and death resulting from resistance of an illegal arrest as adequate provocation for mitigation to manslaughter. Those acts mitigate homicide to manslaughter because they create passion in the defendant and are not considered the product of free will.

In order to determine whether murder should be mitigated to manslaughter we look to the circumstances surrounding the homicide and try to discover if it was provoked by the victim. Over the facts of the case we lay the template of the so-called "Rule of Provocation." The courts of this State have repeatedly set forth the requirements of the Rule of Provocation:

1. There must have been adequate provocation;

2. The killing must have been in the heat of passion;

3. It must have been a sudden heat of passion—that is, the killing must have followed the provocation before there had been a reasonable opportunity for the passion to cool;

4. There must have been a causal connection between the provocation, the passion, and the fatal act.

We shall assume without deciding that the second, third, and fourth of the criteria listed above were met in this case. We focus our attention on an examination of the ultimate issue in this case, that is, whether the provocation of Steven by Joyce was enough in the eyes of the law so that the murder charge against Steven should have been mitigated to voluntary manslaughter. For provocation to be "adequate," it must be "'calculated to inflame the passion of a reasonable man and tend to cause him to act for the moment from passion rather than reason.'" *Carter v. State,* 505 A.2d 545. The issue we must resolve, then, is whether the taunting words uttered by Joyce were enough to inflame the passion of a *reasonable* man so that that man would be sufficiently infuriated so as to strike out in hot-blooded blind passion to kill her. Although we agree with the trial judge that there was needless provocation by Joyce, we also agree with him that the provocation was not adequate to mitigate second degree murder to voluntary manslaughter.

Although there are few Maryland cases discussing the issue at bar, those that do hold that words alone are not adequate provocation. Most recently, in *Sims v. State,* 573 A.2d 1317, we held that "insulting words or gestures, no matter how opprobrious, do not amount to an affray, and standing alone, do not constitute adequate provocation." That case involved the flinging of racial slurs and derogatory comments by the victim at the defendant. That conduct did not constitute adequate provocation.

In *Lang v. State*, 250 A.2d 276 (1969), the Court of Special Appeals stated that it is "generally held that mere words, threats, menaces or gestures, however offensive and insulting, do not constitute adequate provocation." Before the shooting, the victim had called the appellant "a chump" and "a chicken," dared the appellant to fight, shouted obscenities at him and shook his fist at him. The provocation, again, was not enough to mitigate murder.

The court in *Lang* did note, however, that words can constitute adequate provocation if they are accompanied by conduct indicating a present intention and ability to cause the defendant bodily harm. Clearly, no such conduct was exhibited by Joyce in this case. While Joyce did step on Steven's back and pull his hair, he could not reasonably have feared bodily harm at her hands. This, to us, is certain based on Steven's testimony at trial that Joyce was about 5'1" tall and weighed 115 pounds, while he was 6'2" tall, weighing over 200 pounds. Joyce simply did not have the size or strength to cause Steven to fear for his bodily safety. Thus, since there was no ability on the part of Joyce to cause Steven harm, the words she hurled at him could not, under the analysis in *Lang,* constitute legally sufficient provocation.

Other jurisdictions overwhelmingly agree with our cases and hold that words alone are not adequate provocation.

. . . .

We are unpersuaded by that one case awash in a sea of opposite holdings, especially since a Maryland case counters [*Commonwealth v. Nelson*, 514 Pa. 262 (1987),] by stating that "the long-smoldering grudge . . . may be psychologically just as compelling a force as the sudden impulse but it, unlike the impulse, is a telltale characteristic of premeditation." *Tripp v. State*, 374 A.2d 384. Aside from the cases, recognized legal authority in the form of treatises supports our holding. *Perkins on Criminal Law*, at p. 62, states that it is "with remarkable uniformity that even words generally regarded as 'fighting words' in the community have no recognition as adequate provocation in the eyes of the law." It is noted that

> mere words or gestures, however offensive, insulting, or abusive they may be, are not, according to the great weight of authority, adequate to reduce a homicide, although committed in a passion provoked by them, from murder to manslaughter, especially when the homicide was intentionally committed with a deadly weapon.

Thus, with no reservation, we hold that the provocation in this case was not enough to cause a reasonable man to stab his provoker 19 times. Although a psychologist testified to Steven's mental problems and his need for acceptance and love, we agree with the Court of Special Appeals speaking through Judge Moylan that "there must be not simply provocation in psychological fact, but one of certain fairly well-defined classes of provocation recognized as being adequate as a matter of law." *Tripp v. State*, 374 A.2d 384. The standard is one of reasonableness; it does not and should not focus on the peculiar frailties of mind of the Petitioner. That standard of reasonableness has not been met here. We cannot in good conscience countenance holding that a verbal domestic argument ending in the death of one spouse can result in a conviction of manslaughter. We agree with the trial judge that social necessity dictates our holding. Domestic arguments easily escalate into furious fights. We perceive no reason for a holding in favor of those who find the easiest way to end a domestic dispute is by killing the offending spouse.

We will leave to another day the possibility of expansion of the categories of adequate provocation to mitigate murder to manslaughter. The facts of this case do not warrant the broadening of the categories recognized thus far.

Notes & Questions

1. Because malice is the mens rea element for murder, once evidence of sudden heat of passion is introduced, the prosecution bears the burden of disproving sudden heat of passion. Why? Because unless the prosecution *disproves* sudden heat of passion, the evidence cannot *prove* malice. This means that the jury is instructed on the elements of the defense theory, but unlike elements of an offense, the prosecutor need only disprove one of these elements. Consider the following Alaska jury instruction:

It is a defense to the charge of murder in the [first] [second] degree that the defendant acted in a heat of passion.

If you find that the state has proved the elements of the crime of murder in the [first] [second] degree, you must then decide whether the defendant acted with intense passion before there had been a reasonable opportunity for the passion to cool, when the intense passion resulted from a serious provocation from the intended victim.

To prove that the defendant did not act in the heat of passion, the state must prove beyond a reasonable doubt one or more of the following elements:

(1) the defendant did not act with intense passion; or

(2) there was a reasonable opportunity for the defendant's intense passion to cool; or

(3) the intense passion did not result from serious provocation by the intended victim.

If you find that the state has not proved beyond a reasonable doubt that the defendant did not act in the heat of passion, then you must find the defendant not guilty of the charge of murder in the [first] [second] degree and find [him] [her] guilty of manslaughter.

"Passion" includes anger, rage, fear, terror, and other intense emotions.

"Serious provocation" means conduct that is sufficient to excite an intense passion in a reasonable person in the defendant's situation[, other than a person who is intoxicated,] under the circumstances as the defendant reasonably believed them to be. Insulting words, insulting gestures, or hearsay reports of conduct engaged in by the intended victim do not, alone or in combination with each other, constitute serious provocation.

"Intended victim" means a person whom the defendant was attempting to kill or to whom the defendant was attempting to cause serious physical injury when the defendant caused the death of the person the defendant is charged with killing.

2. "I'm not saying I agree, but I understand." Some of you may remember this as a line Chris Rock would use in his standup shows. It also offers a useful approach to better understand voluntary manslaughter. When a defendant intends to kill pursuant to a legal justification such as self-defense or defense of others, a jury not only understands the decision, but agrees it was legally justified. When the jury agrees with such justification, it "erases" the word unlawful and the killing is not criminal. However, when the killing is the result of a sudden heat of passion, the jury does not "agree" that it was justified, but the relationship between the provocation, the sudden homicidal rage, and the formation of the intent to kill allows the jury to "understand" why the defendant lost self-control. Hence the middle ground option between not guilty and murder: voluntary manslaughter.

3. The court notes that being the victim of a serious assault or battery qualifies as an adequate provocation. But why wouldn't the response to such an attack qualify as self-defense? The answer requires a cursory understanding of the requirements for self-defense (addressed in detail in a later chapter). One essential requirement is that the defendant responded to an actual or imminent threat of unlawful violence. Thus, if the victim of a serious assault or battery uses force to prevent the attack, a claim of self-defense may be valid. But it is not uncommon for such a victim to act in revenge against the aggressor; in other words, after the assault or battery is complete and the initial aggressor no longer represents an imminent threat to the defendant. In that situation, the use of deadly force would not be legally justified, but a defendant could offer evidence of the initial assault or battery as an adequate provocation to support a claim of sudden heat of passion. Another requirement for a valid self-defense claim is that the defendant respond to the threat with proportional force. Thus, if the victim of a serious assault or battery responds with deadly force but that level of force is deemed excessive, the claim of self-defense will fail, but the assault or battery would support a claim of sudden heat of passion.

4. Imagine a defendant employs deadly force during a sudden heat of passion triggered by an adequate provocation, but accidentally kills the wrong person. What result? Certainly, the intent to kill the intended victim "transfers" to the unintended victim, but does the mitigating effect of the sudden heat of passion also transfer? The answer is yes, so long as there was a causal connection between the intended victim and the provocation; the critical question is not whether the intended victim was in fact killed, but whether the intent to kill was the result of the sudden heat of passion.

5. Expanding the list of adequate provocations. Note how the court leaves to "another day" the possibility of expanding the categories of what qualifies as a

sudden heat of passion. This could be especially important when a provocation is the result of discovery of sexual infidelity with someone to whom the defendant is not married, or witnessing the death or serious injury of someone the defendant is close with but is not an immediate family member. There is no consensus on such proffered provocations. However, in common-law jurisdictions, the line is relatively solid that mere words, no matter how offensive, do not qualify.

6. If the mitigating doctrine of sudden heat of passion is premised on a recognition that reasonable or ordinary people may reach a limit of tolerance for some provocation, is it logical or fair to impose the restrictive requirements of the common law? For example, why shouldn't words alone be sufficient to explain a loss of self-control, or perhaps more importantly, why should the law deprive the jury from the opportunity to make that assessment and partially forgive a defendant for what is alleged as murder? The next case illustrates how the Model Penal Code sought to vest more discretion in juries to mitigate an intentional killing from murder to manslaughter and highlights some of the challenges that evolution of the law creates.

People v. Casassa

404 N.E.2d 1310 (N.Y. 1980)
New York Court of Appeals

The significant issue on this appeal is whether the defendant, in a murder prosecution, established the affirmative defense of "extreme emotional disturbance" which would have reduced the crime to manslaughter in the first degree.

On February 28, 1977, Victoria Lo Consolo was brutally murdered. Defendant Victor Casassa and Miss Lo Consolo had been acquainted for some time prior to the latter's tragic death. They met in August, 1976 as a result of their residence in the same apartment complex. Shortly thereafter, defendant asked Miss Lo Consolo to accompany him to a social function and she agreed. The two apparently dated casually on other occasions until November, 1976 when Miss Lo Consolo informed defendant that she was not "falling in love" with him. Defendant claims that Miss Lo Consolo's candid statement of her feelings "devastated him."

Miss Lo Consolo's rejection of defendant's advances also precipitated a bizarre series of actions on the part of defendant which, he asserts, demonstrate the existence of extreme emotional disturbance upon which he predicates his affirmative defense. Defendant, aware that Miss Lo Consolo maintained social relationships with others, broke into the apartment below Miss Lo Consolo's on several occasions to eavesdrop. These eavesdropping sessions allegedly caused him to be under great emotional stress. Thereafter, on one occasion, he broke into Miss Lo Consolo's apartment while she was out. Defendant took nothing, but, instead, observed the apartment, disrobed and lay for a time in Miss Lo Consolo's bed. During this break-in, defendant was armed with a knife which, he later told police, he carried "because he knew that he was either going to hurt Victoria or Victoria was going to cause him to commit suicide."

Defendant's final visit to his victim's apartment occurred on February 28, 1977. Defendant brought several bottles of wine and liquor with him to offer as a gift. Upon Miss Lo Consolo's rejection of this offering, defendant produced a steak knife which he had brought with him, stabbed Miss Lo Consolo several times in the throat, dragged her body to the bathroom and submerged it in a bathtub full of water to "make sure she was dead."

The following day the police investigation of Miss Lo Consolo's death began. On the evening of March 1, 1977, Nassau County Police detectives came to the apartment building in which the crime had occurred. They were in the process of questioning several of the residents of the building when defendant presented himself to the police and volunteered that he had been in the victim's apartment on the night of the murder. While denying any involvement in the murder of Miss Lo Consolo, he professed a willingness to co-operate in the investigation.

The police accepted his offer of co-operation and requested that he accompany them to the Nassau County police headquarters in Mineola to discuss the matter further. On the way to Mineola, defendant was informed of his constitutional rights. He indicated that he understood his rights and that he nonetheless wished to co-operate. Defendant was interrogated by police for some nine and one-half hours thereafter and at 5:00 A.M. on the morning of March 2, 1977, he fully confessed to the murder of Victoria Lo Consolo, giving the police several oral and written statements detailing his involvement in the crime.

. . .

On March 8, 1977, defendant was indicted and charged with murder in the second degree. Defendant made several pretrial motions seeking to suppress his statements to police and several pieces of real evidence which had been given to police during questioning. After a hearing, the motions were denied.

Defendant waived a jury and proceeded to trial before the County Court. The minutes of the suppression hearing were incorporated into the trial transcript and defendant's confessions were received into evidence. The defendant did not contest the underlying facts of the crime. Instead, the sole issue presented to the trial court was whether the defendant, at the time of the killing, had acted under the influence of "extreme emotional disturbance." (Penal Law, § 125.25) The defense presented only one witness, a psychiatrist, who testified, in essence, that the defendant had become obsessed with Miss Lo Consolo and that the course which their relationship had taken, combined with several personality attributes peculiar to defendant, caused him to be under the influence of extreme emotional disturbance at the time of the killing.

In rebuttal, the People produced several witnesses. Among these witnesses was a psychiatrist who testified that although the defendant was emotionally disturbed, he was not under the influence of "extreme emotional disturbance" within the meaning of section 125.25 of the Penal Law because his disturbed state was not the product of external factors but rather was "a stress he created from within himself, dealing mostly with a fantasy, a refusal to accept the reality of the situation."

The trial court in resolving this issue noted that the affirmative defense of extreme emotional disturbance may be based upon a series of events, rather than a single precipitating cause. In order to be entitled to the defense, the court held, a defendant must show that his reaction to such events was reasonable. In determining whether defendant's emotional reaction was reasonable, the court considered the appropriate test to be whether in the totality of the circumstances the finder of fact could understand how a person might have his reason overcome. Concluding that the test was not to be applied solely from the viewpoint of defendant, the court found that defendant's emotional reaction at the time of the commission of the crime was so peculiar to him that it could not be considered reasonable so as to reduce the conviction to manslaughter in the first degree. Accordingly, the trial court found defendant guilty of the crime of murder in the second degree. The Appellate Division affirmed, without opinion.

On this appeal defendant contends that the trial court erred in failing to afford him the benefit of the affirmative defense of "extreme emotional disturbance." It is argued that the defendant established that he suffered from a mental infirmity not arising to the level of insanity which disoriented his reason to the extent that his emotional reaction, from his own subjective point of view, was supported by a reasonable explanation or excuse. Defendant asserts that by refusing to apply a wholly subjective standard the trial court misconstrued section 125.25 of the Penal Law. We cannot agree.

Section 125.25 of the Penal Law provides that it is an affirmative defense to the crime of murder in the second degree where "[t]he defendant acted under the influence of extreme emotional disturbance for which there was a reasonable explanation or excuse." This defense allows a defendant charged with the commission of acts which would otherwise constitute murder to demonstrate the existence of mitigating factors which indicate that, although he is not free from responsibility for his crime, he ought to be punished less severely by reducing the crime upon conviction to manslaughter in the first degree.

In enacting section 125.25 of the Penal Law, the Legislature adopted the language of the manslaughter provisions of the Model Penal Code (see § 201.3,). The only substantial distinction between the New York statute and the Model Penal Code is the designation by the Legislature of "extreme emotional disturbance" as an "affirmative defense," thus placing the burden of proof on this issue upon defendant. The Model Penal Code formulation, however, as enacted by the Legislature, represented a significant departure from the prior law of this State.

The "extreme emotional disturbance" defense is an outgrowth of the "heat of passion" doctrine which had for some time been recognized by New York as a distinguishing factor between the crimes of manslaughter and murder. However, the new formulation is significantly broader in scope than the "heat of passion" doctrine which it replaced.

For example, the "heat of passion" doctrine required that a defendant's action be undertaken as a response to some provocation which prevented him from reflecting upon his actions. Moreover, such reaction had to be immediate. The existence of a "cooling off" period completely negated any mitigating effect which the provocation might otherwise have had. In [*People v Patterson*, 39 N.Y.2d 288], however, this court recognized that "[a]n action influenced by an extreme emotional disturbance is not one that is necessarily so spontaneously undertaken. Rather, it may be that a significant mental trauma has affected a defendant's mind for a substantial period of time, simmering in the unknowing subconscious and then inexplicably coming to the fore." This distinction between the past and present law of mitigation, enunciated in *Patterson*, was expressly adopted by the trial court and properly applied in this case.

The thrust of defendant's claim, however, concerns a question arising out of another perceived distinction between "heat of passion" and "extreme emotional disturbance" which was not directly addressed in *Patterson*, to wit: whether, assuming that the defense is applicable to a broader range of circumstances, the standard by which the reasonableness of defendant's emotional reaction is to be tested must be an entirely subjective one. Defendant relies principally upon our decision in *Patterson* and upon the language of the statute to support his claim that the reasonableness of his "explanation or excuse" should be determined solely with reference to his own subjective viewpoint. Such reliance is misplaced.

In *Patterson*, this court was concerned with the question of whether the defendant could properly be charged with the burden of proving the affirmative defense of "extreme emotional disturbance." In deciding that the defendant could constitutionally be required to carry such a burden, we noted that "[t]he purpose of the extreme emotional disturbance defense is to permit the defendant to show that his actions were caused by a mental infirmity not arising to the level of insanity, and that he is less culpable for having committed them." We also noted that "[t]he differences between the present New York statute and its predecessor can be explained by the tremendous advances made in psychology since 1881 and a willingness on the part of the courts, legislators, and the public to reduce the level of responsibility imposed on those whose capacity has been diminished by mental trauma." These comments, however, were relevant to our decision only insofar as they demonstrated that the affirmative defense of "extreme emotional disturbance" is a mitigating factor which the defendant must prove as opposed to a substantive element of the crime of murder which the People must prove.

Defendant, however, would read *Patterson* as holding that all mental infirmity, short of insanity, must constitute "extreme emotional disturbance" if such infirmity causes the defendant to become emotionally disturbed and the defendant subjectively believed his disturbance had a reasonable explanation or excuse. While it is true that the court in *Patterson* recognized that "extreme emotional disturbance" as contemplated by the statute is a lesser form of mental infirmity than insanity, the court did not hold that all mental infirmities not arising to the level of insanity constitute "extreme emotional disturbance" within the meaning of the statute. This question was not presented to us in *Patterson* and we did not decide it. Defendant's attempt to further extend our holding in *Patterson* to support the proposition that the reasonableness of the explanation or excuse for defendant's emotional disturbance must be tested from the subjective viewpoint of defendant is completely unavailing, for that case had nothing whatever to do with this issue.

Having determined that our decision in *Patterson* does not require that reasonableness be tested with a completely subjective standard, we must now determine whether the language of the statute or the legislative history of the statute indicates that such a standard is required.

Section 125.25 of the Penal Law states it is an affirmative defense to the crime of murder that "[t]he defendant acted under the influence of extreme emotional disturbance for which there was a reasonable explanation or excuse, the reasonableness of which is to be determined from the viewpoint of a person in the defendant's situation under the circumstances as the defendant believed them to be." Whether the language of this statute requires a completely subjective evaluation of reasonableness is a question that has never been decided by this court, although it has been raised in our lower courts with diverse results. Moreover, although several States have enacted identical or substantially similar statutes, only one decision of the highest court of any of our sister States which has addressed this question has been called to our attention and that court expressly followed Justice Bentley Kassal's well-reasoned opinion in *People v. Shelton* (88 Misc 2d 136).

Consideration of the Comments to the Model Penal Code, from which the New York statute was drawn, are instructive. The defense of "extreme emotional disturbance" has two principal components—(1) the particular defendant must have "acted under the influence of extreme emotional disturbance," and (2) there must have been "a reasonable explanation or excuse" for such extreme emotional disturbance, "the reasonableness of which is to be determined from the viewpoint of a person in the defendant's situation under the circumstances as the defendant believed them to be." The first requirement is wholly subjective—i.e., it involves a determination that the particular defendant did in fact act under extreme emotional disturbance, that the claimed explanation as to the cause of his action is not contrived or sham.

The second component is more difficult to describe—i.e., whether there was a reasonable explanation or excuse for the emotional disturbance. It was designed to sweep away "the rigid rules that have developed with respect to the sufficiency of particular types of provocation, such as the rule that words alone can never be enough," and "avoids a merely arbitrary limitation on the nature of the antecedent circumstances that may justify a mitigation." "The ultimate test, however, is objective; there must be 'reasonable' explanation or excuse for the actor's disturbance." In light of these comments and the necessity of articulating the defense in terms comprehensible to jurors, we conclude that the determination whether there was reasonable explanation or excuse for a particular emotional disturbance should be made by viewing the subjective, internal situation in which the defendant found himself and the external circumstances as he perceived them at the time, however inaccurate that perception may have been, and assessing from that standpoint whether the explanation or excuse for his emotional disturbance was reasonable, so as to entitle him to a reduction of the crime charged from murder in the second degree to manslaughter in the first degree. We recognize that even such a description of the defense provides no precise guidelines and necessarily leaves room for the exercise of judgmental evaluation by the jury. This, however, appears to have been the intent of the draftsmen. "The purpose was explicitly to give full scope to what amounts to a plea in mitigation based upon a mental or emotional trauma of significant dimensions, with the jury asked to show whatever empathy it can."

By suggesting a standard of evaluation which contains both subjective and objective elements, we believe that the drafters of the code adequately achieved their dual goals of broadening the "heat of passion" doctrine to apply to a wider range of circumstances while retaining some element of objectivity in the process. The result of their draftsmanship is a statute which offers the defendant a fair opportunity to seek mitigation without requiring that the trier of fact find mitigation in each case where an emotional disturbance is shown—or as the drafters put it, to offer "room for argument as to the reasonableness of the explanations or excuses offered."

We note also that this interpretation comports with what has long been recognized as the underlying purpose of any mitigation statute. In the words of Mr. Justice Cardozo, referring to an earlier statute: "What we have is merely a privilege offered to the jury to find the lesser degree when the suddenness of the intent, the vehemence of the passion, seems to call irresistibly for the exercise of mercy. I have no objection to giving them this dispensing power, but it should be given to them directly and not in a mystifying cloud of words." In the end, we believe that what the Legislature intended in enacting the statute was to allow the finder of fact the discretionary power to mitigate the penalty when presented with a situation which, under the circumstances, appears to them to have caused an understandable weakness in one of their fellows. Perhaps the chief virtue of the statute is that it allows such discretion without engaging in a detailed explanation of individual circumstances in which the statute would apply, thus avoiding the "mystifying cloud of words" which Mr. Justice Cardozo abhorred.

We conclude that the trial court, in this case, properly applied the statute. The court apparently accepted, as a factual matter, that defendant killed Miss Lo Consolo while under the influence of "extreme emotional disturbance," a threshold question which must be answered in the affirmative before any test of reasonableness is required. The court, however, also recognized that in exercising its function as trier of fact, it must make a further inquiry into the reasonableness of that disturbance. In this regard, the court considered each of the mitigating factors put forward by defendant, including his claimed mental disability, but found that the excuse offered by defendant was so peculiar to him that it was unworthy of mitigation. The court obviously made a sincere effort to understand defendant's "situation" and "the circumstances as defendant believed them to be," but concluded that the murder in this case was the result of defendant's malevolence rather than an understandable human response deserving of mercy. We cannot say, as a matter of law, that the court erred in so concluding. Indeed, to do so would subvert the purpose of the statute.

In our opinion, this statute would not require that the jury or the court as trier of fact find mitigation on any particular set of facts, but, rather, allows the finder of fact the opportunity to do so, such opportunity being conditional only upon a finding of extreme emotional disturbance in the first instance. In essence, the statute requires mitigation to be afforded an emotionally disturbed defendant only when the trier of fact, after considering a broad range of mitigating circumstances, believes that such leniency is justified. Since the trier of fact found that defendant failed to establish that he was acting "under the influence of extreme emotional disturbance for which there was a reasonable explanation or excuse," defendant's conviction of murder in the second degree should not be reduced to the crime of manslaughter in the first degree.

Accordingly, the order of the Appellate Division should be affirmed.

Notes & Questions

1. What are the primary differences between sudden heat of passion and extreme emotional disturbance?

2. The court notes that "The only substantial distinction between the New York statute and the Model Penal Code is the designation by the Legislature of 'extreme emotional disturbance' as an 'affirmative defense,' thus placing the burden of proof on this issue upon defendant." Why is it permissible to place the burden of proving extreme emotional disturbance on the defendant (normally by a preponderance of the evidence), but it violates due process to place the burden of proving sudden heat of passion on a defendant charged with murder? As you ponder this, consider whether purpose to kill and extreme emotional disturbance are incompatible in the same way malice and sudden heat of passion are incompatible.

Formative Assessments

1. Defendant and his friend Victim got into a huge fight in a nightclub. Victim screamed extremely humiliating insults at Defendant in front of a group friends. Defendant was becoming obviously enraged, but Victim just kept humiliating him. According to witnesses, the Defendant then just seemed to "lose it" and attacked Victim with a knife he grabbed off a nearby table. Defendant stabbed Victim multiple times in the shoulder and chest area. Victim died from these wounds several days later. In a common law jurisdiction, what is the most serious offense supported by this evidence?

A. Murder.

B. Voluntary Manslaughter.

    C. Involuntary Manslaughter.

    D. Negligent Homicide.

2. Would your answer change in an MPC jurisdiction?

3. John was furious with a co-worker because he learned the co-worker had provided a very negative reference for a promotion John was counting on receiving. After being passed over, John plotted to punish the co-worker by beating him severely in the parking lot when he left work after a late-night shift. John would make it look like a mugging by taking the co-worker's backpack and cell phone. John waited in the parking lot on the night he planned the attack, and when the co-worker walked to his car, John attacked him from behind, hitting him on the back with a baseball bat so hard it knocked the co-worker to the ground. John then hit the victim's legs repeatedly with the bat. As the victim was screaming, John said, "Good, now you will know how it feels to suffer for a while." John took the backpack and left. The victim died as a result of the beating. The autopsy concluded the victim died as the result of a pulmonary embolism caused by a blood clot in the leg resulting from the beating. What is the most serious offense supported by this evidence?

    A. First-degree murder.

    B. Second-degree murder.

    C. Voluntary manslaughter.

    D. Involuntary manslaughter.

4. Defendant wanted to be on the travel team for his high school football team. He was a senior who had lettered all three previous years, but a change in coach and knee injury had put him in a position of possibly not making the travel team, and he feared that this would hurt his chances of obtaining a college scholarship. He decided to injure one of the sophomore players, because they had two more years to play, and their future opportunities would not be as seriously impacted by an injury. After practice, he waited in the locker room and, when the last player was in the shower, rushed in and slashed him several times with a straight razor. Unfortunately, during the slashing, he accidentally cut the victim's jugular vein. Despite Defendant's efforts to obtain help, the victim bled to death. What is the most serious crime you believe Defendant may be convicted of?

5. Two brothers who were in need of money approached their wealthy uncle's housekeeper and asked her to poison the uncle. The brothers would inherit the uncle's estate when he died. The housekeeper agreed, but on the condition that they would pay her $10,000 from their inheritance. After the brothers agreed to her demand, the housekeeper decided to place some cyanide in the uncle's tea one morning. As the housekeeper was preparing the tea, the uncle was visited by his personal physician. When the housekeeper was ready to serve the tea, the uncle asked her to fix some tea for his physician also. The housekeeper did so and then carefully set the tea on the

table so that the uncle's cup was facing him. However, when the physician reached over to get some sugar, he inadvertently took the uncle's cup with the cyanide and drank it. Seconds later, the physician died from the poison.

First-degree murder requires proof of premeditation and deliberation. All other murder is second-degree murder. What would you charge the housekeeper with and why?

Chapter 8

Unintentional Criminal Homicide

I. Introduction

Unintentional killings are not immune from criminal sanction. In fact, unintentional killings may qualify as murder, manslaughter, or in many jurisdictions, negligent homicide. Where a defendant's criminal act or omission creates an unjustified risk (a risk a reasonable person would not have created) and that risk results in the death of a victim, the ingredients for a criminal homicide exist. Of course, intent to kill certainly creates an unjustified risk. However, in many cases, the evidence will indicate that while the defendant created an unjustified risk, she did so without intent to kill or even to inflict deadly injury, but instead either expected that the risk would not result in harm (meaning she was reckless) or didn't even realize she was creating the risk (meaning she was negligent). Accordingly, it is useful to begin homicide analysis by asking whether the evidence indicates the defendant *expected* her act or omission would result in the death of a victim—meaning the defendant acted with purpose to kill or knowledge of substantial certainly the act or omission would cause death; or whether the death of the victim was *unexpected*—meaning the defendant intended to inflict non-deadly injury, or knew she was creating the risk but expected to "get away with it," or didn't even realize she was creating the risk. Where the evidence suggests the homicide was *unexpected*, it should be analyzed within the framework of unintentional killings.

In practical terms, whereas intentional killings are very likely to qualify as murder, unintentional killings are more likely to qualify as either manslaughter or negligent homicide. Of course, this is not an ironclad rule: where intent is formed during a sudden heat of passion triggered by an adequate provocation (or there is some other impediment to proving malice such as *imperfect* self-defense), what is normally murder will be "downgraded" to voluntary manslaughter; and where an unjustified risk creation is so objectively extreme that it manifests a wanton disregard or depraved indifference for human life, what is normally involuntary manslaughter will be "upgraded" to murder. Each level of unintentional criminal homicide is therefore indicated by the mens rea that actuates the deadly act or omission.

A. Negligent Killings

At common law, killings resulting from ordinary or "civil" negligence were not *criminal* homicides. Such negligence could support the tort of wrongful death, but not a crime. This is because the minimum state of mind necessary to support a criminal homicide was known as criminal or gross negligence. While there was no formula for distinguishing ordinary from gross negligence, a jury would be instructed that they had to find the risk creation was greater than that associated with ordinary negligence—a gross deviation from the reasonable standard of care. An example of such a gross deviation would be playing with a loaded firearm in close proximity to others while erroneously assuming it is unloaded.

In common law jurisdictions, a finding of gross or criminal negligence supported a conviction for involuntary manslaughter. Because, however, this same offense was supported by a finding of recklessness, many jurisdictions consider a killing resulting from gross negligence as a less aggravated form of criminal homicide. Following the Model Penal Code, these jurisdictions codified a lower level of criminal homicide normally defined as *negligent homicide: the unlawful killing of a human being resulting from criminal negligence.* A small number of jurisdictions define negligent homicide as an unlawful killing resulting from *ordinary* negligence, with gross negligence resulting in an involuntary manslaughter conviction.

B. Reckless Killings

In both the common law and MPC, a killing resulting from a reckless criminal act or omission is defined as *involuntary manslaughter: the unlawful **unintentional** killing of a human being as the result of recklessness.* While (as noted above) some jurisdictions still allow a grossly negligent killing to qualify as involuntary manslaughter, recklessness is the most common basis for this offense. In such cases, a jury would be required to find that the victim's death was legally caused by the defendant's reckless act or omission, meaning the defendant was subjectively aware of the risk creation, ignored that risk, and that the risk was objectively unreasonable.

C. Unintentional Murder

In both common law and MPC jurisdictions, unintentional killings may qualify as murder. In the common law, recall that malice is the essential criminal state of mind to support the crime of murder. Malice may be established for both intentional and unintentional killings. In common law jurisdictions, either an intent to inflict grievous or serious bodily injury (but not death), or unjustified risk creation that was sufficiently extreme to demonstrate a wanton disregard for the value of human life, established malice. Model Penal Code jurisdictions may have dispensed with the term malice, but they nonetheless recognize an analogous theory of unintentional murder: a killing resulting from recklessness that manifests an extreme indifference to the value of human life qualifies as murder. And while intent to inflict grievous or serious bodily injury is not explicitly recognized as establishing murder, such an intent would easily fall within the definitions of knowledge that the conduct would cause death or extreme recklessness.

Because an unintentional killing may qualify as either involuntary manslaughter or murder, students often struggle to distinguish these offenses. The critical difference between a reckless killing that qualifies as manslaughter and one that qualifies as murder is proof that the risk the defendant created manifested what the common law called a wanton disregard for the value of human life and what the Model Penal Code calls an extreme indifference to the value of human life. This is not a subjective finding; the question is not whether the defendant subjectively recognized the extremity of the risk creation. Indeed, if a jury is persuaded that a defendant recognized this level of risk creation, it would very likely justify a finding of *knowledge* that the act or omission would result in death of a human being. Instead, this is an objective assessment: the jury is asked to look at the true nature of the risk the defendant created and decide whether it was so extreme or outrageous that it justifies holding the defendant accountable for murder even when she did not expect the risk creation to result in death.

The common law had many colorful terms for this category of murder: depraved heart murder; black heart murder; murder as the result of an "abandoned and malignant" heart. But these characterizations were all based on the same underlying premise: some defendants are so indifferent to the consequences of their risk creation that when they cause death, they should be condemned for murder.

Assessing if and when an unintentional killing qualifies as murder therefore follows a logical process. First, ensure the defendant's act or omission was the legal cause of a victim's death. Second, ensure that the proof establishes the risk the defendant created was objectively unreasonable, and therefore unjustified. Third, ask if the defendant acted with a subjective intent to inflict grievous or serious bodily injury. If so, that intent establishes malice in a common law jurisdiction and supports a murder conviction; in an MPC jurisdiction, that intent will normally establish either knowledge the conduct would cause death even if it was not the defendant's purpose or recklessness manifesting an extreme indifference to the value of human life, thereby supporting a murder conviction. Fourth, if the defendant *did not* intend to inflict grievous or serious bodily injury, ask whether the risk the defendant created was objectively extreme, meaning substantially greater than what in practical terms is ordinary recklessness.

In making this assessment, it will be useful to consider a common sense question: if you saw the defendant engaged in the risk creating behavior, would you turn to the person next to you and say, "That looks dangerous," or would you say, "That idiot is going to get someone killed"? If the former, it is probably ordinary recklessness or gross negligence. But if the latter, it is a pretty good indicator the risk was sufficiently extreme to escalate what is normally involuntary manslaughter to murder as the result of a wanton disregard or extreme indifference to the value of human life. Just consider a few contrasting examples. While driving on a busy highway, you observe another driver texting. Most of us would recognize this is reckless conduct, but in most cases, our instinct would not be that the driver is about to get someone killed. Now imagine it is a driver engaged in a "Fast and Furious" race through highway traffic at excessive speed swerving in and out of lanes. That conduct would likely trigger a "get someone killed" reaction. If both incidents resulted in a deadly accident, the first driver would likely be guilty of involuntary manslaughter, but the second would face a real risk of a murder conviction. Or imagine it is New Year's Eve. Some friends are gathered at a bonfire out in the woods with no one else around. At midnight, one of them takes out a pistol and shoots a few rounds into the woods to celebrate. If one of those rounds ricochets and hits and kills a friend, the discharge of the weapon *in that context* would likely be considered reckless and support a manslaughter conviction. However, if the same conduct occurred in a heavily populated city with surrounding balconies, watching the defendant pull out the pistol would likely lead to an "about to get someone killed" reaction by other bystanders. The context renders the risk creation substantially more extreme, and if a stray round hits and kills a victim, murder would be an appropriate charge.

D. Faultless Killings

As should be relatively clear to you by now, not all homicides qualify as *criminal* homicides. In order to reach that conclusion, there must be evidence to prove the requisite criminal mens rea/mental state beyond a reasonable doubt. It is unfortunately not uncommon that the killing of one person by another is not the result of any criminal mens rea. These are truly accidents in the legal sense, because they do not result from the deviation from a reasonable or ordinary standard of care. This is why a finding of criminal negligence for an unintentional killing is the minimum necessary mental state to transform a homicide into a criminal homicide. The following jury instruction on "accident" explains this requirement; the instruction is tailored to the killing of a victim as the result of a car collision:

> The evidence has raised the issue of accident in relationship to the offense of Criminally Negligent Homicide. In determining this issue, you must consider all the relevant facts and circumstances (including, but not limited to: evidence the defendant was suffering from excessive fatigue; evidence the defendant was an experienced and properly licensed driver; evidence the defendant had never been in a serious accident previously; evidence the weather was clear and the roads were dry).
>
> Accident is a complete defense to the offense of Criminally Negligent Homicide. If the accused was doing a lawful act in a lawful manner free of any negligence on his part, and an unexpected death occurs, the accused is not criminally liable.
>
> The defense of accident has three parts. First, the accused's (act(s)) (and) (or) (failure to act) resulting in the death must have been lawful. Second, the accused must not have been negligent. In other words, the accused must

have been acting with the amount of care for the safety of others that a reasonably prudent person would have used under the same or similar circumstances. Third, the death must have been unforeseeable and unintentional.

The burden is on the prosecution to establish the guilt of the accused. Consequently, unless you are convinced beyond a reasonable doubt that the death was not the result of an accident, the accused may not be convicted of Criminally Negligent Homicide.

Practice Pointer

Proving unintentional murder is never easy. This is because of the powerful lay instinct that murder requires intent to kill. Indeed, this may have been your instinct when you began your study of criminal law. In many cases a charge of "extreme reckless" murder will result in conviction for the lesser included offense of involuntary manslaughter, indicating the jury was not persuaded that the risk creation was sufficiently extreme to justify imposition of a murder conviction. For example, a prosecutor may seek a murder conviction for a young nanny who shakes a baby to death, conceding there was no intent to kill or even intent to inflict grievous bodily injury, but that the extent of the shaking resulted in a risk creation that was sufficiently extreme to qualify as murder. Such evidence *would* support a murder conviction, but there is also a strong possibility that the jury will be unpersuaded that the defendant should be condemned as a murderer and settle on an involuntary manslaughter conviction. Persuading a jury to "imply" malice or to conclude that the risk creation manifested an extreme indifference to the value of human life therefore involves leveraging all of the relevant facts and circumstances and effective advocacy to reach that essential finding. One such relevant circumstance is the *reason* the defendant created the risk. Some opinions have referred to risk creation resulting from a *base antisocial motive*, suggesting that where the defendant placed others at risk for some illicit motive—for example, to perpetrate or escape from a different crime—it supports the essential "indifference" finding.

II. Application

A. Negligent Killings

At common law, a killing resulting from what was known as criminal negligence or culpable negligence resulted in a conviction for involuntary manslaughter. Today, following the lead of the MPC, many jurisdictions distinguish negligent killings from reckless killings by creating a less aggravated category of criminal homicide aligned with criminal negligence: Negligent Homicide. However, whether assessing culpability for involuntary manslaughter based on criminal negligence pursuant to the common law approach or negligent homicide based on criminal negligence pursuant to the MPC approach, almost all jurisdictions require proof of more than civil negligence or ordinary carelessness. Criminal negligence requires a finding of a *gross* deviation from the ordinary or reasonable standard of care. The next decision illustrates the challenge of drawing this critically important line.

Queeman v. State
520 S.W.3d 616 (2017)
Texas Court of Criminal Appeals

Opinion

In reviewing the sufficiency of the evidence to support this criminally negligent homicide judgment, we address whether a death caused by two driving errors—the failure to control speed and the failure to maintain a proper distance between vehicles—proves a gross deviation from the standard of care that an ordinary person would exercise under the circumstances. Robert Alan Queeman, appellant, was convicted of criminally negligent homicide after failing to prevent his van from colliding with another vehicle, which resulted in the death of a passenger in the other vehicle. The court of appeals reversed the jury's verdict of guilt after finding that the evidence was legally insufficient to sustain the conviction. We agree with the court of appeal's ultimate conclusion that the evidence in this case is legally insufficient to establish criminally negligent homicide because the evidence presented at trial does not show that appellant's failure to maintain a safe driving speed and keep a proper distance from other vehicles was a gross deviation from the standard of care that an ordinary driver would exercise under all the circumstances as viewed from appellant's standpoint at the time of his conduct. We affirm the judgment of the court of appeals.

I. Background

Appellant was driving eastbound on a two-lane highway when his van rear-ended an SUV that was making a left turn off the highway onto an intersecting street. The collision caused the SUV to roll over into the westbound lane where it collided with an oncoming truck before coming to a stop upside down approximately fifty feet from the initial point of impact. Appellant's vehicle traveled approximately another 130-150 feet before coming to a stop. The SUV was occupied by three women: Maria del Rosario Luna was driving, Josefa Payne was in the front passenger seat, and Olga Deleon was in the back seat. Olga Deleon died as a result of injuries sustained in the collision.

Appellant was later charged in a two-count indictment for manslaughter and criminally negligent homicide. A jury acquitted him of manslaughter but found him guilty of criminally negligent homicide. Subsequently, the trial court sentenced him to eighteen months' confinement in a state jail facility.

At trial, Luna testified that she did not remember the details surrounding the accident except that she recalled that she and her passengers were driving home, which meant that she likely would have been making a left turn off the highway where the accident occurred. She could not recall whether her vehicle was stopped or still moving at the moment of impact. She stated that she believed she used her turn signal but could not recall for certain. However, in a statement given to investigators several days after the accident, she stated that she did not use her turn signal.

Appellant's theory about the cause of the accident, which was introduced through Trooper Welch's testimony, was that appellant accidently struck the SUV because it suddenly slowed down to make a left turn without using its turn signal. Appellant claimed that he was driving approximately 36 to 37 miles per hour, which was within the 40 miles-per-hour speed limit, at the time of the collision. Appellant maintained that, when he saw the SUV, he attempted to avoid hitting it but was unable to completely evade it. Appellant suggested that this corrective action resulted in the front-left side of his vehicle striking the right-rear side of the SUV.

Trooper Welch, who was in charge of the accident investigation, issued citations to Luna and appellant for their roles in the collision. Welch issued Luna a traffic ticket for failing to use her turn signal. He cited appellant for failure to maintain control of his speed but did not cite him for speeding. Additionally, Welch did not suspect appellant was intoxicated or impaired before the accident.

In his investigation, Welch determined that the SUV was stopped or nearly stopped at the time of the collision, that the SUV's brake lights were illuminated, and that appellant did not brake until just before or at the time that he struck the SUV.

Rejecting appellant's claim about his speed at the time of the collision, Welch determined that appellant was traveling "significantly" faster than 36 to 37 miles per hour. Welch opined that appellant was exceeding the 40 miles-per-hour speed limit. Welch made that determination based on his calculation of appellant's post-impact speed, which he concluded was approximately 34 miles per hour based on the length of yaw marks left by appellant's vehicle. This calculation required an assumption concerning the coefficient of friction between the tires and pavement because Welch did not have the necessary training to measure the actual friction coefficient for the formula. Welch testified that varying the coefficient of friction by ten percent changed the answer nominally between 32 miles per hour for a friction coefficient of sixty percent and 37 miles per hour for a friction coefficient of eighty percent. Welch stated that the coefficient of friction depends on a number of variables, including the weather and the pavement or surface type, but that his baseline assumption of a seventy-percent friction coefficient for dry asphalt on a clear day is "pretty well accepted." Welch indicated that the collision occurred on a clear, dry day. Furthermore, Welch opined that, based on his experience, appellant's vehicle would have been substantially slowed by a collision with a stationary car, like Luna's SUV. On the other hand, Welch conceded that he had no way of knowing specifically appellant's actual pre-accident speed.

On appeal, appellant challenged the sufficiency of the evidence to support his conviction. *Queeman v. State*, 486 S.W.3d 70 (Tex. App.—San Antonio 2016). The court of appeals reversed the trial court's judgment and rendered a judgment of acquittal. *Id.* at 71. The court of appeals found that the evidence presented could not have provided the jury a basis from which to reasonably infer that appellant was traveling at an "excessive rate of speed." *Id.* at 77. The court of appeals noted that Welch could not quantify appellant's pre-impact speed and also did not cite appellant for speeding. *Id.* Therefore, the court of appeals found that any inference by the jury that appellant was traveling at an excessive speed would be impermissible speculation. *Id.* Additionally, the evidence that appellant's vehicle hit Luna's SUV at an angle rather than straight from behind indicated that appellant tried to swerve to avoid the accident. *Id.* Furthermore, the court of appeals found that the evidence adduced at trial "[did] not show that [appellant] was engaged in any criminally culpable risk-creating conduct—e.g., dangerous speeding, racing, failure to obey traffic signals, or any other misconduct that created or contributed to a 'substantial and unjustifiable' risk of death." *Id.* (quoting *People v. Boutin*, 555 N.E.2d 253, 255-56 (N.Y. 1990)). Nor did the evidence establish that appellant engaged in other types of "serious, blameworthy conduct like distracted driving due to cell phone use and an abrupt, aggressive, unsafe lane change" or intoxicated driving. Id. Instead, the evidence "'establishe[d] only that [appellant] inexplicably failed to see [Luna's] vehicle until he was so close that he could not prevent the collision.'" *Id.* (quoting *Boutin*, 555 N.E.2d at 256). Thus, the court of appeals found the evidence legally insufficient to support appellant's conviction. *Id.*

In its petition for discretionary review, the State challenges the court of appeals's judgment on two grounds. It asks,

> (1) Is failing to maintain a safe speed and keep a proper distance the sort of "unexplained failure" that this Court suggested in *Tello v. State*, 180 S.W.3d 150 (Tex. Crim. App. 2005), would be unworthy of criminal sanction?

> (2) Did the court of appeals ignore basic rules of sufficiency review when it disregarded evidence that supported the verdict and drew inferences contrary to those presumably drawn by the jury?

II. Analysis

After describing the applicable law, we address the State's two arguments. We begin with the State's second ground that asserts that the court of appeals's analysis was flawed by failing to view the facts in a light most favorable to the jury's verdict. After that, we address the State's first ground that the court of appeals erred by deciding that no rational jury could decide that these facts establish criminal negligence.

A. Applicable Law for Establishing Criminal Negligence

... The duty of the reviewing court is simply to ensure that the evidence presented supports the jury's verdict and that the State has presented a legally sufficient case of the offense charged.... "Under this standard, evidence may be legally insufficient when the record contains either no evidence of an essential element, merely a modicum of evidence of one element, or if it conclusively establishes a reasonable doubt." *Britain v. State*, 412 S.W.3d 518, 520 (Tex. Crim. App. 2013) (citing *Jackson* [*v. Virginia*], 443 U.S. at 320).

A legally sufficient showing of criminally negligent homicide requires the State to prove that (1) the defendant's conduct caused the death of an individual; (2) the defendant ought to have been aware that there was a substantial and unjustifiable risk of death from his conduct; and (3) his failure to perceive the risk constituted a gross deviation from the standard of care an ordinary person would have exercised under like circumstances. . . . "Criminal negligence does not require proof of [a defendant's] subjective awareness of the risk of harm, but rather [the defendant's] awareness of the attendant circumstances leading to such a risk." "The key to criminal negligence is not the actor's being aware of a substantial risk and disregarding it, but rather it is the failure of the actor to perceive the risk at all."

This Court has acknowledged that, under the law, criminal negligence is different from ordinary civil negligence. "Civil or 'simple' negligence 'means the failure to use ordinary care, that is, failing to do that which a person of ordinary prudence would have done under the same or similar circumstances or doing that which a person of ordinary prudence would not have done under the same or similar circumstances.'" *Tello*, 180 S.W.3d at 158 (Cochran, J., concurring). Conversely, "[c]onduct that constitutes criminal negligence involves a greater risk of harm to others, without any compensating social utility, than does simple negligence." *Montgomery* [v. *State*], 369 S.W.3d at 193. "The carelessness required for criminal negligence is significantly higher than that for civil negligence; the seriousness of the negligence would be known by any reasonable person sharing the community's sense of right and wrong." *Id.* The risk must be "substantial and unjustifiable," and the failure to perceive it must be a "gross deviation" from reasonable care as judged by general societal standards by ordinary people. *Id.* "In finding a defendant criminally negligent, a jury is determining that the defendant's failure to perceive the associated risk is so great as to be worthy of a criminal punishment." *Id.* . . . . "Nor can criminal liability be predicated on every careless act merely because its carelessness results in death or injury to another." *Id.*

B. Review of Facts in a Light Most Favorable to the Verdict

In its second ground for review, the State suggests that the court of appeals erred by disregarding or discounting evidence establishing that appellant drove at an excessive speed that prevented him from being able to maintain a safe distance and that his inattention caused the accident. As we explain in more detail below, viewing the evidence in a light most favorable to the jury's verdict, we agree with the court of appeals that (1) appellant did fail to maintain a proper speed and safe distance, (2) he was speeding but no evidence shows that he was grossly negligent by speeding excessively over the speed limit, and (3) he was inattentive but no evidence shows that he was grossly negligent in terms of the length of or reason for his inattention. We note here that the court of appeals's analysis of the facts agreed that appellant was negligent, but it disagreed that he was grossly negligent, and thus its focus was on whether appellant's speed was excessive and whether his inattention was extreme. . . .

The evidence, viewed in a light most favorable to the verdict, establishes the acts that the State pleaded in the indictment, specifically, that appellant failed to maintain a safe operating speed and that he did not keep a proper distance. . . .

. . . The State argues that the court of appeals erred by deciding that the jury could not have rationally determined that appellant was excessively speeding, and it argues in its brief that "appellant was traveling at a speed well above the legal limit and high enough to be lethal when the collision occurred." We disagree with the State because the evidence of appellant's speed, even when viewed in a light most favorable to the jury's verdict, would not permit a rational jury to determine that he was excessively speeding. Although it is true that Welch used the word "significantly" when he said that he believed appellant was driving "significantly" faster than the approximately 36 to 37 miles per hour claimed by appellant, it would be irrational under the record in this case for the jury to determine that this testimony meant that appellant drove excessively over the speed limit. . . . Welch further testified that he was unable to ascertain appellant's specific pre-impact speed based on the facts that were available to him. . . .

3. Appellant Was Inattentive But No Evidence of Reason for or Length of Inattention

The State argues that the court of appeals erred by considering appellant's van's collision with the back corner of the SUV as evidence of his efforts to avoid the accident rather than as evidence of his inattentiveness. We agree with the State that, viewed in a light most favorable to the jury's verdict, it would be improper to view that evidence as establishing that appellant made an effort to avoid the accident because the record is silent as to the reason why appellant struck the back corner rather than the back middle of the SUV. We, therefore, disagree with the determination by the court of appeals that the evidence "establish[ed] that [appellant] observed Luna's vehicle in time to swerve and hit the right passenger end of her vehicle." *Queeman*, 486 S.W.3d at 77.

. . . .

Although we agree with the State that the jury rationally could have determined that appellant did not swerve to avoid striking the SUV, we note here that there is no evidence in the record about the length of time that appellant was inattentive before colliding with the SUV or the reasons for his inattentiveness. Although the State suggests that "appellant was speeding without even looking up to see if there was anyone or anything to avoid on a highway going thru a town and lined with businesses," that statement is speculative because there is nothing in the record to show where appellant was looking, the reason for his inattentiveness, or the length of time that he was inattentive. Thus, although the record supports a rational conclusion that appellant was inattentive long enough for him to collide with the back corner of Luna's SUV, nothing in the record demonstrates whether this was ordinary or gross inattentiveness that contributed to the collision.

C. Facts In the Record Do Not Establish Criminal Negligence

The State's first ground suggests that appellant's conduct—his inattention to traffic that caused him to fail to maintain a proper distance and his failure to maintain a safe speed—is worthy of a criminal sanction because "the excessive speed and prolonged inattention required to hit a stationary vehicle in one's lane under good driving conditions involves a greater risk of harm than a simple fender bender without any compensating social utility." . . . The State argues that appellant knew that he was speeding and that he was not watching the road for an extended period of time, and that as a result, appellant collided with a stationary vehicle and killed one of its occupants. . . . The State asserts that, because the precise meanings of "gross deviation" and "substantial and unjustifiable risk" are necessarily vague, criminal negligence is an ad hoc, fact-intensive determination that must be left to juries, as society's representatives, to decide whether conduct deserves criminal liability. . . .

We compare the facts of appellant's case to two recent cases in which this Court has reviewed the sufficiency of the evidence for criminal negligence.

1. Montgomery

In *Montgomery v. State*, this Court upheld a conviction for criminally negligent homicide. 369 S.W.3d at 191. The facts in that case showed that Montgomery drove in the center lane of a three-lane service road adjacent to the interstate while talking on her cell phone. *Id*. After hanging up the phone, Montgomery realized that she had missed the entrance ramp to the interstate that diverged from the left lane, and she abruptly swerved into the left lane in an attempt to exit the service road onto the interstate. *Id*. This lane change occurred some distance after passing the "safety barrier"—the beginning of the solid-white-lined area on the pavement between the ramp and the service road. *Id*. As a result of the abrupt, late lane change, a three-vehicle accident ensued in which a passenger in one of the vehicles was killed. *Id*. Montgomery was convicted of criminally negligent homicide based on the State's evidence of her use of a cell phone, her unsafe lane change, and her failure to maintain a proper lookout. *Id*. In upholding Montgomery's conviction, we observed that she was driving slower than surrounding traffic, was past the "safety barrier" when she abruptly changed lanes, did not signal her lane change or look for surrounding traffic, and attempted to enter an on-ramp past its entrance. *Id*. at 194. We held that a jury could have reasonably concluded that, under these circumstances, Montgomery was criminally negligent in that she "ought to have been aware of the substantial and unjustifiable risk created by her actions." *Id*. We noted that it was "common knowledge that failing to maintain a proper lookout and making an unsafe lane change without signaling or checking for upcoming traffic poses a great risk to other drivers on that road and that anyone sharing the general community's sense of right and wrong would be aware of the seriousness of doing so." *Id*. Further, we held that a jury could have reasonably found that Montgomery's failure to appreciate that substantial and unjustifiable risk, given the circumstances known to her at the time, was a gross deviation from a standard of care that an ordinary person would exercise under the same circumstances. . . .

In contrast to *Montgomery*, here the accident did not include circumstances suggesting that appellant was engaging in any activity while driving that a reasonable person would know might distract him. Further, the evidence does not show that appellant made any particular driving maneuver, such as a late lane change without signaling, that a reasonable driver would recognize as being inherently unsafe. . . . We conclude that this case is distinguishable from *Montgomery* because, as compared to that case, here there is no evidence that appellant was excessively speeding or undertaking some unreasonable activity that caused his inattention and failure to gauge his distance, and his failures that are shown in this record cannot be characterized as a "gross deviation" from the ordinary standard of care. *Id.*

[The court then contrasted the defendant's conduct with the facts of another case, *Tello v. State*, concluding that speeding was not analogous to the level of risk created by failing to properly secure a homemade trailer to a truck resulting in the trailer becoming disconnected and killing a pedestrian].

Driving is a common activity that has risks about which a reasonable person would be cognizant. Failure to appreciate those risks and the circumstances that create them can support ordinary negligence. Criminal negligence, however, requires a greater showing—that the risk is "substantial and unjustifiable" and that the failure to perceive the circumstances creating the risk is a "gross deviation" from the usual standard of care. . . . As the court of appeals essentially determined, the facts in this case satisfy the ordinary civil standard of negligence based on appellant's failure to control his speed and following the SUV without maintaining a safe distance between the vehicles. These types of driving errors are often made by many drivers who also accept these same risks from other drivers because of the great social utility afforded by automotive transportation. Absent more egregious conduct, however, these errors alone fail to show a gross deviation from the usual standard of care in driving. . . .

We hold that there is no evidence of a failure to perceive a substantial and unjustifiable risk that constituted a gross deviation from the standard of care that an ordinary person would have exercised under the circumstances, and, thus, the evidence is legally insufficient to establish criminal negligence. . . .

Notes and Questions

1. How does the court define or "quantify" the line between ordinary and gross/criminal negligence?

2. Notice how the court emphasizes that what makes negligence gross/criminal is not related to whether the defendant recognized the risk. Does this help explain why many states have adopted the crime of negligent homicide?

3. Not all jurisdictions require gross negligence to support conviction for criminal homicide. For example, in *State v. Ramser*, 17 Wash. 2d 581, 136 P.2d 1013 (1943), the Washington Supreme Court upheld a conviction for involuntary manslaughter based on a standard of ordinary negligence pursuant to its interpretation of the state statute. In that case, the defendant was moving a house on a public road. The truck towing the house broke down around dusk, and defendant learned that his flares and lighting equipment were inoperable. While searching for some lights, a car collided with the obstruction, and the two occupants were killed. Ramser was tried for involuntary manslaughter based on an allegation he was negligent in the manner in which he moved the house and in his failure to properly mark it with lighting. He argued on appeal that his motion for acquittal at the close of the prosecution case should have been granted, because the evidence did not rationally support a finding of gross negligence as required by the common law, but only ordinary negligence. According to the Court,

> The argument and the cases cited in support of it are met by the case of *State v. Hedges*, 8 Wn.2d 652, 113 P.2d 530, in which it is said that one may be convicted of manslaughter if he causes the death of another by doing some act in a negligent manner, and that it is not necessary for the jury to find that the accused was guilty of gross negligence before a conviction may be had, but a finding that he failed to exercise ordinary care under the circumstances is sufficient to support a conviction. The case refers to our statute defining manslaughter (Rem. Rev. Stat., § 2395 [P.C. § 9000]), and cites and discusses our recent cases. We said there, p. 666:
>
> > "After careful consideration, we are convinced that the statute referred to does not require a finding by the jury that the accused was guilty of gross negligence, before a conviction may be had. Under this statute, a finding that an accused was guilty of ordinary negligence supports a conviction. If it be desirable that the law be amended by requiring a finding of gross negligence, that matter is within the province of the legislature."
>
> The case is decisive of the question raised and discussed by this assignment of error. The trial court did not err in denying the motion to dismiss the case at the close of the respondent's case.

4. Would the facts of *Queeman* have supported an involuntary manslaughter conviction in Washington?

B. Reckless Manslaughter

While some jurisdictions still allow gross negligence (or even ordinary negligence) to support an involuntary manslaughter conviction, many require that death result from recklessness for this offense. The following case illustrates why negligence, even if gross, is insufficient in many jurisdictions to prove involuntary manslaughter.

State v. Olsen

462 N.W.2d 474 (1990)
South Dakota Supreme Court

SABERS, Justice.

The State appeals a magistrate court order dismissing a charge of manslaughter in the second degree against Michael K. Olsen.

Facts

About 5:00 p.m. on May 24, 1989, Olsen was driving a tractor west on Highway 46, approximately one mile east of the Beresford city limits. Visibility was good as it was a clear, sunny day. Olsen entered the highway from a field where he had been working and was travelling between five and fifteen miles per hour. After travelling approximately one-half mile on the highway, Olsen pulled over to the side of the road to allow a car that was following him to pass. A second vehicle, driven by Lloyd Saugstad, was a short distance farther back.

Shortly after pulling over to the side of the road, Olsen turned left toward a gravel road leading to his parents' home. As he was crossing the eastbound lane of the highway, the front of the tractor was struck by a car travelling east in that lane. The collision resulted in the immediate death of the driver of the eastbound vehicle. When Saugstad approached the accident scene, Olsen ran from the tractor saying "I didn't see it." After rescue personnel arrived, Olsen was taken to the Beresford clinic and treated for shock.

The State filed a complaint against Olsen on May 30, 1989, charging him with one count of manslaughter in the second degree. A preliminary hearing was held on July 27, 1989. At the hearing, Saugstad testified that he saw the eastbound vehicle coming and knew that a crash was imminent when Olsen turned his tractor. The South Dakota highway patrol trooper who investigated the accident testified that he interviewed Olsen the evening of the accident. Olsen told the trooper that before attempting to make his turn he looked both behind and forward, but did not see the approaching vehicle.

Following the presentation of the State's case at the preliminary hearing, Olsen moved to dismiss the complaint against him. The magistrate granted Olsen's motion and dismissed the manslaughter charge because "the factual situation fails to meet the burden to sustain a charge of felony manslaughter." The State petitioned this court for permission to appeal the intermediate order of the magistrate court. We granted the petition, but deny the relief sought.

[The court first explained that the purpose of a preliminary hearing is to test whether the evidence presented by the state is sufficient to establish probable cause the defendant committed the alleged offense, and that a judge should dismiss the complaint (charge) if the evidence insufficient.]

Recklessness requires a conscious disregard of a risk. SDCL 22-16-20 treats "[a]ny reckless killing" as manslaughter in the second degree. The definition of "reckless" for the purpose of this statute is set forth in SDCL 22-1-2(1)(d). *State v. Martin*, 449 N.W.2d 29 (S.D.1989). That definition states:

> The words "reckless, recklessly" and all derivatives thereof, import a conscious and unjustifiable disregard of a substantial risk that the offender's conduct may cause a certain result or may be of a certain nature. A person is reckless with respect to circumstances when he consciously and unjustifiably disregards a substantial risk that such circumstances may exist[.]

In other words, for someone's conduct to be deemed reckless, they must consciously disregard a substantial risk. Consequently, someone cannot be reckless if they are unaware of the risk their behavior creates as they cannot disregard that risk if they are unaware of it. . . .

Recklessness requires more than ordinary negligent conduct. Evidence of carelessness, inadvertence or other similar behavior is insufficient to sustain a conviction where reckless conduct is required. . . . The difference between reckless behavior and negligent behavior is primarily measured by the state of mind of the individual. As explained in 1 C. Torcia, Wharton's Criminal Law § 27 at 140 (1978):

> The difference between the terms "recklessly" and "negligently", as usually defined, is one of kind, rather than of degree. Each actor creates a *risk* of harm. The reckless actor is *aware* of the risk and disregards it; the negligent actor is *not aware* of the risk but should have been aware of it.

(Emphasis in original). The same idea is expressed in Treiman, *Recklessness and the Model Penal Code*, 9 Am.J.Crim.L. 281, 351 (1981):

> It is the concept of conscious disregard that distinguishes recklessness from negligence. The negligent actor fails to perceive a risk that he ought to perceive. The reckless actor perceives or is conscious of the risk, but disregards it.

Consequently, outwardly identical actions by two people may be reckless behavior for one, but only negligent behavior for the other.

Although it is not always possible for the State to directly establish that a defendant was aware of a risk, it can be done indirectly through the defendant's conduct. Awareness can be established if the defendant acts in a manner that indicates a reckless disregard for the safety of others. However, the operation of a motor vehicle in violation of the law is not in and of itself sufficient to constitute reckless conduct, even if a person is killed as a result thereof. . . . As explained in *Commonwealth v. Kaulback*, 256 Pa.Super. 13, 389 A.2d 152, 154–155 (1978), the evidence must show more than a mere violation of the law before criminal responsibility for a death will arise:

> [N]ot every violation of law or unlawful act in the operation of a motor vehicle will render the operator criminally responsible for deaths which may result. Such an operator, to be criminally responsible, must evidence a disregard of human life or an indifference to the consequences of his acts. This is based on the sound principle that there must be found from the evidence

some degree of culpable behavior or reckless disregard for the safety of others before a conviction may be sustained.

. . . .

In the present case, the State has failed to introduce evidence of Olsen's conduct that would rise above the level of negligence. Nothing in the evidence of Olsen's behavior suggests that he was in any way aware of the risk he was creating when he turned his tractor towards the gravel road. . . . The State has failed to offer evidence indicating that Olsen's failure to yield the right-of-way was done in such a manner as to suggest a reckless disregard for the safety of others. While the State need not introduce evidence that Olsen could foresee a death resulting from his conduct, the State must introduce evidence that would allow a trier of fact to conclude that Olsen was aware of the dangerous nature of his conduct. Since the State has failed to introduce such evidence, we cannot say that the magistrate court abused its discretion in dismissing the complaint against Olsen. . . .[4]

WUEST, Justice (concurring specially).

I concur. The key in this case was factual. Did Olsen see the oncoming vehicle and try to beat it across the highway, or did he fail to see it? If it was the former, he should have been held for trial on manslaughter charges. If the latter, the dismissal was correct.

Magistrates are not the finders of fact (i.e. jury) in criminal prosecutions. Conflicting facts or inferences are for the trier of fact to resolve. *State v. Dunn*, 121 Wis.2d 389, 359 N.W.2d 151 (1984). However, a magistrate must necessarily ascertain the facts to decide probable cause. In performing this function he may assess the weight and competency of the evidence and the credibility of the witnesses. *People v. Paille*, 383 Mich. 621, 178 N.W.2d 465 (1970).

In this case the spontaneous statement at the accident scene by defendant he did not see the oncoming vehicle is credible. It does not appear to be a statement conceived after the fact to exculpate himself from a manslaughter charge. The magistrate apparently determined from the spontaneity of the remark Olsen did not see the oncoming vehicle, hence no manslaughter charge. Under that scenario, it was not an abuse of discretion to dismiss the charges.

---

4. In this case, the magistrate did not choose between conflicting facts, but merely determined that the facts, as presented by the State, did not establish each element of the crime charged. It is settled law that such a decision is within the magistrate's discretion:

> [I]f the inference that the accused committed a felony is so weak that drawing it still does not establish a plausible account of probable guilt, *it is within the discretion of the magistrate* to decline to find probable cause to bind him over for trial.

State v. Dunn, 121 Wis.2d 389, 359 N.W.2d 151, 155 (1984) (quoting from State's brief) (emphasis added). The inference that Olsen consciously disregarded a substantial risk because it was a clear day and somebody else was able to see the decedent's vehicle is too weak to establish a plausible account of probable guilt.

Notes and Questions

1. Based on the foregoing opinion, write an instruction for a jury explaining recklessness and negligence and highlight for the jury what distinguishes these two criminal mental states.

2. If you had been trying this case, what evidence might you have attempted to present to satisfy the definition of recklessness?

C. Unintentional Murder

As noted in the Introduction, murder has never required proof the defendant intended to kill. Instead, at common law, the malice aforethought requirement for murder could be established for an unintentional killing where the defendant manifested a wanton disregard for the value of human life. This type of "implied" malice may be more challenging to prove, but allows the extremity of the risk created by a defendant to result in a murder conviction.

Imagine a scenario where U.S. soldiers "stage" a firefight that results in the unintentional death of a civilian during security operations in a crowded foreign city in order to cover up their loss of a pistol when they violated orders and visited a brothel during a patrol. Hard to believe? Well, this is exactly what led to a murder conviction of a U.S. soldier who participated in Operation Just Cause, the 1989 U.S. invasion of Panama. The accused was convicted of a violation of Article 118(3) of the Uniform Code of Military Justice, which defines murder as, *inter alia*, a killing resulting from an inherently dangerous act that manifests as wanton disregard for the value of human life, which is defined in the Manual for Courts-Martial as heedless indifference to the risk to human life and is "is not measured subjectively by the state of an accused's mind but is measured objectively by a 'qualitative judgment' of the circumstances of his conduct." The military jury that decided the case rejected a finding of guilt based on an intent to inflict serious bodily injury but nonetheless convicted the accused soldier of murder for this unintentional killing. Firing off a clip of military ammunition in a fake firefight among buildings crowded with civilians in order to cover up serious misconduct is a classic example of "wanton disregard" or "depraved indifference" for the consequences of the reckless conduct. However, because the military judge presiding over the case failed to instruct the military jury that an *honest and reasonable* belief that the shooting was justified in response to a hostile threat—something the accused said in a statement to criminal investigators—would negate the unlawfulness of the killing, the military appeals court reversed the conviction. *See United States v. McMonagle*, 38 M.J. 53 (1993)

Berry v. Superior Court

256 Cal. Rptr. 344 (1989)
California Court of Appeals

The People have charged Michael Patrick Berry, defendant, with the murder of two and one half year old James Soto who was killed by Berry's pit bull dog . . . By this statutorily authorized petition for a writ of prohibition (Pen.Code, § 999a), defendant seeks dismissal of the charges of murder and Penal Code section 399. He claims the evidence taken at the preliminary hearing falls legally short of establishing implied malice sufficient to bind over for murder. . . .

The test whether evidence is sufficient to allow a prosecution to proceed to trial is whether "'a man of ordinary caution or prudence would be led to believe and conscientiously entertain a strong suspicion of the guilt of the accused.'" An information will not be set aside or a prosecution thereon prohibited if there is some rational ground for assuming the possibility that an offense has been committed and the accused is guilty of it. . . .

We have concluded, for reasons we shall state, that judged by this standard of review the record here will support a prosecution for murder. The other charges may also go forward.

Record of the Preliminary Hearing

. . . .

The record shows that on June 13, 1987, James Soto, then aged two years and eight months, was killed by a pit bull dog named "Willy" owned by defendant. The animal was tethered near defendant's house but no obstacle prevented access to the dog's area. The victim and his family lived in a house which stood on the same lot, sharing a common driveway. The Soto family had four young children. . . .

On the day of the child's death, his mother, Yvonne Nunez, left the child playing on the patio of their home for a minute or so while she went into the house, and when she came out the child was gone.   She was looking for him when within some three to five minutes her brother-in-law, Richard Soto, called her and said defendant's dog had attacked James. Meanwhile the father, Arthur Soto, had come upon the dog Willy mauling his son. He screamed for defendant to come get the dog off the child; defendant did so. The child was bleeding profusely. Although an on-call volunteer fireman with paramedical training who lived nearby arrived within minutes and attempted to resuscitate the child, James died before an emergency crew arrived at the scene.

There was no evidence that Willy had ever before attacked a human being, but there was considerable evidence that he was bred and trained to be a fighting dog and that he posed a known threat to people. Defendant bought Willy from a breeder of fighting dogs, who informed defendant of the dog's fighting abilities, his gameness, wind, and exceptionally hard bite. The breeder told defendant that in a dog fight "a dog won't go an hour with Willy and live."

The police searched defendant's house after the death of James and found many underground publications about dog fighting; a pamphlet entitled "42 day keep" which set out the 6-week conditioning procedures used to prepare a dog for a match; a treadmill used to condition a dog and increase its endurance; correspondence with Willy's breeder, Gene Smith; photographs of dog fights; and a "break stick," used to pry fighting dogs apart since they will not release on command. One of Smith's letters dated December 7, 1984, described Willy as having an exceptionally hard bite.

Two women who knew defendant testified he told them he had raised dogs for fighting purposes and had fought pit bulls.

Richard Soto testified defendant told him he used the treadmill to increase the strength and endurance of his dogs. Defendant also told both Arthur and Richard Soto that he would not fight his dogs for less than $500 and he told Richard Willy had had matches as far away as South Carolina.

The victim's mother testified defendant had several dogs. He told her not to be concerned about the dogs, that they would not bother her children, except for "one that he had on the side of the house" which was behind a six foot fence. Defendant further said this dangerous dog was Willy but that she need not be concerned since he was behind a fence. There was a fence where the dog was tethered on the west side of defendant's house, but the fence was not an enclosure and did not prevent access to the area the dog could reach.

The police found some 243 marijuana plants growing behind defendant's house. Willy was tethered in such location that anyone wanting to approach the plants would have to cross the area the dog could reach. That area was readily accessible to anyone.

An animal control officer qualified as an expert on fighting dogs testified. He said pit bull dogs are selectively bred to be aggressive towards other animals. They give no warning of their attack, attack swiftly, silently and tenaciously. Although many recently bred pit bulls have good dispositions near human beings and are bred and raised to be pets, there are no uniform breeding standards for temperament and the animal control officers consider a pit bull dangerous unless proved otherwise.

Defendant's counsel placed great emphasis on certain testimony of the animal control officer, Miller. Counsel claimed that Miller testified Willy's attack on James was completely unpredictable, and that the People are bound by this testimony and therefore cannot argue that defendant ought to have foreseen what would happen. The testimony occurred during cross examination, as follows: defendant's counsel asked Miller whether he knew of any prior attacks by Willy, and he said no. Then counsel quoted from an article written by Miller saying that even pit bulls with no prior history of aggression have been known to become highly aggressive "when at large, when in a pack, when confronted by any aggressive dog or under other unpredictable situations." Miller affirmed he believed this. Then counsel ruled out such factors as the dog being at large, in a pack, and so forth, and then said the dog being confronted by the little boy "would come under this unpredictable situation then, wouldn't he?" and Miller said yes. Counsel then asked, "So then what you are saying is is [sic] that without any prior knowledge of unpredictability, Willy could cause an attack such as this, isn't that true?" and Miller said yes.

When testifying, Arthur Soto denied having told any investigator that defendant had warned him about Willy. Counsel interrogating him insinuated that he was afraid to testify about prior warnings because he might jeopardize his civil lawsuit against defendant. Later an officer who had investigated the death and had interviewed Arthur testified pursuant to Evidence Code section 1237 that Arthur had told the officer defendant had warned Arthur to "keep the kids away from the killer dog," meaning Willy.

Discussion

Whether Evidence Is Sufficient To Bind Over on Murder Charge

First, defendant claims that as a matter of law the record does not show implied malice sufficient to require him to stand trial for a charge of second degree murder. As stated above, the issue at this stage of the proceedings is not whether the evidence establishes guilt beyond a reasonable doubt, but rather whether the evidence is sufficient to lead a man of ordinary caution or prudence to believe and conscientiously entertain a strong suspicion of his guilt of this offense, or whether there is some rational ground for assuming the possibility of his guilt.   (*Rideout v. Superior Court*, *supra*, 67 Cal.2d 471, 62 Cal.Rptr. 581, 432 P.2d 197.)

. . . .

The recent decision in *People v. Protopappas* (1988) 201 Cal.App.3d 152, 246 Cal. Rptr. 915 further elaborates the definition of implied malice. That case found sufficient evidence of implied malice to support the defendant dentist's convictions of the murders of three of his patients, who died because of his recklessness. He clearly did not intend to kill them; as the decision pointed out, it was in his interests to keep them alive so that he could continue to collect fees from them. Further, his failure to provide proper treatment for them could be characterized as an act of omission or neglect rather than an affirmative act of homicide. But the appellate court found sufficient evidence of malice because the jury could infer from his conduct that he actually appreciated the risk to his patients and exhibited extreme indifference to their welfare in failing to provide the proper treatment and care and in administering anaesthesia to them in grossly negligent fashion. The court found substantial evidence Protopappas's treatment of his patients was " ' "aggravated, culpable, gross, or reckless" neglect [which] involved such a high degree of probability that it would result in death that it constituted "a wanton disregard for human life" making it second degree murder.' " (*People v. Protopappas, supra*, at p. 167, 246 Cal.Rptr. 915, citing *People v. Burden* (1977) 72 Cal.App.3d 603, 615, 140 Cal.Rptr. 282.) The *Protopappas* court further elaborated the requirements of implied malice thus: "wantonness, an extreme indifference to [the victim's] life, and subjective awareness of the very high probability of her death." (*Id.* 201 Cal.App.3d at p. 168, 246 Cal.Rptr. 915.)

Interestingly, the court in *Protopappas* referred to the dentist's conduct as "the health care equivalent of shooting into a crowd or setting a lethal mantrap in a dark alley." (*Id.* at p. 167, fn. 9, 246 Cal.Rptr. 915.) Similarly here, the People seek to analogize defendant's manner of keeping Willy as the equivalent of setting a lethal mantrap, since anyone could have approached the dog and been at risk of attack. (Cases holding second degree murder may rest on the setting of a lethal trap include *People v. Ceballos* (1974) 12 Cal.3d 470, 477, 116 Cal.Rptr. 233, 526 P.2d 241.)

Another decision which thoughtfully explores the nature of implied malice is *People v. Love* (1980) 111 Cal.App.3d 98, 168 Cal.Rptr. 407. The facts of that case may be considered more aggravated than in this case or in *Protopappas, supra,* since in *Love* the defendant put a gun to the victim's temple and then claimed it went off accidentally. The analysis is nonetheless useful. The court discusses the "fine line between cases involving conduct consonant with the punishment to be imposed for second degree murder and those which are properly lesser crimes" (*id.* at p. 106, 168 Cal.Rptr. 407) and points out that the former cases all involve "an element of viciousness—an extreme indifference to the value of human life." (*Id.* at p. 105, 168 Cal.Rptr. 407.) Examples given of such conduct include the striking of a child, assault with a deadly weapon, or a father's neglect in caring for his son. (*Ibid.*, citing *People v. Atkins* (1975) 53 Cal.App.3d 348, 359, 125 Cal.Rptr. 855; *People v. Goodman* (1970) 8 Cal.App.3d 705, 708, 87 Cal.Rptr. 665; *People v. Burden, supra,* 72 Cal.App.3d 603, 619–620, 140 Cal.Rptr. 282.)

Love observes that the "continuum of death-causing behavior for which society imposes sanctions is practically limitless with the gradations of more culpable conduct imperceptibly shading into conduct for the less culpable. Our high court has drawn this line placing in the more culpable category not only those deliberate life-endangering acts which are done with a subjective awareness of the risk involved, but also life-endangering conduct which is 'only' done with the awareness the conduct is contrary to the laws of society. Although behavior in the latter category may not be as morally heinous as the former, the difference in culpability does not require the latter crime to be legally shifted into manslaughter slots. The blameworthiness of death-causing conduct which can legitimately be described as involving a high degree of probability that it will result in death where accomplished with an awareness of one's societal duties is not disproportionate to the sanctions which may be imposed for second degree murder. One's felt sense of justice is not moved, much less outraged, when such life-endangering and death-causing conduct is labeled as second degree murder." (*Id.* 111 Cal.App.3d at pp. 107–108, 168 Cal.Rptr. 407.)

The decision in *Love* sets forth two prerequisites for affixing second degree murder liability upon an unintentional killing. One requirement is the defendant's extreme indifference to the value of human life, a condition which must be demonstrated by showing the probability that the conduct involved will cause death. Another requirement is awareness either (1) of the risks of the conduct, or (2) that the conduct is contrary to law. Here, evidence of the latter requirement is first, that the very possession of Willy may have constituted illegal keeping of a fighting dog. (Pen.Code, § 597.5.) Second, there is evidence that defendant kept Willy to guard marijuana plants, also conduct with elements of illegality and antisocial purpose. Thus the second element which *Love* required could be satisfied here in a number of ways.

Defendant argues that the elements posited in *Love*—awareness of high risk or antisocial or illegal conduct—are insufficient. He says a further requirement is that the defendant have actively killed the victim, rather than being guilty of passive omissions which result in the death. He contends the cases involving implied malice all exhibit a physical act of commission, such as an aggressive act with a weapon or an automobile. In support of his interpretation of the precedent he cites a law review article which makes the observation that a physical act requirement is a "key element" in deciding whether actions create a high probability that death will occur. (71 Cal.L.Rev. 1298, 1303 (1983).) He also lists many cases where implied malice was grounded on such aggressive acts as reckless driving under the influence. . . .

However, despite defendant's argument that all second degree murders involve acts of commission rather than omission, at least two cases of second degree murder, *Protopappas* and *Burden, supra,* arguably rest on reckless failure to provide proper care or treatment. The *Protopappas* court described the defendant's conduct there in precisely those terms. *Burden* rests on a father's neglect in caring for his son, namely, allowing him to starve to death. The *Burden* court said that "the common law does not distinguish between homicide by act and homicide by omission."

. . . .

Have we here evidence of the elements of second degree murder as described in these decisions, namely, the high probability the conduct will result in the death of a human being, a subjective appreciation of the risk, and a base antisocial purpose or motive? The People point to these facts: The homes of defendant and the victim's family shared a lot and were in close proximity, the Soto family had four very young children and defendant knew this; defendant knew the dog Willy was dangerous to the children, as evidenced by the mother's testimony that he told her that dog could be dangerous but was behind a fence; defendant in fact lulled Yvonne into a false sense of security by assuring her the dangerous dog was behind a fence when he was in fact accessible; defendant bred fighting dogs and had knowledge of the nature and characteristics of fighting pit bulls; defendant had referred to Willy as a "killer dog"; pit bulls in fact are sometimes dangerous and will attack unpredictably and without warning; and Willy was a proven savage fighting dog.

From this mass of evidence it is possible to isolate facts which standing alone would not suffice as the basis of a murder charge. For example, we do not believe that a showing that Willy was dangerous to other dogs, without more, would be sufficient to bind over his owner on a murder charge; there is no evidence in this record that dogs who are dangerous to their own kind are ipso facto dangerous to human beings and therefore there is no support for an inference that the owner of such a dog should be aware of any such danger. But the evidence amassed here goes beyond demonstrating that Willy was aggressive towards his own kind. We believe this record shows first, that Willy's owner may have been actually aware of the dog's potential danger to human beings. This mental state may be proved by showing he kept the dog chained, he warned the child's parents that the dog was dangerous to children, and he spoke of the dog as dangerous. Second, the testimony of the animal control officer could support an inference that fighting pit bull dogs are dangerous to human beings, and the record of defendant's extensive knowledge of the breed could support an inference that he knew such dogs are dangerous.

Defendant argues that the testimony of the animal control officer, Miller, regarding the dangerousness of pit bulls, conclusively establishes that Willy's attack was "unpredictable" in the sense that it could not reasonably have been anticipated. This interpretation is not compelled. Some of that testimony consists of responses to ungrammatical questions and as such does not establish any proposition with certainty.[1] But a possible fair reading of Miller's testimony is that he used "unpredictable" not in the sense that no one could predict whether the dog would ever attack, but rather, in the sense that the dog could be expected to attack without advance warning or apparent cause. Thus Miller's testimony could support an inference that pit bulls are known to be liable to attack human beings. There is also evidence, consisting mainly of physical evidence seized from defendant's home, showing that defendant is a connoisseur of fighting pit bull dogs and had sought out a vicious dog in order to have him fight successfully.

Thus there is a basis from which the trier of fact could derive the two required elements of implied malice, namely existence of an objective risk and subjective awareness of that risk. Additionally, there is arguably some base and antisocial purpose involved in keeping the dog (1) because harboring a fighting dog is illegal and (2) because there is some evidence the dog was kept to guard an illegal stand of marijuana. Illegality of the underlying conduct is not an element of the charge, but may be relevant on the issue of subjective intent. (See discussion of *Love, supra*.)

We do not know the actual probability that a death could result from defendant's conduct in keeping the dog. Presumably that is a question of fact to be submitted to the court or jury upon appropriate instructions requiring that it find a high probability that death would result from the circumstances before it can convict of murder.

. . . .

We conclude that it is for the jury to resolve the factual issues of probability of death and subjective mental state. There is sufficient evidence to justify trial for murder on an implied malice theory.

---

1. The question counsel asked Miller was "So then what you are saying is is [sic] that without any prior knowledge of unpredictability, Willy could cause an attack such as this, isn't that true?" to which he said yes. As a matter of English grammar there is no reliable inference that can be based on this interrogation.

Notes & Questions

1. On this evidence, would you have voted to convict Berry for murder or for involuntary manslaughter? Does the fact that he appears to have kept Willy to deter others from interfering or discovering his marijuana grove impact your judgment?

2. Berry went to trial on the murder charge, but was convicted of involuntary manslaughter and sentenced to 3 years and 8 months of confinement.

3. Almost all cases of unintentional murder reference the requirement to prove a "high probability" of death. But does the defendant have to be aware of that probability, or only that his conduct creates *a risk* of death? It seems requiring proof the defendant was subjectively aware his conduct created a high probability of death would conflate extreme reckless murder with murder based on knowledge. Berry certainly didn't expect Willy would kill someone, nor is it likely Fleming (see Chapter 4) expected to kill someone when he was driving drunk and recklessly. Even the soldier in the Panama scenario was unlikely expecting his shooting would result in a death. Accordingly, the "high probability of death" element of implied malice/extreme recklessness is best understood as an objective standard: the defendant is aware he is creating *some* risk to others, but the jury concludes the risk was *objectively* extreme.

4. *Berry* refers to a "base antisocial motive" as a requirement for proving implied malice. However, in a subsequent decision involving another killing by a dangerous dog, the California Supreme Court clarified the meaning of implied malice:

> The statutory definition of implied malice, a killing by one with an "abandoned and malignant heart," is far from clear in its meaning. Indeed, an instruction in the statutory language could be misleading, for it "could lead the jury to equate the malignant heart with an evil disposition or a despicable character" instead of focusing on a defendant's awareness of the risk created by his or her behavior. "Two lines of decisions developed, reflecting judicial attempts 'to translate this amorphous anatomical characterization of implied malice into a tangible standard a jury can apply.'" Under both lines of decisions, implied malice requires a defendant's awareness of the risk of death to another.
>
> The earlier of these two lines of decisions ... originated in Justice Traynor's concurring opinion in *People v. Thomas*, 41 Cal. 2d 470, 480 (1953), which stated that malice is implied when "the defendant for a base, antisocial motive and with wanton disregard for human life, does an act that involves a high degree of probability that it will result in death." The later line dates from this court's 1966 decision in *People v. Phillips*, 51 Cal. Rptr. 225: Malice is implied when the killing is proximately caused by "an act, the natural consequences of which are dangerous to life, which act was deliberately performed by a person who knows that his conduct endangers the life of another and who acts with conscious disregard for life."

People v. Knoller, 59 Cal. Rptr. 3d 157, 41 Cal. 4th 139, 158 P.3d 731 (2007).

This clarification indicates that base antisocial motive is not required for a finding of implied malice. However, this does not mean such a motive is irrelevant. Instead, it is better understood as a factor among the totality of the evidence a jury will consider to decide whether the defendant acted with a wanton disregard for the value of human life.

D. The Model Penal Code and Extreme Reckless Murder

As introduced above, the MPC dispensed with the term malice; unlike the common law, unintentional murder cannot be based on implied malice. However, as the following case indicates, the same basic equation is utilized to assess when a killing is the result of recklessness that manifests an extreme indifference to human life and is therefore murder; what New York defines as "depraved indifference" murder.

People v. Snyder
937 N.Y.S.2d 429 (2012)
New York Supreme Court

GARRY, J.

[Snyder] Appeals (1) from a judgment of the County Court of Franklin County (Rogers, J.), rendered July 30, 2001, upon a verdict convicting defendant of the crimes of murder in the second degree. . . .

After the January 1996 death of her daughter (born in 1993), defendant was arrested and charged with, among other things, three counts of murder in the second degree, including intentional murder, depraved indifference murder, and depraved indifference murder of a person under 11 years old. She was also charged with attempted intentional murder of her son (born in 1992), and multiple counts of both assault in the first degree and reckless endangerment. In 2001, defendant was convicted by jury verdict of depraved indifference murder, assault in the first degree (four counts) and reckless endangerment in the first degree (eight counts), and was thereafter sentenced to an aggregate prison term of 50 years to life. . . .

A person is guilty of depraved indifference murder when, "[u]nder circumstances evincing a depraved indifference to human life, he [or she] recklessly engages in conduct which creates a grave risk of death to another person, and thereby causes the death of another person" (Penal Law § 125.25 [2]). . . .

Although defendant advances a variety of challenges to her convictions, her primary challenge on appeal relates to the legal sufficiency and weight of the evidence. She argues that the evidence does not support a finding . . . that she possessed the necessary mens rea. . . . We reject these contentions. . . .

The People's case was based entirely on the theory that defendant attempted to cause breathing problems in both of her children by suffocating them for the purpose of collecting government benefits. To that end, the People presented extensive testimony from the numerous pediatricians, specialists, nurses, emergency personnel and social workers who cared for the children or otherwise interacted with defendant and her children from the birth of defendant's son in 1992 until the death of defendant's daughter in 1996. The mostly circumstantial evidence established that both children were admitted to the hospital—after experiencing difficulty breathing and being rushed to the emergency room—on numerous occasions following their births for what appeared to be apnea episodes. Each episode occurred during daytime hours, defendant was the only person present when the symptoms began and she was the sole source of information as to what occurred. Although numerous tests were performed, the results were routinely normal and medical personnel were unable to determine any organic cause for the children's identical breathing problems. One such test performed on defendant's daughter revealed that her apnea originated in the lung area, rather than in the brain, indicating that it was caused by something blocking her airway. According to various medical witnesses, there were other indicators that the children's problems were caused by suffocation, including reports of blood in their noses or mouths and certain recorded information on heart and respiratory rate monitors, which signified that their lungs were healthy but that the oxygen flow had been interrupted for a period of time.

Medical personnel who came in contact with defendant and her children at the hospital observed more than one incident that caused them to suspect that defendant was suffocating them. After one such incident, Donald Swartz, the pediatric pulmonologist for defendant's son, directed that defendant not be left alone with the child while he was in the hospital, and he experienced no further apnea episodes during the remainder of his hospital stay. Swartz thereafter discharged the son with orders that he not be left alone at home with defendant and made arrangements for nurses to regularly visit the home. When the son was later readmitted to the hospital, defendant and the child's father requested that Swartz not be involved in caring for him.

This person was also referred to as defendant's boyfriend or husband.

Subsequently, defendant's daughter was referred to Daniel Shannon, a pediatrician at Massachusetts General Hospital, who diagnosed her with a sinus node dysfunction with a possible seizure disorder and recommended surgery to implant a pacemaker. Despite such surgery, the daughter's apnea episodes continued and she was admitted to the emergency room several times thereafter with reported seizures. No seizures were ever documented during her hospital stays and none were actually witnessed by medical personnel.

This recommendation was in direct conflict with the opinion of Thomas Truman, the director of the pediatric intensive care unit of Massachusetts General Hospital, who also had an opportunity to examine defendant's daughter prior to her pacemaker surgery and opined that her life threatening events were occurring because she was being suffocated.

Ultimately, in January 1996, defendant's daughter was rushed to the local hospital emergency room in respiratory and cardiac arrest. She was transferred to another hospital, where she died a few days later. Her death was determined to have resulted from a lack of oxygen and inadequate blood flow to the brain. The chief medical examiner who performed the autopsy on defendant's daughter testified that he was unable to rule out suffocation as the cause of death, and that he believed that the manner of death was "consistent with a homicide." The People's expert witness similarly testified that, in her opinion, both children's frequent hospitalizations resulted from suffocation, which carried a significant risk of death, and that the death of defendant's daughter was, in fact, caused by suffocation.

Pamela Marshall, an inmate at the Franklin County Jail when defendant was incarcerated there after her arrest, also testified for the People. According to Marshall, defendant spoke with her about the case on one occasion and told Marshall that she and her husband had been having financial difficulties and decided to try to get disability benefits for her children after learning that a friend had received such benefits for a child who was having breathing problems. During that conversation, defendant described several incidents—which were consistent with the testimony of other witnesses—in which she had attempted to induce such breathing problems in her children. Defendant also told Marshall that, on the day her daughter was taken to the hospital just prior to her death, she had attempted several times to put a pillow over her face in order to cause breathing problems in anticipation of the arrival of a home health nurse that day. Defendant stated that she "didn't mean for it to go as far as it did," but that the nurse who was scheduled to come to the house had arrived late.

Defendant also admitted to a police investigator that she had attempted to smother her daughter once shortly after her birth. She was not charged with any crime occurring on that earlier date.

In addition, a claims representative for the Supplemental Security Income (hereinafter SSI) program testified regarding defendant's applications for disability benefits on behalf of her children based upon alleged lung problems/obstructive apnea, which applications were ultimately successful. The People attempted to demonstrate a correlation between the timing of various aspects of the application process—including reviews of entitlement to benefits and payments made—and the occurrence or "remission" of the children's apnea events in order to prove that defendant induced their problems at particular times in her effort to obtain or maintain eligibility for such benefits.

Dapheny Wright, a salesperson for a mobile home company, testified that she first encountered defendant and her boyfriend in 1995 when they purchased a mobile home. Wright was concerned about their ability to secure financing for the purchase, as their income consisted of public assistance and SSI benefits. When Wright asked defendant whether the SSI benefits were permanent, defendant responded that the benefits were for her daughter, who was disabled due to "respiratory problems and weak blood," that she anticipated the condition to be a long-term disability and that the benefits would continue for the rest of the child's life. . . .

. . . .

Mens rea may be demonstrated by circumstantial evidence (*see People v. Manos,* 73 A.D.3d 1333, 1334, 901 N.Y.S.2d 408 [2010], *lv. denied* 15 N.Y.3d 807, 908 N.Y.S.2d 166, 934 N.E.2d 900 [2010]). In the event of an unintentional killing of a single individual, depraved indifference may be established, as relevant here, where the "'defendant—acting with a conscious objective not to kill but to harm—engages in torture or a brutal, prolonged and ultimately fatal course of conduct against a particularly vulnerable victim'" (*People v. Taylor,* 15 N.Y.3d 518, 523, 914 N.Y.S.2d 76, 939 N.E.2d 1206 [2010], quoting *People v. Suarez,* 6 N.Y.3d at 212, 811 N.Y.S.2d 267, 844 N.E.2d 721; *see People v. Smith,* 41 A.D.3d 964, 966, 838 N.Y.S.2d 690 [2007], *lv. denied* 9 N.Y.3d 881, 842 N.Y.S.2d 793, 874 N.E.2d 760 [2007]). The defendant's actions must "reflect wanton cruelty, brutality or callousness [and be] combined with utter indifference to the life or safety" of the victim (*People v. Varmette,* 70 A.D.3d 1167, 1169, 895 N.Y.S.2d 239 [2010], *lv. denied* 14 N.Y.3d 845, 901 N.Y.S.2d 152, 927 N.E.2d 573 [2010] [internal quotation marks and citations omitted]; *see People v. Ford,* 43 A.D.3d 571, 573, 840 N.Y.S.2d 668 [2007], *lv. denied* 9 N.Y.3d 1033, 852 N.Y.S.2d 19, 881 N.E.2d 1206 [2008]). The Court of Appeals has stated that "'depraved indifference is best understood as an utter disregard for the value of human life—a willingness to act not because one intends harm, but because one simply doesn't care whether grievous harm results or not'" (*People v. Feingold,* 7 N.Y.3d at 296, 819 N.Y.S.2d 691, 852 N.E.2d 1163, quoting *People v. Suarez,* 6 N.Y.3d at 214, 811 N.Y.S.2d 267, 844 N.E.2d 721). As set forth above, the proof here revealed that defendant repeatedly suffocated her two helpless children and forced them to undergo unnecessary medical procedures, callously causing repeated injury to each of them without regard to the risk of grievous harm posed by her actions, which ultimately resulted in her daughter's death. Defendant's indifference to the lives and safety of her children was further demonstrated in the testimony describing her behavior on the day that she last suffocated her daughter; the person whom defendant later described as a "home health nurse" arrived at defendant's home to find that the child was not breathing, had no pulse, was limp, colorless and "ice cold," and that defendant had not called for help. This individual, a parent monitor, testified at trial that although she repeatedly instructed defendant to perform rescue breathing, defendant did not do so. Instead, defendant "just [sat] there," tearless and doing nothing, while the monitor summoned rescue personnel and tended to the child. Defendant's state of apparent unconcern continued at the hospital; while medical personnel attempted to resuscitate her daughter, defendant remained outside the treatment room, calmly eating snacks.

The evidence revealed that defendant's sole reason for wishing that her children would not die as a result of her repeated, brutal acts was so that she might continue to torture them, and thereby continue to receive disability benefits. This wish—to be able to indefinitely continue brutalizing her children for financial gain—does not and cannot constitute anything but the most "'utter disregard for the value of human life'" . . . and for her children's lives. Indeed, defendant's wish to continue to profit from her children's pain and suffering was cruelly depraved. Her desire for her children to continue living only to serve her cruel purpose cannot legally be deemed to constitute even the smallest shred of concern for their lives or safety. Thus, we find that the evidence of depraved indifference is legally sufficient to support defendant's convictions. . . .

Notes & Questions

1. Notice how Snyder's motive contradicted the assertion that she intended to kill—either had the purpose to kill or knew with substantial certainty her conduct would cause death. Her motive to continue to defraud the government necessitated keeping the child victim alive. As a result, while the risk to human life she created was unquestionably extreme, and while it was easily inferred that she knew she was creating *some* risk of death, it is unlikely she was subjectively aware of a substantial certainty she would kill her child. Her depravity, however, justified the murder conviction.

2. Do you think her base anti-social motive—to commit felony fraud against the government—serves to aggravate the level of depravity? It was obviously terrible that she subjected her children to this abuse, but doing so to reap a criminally fraudulent windfall seems to make her misconduct even more depraved.

3. The MPC defines unintentional murder as a killing caused by reckless conduct that manifests an extreme indifference to human life; the New York statute uses the term depraved indifference to human life; the common law uses wanton disregard for human life. While terminology varies among jurisdictions, the basic equation is constant: a finding that the extremity of risk created by the defendant was sufficiently extreme to warrant a murder conviction.

III. A Graphic Approach to "Expected" vs. "Unexpected" Killings

Having now studied intentional and unintentional killings, it should be clear that either may qualify as murder or manslaughter. What is useful is to consider *what to look for* in a factual situation to properly assess the level of culpability. For intentional killings, look for evidence of a sudden heat of passion (or imperfect self-defense) that may prevent proof of malice (in an MPC jurisdiction, extreme emotional disturbance) and "downgrade" the intentional killing from murder to manslaughter. For an unintentional killing, look for evidence of extreme risk creation—the "he's going to get someone killed" facts—that "upgrade" the unintentional killing from involuntary manslaughter to implied malice murder (in an MPC jurisdiction, extreme indifference murder).

DEATH AS AN EXPECTED OUTCOME OF DEF'S CONDUCT: THINK MURDER, THEN LOOK FOR AN ERASER	
Common Law	**Model Penal Code**

Murder
Unlawful killing **WITH** malice
Express malice
  Intent to kill
  Intent to inflict grievous bodily harm
	Murder
	Killing done with "purpose"
	Killing done with "knowledge of substantial probability of death"

1st Degree Murder: An express malice murder PLUS
 	
  Premeditation & Deliberation (P&D) OR
  Proof murder falls into statutory category of 1st degree
  *Remember voluntary intoxication may erase P&D
	No degrees of murder
	
	Gravity of murder is determined on a case by case basis

Voluntary Manslaughter
A presumptive murder **DOWNGRADED** because malice is erased by:
  Provocation producing sudden heat of passion
  Diminished mental capacity
  Imperfect self-defense
	Manslaughter
	A presumptive murder **DOWNGRADED** due to evidence of EXTREME EMOTIONAL DISTURBANCE (EED)

DEATH AS AN UNEXPECTED OUTCOME OF DEF'S UNJUSTIFIED RISK CREATION: THINK MANSLAUGHTER, THEN LOOK FOR AN ESCALATOR	

Murder
Implied malice
  Reckless (knew risk and ignored)
  PLUS evidence proving a
WANTON DISREGARD FOR THE VALUE OF HUMAN LIFE (WDVHL)
	Murder
	Killing resulting from:
	  Reckless conduct *PLUS* evidence proving an
	EXTREME INDIFFERENCE TO HUMAN LIFE (EIHL)

Involuntary Manslaughter
Unlawful killing **WITHOUT** malice
  A killing resulting from reckless conduct *THAT DOES NOT* manifest a WDVHL
  A killing that results from criminal/culpable negligent conduct
  (criminal/gross negligence)
	Manslaughter
	A killing resulting from reckless conduct *THAT DOES NOT* manifest EIHL
	
	Negligent Homicide: Killing caused by criminal/gross negligence

Formative Assessments

1. Defendant is the supervisor of a team that is doing some renovations on a home. The worker is installing a very large ceiling light fixture/fan. The ceiling is 18 feet high, and the fixture/fan weighs about 90 pounds, and is being installed above the center point of the living room. During the installation, another worker notices that one of the anchor parts is missing. He tells Defendant that he is worried the fixture might not be properly secured. Defendant responds, "Don't worry about it. It will be fine." The other worker responds that he is worried it might fall out of the ceiling, but the Defendant tells him to shut up and get back to work. Two weeks later, the fixture falls from the ceiling and kills one of the children who lives in the home when it lands on him. Based on this evidence, would you charge the Defendant with a criminal homicide? If so, what crime do you think you could prove?

2. Defendant gets drunk while hanging out in his local pub for an evening. After drinking for about 3 hours, he pulls out a pistol and tells the bartender, "Hey, check out what I bought today." The bartender says, "Put that away, and be careful with it." Defendant responds, "Stop worrying, it isn't loaded." He then starts tossing the pistol from one hand to the other. The pistol falls from his hand, and when it hits the floor,

it discharges a round, which hits and kills another customer. Defendant is shocked and says, "But I thought it wasn't loaded." Defendant is tried for involuntary manslaughter. He testifies that he was so drunk, he forgot that he had loaded the pistol earlier that day and honestly believed it was unloaded. If the jury believes Defendant, he should be convicted of:

A. Involuntary manslaughter.

B. Negligent homicide.

3. Homer lived on the second floor of a small convenience store/gas station that he owned. One night, he refused to sell Augie a six-pack of beer after hours, saying he could not violate the state laws. Augie became enraged and deliberately drove his car into one of the gasoline pumps, severing it from its base. There was an ensuing explosion causing a ball of fire to go from the underground gasoline tank into the building. As a result, the building burned to the ground and Homer was killed. In a common law jurisdiction, what is the most serious crime you believe is supported by these facts?

4. Adam and Greg were attending the Texas Longhorns vs. Oklahoma Sooners game held at Dallas Cowboys Stadium. They did not know each other, but were seated near each other in the stadium when a brawl broke out between Longhorn and Sooner fans. Adam decided to partake in the action, swung wildly and punched Greg on the side of his head. Greg was not even knocked down, but started complaining of a headache about 30 minutes later. Greg collapsed soon after and died at the stadium. An autopsy revealed that Greg suffered from an unknown illness that made his skull unusually weak, which contributed substantially to his death from the blow to his head. What is the most likely outcome if Adam is tried on a charge of murder?

A. Guilty of murder.

B. Guilty of voluntary manslaughter.

C. Guilty of involuntary manslaughter.

D. Guilty of battery.

5. Defendant is celebrating New Year's Eve in downtown Big City in an area with lots of high-rise apartment buildings. Many other celebrants are out on their apartment porches. Defendant suddenly takes out his 9mm pistol and starts firing celebratory shots into the air. One of the shots ricochets off the side of an apartment building and hits a woman on a porch, killing her instantly. What is the most serious crime supported by this evidence?

A. Murder.

B. Involuntary manslaughter.

C. Negligent homicide.

D. Unlawful discharge of a firearm.

6. Jane is a nurse on night shift in the hospital. She is responsible for administering medications to patients in the intensive care unit. One night, during an especially busy shift, Jane mistakenly gives a patient the wrong dose of medication. Sadly, the patient dies as a result. When questioned, Jane admits she was in such a rush she overlooked a change in the doctor's order that went into effect earlier that day. Jane is charged with criminally negligent homicide. What is the best argument you could make in her defense?

Chapter 9

Felony Murder

I. The Felony Murder Rule

One of the most controversial doctrines in criminal law is the felony murder rule. In its broadest form, the felony murder doctrine allows the defendant to be convicted of murder for any killing proximately connected to the attempt, commission, or immediate flight from the alleged felony. In common law jurisdictions, malice is automatically established by this equation; in jurisdictions that define murder with a different criminal mental state, felony murder is an established form of murder. Accordingly, the controversy stems from the fact that the defendant can be convicted of murder without proof of a defined criminal mental state that set in motion the act which caused the death, as proof of the attempted or completed felony serves as a substitute for that mens rea.

Every other criminal homicide conviction requires proof beyond a reasonable doubt of concurrence between the requisite mens rea for the homicide offense and the killing: that the defendant acted with malice or some other defined mens rea element. The felony murder rule dispenses with this proof requirement. To obtain a conviction, the prosecution need only prove the mens rea required for conviction of the underlying felony. Once the underlying felony is proven, the offender is strictly liable for the death that was proximately caused by the felony. For instance, suppose that D robs a bank, and during the robbery, the teller dies of a heart attack caused by the fright of the event. If D is charged with felony murder, with robbery being the predicate felony, then D will be guilty of felony murder if the prosecution proves the elements of robbery, since the heart attack was the direct result of the robbery. The felony murder rule would apply even if the victim had a preexisting heart condition, as long as the robbery facilitated the heart attack. *See People v. Stamp,* 82 Cal. Rptr. 598 (1969). Or imagine a defendant is robbing a convenience store and gets frightened and drops his pistol to run. If the pistol goes off and kills a bystander, even if accidentally, the defendant is guilty of murder pursuant to the felony murder rule.

Because of the controversial nature of the felony murder rule a few states, including Kentucky, Hawaii and Michigan, have no felony murder rule at all. Furthermore, the MPC rejects the felony murder rule:

> Punishment for homicide obtains only when the deed is done with a state of mind that makes it reprehensible as well as unfortunate. Murder is invariably

punished as a heinous offense. . . . Sanctions of such gravity demand justification, and their imposition must be premised on the confluence of conduct
and culpability. Thus, under the Model Code, as at common law, murder
occurs if a person kills purposely, knowingly, or with extreme recklessness.
Lesser culpability yields lesser liability, and a person who inadvertently kills
another under circumstances not amounting to negligence is guilty of no
crime at all. The felony-murder rule contradicts this scheme. It bases conviction of murder not on any proven culpability with respect to homicide but on
liability for another crime. The underlying felony carries its own penalty and
the additional punishment for murder is therefore gratuitous.

See Model Penal Code § 210.2, Commentary.

II. The Basic Rule: Killing in Furtherance of a Felony

The felony murder rule seems simple at first blush. However, it is not as simple as
it seems. The prosecution must prove a connection between the death and the felony.
To obtain a felony murder conviction, a prosecutor must prove beyond a reasonable
doubt that the defendant was engaged in a felony upon which felony murder may be
predicated and that the death resulted from the felony. If the killing has no connection to the felony, then a felony murder conviction will not be possible. For instance,
if the defendant's intent is to kill the victim for cheating on his wife, and after killing
him, the defendant decides to steal his car, then he is not guilty of felony murder,
since the robbery was an afterthought formed after the killing had already occurred.
Furthermore, in order to be convicted of felony murder, the prosecution must prove
that the death occurred during the commission or attempted commission of the
felony. Once the defendant has completed the felony or has terminated the attempt
to commit the felony and reaches a point of temporary safety, then he is no longer
liable for felony murder.

People v. Fuller

150 Cal. Rptr. 515 (1978)
California Court of Appeals

FRANSON, J.

This appeal challenges the California felony-murder rule as it applies to an unintentionally caused death during a high speed automobile chase following the commission of a nonviolent, daylight burglary of an unattended motor vehicle. Solely by
force of precedent we hold that the felony-murder rule applies and respondents can
be prosecuted for first degree murder. . . .

The pertinent facts are as follows: On Sunday, February 20, 1977, at about 8:30 a.m.,
uniformed Cadet Police Officer Guy Ballesteroz was on routine patrol in his vehicle,

proceeding southbound on Blackstone Avenue in the City of Fresno. As the officer approached the Fresno Dodge car lot, he saw an older model Plymouth parked in front of the lot. He also saw respondents rolling two tires apiece toward the Plymouth. His suspicions aroused, the officer radioed the dispatcher and requested that a police unit be sent.

Officer Ballesteroz kept the respondents under observation as he proceeded past the car lot and stopped at the next intersection. As he reached that point he saw the respondents stop rolling the tires and walk to the Plymouth on the street. Ballesteroz made a U-turn and headed northbound on Blackstone. The respondents got into the Plymouth and drove away "really fast." Thereafter, a high speed chase ensued which eventually resulted in respondents' car running a red light at the intersection of Blackstone and Barstow Avenues and striking another automobile which had entered the intersection. The driver of the other automobile was killed. Respondents were arrested at the scene. The chase from the car lot covered some 7 miles and lasted approximately 10 to 12 minutes. During the chase the respondents' car narrowly missed colliding with several other cars including two police vehicles that were positioned to block their escape.

Later investigation revealed that four locked Dodge vans at the car lot had been forcibly entered and the spare tires removed. Fingerprints from both of the respondents were found on the jack stands in some of the vans. . . .

Penal Code section 189 provides, in pertinent part: "All murder . . . which is committed *in the perpetration of,* or attempt to perpetrate, arson, rape, robbery, *burglary,* mayhem, or [lewd acts with a minor], is murder of the first degree; . . . ." (Italics added.) This statute imposes strict liability for deaths committed in the course of one of the enumerated felonies whether the killing was caused intentionally, negligently, or merely accidentally. Malice is imputed and need not be shown. The purpose of the felony-murder rule is to deter felons from killing negligently or accidentally.

Burglary falls expressly within the purview of California's first degree felony-murder rule. Any burglary within Penal Code section 459 is sufficient to invoke the rule. Whether or not the particular burglary was dangerous to human life is of no legal import.

The meaning of murder committed "in the perpetration of" a felony within Penal Code section 189 also is clear. The Supreme Court has stated that this language does not require a strict causal relation between the felony and the killing; it is sufficient if both are "parts of one continuous transaction." Flight following a felony is considered part of the same transaction as long as the felon has not reached a "place of temporary safety." Whether the defendant has reached such a place of safety is a question of fact for the jury.

We deem it appropriate, however, to make a few observations concerning the irrationality of applying the felony-murder rule in the present case. In *People v. Washington, supra,* 62 Cal.2d 777, 783, a case limiting the rule's application to killings committed by the defendant or his accomplice, our Supreme Court stated: "The felony-murder rule has been criticized on the grounds that in almost all cases in which it is applied it is unnecessary and that it erodes the relation between criminal liability and moral culpability. Although it is the law in this state, *it should not be extended beyond any rational function that it is designed to serve.*" (Italics added.) In *People v. Phillips* (1966) 64 Cal.2d 574 [51 Cal. Rptr. 225, 414 P.2d 353], the court elaborated: "We have thus recognized that the felony-murder doctrine expresses a highly artificial concept that deserves no extension beyond its required application. Indeed, the rule itself has been abandoned by the courts of England, where it had its inception. It has been subjected to severe and sweeping criticism." The *Phillips* court explained, "The felony-murder doctrine has been censured not only because it artificially imposes malice as to one crime because of defendant's commission of another but because it anachronistically resurrects from a bygone age a 'barbaric' concept that has been discarded in the place of its origin. . . ."

The Supreme Court has recently reaffirmed its dislike of the felony-murder rule. . . . The literature is replete with criticism of the rule . . . Nonetheless, as previously explained the force of precedent requires the application of the first degree felony-murder rule to the instant case. . . .

Notes and Questions

1. Why can Fuller be convicted of felony murder despite the fact that the death occurred at least 7 miles and 10-12 minutes from the scene of the burglary?

2. Suppose Fuller and his accomplices had made it home without killing anyone, but thereafter the officer recognized him as the perpetrator of the earlier burglary, and while evading the officer, Fuller hit another, car and that driver died. Would he be guilty of felony murder?

3. Unlike common law burglary, which restricts the crime to the breaking and entering of a dwelling, California's burglary definition is much more expansive. In California, a burglary can occur by entering any "house, room apartment . . . , or vehicle . . . when the doors are locked. . . ."

4. Why, according to the court, is it "of no legal import" whether the burglary was inherently dangerous to life?

5. Given how critical the court is of the felony murder rule, why didn't it just affirm the lower court's order overturning Fuller's conviction?

6. Although proof of mens rea with regard to the killing is not required to obtain a felony murder conviction, some states do enhance the punishment in the event that the killing was done intentionally. For instance, in Texas, a person who "intentionally commits the murder in the course of committing or attempting to commit kidnapping, burglary, robbery, aggravated sexual assault, arson, obstruction for retaliation, or terroristic threat . . ." is guilty of capital murder and may be sentenced to death, whereas an offender who commits felony murder but does not intentionally kill faces a prison term between 5 and 99 years.

7. Note that the court indicates the rationale of felony murder is to deter negligent killings during the course of committing a felony. Is it logical to seek to deter negligence?

8. Defendant is charged with felony murder based on the following statute: "All unlawful killings during the attempt, commission, or immediate flight from burglary, arson, rape, robbery, kidnapping, or felony use of an explosive device is murder in the first degree." The facts indicate defendant, who lives on a remote farm by himself, was experimenting with different explosives because he needed to clear a field and wanted to use a small explosive to break up some massive rocks. On the day of the alleged offense, a hiker who got lost happened to be in a ravine below the area where defendant set off one of his experimental explosives. When he set it off, he heard a scream, and rushed to the ravine to find the victim mortally wounded from a tree branch blown off by the explosion. Any use of an improvised explosive device without a permit is a felony in the jurisdiction. Defendant moves to dismiss the first degree murder charge. You are the judge. Do you grant the motion?

Practice Pointer

Prosecutors typically will opt to seek a felony murder conviction over other murder convictions or even manslaughter convictions, because a felony murder charge relieves them of the burden of proving the defendant's mens rea with respect to the death that resulted from the felony. There's no downside to seeking a felony murder conviction for the prosecutor, since the penalty for felony murder is at least equal to other murder charges and often might be more severe. For instance, in many jurisdictions, felony murder is designated as first-degree murder, and in those that have retained the death penalty, felony murder is a capital crime which subjects the defendant to a possible death sentence upon conviction.

Does this mean felony murder is a strict liability crime? No. While the prosecutor need not allege or prove mens rea related to the killing, felony murder always requires proof beyond a reasonable doubt that the defendant committed or attempted to commit the alleged felony upon which the felony murder charge is predicated. This is known as the *predicate* felony. If the prosecutor can't prove the alleged felony, either because of a failure to prove the requisite elements or because of an affirmative defense *to the felony*, there is no basis for a felony murder conviction. This means any defense to the alleged predicate felony is *ipso facto* a defense to the felony murder. It also means that conviction (or acquittal) for felony murder is considered a final verdict on the alleged felony as well, meaning double jeopardy bars subsequently trying the defendant for just the felony.

III. Limitations

Because of the potentially overbroad impact of the felony murder rule—a murder conviction absent proof of actual mens rea related to the killing—most jurisdictions that have adopted the felony murder rule have limited its application so that it does not apply to every death that results from or attempted commission of every felony. In order to obtain a felony murder conviction, a prosecutor must overcome five obstacles. First, the felony murder rule is limited by the felonies that may be properly alleged as the predicate felony. The prosecutor may only allege felony murder based on the "right" type of felony. If the statutory definition of murder enumerates, or indicates, the felonies that result in felony murder, these are the "right" type because the legislature has made that decision. In some cases, however, there will be no such enumeration, which allows conviction only based on felonies that are "inherently dangerous to human life." While some felonies are obviously "inherently dangerous"—which includes almost all original common law felonies—the inclusion of many *malum prohibitum* felonies in modern criminal statutes means the line is not always easy to draw, as the cases below illustrate. Some jurisdictions consider only the elements of the felony in determining whether it is dangerous, while others consider the circumstances of the commission of the felony in determining whether it is inherently dangerous.

Second, in many jurisdictions, the alleged felony must be "independent" from the killing. This means that if the offender's only purpose is to physically harm the victim—in other words, if the primary felonious motive is assaultive in nature—then the felony is too intertwined with the homicide and cannot be the predicate felony for felony-murder purposes. While this may seem odd (excluding, for example, aggravated battery from the "right" type of felony category), it is a limitation intended to bar the prosecutor from transforming a crime where assaultive conduct was the primary motive into murder *automatically* whenever the victim dies. Such a rule would effectively nullify the crime of manslaughter.

Third, the deadly act must be inflicted during the attempt, commission, or immediate flight from the felony. As noted above, this is what is meant by "in furtherance" of the felony. Notably, however, there is no requirement that an attempted felony be completed (obviously, all completed crimes begin with an attempt). So long as the deadly injury was inflicted during the attempt, it is irrelevant whether the defendant completed the target offense.

Fourth, there must be a proximate causal connection between the felony and the death. Traditionally, this rule has been liberally applied, but it does limit liability where the death is unrelated to the felony or is such an abnormal outcome of the felony that it was not foreseeable. For example, if a defendant is in the midst of a bank robbery when the bank manager, completely unaware of the robbery, dies of a heart attack, there would be no proximate causal connection between the felony and the death.

Fifth, the killing must be attributed to the defendant. If the victim dies at the defendant's hand, the killing will be attributed to him so long as it was proximately caused by the felony. However, where the victim dies at the hand of someone *other than* the defendant (in other words, there is a third-party killer), jurisdictions are split on whether the killing may be attributed to the defendant. Under the original felony murder doctrine, all felons were responsible for any killing by any person so long as the death was proximately caused by the felony. In this sense, jurisdictions that retain this proximate cause rule have only four steps to felony murder. But in a slight majority of jurisdictions, the liability of a surviving felon for a killing at the hand of a third-party during the felony is limited. In these jurisdictions, the prosecutor must prove that the killing was committed by one of the parties to the felony—in other words, that the third-party killer was acting as an "agent" of the defendant. For instance, if during a robbery, a police officer or innocent bystander kills either an innocent bystander, another officer or one of the co-felons, then defendant is not guilty of felony murder, since neither he nor one of his "agents" committed the killing. Finally, in some jurisdictions, the death of a co-felon is excluded from the scope of felony murder liability.

If the prosecutor satisfies these requirements—proof beyond a reasonable doubt the defendant attempted or committed a felony that may be alleged for felony murder; that the deadly act occurred during the attempt, commission, or immediate flight from the felony; that the death was proximately caused by the felony; and that the killing is properly attributable to the defendant—a felony murder conviction is appropriate. It is important, however, to bear in mind that *if* felony murder is blocked by one of these obstacles, it does not mean a murder conviction is barred. The evidence may still be sufficient to convict a defendant and his co-felons for murder by proving the mens rea required for murder (for example, depraved heart murder) or for a lesser homicide offense such as involuntary manslaughter.

A. Inherently Dangerous Felony Limitation

1. Enumerated versus Unenumerated Felonies

In every jurisdiction that employs the felony murder rule, the underlying felony must be dangerous to human life. Some jurisdictions specifically enumerate the felonies which the legislature has defined as inherently dangerous and, therefore, which can be the predicate felony in a felony murder prosecution. For instance, in California, the felonies that can be the subject of a first-degree felony murder prosecution are specifically enumerated:

California Penal Code § 189(a):

> All murder . . . that is committed in the perpetration of, or attempt to perpetrate, arson, rape, carjacking, robbery, burglary, mayhem, kidnapping, train wrecking, . . . is murder of the first degree.

In jurisdictions such as California, only those specifically enumerated felonies may be the predicate of a first-degree felony murder prosecution. By contrast, in some states, the felony murder statutes do not enumerate the felonies that may be alleged as the predicate felony. Indeed, even in states like California that enumerate felonies for first-degree felony murder, other felonies may be alleged for a second-degree felony murder prosecution. When the felony is not enumerated, it must be "dangerous" or "serious." The Texas felony murder statute is an example:

Texas Penal Code § 19.02(b)(3):

> A person commits [murder] if he . . . (3) commits or attempts to commit a felony, other than manslaughter, and in the course of and in furtherance of the commission or attempt or in immediate flight from the commission or attempt, he commits or attempts to commit an act clearly dangerous to human life that causes the death of an individual.

In jurisdictions that do not enumerate the predicate felonies, it is up to the courts to determine which felonies qualify as the "right" type of felony for felony murder. This is a legal question: has the prosecution properly alleged the crime? If the court determines that the felony *is not* inherently dangerous, it should dismiss the felony murder charge.

Courts in these jurisdictions use one of two approaches in determining whether a felony is inherently dangerous. Some jurisdictions use the "abstract" approach. Courts in these jurisdictions consider the elements of a felony in the abstract and determine whether, based on the elements of the crime alone, the felony is one clearly dangerous to human life. This is done by asking whether it is plausible that the felony *could* be committed in a way that *does not* create an inherent or serious danger to life. If the answer is yes, it means the felony is not *always* inherently dangerous and therefore cannot be alleged as a felony murder predicate. Note that courts in these jurisdictions do not consider the facts of the particular killing in determining whether the felony is inherently dangerous to human life. Other jurisdictions use the "circumstance" approach. Courts in these jurisdictions consider not only the abstract definition of the felony but also the circumstances in which it was committed in determining whether the felony was sufficiently dangerous for felony murder purposes. This is obviously a far more permissive test considering that any application will involve a death resulting from the felony.

The following two cases illustrate the application of the two approaches.

a. Abstract Approach

People v. Burroughs

35 Cal. 3d 824 (1984)
California Supreme Court

GRODIN, J.

Defendant Burroughs, a 77-year-old self-styled "healer," appeals from a judgment convicting him of unlawfully selling drugs, compounds, or devices for alleviation or cure of cancer; felony practicing medicine without a license, now; and second degree felony murder in the treatment and death of Lee Swatsenbarg.

Burroughs challenges his second degree murder conviction by contending the felonious unlicensed practice of medicine is not an "inherently dangerous" felony, as that term has been used in our previous decisions to describe and limit the kinds of offenses which will support application of the felony-murder rule. We conclude that while the felonious unlicensed practice of medicine can, in many circumstances, pose a threat to the health of the individual being treated, commission of that crime as defined by statute does not inevitably pose danger to human life. Under well-established principles it cannot, therefore, be made the predicate for a finding of murder, absent proof of malice. As a consequence, we must reverse defendant's second degree felony-murder conviction. . . .

Lee Swatsenbarg had been diagnosed by the family physician as suffering from terminal leukemia. Unable to accept impending death, the 24-year-old Swatsenbarg unsuccessfully sought treatment from a variety of traditional medical sources. He and his wife then began to participate in Bible study, hoping that through faith Lee might be cured. Finally, on the advice of a mutual acquaintance who had heard of defendant's ostensible successes in healing others, Lee turned to defendant for treatment.

During the first meeting between Lee and defendant, the latter described his method of curing cancer. This method included consumption of a unique "lemonade," exposure to colored lights, and a brand of vigorous massage administered by defendant. Defendant remarked that he had successfully treated "thousands" of people, including a number of physicians. He suggested the Swatsenbargs purchase a copy of his book, *Healing for the Age of Enlightenment*. If after reading the book Lee wished to begin defendant's unorthodox treatment, defendant would commence caring for Lee immediately. During the 30 days designated for the treatment, Lee would have to avoid contact with his physician.

Lee read the book, submitted to the conditions delineated by defendant, and placed himself under defendant's care. Defendant instructed Lee to drink the lemonade, salt water, and herb tea, but consume nothing more for the ensuing 30 days. At defendant's behest, the Swatsenbargs bought a lamp equipped with some colored plastic sheets, to bathe Lee in various tints of light. Defendant also agreed to massage Lee from time to time, for an additional fee per session.

Rather than improve, within two weeks Lee's condition began rapidly to deteriorate. He developed a fever, and was growing progressively weaker. Defendant counseled Lee that all was proceeding according to plan, and convinced the young man to postpone a bone marrow test urged by his doctor.

During the next week Lee became increasingly ill. He was experiencing severe pain in several areas, including his abdomen, and vomiting frequently. Defendant administered "deep" abdominal massages on two successive days, each time telling Lee he would soon recuperate.

Lee did not recover as defendant expected, however, and the patient began to suffer from convulsions and excruciating pain. He vomited with increasing frequency. Despite defendant's constant attempts at reassurance, the Swatsenbargs began to panic when Lee convulsed for a third time after the latest abdominal massage. Three and a half weeks into the treatment, the couple spent the night at defendant's house, where Lee died of a massive hemorrhage of the mesentery in the abdomen. The evidence presented at trial strongly suggested the hemorrhage was the direct result of the massages performed by defendant.

Defendant's conviction of second degree felony murder arose out of the jury's determination that Lee Swatsenbarg's death was a homicide committed by defendant while he was engaged in the felonious unlicensed practice of medicine. The trial court ruled that an underlying felony of unlicensed practice of medicine could support a felony-murder conviction because such practice was a felony "inherently dangerous to human life." Consequently, the trial judge instructed the jury that if the homicide resulted directly from the commission of this felony, the homicide was felony murder of the second degree. This instruction was erroneous as a matter of law.

When an individual causes the death of another in furtherance of the perpetration of a felony, the resulting offense may be felony murder. This court has long held the felony-murder rule in disfavor. "We have repeatedly stated that felony murder is a 'highly artificial concept' which 'deserves no extension beyond its required application.'" . . . For the reasons stated below, we hold that to apply the felony-murder rule to the facts of the instant case would be an unwarranted extension of this highly "anachronistic" notion.

At the outset we must determine whether the underlying felony is "inherently dangerous to human life." We formulated this standard because "[if] the felony is not inherently dangerous, it is highly improbable that the potential felon will be deterred; he will not anticipate that any injury or death might arise solely from the fact that he will commit the felony."

In assessing whether the felony is inherently dangerous to human life, "we look to the elements of the felony in the abstract, not the particular 'facts' of the case." This form of analysis is compelled because there is a killing in every case where the rule might potentially be applied. If in such circumstances a court were to examine the particular facts of the case prior to establishing whether the underlying felony is inherently dangerous, the court might well be led to conclude the rule applicable despite any unfairness which might redound to the defendant by so broad an application: the existence of the dead victim might appear to lead inexorably to the conclusion that the underlying felony is exceptionally hazardous. We continue to resist such unjustifiable bootstrapping.

In our application of the second degree felony-murder analysis we are guided by the bipartite standard articulated by this court in *People v. Henderson, supra*, 19 Cal.3d 86. In *Henderson*, we stated a reviewing court should look first to the primary element of the offense at issue, then to the "factors elevating the offense to a felony," to determine whether the felony, taken in the abstract, is inherently dangerous to human life, or whether it possibly could be committed without creating such peril. In this examination we are required to view the statutory definition of the offense as a whole, taking into account even nonhazardous ways of violating the provisions of the law which do not necessarily pose a threat to human life.

The primary element of the offense in question here is the practice of medicine without a license. The statute defines such practice as "treating the sick or afflicted." One can certainly conceive of treatment of the sick or afflicted which has quite innocuous results—the affliction at stake could be a common cold, or a sprained finger, and the form of treatment an admonition to rest in bed and drink fluids or the application of ice to mild swelling. Thus, we do not find inherent dangerousness at this stage of our investigation.

The next level of analysis takes us to consideration of the factors which elevate the unlicensed practice of medicine to a felony: "circumstances or conditions which cause or create a risk of great bodily harm, serious mental or physical illness, *or death*." That the Legislature referred to "death" as a separate risk, and in the disjunctive, strongly suggests the Legislature perceived that one may violate the proscription against the felonious practice of medicine without a license and yet not necessarily endanger human life. . . .

Moreover, our analysis of precedent in this area reveals that the few times we have found an underlying felony inherently dangerous (so that it would support a conviction of felony murder), the offense has been tinged with malevolence totally absent from the facts of this case. In *People v. Mattison* (1971) 4 Cal.3d 177 [93 Cal. Rptr. 185, 481 P.2d 193], we held that poisoning food, drink, or medicine with intent to injure was inherently dangerous. The wilful [*sic*] and malicious burning of an automobile (located in a garage beneath an occupied home) was ruled inherently dangerous in *People v. Nichols* (1970) 3 Cal.3d 150, 162-163 [89 Cal. Rptr. 721, 474 P.2d 673]. Finally, we held kidnaping to be such an offense in *People v. Ford, supra*, 60 Cal.2d 772, 795 . . . .

To hold, as we do today, that a violation of section 2053 [practicing medicine without a license] is not inherently so dangerous that by its very nature, it cannot be committed without creating a substantial risk that someone will be killed, is consistent with our previous decisions in which the underlying felony has been held not inherently hazardous. We have so held where the underlying felony was felony false imprisonment (*People v. Henderson, supra*, 19 Cal.3d 86), possession of a concealable firearm by an ex-felon (*People v. Satchell, supra*, 6 Cal.3d 28), escape from a city or county penal facility (*People v. Lopez, supra*, 6 Cal.3d 45), and in other, less potentially threatening circumstances.

Finally, the underlying purpose of the felony-murder rule, to encourage felons to commit their offenses without perpetrating unnecessary violence which might result in a homicide, would not be served by applying the rule to the facts of this case. Defendant was or should have been aware he was committing a crime by treating Swatsenbarg in the first place. Yet, it is unlikely he would have been deterred from administering to Lee in the manner in which he did for fear of a prosecution for murder, given his published beliefs on the efficacy of massage in the curing of cancer. Indeed, nowhere is it claimed that defendant attempted to perform any action with respect to Swatsenbarg other than to heal him—and earn a fee for doing so.

This clearly is a case in which conviction of felony murder is contrary to our settled law, as well as inappropriate as a matter of sound judicial policy. The instruction regarding felony murder was erroneous.

Accordingly, defendant's second degree murder conviction is reversed.

b. Circumstance Approach

State v. Stewart

663 A.2d 912 (1995)
Rhode Island Supreme Court

WEISBERGER, Chief Justice.

This case comes before us on the appeal of the defendant, Tracy Stewart, from a judgment of conviction entered in the Superior Court on one count of second-degree murder in violation of G.L. 1956 (1981 Reenactment) § 11-23-1. We affirm the judgment of conviction. The facts insofar as pertinent to this appeal are as follows.

On August 31, 1988 twenty-year-old Tracy Stewart (Stewart or defendant) gave birth to a son, Travis Young (Travis). Travis's father was Edward Young, Sr. (Young). Stewart and Young, who had two other children together, were not married at the time of Travis's birth. Travis lived for only fifty-two days, dying on October 21, 1988, from dehydration.

During the week prior to Travis's death, Stewart, Young, and a friend, Patricia McMasters (McMasters), continually and repeatedly ingested cocaine over a two- to three-consecutive-day period at the apartment shared by Stewart and Young. The baby, Travis, was also present at the apartment while Stewart, Young, and McMasters engaged in this cocaine marathon. Young and McMasters injected cocaine intravenously and also smoked it while Stewart ingested the cocaine only by smoking it. The smoked cocaine was in its strongest or base form, commonly referred to as "crack." When the three exhausted an existing supply of cocaine, they would pool

their money and Young and McMasters would go out and buy more with the accu-
mulated funds. . . .

The cocaine binge continued uninterrupted for two to three days. McMasters testified that during this time neither McMasters nor Stewart slept at all. McMasters
testified that defendant was never far from her during this entire two- to three-day
period except for the occasions when McMasters left the apartment to buy more
cocaine. During this entire time, McMasters saw defendant feed Travis only once.
Travis was in a walker, and defendant propped a bottle of formula up on the walker,
using a blanket, for the baby to feed himself. McMasters testified that she did not see
defendant hold the baby to feed him nor did she see defendant change Travis's diaper
or clothes during this period.

Ten months after Travis's death defendant was indicted on charges of second-
degree murder, wrongfully causing or permitting a child under the age of eighteen
to be a habitual sufferer for want of food and proper care (hereinafter sometimes
referred to as "wrongfully permitting a child to be a habitual sufferer"), and manslaughter. The second-degree-murder charge was based on a theory of felony murder.
The prosecution did not allege that defendant intentionally killed her son but rather
that he had been killed during the commission of an inherently dangerous felony,
specifically, wrongfully permitting a child to be a habitual sufferer. Moreover, the
prosecution did not allege that defendant intentionally withheld food or care from
her son. Rather the state alleged that because of defendant's chronic state of cocaine
intoxication, she may have realized what her responsibilities were but simply could
not remember whether she had fed her son, when in fact she had not.

. . . .

The defendant was found guilty of both second-degree murder and wrongfully
permitting a child to be a habitual sufferer. A subsequent motion for new trial was
denied. This appeal followed.

. . . .

Whether Wrongfully Permitting a Child to Be a Habitual Sufferer is an Inherently Dangerously Felony

Rhode Island's murder statute, § 11-23-1, enumerates certain crimes that may serve
as predicate felonies to a charge of first-degree murder. A felony that is not enumerated in § 11-23-1 can, however, serve as a predicate felony to a charge of second-degree
murder. *See In re Leon,* 122 R.I. 548, 410 A.2d 121 (1980); *State v. Miller,* 52 R.I. 440, 1
61 A. 222 (1932). Thus the fact that the crime of wrongfully permitting a child to be a
habitual sufferer is not specified in § 11-23-1 as a predicate felony to support a charge
of first-degree murder does not preclude such crime from serving as a predicate to
support a charge of second-degree murder.

In Rhode Island second-degree murder has been equated with common-law
murder. *In re Leon,* 122 R.I. at 553, 410 A.2d at 124. At common law, where the
rule is unchanged by statute, "[h]omicide is murder if the death results from the

perpetration or attempted perpetration of an inherently dangerous felony." *Id.* (quoting Perkins, *Criminal Law* 44 (2d ed. 1969)). To serve as a predicate felony to a charge of second-degree murder, a felony that is not specifically enumerated in § 11-23-1 must therefore be an inherently dangerous felony. *Id.*

The defendant contends that wrongfully permitting a child to be a habitual sufferer is not an inherently dangerous felony and cannot therefore serve as the predicate felony to a charge of second-degree murder. In advancing her argument, defendant urges this court to adopt the approach used by California courts to determine if a felony is inherently dangerous. This approach requires that the court consider the elements of the felony "in the abstract" rather than look at the particular facts of the case under consideration. *See, e.g., People v. Patterson,* 49 Cal. 3d 615, 620-21, 778 P.2d 549, 553, 262 Cal. Rptr. 195, 199 (1989). With such an approach, if a statute can be violated in a manner that does not endanger human life, then the felony is not inherently dangerous to human life. *People v. Burroughs,* 35 Cal.3d 824, 830-33, 678 P.2d 894, 898-900, 201 Cal. Rptr. 319, 323–25 (1984); *People v. Caffero,* 207 Cal. App. 3d 678, 683-84, 255 Cal. Rptr. 22, 25 (1989). Moreover, the California Supreme Court has defined an act as "inherently dangerous to human life when there is 'a *high probability* that it will result in death.'" *Patterson,* 49 Cal.3d at 627, 262 Cal. Rptr. at 204, 778 P.2d at 558.

In *Caffero, supra,* a two-and-one-half week-old baby died of a massive bacterial infection caused by lack of proper hygiene that was due to parental neglect. The parents were charged with second-degree felony murder and felony-child abuse, with the felony-child-abuse charge serving as the predicate felony to the second-degree-murder charge. Examining California's felony child abuse statute in the abstract, instead of looking at the particular facts of the case, the court held that because the statute could be violated in ways that did not endanger human life, felony-child abuse was not inherently dangerous to human life. . . .

The defendant urges this court to adopt the method of analysis employed by California courts to determine if a felony is inherently dangerous to life. Aside from California, it appears that Kansas is the only other state which looks at the elements of a felony in the abstract to determine if such felony is inherently dangerous to life. *See, e.g., State v. Wesson,* 247 Kan. 639, 647, 802 P.2d 574, 581 (1990) (holding that the sale of crack cocaine when viewed in the abstract is not inherently dangerous to human life); *State v. Underwood,* 228 Kan. 294, 303, 615 P.2d 153, 161 (1980) (holding that the unlawful possession of a firearm by an ex-felon when viewed in the abstract is not inherently dangerous to human life). . . .

We decline defendant's invitation to adopt the California approach in determining whether a felony is inherently dangerous to life and thus capable of serving as a predicate to a charge of second-degree felony murder. We believe that the better approach is for the trier of fact to consider the facts and circumstances of the particular case to determine if such felony was inherently dangerous in the manner and the circumstances in which it was committed, rather than have a court make the determination by viewing the elements of a felony in the abstract. We now join a number of states that have adopted this approach. . . .

A number of felonies at first glance would not appear to present an inherent danger to human life but may in fact be committed in such a manner as to be inherently dangerous to life. The crime of escape from a penal facility is an example of such a crime. On its face, the crime of escape is not inherently dangerous to human life. But escape may be committed or attempted to be committed in a manner wherein human life is put in danger. Indeed in *State v. Miller, supra,* this court upheld the defendant's conviction of second degree murder on the basis of the underlying felony of escape when a prison guard was killed by an accomplice of the defendant during an attempted escape from the Rhode Island State prison. By way of contrast, the California Supreme Court has held that the crime of escape, viewed in the abstract, is an offense that is not inherently dangerous to human life and thus cannot support a second-degree felony-murder conviction. *People v. Lopez,* 6 Cal. 3d 45, 51, 489 P.2d 1372, 1376, 98 Cal. Rptr. 44, 48 (1971) (In Bank).

The amendment of our murder statute to include any unlawful killing "committed during the course of the perpetration, or attempted perpetration, of felony manufacture, sale, delivery, or other distribution of a controlled substance otherwise prohibited by the provisions of chapter 28 of title 21" lends further support for not following California's approach to determining the inherent dangerousness of a felony. G.L.1956 (1981 Reenactment) § 11-23-1, as amended by P.L. 1990, ch. 284, § 4. According to the statute a person who delivers phencyclidine (PCP), a controlled substance under section (e)(5) of schedule II of G.L.1956 (1989 Reenactment) § 21-28-2.08, as amended by P.L.1991, ch. 211, § 1, to another person who then dies either as a result of an overdose or as a result of behavior precipitated by the drug use (such as jumping off a building because of the loss of special [*sic*] perception) could be charged with first-degree murder under § 11-23-1. Conversely, the California Court of Appeal has held that when viewed in the abstract, the standard used by California courts to determine whether a felony is inherently dangerous, the furnishing or selling of PCP is not a felony that carries a high probability that death will result. *People v. Taylor,* 6 Cal. App. 4th 1084, 1100, 8 Cal. Rptr. 2d 439, 449 (1992). Consequently, the California Court of Appeal held that the felony of furnishing PCP could not serve as a predicate to a charge of second-degree felony murder. *Id.* at 1101, 8 Cal. Rptr. 2d at 450. It is clear that there is a profound ideological difference in the approach of the Rhode Island Legislature from the holdings of the courts of the State of California concerning appropriate criminal charges to be preferred against one who furnishes PCP (and presumably a host of other controlled substances) to another person with death resulting therefrom. The lawmakers of the State of Rhode Island have deemed it appropriate to charge such a person with the most serious felony in our criminal statutes first-degree murder. It appears that the appellate court of California, however, would hold that the most serious charge against one who furnishes PCP to another person with death resulting therefrom would be involuntary manslaughter. *See id.*

The Legislature's recent amendment to our murder statute as well as this court's prior jurisprudence concerning second-degree felony murder (*In re Leon, supra; State v. Miller, supra*) reinforces our belief that we should not adopt the California approach to determine whether a felony is inherently dangerous. The proper procedure for making, such a determination is to present the facts and circumstances of the particular case to the trier of fact and for the trier of fact to determine if a felony is inherently dangerous in the manner and the circumstances in which it was committed. This is exactly what happened in the case at bar. . . .

. . . [W]e are of the opinion that the evidence offered by the state was sufficient to prove beyond a reasonable doubt each of the elements of second-degree felony murder, including that the crime of wrongfully permitting a child to be a habitual sufferer was an inherently dangerous felony in its manner of commission. The defendant's motions for judgment of acquittal on the felony-murder charge on the ground that wrongfully permitting a child to be a habitual sufferer is not an inherently dangerous felony were properly denied.

Notes and Questions

1. Do you agree with the court in *Burroughs* that the prospect of a murder conviction would not deter doctors from practicing medicine without a license?

2. It might appear that the circumstances test for inherent dangerousness is a fig leaf, as it would appear to apply to any felony that resulted in a death. However, there may be situations where the circumstances of the commission of a felony were simply not inherently dangerous, with death resulting as a completely unpredictable coincidence. For example, in *Ford v. State*, 423 S.E.2d 255 (Ga. 1992), the defendant was convicted of felony murder based on commission of a violation of a Georgia statute making it a felony for any convicted felon to possess a firearm. Defendant, a convicted felon, had possession of a firearm. While visiting his girlfriend, defendant attempted to unload the pistol. The pistol accidentally went off, and the bullet went through the floor into the apartment below, killing the victim instantly. The Georgia Supreme Court reversed Ford's felony murder conviction. The court noted that there are many situations where a violation of this felony would create an inherent danger, but in this instance, nothing about Ford's violation indicated the circumstances of the felony were inherently dangerous.

3. On January 6, 2021, rioters stormed the U.S. Capitol in what appears to have been an attempt to prevent the certification of electoral college votes. A Capitol Hill police officer died after being hit in the head by a fire extinguisher by one of the rioters. The U.S. Attorney is considering felony murder charges. 18 U.S.C. § 2384 defines "Seditious Conspiracy" as follows:

> If two or more persons in any State or Territory, or in any place subject to the jurisdiction of the United States, conspire to overthrow, put down, or to destroy by force the Government of the United States, or to levy war against

them, or to oppose by force the authority thereof, or by force to prevent, hinder, or delay the execution of any law of the United States, or by force to seize, take, or possess any property of the United States contrary to the authority thereof, they shall each be fined under this title or imprisoned not more than twenty years, or both.

Assume you are the federal judge in a case involving a felony murder allegation based on Seditious Conspiracy. Is this an inherently dangerous felony pursuant to the abstract test such that it could be the predicate felony in a felony murder prosecution? Would your answer change if your jurisdiction followed the circumstances test?

Now imagine the alleged felony murder is based on a violation of this statute:

Whoever incites, sets on foot, assists, or engages in any rebellion or insur-rection against the authority of the United States or the laws thereof, or gives aid or comfort thereto, shall be fined under this title or imprisoned not more than ten years, or both; and shall be incapable of holding any office under the United States.

Assume your jurisdiction follows the abstract test. Would you grant or deny a motion to dismiss for failing to properly allege felony murder?

4. In *Lomax v. State,* 233 S.W.3d 302 (Tex. Crim. App. 2007), the defendant was charged with felony murder with Driving While Intoxicated ("DWI"), a third-degree felony, as the predicate felony. Because Texas is a circumstance state, there was no issue with respect to the dangerousness of the felony. However, in Texas, DWI is a strict liability offense. Thus, in order to obtain a felony murder conviction, the prosecutor would not be required to prove mens rea for either the predicate felony or the murder. The court upheld the felony murder conviction, finding that the clear legislative intent was to dispense with a culpable mental state.

B. Independent Felonious Purpose Limitation

Felonies such as burglary, arson, rape, robbery, and kidnapping (BARRK) are considered not only "inherently dangerous," but also "independent" of the homi-cide. Accordingly, even when not enumerated in the definition of murder, and even in an abstract jurisdiction, these felonies will almost always qualify as a predicate for felony murder. Felonies such as manslaughter cannot be the predicate felony. If this were not the case, every factual manslaughter would be charged as felony murder and manslaughter would cease to exist as a crime. In most jurisdictions, assaultive con-duct—crimes such as assault, battery, and mayhem (a battery resulting in permanent physical disability)—are also not sufficiently independent from the killing to qualify as a permissible predicate felony for a felony murder charge. Instead, these crimes "merge" into the killing. Thus, should D set out to assault V, resulting in the death of V, a felony murder charge would be invalid because D did not have a felonious purpose *other than assaultive* that was independent of the killing. If the merger rule did not exist and felonies with a primary assaultive purpose qualified as predicates for felony murder, every assault that results in death would be prosecuted as felony murder. Prosecutors would be relieved of the burden of proving that the killing was the result of malice or any other defined criminal mental state for murder.

There are two important qualifications to this "independent" felony requirement. First, if the felony is enumerated in the definition of murder, whether or not it is independent is irrelevant; once the legislature indicates the felony supports felony murder, there is no further inquiry. For example, note that in the California murder provision excerpted above, mayhem is an enumerated felony. Mayhem is certainly not an independent felony, but it nonetheless qualifies as the "right" type of felony for felony murder because it is enumerated. Second, not all states follow this independent felony limitation for unenumerated felonies. In those states, the only question is whether the felony is inherently dangerous.

State v. Lucas

759 P.2d 90 (1988)
Kansas Supreme Court

McFARLAND, J.

Robert Lynn Lucas appeals his jury trial convictions of two counts of child abuse, (one count as to victim Shannon Woodside and one count as to victim Shaina Woodside) and one count of felony murder, as to victim Shaina Woodside. Lucas was sentenced to three to eight years' imprisonment on each count of child abuse and to life imprisonment for felony murder.

At the times of the crimes of which defendant was convicted, he was living in Olathe with Jean Woodside and her two daughters, Shaina (age 18 months at the time of her death) and Shannon (age 3 years). Mrs. Woodside worked three evenings a week and attended school the other four evenings. Defendant had the children in his care every evening and frequently in the daytime. At approximately 10:30 p.m. on July 6, 1986, defendant called 911, . . . to request medical assistance for Shaina. First on the scene was Officer James Stover. He found the defendant in an upstairs bathroom standing over the unconscious body of Shaina. Shannon was in the bathtub. . . . Officer Stover asked defendant what had happened and defendant gave a lengthy detailed account of how he had placed the two little girls in the tub for their evening bath, shut the glass shower doors, and gone downstairs to watch television. Sometime later he had returned upstairs to check on the children and had found Shaina floating face down in the tub. . . .

The child was pronounced dead at the hospital. A number of suspicious injuries were observed on her body at the hospital, including patterned burns on her buttocks, three burns resembling cigarette burns on other parts of her body, severe fresh lacerations to her nipples, and numerous bruised areas on many different parts of her body. . . . [A]n autopsy was performed which showed Shaina had suffered severe multiple blows to the head. . . . The coroner testified Shaina's body showed injuries which were the "characteristic stigmata that one sees in child abuse." He found it probable Shaina had met her death by losing consciousness in a body of water and drowning. . . .

Further investigation and trial evidence revealed a real-life horror story of abuse inflicted by the defendant on both little girls over a period of time, directed particularly at Shaina. . . . There was evidence that defendant had, prior to July 6, 1986, beaten Shaina severely with a heavy leather belt, poured Tabasco sauce down her throat, set her down on a hot stove burner, and repeatedly pinched and bitten the child. While in his care Shaina's arm had been broken. A few days before Shaina's death, Mrs. Woodside had observed Shaina in a dazed condition while in the bathroom with defendant. Defendant told her that he had "tranked" the child. He explained this consisted of holding his hand over the child's face until she passed out from lack of oxygen. . . . He generally explained Shaina's injuries, when observed by others, as arising from accidents or efforts at discipline. . . .

Defendant was charged with and convicted [of] . . . child abuse and felony murder as to Shaina. . . . [D]efendant contends the district court erred in failing to dismiss the charge of felony murder as the child abuse charge merged into the felony murder and could not constitute the requisite collateral felony to support the felony-murder charge. . . . In Kansas, as in many other states, the application of felony murder has been limited by judicial decision to situations where: (1) the underlying felony is inherently dangerous to human life; and (2) the elements of the underlying felony are so distinct from the homicide as not to be an ingredient of the homicide. . . .

K.S.A. 1987 Supp. 21-3609 provides: "Abuse of a child is willfully torturing, cruelly beating or inflicting cruel and inhuman corporal punishment upon any child under the age of 18 years."

Clearly, abuse of a child as defined [above] is a felony inherently dangerous to human life and no contrary assertion is made herein. Rather, the issue herein is whether the underlying or collateral felony is so distinct from the homicide as not to be an ingredient of the homicide. If the underlying felony does not meet this test it is said to merge with the homicide and preclude the application of felony murder. . . . Otherwise, all degrees of homicide would constitute murder in the first degree, regardless of the defendant's intention or premeditation. . . .

It was the State's theory that Shaina died as a result of a severe beating to her head administered by the defendant from which she lost consciousness and drowned in the bathtub. There was no claim that any of the other acts of abuse caused or contributed to her death. The defendant could have been found guilty of abuse of a child based solely on the fatal beating and convicted of felony murder solely on the fatal beating. . . .

Had an adult been beaten on the head, lost consciousness as a result thereof, . . . we would have no hesitancy in holding that the aggravated battery (the beating) was an integral part of the homicide and that it merged therewith and could not serve as the underlying felony. Can a different result logically be reached by designating the beating as abuse of a child rather than aggravated battery? We believe not. . . . If additional protection for children is desired, the Kansas Legislature might well consider legislation which would make the death of a child occurring during the commission of the crime of abuse of a child, or aggravated battery against a child, first- or second-degree felony murder. . . .

Notes and Questions

1. In *Lucas*, the court closes its opinion by indicating that the Kansas Legislature may choose to increase the criminal consequence of causing death of a child as the result of child abuse. This should reveal to you that the court was in no way condoning the brutal treatment of the victim in the case, but instead respecting the principle of legality. For the court, it was the function of the legislature to decide whether such a felony should serve as a predicate for felony murder. Perhaps unsurprisingly, the legislature did just that, adding felony child abuse to the very extensive list of enumerated felonies in the Kansas murder statute as reflected below:

(a) Murder in the first degree is the killing of a human being committed:

    (1) Intentionally, and with premeditation; or

    (2) in the commission of, attempt to commit, or flight from any inherently dangerous felony.

(b) Murder in the first degree is an off-grid person felony.

(c) As used in this section, an "inherently dangerous felony" means:

    (1) Any of the following felonies, whether such felony is so distinct from the homicide alleged to be a violation of subsection (a)(2) as not to be an ingredient of the homicide alleged to be a violation of subsection (a)(2):

        (A) Kidnapping, as defined in K.S.A. 21-5408(a), and amendments thereto;

        (B) aggravated kidnapping, as defined in K.S.A. 21-5408(b), and amendments thereto;

        (C) robbery, as defined in K.S.A. 21-5420(a), and amendments thereto;

        (D) aggravated robbery, as defined in K.S.A. 21-5420(b), and amendments thereto;

        (E) rape, as defined in K.S.A. 21-5503, and amendments thereto;

        (F) aggravated criminal sodomy, as defined in K.S.A. 21-5504(b), and amendments thereto;

        (G) abuse of a child, as defined in K.S.A. 21-5602, and amendments thereto;

        (H) felony theft of property, as defined in K.S.A. 21-5801(a)(1) or (a)(3), and amendments thereto;

(I) burglary, as defined in K.S.A. 21-5807(a), and amendments thereto;

(J) aggravated burglary, as defined in K.S.A. 21-5807(b), and amendments thereto;

(K) arson, as defined in K.S.A. 21-5812(a), and amendments thereto;

(L) aggravated arson, as defined in K.S.A. 21-5812(b), and amendments thereto;

(M) treason, as defined in K.S.A. 21-5901, and amendments thereto;

(N) any felony offense as provided in K.S.A. 21-5703, 21-5705 or 21-5706, and amendments thereto;

(O) any felony offense as provided in K.S.A. 21-6308(a) or (b), and amendments thereto;

(P) endangering the food supply, as defined in K.S.A. 21-6317(a), and amendments thereto;

(Q) aggravated endangering the food supply, as defined in K.S.A. 21-6317(b), and amendments thereto;

(R) fleeing or attempting to elude a police officer, as defined in K.S.A. 8-1568(b), and amendments thereto;

(S) aggravated endangering a child, as defined in K.S.A. 21-5601(b)(1), and amendments thereto;

(T) abandonment of a child, as defined in K.S.A. 21-5605(a), and amendments thereto;

(U) aggravated abandonment of a child, as defined in K.S.A. 21-5605(b), and amendments thereto; or

(V) mistreatment of a dependent adult or mistreatment of an elder person, as defined in K.S.A. 21-5417, and amendments thereto; . . .

K.S.A. § 21-5402.

2. Any legislation subsequently enacted by the Kansas legislature could not be applied to Lucas, because doing so would violate the Due Process Clause of the Fourteenth Amendment to the U.S. Constitution as an ex post facto law. Does that mean that the prosecutor is powerless to hold the defendant responsible for Shaina's death? Are there other homicide charges that could have been brought against him?

3. As noted above, some states have not adopted the independent felony/merger limitation and thus allow assaultive felonies to be the underlying felony. For instance, Washington R.C.W. § 9A.32.050 provides:

(a) A person is guilty of murder in the second degree when: . . .

(b) He or she commits or attempts to commit any felony, *including assault*, . . . and in the course of and in furtherance of such crime or in immediate flight therefrom, he or she, or another participant, causes the death of a person other than one of the participants [emphasis added].

See also Texas Penal Code § 19.02(b) in the previous section.

4. An example of the consequence of *not* following the independent felony limitation was the 2020 murder charge against Derek Chauvin, the Minneapolis police officer found guilty of murdering George Floyd. Chauvin's second-degree murder conviction was based on a felony murder theory with assault alleged as the predicate felony. According to the Minnesota Criminal Code, second-degree murder is defined to include any unintentional killing where the defendant:

(1) causes the death of a human being, without intent to effect the death of any person, while committing or attempting to commit a felony offense other than criminal sexual conduct in the first or second degree with force or violence or a drive-by shooting;

C. Attribution of Killings at the Hand of a Third Party and the Agency Limitation

In most jurisdictions, felony murder liability depends both on who kills and who is killed. At common law, any killing of any victim that was proximately caused by the felony was attributed to all surviving felons. But in a majority of states, as the next case illustrates, a felony murder conviction requires that the killing be done by the defendant or one of his co-felons. Accordingly, if the victim dies at the hand of someone *other than* the defendant, the killing will be attributed to the defendant only if the killer was a co-felon. In addition, in many states, the felony murder rule is inapplicable when the person killed is a co-felon, even if killed by another co-felon.

State v. Sophophone
19 P.3d 70 (2001)
Kansas Supreme Court

LARSON, J.

This is Sanexay Sophophone's direct appeal of his felony-murder conviction for the death of his co-felon during flight from an aggravated burglary in which both men participated.

The facts are not in dispute. Sophophone and three other individuals conspired to and broke into a house in Emporia. The resident reported the break-in to the police.

Police officers responded to the call, saw four individuals leaving the back of the house, shined a light on the suspects, identified themselves as police officers, and ordered them to stop. The individuals, one being Sophophone, started to run away. One officer ran down Sophophone, hand-cuffed him, and placed him in a police car.

Other officers arrived to assist in apprehending the other individuals as they were running from the house. An officer chased one of the suspects later identified as Somphone Sysoumphone. Sysoumphone crossed railroad tracks, jumped a fence, and then stopped. The officer approached with his weapon drawn and ordered Sysoumphone to the ground and not to move. Sysoumphone was lying face down but raised up and fired at the officer, who returned fire and killed him. It is not disputed that Sysoumphone was one of the individuals observed by the officers leaving the house that had been burglarized.

Sophophone was charged with conspiracy to commit aggravated burglary; aggravated burglary; obstruction of official duty; and felony murder.

Sophophone moved to dismiss the felony-murder charges, contending the complaint was defective because it alleged that he and not the police officer had killed Sysoumphone and further because he was in custody and sitting in the police car when the deceased was killed and therefore not attempting to commit or even fleeing from an inherently dangerous felony. His motion to dismiss was denied by the trial court.

Sophophone was convicted by a jury of all counts. His motion for judgment of acquittal was denied. He was sentenced on all counts. He appeals only his conviction of felony murder.

We consider only the question of law, upon which our review is unlimited, of whether Sophophone can be convicted of felony murder for the killing of a co-felon not caused by his acts but by the lawful acts of a police officer acting in self-defense in the course and scope of his duties in apprehending the co-felon fleeing from an aggravated burglary.

The applicable provisions of K.S.A. 21-3401 read as follows:

"Murder in the first degree is the killing of a human being committed:

"(b) in the commission of, attempt to commit, or flight from an inherently dangerous felony. . . ."

Aggravated burglary is one of the inherently dangerous felonies as enumerated by K.S.A. 21-3436(10). . . .

With this brief background of our prior Kansas cases, we look to the prevailing views concerning the applicability of the felony-murder doctrine where the killing has been caused by the acts of a third party. The two different approaches applicable are succinctly set forth in Comment Kansas Felony Murder: Agency or Proximate Cause? 48 Kan. L. Rev. 1047, 1051–52 (2000), in the following manner:

"There are two basic approaches to application of the felony-murder doctrine: the agency and proximate cause theories. The agency approach, which is the majority view, limits application of the doctrine to those homicides committed by the felon or an agent of the felon. Under such an approach, 'the identity of the killer becomes the threshold requirement for finding liability under the felony-murder doctrine.'

"The proximate cause approach provides that 'liability attaches "for **any** death proximately resulting from the unlawful activity—even the death of a co-felon—notwithstanding the killing was by one resisting the crime.'" [emphasis in original] Under the proximate cause approach, felony murder may preclude consideration of the deceased's identity, which would make a defendant liable for all deaths caused by others during the crime. Application of the proximate cause varies greatly by jurisdiction because the statutes differ substantially. The proximate cause approach becomes controversial when the homicide is committed by someone other than the felons, but only a minority of jurisdictions follow this approach."

In Dressler, Understanding Criminal Law, § 31.07[4] Killing by a Non-Felon, pp. 471–72 (1987), the question is posed of whether the felony-murder rule should apply when the fatal act is performed by a non-felon. Dressler states:

"This issue has perplexed courts. Two approaches to the question have been considered and applied by the courts.

"The majority rule is that the felony-murder doctrine does not apply if the person who directly causes the death is a non-felon. . . .

"The reasoning of this approach stems from accomplice liability theory. Generally speaking, the acts of the primary party (the person who directly commits the offense) are imputed to an accomplice on the basis of the agency doctrine. It is as if the accomplice says to the primary party: 'Your acts are my acts.' It follows that [a co-felon] cannot be convicted of the homicides because the primary party was not the person with whom she was an accomplice. It is not possible to impute the acts of the antagonistic party—[the non-felon or] the police officer—to [a co-felon] on the basis of agency.

"An alternative theory, followed by a few courts for awhile [*sic*], holds that a felon may be held responsible under the felony-murder rule for a killing committed by a non-felon if the felon set in motion the acts which resulted in the victim's death.

"Pursuant to this rule, the issue becomes one of proximate causation: if an act by one felon is the proximate cause of the homicidal conduct by [the non-felon] or the police officer, murder liability is permitted."

In 2 LaFave & Scott, Substantive Criminal Law, § 7.5(d), pp. 217–18 (1986), the author opines: "Although it is now generally accepted that there is no felony-murder liability when one of the felons is shot and killed by the victim, a police officer, or a bystander, it is not easy to explain why this is so." . . .

The leading case adopting the agency approach is *Commonwealth v. Redline*, 391 Pa. 486, 495, 137 A.2d 472 (1958), where the underlying principle of the agency theory is described as follows:

"In adjudging a felony-murder, it is to be remembered at all times that the thing which is imputed to a felon for a killing incidental to his felony is malice and not the act of killing. The mere coincidence of homicide and felony is not enough to satisfy the felony-murder doctrine."

The following statement from *Redline* is more persuasive for Sophophone:

"In the present instance, the victim of the homicide was one of the robbers who, while resisting apprehension in his effort to escape, was shot and killed by a policeman in the performance of his duty. Thus, the homicide was justifiable and, obviously, could not be availed of, on any rational legal theory, to support a charge of murder. How can anyone, no matter how much of an outlaw he may be, have a criminal charge lodged against him for the consequences of the lawful conduct of another person? The mere question carries with it its own answer." . . .

It should be mentioned that some courts have been willing to impose felony-murder liability even where the shooting was by a person other than one of the felons in the so-called "shield" situations where it has been reasoned "that a felon's act of using a victim as a shield in compelling a victim to occupy a place or position of danger constitutes a direct lethal act against the victim." *Campbell v. State*, 293 Md. 438, 451 n. 3, 444 A.2d 1034 (1982). . . .

The overriding fact which exists in our case is that neither Sophophone nor any of his accomplices "killed" anyone. The law enforcement officer acted lawfully in committing the act which resulted in the death of the co-felon. . . .

It appears to the majority that to impute the act of killing to Sophophone when the act was the lawful and courageous one of a law enforcement officer acting in the line of his duties is contrary to the strict construction we are required to give criminal statutes. There is considerable doubt about the meaning of [Kansas felony murder statute] as applied to the facts of this case, and we believe that making one criminally responsible for the lawful acts of a law enforcement officer is not the intent of the felony-murder statute as it is currently written. . . .

We hold that under the facts of this case where the killing resulted from the lawful acts of a law enforcement officer in attempting to apprehend a co-felon, Sophophone is not criminally responsible for the resulting death of Somphone Sysoumphone, and his felony-murder conviction must be reversed. . . .

Notes and Questions

1. In *People v. Hernandez*, 604 N.Y.S.2d 524 (1993), the court summarized the reasons most jurisdictions do not hold the defendant liable when the shooter is someone other than a co-felon:

The rationale for requiring that one of the cofelons be the shooter (or, more broadly, the person who commits the final, fatal act) has been framed in several ways. Some courts have held that when the victim or a police officer or a bystander shoots and kills, it cannot be said that the killing was in furtherance of a common criminal objective. Others have concluded that under such circumstances the necessary malice or intent is missing. Under the traditional felony murder doctrine, the malice necessary to make the killing murder was constructively imputed from the *mens rea* incidental to perpetration of the underlying felony. Thus, in *Wooden,* the Virginia Supreme Court concluded that where a nonparticipant in the felony is the shooter, there can be no imputation of the necessary malice to him, and no party in the causal chain has both the requisite *mens rea* and culpability for the *actus reus.* [*Wooden v Commonwealth*, 222 Va. 758, 284 S.E.2d 811.] Still other courts have expressed policy concerns about extending felony murder liability. They have asserted that no deterrence value attaches when the felon is not the person immediately responsible for the death, or have contended that an expansive felony murder rule might unreasonably hold the felons responsible for the acts of others—for instance, when an unarmed felon is fleeing the scene and a bystander is hit by the bad aim of the armed victim.

2. Some jurisdictions impose other limitations on the felony murder rule by statute or by judicial precedent. For example, in *People v. Hernandez, supra,* the court rejected the agency limitation and upheld a felony murder conviction when the victim was killed at the hand of a third-party non-felon (a police officer) based on the holding that the New York felony murder statute extended liability to all deaths proximately cause by the felony, which is the original common law rule. However, the court also explained that the New York felony murder statute included a defense that limited the potential overbreadth of imposing felony murder liability based on this proximate cause rule. This affirmative defense is available for a non-violent accomplice/co-felon who (a) does not cause the death, (b) is unarmed, (c) has no reason to believe that the co-felon is armed and (d) has no reason to believe that the co-felon will "engage in conduct likely to result in death or serious physical injury." This "nonviolent co-felon" exemption is not unique to New York State. The court in *People v. Hernandez* also noted that New York's felony murder statue applied when "either the defendant or an accomplice causes the death of a person other than one of the participants." Accordingly, the death of a co-felon cannot result in felony murder liability. This limitation, like the non-violent accomplice limitation, is also not unique to New York State.

3. The court held that Sophophone cannot be convicted of felony murder based on a shooting by a police officer who obviously was not his agent. The prosecutor may still want to hold Sophophone responsible for the death that occurred since his actions set in motion the events that led to the death of his co-felon. Is there another homicide charge that can be brought that could result in a conviction?

4. What would the result be if the victim had been shot and killed by Sophophone?

5. As the court mentioned in its decision, even those jurisdictions that have adopted the agency rule do not apply it in "shield" cases. A defendant who commits a felony and then uses another person as a shield to protect himself from being killed that results in the death of the shield can still be convicted of felony murder even though a third party killed the shield. What is the rationale of this exception?

Many common law jurisdictions have recognized a misdemeanor variant of the felony murder rule: misdemeanor manslaughter. Under this rule, a death proximately caused during the attempt or commission of a *malum in se* misdemeanor is involuntary manslaughter, with no requirement to prove a criminal state of mind other than that required to prove the predicate misdemeanor. Some jurisdictions even allow the use of a non-inherently dangerous felony to support such a conviction. Importantly, however, not all misdemeanors support misdemeanor manslaughter, in recognition that there are numerous *malum prohibitum* misdemeanors codified in criminal statutes. Nonetheless, in a state that retains this rule, even a relatively minor offense that results in an unintended death, like misdemeanor battery, will support an involuntary manslaughter conviction.

Felony Murder

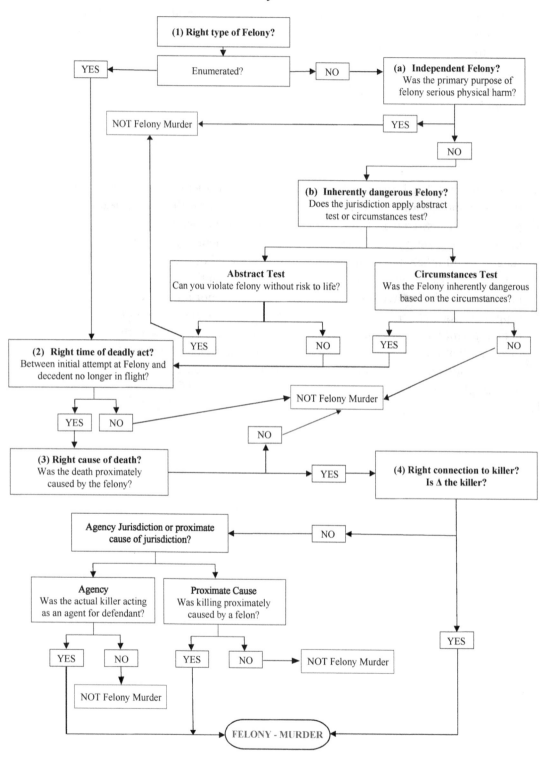

Formative Assessments

1. D is a night watchman who sleeps during the day. D's neighbor recently began some renovations on his house. During the past week, the workers arrived very early each morning, beginning around 7AM. D is struggling to get to sleep as a result of the construction noise. D visits his neighbor who is new to the area and asks him if he can delay the work until at least around 9AM so D can fall asleep. The neighbor responds, "Sorry, but it's not my fault you work at night. Deal with it." The construction continues to commence early each morning, and after about a week of getting very little sleep, D decides he has to send a message. D decides to sneak over to the worksite at night and sabotage some of the equipment. He uses an icepick to punch some holes in the bottom of the generator fuel tank, hoping it will make it inoperable. When the workers arrive the next morning, one of them goes to start the generator. He is smoking a cigarette, and not knowing that fuel has leaked on the ground, he tosses the cigarette away as he approaches the turn on switch. The burning butt immediately ignites the fuel-soaked grass and causes an explosion of the fuel tank. The worker is killed from the fire.

The jurisdiction includes the following statute: "Any killing during the commission of an inherently dangerous felony shall be murder in the second degree." The jurisdiction follows the "abstract" doctrine. If D is charged with felony murder based on the felony of "Trespass Resulting in Damage to Property," will the charge survive a motion to dismiss?

2. Defendant was driving his automobile at a legal speed in a residential zone. A child darted out in front of him. Defendant was unable to brake in time and hit and killed the child. Defendant's blood alcohol level was slightly above the legal limit, and he was cited for driving while intoxicated, a misdemeanor in the jurisdiction. On a charge of manslaughter, Defendant should be found

A. Guilty under the misdemeanor manslaughter rule.

B. Guilty, because he was grossly negligent.

C. Not guilty, because evidence is insufficient to support the conviction.

D. Not guilty, because there is no evidence defendant intended to kill.

3. Defendant, an avid fan of his home town football team, shot at the leg of a star player for a rival team, intending to injure his leg enough to hospitalize him for a few weeks, but not to kill him. The victim died of loss of blood. Will defendant's intentional battery using a dangerous weapon support a felony murder charge?

4. Shore decided to destroy his dilapidated home in order to file a false insurance claim. He hired Parsons to burn down the building. Parsons broke into the building and carefully searched it to make sure no one was inside. He failed, however, to realize there was a basement where a vagrant was asleep. He started a fire. The building was destroyed, and the person in the basement died from burns a week later. Two days after the fire, Shore filed an insurance claim in which he stated that he had no

information about the cause of the fire. The jurisdiction defines felony arson as, "Any intentional destruction by fire or explosive of a dwelling house of another, or of any house for purposes of insurance fraud." The jurisdiction follows the abstract doctrine of inherent dangerousness. Explain which, if any, of the felonies listed below will support a felony murder charge against Shore.

A. Felony arson.

B. Felony fraud.

C. Felony conspiracy.

D. Felony solicitation.

Chapter 10

Capital Punishment in the United States

I. Introduction

This chapter will cover four important aspects of capital punishment. First, there will be a review of the constitutionality of the death penalty. Specifically, the reasons why a majority of the Supreme Court ultimately ruled that the death penalty does not violate the Eighth Amendment ban on cruel and unusual punishments. Despite the Court's ruling upholding the death penalty there continue to be concerns expressed by members of the Court regarding the constitutionality of the death penalty, such as the arbitrary manner in which it is inflicted, and these concerns will be discussed. Second, not all killers are subject to the death penalty. The next section reviews the state of mind that is required for the death penalty to be inflicted. Third, the Supreme Court has imposed numerous limitations on classes of individuals who cannot be sentenced to death regardless of the severity of their crimes. These limitations include juveniles, intellectually disabled individuals and those who do not kill. Finally, the death penalty has been infected since its inception by race. Throughout the death penalty's history and continuing today, this unique punishment has been inflicted disproportionately on African Americans. Race also matters in terms of the victim: the death penalty is much more likely to be imposed upon those who kill whites than upon those who kill other races.

II. Constitutionality

Capital punishment was practiced in England before English settlers arrived in America, and they brought the death penalty with them when they came to America. The first recorded American execution occurred in 1608, and the practice of executing offenders continued and was largely unregulated by the U.S. Supreme Court until its 1972 decision in *Furman v. Georgia*. In *Furman*, 408 U.S. 238 (1972), the Court held, over the strong dissents of four justices, that the manner in which the death penalty was being imposed in the United States was arbitrary and therefore a violation of the Eighth Amendment which prohibits cruel and unusual punishment. The effect of the Court's decision was to invalidate the death penalty statutes of every state which retained the death penalty. The public reaction to the *Furman* decision was overwhelmingly negative, especially in the law enforcement community. In reaction to the decision, 35 states and the Federal government enacted new death penalty statutes which attempted to address the arbitrary application which led to the Court's decision. The Court ruled on the constitutionality of these statutes in *Gregg v. Georgia.*

Gregg v. Georgia
428 U.S. 153 (1976)
U.S. Supreme Court

STEWART, J.

The issue in this case is whether the imposition of the sentence of death for the crime of murder under the law of Georgia violates the Eighth and Fourteenth Amendments.

The petitioner, Troy Gregg, was charged with committing armed robbery and murder. In accordance with Georgia procedure in capital cases, the trial was in two stages, a guilt stage and a sentencing stage. The evidence at the guilt trial established that on November 21, 1973, the petitioner and a traveling companion, Floyd Allen, while hitchhiking north in Florida were picked up by Fred Simmons and Bob Moore. Their car broke down, but they continued north after Simmons purchased another vehicle with some of the cash he was carrying. While still in Florida, they picked up another hitchhiker, Dennis Weaver, who rode with them to Atlanta, where he was let out about 11 p.m. A short time later the four men interrupted their journey for a rest stop along the highway. The next morning the bodies of Simmons and Moore were discovered in a ditch nearby.

. . . [T]he judge instructed the jury that it "would not be authorized to consider [imposing] the penalty of death" unless it first found beyond a reasonable doubt one of these aggravating circumstances:

> "One—That the offense of murder was committed while the offender was engaged in the commission of two other capital felonies, to-wit the armed robbery of [Simmons and Moore].

> "Two—That the offender committed the offense of murder for the purpose of receiving money and the automobile described in the indictment.

> "Three—The offense of murder was outrageously and wantonly vile, horrible and inhuman, in that they *[sic]* involved the depravity of [the] mind of the defendant." Tr. 476-477.1

Finding the first and second of these circumstances, the jury returned verdicts of death on each count.

We address initially the basic contention that the punishment of death for the crime of murder is, under all circumstances, "cruel and unusual" in violation of the Eighth and Fourteenth Amendments to the Constitution. . . . We now hold that the punishment of death does not invariably violate the Constitution.

[Precedent establishes] that the Eighth Amendment has not been regarded as a static concept. As Mr. Chief Justice Warren said, in an often-quoted phrase, "[t]he Amendment must draw its meaning from the evolving standards of decency that mark the progress of a maturing society." Thus, an assessment of contemporary values concerning the infliction of a challenged sanction is relevant to the application of the Eighth Amendment. . . .

It is apparent from the text of the Constitution itself that the existence of capital punishment was accepted by the Framers. . . . Despite the continuing debate, dating back to the 19th century, over the morality and utility of capital punishment, it is now evident that a large proportion of American society continues to regard it as an appropriate and necessary criminal sanction. . . . The most marked indication of society's endorsement of the death penalty for murder is the legislative response to *Furman.* The legislatures of at least 35 States have enacted new statutes that provide for the death penalty for at least some crimes that result in the death of another person. And the Congress of the United States, in 1974, enacted a statute providing the death penalty for aircraft piracy that results in death. . . .

The death penalty is said to serve two principal social purposes: retribution and deterrence of capital crimes by prospective offenders. . . .

In part, capital punishment is an expression of society's moral outrage at particularly offensive conduct. This function may be unappealing to many, but it is essential in an ordered society that asks its citizens to rely on legal processes rather than self-help to vindicate their wrongs.

> "The instinct for retribution is part of the nature of man, and channeling that instinct in the administration of criminal justice serves an important purpose in promoting the stability of a society governed by law. When people begin to believe that organized society is unwilling or unable to impose upon criminal offenders the punishment they 'deserve,' then there are sown the seeds of anarchy—of self-help, vigilante justice, and lynch law." *Furman v. Georgia,* 408 U.S., at 308 (Stewart, J., concurring).

. . . Indeed, the decision that capital punishment may be the appropriate sanction in extreme cases is an expression of the community's belief that certain crimes are themselves so grievous an affront to humanity that the only adequate response may be the penalty of death. . . .

[As for the deterrence purpose] [s]tatistical attempts to evaluate the worth of the death penalty as a deterrent to crimes by potential offenders have occasioned a great deal of debate. The results simply have been inconclusive. . . .

Although some of the studies suggest that the death penalty may not function as a significantly greater deterrent than lesser penalties, there is no convincing empirical evidence either supporting or refuting this view. We may nevertheless assume safely that there are murderers, such as those who act in passion, for whom the threat of death has little or no deterrent effect. But for many others, the death penalty undoubtedly is a significant deterrent. There are carefully contemplated murders, such as murder for hire, where the possible penalty of death may well enter into the cold calculus that precedes the decision to act. And there are some categories of murder, such as murder by a life prisoner, where other sanctions may not be adequate. . . .

We hold that the death penalty is not a form of punishment that may never be imposed, regardless of the circumstances of the offense, regardless of the character of the offender, and regardless of the procedure followed in reaching the decision to impose it.

Notes and Questions

1. Why did the Court reverse course in *Gregg?*

2. On the same day that the Court decided *Gregg,* it also decided *Woodson v. North Carolina,* 428 U.S. 280 (1976). In response to the *Furman* decision, North Carolina enacted a mandatory death penalty statute for first degree murder. The Court invalidated the North Carolina statute. First, the Court was concerned that discretion would still be available under mandatory death penalty statutes like North Carolina's. The Court pointed out that before murder was separated into degrees, it was a capital crime automatically punishable by death. However, juries could, and often did, avoid imposing the death penalty by failing to convict the offender. Furthermore, prosecutors could continue to exercise discretion through their charging decisions. Second, the Court was concerned that mandatory death sentences did not provide an opportunity for the jury to consider the defendant's humanity. "A process that accords no significance to [mitigating circumstances] excludes . . . the possibility of compassionate or mitigating factors stemming from the diverse frailties of humankind. It treats all persons convicted of a designated offense not as uniquely human beings, but as members of a faceless, undifferentiated mass to be subjected to the blind infliction of the penalty of death." What evidence might convince a jury not to sentence a defendant to death?

3. In a dissenting opinion in *Glossip v. Gross,* 576 U.S. 863 (2015), Justice Stephen Breyer, joined by Justice Ruth Bader Ginsburg, called on the Court to reexamine its holding in *Gregg.* "Nearly 40 years ago, this Court upheld the death penalty under statutes that, in the Court's view, contained safeguards sufficient to ensure that the penalty would be applied reliably and not arbitrarily. . . . The circumstances and the evidence of the death penalty's application have changed radically since then." According to Justice Breyer, "those changes, taken together with my own 20 years of experience on this Court . . . lead me to believe that the death penalty, in an of itself, now likely constitutes a legally prohibited 'cruel and unusual punishment.'" First, he cited the "serious unreliability" of the death penalty as evidenced by the number of wrongly convicted and executed inmates. Second, he noted the continued arbitrariness as the death penalty fails to distinguish between the worse crimes and worse murderers and the fact that race continues to be a contributing factor. Third, he believed the death penalty was cruel because of the long delays in carrying out

executions and that it was unusual because most of the United States has discontinued the practice. Justice Breyer noted that prosecutors, except for a handful of jurisdictions, rarely seek death and juries rarely impose it when it is sought. Justice Scalia believed that the question regarding the future viability of the death penalty should be left up to states to decide. Do you agree with Justice Breyer or Scalia?

4. According to the Death Penalty Information Center, "[s]ince 1973, 186 former death-row prisoners have been exonerated of all charges related to the wrongful convictions that had put them on death row." *See* Death Penalty Information Center, at https://deathpenaltyinfo.org/policy-issues/innocence. According to Justice Souter, "[m]ost of these wrongful convictions and sentences resulted from eyewitness misidentification, false confession, and (most frequently) perjury, and the total shows that among all prosecutions homicide cases suffer an unusually high incidence of false conviction, probably owing to the combined difficulty of investigating without help from the victim, intense pressure to get convictions in homicide cases, and the corresponding incentive for the guilty to frame the innocent." *Kansas v. Marsh*, 548 U.S. 163, 210 (2006) (Souter, J. dissenting). According to Justice Scalia, "[r]eversal of an erroneous conviction on appeal or on habeas, or the pardoning of an innocent condemnee through executive clemency, demonstrates not the failure of the system but its success." *Id.* at 193 (Scalia, J., concurring). Do the large number of exonerations prove that the system is flawed or that it is successful?

5. The predominant execution method in the United States is lethal injection. Traditionally, those inmates executed by lethal injection have been administered a three-drug cocktail. The first drug administered was sodium thiopental, a common barbiturate which puts patients quickly to sleep. The second drug administered is pavilion, a common muscle relaxant which stops the inmate's breathing. A third drug, potassium chloride, was subsequently administered in order to relax the heart and stop it from pumping. Inmates have challenged lethal injection based on the Eighth Amendment prohibition on cruel and unusual punishment. First, they argue that it is cruel because lethal injection frequently doesn't result in instantaneous death. Rather it causes "torture or lingering death" which the Eighth Amendment forbids. *See Wilkerson v. Utah*, 99 U.S. 130, 135–136 (1879). Second, active death penalty states such as Texas and Oklahoma have experienced difficulty in obtaining the three drugs, since pharmaceutical companies are reluctant to sell the drugs for purposes of carrying out executions. States have been forced to use substitutes instead, which inmates argue have not been tested for their reliability and which also cause "lingering death." Challenges to lethal injections based on "lingering death" and drug substitutes have been rejected. *See Glossip v. Gross*, 135 S. Ct. 2726 (2015).

6. Other methods of execution still on the books are the electric chair, hanging, gas chamber and firing squad. The U.S. Supreme Court has not ruled that any method of execution violates the Eighth Amendment. However, the Supreme Courts of Georgia and Nebraska have ruled that the electric chair violates their state constitutions. *See Dawson v. State*, 554 S.E.2d 137 (Ga. 2001); *State v. Mata*, 745 N.W.2d 229 (Neb. 2008)

III. State of Mind

All murderers don't deserve to be sentenced to death and executed. One way to distinguish those more deserving of a death sentence is the mens rea of the actor. In *Enmund v. Florida*, 458 U.S. 782 (1982), the Court held that the death penalty could not be imposed on a defendant who did not kill, attempt to kill or intend to kill anyone. However, the Court has held that certain defendants who did not intend to kill can nevertheless be sentenced to death.

Tison v. Arizona
481 U.S. 137 (1987)
U.S. Supreme Court

O'CONNOR, J.

The question presented is whether the petitioners' participation in the events leading up to and following the murder of four members of a family makes the sentences of death imposed by the Arizona courts constitutionally permissible although neither petitioner specifically intended to kill the victims and neither inflicted the fatal gunshot wounds. We hold that the Arizona Supreme Court applied an erroneous standard in making the findings required by *Enmund v. Florida*, 458 U.S. 782 (1982), and, therefore, vacate the judgments below and remand the case for further proceedings not inconsistent with this opinion.

Gary Tison was sentenced to life imprisonment as the result of a prison escape during the course of which he had killed a guard. After he had been in prison a number of years, Gary Tison's wife, their three sons Donald, Ricky, and Raymond, Gary's brother Joseph, and other relatives made plans to help Gary Tison escape again. The Tison family assembled a large arsenal of weapons for this purpose. Plans for escape were discussed with Gary Tison, who insisted that his cellmate, Randy Greenawalt, also a convicted murderer, be included in the prison break. . . .

On July 30, 1978, the three Tison brothers entered the Arizona State Prison at Florence carrying a large ice chest filled with guns. The Tisons armed Greenawalt and their father, and the group, brandishing their weapons, locked the prison guards and visitors present in a storage closet. The five men fled the prison grounds in the Tisons' Ford Galaxy automobile. No shots were fired at the prison.

After leaving the prison, the men abandoned the Ford automobile and proceeded on to an isolated house in a white Lincoln automobile that the brothers had parked at a hospital near the prison. At the house, the Lincoln automobile had a flat tire; the only spare tire was pressed into service. After two nights at the house, the group drove toward Flagstaff. As the group traveled on back roads and secondary highways through the desert, another tire blew out. The group decided to flag down a passing motorist and steal a car. Raymond stood out in front of the Lincoln; the other four armed themselves and lay in wait by the side of the road. One car passed by without stopping, but a second car, a Mazda occupied by John Lyons, his wife Donnelda, his 2-year-old son Christopher, and his 15-year-old niece, Theresa Tyson, pulled over to render aid.

As Raymond showed John Lyons the flat tire on the Lincoln, the other Tisons and Greenawalt emerged. The Lyons family was forced into the backseat of the Lincoln. Raymond and Donald drove the Lincoln down a dirt road off the highway and then down a gas line service road farther into the desert; Gary Tison, Ricky Tison, and Randy Greenawalt followed in the Lyons' Mazda. The two cars were parked trunk to trunk and the Lyons family was ordered to stand in front of the Lincoln's headlights. The Tisons transferred their belongings from the Lincoln into the Mazda. They discovered guns and money in the Mazda which they kept, and they put the rest of the Lyons' possessions in the Lincoln.

Gary Tison then told Raymond to drive the Lincoln still farther into the desert. Raymond did so, and, while the others guarded the Lyons and Theresa Tyson, Gary fired his shotgun into the radiator, presumably to completely disable the vehicle. The Lyons and Theresa Tyson were then escorted to the Lincoln and again ordered to stand in its headlights. Ricky Tison reported that John Lyons begged, in comments "more or less directed at everybody," "Jesus, don't kill me." Gary Tison said he was "thinking about it." John Lyons asked the Tisons and Greenawalt to "give us some water . . . just leave us out here, and you all go home." Gary Tison then told his sons to go back to the Mazda and get some water. Raymond later explained that his father "was like in conflict with himself. . . . What it was, I think it was the baby being there and all this, and he wasn't sure about what to do."

The petitioners' statements diverge to some extent, but it appears that both of them went back towards the Mazda, along with Donald, while Randy Greenawalt and Gary Tison stayed at the Lincoln guarding the victims. Raymond recalled being at the Mazda filling the water jug "when we started hearing the shots." Ricky said that the brothers gave the water jug to Gary Tison who then, with Randy Greenawalt went behind the Lincoln, where they spoke briefly, then raised the shotguns and started firing. In any event, petitioners agree they saw Greenawalt and their father brutally murder their four captives with repeated blasts from their shotguns. Neither made an effort to help the victims, though both later stated they were surprised by the shooting. The Tisons got into the Mazda and drove away, continuing their flight. Physical evidence suggested that Theresa Tyson managed to crawl away from the bloodbath, severely injured. She died in the desert after the Tisons left.

Several days later the Tisons and Greenawalt were apprehended after a shootout at a police roadblock. Donald Tison was killed. Gary Tison escaped into the desert where he subsequently died of exposure. Raymond and Ricky Tison and Randy Greenawalt were captured and tried jointly for the crimes associated with the prison break itself and the shootout at the roadblock; each was convicted and sentenced.

The State then individually tried each of the petitioners for capital murder of the four victims as well as for the associated crimes of armed robbery, kidnaping, and car theft. The capital murder charges were based on Arizona felony-murder law providing that a killing occurring during the perpetration of robbery or kidnaping is capital murder, and that each participant in the kidnaping or robbery is legally responsible for the acts of his accomplices. Each of the petitioners was convicted of the four murders under these accomplice liability and felony-murder statutes.

. . . the judge sentenced both petitioners to death. . . . On direct appeal, the Arizona Supreme Court affirmed.

[Petitoners contend that their death sentences had to be set aside in light of *Enmund v. Florida*, 458 U.S. 782 (1978).] In *Enmund v. Florida*, this Court reversed the death sentence of a defendant convicted under Florida's felony-murder rule. Enmund was the driver of the "getaway" car in an armed robbery of a dwelling. The occupants of the house, an elderly couple, resisted and Enmund's accomplices killed them. . . . This Court, citing the weight of legislative and community opinion, found a broad societal consensus, with which it agreed, that the death penalty was disproportional to the crime of robbery-felony murder "in these circumstances." . . . Since Enmund's own participation in the felony murder was so attenuated and since there was no proof that Enmund had any culpable mental state, the death penalty was excessive retribution for his crimes.

Enmund's sentence was disproportional under the Eighth Amendment. At one pole was Enmund himself: the minor actor in an armed robbery, not on the scene, who neither intended to kill nor was found to have had any culpable mental state. Only a small minority of States even authorized the death penalty in such circumstances and even within those jurisdictions the death penalty was almost never exacted for such a crime. The Court held that capital punishment was disproportional in these cases. *Enmund* also clearly dealt with the other polar case: the felony murderer who actually killed, attempted to kill, or intended to kill. The Court clearly held that the equally small minority of jurisdictions that limited the death penalty to these circumstances could continue to exact it in accordance with local law when the circumstances warranted. The Tison brothers' cases fall into neither of these neat categories. . . .

The issue raised by this case is whether the Eighth Amendment prohibits the death penalty in the intermediate case of the defendant whose participation is major and whose mental state is one of reckless indifference to the value of human life. *Enmund* does not specifically address this point. . . .

A critical facet of the individualized determination of culpability required in capital cases is the mental state with which the defendant commits the crime. Deeply ingrained in our legal tradition is the idea that the more purposeful is the criminal conduct, the more serious is the offense, and, therefore, the more severely it ought to be punished. The ancient concept of malice aforethought was an early attempt to focus on mental state in order to distinguish those who deserved death from those who through "Benefit of . . . Clergy would be spared. Over time, malice aforethought came to be inferred from the mere act of killing in a variety of circumstances; in reaction, Pennsylvania became the first American jurisdiction to distinguish between degrees of murder, reserving capital punishment to "wilful, deliberate and premeditated" killings and felony murders. More recently, in *Lockett v. Ohio*, 438 U.S. 586 (1978), the plurality opinion made clear that the defendant's mental state was critical to weighing a defendant's culpability under a system of guided discretion, vacating a death sentence imposed under an Ohio statute that did not permit the sentencing authority to take into account "the absence of direct proof that the defendant intended to cause the death of the victim." In *Enmund v. Florida*, the Court recognized again the importance of mental state, explicitly permitting the death penalty in at least those cases where the felony murderer intended to kill and forbidding it in the case of a minor actor not shown to have had any culpable mental state.

A narrow focus on the question of whether or not a given defendant "intended to kill," however, is a highly unsatisfactory means of definitively distinguishing the most culpable and dangerous of murderers. Many who intend to, and do, kill are not criminally liable at all—those who act in self-defense or with other justification or excuse. Other intentional homicides, though criminal, are often felt undeserving of the death penalty—those that are the result of provocation. On the other hand, some nonintentional murderers may be among the most dangerous and inhumane of all—the person who tortures another not caring whether the victim lives or dies, or the robber who shoots someone in the course of the robbery, utterly indifferent to the fact that the desire to rob may have the unintended consequence of killing the victim as well as taking the victim's property. This reckless indifference to the value of human life may be every bit as shocking to the moral sense as an "intent to kill." Indeed it is for this very reason that the common law and modern criminal codes alike have classified behavior such as occurred in this case along with intentional murders. *Enmund* held that when "intent to kill" results in its logical though not inevitable consequence—the taking of human life—the Eighth Amendment permits the State to exact the death penalty after a careful weighing of the aggravating and mitigating circumstances. Similarly, we hold that the reckless disregard for human life implicit in knowingly engaging in criminal activities known to carry a grave risk of death represents a highly culpable mental state, a mental state that may be taken into account in making a capital sentencing judgment when that conduct causes its natural, though also not inevitable, lethal result.

The petitioners' own personal involvement in the crimes was not minor, but rather, as specifically found by the trial court, "substantial." Far from merely sitting in a car away from the actual scene of the murders acting as the getaway driver to a robbery, each petitioner was actively involved in every element of the kidnaping-robbery and was physically present during the entire sequence of criminal activity culminating in the murder of the Lyons family and the subsequent flight. The Tisons' high level of participation in these crimes further implicates them in the resulting deaths. Accordingly, they fall well within the overlapping second intermediate position which focuses on the defendant's degree of participation in the felony.

Only a small minority of those jurisdictions imposing capital punishment for felony murder have rejected the possibility of a capital sentence absent an intent to kill, and we do not find this minority position constitutionally required. We will not attempt to precisely delineate the particular types of conduct and states of mind warranting imposition of the death penalty here. Rather, we simply hold that major participation in the felony committed, combined with reckless indifference to human life, is sufficient to satisfy the *Enmund* culpability requirement. The Arizona courts have clearly found that the former exists; we now vacate the judgments below and remand for determination of the latter in further proceedings not inconsistent with this opinion.

Notes and Questions

1. Most death penalty states permit the death penalty for felony murder. Some permit the death penalty to be imposed only if the killing was committed intentionally or knowingly. *See* Texas Penal Code §19.03 (the person "intentionally commits the murder in the course of committing or attempting to commit kidnapping, burglary, robbery, aggravated sexual assault, arson, obstruction or retaliation, or terroristic threat . . ."). Others permit death to be imposed even though the offender had no intent to kill or to inflict serious bodily injury. *See State v. Carlson*, 351 P.3d 1079 (Arizona 2015) ("To be eligible for the death penalty, a defendant must have actually killed, intended that a killing take place, or been a major participant in the underlying felony and recklessly indifferent to another person's life.").

2. Suppose A, B and C agree to rob a bank. They also agree that no one will be killed. A and B enter the bank, while C remains as the lookout. A deliberately shoots and kills the teller. Can B and C be sentenced to death in Texas? Arizona?

3. How were the Tisons recklessly indifferent to the value of human life?

IV. Limitations on Death Eligibility

Certain classes of offenders are categorically excluded from being sentenced to death. The Court has held that offenders who are intellectually disabled and juveniles cannot be sentenced to death. According to the Supreme Court, their executions would not serve the purposes of either deterrence or retribution. The Court has also prohibited the death penalty for rape and other non-homicides.

A. Intellectual Disability

The American Psychological Association defines intellectual disability as a person with deficits in intellectual functioning, typically an IQ score of 70 or below, and deficits in adaptive functioning, the skills needed to live in an independent and responsible manner.

Atkins v. Virginia

536 U.S. 304 (2002)

U.S. Supreme Court

STEVENS, J.

Those mentally retarded persons who meet the law's requirements for criminal responsibility should be tried and punished when they commit crimes. Because of their disabilities in areas of reasoning, judgment, and control of their impulses, however, they do not act with the level of moral culpability that characterizes the most serious adult criminal conduct. Moreover, their impairments can jeopardize the reliability and fairness of capital proceedings against mentally retarded defendants. Presumably for these reasons, in the 13 years since we decided *Penry v. Lynaugh*, 492 U.S. 302 (1989), the American public, legislators, scholars, and judges have deliberated over the question whether the death penalty should ever be imposed on a mentally retarded criminal. The consensus reflected in those deliberations informs our answer to the question presented by this case: whether such executions are "cruel and unusual punishments" prohibited by the Eighth Amendment to the Federal Constitution.

Petitioner, Daryl Renard Atkins, was convicted of abduction, armed robbery, and capital murder, and sentenced to death. At approximately midnight on August 16, 1996, Atkins and William Jones, armed with a semiautomatic handgun, abducted Eric Nesbitt, robbed him of the money on his person, drove him to an automated teller machine in his pickup truck where cameras recorded their withdrawal of additional cash, then took him to an isolated location where he was shot eight times and killed. . . .

In the penalty phase, the defense relied on one witness, Dr. Evan Nelson, a forensic psychologist who had evaluated Atkins before trial and concluded that he was "mildly mentally retarded." His conclusion was based on interviews with people who knew Atkins, a review of school and court records, and the administration of a standard intelligence test which indicated that Atkins had a full scale IQ of 59.

The jury sentenced Atkins to death, but the Virginia Supreme Court ordered a second sentencing hearing because the trial court had used a misleading verdict form. At the resentencing, Dr. Nelson again testified. The State presented an expert rebuttal witness, Dr. Stanton Samenow, who expressed the opinion that Atkins was not mentally retarded, but rather was of "average intelligence, at least," and diagnosable as having antisocial personality disorder. The jury again sentenced Atkins to death. . . .

The Eighth Amendment succinctly prohibits "excessive" sanctions. It provides: "Excessive bail shall not be required, nor excessive fines imposed, nor cruel and unusual punishments inflicted." . . .

A claim that punishment is excessive is judged not by the standards that prevailed in 1685 when Lord Jeffreys presided over the "Bloody Assizes" or when the Bill of

Rights was adopted, but rather by those that currently prevail. As Chief Justice Warren explained in his opinion in *Trop v. Dulles*, 356 U.S. 86 (1958): "The basic concept underlying the Eighth Amendment is nothing less than the dignity of man. . . . The Amendment must draw its meaning from the evolving standards of decency that mark the progress of a maturing society."

Proportionality review under those evolving standards should be informed by "'objective factors to the maximum possible extent.'" We have pinpointed that the "clearest and most reliable objective evidence of contemporary values is the legislation enacted by the country's legislatures." Relying in part on such legislative evidence, we have held that death is an impermissibly excessive punishment for the rape of an adult woman, *Coker v. Georgia*, 433 U.S. 584, 593–596 (1977), or for a defendant who neither took life, attempted to take life, nor intended to take life, *Enmund v. Florida*, 458 U.S. 782, 789–793 (1982).

The parties have not called our attention to any state legislative consideration of the suitability of imposing the death penalty on mentally retarded offenders prior to 1986. In that year, the public reaction to the execution of a mentally retarded murderer in Georgia apparently led to the enactment of the first state statute prohibiting such executions. In 1988, when Congress enacted legislation reinstating the federal death penalty, it expressly provided that a "sentence of death shall not be carried out upon a person who is mentally retarded." In 1989, Maryland enacted a similar prohibition. It was in that year that we decided *Penry*, and concluded that those two state enactments, "even when added to the 14 States that have rejected capital punishment completely, do not provide sufficient evidence at present of a national consensus."

Much has changed since then. Responding to the national attention received by the Bowden execution and our decision in *Penry*, state legislatures across the country began to address the issue. In 1990 Kentucky and Tennessee enacted statutes similar to those in Georgia and Maryland, as did New Mexico in 1991, and Arkansas, Colorado, Washington, Indiana, and Kansas in 1993 and 1994. In 1995, when New York reinstated its death penalty, it emulated the Federal Government by expressly exempting the mentally retarded. Nebraska followed suit in 1998. There appear to have been no similar enactments during the next two years, but in 2000 and 2001 six more States—South Dakota, Arizona, Connecticut, Florida, Missouri, and North Carolina—joined the procession. The Texas Legislature unanimously adopted a similar bill, and bills have passed at least one house in other States, including Virginia and Nevada.

It is not so much the number of these States that is significant, but the consistency of the direction of change. Given the well-known fact that anticrime legislation is far more popular than legislation providing protections for persons guilty of violent crime, the large number of States prohibiting the execution of mentally retarded persons (and the complete absence of States passing legislation reinstating the power to conduct such executions) provides powerful evidence that today our society views mentally retarded offenders as categorically less culpable than the average criminal.

The evidence carries even greater force when it is noted that the legislatures that have addressed the issue have voted overwhelmingly in favor of the prohibition. Moreover, even in those States that allow the execution of mentally retarded offenders, the practice is uncommon. Some States, for example New Hampshire and New Jersey, continue to authorize executions, but none have been carried out in decades. Thus there is little need to pursue legislation barring the execution of the mentally retarded in those States. And it appears that even among those States that regularly execute offenders and that have no prohibition with regard to the mentally retarded, only five have executed offenders possessing a known IQ less than 70 since we decided *Penry*. The practice, therefore, has become truly unusual, and it is fair to say that a national consensus has developed against it.

This consensus unquestionably reflects widespread judgment about the relative culpability of mentally retarded offenders, and the relationship between mental retardation and the penological purposes served by the death penalty. Additionally, it suggests that some characteristics of mental retardation undermine the strength of the procedural protections that our capital jurisprudence steadfastly guards.

As discussed above, clinical definitions of mental retardation require not only subaverage intellectual functioning, but also significant limitations in adaptive skills such as communication, self-care, and self-direction that became manifest before age 18. Mentally retarded persons frequently know the difference between right and wrong and are competent to stand trial. Because of their impairments, however, by definition they have diminished capacities to understand and process information, to communicate, to abstract from mistakes and learn from experience, to engage in logical reasoning, to control impulses, and to understand the reactions of others. There is no evidence that they are more likely to engage in criminal conduct than others, but there is abundant evidence that they often act on impulse rather than pursuant to a premeditated plan, and that in group settings they are followers rather than leaders. Their deficiencies do not warrant an exemption from criminal sanctions, but they do diminish their personal culpability.

In light of these deficiencies, our death penalty jurisprudence provides two reasons consistent with the legislative consensus that the mentally retarded should be categorically excluded from execution. First, there is a serious question as to whether either justification that we have recognized as a basis for the death penalty applies to mentally retarded offenders. *Gregg v. Georgia*, 428 U.S. 153, 183 (1976), identified "retribution and deterrence of capital crimes by prospective offenders" as the social purposes served by the death penalty. Unless the imposition of the death penalty on a mentally retarded person "measurably contributes to one or both of these goals, it 'is nothing more than the purposeless and needless imposition of pain and suffering,' and hence an unconstitutional punishment."

With respect to retribution—the interest in seeing that the offender gets his "just deserts"—the severity of the appropriate punishment necessarily depends on the culpability of the offender. Since *Gregg*, our jurisprudence has consistently confined the imposition of the death penalty to a narrow category of the most serious crimes. For example, in *Godfrey v. Georgia*, 446 U.S. 420 (1980), we set aside a death sentence because the petitioner's crimes did not reflect "a consciousness materially more 'depraved' than that of any person guilty of murder." If the culpability of the average murderer is insufficient to justify the most extreme sanction available to the State, the lesser culpability of the mentally retarded offender surely does not merit that form of retribution. Thus, pursuant to our narrowing jurisprudence, which seeks to ensure that only the most deserving of execution are put to death, an exclusion for the mentally retarded is appropriate.

With respect to deterrence—the interest in preventing capital crimes by prospective offenders—"it seems likely that 'capital punishment can serve as a deterrent only when murder is the result of premeditation and deliberation.'" Exempting the mentally retarded from that punishment will not affect the "cold calculus that precedes the decision" of other potential murderers. Indeed, that sort of calculus is at the opposite end of the spectrum from behavior of mentally retarded offenders. The theory of deterrence in capital sentencing is predicated upon the notion that the increased severity of the punishment will inhibit criminal actors from carrying out murderous conduct. Yet it is the same cognitive and behavioral impairments that make these defendants less morally culpable—for example, the diminished ability to understand and process information, to learn from experience, to engage in logical reasoning, or to control impulses—that also make it less likely that they can process the information of the possibility of execution as a penalty and, as a result, control their conduct based upon that information. Nor will exempting the mentally retarded from execution lessen the deterrent effect of the death penalty with respect to offenders who are not mentally retarded. Such individuals are unprotected by the exemption and will continue to face the threat of execution. Thus, executing the mentally retarded will not measurably further the goal of deterrence.

The reduced capacity of mentally retarded offenders provides a second justification for a categorical rule making such offenders ineligible for the death penalty. The risk "that the death penalty will be imposed in spite of factors which may call for a less severe penalty," is enhanced, not only by the possibility of false confessions, but also by the lesser ability of mentally retarded defendants to make a persuasive showing of mitigation in the face of prosecutorial evidence of one or more aggravating factors. Mentally retarded defendants may be less able to give meaningful assistance to their counsel and are typically poor witnesses, and their demeanor may create an unwarranted impression of lack of remorse for their crimes. . . .

Notes and Questions

1. The American Psychiatric Association has replaced the term "mental retardation" with "intellectual disability."

2. In the first sentence of the majority opinion, Justice Stevens states "[t]hose [intellectually disabled] persons who meet the law's requirements for criminal responsi-

bility should be tried and punished when they commit crimes." Why shouldn't they be completely excused from criminal liability?

3. According to the majority opinion, executing intellectually disabled offenders serves neither deterrence nor retribution. Why not? Why is this important?

4. Justice Stevens goes through the number of states which have excluded intellectually disabled offenders from receiving death sentences. Why is this important?

5. Does it make sense to leave the task of defining intellectual disability to the states?

6. Although the Court left it to the states to define intellectual disability, there are limits. In *Hall v. Florida*, 572 U.S. 701 (2014), the Court held that given the fact that IQ test scores are not infallible, Florida's threshold requirement of a 70 IQ score or below before an inmate is able to submit additional evidence of intellectual disability is unconstitutional.

7. Justice Scalia argues that, given that there are degrees of intellectual disability, whether an intellectually disabled offender should be sentenced to death should be determined on a case by case basis. Do you agree or disagree?

B. Juveniles

Whether an offender who kills before he reaches his 18th birthday should be executed was the subject of intense debate before the Supreme Court decided *Roper*.

Roper v. Simmons
543 U.S. 551 (2005)
U.S. Supreme Court

KENNEDY, J.

This case requires us to address, for the second time in a decade and a half, whether it is permissible under the Eighth and Fourteenth Amendments to the Constitution of the United States to execute a juvenile offender who was older than 15 but younger than 18 when he committed a capital crime. . . .

At the age of 17, when he was still a junior in high school, Christopher Simmons, the respondent here, committed murder. About nine months later, after he had turned 18, he was tried and sentenced to death. There is little doubt that Simmons was the instigator of the crime. Before its commission Simmons said he wanted to murder someone. In chilling, callous terms he talked about his plan, discussing it for the most part with two friends, Charles Benjamin and John Tessmer, then aged 15 and 16 respectively. Simmons proposed to commit burglary and murder by breaking and entering, tying up a victim, and throwing the victim off a bridge. Simmons assured his friends they could "get away with it" because they were minors.

The three met at about 2 a.m. on the night of the murder, but Tessmer left before the other two set out. (The State later charged Tessmer with conspiracy, but dropped the charge in exchange for his testimony against Simmons.) Simmons and Benjamin entered the home of the victim, Shirley Crook, after reaching through an open window and unlocking the back door. Simmons turned on a hallway light. Awakened, Mrs. Crook called out, "Who's there?" In response Simmons entered Mrs. Crook's bedroom, where he recognized her from a previous car accident involving them both. Simmons later admitted this confirmed his resolve to murder her.

Using duct tape to cover her eyes and mouth and bind her hands, the two perpetrators put Mrs. Crook in her minivan and drove to a state park. They reinforced the bindings, covered her head with a towel, and walked her to a railroad trestle spanning the Meramec River. There they tied her hands and feet together with electrical wire, wrapped her whole face in duct tape and threw her from the bridge, drowning her in the waters below.

By the afternoon of September 9, Steven Crook had returned home from an overnight trip, found his bedroom in disarray, and reported his wife missing. On the same afternoon fishermen recovered the victim's body from the river. Simmons, meanwhile, was bragging about the killing, telling friends he had killed a woman "because the bitch seen my face." . . .

The evidence of national consensus against the death penalty for juveniles is similar, and in some respects parallel, to the evidence *Atkins* held sufficient to demonstrate a national consensus against the death penalty for the mentally retarded. When *Atkins* was decided, 30 States prohibited the death penalty for the mentally retarded. This number comprised 12 that had abandoned the death penalty altogether, and 18 that maintained it but excluded the mentally retarded from its reach. By a similar calculation in this case, 30 States prohibit the juvenile death penalty, comprising 12 that have rejected the death penalty altogether and 18 that maintain it but, by express provision or judicial interpretation, exclude juveniles from its reach. *Atkins* emphasized that even in the 20 States without formal prohibition, the practice of executing the mentally retarded was infrequent. . . .

As in *Atkins*, the objective indicia of consensus in this case—the rejection of the juvenile death penalty in the majority of States; the infrequency of its use even where it remains on the books; and the consistency in the trend toward abolition of the practice—provide sufficient evidence that today our society views juveniles, in the words *Atkins* used respecting the mentally retarded, as "categorically less culpable than the average criminal."

A majority of States have rejected the imposition of the death penalty on juvenile offenders under 18, and we now hold this is required by the Eighth Amendment.

Because the death penalty is the most severe punishment, the Eighth Amendment applies to it with special force. Capital punishment must be limited to those offenders who commit "a narrow category of the most serious crimes" and whose extreme culpability makes them "the most deserving of execution." This principle is implemented throughout the capital sentencing process. States must give narrow and precise definition to the aggravating factors that can result in a capital sentence. In any capital case a defendant has wide latitude to raise as a mitigating factor "any aspect of [his or her] character or record and any of the circumstances of the offense that the defendant proffers as a basis for a sentence less than death." There are a number of crimes that beyond question are severe in absolute terms, yet the death penalty may not be imposed for their commission. The death penalty may not be imposed on certain classes of offenders, such as juveniles under 16, the insane, and the mentally retarded, no matter how heinous the crime. These rules vindicate the underlying principle that the death penalty is reserved for a narrow category of crimes and offenders.

Three general differences between juveniles under 18 and adults demonstrate that juvenile offenders cannot with reliability be classified among the worst offenders. First, as any parent knows and as the scientific and sociological studies respondent and his amici cite tend to confirm, "[a] lack of maturity and an underdeveloped sense of responsibility are found in youth more often than in adults and are more understandable among the young. These qualities often result in impetuous and ill-considered actions and decisions." It has been noted that "adolescents are overrepresented statistically in virtually every category of reckless behavior." In recognition of the comparative immaturity and irresponsibility of juveniles, almost every State prohibits those under 18 years of age from voting, serving on juries, or marrying without parental consent.

The second area of difference is that juveniles are more vulnerable or susceptible to negative influences and outside pressures, including peer pressure. This is explained in part by the prevailing circumstance that juveniles have less control, or less experience with control, over their own environment.

The third broad difference is that the character of a juvenile is not as well formed as that of an adult. The personality traits of juveniles are more transitory, less fixed.

These differences render suspect any conclusion that a juvenile falls among the worst offenders. The susceptibility of juveniles to immature and irresponsible behavior means "their irresponsible conduct is not as morally reprehensible as that of an adult." Their own vulnerability and comparative lack of control over their immediate surroundings mean juveniles have a greater claim than adults to be forgiven for failing to escape negative influences in their whole environment. The reality that juveniles still struggle to define their identity means it is less supportable to conclude that even a heinous crime committed by a juvenile is evidence of irretrievably depraved character. From a moral standpoint it would be misguided to equate the failings of a minor with those of an adult, for a greater possibility exists that a minor's character deficiencies will be reformed. Indeed, "[t]he relevance of youth as a mitigating factor derives from the fact that the signature qualities of youth are transient; as individuals mature, the impetuousness and recklessness that may dominate in younger years can subside." . . .

Once the diminished culpability of juveniles is recognized, it is evident that the penological justifications for the death penalty apply to them with lesser force than to adults. We have held there are two distinct social purposes served by the death penalty: "'retribution and deterrence of capital crimes by prospective offenders.'" As for retribution, we remarked in *Atkins* that "[i]f the culpability of the average murderer is insufficient to justify the most extreme sanction available to the State, the lesser culpability of the mentally retarded offender surely does not merit that form of retribution." The same conclusions follow from the lesser culpability of the juvenile offender. Whether viewed as an attempt to express the community's moral outrage or as an attempt to right the balance for the wrong to the victim, the case for retribution is not as strong with a minor as with an adult. Retribution is not proportional if the law's most severe penalty is imposed on one whose culpability or blameworthiness is diminished, to a substantial degree, by reason of youth and immaturity.

As for deterrence, it is unclear whether the death penalty has a significant or even measurable deterrent effect on juveniles, as counsel for petitioner acknowledged at oral argument. In general we leave to legislatures the assessment of the efficacy of various criminal penalty schemes. Here, however, the absence of evidence of deterrent effect is of special concern because the same characteristics that render juveniles less culpable than adults suggest as well that juveniles will be less susceptible to deterrence. . . .

Our determination that the death penalty is disproportionate punishment for offenders under 18 finds confirmation in the stark reality that the United States is the only country in the world that continues to give official sanction to the juvenile death penalty. This reality does not become controlling, for the task of interpreting the Eighth Amendment remains our responsibility. Yet at least from the time of the Court's decision in Trop, the Court has referred to the laws of other countries and to international authorities as instructive for its interpretation of the Eighth Amendment's prohibition of "cruel and unusual punishments."

As respondent and a number of amici emphasize, Article 37 of the United Nations Convention on the Rights of the Child, which every country in the world has ratified save for the United States and Somalia, contains an express prohibition on capital punishment for crimes committed by juveniles under 18. No ratifying country has entered a reservation to the provision prohibiting the execution of juvenile offenders. Parallel prohibitions are contained in other significant international covenants.

Respondent and his amici have submitted, and petitioner does not contest, that only seven countries other than the United States have executed juvenile offenders since 1990: Iran, Pakistan, Saudi Arabia, Yemen, Nigeria, the Democratic Republic of Congo, and China. Since then each of these countries has either abolished capital punishment for juveniles or made public disavowal of the practice. In sum, it is fair to say that the United States now stands alone in a world that has turned its face against the juvenile death penalty. . . .

It is proper that we acknowledge the overwhelming weight of international opinion against the juvenile death penalty, resting in large part on the understanding that the instability and emotional imbalance of young people may often be a factor in the crime. The opinion of the world community, while not controlling our outcome, does provide respected and significant confirmation for our own conclusions.

Over time, from one generation to the next, the Constitution has come to earn the high respect and even, as Madison dared to hope, the veneration of the American people. The document sets forth, and rests upon, innovative principles original to the American experience, such as federalism; a proven balance in political mechanisms through separation of powers; specific guarantees for the accused in criminal cases; and broad provisions to secure individual freedom and preserve human dignity. These doctrines and guarantees are central to the American experience and remain essential to our present-day self-definition and national identity. Not the least of the reasons we honor the Constitution, then, is because we know it to be our own. It does not lessen our fidelity to the Constitution or our pride in its origins to acknowledge that the express affirmation of certain fundamental rights by other nations and peoples simply underscores the centrality of those same rights within our own heritage of freedom. . . .

Notes and Questions

1. According to the majority, juveniles are not as deterrable as adults and therefore the retributive purpose is not served by executing them. Why? Do you agree?

2. Was the Court right in drawing the age line at 18? Should the line have been left at 16? Should there be any line? If so, what should it be?

3. The Court indicated that the United States was one of the few nations in the world that continued to execute juveniles in violation of international law and cited to the United Nations Convention on the Rights of the Child which prohibits the execution of juveniles. Was this relevant in interpreting the Eighth Amendment?

4. Is Justice Scalia right that juveniles should not be categorically excluded but instead that the issue should be decided on a case-by-case basis?

C. Non-Homicide

The Supreme Court has precluded the death penalty for crimes other than murder, although it did leave the door open for crimes that it called "offenses against the State."

Kennedy v. Louisiana
554 U.S. 407 (2008)
U.S. Supreme Court

KENNEDY, J.

Petitioner's crime was one that cannot be recounted in these pages in a way sufficient to capture in full the hurt and horror inflicted on his victim or to convey the revulsion society, and the jury that represents it, sought to express by sentencing petitioner to death. At 9:18 a.m. on March 2, 1998, petitioner called 911 to report that his stepdaughter, referred to here as L.H., had been raped. He told the 911 operator that L.H. had been in the garage while he readied his son for school. Upon hearing loud screaming, petitioner said, he ran outside and found L.H. in the side yard. Two neighborhood boys, petitioner told the operator, had dragged L.H. from the garage to the yard, pushed her down, and raped her. Petitioner claimed he saw one of the boys riding away on a blue 10-speed bicycle.

When police arrived at petitioner's home between 9:20 and 9:30 a.m., they found L.H. on her bed, wearing a T-shirt and wrapped in a bloody blanket. She was bleeding profusely from the vaginal area. Petitioner told police he had carried her from the yard to the bathtub and then to the bed. Consistent with this explanation, police found a thin line of blood drops in the garage on the way to the house and then up the stairs. Once in the bedroom, petitioner had used a basin of water and a cloth to wipe blood from the victim. This later prevented medical personnel from collecting a reliable DNA sample.

L.H. was transported to the Children's Hospital. An expert in pediatric forensic medicine testified that L.H.'s injuries were the most severe he had seen from a sexual assault in his four years of practice. A laceration to the left wall of the vagina had separated her cervix from the back of her vagina, causing her rectum to protrude into the vaginal structure. Her entire perineum was torn from the posterior fourchette to the anus. The injuries required emergency surgery. . . .

Eight days after the crime, and despite L.H.'s insistence that petitioner was not the offender, petitioner was arrested for the rape. The State's investigation had drawn the accuracy of petitioner and L.H.'s story into question. Though the defense at trial proffered alternative explanations, the case for the prosecution, credited by the jury, was based upon the following evidence: An inspection of the side yard immediately after the assault was inconsistent with a rape having occurred there, the grass having been found mostly undisturbed but for a small patch of coagulated blood. Petitioner said that one of the perpetrators fled the crime scene on a blue 10-speed bicycle but gave inconsistent descriptions of the bicycle's features, such as its handlebars. Investigators found a bicycle matching petitioner and L.H.'s description in tall grass behind a nearby apartment, and petitioner identified it as the bicycle one of the perpetrators was riding. Yet its tires were flat, it did not have gears, and it was covered in spider webs. In addition police found blood on the underside of L.H.'s mattress. This convinced them the rape took place in her bedroom, not outside the house.

Police also found that petitioner made four telephone calls on the morning of the rape. Sometime before 6:15 a.m., petitioner called his employer and left a message that he was unavailable to work that day. Petitioner called back between 6:30 and 7:30 a.m. to ask a colleague how to get blood out of a white carpet because his daughter had "'just become a young lady.'" Brief for Respondent 12. At 7:37 a.m., petitioner called B & B Carpet Cleaning and requested urgent assistance in removing bloodstains from a carpet. Petitioner did not call 911 until about an hour and a half later.

About a month after petitioner's arrest L.H. was removed from the custody of her mother, who had maintained until that point that petitioner was not involved in the rape. On June 22, 1998, L.H. was returned home and told her mother for the first time that petitioner had raped her. And on December 16, 1999, about 21 months after the rape, L.H. recorded her accusation in a videotaped interview with the Child Advocacy Center. . . .

The Eighth Amendment, applicable to the States through the Fourteenth Amendment, provides that "[e]xcessive bail shall not be required, nor excessive fines imposed, nor cruel and unusual punishments inflicted." The Amendment proscribes "all excessive punishments, as well as cruel and unusual punishments that may or may not be excessive." The Court explained in *Atkins* and *Roper* that the Eighth Amendment's protection against excessive or cruel and unusual punishments flows from the basic "precept of justice that punishment for [a] crime should be graduated and proportioned to [the] offense." Whether this requirement has been fulfilled is determined not by the standards that prevailed when the Eighth Amendment was adopted in 1791 but by the norms that "currently prevail." The Amendment "draw[s] its meaning from the evolving standards of decency that mark the progress of a maturing society." This is because "[t]he standard of extreme cruelty is not merely descriptive, but necessarily embodies a moral judgment. The standard itself remains the same, but its applicability must change as the basic mores of society change."

Evolving standards of decency must embrace and express respect for the dignity of the person, and the punishment of criminals must conform to that rule. As we shall discuss, punishment is justified under one or more of three principal rationales: rehabilitation, deterrence, and retribution. It is the last of these, retribution, that most often can contradict the law's own ends. This is of particular concern when the Court interprets the meaning of the Eighth Amendment in capital cases. When the law punishes by death, it risks its own sudden descent into brutality, transgressing the constitutional commitment to decency and restraint.

For these reasons we have explained that capital punishment must "be limited to those offenders who commit 'a narrow category of the most serious crimes' and whose extreme culpability makes them 'the most deserving of execution.'" Though the death penalty is not invariably unconstitutional, the Court insists upon confining the instances in which the punishment can be imposed. . . .

Based both on consensus and our own independent judgment, our holding is that a death sentence for one who raped but did not kill a child, and who did not intend to assist another in killing the child, is unconstitutional under the Eighth and Fourteenth Amendments.

The existence of objective indicia of consensus against making a crime punishable by death was a relevant concern in *Roper, Atkins, Coker* and *Enmund,* and we follow the approach of those cases here. The history of the death penalty for the crime of rape is an instructive beginning point.

In 1925, 18 States, the District of Columbia, and the Federal Government had statutes that authorized the death penalty for the rape of a child or an adult. Between 1930 and 1964, 455 people were executed for those crimes. To our knowledge the last individual executed for the rape of a child was Ronald Wolfe in 1964.

In 1972, *Furman* invalidated most of the state statutes authorizing the death penalty for the crime of rape; and in *Furman*'s aftermath only six States reenacted their capital rape provisions. Three States—Georgia, North Carolina, and Louisiana—did so with respect to all rape offenses. Three States—Florida, Mississippi, and Tennessee—did so with respect only to child rape. All six statutes were later invalidated under state or federal law.

Louisiana reintroduced the death penalty for rape of a child in 1995. Under the current statute, any anal, vaginal, or oral intercourse with a child under the age of 13 constitutes aggravated rape and is punishable by death. Mistake of age is not a defense, so the statute imposes strict liability in this regard. Five States have since followed Louisiana's lead: Four of these States' statutes are more narrow than Louisiana's in that only offenders with a previous rape conviction are death eligible. Georgia's statute makes child rape a capital offense only when aggravating circumstances are present, including but not limited to a prior conviction.

By contrast, 44 States have not made child rape a capital offense. As for federal law, Congress in the Federal Death Penalty Act of 1994 expanded the number of federal crimes for which the death penalty is a permissible sentence, including certain nonhomicide offenses; but it did not do the same for child rape or abuse. Under 18 U.S.C. § 2245, an offender is death eligible only when the sexual abuse or exploitation results in the victim's death. . . .

The evidence of a national consensus with respect to the death penalty for child rapists, as with respect to juveniles, mentally retarded offenders, and vicarious felony murderers, shows divided opinion but, on balance, an opinion against it. Thirty-seven jurisdictions—36 States plus the Federal Government—have the death penalty. As mentioned above, only six of those jurisdictions authorize the death penalty for rape of a child. Though our review of national consensus is not confined to tallying the number of States with applicable death penalty legislation, it is of significance that, in 45 jurisdictions, petitioner could not be executed for child rape of any kind. . . .

As we have said in other Eighth Amendment cases, objective evidence of contemporary values as it relates to punishment for child rape is entitled to great weight, but it does not end our inquiry. . . .

It must be acknowledged that there are moral grounds to question a rule barring capital punishment for a crime against an individual that did not result in death. These facts illustrate the point. Here the victim's fright, the sense of betrayal, and the nature of her injuries caused more prolonged physical and mental suffering than, say, a sudden killing by an unseen assassin. The attack was not just on her but on her childhood. For this reason, we should be most reluctant to rely upon the language of the plurality in *Coker*, which posited that, for the victim of rape, "life may not be nearly so happy as it was," but it is not beyond repair. Rape has a permanent psychological, emotional, and sometimes physical impact on the child. We cannot dismiss the years of long anguish that must be endured by the victim of child rape.

It does not follow, though, that capital punishment is a proportionate penalty for the crime. The constitutional prohibition against excessive or cruel and unusual punishments mandates that the State's power to punish "be exercised within the limits of civilized standards." Evolving standards of decency that mark the progress of a maturing society counsel us to be most hesitant before interpreting the Eighth Amendment to allow the extension of the death penalty, a hesitation that has special force where no life was taken in the commission of the crime. It is an established principle that decency, in its essence, presumes respect for the individual and thus moderation or restraint in the application of capital punishment.

To date the Court has sought to define and implement this principle, for the most part, in cases involving capital murder. One approach has been to insist upon general rules that ensure consistency in determining who receives a death sentence. At the same time the Court has insisted, to ensure restraint and moderation in use of capital punishment, on judging the "character and record of the individual offender and the circumstances of the particular offense as a constitutionally indispensable part of the process of inflicting the penalty of death." . . .

Our concern here is limited to crimes against individual persons. We do not address, for example, crimes defining and punishing treason, espionage, terrorism, and drug kingpin activity, which are offenses against the State. As it relates to crimes against individuals, though, the death penalty should not be expanded to instances where the victim's life was not taken. . . .

Consistent with evolving standards of decency and the teachings of our precedents we conclude that, in determining whether the death penalty is excessive, there is a distinction between intentional first-degree murder on the one hand and nonhomicide crimes against individual persons, even including child rape, on the other. The latter crimes may be devastating in their harm, as here, but "in terms of moral depravity and of the injury to the person and to the public," they cannot be compared to murder in their "severity and irrevocability." . . .

The goal of retribution, which reflects society's and the victim's interests in seeing that the offender is repaid for the hurt he caused, does not justify the harshness of the death penalty here. In measuring retribution, as well as other objectives of criminal law, it is appropriate to distinguish between a particularly depraved murder that merits death as a form of retribution and the crime of child rape.

There is an additional reason for our conclusion that imposing the death penalty for child rape would not further retributive purposes. In considering whether retribution is served, among other factors we have looked to whether capital punishment "has the potential . . . to allow the community as a whole, including the surviving family and friends of the victim, to affirm its own judgment that the culpability of the prisoner is so serious that the ultimate penalty must be sought and imposed." In considering the death penalty for nonhomicide offenses this inquiry necessarily also must include the question whether the death penalty balances the wrong to the victim.

It is not at all evident that the child rape victim's hurt is lessened when the law permits the death of the perpetrator. . . . Society's desire to inflict the death penalty for child rape by enlisting the child victim to assist it over the course of years in asking for capital punishment forces a moral choice on the child, who is not of mature age to make that choice. The way the death penalty here involves the child victim in its enforcement can compromise a decent legal system; and this is but a subset of fundamental difficulties capital punishment can cause in the administration and enforcement of laws proscribing child rape.

In addition, by in effect making the punishment for child rape and murder equivalent, a State that punishes child rape by death may remove a strong incentive for the rapist not to kill the victim. Assuming the offender behaves in a rational way, as one must to justify the penalty on grounds of deterrence, the penalty in some respects gives less protection, not more, to the victim, who is often the sole witness to the crime. It might be argued that, even if the death penalty results in a marginal increase in the incentive to kill, this is counterbalanced by a marginally increased deterrent to commit the crime at all. Whatever balance the legislature strikes, however, uncertainty on the point makes the argument for the penalty less compelling than for homicide crimes.

Notes and Questions

1. Do you agree that those who rape but do not kill their victims should not be subject to capital punishment?

2. According to the Death Penalty Information Center, between 1930 and 1972, 455 people were legally executed for rape. 405 of those executed were African-American.

3. Should there be an exception for those who rape but do not kill children?

4. Is the Court's concern that intra-family rapes may go unreported if the death penalty is on the table a legitimate concern?

5. In *Kennedy,* the Court stated that its opinion does not "address, for example, crimes defining and punishing treason, espionage, terrorism, and drug kingpin activity, which are offenses against the State." Do you agree that these should potentially be crimes punishable by death when no death results?

6. Are there any non-homicide crimes for which death would be an appropriate punishment?

V. Race and the Death Penalty

The death penalty has been disproportionately imposed on African Americans throughout the history of the United States, and that continues to be the case. The death penalty is more likely to be imposed if the offender is African American and/ or if the victim is white. The Supreme Court addressed the latter issue in *McCleskey*.

McCleskey v. Kemp
481 U.S 279 (1987)
U.S. Supreme Court

POWELL, J.

This case presents the question whether a complex statistical study that indicates a risk that racial considerations enter into capital sentencing determinations proves that petitioner McCleskey's capital sentence is unconstitutional under the Eighth or Fourteenth Amendment.

. . . In support of his claim, McCleskey proffered a statistical study performed by Professors David C. Baldus, Charles Pulaski, and George Woodworth (the Baldus study) that purports to show a disparity in the imposition of the death sentence in Georgia based on the race of the murder victim and, to a lesser extent, the race of the defendant. The Baldus study is actually two sophisticated statistical studies that examine over 2,000 murder cases that occurred in Georgia during the 1970's. The raw numbers collected by Professor Baldus indicate that defendants charged with killing white persons received the death penalty in 11% of the cases, but defendants charged with killing blacks received the death penalty in only 1% of the cases. The raw numbers also indicate a reverse racial disparity according to the race of the defendant: 4% of the black defendants received the death penalty, as opposed to 7% of the white defendants.

Baldus also divided the cases according to the combination of the race of the defendant and the race of the victim. He found that the death penalty was assessed in 22% of the cases involving black defendants and white victims; 8% of the cases involving white defendants and white victims; 1% of the cases involving black defendants and black victims; and 3% of the cases involving white defendants and black victims. Similarly, Baldus found that prosecutors sought the death penalty in 70% of the cases involving black defendants and white victims; 32% of the cases involving white defendants and white victims; 15% of the cases involving black defendants and black victims; and 19% of the cases involving white defendants and black victims.

Baldus subjected his data to an extensive analysis, taking account of 230 variables that could have explained the disparities on nonracial grounds. One of his models concludes that, even after taking account of 39 nonracial variables, defendants charged with killing white victims were 4.3 times as likely to receive a death sentence as defendants charged with killing blacks. According to this model, black defendants were 1.1 times as likely to receive a death sentence as other defendants. Thus, the Baldus study indicates that black defendants, such as McCleskey, who kill white victims have the greatest likelihood of receiving the death penalty.

McCleskey's first claim is that the Georgia capital punishment statute violates the Equal Protection Clause of the Fourteenth Amendment. He argues that race has infected the administration of Georgia's statute in two ways: persons who murder whites are more likely to be sentenced to death than persons who murder blacks, and black murderers are more likely to be sentenced to death than white murderers. As a black defendant who killed a white victim, McCleskey claims that the Baldus study demonstrates that he was discriminated against because of his race and because of the race of his victim. In its broadest form, McCleskey's claim of discrimination extends to every actor in the Georgia capital sentencing process, from the prosecutor who sought the death penalty and the jury that imposed the sentence, to the State itself that enacted the capital punishment statute and allows it to remain in effect despite its allegedly discriminatory application. We agree with the Court of Appeals, and every other court that has considered such a challenge, that this claim must fail.

Our analysis begins with the basic principle that a defendant who alleges an equal protection violation has the burden of proving "the existence of purposeful discrimination." A corollary to this principle is that a criminal defendant must prove that the purposeful discrimination "had a discriminatory effect" on him. Thus, to prevail under the Equal Protection Clause, McCleskey must prove that the decisionmakers in *his* case acted with discriminatory purpose. He offers no evidence specific to his own case that would support an inference that racial considerations played a part in his sentence. Instead, he relies solely on the Baldus study. McCleskey argues that the Baldus study compels an inference that his sentence rests on purposeful discrimination. McCleskey's claim that these statistics are sufficient proof of discrimination, without regard to the facts of a particular case, would extend to all capital cases in Georgia, at least where the victim was white and the defendant is black.

The Court has accepted statistics as proof of intent to discriminate in certain limited contexts. First, this Court has accepted statistical disparities as proof of an equal protection violation in the selection of the jury venire in a particular district. Although statistical proof normally must present a "stark" pattern to be accepted as the sole proof of discriminatory intent under the Constitution, "because of the nature of the jury-selection task, . . . we have permitted a finding of constitutional violation even when the statistical pattern does not approach [such] extremes." Second, this Court has accepted statistics in the form of multiple-regression analysis to prove statutory violations under Title VII of the Civil Rights Act of 1964.

But the nature of the capital sentencing decision, and the relationship of the statistics to that decision, are fundamentally different from the corresponding elements in the venire-selection or Title VII cases. Most importantly, each particular decision to impose the death penalty is made by a petit jury selected from a properly constituted venire. Each jury is unique in its composition, and the Constitution requires that its decision rest on consideration of innumerable factors that vary according to the characteristics of the individual defendant and the facts of the particular capital offense. Thus, the application of an inference drawn from the general statistics to a specific decision in a trial and sentencing simply is not comparable to the application of an inference drawn from general statistics to a specific venire-selection or Title VII case. In those cases, the statistics relate to fewer entities, and fewer variables are relevant to the challenged decisions.

McCleskey also suggests that the Baldus study proves that the State as a whole has acted with a discriminatory purpose. He appears to argue that the State has violated the Equal Protection Clause by adopting the capital punishment statute and allowing it to remain in force despite its allegedly discriminatory application. But "'discriminatory purpose' . . . implies more than intent as volition or intent as awareness of consequences. It implies that the decisionmaker, in this case a state legislature, selected or reaffirmed a particular course of action at least in part 'because of,' not merely 'in spite of,' its adverse effects upon an identifiable group." For this claim to prevail, McCleskey would have to prove that the Georgia Legislature enacted or maintained the death penalty statute *because of* an anticipated racially discriminatory effect. In *Gregg v. Georgia*, this Court found that the Georgia capital sentencing system could operate in a fair and neutral manner. There was no evidence then, and there is none now, that the Georgia Legislature enacted the capital punishment statute to further a racially discriminatory purpose.

Nor has McCleskey demonstrated that the legislature maintains the capital punishment statute because of the racially disproportionate impact suggested by the Baldus study. As legislatures necessarily have wide discretion in the choice of criminal laws and penalties, and as there were legitimate reasons for the Georgia Legislature to adopt and maintain capital punishment, we will not infer a discriminatory purpose on the part of the State of Georgia. Accordingly, we reject McCleskey's equal protection claims.

In light of our precedents under the Eighth Amendment, McCleskey cannot argue successfully that his sentence is "disproportionate to the crime in the traditional sense." He does not deny that he committed a murder in the course of a planned robbery, a crime for which this Court has determined that the death penalty constitutionally may be imposed. His disproportionality claim "is of a different sort." McCleskey argues that the sentence in his case is disproportionate to the sentences in other murder cases.

On the one hand, he cannot base a constitutional claim on an argument that his case differs from other cases in which defendants *did* receive the death penalty. On automatic appeal, the Georgia Supreme Court found that McCleskey's death sentence was not disproportionate to other death sentences imposed in the State. The court supported this conclusion with an appendix containing citations to 13 cases involving generally similar murders. Moreover, where the statutory procedures adequately channel the sentencer's discretion, such proportionality review is not constitutionally required.

On the other hand, absent a showing that the Georgia capital punishment system operates in an arbitrary and capricious manner, McCleskey cannot prove a constitutional violation by demonstrating that other defendants who may be similarly situated did *not* receive the death penalty.

Although our decision in *Gregg* as to the facial validity of the Georgia capital punishment statute appears to foreclose McCleskey's disproportionality argument, he further contends that the Georgia capital punishment system is arbitrary and capricious in *application*, and therefore his sentence is excessive, because racial considerations may influence capital sentencing decisions in Georgia. We now address this claim.

To evaluate McCleskey's challenge, we must examine exactly what the Baldus study may show. Even Professor Baldus does not contend that his statistics *prove* that race enters into any capital sentencing decisions or that race was a factor in McCleskey's particular case. Statistics at most may show only a likelihood that a particular factor entered into some decisions. There is, of course, some risk of racial prejudice influencing a jury's decision in a criminal case. There are similar risks that other kinds of prejudice will influence other criminal trials. The question "is at what point that risk becomes constitutionally unacceptable," McCleskey asks us to accept the likelihood allegedly shown by the Baldus study as the constitutional measure of an unacceptable risk of racial prejudice influencing capital sentencing decisions. This we decline to do.

At most, the Baldus study indicates a discrepancy that appears to correlate with race. Apparent disparities in sentencing are an inevitable part of our criminal justice system. The discrepancy indicated by the Baldus study is "a far cry from the major systemic defects identified in *Furman*." As this Court has recognized, any mode for determining guilt or punishment "has its weaknesses and the potential for misuse." Specifically, "there can be 'no perfect procedure for deciding in which cases governmental authority should be used to impose death.'" Despite these imperfections, our consistent rule has been that constitutional guarantees are met when "the mode [for determining guilt or punishment] itself has been surrounded with safeguards to make it as fair as possible." Where the discretion that is fundamental to our criminal process is involved, we decline to assume that what is unexplained is invidious. In light of the safeguards designed to minimize racial bias in the process, the fundamental value of jury trial in our criminal justice system, and the benefits that discretion provides to criminal defendants, we hold that the Baldus study does not demonstrate a constitutionally significant risk of racial bias affecting the Georgia capital sentencing process.

Two additional concerns inform our decision in this case. First, McCleskey's claim, taken to its logical conclusion, throws into serious question the principles that underlie our entire criminal justice system. The Eighth Amendment is not limited in application to capital punishment, but applies to all penalties. Thus, if we accepted McCleskey's claim that racial bias has impermissibly tainted the capital sentencing decision, we could soon be faced with similar claims as to other types of penalty. Moreover, the claim that his sentence rests on the irrelevant factor of race easily could be extended to apply to claims based on unexplained discrepancies that correlate to membership in other minority groups, and even to gender. Similarly, since McCleskey's claim relates to the race of his victim, other claims could apply with equally logical force to statistical disparities that correlate with the race or sex of other actors in the criminal justice system, such as defense attorneys or judges. Also, there is no logical reason that such a claim need be limited to racial or sexual bias. If arbitrary and capricious punishment is the touchstone under the Eighth Amendment, such a claim could—at least in theory—be based upon any arbitrary variable, such as the defendant's facial characteristics, or the physical attractiveness of the defendant or the victim, that some statistical study indicates may be influential in jury decisionmaking. As these examples illustrate, there is no limiting principle to the type of challenge brought by McCleskey. The Constitution does not require that a State eliminate any demonstrable disparity that correlates with a potentially irrelevant factor in order to operate a criminal justice system that includes capital punishment. As we have stated specifically in the context of capital punishment, the Constitution does not "plac[e] totally unrealistic conditions on its use."

Second, McCleskey's arguments are best presented to the legislative bodies. It is not the responsibility—or indeed even the right—of this Court to determine the appropriate punishment for particular crimes. It is the legislatures, the elected representatives of the people, that are "constituted to respond to the will and consequently the moral values of the people." Legislatures also are better qualified to weigh and "evaluate the results of statistical studies in terms of their own local conditions and with a flexibility of approach that is not available to the courts," Capital punishment is now the law in more than two-thirds of our States. It is the ultimate duty of courts to determine on a case-by-case basis whether these laws are applied consistently with the Constitution. Despite McCleskey's wide-ranging arguments that basically challenge the validity of capital punishment in our multiracial society, the only question before us is whether in his case the law of Georgia was properly applied. We agree with the District Court and the Court of Appeals for the Eleventh Circuit that this was carefully and correctly done in this case.

Notes and Questions

1. According to the Death Penalty Information Center, as of February 2021, U.S. executions by race are as follows:

WHITE—1152 (75%)
BLACK—204 (13%)
LATINO—100 (6%)

2. According to the Death Penalty Information Center, as of February 2021, the racial composition of the death row population and total U.S. executions since 1976 are as follows:

EXECUTIONS SINCE 1976	DEATH ROW POPULATION
TOTAL—1532	TOTAL—2553
WHITE—854 (55%)	WHITE—1076 (42%)
BLACK—523 (34%)	BLACK—1062 (42%)
LATINO—129 (8%)	LATINO—343 (13%)
	OTHER—72 (2.9%)

3. The Court holds that in order to state a prima facie case, the inmate must prove that the decision makers in his specific case—judge, jury, prosecutor—discriminated against him. How does the defendant do this?

4. In his dissent, Justice Brennan says that "[a]t some point in this case, Warren McCleskey doubtless asked his lawyer whether a jury was likely to sentence him to die. A candid response to this question would have been disturbing. First, counsel would have to tell McCleskey that few of the details of the crime or of McCleskey's past criminal conduct were more important than the fact that his victim was white. Furthermore, counsel would feel bound to tell McCleskey that defendants charged with killing white victims in Georgia are 4.3 times as likely to be sentenced to death as defendants charged with killing blacks.... The story could be told in a variety of ways, but McCleskey could not fail to grasp its essential narrative: there was a significant chance that race would play a prominent role in determining if he lived or died."

5. The majority of homicide victims in the United States are African-American yet most of their killers are not sentenced to death. Black Lives Matter was created out of concern that the criminal justice system devalues black lives. Are they right or is there a plausible explanation for why killers of blacks are frequently not sentenced to death while killers of whites are?

6. Jurors in death penalty cases must be "death qualified." This means that they must be open to the possibility of imposing a death sentence. Because many African Americans are opposed to the death penalty, they are often disqualified as jurors by the prosecution.

7. The Capital Jury Project has found that the racial composition of the jury has a big impact on whether a defendant is sentenced to death. Some of the project's findings are as follows:

    a. "African-Americans as a class may be disproportionately excluded from jury service by virtue of the group's disproportionate view of the inappropriateness of capital punishment. Moreover, researchers categorize jurors in capital cases as 'demographically unique' in that they tend to be both white and male. This exclusion of blacks appears to have a significant impact on the outcome of capital cases."

b. In all statistical models, black jurors are significantly more likely to oppose the death penalty than are white jurors.

c. Race is the greatest influence in capital sentencing where there is a black defendant and a white victim.

d. At the guilt phase, whites were three times more likely than blacks to take a pro death stand on punishment.

e. Black jurors were far more likely than their white counterparts to have lingering doubts about the defendant's guilt when making their punishment decisions.

f. Black jurors were much more likely than their white counterparts in black/white cases to see the defendant as remorseful.

g. White jurors were more likely than their black counterparts to see the defendant in black on white cases as dangerous and to regard his dangerousness as a reason for the death penalty.

h. Black males were the most likely, and white males the least likely, to see the defendant as remorseful, and to identify with the defendant's family's situation.

i. The death penalty is more than twice as likely for the defendant in a black defendant/white victim case who draws five or more white male jurors as for a defendant who draws fewer than five. A life sentence is almost twice as likely for the defendant who draws a black male juror than for the one who fails to do so.

j. "Black jurors are significantly more receptive to mitigation than their white counterparts and more receptive overall."

k. "All jurors were significantly more receptive in [b]lack victim cases."

l. "Both [b]lack and [w]hite jurors are more receptive to mitigation in cases where a same-race defendant is charged with killing another-race victim."

Id. at 540. What do you believe explains these findings?

Formative Assessments

1. The United States government authorizes the death penalty for several crimes for which it does not require that death occur. For instance, treason, espionage, and drug trafficking. No one is currently on death row for committing such crimes. If at some point, a defendant is convicted and sentenced to death for one of these crimes, would their death sentences be overturned in light of *Kennedy v. Louisiana* and *Corker v. Georgia*?

2. Which of the following statements is most accurate regarding the death penalty?

A. The death penalty is constitutional for any crime that the legislature deems appropriate.

B. The death penalty cannot be imposed on a person who was an accomplice to a crime.

C. The death penalty can be imposed on an individual who commits multiple rapes.

D. A defendant serving a life sentence without parole who kills a prison guard cannot automatically be sentenced to death.

3. Which of the following death sentenced defendants is most likely to have his death sentence upheld on appeal?

A. The Defendant is 76 years old and in poor health.

B. The Defendant believes that the state is executing him because he is Jesus Christ.

C. The Defendant's attorney is a recent law school graduate and has never worked on a death penalty case before.

D. The Defendant has an IQ of 72, has never held a job, been married and has never had a close friend. He also has a history of committing crimes.

Chapter 11

Rape and Sexual Assault

I. Introduction

> The United States [] does not have a single set of rape laws or a single system for enforcement, but instead 51 different rape statutes and 51 different procedural systems.[1]

The variance in U.S. rape laws is a byproduct of multiple intertwined factors which at times serve as cause and at others effect. The factors include the obvious—different legislative enactments (laws/statutes) and judicial interpretations (legal opinions) in different jurisdictions over time. But there is a subtext to these differences. The laws and case interpretations vary, at least in part, because of differences in social norms, stigmas, and misperceptions about sexuality in general and more specifically sexual assault offenses. This includes a willful blindness towards acknowledging that in the vast majority of cases acquaintances, not strangers, commit rape and other sexual assaults. Similarly, despite better understanding, society and the legal system often fail to recognize that how rape survivors[2] react during the offense, and whether, when and to whom they report, are individualized trauma responses which can—and do—vary.

Additionally, the often-overlooked relationship between the rights and protections afforded to putative sexual assault victims and alleged offenders[3] is another factor which both complicates and explains rape law differences. Modifying the rights and protections of either victim or offender inevitably impacts the other. The oft repeated cycle is a rape (or series of rapes) not handled appropriately in the eyes of the media, the public and victims advocacy groups, who then lobby the legislature for a change

---

1. Donald Dripps, *Rape, Law and American Society, in* RETHINKING RAPE LAW: INTERNATIONAL AND COMPARATIVE PERSPECTIVES, 224 (F.P. Reddington & B.W. Kriesel Eds. 2010) (referring to the fifty States and the District of Columbia).

2. As a general matter, this chapter uses the term victim while acknowledging a growing preference for the term "rape survivor." *See* Jericho M. Hockett et al., *A "Rape Victim" by Any Other Name: The Effects of Labels on Individuals' Rape-Related Perceptions, in* EXPRESSION OF INEQUALITY IN INTERACTION: POWER, DOMINANCE AND STATUS (H. Pishwa & R. Schulze Eds. 2014).

3. Prior to an adjudication, individuals are putative victims and alleged offenders. Following adjudication, they are victims and offenders. This chapter uses victim and offender to refer to both categories.

to the law they believe facilitated injustice.[4] Depending on the jurisdiction's criminal law and process, legislative "fixes" may achieve the objectives of reform advocates but produce unintended negative effects on the administration of justice.[5] An appellate court may then find that the fix infringes on the constitutional or statutory rights of an offender. The law then reverts to either a point of uncertainty or to where it was deemed necessary to revise it, and a host of other cases are reversed and retried—subjecting both victim and offender to another trial process and often causing both to believe the system is at best flawed and at worst biased.

As both a complication and explanation, all of these factors are imbedded in and the byproduct of structural misogyny—ingrained prejudice against women, originating thousands of years ago and perpetuated through English common law. The United States not only incorporated and continued that bias but added racism, further contorting the development and operation of sexual assault laws.

As reflected in the quote at the outset, there is no majority view definition of the offense of rape. Both to ensure clarity and to provide a point of comparison for different formulations, this chapter introduces a definition. Next, the chapter briefly explains the social norms, stigmas, and misperceptions and symbiotic relationship points highlighted above. From there, to understand how rape law developed so differently requires reviewing its origins in English common law and then within different U.S jurisdictions.

There are a variety of ways to define rape, which reflects policy choices and the attitudes and biases discussed above. After reading this chapter, you should be able to examine different formulations of the offense of rape and recognize the significance of the terms both present and absent. At times. this chapter may seem graphic, but a substantive discussion of rape requires specificity in terms of human anatomy and sexual acts.

Finally, it is important to remember that rape *as a crime* triggers the presumptions and burdens associated with any crime: the prosecution must allege the offense; the defendant is presumed not guilty; the prosecution must prove the allegation beyond

---

4. One category of sexual assaults which does not receive much attention is sexual violence inside prisons, which has been labeled "an urgent public health issue." *See* Nancy Woff et al., *Sexual Violence Inside Prisons: Rates of Victimization*, 83 J. URBAN HEALTH 835 (2006). Following the publication by Human Rights Watch of "No Escape: Male Rape in Prison," Congress passed The Prison Rape Elimination Act (PREA) of 2003. But obtaining reliable evidence and statistics, one of PREA's major objectives, has proven challenging, which has limited the ability for informed interventions.

5. "Fixes" may also be under-resourced, which is also problematic. For example, public pressure led police to collect more "rape kits," which is a collection of physical evidence, including DNA, from a sexual assault victim's body, clothes and belongings. But the collected evidence must be tested, and without increased resources and combined with mismanagement, the result has been that "cities and states across the country have discovered DNA evidence from thousands of untested rape kits that were collected by law enforcement or during sexual assault forensic exams, but never sent to crime labs for analysis." *Addressing the Rape Kit Backlog*, RAPE, ABUSE & INCEST NATIONAL NETWORK, *available at* https://www.rainn.org/articles/addressing-rape-kit-backlog (last visited 22 Aug. 2021).

a reasonable doubt. As with any other crime, this means that there are cases where an allegation is *factually* accurate but the evidence is insufficient to prove *legal* guilt. This perceived disconnect between what is true and what is proven is always troubling, but perhaps more so in relation to rape than any other crime. Nonetheless, it is essential that you remember that just as an actual murderer can get away with murder if the evidence doesn't prove guilt beyond a reasonable doubt, an actual rapist may get away with rape.

A. What Is Rape?

In compiling statistics for the Uniform Crime Report, the FBI defines rape as: "the penetration, no matter how slight, of the vagina or anus with any body part or object, or oral penetration by a sex organ of another person, without the consent of the victim."[6] Under this definition, anyone, regardless of gender identity, can commit, or be a victim of, rape.[7]

The FBI definition is useful for several reasons. First, as you read different formulations of the offense of rape, compare them to the FBI version. When presented with a formulation of the offense of rape, consider:

1) What conduct (actus reus) qualifies as rape?

2) May any gender identity commit or be the victim of rape?

3) What, if any, reference does the offense make to "force" or "resistance"?

4) What, if any, reference does the offense make to "consent"? And

5) Is there a criminal mental state (mens rea) in the offense? If so, what does it apply to?

The second reason the FBI definition is useful is that it underscores longstanding challenges in and with defining rape. The FBI definition is from 2012 and *represents the first update or change since 1927.*[8] Prior to 2012, the FBI relied on a common law definition dating back over two-hundred years[9] — "the carnal knowledge [vaginal sexual penetration] of a female [by a male], forcibly and against her will."[10] There are still states that define rape this way and address other sexual assaults covered in the broader FBI definition as distinct crimes (such as forcible sodomy; sexual battery; indecent acts; etc.). Thus, for over eighty-five years extending well into the

---

6. *An Updated Definition of Rape*, DEPARTMENT OF JUSTICE (JAN. 6, 2012) [hereinafter DoJ Rape Definition].

7. In the summer of 2021, the Attorneys General for New Jersey and Massachusetts wrote the director of the FBI requesting that the FBI modify its gender classification in the UCR to include a non-binary gender designation. https://www.nj.gov/oag/newsreleases21/Uniform-Crime-Reporting -Letter-From-21-State-AGs-on-Non-Binary-Gender-Designation.pdf.

8. DoJ Rape Definition, *supra* note 6.

9. *Id.*

10. Theodore J. Grayson, *The Law as to Consent When Pleaded as a Defence to Certain Crimes against the Person*, 42 AM. L. REG. 467, 470 (1903) [hereinafter Grayson].

21st century, the FBI definition of rape only included male penile penetration of a female vagina and, as will be discussed later, added a force requirement beyond penetration and a reference to the (female) victim's will, which as will be discussed, problematically refers to resistance.

B. Social Norms, Stigmas, and Misperceptions

Rape continues to be the most under-reported violent crime in the United States. According to the Department of Justice, in 2018 and 2019, 2/3 to 3/4 of rapes were not reported to the police.[11] The lack of reporting is not because the crime infrequently occurs; far from it. According to a 2015 National Sexual Violence Resource Center report, "[o]ne in five women and one in 71 men will be raped at some point in their life."[12]

There are a variety of reasons why rape isn't reported. One possibility is the flawed belief that rape is committed by a stranger, someone unknown to the victim. This is simply not the case. In 80% of rape cases, the victim knew the person who sexually assaulted them.[13] At colleges and universities, that number increases.

> About 85-90 percent of sexual assaults reported by college women are perpetrated by someone known to the victim; about half occur on a date. The most common locations are the man's or woman's home in the context of a party or a date. The perpetrators may range from classmates to neighbors.[14]

Yet half of the students who reported being sexually assaulted did not characterize the incident as rape.[15] There are a number of unhelpful stigmas at play which likely contribute to the reluctance in reporting in general and to reporting what happened as rape.[16]

---

11. DoJ Rape Definition, *supra* note 6. In 2015, the National Sexual Violence Resource Center reported that, "[a]nnually, rape costs the U.S. more than any other crime ($127 billion), followed by assault ($93 billion), murder ($71 billion), and drunk driving ($61 billion)." NATIONAL SEXUAL VIOLENCE RESOURCE CENTER. *Statistics available at* https://www.nsvrc.org/statistics (last visited 14 August 2021) [hereinafter NSVRC Statistics].

12. NSVRC Statistics, *supra* note 11. Roughly 90% of the victims of rape are female and 10% male.

13. *Id.*

14. *Most Victims Know Their Attacker,* National Institute of Justice, Sept. 30, 2008 https://nij.ojp .gov/topics/articles/most-victims-know-their-attacker [hereinafter NIJ].

15. *Id.* The RAINN (Rape, Abuse & Incest National Network) advises not using the terms "date rape" or "acquaintance rape" as they may create the impression of being somehow different or less serious than rape. Key Terms and Phrases, ABUSE & INCEST NATIONAL NETWORK, *available at* https://www.rainn.org/articles/key-terms-and-phrases (last visited 22 Aug. 2021). *See also* Michelle J. Anderson, *Diminishing the Legal Impact of Negative Social Attitudes toward Acquaintance Rape Victims,* 13 NEW CRIM. L. REV. 644 (2010).

16. *See* D.J. Angelone et al., *Men's perceptions of acquaintance rape: The role of relationship length, victim resistance, and gender role attitudes,* 30 J. INTERPER. VIOL. 278 (2015); E.E. Ayala et al., *Blame attributions of victims and perpetrators: Effects of victim gender, perpetrator gender, and relationship,* 33 J. INTERPER. VIOL. 94 (2018). As with many crimes, there is also a socio-economic component to reporting allegations of sexual assault—the capacity to "take off work, obtain child care [and]

One reason is understandably wanting to avoid what follows reporting rape to law enforcement (or to anyone with a legal duty to relay that report to law enforcement). One early step involves being subjected to a sexual assault forensic exam and law enforcement questioning.[17] Should the report result in a criminal investigation, charge and a trial, victims will be subjected to multiple bouts of questioning: by police continuing to investigate; by prosecutors with the aid of a victim's advocate; by defense counsel perhaps in preparation for the trial but at a minimum through adversarial cross examination at a public trial and in the presence of the alleged offender. Finally, victims don't know to what extent the finder of fact deciding guilt or innocence may believe one or more of the stigmas surrounding rape.[18]

No prosecutor should ever consider a rape case as "easy" due to the trauma and suffering caused by this crime. But some cases are certainly easier *to prove*. Most prosecutors (and defense counsel) would agree that the most likely rape conviction involves cases of "stranger" rape, particularly when the offender denies sexual intercourse occurred and there is DNA evidence to the contrary. That case seldom arises, and when it does, is usually resolved by a guilty plea. The type of case that arises far more frequently involves an offender known to the victim. Such cases are far more difficult to prove. It is not uncommon that the victim and defendant engaged in consensual foreplay prior to the alleged rape; or even engaged in consensual sex prior to the alleged rape and in some cases after. Similarly, it is not uncommon that alcohol or drugs were voluntarily consumed/taken prior to the alleged rape. This is not in any way to suggest that such incidents cannot be rape; they of course can be. But those factors can make proving the elements of rape beyond a reasonable doubt challenging.

C. Symbiotic Relationship Between Offenders and Victims

Another challenge with rape laws is as a byproduct of a cycle whereby existing law is recognized as insufficient[19] (or not effectively enforced) to adequately protect

transportation to meet with police or lawyers, or go to court" serve as boundaries for access to the criminal justice system. Email from South Texas College of Law student Valerie Bass to casebook authors.

17. *What Is a Sexual Assault Forensic Exam?*, RAPE, ABUSE & INCEST NATIONAL NETWORK, *available at* https://www.rainn.org/articles/rape-kit (last visited 19 Aug. 2021).

18. One exceedingly unhelpful stigma is that "real" rape victims immediately report to law enforcement. *See* A.W. Burgess et al., *Delayed Reporting of the Rape Victim*, 33 J. PSYCHOSOC. NURS. MENT. HEALTH. SERV. 21 (1995). We now know to think of rape as a traumatic event. And trauma responses, including memory of events and if and when the incident was reported (and to whom) vary. Yet our ability—or more so willingness—to think and act about rape consistent with what we have learned remains in question.

19. At times, law enforcement aren't even aware of some aspects of their jurisdiction's sexual assault laws, as was the case in Minnesota in 2015. A woman in the midst of a divorce found a videotape which depicted her then husband sexually assaulting her while she lay next to her sleeping four-year-old son. She reported the crime to the police, who arrested and charged her husband with

victims and society more generally. This often leads to modifications in law and/or enforcement, sometimes rushed or not fully thought out, which may infringe on constitutional or statutory protections afforded offenders, obviously to their detriment. The U.S. government and colleges/universities provide examples of simultaneously seeming to do too little and too much in response to rape, further complicating development of the law and social stigmas.

The Department of Defense (DoD) has faced long standing criticism for its handling of rape and other forms of sexual assault.[20] Whether of its own volition or pursuant to Congressional direction, DoD has made a number of changes and improvements, though more is no doubt needed.[21] But one of the changes proved an overcorrection. In 2006, Congress revised the military version of the offense of rape.[22] Among other changes, the law recognized a burden to prove consent to sex and placed that burden on the accused. Five years later, the Court of Appeals for the Armed Forces determined the burden shifting to be an unconstitutional infringement on the due process rights of any service-member accused of rape.[23]

Colleges and universities are not a singular entity like DoD, so in some ways, their experience is more representative of the challenges different states have faced. Many of these institutions have been criticized both for not investigating rape allegations at all as well as not taking the issue seriously when they do investigate. At one college, students who committed laptop theft were punished more severely than those who committed rape, and not a single student found responsible for sexual assault was expelled.[24] Students protested at another college after a school sanctioned a student found to have raped another student by requiring the offender to write a 500-word reflective essay.[25] And in 2021, the Dean of the University of Montana Law School

---

a felony. That same day, the police dropped the charge, as they learned of Minnesota's "voluntary relationship" doctrine, a euphemism for the "spousal exception" discussed later in this chapter, under which as a matter of law, one spouse cannot commit the offense of rape against the other. The husband was charged with misdemeanor "invasion of privacy." The woman contended that everyone except her husband's defense attorney were "dumbfounded" by the voluntary relationship doctrine. According to the woman, "The county attorney's office didn't know it and the judge didn't know that this law existed." In 2019, almost four years after the incident, the Minnesota Legislature repealed the voluntary relationship doctrine. Briana Bierschbach, *Woman's fight for justice ends 'marital rape' exception*, MPR NEWS, May 1, 2019. For a relatively recent survey of the status of spousal rape exemptions around the U.S., see Kennedy Holmes, *Shining Another Light on Spousal Rape Exemptions: Spousal Sexual Violence Laws in the #MeToo Era*, 11 U.C. IRVINE L. REV. 1213 (2021).

20. Melinda Wenner Moyer, *'A Poison in the System': The Epidemic of Military Sexual Assault*, N.Y. TIMES MAG., Aug. 3, 2021.

21. Kristy N. Kamarch & Barbara Salazar Toerreon, *Military Sexual Assault: A Framework for Congressional Oversight*, CONGRESSIONAL RESEARCH SERVICE R44944 (Feb. 26, 2021).

22. Howard H. Hoege III, *"Overshift": The unconstitutional double burden-shift on affirmative defenses in the new article 120*, ARMY LAWYER (May 2007).

23. *See United States v. Prather*, 69 M.J. 338 (C.A.A.F. 2011).

24. Zoe Ridolfi-Starr, *Transformation Requires Transparency: Critical Policy Reforms to Advance Campus Sexual Violence Response*, 125 YALE L.J. (2016) [hereinafter Ridolfi-Starr].

25. *Id.*

resigned following law student complaints that the law school discourged students from filing Title IX complaints concerning alleged sexual misconduct.[26]

Many colleges and universities have modified their sexual assault investigation and hearing processes,[27] leading to the expulsion of a number of offenders.[28] Perhaps unsurprisingly, this produced its own controversy: between 2013 and 2020, over 300 students sanctioned by a college or university for sexual misconduct filed suit, alleging the varied approaches at investigating sexual misconduct and conducting expulsion hearings amounted to violations of due process.[29] In over half the lawsuits, different courts have denied the college/university's motion to dismiss and the issues are being litigated. In several cases, the expelled student has won, meaning that the college/university's investigation and/or hearing process were deemed to violate due process.[30]

The impetuous for these "over corrections" was the laws and processes created over time, both of which incorporated, to varying degrees, systemic culturally ingrained bias against women. As a result, understanding how these factors shaped legal and policy trends necessitates a review of the origins and evolution of rape law, "warts and all."

D. Misogynistic Underpinnings to Rape Law

1. English Common Law

It was not until the 11th or 12th century that rape transitioned from a property offense to being a considered a "violent, sexual crime."[31] By 1250, rape laws in

---

26. Stephanie Francis Ward, *Montana law school dean resigns after complaints about the oversight of Title IX allegations*, ABAJOURNAL.COM, Oct. 7, 2021. Colleges and universities receiving any federal funds must comply with Title IX of the Education Amendments of 1972 ("Title IX"), 20 U.S.C. § 1681 *et seq.*, a Federal civil rights law that prohibits discrimination on the basis of sex in education programs and activities. Discrimination on the basis of sex can include sexual harassment or sexual violence, such as rape, sexual assault, sexual battery, and sexual coercion.

27. In 2011 and again in 2014, the Obama administration issued new Title IX guidance for investigating campus sexual assault. Then the Trump administration significantly revised the guidance in 2020, followed by the Biden administration rescinding that guidance. As of the summer of 2021, the Biden administration had begun a "sweeping rewrite of Title IX Sexual Misconduct Rules." *See* Lauren Camera, *Education Department Begins Sweeping Rewrite of Title IX Sexual Misconduct Rules*, US NEWS, Jun. 7, 2021.

28. *See, e.g.,* Matthew R. Triplett, *Sexual Assault on College Campuses: Seeking the Appropriate Balance Between Due Process and Victim Protection*, 62 DUKE L.J. 487 (2012); Samantha Harris & KC Johnson, *Campus Courts in Court: The Rise in Judicial Involvement in Campus Sexual Misconduct Adjudications*, 22 N.Y.U. J. LEGIS. & PUB. POL'Y 49 (2019).

29. Andrew Kreighbaum, *Title IX Court Decisions Make It Harder for Biden to Rewrite Rules*, BLOOMBERG (Apr. 5, 2021).

30. For one such example, see *Doe v. Brandeis*, 177 F. Supp. 3d 561 (D. Mass. 2016).

31. Kyla Bishop, *A Reflection on the History of Sexual Assault Laws in the United States*, ARKANSAS J. SOC. CHANGE & PUB. SERV. Apr. 15, 2018 [hereinafter Bishop]. The first record of a law criminalizing sexual assault dates to 1900 B.C.E in Babylon and the Code of Hammurabi, "an extensive

the United Kingdom existed and could entail the most severe punishment for the offender. But the severity of the punishment depended on the status (chasteness) of the victim:

> Punishment of [the severe] kind does not follow in the case of every woman, though she is forcibly ravished, but some other severe punishment does follow, according as she is married or a widow living a respectable life, a nun or a matron, a recognized concubine or a prostitute plying her trade without discrimination of person, all of whom the king must protect for the preservation of his peace, though a like punishment will not be imposed for each.[32]

The varying punishments resulted from a trial. But in order for a rape trial to take place, there were a number of preconditions. According to Henri de Bracton, considered the leading legal authority in the Middle Ages:

> When therefore a virgin has been so deflowered and overpowered against the peace of the lord the King, forthwith and whilst the act is fresh, she ought repair with hue and cry to the neighboring vills, and there display to honest men the injury done to her, the blood and her dress stained with blood, and the tearing of her dress, and so she ought to go to the provost of the hundred and to the searjeant of the lord the King, and to the coroners and to the viscount and make her appeal at the first county court.[33]

Built into Bracton's summary were: the chastity requirement (the more chaste the victim, the more credible their rape allegation); the prompt complaint requirement; a requirement for corroboration (a women's claim of rape, by itself, was insufficient as a matter of law); and a requirement for the woman to have resisted.

Those requirements applied when the offender was not the husband of the victim. That's because of the common law spousal exception—"the husband cannot be guilty of a rape committed by himself upon his lawful wife for by their mutual

---

code of civil and criminal laws which were said to have been given to King Hammurabi by the Sun God and which were subsequently published throughout the Mesopotamian world." Sally Gold & Martha Wyatt, *The Rape System: Old Roles and New Times*, 27 CATH. U. L. REV. 695, 696 (1978). This law (and those which would follow for over three thousand years) considered sexual assault a property crime. The property was a woman's virginity, and rape would decrease her market value. As a result, the woman wasn't even considered the victim of rape. The victim (of the loss of value) was the woman's father if she was not yet engaged or her fiancé if she was. This is because the father or the fiancé were considered "the legitimate possessor of the woman." *Id.* This conception aligns with the origins of the word rape, which derives from the Latin word rapere and means "to steal or carry off" property. Kathleen N. Franco et al., *Rape, in* ENCYCLOPEDIA OF WOMEN'S HEALTH (2004). Its property origins and meaning are one reason why some advocates suggest not using the word rape.

32. Barbara J. Baines, *Effacing Rape in Early Modern Representation*, 65 ELH 69, 71 (1998) [hereinafter Baines].

33. Michelle J. Anderson, *Diminishing the Legal Impact of Negative Social Attitudes Toward Acquaintance Rape Victims*, 13 NEW CRIM. L. REV. 644, 648 (2010).

matrimonial consent and contract the wife hath given up herself in this kind unto her husband which she cannot retract."[34]

Lastly, when the offender was not the husband and the victim managed to meet all the requirements above, at trial the judge would instruct jurors to consider a rape complainant's testimony with skepticism.[35]

By the end of the 13th Century, King Edward I enacted the Statutes of Westminster which made considerable improvements, though that's a relative statement to be sure. In tracing the development of the offense of rape, at times, it's difficult to parse misogyny from ignorance. On some level, this was to be expected, every aspect of a rape investigation and prosecution was performed by a man. Men wrote the laws, served as law enforcement, medical doctors, counsel, jurors and as judge. A British legal text written around the time of the Westminster Statutes claimed that "[w]ithout a woman's consent she could not conceive."[36] The import of this bizarre claim was that if a woman became pregnant, she must have consented to intercourse and thus was not raped.

The Statutes of Westminster redefined rape as an "issue of public interest and concern" and not just "merely a family misfortunate and a threat to land and property."[37] The statutes replaced Bracton's "while the act is fresh" reporting requirement with a forty-day time period during which the woman could file suit. If she did not file, then the King could. Under the Statutes of Westminster, it was a crime to have sex with any woman against her will and with an underage girl (under ten) regardless of whether she consented, the predecessor to statutory rape discussed later in this chapter.

The first English rape law appears to be the initial Statute of Westminster in 1275 and combines both force and consent: "the King prohibeth that none do ravish, nor take away by force any maiden within Age (neither by her own consent nor without),

---

34. Baines, *supra* note 32, at 94. *See also* Maria Pracher, *The Marital Rape Exemption: A Violation of a Woman's Right of Privacy*, 11 GOLDEN GATE U. L. REV. (1981).

35. Seventeenth-century English jurist Sir Matthew Hale expressed the widely held concern that rape "is an accusation easily to be made and hard to be proved, and harder to be defended by the party accused, tho' never so innocent." MATTHEW HALE, PLEAS OF THE CROWN 629 (1847).

36. Elise Bennett Histed, *Mediaeval Rape: A Conceivable Defence?*, 63 CAMBRIDGE L.J. 743, 744 (2004). Five hundred years later, the purportedly informed view shifted to somehow linking conception, rape and female orgasm. According to *Elements of Medical Jurisprudence,* published in 1814 by a physician: "without an excitation of lust, or the enjoyment of pleasure in the venereal act, no conception can probably take place. So that if an absolute rape were to be perpetrated, it is not likely she would become pregnant." ANNE LEAH GREENFIELD, INTERPRETING SEXUAL VIOLENCE 1660-1800 30 (2015). Amazingly both more ignorant and offensive, in 2012, Todd Atkin, a Missouri politician campaigning for the U.S. Senate, used the term "legitimate rape" in discussing abortion in the case of rape. Atkin doubled down on ignorance by claiming that "[i]f it's a legitimate rape, the female body has ways to try to shut that whole thing down." John Eligon & Michael Schwirtz, *Senate Candidate Provokes Ire With 'Legitimate Rape' Comment*, N.Y. TIMES, Aug. 19, 2012.

37. Bruce A. MacFarlane, *Historical Development of the Offence of Rape, in* 100 YEARS OF THE CRIMINAL CODE IN CANADA; ESSAYS COMMEMORATING THE CENTENARY OF THE CANADIAN CRIMINAL CODE 11 (Wood & Peck eds 1993) [hereinafter MacFarlane].

nor any Wife or Maiden of full Age, nor any other Woman against her will. . . ."[38] Ten years later, the Second Statute of Westminster removed the force element and focused on consent: "[i]t is provided, That if a Man from henceforth do ravish a Woman married, Maid or other, where she did not consent neither before nor after he shall have Judgement of Life and of Member."[39]

Over time, a modified version of the First Statute of Westminster became the accepted common law definition of rape: "[r]ape is the unlawful carnal knowledge of a woman by force and against her will."[40] At times, British courts struggled to apply that definition in cases where capacity to consent was not present. First in a case involving a developmentally challenged victim and later a severely intoxicated victim, appellate courts considered whether rape was sex against someone's will or was a lack of consent sufficient. In both cases, due to the incapacity of the victim, there was no evidence that sex was against the will of the victim, but there was also no evidence of consent. As one judge explained:

> The question is, what is the proper definition of the crime of rape? Is it carnal knowledge of a woman, against her will, or is it sufficient if it be without the consent of the [victim]? If it must be against her will, then the crime was not proved in this case.[41]

Both courts resurrected the consent portion of the Second Westminster Statute and decided that that "without her consent" was synonymous with "against her will." As both victims did not have the capacity to consent, the appellate courts affirmed the conviction. This interpretation of rape placed the focus directly on consent. But this interpretation only seemed to apply in cases where the victim unequivocally lacked capacity to consent. In most cases, English courts interpreted "without her consent" as meaning something different than "against her will." This interpretation uses the offender's force and victim's resistance as indirect measures of whether the victim consented to sex.

The disparate interpretations migrated to the American colonies and, as in England, the majority interpretation was that the offense of rape contained a force element measured by victim resistance.

---

38. Grayson, *supra* note 10, at 469.

39. *Id.* Of life refers to lifetime incarceration. Judgment of member refers to severing the rapist's penis. Note how the statute allows for consent either before or after intercourse.

40. An interim and longer version built in the age of consent: "Rape is felony by the common law, declared by parliament for the unlawful and carnal knowledge and abuse of any woman above the age of ten years against her will, or of a woman child under the age of ten years with her will, or against her will. . . ." Grayson, *supra* note 10, at 469. As this book's publication in 2022, the U.S. State of Georgia utilizes almost exactly the same formulation: "A person commits the offense of rape when he has carnal knowledge of: (1) A female forcibly and against her will; or (2) A female who is less than ten years of age." Georgia Criminal Code § 16-6-1.

41. Grayson, *supra* note 10, at 470.

a. United States

i. Racism

In addition to perpetuating the structural misogyny of English common law regarding rape, it is undeniable that racism also impacted the law's development in the United States. However biased the criminal justice system has been towards women, it has been much more so towards women of color. Prior to the Civil War, it was not even a crime to rape an African American woman.[42] "In the few places where the rape of a African American woman was technically criminalized, rules of procedure prevented African American women from testifying about their victimization."[43] Particularly in the South, efforts to reform rape laws lagged, at least in part "because legislators explicitly feared that it 'would enable [African American] girls to sue white men' and thus put the '[African American] female on the same plane with the white female.'"[44]

In addition to the racism imbedded in the notion that that rape was only committed against a white "chaste" woman is the trope that African American men were pervasive perpetrators of rape. While not trying to compare experiences, African American men suffered immensely as a result. Prior to the Civil War, "statutes in many jurisdictions provided the death penalty or castration for rape when the convicted man was Black or mulatto and the victim white[,]" penalties which were "frequently imposed" and before conviction.[45] Some of the worst days in American history involve mobs breaking into jails and even courtrooms and lynching (murdering) African American men *alleged* to have raped white women.

ii. American Common Law of Rape

More broadly, judicial interpretations of the inherited definition of the offense of rape in the United States mirrored the disparity in English courts. In an 1865 Michigan case, a judge ruled that "[w]e are aware of no adjudged case that will justify us in construing the words 'against her will' as equivalent in meaning with 'without her intelligent assent'; nor do we think sound reason will sanction it."[46] Yet five years later and still in Michigan, a different judge determined that consent and will *must* be synonymous because:

> If it were otherwise, any woman in a state of utter stupefaction, whether caused by drunkenness, sudden disease, the blow of a third person, or

---

42. *See* Jeffrey J. Pokorak, *Rape as a Badge of Slavery: The Legal History of, and Remedies for, Prosecutorial Race-of-Victim Charging Disparities*, 7 NEVADA L.J. 1 (2006) [hereinafter Pokorak].

43. *Id.* at 6.

44. Estelle B. Freedman, *Women's long battle to define rape*, WASH. POST (Aug. 24, 2012).

45. Jennifer Wriggins, *Rape, Racism, and the Law*, 6 HARV. WOMEN'S L.J. 103, 105 (1983). One of the more prominent and notorious incidents involved the "Scottsboro Boys," a group of young African American men falsely accused of trying to rape two white women. *See* JAMES GOODMAN, STORIES OF SCOTTSBORO (1994).

46. Grayson, *supra* note 10, at 472.

drugs which she had been persuaded to take, even by the defendant himself, would be unprotected from personal dishonor. The law is not open to such a reproach.[47]

By 1897, the U.S. Supreme Court unhelpfully resolved the force question in *Mills v. U.S.* The *Mills* case is in some ways the origin of both the problems with rape law in the U.S. and the divergent paths states have taken in response. In *Mills*, the Supreme Court reviewed a jury instruction from a rape case:

> The fact is that all the force that need be exercised, if there be no consent, is the force incident to the commission of the act. If there is nonconsent of the woman, the force, I say, incident to the commission of the crime is all the force that is required to make out this element of the crime.[48]

The jury instruction reflected what is known as the "intrinsic force" standard: vaginal penetrative force (however slight), in other words, the force inherent in sexual intercourse, satisfies the force element of rape.

The Supreme Court reversed Mills' conviction, holding that

> In this charge [the jury instruction] we think the court did not explain fully enough so as to be understood by the jury what constitutes in law nonconsent on the part of the woman, and what is the force necessary in all cases of non-consent to constitute the crime. He merely stated that if the woman did not give consent the only force necessary to constitute the crime in that case was that which was incident to the commission of the act itself. That is true in a case where the woman's will or her resistance had been overcome by threats or fright, or she had become helpless or unconscious, so that while not consenting she still did not resist. But the charge in question covered much more extensive ground. It covered the case where no threats were made; where no active resistance was overcome; where the woman was not unconscious, but where there was simply nonconsent on her part and no real resistance whatever. Such nonconsent as that is no more than a mere lack of acquiescence, and is not enough to constitute the crime of rape. Taking all the evidence in the case, the jury might have inferred just that amount of nonconsent in this case. Not that they were bound to do so, but the question was one for them to decide. The mere nonconsent of a female to intercourse where she is in possession of her natural, mental, and physical powers, is not overcome by numbers or terrified by threats, or in such place and position that resistance would be useless, does not constitute the crime of rape on the part of the man who has connection with her under such circumstances. More force is necessary when that is the character of nonconsent than was stated by the court to be necessary to make out the element of the crime. That kind of nonconsent is not enough, nor is the force spoken of then sufficient, which is only incidental

---

47. *Id.*
48. *Mills v. United States*, 164 U.S. 644 (1897).

to the act itself. . . . [W]*here a woman is awake, of mature years, of sound mind and not in fear, a failure to oppose the carnal act is consent; and though she object verbally, if she make no outcry and no resistance, she by her conduct consents, and the act is not rape in the man.*[49]

The Court ruled that rape requires the use of force above and beyond the intrinsic force standard. This is known as the extrinsic force standard.

Following *Mills*, lower courts developed a standard against which to evaluate women's actions.[50] That standard was how much the woman resisted. There have been gradations of the resistance standard, beginning with "utmost" resistance, then "earnest," and more recently "reasonable."

Under the utmost resistance standard:

(1) a woman must have struggled to the utmost of her physical capacity and

(2) her resistance must not have subsided until after penetration.

Under this requirement, if a woman did not resist the rape to the utmost of her physical capacity, she was not raped. If a woman struggled to the utmost of her physical capacity until doing so appeared futile to her, and only then acquiesced to the rapist's advances, she also was not raped.[51]

Built into this standard were both misogyny and ignorance. The medical community around the time of the 1897 *Mills* decision impliedly offered support for the utmost resistance standard, claiming that

women have the physical means to stop rape if they so desire, by using hands, limbs and pelvic muscles. . . . [A]ny woman who wasn't willing to have sex could stop any man regardless of size from penetrating her.[52]

The utmost resistance standard "became impossibly difficult to satisfy and dangerous to any victim who tried."[53]

In contrast, earnest resistance is "genuine physical effort." Continuing on the spectrum, the reasonable resistance standard requires "reasonable resistance under the circumstances." This includes that the woman "was not required to resist if she reasonably believe[d] that resistance would be useless and would result in serious bodily injury."[54]

Depending on how extrinsic force and resistance are interpreted and applied, they present an impossible dilemma for victims—don't physically resist, thus increasing the chances of the sexual assault but also survival while precluding the possibility of

---

49. *Id.* at 647-48.

50. *See* Michelle J. Anderson, *Reviving Resistance in Rape Law*, 1998 U. ILL. L. REV. 953, 963 (1998) [hereinafter Anderson].

51. *Id.* at 963.

52. JOAN MCGREGOR, HANDBOOK ON SEXUAL VIOLENCE 74 (2011) [hereinafter McGregor].

53. *Id.*

54. Anderson, *supra* note 50, at 963.

a rape charge; or physically resist, perhaps decreasing the chance of the sexual assault while increasing the possibility of a rape charge but also the risk of additional injury or even death.

Almost all states have moved away from the utmost resistance standard,[55] but many still require external force and some quantum of physical resistance. Alabama for example maintains an earnest resistance standard.[56] By contrast, New Jersey requires extrinsic force, but almost any extrinsic force qualifies—basically *any* physical contact (other than penetration) between offender and victim.[57]

Other states have removed the force requirement or treat the act of intercourse as satisfying this requirement and don't require resistance for a rape conviction. But several of those states, while not requiring resistance, instruct the jury to consider a lack of resistance in determining consent. In these jurisdictions, although "the victim is no longer required to resist, [they are] effectively penalized for not attempting to repel [their] attacker's advances."[58]

Extrinsic force standards and requiring physical resistance fundamentally and dangerously misunderstand the manner by which rape occurs. The fundamental misunderstanding is in assuming there is one response to rape, when we know there is a constellation of responses to rape, including "tonic immobility," a form of involuntary paralysis.[59] Obviously someone who is involuntarily paralyzed would not be able to move or even speak. But without the victim doing or saying something, the offender's actions may not constitute rape depending on the jurisdiction. The dangerous misunderstanding is in requiring resistance when few individuals are trained or prepared to do so.

The different roles of victim resistance have created a number of difficulties and further confused matters. Using victim resistance as a measure of force ignores threats or constructive force to compel sex. Using victim resistance as evidence of nonconsent risks equating the absence of resistance with consent. When that occurs, the bizarre outcome can and has been that verbal resistance (saying no/stop) is not considered a lack of consent.

Left out of the discussion thus far is the MPC. That's because, while progressive in some areas of the law, like mental responsibility, in terms of the offense of rape, the

55. *See Consent Laws*, Louisiana, Rape, Abuse & Incest National Network (March 2020), *available at* https://apps.rainn.org/policy/compare/consent-laws.cfm

56. *See* Katie J.M. Baker, *A College Student Accused a Powerful Man of Rape. Then She Became a Suspect*, BuzzFeed (Jun. 22, 2017); *see also* Bethy Squires, *Why Do We Still Have Laws that Say It's Not Rape Unless the Victim Fights Back?* Vice Jul. 27, 2017.

57. *See State in the Interest of M.T.S.*, 609 A.2d 1266 (N.J. 1992).

58. Joshua Mark Fried, *Forcing the Issue: An Analysis of the Various Standards of Forcible Compulsion in Rape*, 23 Pepp. L. Rev. 1277, 1283 (1996).

59. Francine Russo, *Sexual Assault May Trigger Involuntary Paralysis*, Scientific America Aug. 4, 2017.

initial 1962 MPC was decidedly not.[60] As the American Law Institute (ALI), which developed the MPC recently noted, the MPC's sexual assault provisions are "no longer a reliable guide for legislatures and courts."[61] For example, the MPC defined rape as a crime committed by men against women—women who were not the offender's wife, implicitly recognizing the spousal rape "exception."

It should be noted that the MPC did effectuate some progress. The MPC formulation of rape recognized threat of harm in addition to actual force and provided for involuntary intoxication or lack of consciousness of the victim. But on the whole, the MPC codified several aspects of the misogynistic common law. The MPC incorporated degrees of rape, which itself could have been progress, but the manner of delineation was problematic and continued both misunderstandings and stigmas. Under the MPC, committing first degree rape required either inflicting serious bodily injury or a victim who was not the offender's "voluntary social companion" who had "previously permitted him sexual liberties." A man could commit first degree rape against a stranger but not someone with whom he had previously had sex, aka been "permitted sexual liberties."[62]

There were more negatives than positives in the MPC. It contained a prompt complaint requirement for sexual offenses—but for no other crime.[63] Similarly, the MPC perpetuated the "hysterical victim" mythology by including a corroboration requirement—the testimony of a rape victim alone was insufficient as a matter of law.[64] Under the MPC, a defendant may be found guilty of any offense based on the credible but uncorroborated testimony of one person—except rape. Victims of rape

---

60. Under the MPC § 213.1,
    A male who has sexual intercourse with a female not his wife is guilty of rape if:
    (a) he compels her to submit by force or by threat of imminent death, serious bodily injury, extreme pain or kidnapping, to be inflicted on anyone; or
    (b) he has substantially impaired her power to appraise or control her conduct by administering or employing without her knowledge drugs, intoxicants or other means for the purpose of preventing resistance; or
    (c) the female is unconscious; or
    (d) the female is less than 10 years old.

61. American Law Institute, Model Penal Code Sexual Assault Provisions, *available at* https://www.ali.org/publications/show/sexual-assault-and-related-offenses/ (last visited Sept. 7, 2021). It is by no means clear that the bulk of MPC's sexual assault provisions were ever "a reliable guide for legislatures and courts." No state adopted the MPC's sexual assault provisions in their entirety, and only five states adopted portions. *See* Lawrence K. Furbish et al., *Model Penal Code Sexual Assault Provision*, OFFICE OF LEGISLATIVE RESEARCH, Dec. 18, 1998.

62. Deborah W. Denno, *Why the Model Penal Code's Sexual Offense Provisions Should Be Pulled and Replaced*, 1 OHIO ST. J. CRIM. L. 207, 209 (2003).

63. *See* Anderson, *supra* note 50, at 648 (quoting the MPC's prompt complaint requirement that "[n]o prosecution may be instituted or maintained under this Article [for sexual offenses] unless the alleged offense was brought to the notice of public authority within [3] months of its occurrence").

64. *See id.* (quoting the MPC's corroboration requirement that "[n]o person shall be convicted of any felony under this Article [for sexual offenses] upon the uncorroborated testimony of the alleged victim").

were deemed to be "emotionally involved" in the case such that the MPC perpetuated the common law tradition of a cautionary instruction regarding victim testimony.[65] And yet again, for no other crime does the MPC require a cautionary jury instruction regarding the victim.

The approach the MPC took to sexual assault offenses was on the whole backward looking.[66] By the start of the 1970s, considerable momentum began to form around changing norms and laws regarding rape. While commentators identified problems with the MPC's rape provisions relatively early on, it was not until 2012 that ALI began a revision effort, which was completed in the summer of 2021. It's not clear what influence the 2021 revisions will have on state laws. While the MPC went fifty years without revision, for better and for worse, state laws and processes have repeatedly changed since 1962.

While there has been considerable change and progress with U.S. rape laws and trial processes,[67] similar to the Statutes of Westminster, that is a relative statement.[68]

---

65. *See id* (quoting the MPC's jury instruction requirement that "[i]n any prosecution before a jury for an offense under this Article [for sexual offenses], the jury shall be instructed to evaluate the testimony of a victim or complaining witness with special care in view of the emotional involvement of the witness and the difficulty of determining the truth with respect to alleged sexual activities carried out in private").

66. The ALI revisions to the MPC's sexual assault provisions spans 659 pages. The revised version makes rape (a term the MPC doesn't use, opting for penetration) gender neutral and removes the legacy common law-based preconditions and qualifications, including the corroboration requirement, the spousal rape exception and the jury instruction. *See* American Law Institute, *Model Penal Code: Sexual Assault and Related Offenses Tentative Draft #5* (May 4, 2021). The majority of jurisdictions made most and in some cases all those changes decades ago.

67. Arguably the most significance developments were in the form of new federal evidence rules, including FRE 412, known as the "Rape Shield" rule as it limits the questioning of a victim's sexual behavior, which was previously often deemed relevant and admissible.

68. By way of example of how mixed American progress has been, returning to the English common law conditions and limitations on rape, there is a tendency to assume that of course they are historical vestiges from a bygone era. They should be, but they are not. All the conditions and limitations became part of American common law and were widely employed until disturbingly recently. Worse, they still have not been completely eliminated. For the chastity requirement, factoring in virginity and marital status into rape law remained in a number of states until the 1990s, with Mississippi being the last to remove the requirement in 1998. *See* CAROLYN E. COCCA, JAILBAIT: THE POLITICS OF STATUTORY RAPE LAWS IN THE UNITED STATES 12 (2007). While eliminated in almost all states, the prompt complaint requirement remains today in three states, as does the corroboration requirement, though in three different states. *See* Michele J. Anderson, *The Legacy of the Prompt Complaint Requirement, Corroboration Requirement, and Cautionary Instructions on Campus Sexual Assault,* Working Paper Series 20 (2004). On "cautionary instructions" to the jury regarding rape victim testimony, no U.S. state still requires them. But thirteen states still allow them. *Id.* Saving the worst for last, on the politely worded "spouse exception," not a single state criminalized marital rape until 1976, and it took until 1993 before marital rape was recognized as rape in all fifty states. *See* Bishop, *supra* note 31. Even still, as of 2019, "[i]n 17 states, a spouse can't be convicted of raping a partner who was unconscious, drugged, or otherwise incapacitated." Madison Pauly, *It's 2019, And States Are Still Making Exceptions for Spousal Rape,* MOTHER JONES, Nov. 21, 2019.

The issues of whether the offense of rape should include a force and resistance element or be based on consent and what consent means, continue to vex jurisdictions.

Defining the offense of rape tends to be a series of tradeoffs, and there are different pros/cons between the common law and the MPC. As discussed above, common law jurisdictions incorporate a wide range of force requirements in defining the offense of rape. The more the definition relies on force, and resistance as a measure of force, the more dangerous it is for victims. Because of this extrinsic force requirement, the law almost never recognized the relevance of mistake of fact as to consent: proof that the defendant compelled the victim to submit by force or threat of force *ipso facto* proved the defendant knew the victim did not consent. But you should also recognize that the *mens rea* required for rape is unclear. Is it merely the intent to engage in sexual intercourse? Or is there any requirement to prove the defendant knew the victim had not consented? Pursuant to the extrinsic force notion of rape, rape is considered a general intent crime, with intent referring to the act of intercourse. Consent is an attendant circumstance.[69] This means that a defendant cannot raise mistake of fact regarding consent.

That jurisdictions increasingly are removing or lessening the extrinsic force and resistance requirements is largely but not exclusively a positive. It's an obvious safety benefit to victims, and certainly better aligns the crime of rape with the reality of rape. While these formulations don't technically change the status of consent as an attendant circumstance, eliminating the extrinsic force requirement or allowing the force of the sexual act to satisfy that requirement eliminated the obvious indication that the defendant knew the victim had not consented. As a result, jurisdictions that have so reformed their law now allow a defendant to raise mistake of fact as to consent based on the theory that the mens rea for rape is intent to engage in *non-consensual* sexual intercourse. This seems to be out of a concern that not allowing a defendant to do so may violate due process.[70] Importantly, however, this mens rea is almost universally treated as "general intent," meaning the prosecutor may satisfy that mental state either by proving the defendant actually knew the victim did not consent *or* that a reasonable person in that situation would have realized the victim did not consent. In other words, only an honest and reasonable mistaken assumption of consent is a defense.

The following cases illustrate the difficulties in drafting and applying rape laws. The cases begin with a focus on force and resistance and then shift to consent and

---

69. The mens rea of rape has led to considerable confusion. The mens rea applies to the actus reus, intercourse. But rape is not just intercourse but nonconsensual intercourse. The confusion often centers on whether and how the mens rea applies to the issue of consent. That issue is further discussed in the *Barela* case below. *See also* Kit Kinports, *Rape and Force: The Forgotten Mens Rea*, 4 Buff. Crim. L. Rev. 755 (2011).

70. Some jurisdictions express concern that not allowing a rape defendant to assert mistake of fact may render rape almost a strict liability offense. How legitimate is that concern?

capacity to consent. As you will see, the line between force and consent has become muddled, as well as how its interpreted both initially at trial and later on appeal.

II. Consent

Similar to the lack of consensus on force and resistance standards, "there's no universal definition of consent in the United States. Each state defines it differently, if it defines it at all."[71] This is yet another reason for the differences in state approaches—and the disparity in results. Identical events might constitute rape in one jurisdiction and not in another. With the evolution of force standards, the disparity is now often due to differences in viewing and applying consent.

Defining what constitutes consent has been a challenge, a challenge made harder the more we learn more about the different responses to rape. Moreover, any definition of consent needs to also consider the defendant's constitutional rights and protections.

As discussed in the introduction, the vast majority of rapes involve offenders known to the victim. When those cases reach the courtroom, the defendant will often acknowledge having had sex with the victim but claim that either the sex was consensual or, alternatively, if it was not consensual, that the defendant honestly and reasonably believed the victim consented.

One commentator acknowledges the challenges in defining and applying consent, but claims the courts make the issue more confusing:

> Courts have sought to enunciate legal standards for consent with respect to allegations of rape, rather than leaving the issue as a question of fact for the jury. Thus, judges have intruded into an area which in terms of the common law definition of rape should be dealt with by the jury. This appears to suggest that juries are incompetent to do their job, that is, to review the facts as impartially as possible, and to make findings beyond a reasonable doubt without being led astray by prejudices or irrelevancies. The jury is indispensable to the common law justice system. If rape is defined as "carnal knowledge of a woman without her consent," then it makes nonsense of the proposition that the jury is the trier of fact if the judge takes it upon himself to tell the jury what is or is not consent. If the purpose of the law is to protect women from acts of sexual intercourse to which they have not in fact consented, whether by reason of force actually applied, physical or other threat, or fear induced by accused or by others, then the relevant question would appear to be: Did this particular woman, in these particular circumstances, submit to this particular man; or did she in fact freely consent to have intercourse with him? If, on the contrary, the law requires a woman to react in a

---

71. Abby Ellin, *Is Sex by Deception a Form of Rape?*, N.Y. Times, Apr. 23, 2019.

particular way, that is, by fighting back against her attacker and sustaining a certain degree of damage inflicted by the accused in order to signify the lack of consent, and if the law deems the woman to have consented to the act despite ample evidence of threats which rendered her submissive but non-consenting, then the law cannot be said to be serving its true function of protecting individuals from the imposition of non-consensual sexual inter-course. Whether the relevant threats do or do not measure up to standards which appear to be set in current rape cases that the threat be immediate, physical, violent, interpreted on a reasonable-man standard the accused is amply protected. He cannot be convicted unless the prosecution has proved beyond a reasonable doubt the requisite state of mind: that he intended to have intercourse with the woman without her consent, and did so; or that he was reckless thereto. By imposing an artificial standard of consent, by requiring the woman concerned to resist or at least not simply to suffer the imposition of the act as a lesser evil, the criminal law would seem to require a measure of "self-help" which it does not require in any other area of criminal law and indeed which is usually frowned upon by the law.[72]

Whether a jurisdiction follows the original common law approach to rape requir-ing a close nexus between extrinsic force or threat of force and the victim's submis-sion, or has reformed its law to eliminate or substantially reduce this requirement (allowing verbal resistance to satisfy the element or allowing the force of the sexual act to satisfy the element), consent is *always* a complete defense to rape. This means the prosecution must convince the fact-finder beyond a reasonable doubt that the victim in fact did not consent.

At common law, once this fact was proven, the culpability focus shifted to whether the defendant had to use force or a threat of force to overcome the victim's resistance. As noted in the introduction, this *ipso facto* proved the defendant must have known of the victim's lack of consent. But this near-conclusive inference is nullified once that common law force/resistance equation is modified. And this in turn raises an important question: what exactly is the mens rea for rape? Is it merely the intent to engage in the sexual act? Or is there an implied requirement to prove the defendant knew or reasonably should have known the intentional act was "against the victim's will"?

The next case illustrates why this is such an important question. As you read *Barela*, notice how Utah's sexual assault law implicates both common law and MPC mens rea. The case focuses on whether the mens rea of a rape offense applies only to intercourse or also to consent. Once again, we see the challenge of distilling compli-cated—and, with rape, convoluted—law into jury instructions.

---

72. *State v. Rusk*, 289 Md. 230, 424 A.2d 720 (1981) (J. Wilner dissent, quoting from 13 WESTERN AUSTRALIAN L. REV. at 75 (1977)).

State v. Barela

2015 UT 22 (2012)
Utah Supreme Court

JUSTICE LEE, opinion of the Court:

This is an appeal from a conviction of Robert Barela of first-degree rape. Barela claims that his trial counsel was ineffective in a variety of ways. . . . He also challenges the sufficiency of the evidence to establish that the victim of the alleged rape had not consented to sex, an issue that requires us to interpret the statutes defining nonconsent in the context of a rape charge.

We reverse, finding ineffective assistance in counsel's failure to object to a jury instruction misstating the requirement of mens rea as applied to the elements of first-degree rape. In reversing on this ground, we decline to reach a number of alternative grounds raised by Barela. . . . .

Barela had sex with K.M. at a Massage Envy studio, where Barela was employed as a massage therapist and K.M. was a client. K.M. had received one previous massage from Barela at the studio. And when she arrived on the date in question, she had not requested Barela as her therapist. K.M. removed all of her clothing for the massage. During the massage she was covered only by a sheet and blanket.

That much is undisputed. But as to other details of the events leading to the sexual encounter, the jury heard two very different stories. In Barela's version of the encounter, K.M. became aroused and initiated sexual contact by humping the table and grabbing Barela's crotch. The two then began having sex, in which K.M. showed active engagement by giving him oral sex, rolling over on the table, and playing with her breasts.

In contrast, K.M. told the jury that she was receiving a massage from Barela when he unexpectedly started massaging her inner thigh. She testified that she felt "very uncomfortable" because she had never had a massage therapist do that in previous massages, and she "didn't know how to respond." Then, "before [she] knew it," Barela pulled her to the end of the table, dropped his pants and penetrated her vagina with his penis. K.M. testified that "everything happened very fast" and that Barela may have touched or penetrated her vagina with his finger, but that she wasn't sure. She testified that Barela went from rubbing her thigh to penetrating her vagina within "a matter of seconds."

K.M. testified that she had not "flirt[ed]" with Barela, and did not say or do anything to suggest that she wanted to have sex with him. She also testified that she did not physically resist or verbally tell Barela "no"; she said nothing at all. Instead, she clung to the blanket and "just froze." She said she felt fearful because she was alone, and because the only other person in the massage parlor was a male receptionist. She repeatedly stressed that "everything happened very fast." She elaborated that she "checked out," "kind of withdrew," and "was scared." When asked to explain what "checked out" meant, K.M. said she just "kind of froze."

K.M. testified that she heard Barela make an alarmed (and profane) exclamation, and then saw him looking at semen in his hand. Then he told her "this concludes your massage" and left the room. K.M. got up as "quickly as [she] could," wiped herself with a towel, and got dressed. She testified that her main concern was "getting out of Massage Envy" as quickly as she could. Barela met her in the hallway, where he offered her water, which she accepted. She "checked out as normal," told the receptionist the massage was "fine," paid her bill (including a tip), and took a mint.

K.M. testified that she then drove away from the massage studio but pulled over a few blocks away. At that point she telephoned her friend, who described her as "frantic" and "very upset." She returned home to her partner, Trista, who said K.M. was sobbing, shaking, and hysterical. Trista drove K.M. to the hospital. At the hospital, K.M. was examined by a nurse trained in examining sexual assault victims. The nurse found semen in K.M.'s vagina, which was identified as Barela's through DNA testing. According to the nurse, K.M.'s physical condition was consistent with K.M.'s account. But she conceded that K.M.'s condition was also "consistent with consensual sex," as there was no genital injury, while explaining that only twenty to thirty percent of assault victims display genital injuries. The nurse also testified that sometimes victims of sexual assault or other shocks have a difficult time remembering the details of the event.

The defense's primary theory at trial was that K.M. had been the instigator and that the sex was consensual. In addition, the defense also asserted that K.M. had lied about the encounter in an effort to protect her relationship with Trista. In further explanation of this theory, the defense presented evidence that K.M. and Trista had one child together (conceived by K.M. through artificial insemination), and that at the time of the massage K.M. was taking fertility medication and had been artificially inseminated only a few days earlier. The evidence also indicated that the sperm donor was an African American friend of K.M. and Trista. Thus, the defense theory was that K.M. had consensual sex with Barela, worried that she had conceived and that the baby would resemble him (a "light-skinned Hispanic"), and that a "serious problem" would ensue when Trista realized that the baby did not resemble their African American donor.

The defense also challenged the plausibility of K.M.'s version of events. First, the defense highlighted elements of K.M.'s testimony that were allegedly inconsistent with her previous ac- counts of the rape: (a) that K.M. had told the nurse that Barela had massaged her genitals and told the police that he had penetrated her vagina with his finger, but at the preliminary hearing she could not remember whether he had penetrated her with his finger or with his penis and at trial could not remember whether he had touched her vagina at all; and (b) that K.M. had explained her freezing reaction in different ways at different times, characterizing it alternatively as a result of fear, surprise, or drowsiness.

The defense also asserted that K.M.'s actions after the sexual encounter were inconsistent with rape. It noted that K.M. had accepted water from Barela and checked out of the massage studio as normal and left a tip, without appearing (to the receptionist) to be upset. And the defense emphasized that K.M. had told Trista that she didn't know if she was raped because she didn't resist, a point arguably consistent with a statement she made to a police detective—that she didn't "necessarily . . . even care if he's convicted of a crime." Counsel also reminded the jury that there was no evidence of vaginal trauma. And the defense argued that if the rape occurred quickly as K.M. had indicated, it would stand to reason that she would have suffered genital injury.

After closing arguments, the jury was given its instructions. Instruction 13 enumerated the elements of the offense of rape. It indicated that in order to find Barela guilty of rape the jury would have to find the following:

1. The defendant, Robert K. Barela,

2. Intentionally or knowingly;

3. Had sexual intercourse with K.M.;

4. That said act of intercourse was without the consent of K.M.

Instruction 14 quoted a large portion of Utah Code section 76-5-406, which lists "circumstances" in which "[a]n act of sexual intercourse . . . is without the consent of the victim." The list in Instruction 14 did not make express reference to a circumstance in which the victim "freezes." But in closing argument the prosecutor asserted that Instruction 14 was not an "exhaustive list" that "tells you where as a matter of law consent doesn't exist." And the prosecutor told the jury that "ultimately it is up to you to determine if after listening to the facts consent exists in this case."

On the [failure to object to the jury instruction claim], we find reversible error, as we conclude that reasonable counsel should have objected to a defect in the instruction and that defect was reasonably likely to have affected the verdict.

. . . .

This instruction was in error. In asking the jury to consider whether Barela "intentionally or knowingly" "had sexual intercourse with K.M." and whether the intercourse was "without [her] consent," the instruction implied that the mens rea requirement ("intentionally or knowingly") applied *only* to the act of sexual intercourse, and not to K.M.'s nonconsent. It conveyed that idea by coupling the mens rea requirement directly with the element of sexual intercourse, and by articulating the element of K.M.'s nonconsent without any apparent counterpart requirement of mens rea. That implication was error. After all, our criminal code requires proof of mens rea for each element of a non-strict liability crime, and the crime of rape unmistakably includes the element of nonconsent. So, as our court of appeals has held, the crime of rape requires proof not only that a defendant "knowingly, intentionally, or recklessly had sexual intercourse," but also that he had the requisite mens rea as to the victim's nonconsent. *State v. Marchet*, 2009 UT App 262, ¶ 23, 219 P.3d 75.

. . . [A] reasonable lawyer could well have decided not to present alternative theories to the jury—particularly where (as here) the fallback theory (reasonable mistake as to nonconsent) could have undermined the primary one (the victim was the instigator). But no reasonable lawyer would have found an advantage in understating the mens rea requirement as applied to the victim's nonconsent. There is only upside in a complete statement of the requirement of mens rea, particularly in a case like this one where the jury could reasonably have decided to reject both the prosecution's case and the defense's case in a manner that could have led to an acquittal. Thus, trial counsel was ineffective in failing to object to Instruction 13. . . .

If Instruction 13 had clearly and correctly required the jury to find mens rea as to K.M.'s nonconsent, the jury could reasonably have acquitted Barela on the basis of a determination that he mistook K.M.'s reaction for consent. And on this record we conclude that that was reasonably likely.

The jury heard two different accounts of the events leading to Barela's sexual intercourse with K.M.—Barela's and K.M.'s. Barela painted K.M. as the instigator. K.M. had it the other way around (Barela as the instigator). But even in K.M.'s account, she never explicitly (in words) or openly (in physical resistance) rebuffed Barela's advances. Instead K.M. testified that she "froze"—neither actively participating in sex nor speaking any words.

. . . Because the instructions required mens rea only as to sexual intercourse, all we know from the jury's verdict is that it concluded (a) that Barela's intercourse with K.M. was intentional or knowing, and (b) that K.M. did not consent. But that does not at all mean that the jury accepted K.M.'s story lock, stock, and barrel. The jury could easily have thought that the truth fell somewhere in between the two accounts—that K.M. was some- what flirtatious but not the clear instigator (and did not ultimately consent). And even in that event, the jury (as incorrectly instructed) could still have found Barela guilty upon a mere finding of intercourse that was intentional and nonconsensual—but without ever considering Barela's state of mind as to K.M.'s consent.

. . . .

[Reversed and Remanded]

JUSTICE DURHAM, dissenting:

I agree that Mr. Barela's counsel provided ineffective representation by failing to object to the jury instructions. The instructions were erroneous because they implied that the State had to prove only that K.M. did not consent to sexual intercourse rather than prove that Mr. Barela had the requisite mens rea as to the victim's lack of consent. In other words, the instructions did not convey the requirement that the State prove Mr. Barela's intentional, knowing, or reckless state of mind regarding the absence of K.M.'s consent. *See State v. Calamity*, 735 P.2d 39, 43 (Utah 1987) (crime of rape "may be proved by an intentional, knowing, or reckless mental state"); Utah Code § 76-2-102 ("[W]hen the definition of [an] offense does not specify a culpable mental state and the offense does not involve strict liability, intent, knowledge, or recklessness shall suffice to establish criminal responsibility.").

I disagree, however, with the majority's conclusion that Mr. Barela satisfied the second step of a *Strickland* ineffective assistance of counsel claim. [*Strickland v. Washington*, 466 U.S. 668 (1984).] In my view, Mr. Barela cannot show a reasonable probability that, but for the deficiency of trial counsel in failing to object to the instructions, the jury's verdict would have been different.

. . . .

In this case, Mr. Barela asserted that he was innocent because K.M. actively solicited a sexual encounter. Although the verdict demonstrates that the jury did not believe Mr. Barela's testimony, we must still evaluate the likelihood that a correctly instructed jury would have found that Mr. Barela lacked the required mens rea given K.M.'s version of what happened. *See* [*State v.*] *Hutchings*, 2012 UT 50, (evaluating the likelihood of a defense verdict if the jury had been correctly instructed where the jury had clearly rejected the defendant's testimony); [*State v.*] *Powell*, 2007 UT 9 (same).

. . . .

Given [] evidence [of the encounter as described by the majority], it is highly probable that a properly instructed jury would have concluded that Mr. Barela knew that K.M. had not consented to sex when he penetrated her vagina with his penis. And it is even more likely that a jury would conclude that Mr. Barela acted with criminal recklessness. . . .

According to K.M.'s testimony . . . Mr. Barela inserted his penis into the vagina of a client who was a near-stranger to him within a matter of seconds of massaging her inner thigh. K.M. did not indicate her consent to Mr. Barela's actions in any way or even engage in conversation with him. The most that can be said is that K.M. did not actively object to Mr. Barela massaging her inner thigh within seconds of his doing so. Thus the question presented to a correctly instructed jury would have been (1) whether Mr. Barela was "aware of but consciously disregarded a substantial and unjustifiable risk that" K.M. had not consented to sex and, if so, (2) whether Mr. Barela's assumption of the risk of being wrong about any conjecture that K.M. had consented to sex under these facts "constitute[d] a gross deviation from the standard of care that an ordinary person would exercise." *Id.*

. . . .

I conclude that the probability that a properly instructed jury would acquit Mr. Barela of rape is not sufficient to undermine my confidence in the verdict. I would, therefore, . . . affirm his conviction.

Notes and Questions

1. If you were the judge. would you have instructed the jury on mistake of fact? At first glance, this might appear like a "disagreement" of fact case: divergent testimony on the question of consent. But notice that there is no evidence the victim ever verbally indicated her lack of consent. This is why the majority indicates the defense

could have adopted an alternative theory had the jury been properly instructed: argue first that the prosecution failed to prove a lack of consent beyond a reasonable doubt, and, in the alternative, that even if the prosecution did meet that burden, they did not prove the defendant's mistaken assumption of consent was objectively unreasonable.

2. Historically, mistake of fact was not relevant in a rape case in common law because of the inherent invalidity of mistake once the prosecutor proved extrinsic force (the force or threat of force used by the defendant to compel the victim to submit). As discussed above, some common law jurisdictions, in modifying or removing the extrinsic force requirement, allow a defendant to introduce mistake of fact evidence as to consent, but require the mistake to be honestly held and objectively reasonable. *See Commonwealth v. Sherry*, 386 Mass. 682 (1982) (discussing how the jury instruction for rape, that "[t]he act of the defendant must have been against the will, that is without the woman's consent, and there must have been sufficient force used by him to accomplish his purpose" arguably rendered mistake of fact as to consent irrelevant). In *Sherry*, the Massachusetts Supreme Court acknowledged that "[w]hether a reasonable good faith mistake of fact as to the fact of consent is a defense to the crime of rape has never, to our knowledge, been decided in [Massachusetts]" and that the court was not aware of any "American court of last resort that recognizes mistake of fact, without consideration of its reasonableness."

3. If an honest but objectively unreasonable mistaken belief of consent is sufficient to prove guilt for rape, does this mean a defendant can be guilty of rape by recklessness? And if a mistaken but objectively reasonable belief of consent is a defense to rape, does this mean the victim was not raped?

4. Were you persuaded by Justice Durham's dissent in *Barela*? In part he identifies the circumstantial evidence the prosecutor may have used and which the jury found persuasive. Circumstantial evidence and placing events and actions in context are critically important tools for prosecutors. *See* Allison Leotta, *I Was a Sex-Crimes Prosecutor. Here's Why 'He Said, She Said' Is a Myth,* TIME (Oct. 3, 2018). As Leotta points out, rape is the only violent crime subjected to the claim of "he said she said" and that "there are methods of discerning the truth in a court of law. We need to understand that when two people tell different stories—whether about a sex crime or an armed robbery—we *can* use common sense, reasoning and investigation to figure out what happened." Leota also makes the important point that "studies show that rape claims are false at exactly the same rate as claims of any other crime, about 2–6% of the time. You're just as likely to be falsely accused of mugging someone as raping them."

5. At one point, the ALI proposed an "affirmative consent" standard. Affirmative consent has its supporters as well as detractors. *See* Christina M. Tchen, *Rape Reform and a Statutory Consent Defense*, 74 J. CRIM. L & CRIMINOLOGY 1518 (1983) (proposing an affirmative consent requirement); *but see* Megan McArdle, *'Affirmative Consent' Will Make Rape Laws Worse*, BLOOMBERG (Jul. 1, 2015) (responding

to the ALI's affirmative consent proposal which McArdle claims was "[a]n effort to reduce confusion and fear" but which "would actually add both"). Ultimately the ALI did not adopt the proposal. Would requiring affirmative consent help or worsen sexual assault laws?

6. Revoking or withdrawing consent. Where an individual consents to a sexual act, unlike the English common law, that consent is not irrevocable. Consent may be revoked at any time, rendering subsequent sexual acts nonconsensual. *See In re John Z.*, 29 Cal. 4th 756, 128 Cal. Rptr. 2d 783, 60 P.3d 183 (2003) (stressing that a woman has an absolute right to say "no" to an act of sexual intercourse. After intercourse has commenced, she has the absolute right to call a halt and say "no more," and if she is compelled to continue, a forcible rape is committed).

Practically speaking, cases involving revoked consent can be difficult to establish. In one high profile case a Colombia university student, (Emma) accused a fellow Colombia student, (Paul) of rape for some but not all the sexual acts in which the two engaged. Emma claimed essentially that she consented to sexual acts "a" and "b". At some point during act "b", Paul talked about sexual act "c", to which Emma claims to have clearly and unambiguously said no. According to Emma, Paul ignored her voicing nonconsent and forcibly engaged in act "c". A Colombia university investigation did not substantiate Emma's claims. She then turned the experience into a thesis project and carried the mattress on which she claimed Paul raped her around campus, including to graduation. While not being found to having raped Emma, Paul claimed he was shunned and shamed (and his name published in the campus newspaper) as if he had. Paul went on to sue Colombia, which settled the case. If events occurred as Emma claimed, Paul committing sexual act "c" was rape. But practically speaking, proving lack of consent beyond a reasonable doubt when it has already been given is possible but can be challenging. *See* Emily Bazelon, *Have We Learned Anything From the Columbia Rape Case?*, N.Y. Times, May 29, 2015.

7. Rape by Fraud. Rape by fraud encompasses "an action whereby a person obtains sexual consent and has sexual intercourse of any type by fraud, deception, misrepresentation, or impersonation." *See* Michael Mullen, *Rape by Fraud: Eluding Washington Rape Statutes*, 41 Seattle U. L. Rev. 1035 (2018). Mullen describes different types of fraud, which, depending on a given jurisdiction's laws, may or may not be a crime. The types include:

> Fraudulent treatment is characterized by fraudulent medical, psychological, psychiatric, and religious treatment used to obtain sexual intercourse. Many of the most infamous rape by deception cases involve unscrupulous physicians convincing patients that sexual complicity is essential to or helpful in providing a needed medical operation or diagnosis. [This known as *fraud in the factum*.]
>
> Sexual impersonation involves someone who pretends to be someone else to fraudulently obtain sexual intercourse. Impersonation of a significant

other is characteristic of this category; however, case law also provides examples of defendants impersonating famous people to obtain sexual intercourse.

Sexual scams typically involve fraudsters targeting vulnerable people, often impersonating agents or producers within the entertainment industry, especially pornographic content production. Sexual scammers sometimes use other techniques to fraudulently induce sexual complicity, including operating under the guise of (bogus) scientific research and, in one particularly bizarre case, posing as an entranced psychic and demanding sex during a séance. [*This is known as fraud in the inducement.*]

Under the common law, a defendant who induced the victim to consent to sex through a fraud (fraud in the inducement) did not commit rape. This was because the victm knew what she was consenting to (sex) and therefore the consent was considered valid and a complete defense. In contrast, a defendant who induced the victim to submit to sex by fraudulently indicating the victim was consenting to something other than sex (fraud in the factum), the consent was considered invalid, and the defendant was convicted of rape. In short, so long as the victim knew she was consenting to sex, the consent was treated as valid, even if the victim was tricked into giving that consent. But if the victim did not know what she was consenting to the consent was invalid, and the defendant committed rape.

One situation that created great confusion in applying this equation was a defendant who induced the victim to consent to sex by posing as the victim's normal sexual partner, for example, a husband's male friend who poses as the husband and climbs into bed with the wife/victim. This seems like a fraudulent inducement, because the victim did in fact consent to sex. Some courts treated it, however, as fraud in the factum by concluding the victim consent to *marital* sex and not adulterous sex, thereby invalidating the consent and rendering the defendant guilty of rape.

8. Consider the following:

In her freshman year at Purdue University, Abbi Finney was visiting her boyfriend in his dorm room. . . . By 2 a.m. Finney had fallen asleep in bed with her boyfriend. His friends had sacked out on a futon below. At some point, Finney woke up to the realization that someone was fondling her. The fondling led to sex. Only later did she realize the man in bed with her was not her boyfriend. To her, what had happened was clear. She had been raped. . . . She went to the hospital for a rape exam. She reported the assault to police. . . . Questioned about the incident by police, Finney's assailant, Donald Grant Ward, admitted he had waited for her boyfriend to leave the room and then climbed into bed with Finney. "Ward indicated he had sexual intercourse with (the) victim . . . knowing she believed him to be her boyfriend," police said in an affidavit supporting the rape charge.

Elsewhere: Rape by deception should be a crime, THE GOSHEN NEWS, Mar 8, 2021.

The police have brought you their investigation file and need a decision on whether to pursue a criminal charge. In your jurisdiction (Indiana), there are three ways to commit the offense of rape: "[t]he first is when a victim is compelled by force or threat of force. The second is when the victim is unconscious or unaware of the attack. And the third is when the victim is mentally disabled to a degree that makes consent impossible." *Id.* Can you charge Ward with rape?

9. App for that? In 2014 a company released the "Good2Go" app, which records mutual consent before sex. Assume you work for a sexual assault victim's advocacy group. The company has sent you the following description of the app and has requested your group's endorsement.

> After deciding that you would like to have sex with someone, launch the Good2Go app (free on iTunes and Google Play), hand the phone off to your potential partner, and allow him or her to navigate the process to determine if he or she is ready and willing. "Are We Good2Go?" the first screen asks, prompting the partner to answer "No, Thanks," "Yes, but . . . we need to talk," or "I'm Good2Go." If the partner chooses door No. 1, a black screen pops up that reads "Remember! No means No! Only Yes means Yes, BUT can be changed to NO at anytime!" If he or she opts instead to have a conversation before deciding—imagine, verbally communicating with someone with whom you may imminently engage in sexual intercourse—the app pauses to allow both parties to discuss.
>
> If the partner—let's assume the partner is a she—indicates that she is "Good2Go," she's sent to a second screen that asks if she is "Sober," "Mildly Intoxicated," "Intoxicated but Good2Go," or "Pretty Wasted." If she chooses "Pretty Wasted," the app informs her that she "cannot consent" and she's instructed to return the phone back to its owner (and presumably, not have sex under any circumstances, young lady). All other choices lead to a *third* screen, which asks the partner if she is an existing Good2Go user or a new one. If she's a new user, she's prompted to enter her phone number and a password, confirm that she is 18 years old, and press submit. (Minors are out of luck—the app is only for consenting *adults*.) Then, she'll fill out a *fourth* prompt, which asks her to input a six-digit code that's just been texted to her *own* cellphone to verify her identity with that app. (Previous users can just type in their phone number—which serves as their Good2Go username—and password.) Once that level is complete, she returns the phone to its owner, who can view a message explaining the terms of the partner's consent. (For example, the "Partner is intoxicated but is Good2Go.") *Then*, the instigator presses a button marked "Ok," which reminds him again that yes can be changed to "NO at anytime!" Then you get to have sex.

Amanda Hess, *Consensual Sex: There's an App for That*, SLATE, Sept. 29, 2014. Will you recommend to your boss that the advocacy group endorse the app? Why or why not?

III. Capacity to Consent

Consenting to sexual intercourse requires the capacity to form consent. There are several different circumstances where that capacity may be lacking. These include intellectual disabilities which call into question an individual's ability to meaningfully consent to sex.[73] Also included, and discussed at the end of this section, are individuals who have not yet reached the age in their jurisdiction to be able to legally consent to having sex.[74] Depending on the jurisdiction and the ages and age range of the individuals involved, the result of seemingly consensual underage sex may be the offense of statutory rape.

The most frequently arising capacity to consent issue is where someone is intoxicated by drugs and/or alcohol. Intoxication in the rape context may involve administering drugs, including by surreptitiously placing the substance in a beverage. The most commonly used substances are Rohypnol, GHB (Gamma Hydroxybutyric Acid), GBL (Gamma-Butyrolactone), and ketamine. As the Drug Enforcement Agency explains:

> These substances make it easier for a perpetrator to commit sexual assault because they inhibit a person's ability to resist and can prevent them from remembering the assault. Drug-facilitated sexual assault can happen to anyone, by anyone, whether the perpetrator is a date, a stranger, an acquaintance, or someone you have known a long time.[75]

But alcohol "remains the most commonly used drug in crimes of sexual assault."[76] Alcohol intoxication can lead to "blackouts"—periods of memory loss. According to one expert,

> Blackouts tend to start at blood alcohol levels of at least 0.15 percent, about twice the legal limit for driving, especially when a person hits that level quickly. When alcohol floods the hippocampus—a brain region that records our lives as they unfold—neurons stop talking to each other and capturing memories.[77]

---

73. According to DoJ research obtained by National Public Radio, "people with intellectual disabilities—women and men—are the victims of sexual assaults at rates more than seven times those for people without disabilities." Joseph Shapiro, *The Sexual Assault Epidemic No One Talks About*, NPR ALL THINGS CONSIDERED, Jan. 8, 2018.

74. *Statutory Rape: A Guide to State Laws and Reporting Requirements*, Health & Human Services, Dec. 14, 2004 [hereinafter *Statutory Rape*].

75. Drug Facilitated Sexual Assault, Drug Enforcement Agency, *available at* https://www.dea.gov /sites/default/files/2018-07/DFSA_0.PDF (last visited Aug. 22, 2021) [hereinafter DEA]; *see also* RH Schwartz et al., *Drug-facilitated sexual assault ('date rape')*, 93 S. MED. J. 558 (2000).

76. DEA, *supra* note 75.

77. John Eligon, *Maybe Just Drunk Enough to Remember*, N.Y. TIMES, Apr. 23, 2011 (quoting Dr. Aaron White) [hereinafter Eligon]; *see also* Aaron M. White, *What Happened? Alcohol, Memory Blackouts, and the Brain*, 27 ALCOHOL RESEARCH & HEALTH 186 (2003).

Essentially, "when the hippocampus is off, no matter how hard one tries, a memory will not be recalled because it will not have been recorded in the first place."[78] At the same time, [the] person may still be conscious and "interacting with people, talking, driving a car, having sex, engaging in all kinds of complex behavior. . . ."[79]

Intoxication may be raised in rape cases in several different contexts.[80] At common law, the defendant's voluntary intoxication would not be of use during the guilt phase, as rape is a general intent crime. Furthermore, the extrinsic force proof requirement essentially nullified the credibility of any claim intoxication explained why the defendant that mistakenly believed the victim consented. But voluntary intoxication could be of use to negate the specific intent of attempted rape or any form of assault aggravated by an intent to commit rape or some other sexual offense. For MPC jurisdictions, voluntary intoxication is of use to the offender only if the offense requires proof of a purely subjective mens rea element.

For victims, some jurisdictions include voluntary intoxication as a form of mental incapacitation meaning they could not consent. The victim's voluntary intoxication was raised in the *Khalil* case below. As you read *Khalil*, consider what effect, if any, you think voluntary intoxication should have on the ability to consent to sex—and to prosecute those who engage in sex with visibly, voluntarily, intoxicated individuals.

State v. Khalil

956 N.W.2d 627 (2021)
Minnesota Supreme Court

THISSEN, Justice.

This case arises from an experience no person should ever have to endure. J.S. was intoxicated after drinking alcohol and taking a prescription narcotic. She went to a bar with a friend but was denied entry due to her intoxication. Appellant Francios Momolu Khalil approached J.S. outside of the bar and invited her to accompany him to a supposed party at a house. After arriving at the house, J.S. passed out and woke up to find Khalil penetrating her vagina with his penis. The question before us is whether Khalil's conduct is third-degree criminal sexual conduct: sexual penetration with another person when the actor knows or has reason to know that the complainant is "mentally incapacitated."

Our decision turns on the meaning of mentally incapacitated as defined by the Legislature in Minn. Stat. § 609.341, subd. 7 (2020). The statute provides: "Mentally incapacitated" means that a person under the influence of alcohol, a narcotic, anesthetic, or any other substance, administered to that person without the person's

78. *Id.*
79. *Id.*
80. *See* Mitchell Keiter, *Just Say No Excuse: The Rise and Fall of the Intoxication Defense*, 87 J. Crim. L. & Criminology 482 (1997).

agreement, lacks the judgment to give a reasoned consent to sexual contact or sexual penetration. *Id.* Specifically, we are asked to determine whether the phrase "administered to that person without the person's agreement" applies to alcohol. *Id.* In other words, we must decide whether a person can be mentally incapacitated under the statute when the person voluntarily ingests alcohol, or whether the alcohol must be administered to the person without his or her agreement.

We hold that a person is mentally incapacitated under the definition adopted by the Legislature in section 609.341, subdivision 7, when that person is "under the influence of alcohol administered to that person without the person's agreement." Consequently, we reverse the decision of the court of appeals and remand to the district court for a new trial.

Facts

The parties do not dispute the relevant facts. On the evening of May 13, 2017, J.S. consumed approximately five shots of vodka and one pill of a prescription narcotic. She then traveled to the Dinkytown neighborhood of Minneapolis with her friend S.L. Upon arriving, J.S. attempted to enter a local bar but was denied entry by the bouncer because she was intoxicated. Shortly thereafter, Khalil and two other men approached J.S. and S.L. outside the bar and invited them to a party. Khalil then drove the group to a house in North Minneapolis, arriving in the early morning hours of May 14, 2017. There was no party at the house.

S.L. testified that, after walking into the house, J.S. immediately laid down on the living room couch and soon fell asleep. J.S. testified that she "blacked out" due to her intoxication shortly after arriving at the house and did not clearly remember lying down on the couch. J.S. woke up some time later to find Khalil penetrating her vagina with his penis. She said, "No, I don't want to," to which he replied, "But you're so hot and you turn me on." J.S. then lost consciousness and woke up at some point between 7 and 8 a.m. with her shorts around her ankles. She retrieved S.L. from another room and the two called a Lyft and left the house. During the ride, J.S. told S.L. that she had been raped. Later that day, J.S. went to Regions Hospital in St. Paul to have a rape kit done.

On May 18, 2017, J.S. contacted the Minneapolis police department to report the incident. The police conducted an investigation and the State charged Khalil with one count of third-degree criminal sexual conduct involving a mentally incapacitated or physically helpless complainant. . . .

At trial, the district court issued jury instructions, which stated in part:

> A person is mentally incapacitated if she lacks the judgment to give reasoned consent to sexual penetration due to the influence of alcohol, a narcotic, or any other substance administered without her agreement.

. . . .

[T]he jury sought to clarify whether it was sufficient that J.S. voluntarily consumed the alcohol or whether Khalil or another person had to have administered the alcohol to J.S. without her agreement for her to qualify as mentally incapacitated under Minn. Stat. § 609.341, subd. 7. Over Khalil's objection, the district court instructed the jury that the first reading of the statute was correct, stating: "[Y]ou can be mentally incapacitated following consumption of alcohol that one administers to one's self or narcotics that one administers to one's self or separately something else that's administered without someone's agreement." The jury then found Khalil guilty of third-degree criminal sexual conduct.

On appeal, Khalil challenged the validity of the jury instructions, arguing that the district court erred by instructing the jury on the definition of mentally incapacitated the way it did.... The court of appeals rejected Khalil's argument and affirmed his conviction.... We granted review.

Analysis

The jury convicted Khalil of third-degree criminal sexual conduct under Minn. Stat. § 609.344, subd. 1(d), which states in relevant part:

> A person who engages in sexual penetration with another person is guilty of criminal sexual conduct in the third degree if any of the following circumstances exists: . . .

> (d) the actor *knows or has reason to know* that the complainant is mentally impaired, *mentally incapacitated*, or physically helpless[.]

(Emphasis added.) Consequently, to convict Khalil of third-degree criminal sexual conduct under section 609.344, subdivision 1(d), the State was required to prove that when Khalil sexually penetrated J.S., he knew or had reason to know that J.S. was in a particular state; namely, that J.S. was mentally incapacitated.

It is certainly true that a commonsense understanding of the term mentally incapacitated could include a person who cannot exercise judgment sufficiently to express consent due to intoxication resulting from the voluntary consumption of alcohol. But here, we do not look at the ordinary, commonsense understanding of mentally incapacitated because the Legislature expressly defined the term in the general definitions section of Minnesota's criminal sexual conduct statutes.... For the purpose of criminal sexual conduct offenses, "'[m]entally incapacitated' means that a person under the influence of alcohol, a narcotic, anesthetic, or any other substance, administered to that person without the person's agreement, lacks the judgment to give a reasoned consent to sexual contact or sexual penetration." Minn. Stat. § 609.341, subd. 7.

The State does not claim that Khalil knew or had reason to know that J.S. was under the influence of alcohol administered to J.S. *without* her agreement. There is no evidence to support such a claim. On the other hand, Khalil does not dispute that there is sufficient evidence in the record that he knew or had reason to know that J.S. was under the influence of alcohol. Accordingly, our decision in this appeal turns on whether the *Legislature's* definition of mentally incapacitated includes a state of mental incapacitation caused by the consumption of alcohol, voluntary or not, or whether it is limited to circumstances where the state of mental incapacitation results from consumption of alcohol administered to the complainant involuntarily without her agreement.

The State urges us to read the definition of mentally incapacitated like the district court did when it instructed the jury in response to the jury's questions: mentally incapacitated means that a person under the influence of alcohol, however consumed, lacks the judgment to give a reasoned consent to sexual contact or sexual penetration. In contrast, Khalil challenges the district court's interpretation of the Legislature's definition of mentally incapacitated and urges us to read the statute as follows: mentally incapacitated means that a person under the influence of alcohol, administered to that person without the person's agreement, lacks the judgment to give a reasoned consent to sexual contact or sexual penetration.

. . . .

A good example of the unique institutional capacity of the Legislature (as compared with the judiciary) to sort out complex policy issues is the work currently underway to amend Minnesota's criminal sexual conduct statutes, including revisions to address the Legislature's concern about a potential gap concerning sexual penetration of, or sexual contact with, voluntarily intoxicated persons.

If the Legislature's intended meaning is clear from the text of the statute, we apply that meaning and not what we may wish the law was or what we think the law should be. . . . We hold that the definition of "mentally incapacitated" in section 609.341, subd. 7, is susceptible to only one reasonable interpretation; namely, that alcohol causing a person to lack judgment to give a reasoned consent must be administered to the person without the person's agreement.

In summary, we read the Legislature's definition of "mentally incapacitated" to unambiguously mean that substances (including alcohol) which cause a person to lack judgment to give a reasoned consent must be administered to the person without the person's agreement. The State's contrary interpretation unreasonably strains and stretches the plain text of the statute. Accordingly, we conclude that section 609.341, subdivision 7, means that a person under the influence of alcohol is not mentally incapacitated unless the alcohol was administered to the person under its influence without that person's agreement.

Of course, we offer no judgment as to whether the Legislature's choice about the level of criminal liability and punishment that should be imposed on a person who sexually penetrates another person knowing (or negligently unaware) that the other person lacks the judgment to consent due to voluntary intoxication is appropriate. If the Legislature intended for the definition of mentally incapacitated to include voluntarily intoxicated persons, "it is the Legislature's prerogative to reexamine the . . . statute and amend it accordingly." . . .

Reversed and remanded.

Notes and Questions

1. In a footnote at the start of the unanimously decided *Khalil* decision, the court laid out the limited nature of their role:

> We are mindful of and concerned with the fact that, as the Minnesota County Attorneys Association points out in its amicus brief, nearly half of all women in the United States have been the victim of sexual violence in their lifetime—including an estimated 10 million women who have been raped while under the influence of alcohol or drugs. With this level of sexual violence, legislatures across the country have enacted statutes aimed at prioritizing consent and protecting intoxicated victims of rape and sexual assault, regardless of how the victim became intoxicated. *See, e.g.,* Wash. Rev. Code § 9A.44.010 (defining "mental incapacity"—for the purpose of second-degree rape under Wash. Rev. Code § 9A.44.050—as a "condition existing at the time of the offense which prevents a person from understanding the nature or consequences of the act of sexual intercourse whether that condition is produced by illness, defect, the influence of a substance or from some other cause"). These statutory definitions protect intoxicated victims of rape regardless of how they became intoxicated. But today we undertake the task of interpreting the definition of "mentally incapacitated" that the Minnesota Legislature enacted in Minn. Stat. § 609.341, subd. 7 (2020).

2. The Minnesota Supreme Court issued the *Kahlil* decision in March 2021. By the end of June, the Minnesota legislature enacted a series of changes to Minnesota sexual assault laws including voluntary intoxication in the definition of mentally incapacitated. In August, Khalil pled guilty to the misdemeanor offense of nonconsensual touching and was sentenced to time served (he had already served two years confinement) and the requirement to register as a sexual predator for ten years. Neither Kahlil nor the victim were satisfied with the outcome. The victim issued a statement through the prosecutor contending that

> It is nearly impossible for me to accept this plea as a consequence for Mr. Khalil as it shows just how heavily the system itself fails me, victims and survivors from all over the world, of all sorts of forms of abuse. . . . We need to do better as individuals. We need to do better as a state and we need to do better as a system.

The victim was purportedly not satisfied that Kahlil's plea did not include a no-contact order. The victim acknowledged wanting to avoid "another traumatic trial" and that she had suffered a panic attack when she learned of Kahlil's release from jail. The victim's statement ended by noting that "[a]ll of us have already endured and processed an enormous amount of effort, time and support that was necessary for this case, yet the system continues to ask for more." Kahlil continued to deny he had done anything wrong, and his lawyer said in that court that "[r]egret is not rape," that Kahlil had never raped the victim and that he spent two years in prison because of the trial court's error. *See* Rochelle Olson, *Attacker at center of Minnesota rape law change pleads guilty to unwanted sexual touching*, STAR TRIBUNE, Aug. 2, 2021.

3. One commentator claims that Minnesota (prior to the summer 2021 changes) was one of about 40 states that do not explicitly prohibit sex with a voluntarily intoxicated victim. *See* Michal Buchhandler-Raphael, *The Conundrum of Voluntary Intoxication and Sex*, 83 BROOKLYN L. REV. 1031 (2017). One of those states is New York, whose mental incapacitation statute is nearly identical to the one in Minnesota as of the *Kahlil* case. For several years, there have been unsuccessful legislative efforts in New York to revise its law. The *Kahlil* decision appears to have provided the necessary impetus, as in the summer of 2021, the New York Senate passed a bill to include voluntary intoxication in mental incapacitation. However, as of January 2022, the New York Assembly had yet to take up the legislation.

4. In 2007, a UK appellate court overturned a conviction in a case the facts of which were similar to *Kahlil*. The UK court also reversed, rejecting the claim that intoxication necessarily precluded capacity to consent. The UK court suggested a more nuanced or at least individualized approach:

> If, through drink (or for any other reason) the complainant has temporarily lost her capacity to choose whether to have intercourse on the relevant occasion, she is not consenting, and subject to questions about the defendant's state of mind, if intercourse takes place, this would be rape. However, where the complainant has voluntarily consumed even substantial quantities of alcohol, but nevertheless remains capable of choosing whether or not to have intercourse, and in drink agrees to do so, this would not be rape. We should perhaps underline that, as a matter of practical reality, capacity to consent may evaporate well before a complainant becomes unconscious. Whether this is so or not, however, is fact specific, or more accurately, depends on the actual state of mind of the individuals involved on the particular occasion.

> Considerations like these underline the fact that it would be unrealistic to endeavor to create some kind of grid system which would enable the answer to these questions to be related to some prescribed level of alcohol consumption. Experience shows that different individuals have a greater or lesser capacity to cope with alcohol than others, and indeed the ability of a single individual to do so may vary from day to day. The practical reality is that there are some areas of human behavior which are inapt for detailed legislative structures. In this context, provisions intended to protect women from sexual assaults might very well be conflated into a system which would provide patronizing interference with the right of autonomous adults to make personal decisions for themselves.

Do you agree or like the UK court's approach? Is it practically workable? What do you think of the contention that blanket rules on intoxication would "provide patronising interference with the right of autonomous adults to make personal decisions for themselves"?

5. Notice that the statute provides that guilt requires proof that, "(d) the actor *knows or has reason to know* that the complainant is mentally impaired, *mentally incapacitated*, or physically helpless[.]" Does this mean a negligent failure to realize the victim is mentally incapacitated is sufficient to support a rape conviction?

IV. Force

Combining requirements for some quantum of external force and a lack of consent, while using the victim's resistance as a measure for both, sets the conditions for confused applications of rape laws. As one judge explained:

> Unfortunately, courts . . . often tend to confuse these two elements force and lack of consent and to think of them as one. They are not. They mean, and require, different things. . . . What seems to cause the confusion, what, indeed, has become a common denominator of both elements is the notion that the victim must actively resist the attack upon her. If she fails to offer sufficient resistance (sufficient to the satisfaction of the judge), a court is entitled, or at least presumes the entitlement, to find that there was no force or threat of force, or that the act was not against her will, or that she actually consented to it, or some unarticulated combination or synthesis of these elements that leads to the ultimate conclusion that the victim was not raped. Thus it is that the focus is almost entirely on the extent of resistance, the victim's acts, rather than those of her assailant. Attention is directed not to the wrongful stimulus, but to the victim's reactions to it.[81]

As you read *Touchet*, attempt to determine the problem the majority has with the conviction. Is it that force was threatened but the victim never actually battered? Or is it that the victim did not physically resist?

Louisiana v. Touchet
897 So. 2d 900 (2005)
Louisiana Court of Appeals

Facts

The State of Louisiana alleges that the Defendant struck the victim with his fists, forced her to remove her clothing at knife point, and had sexual intercourse with the victim against her will.

The Defendant, Wilbert Touchet, Jr., was charged with aggravated rape committed in violation of La.R.S. . . . The trial court sentenced the Defendant to a mandatory

---

81. *State v. Rusk*, 289 Md. 230, 424 A.2d 720 (1981) (J. Wilner dissent). Following the Maryland Court of Appeals decision reversing Rusk's conviction, the Maryland Supreme Court essentially adopted Judge Wilner's cogent dissenting opinion and reversed the Court of Appeals.

sentence of life imprisonment on the charge of aggravated rape.... The Defendant appeals [that] conviction[].

Sufficiency of the Evidence

The Defendant sets forth one assignment of error alleging the evidence submitted by the State is insufficient to support conviction of the three offenses charged.

. . . .

In order for the State to obtain a conviction, it must prove the elements of the crime beyond a reasonable doubt. In order for this court to affirm a conviction, the record must reflect that the State has satisfied this burden of proving the elements of the crime beyond a reasonable doubt. *State v. Kennerson*, 96-1518 (La.App. 3 Cir. 5/7/97), 695 So.2d 1367.

Aggravated Rape

The trial court found the Defendant guilty of aggravated rape in violation of La.R.S. 14:42(A)(3), which states, in pertinent part:

> A. Aggravated rape is a rape committed upon a person sixty-five years of age or older or where the anal, oral, or vaginal sexual intercourse is deemed to be without lawful consent of the victim because it is committed under any one or more of the following circumstances:
>
> . . . .
>
> (3) When the victim is prevented from resisting the act because the offender is armed with a dangerous weapon.

The victim testified that she met the Defendant around Mardi Gras 2002. The two subsequently spent several nights together. At some point, the Defendant left to go to work offshore. While he was offshore, the victim rented a house for the two to live in together when he returned. All of this happened between Mardi Gras and the first week of March 2002. When the Defendant returned from working offshore, he moved in with the victim. The two slept together in a small bedroom in the rented house.

The victim stated that about two weeks after they had moved in together, she and the Defendant had gone on an outing and when they returned, the Defendant told the victim that she had been acting like a whore. Upon arriving at their home, they entered the home, and the Defendant locked the front door. The victim proceeded to go to the bathroom, which was through the bedroom. The Defendant met the victim and told her, "[i]f you want to act like a whore, I'm going to treat you like a whore," and told the victim to remove her clothing. The victim testified that she told the Defendant no at first. At that point, the Defendant pulled out a pocket knife. Then the victim testified that she did not remember the knife being very close to her, but "he came to [her] with it." The victim stated that she believed that he was capable of using the knife and that she was scared that if she tried to get away, the Defendant would catch up to her.

After refusing once or twice, the victim removed her own clothing at the Defendant's prompting. She stated she probably would have removed her clothing even if he had not had the knife because she was the "underdog." After she removed her clothing, the Defendant "set the knife down" and "proceeded to come up on [her]." At that point the two had sexual intercourse.

The victim testified that she did not want to have sex. The victim stated that she resisted the Defendant verbally, but did not get up and leave the room because she was scared. On cross-examination, the victim stated that other than saying no, she did not resist the Defendant in any way.

The Defendant testified that he never held a knife to the victim's throat and raped her. The Defendant further testified that the victim never indicated to him that she did not want to have sex with him.

In *State v. Jackson*, 03-1079 (La.App. 3 Cir. 2/4/04), 866 So.2d 358, *writ denied*, 04-1126 (La. 10/8/04), 883 So.2d 1027, this court upheld the defendant's conviction of aggravated rape. In *Jackson*, the defendant forced two women upstairs at knife point, tied one of the women up with an electrical cord and put her in a hall closet. The victim testified that while he was tying up the other woman, the defendant told her to shut up "that he had killed a woman in Houston and he would not hesitate killing two more." *Id.* at 363. Then Jackson told the victim to go into a room. He approached the victim, twisted her shirt around her neck, placed the knife at her throat and said, "you do it or I do it." *Id.* at 364. The victim then requested that they go into another room, which she testified contained items that she could have used as a weapon. During the rape, the victim testified that Jackson did not have the knife, but still had a pair of scissors, which were either in his hand or on the floor near the victim's head during the rape. The victim stated that during the attack the defendant had one hand on his penis and the other hand on her shoulder holding her down; the scissors were on the floor next to her head. After raping the victim, Jackson forced her into a bathroom, took her shoes, tied the door shut from the outside and left in the victim's vehicle. In affirming Jackson's conviction, this court stated:

> In the present case, the occurrence of sexual intercourse is undisputed; the contested issue is whether the sex was consensual. R.M. testified the defendant had a knife to her throat when he ordered her to undress. Although the defendant put the knife down prior to the rape, R.M. testified the defendant had one hand on her shoulder and the scissors were near her head. Although it is not clear whether the scissors were actually in the defendant's hand during the perpetration of the rape, the jury was reasonable in determining that they were easily accessible to him.

In the case at bar, unlike *Jackson*, the victim testified that the Defendant did not get near her with the knife. Also, unlike *Jackson*, the victim did not testify that the knife or any other weapon was accessible to the Defendant during the commission of the sexual act. Accordingly, we find that the evidence viewed in the light most favorable to the prosecution is not sufficient to uphold a conviction of aggravated rape.

. . . .

In *State v. Powell*, 438 So.2d 1306 (La.App. 3 Cir.), *writ denied*, 443 So.2d 585 (La. 1983), this court held that the evidence was insufficient to uphold the Defendant's conviction for forcible rape. In *Powell*, the defendant picked the victim up on the street corner where she was waiting for her ride. The victim testified that after getting into the defendant's car, he brought her to a secluded area and threatened to kill her when she refused to have sexual intercourse with him. The defendant struck the victim several times in the face while threatening to kill her with a weapon that he claimed was underneath the seat. The victim testified that she never saw a weapon. After being struck and threatened, the victim removed her own pants and engaged in sexual intercourse with the defendant. In reversing Powell's conviction, this court stated:

> The only evidence concerning the act of sexual intercourse is the testimony of the victim. There was no other factual evidence to corroborate her testimony. Nevertheless, we find that any rational trier of fact could have reasonably concluded that the evidence taken in the light most favorable to the prosecution, showed beyond a reasonable doubt sufficient proof of the element. Under the Jackson test we feel that the jury (fact finder) could have reasonably accorded great weight to the victim's testimony to the extent that this element of the crime was proven beyond a reasonable doubt.
>
> There was no showing, however, of resistance on the part of the victim and very little evidence that she was prevented from resisting by force or threats of physical violence under the circumstances. Construing the evidence in a light most favorable to the prosecution, we do not feel that any rational trier of fact could find beyond a reasonable doubt that there was force or threats of physical violence where the victim reasonably believed that resistance to the act would be to no avail.

. . . .

After a thorough review of the record we find that the evidence is insufficient to convince a reasonable fact finder beyond a reasonable doubt that the victim was prevented from resisting the act by threats of force or physical violence under the circumstances. We recognize that there are cases holding that the victim's testimony is sufficient to establish an essential element of a crime. *State v. Rives*, 407 So.2d 1195 (La. 1981). However, it is clear, that the victim's testimony in this case, even when construed in a light most favorable to the prosecution, leaves reasonable doubt in the minds of reasonable men as to the commission of an essential element of the crime. Therefore, the State has failed to carry its burden of proof under *Jackson v. Virginia*, [443 U.S. 307 (1979),] as to an essential element of the crime. *Id.* at 1308-09.

While the victim in this case actually saw the weapon the Defendant possessed, the victim did not testify that the Defendant actually verbally threatened her with the weapon. The victim in *Powell* was struck several times in the face; the victim in the case at bar did not testify that she was struck the Defendant during this incident. Like *Powell* there is little showing of resistance on the part of the victim and little evidence that she was precluded from resisting by force or threats of force. The victim stated that the Defendant pulled the knife out and opened it, but did not remember the knife being very close to her; she stated that she removed her own clothing and that the Defendant put the weapon down before approaching her. The victim also stated that other than saying no to removing her clothing, she offered no other resistance to the attack. In *Powell*, the defendant and the victim were at most acquaintances. In the case at bar, the victim and the Defendant were involved in an intimate relationship both before and after the incident.

. . . .

Accordingly, we reverse the Defendant's conviction of aggravated rape and substitute a conviction for sexual battery, a statutory responsive verdict pursuant to La. Code Crim.P. art. 814(A)(8), and remand this case for re-sentencing in conformity with the conviction of sexual battery.

. . . .

Notes and Questions

1. *Touchet* represents the traditional common law requirement that the evidence establish a nexus between the force or threat of force used by the defendant and the victim's submission. There are differing views on how close the nexus must be. For example, in *Alston v. North Carolina*, 310 N.C. 399 (1984), the North Carolina Supreme Court overturned a jury verdict finding Alston guilty of raping his former girlfriend. The court acknowledged that the victim had expressed her lack of consent and that the defendant had threatened to "fix her face" if she refused to have sex with him. But the court concluded that because this threat preceded the actual sexual intercourse and that the threat was not made when the defendant undressed the victim and engaged in sex with her, the evidence failed to satisfy the force element of rape. Obviously, the jury in *Alston* thought otherwise, as in *Touchet*. This troubling aspect of traditional rape jurisprudence has thankfully become increasingly less common. Even in *Touchet*, note that the court substituted a conviction for un-aggravated sexual assault, apparently based on the conclusive evidence of the victim's lack of consent.

2. Regarding determining what are and are not facts and assessing witness credibility and demeanor, what role do trial juries and the trial judge play vs. appellate courts? Is the appellate court in *Touchet* performing that role or something different?

3. Do you think the evidence was sufficient to support at least *a* rational finding of aggravated rape? Towards the end of the opinion, the court indicates that the evidence was insufficient to satisfy the *Jackson v. Virginia* standard. Did the court really

apply that standard? Early in the case, the court noted that, "[I]n order for this court to affirm a conviction, the record must reflect that the State has satisfied this burden of proving the elements of the crime beyond a reasonable doubt." *State v. Kennerson*, 695 So. 2d 1367 (La. Ct. App. 1997). Is this the *Jackson* standard of review? Or did the court apply a more demanding standard?

4. In *Touchet*, the victim several times refused to take off her clothes as instructed and offered verbal resistance. Why wasn't that sufficient resistance?

5. Many states have modified their rape statutes to include constructive force and placing the victim in fear of force. *See Kansas v. Brooks*, 317 P.3d 54 (Kan. 2014). What is the required temporal nexus between constructive force and the sexual act? In *State v. Rusk*, 289 Md. 230 (1981), the Maryland Court of Appeals reversed Rusk's conviction for second-degree rape. At trial, the victim testified that she had just met Rusk while out with a friend and agreed to drive him to his apartment by herself, telling Rusk that "I'm just giving you a ride home." Rusk lived in a part of town unfamiliar to the victim, and upon their arrival, Rusk took the victim's keys out of the ignition and kept them. He then asked her to come up to his apartment. Once there, the victim did not make noise or attempt to leave. Rusk undressed the victim following which the victim asked him "[i]f I do what you want, will you let me go without killing me?" Rusk responded, "yes," the victim began crying, and Rusk initiated sexual intercourse, after which he returned the victim's keys, and she left. Rusk testified that the victim voluntarily turned her car off, came up to his apartment and had sex. The Court of Appeals ruled that even based on the victim's version, there was not sufficient evidence of rape, which at the time was defined as:

> A person is guilty of rape in the second degree if the person engages in vaginal intercourse with another person:

> (1) By force or threat of force against the will and without the consent of the other person. . . .

That there was intercourse is not in question. Do you agree with the Court of Appeals that the intercourse was not, as a matter of law, by "threat of force against the will" of the victim? Must threats of force be verbalized?

6. Asher and Bailey are dating, though their relationship has taken a series of problematic turns. When they began dating, they were both employed. Several months into the relationship, Asher was let go from her job due to the COVID pandemic and was unable to find steady work. Asher moved in with Bailey, which went well for a while. But as Asher's self-esteem began to suffer from going without a job, Asher became less and less interested in being intimate with Bailey. At the same time, Bailey was growing increasing frustrated at paying all their expenses. Things escalated one Friday night after both had consumed considerable amounts of wine. Bailey began berating Asher about everything but focused on the lack of interest in have sex. Bailey, jabbing an index forward towards (but never touching) Asher, said: "Let me make this clear for you. You either have sex with me right now or I'm tossing

you and your stuff on the street." Confused and angry, Asher initially said no. After an awkward silence, Asher, with no money or access to money without Bailey, turned and walked to their bedroom and had sex with Bailey. Several hours later, Asher, now sobbing, walked to the police station and reported what happened. You are the prosecutor. Applying the definition of the offense of rape used in *Touchet*, are you able to charge Bailey with rape?

Now assume you are using the Kansas law referenced in note 5 above. Does your answer change?

V. Statutory Rape

As discussed in the introduction, statutory rape is an offense in many jurisdictions. Statutory rape involves consensual sex in the general but not legal sense. That is because with statutory rape one of the participants is below the jurisdiction's age of consent. Different jurisdictions have different age limitations on when someone is deemed to have the capacity to legally consent to have sex. In most states, the age of consent is sixteen; in others, it is either seventeen or eighteen.[82] So while a fifteen-year-old may agree to have sex and even initiate the act, any resulting sexual intercourse is considered nonconsensual.

As you will remember from Chapter 5 (Mens Rea), statutory rape is controversial, because it is one of the rare offenses which does not require proof of mens rea but results in serious penal consequences, including confinement. While the wording of statutory rape offenses varies, to commit the crime only requires that the prosecution prove two elements: 1) sexual intercourse occurred and 2) the age of one of the parties at the time of the intercourse was below the jurisdiction's age of consent.

Defendants are often particularly challenged when facing a strict liability charge like statutory rape. While defendants are able to present a case, any evidence they wish to introduce must be relevant to either sex or age. What is not relevant is the defendant's mistaken belief as to the age of the sexual partner no matter how reasonable the mistake may have been. Recall that mistake of fact is where a defendant attempts to "block" or obstruct proof of the mens rea of an offense. But as there is no mens rea in a statutory rape offense, a defendant's mistake as to age, however honestly and reasonably held, is irrelevant and thus inadmissible.

As you read the *Holmes* case, note the court's strict view about its role in interpreting and not creating law. In several of the cases in this chapter, appellate courts appear to have substituted their views for that of the finder of fact at trial. Think about which approach you prefer and why. Is it better to have outcomes in individual cases which are deemed fair or to have predictability in how the law operates? Can we have both?

---

82. *Statutory Rape, supra* note 74.

New Hampshire v. Holmes

920 A.2d 632 (2007)
Supreme Court of New Hampshire

DALIANIS, J.

The defendant, Martin Holmes, appeals his conviction by a jury for felonious sexual assault for engaging in sexual penetration with a person who was thirteen years of age or older but less than sixteen years of age. . . . He argues that the Superior Court [] erred when it ruled that the State did not have to prove that he knew that the victim was under the age of legal consent. We affirm.

The parties do not dispute the following facts: The defendant is twenty-four years old. The victim met the defendant while walking with a friend in Rochester. Although she was fifteen years old, she told the defendant that she was seventeen. The victim and the defendant exchanged telephone numbers and spoke on the phone a few days later. Approximately a week later, after consuming alcohol, the victim phoned the defendant and arranged to meet him at a local park, where they eventually had sexual intercourse.

The defendant was charged by grand jury indictment with felonious sexual assault for having engaged in sexual penetration with a person, other than his legal spouse, who was then fifteen years old. See RSA 632-A:3, II. At the close of the State's case, he moved to dismiss the charge on the ground that the State had failed to prove that he knew that the victim was less than sixteen years of age. Relying upon our prior case law, the trial court denied the motion, ruling that the State did not have to prove beyond a reasonable doubt that the defendant knew that the victim was less than sixteen years old. See *Goodrow v. Perrin*, 119 N.H. 483, 488-89, 403 A.2d 864 (1979).

On appeal, the defendant invites us to overrule our prior precedent, which holds that the offense of felonious sexual assault with a person who is under the age of legal consent (statutory rape) "is a strict liability crime in that an accused cannot assert as a legal defense that he did not know the complainant was under the age of legal consent when penetration occurred." *State v. Carlson*, 146 N.H. 52, 58-59, 767 A.2d 421 (2001); see *Goodrow*, 119 N.H. at 488-89, 403 A.2d 864. For the reasons that follow, we decline his invitation.

. . . .

I. Development of Related Principles of Law

. . . .

[W]e had previously held, in effect, that a defendant's knowledge of the victim's age is not a material element of statutory rape. See *Goodrow*, 119 N.H. at 488-89, 403 A.2d 864. The plaintiff in Goodrow challenged the constitutionality of our statutory rape law, contending, in part, that the statute was invalid because it lacked the requirement of scienter. *Id.* at 487, 403 A.2d 864. We observed first that the statutory rape provision did not allow a defense of honest or reasonable mistake as to the victim's age. *Id.* at 488-89, 403 A.2d 864. We then ruled that the statute was not unconstitutional because it did not allow for such a defense. *Id.* at 489, 403 A.2d 864. We rejected the plaintiff's assertion that such a defense was constitutionally required, explaining that the United States Supreme Court "has never held that an honest mistake as to the age of the [complainant] is a constitutional defense to statutory rape." *Id.* (quotation omitted).

Since we decided *Goodrow* in 1979, the legislature has amended the statutory rape law numerous times, but has not seen fit to add a mens rea or to make reasonable mistake of age a defense. See Laws 1981, 415:4; Laws 1985, 228:4; Laws 1997, 220:3; Laws 2003, 226:3, 4. The legislature most recently amended the statutory rape provision during this past legislative session. See Laws 2006, 162:1. As amended, the statutory rape provision makes it a felony to engage in sexual penetration with a person other than one's legal spouse who is thirteen years of age or older and less than sixteen years of age only where the age difference between the actor and the other person is three years or more. See *id.*

By amending the statutory rape provision, but failing to insert a mens rea or provide a reasonable mistake of age defense, the legislature has impliedly accepted our construction of that provision. See *Del Norte, Inc. v. Provencher*, 142 N.H. 535, 539, 703 A.2d 890 (1997). It is well settled that "when the legislature reenacts a statute on which a repeated practical construction has been placed by the Bench and Bar, that reenactment constitutes a legislative adoption of the longstanding construction." *Id.* (quotation and brackets omitted); see also *Com. v. Miller*, 385 Mass. 521, 432 N.E.2d 463, 465 (1982). . . .

The defendant next asserts that because adult consensual sexual relationships are not as regulated as they were when we decided our prior cases, there is no longer any justification for permitting strict liability for statutory rape. . . .

As we explained in *Goodrow*:

> The State, by enacting [the statutory rape provision], has fixed the age at which a minor person may consent to sexual intercourse. In essence, this provision prohibits an adult, such as the plaintiff, from engaging in sexual intercourse with a person who is below the fixed age of consent. It is well established that the State has an independent interest in the well-being of its youth. One reason for this heightened interest is the vulnerability of children to harm. Another reason for the State's concern is that minors below a certain age are unable to make mature judgments about important matters.

Goodrow, 119 N.H. at 486, 403 A.2d 864 (quotation and citations omitted). This justification for making statutory rape a strict liability crime remains viable, despite decreased regulation of adult consensual sexual activity.

Statutory rape laws are based upon "a policy determination by the legislature that persons under the age of sixteen are not competent to consent to sexual contact or sexual intercourse." *State v. Jadowski*, 272 Wis.2d 418, 680 N.W.2d 810, 817

(2004); see *Collins* [*v. State*], 691 So.2d at 923. "The statutes are designed to impose the risk of criminal penalty on the adult, when the adult engages in sexual behavior with a minor." *Jadowski*, 680 N.W.2d at 817; see also *Carlson*, 146 N.H. at 59, 767 A.2d 421 (defendant placed himself in risky circumstances, relying upon victim's mature behavior to substantiate her representation of her age). In this way, these statutes accomplish deterrence. *Owens v. State*, 352 Md. 663, 724 A.2d 43, 54(Md.), cert. denied, 527 U.S. 1012, 119 S.Ct. 2354, 144 L.Ed.2d 250 (1999). "The reason that mistake of fact as to the [child]'s age constitutes no defense is, not that these crimes like public welfare offenses require no mens rea, but that a contrary result would strip the victims of the protection which the law exists to afford." *State v. Yanez*, 716 A.2d 759, 769 (R.I.1998) (quotation omitted); see *Owens*, 724 A.2d at 54 ("The legislature's decision to disallow a mistake-of-age defense to statutory rape furthers its interest in protecting children in ways that may not be accomplished if the law were to allow such a defense."). "If reasonable mistake were recognized as a defense, the very purpose of the [statutory rape] statute would be frustrated and the deterrent effect considerably diminished." *Collins*, 691 So.2d at 923.

The defendant next suggests that *Goodrow* is contrary to the modern trend of judicial decisions in this area. He notes that "several state courts have overruled prior precedent and have required either a culpable mens rea or have allowed for some kind of reasonable mistake of age defense." To the contrary, "[i]n most states. a mistake of age, no matter how reasonable, is no defense." Loewy, *Statutory Rape in a Post* Lawrence v. Texas *World*, 58 SMU L.Rev. 77, 88-89 (Winter 2005); see Carpenter, *On Statutory Rape, Strict Liability, and the Public Welfare Offense Model*, 53 Am. U.L.Rev. 313, 316–17 (2003). While "mistake of age" "has been asserted successfully as a defense in several states and is recognized by the Model Penal Code when the child is over the age of ten years, ... this defense remains the minority view. Far more states have rejected [it]." *Collins*, 691 So.2d at 923.

To the extent that a reasonable mistake of age defense exists in certain states, it is generally because the legislature has amended the applicable statute, not because the judiciary has engrafted this defense onto a statute that does not contain it. Indeed, at oral argument, the defendant conceded that hardly any states have a reasonable mistake of age defense. See Carpenter, *supra* at 385-91 (legislatures in three states have enacted statutes in which reasonable mistake of age is a defense regardless of age of victim; legislatures in eighteen states have enacted statutes providing for defense of reasonable mistake of age depending upon relative age of victim and perpetrator; in remaining twenty-nine states, reasonable mistake of age is no defense to statutory rape). As one commentator has noted, "[I]n more recent times it has been recognized that [whether there should be a reasonable mistake of age defense to statutory rape] is a policy matter that ought to be specifically addressed in the statutory definition of the crime." W. LaFave, Substantive Criminal Law § 17.4(c) at 650 (2d ed. 2003).

For all of the above reasons, we conclude that the defendant has failed to demonstrate that our decision in *Goodrow* is "no more than a remnant of abandoned doctrine." *Jacobs [v. Director, N.H. Div. of Motor Vehicles]*, 149 N.H. at 505, 823 A.2d 752 (quotation omitted).

. . . .

Affirmed.

Notes and Questions

1. According to somewhat dated DoJ statistics, in 2000, there was one statutory rape for every three rapes involving a juvenile victim reported to law enforcement. Ninety-nine percent of offenders of statutory rape were male. *See* Karyl Troup-Leasure & Howard N. Snyder, *Statutory Rape Known to Law Enforcement*, U.S. Department of Justice Office of Justice Programs Office of Juvenile Justice and Delinquency Prevention, Aug. 2005.

2. Often times, states criminalizing statutory rape also have a "Romeo & Juliet" provision accounting for teenagers in a relationship but who would otherwise meet the age level and disparity for statutory rape. For example, Texas provides an affirmative defense to sexual assault where there is not more than a three-year age gap between individuals, both individuals are over the age of fourteen and consented to the act in question, and neither are registered sex offenders. *See* Texas Penal Code § 22.011.(e). Absent such a provision, when two fifteen-year-olds have sex, they are technically simultaneously committing, and the victim of, statutory rape.

3. Statutory rape is not included in the MPC. Nonetheless, some states that have adopted the MPC retained this crime in their statutes.

Formative Assessments

1. The offender in most sexual assaults is unknown to the victim.

A. True.

B. False.

2. A sexual assault offense without an extrinsic force requirement most likely places the focus on:

A. Consent.

B. Past dating history, if any, between alleged offender and victim.

C. Voluntary ingestion of drugs/alcohol by alleged offender.

D. Voluntary ingestion of drugs/alcohol by alleged victim.

3. You are a prosecutor in the newly formed jurisidction of TexaHoma. You are prosecuting Bevan, an eighteen-year-old, charged with raping Carey, who is fifteen. The two have been in a romantic relationship for some time. Carey has just given birth to Bevan's son. The age of consent in Texahoma is sixteen. The TexaHoma criminal code contains a statutory rape offense. Which of the following most accurately describes Bevan's criminal liability ?

A. Bevan has committed statutory rape.

B. Bevan has committed statutory rape, but only if TexaHoma is an extrinsic force jurisdiction.

C. Bevan has committed statutory rape, but only if TexaHoma is an intrinsic force jurisdiction.

D. Bevan has not committed statutory rape so long as Carey unequivocally consented to sex.

Chapter 12

Other Crimes Against Persons

I. Introduction

Crimes against persons range from minor offenses, such as misdemeanor battery, to extremely serious offenses, such as kidnapping. This chapter will cover the most common of these crimes: battery, assault, and kidnapping. While there are significant statutory variations to terminology and definitions of these crimes across jurisdictions, common law definitions provide a relatively consistent foundation.

Terminology for assault and battery can be somewhat confusing. This is because many jurisdictions use the term "assault" to cover both common-law battery *and* assault. Under the common law, if a victim was actually "battered"—meaning a defendant's actus reus resulted in corporeal (physical) harmful or offensive touching—the defendant would face a charge of battery. In contrast, if the victim was not battered (i.e., there was no contact), the defendant would face a charge of assault. Today, however, what was considered a battery at common law is defined as a type of assault under a general assault provision. For example, a common-law act of battery might be defined today as an assault consummated by battery.

This may be potentially confusing, but it is important to learn these as distinct offenses. In jurisdictions that distinguish these two crimes, an initial assault may be understood as an attempted battery that merges with the battery upon its completion; hence, it would be improper to charge the defendant with an assault and battery for the same actus reus. (Of course, if the defendant engages in two distinct criminal acts, for example, by swinging a punch at a victim and missing but then swinging again and hitting, that would justify two distinct charges: the initial assault and the subsequent battery.) It will therefore be useful to analyze conduct that results in contact with the victim as battery and conduct that does not as assault.

Another complicating factor in analyzing assault and battery is distinguishing between "simple" and "aggravated" versions of these crimes. In almost all jurisdictions, a simple assault or battery (i.e., an assault or battery with no proof of an additional aggravating factor) will qualify as a misdemeanor. Both of these crimes, however, are often elevated to the felony level by proof of an aggravating element, thereby becoming aggravated assault or aggravated battery.

While the additional requirements to elevate a simple assault or battery to an aggravated version vary by jurisdiction, there are some general trends. For battery, common aggravating elements include:

- Use of a means likely to inflict death or great bodily harm (e.g., a deadly weapon or an instrumentality used in a deadly or highly dangerous manner, such as a brick)
- Intent to inflict great bodily harm
- Actual infliction of serious injury or permanent disability
- Battery of a specially protected victim, such as a peace officer or child

For assault, common aggravating elements include:

- Use of a means likely to inflict death or great bodily harm
- Intent to inflict great bodily harm
- Assault of a specially protected victim, such as a peace officer or child

Notice that for assault, actual infliction of serious injury or permanent disability is not an aggravating element. This is because an assault does not result in the battering of a victim.

Three additional considerations are important in assessing a defendant's criminal culpability. First, some jurisdictions retain a modified version of the common law crime of mayhem. Mayhem was originally defined as the intentional mutilation of the victim, and required proof that the criminal act resulted in the victim's loss of a body part that handicapped the victim's ability to defend himself in the future (a useful example from popular culture is when Jaime Lannister lost his hand in *Game of Thrones*). Modern statutes define mayhem as a battery that results in permanent physical disability or disfigurement. For example, California Penal Code § 205 provides:

> A person is guilty of aggravated mayhem when he or she unlawfully, under circumstances manifesting extreme indifference to the physical or psychological well-being of another person, intentionally causes permanent disability or disfigurement of another human being or deprives a human being of a limb, organ, or member of his or her body. For purposes of this section, it is not necessary to prove an intent to kill. Aggravated mayhem is a felony punishable by imprisonment in the state prison for life with the possibility of parole.

In states that have abolished the crime of mayhem, the same criminal misconduct would qualify as aggravated battery.

Second, it is important to be able to distinguish assault or battery from attempted homicide. To convict a defendant for an attempt to commit a "target" offense, it is necessary to prove that the defendant engaged in the act with the specific intent to complete that target crime. This means that if the evidence establishes that the defendant committed assaultive conduct that does not result in the victim's death, the line between assault or battery and attempted homicide (intentional murder or voluntary manslaughter) is indicated by intent. If the evidence establishes the defendant intended to kill the victim and failed, the crime should be classified as an attempted intentional homicide offense; if the evidence fails to establish intent to kill, the crime will fall into the assault or battery category.

Third, in the event that the death of a victim follows a defendant's actus reus, the evidence may be insufficient to prove the defendant is the legal cause of the victim's death, particularly if there is an unforeseeable intervening cause that supersedes the defendant's responsibility. In these situations, the defendant may still be culpable for the underlying battery that set in motion the events leading to the victim's death. In other words, a finding that the defendant is not guilty for a homicide offense because of an intervening superseding cause will often result in a finding of guilt for some form of battery.

The two diagrams embedded in this chapter visually illustrate how these factors impact culpability assessment and should assist in your understanding of how to analyze these offenses.

II. Crimes Against the Person

A. Battery

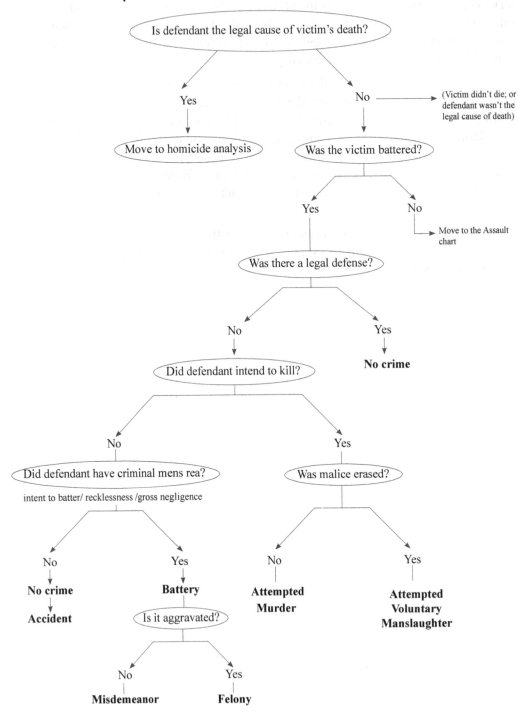

© 2012 Geoffrey S. Corn

The actus reus of common law battery was a criminal act by the defendant that resulted in a harmful or offensive touching of the victim. The defendant did not have to personally touch the victim; setting in motion a force, like a rock or a bullet, that then touches the victim satisfied the actus reus of battery. The corresponding mens rea included intent, recklessness, or criminal negligence. Accordingly, battery is *an intentional, reckless, or grossly negligent harmful or offensive touching of the victim by the defendant.* As noted above, this simple battery may be elevated to an aggravated battery by proving an additional aggravating element as defined in the relevant criminal statute.

But what qualifies as a "touching" for purposes of battery? The next case addresses this question. Note that the expansive definition of "touching" carries greater importance on proving the requisite mens rea. Also note Virginia's requirement that the battery be intentional.

Adams v. Commonwealth

534 S.E.2d 347 (2000)
Virginia Court of Appeals

ROBERT P. FRANK, J.

Jeremy Britt Adams (appellant) appeals his bench trial conviction of an assault and battery on a law enforcement officer in violation of Va. Code Ann. §18.2-57(C). On appeal, appellant contends the evidence was insufficient to prove: (1) a touching and (2) that he had the requisite intent to commit the offense. We disagree and affirm the conviction.

I. Background

On September 22, 1998, while on duty at the Gloucester County High School, Sergeant Steven Giles of the Gloucester County Sheriff's Department was struck in his right eye by a laser light owned by appellant, who was a twelfth-grade student at the school. Giles had been talking with another officer, Sergeant Adams, and the school nurse when he felt a "stinging sensation" in his eye. Sergeant Adams told Giles that appellant had "just lit [him] up," as there was "a red dot" on him.

Giles approached appellant and asked what he had. Appellant said, "It can't hurt you," and handed over the laser light, which was attached to his key chain. Giles gave the laser light to the assistant principal and told appellant he could retrieve it later.

Giles said he "felt a burning sensation" in his eye and "saw red" before looking away, but he did not know how long the laser had been pointed at him. Giles had his eye checked the next morning by a local doctor who found "heavy irritation" but no other injury.

Appellant moved to strike the evidence at the conclusion of the Commonwealth's case-in-chief. He argued that the Commonwealth had not proved the laser light was capable of causing injury, had injured Giles, or appellant knew or should have known the laser was dangerous. The trial court overruled the motion.

Appellant then presented his case. Sergeant Adams testified that appellant was approximately 150 feet from Giles and the laser light had "jump[ed] all around his upper torso and head." Adams did not "actually see the thing strike [Giles'] eye," but he saw Giles flinch when he was hit.

James Brown and Jessica Hubbard, both students, testified that they did not see the laser strike Giles in the face or eyes. They also said they had not been hurt when similarly hit in the eye with a laser light.

Appellant testified that he purchased the laser light for six dollars at a convenience store two days before the offense. He said it had no warning on it regarding use and that he had not been hurt when hit in the eye by the light. Appellant denied hitting Giles in the face or eye and claimed he had not intended to strike Giles with the light but, instead, was "just goofing off" to get Adams' attention by waving the laser around. Adams previously had been the school's resource officer, and appellant had a friendly relationship with him. Appellant, however, did not get along well with Sergeant Giles. He stated that Giles had previously given him a hard time. Appellant acknowledged he had pled guilty to three felonies.

The trial court again overruled appellant's motion to strike the evidence and convicted appellant of assault and battery on a law enforcement officer.

II. Analysis

. . . .

Code § 18.2-57(C) provides that "any person [who] commits an assault or an assault and battery against a law enforcement officer shall be guilty of a Class 6 felony," and shall be sentenced to a mandatory, minimum term of six months in jail.

. . . .

When the injury is actually inflicted, a battery has been committed regardless of how small the injury might be. "Battery is the actual infliction of corporal hurt on another (e.g., the least touching of another's person), willfully or in anger, whether by the party's own hand, or by some means set in motion by him." *Seegars v. Commonwealth*, 445 S.E.2d 720, 722 (1994).

. . . .

A battery is an unlawful touching of another. It is not necessary that the touching result in injury to the person. Whether a touching is a battery depends on the intent of the actor, not on the force applied.

. . . .

"The slightest touching of another, if done in a rude, insolent, or angry manner, constitutes a battery for which the law affords redress." *Crosswhite v. Barnes*, 124 S.E. 242, 244 (1924).

"Where there is physical injury to another person, it is sufficient that the cause is set in motion by the defendant, or that the [victim] is subjected to its operation by means of any act or control which the defendant exerts." "The law upon the subject is intended primarily to protect the sacredness of the person, and, secondarily, to prevent breaches of the peace." *Banovitch v. Commonwealth*, 83 S.E.2d 369, 374 (1954).

A. Touching

Adams contends that shining the laser on Sergeant Giles was insufficient to constitute a touching for the purposes of assault and battery. Touch is defined as to be in contact or to cause to be in contact.

In Virginia, it is abundantly clear that a perpetrator need not inflict a physical injury to commit a battery. The cases that guide our analysis, however, have not addressed circumstances where contact with the corporeal person was accomplished by directing a beam of light at the victim. Because substances such as light or sound become elusive when considered in terms of battery, contact by means of such substances must be examined further in determining whether a touching has occurred. Such a test is necessary due to the intangible nature of those substances and the need to limit application of such a principle (touching by intangible substances) to reasonable cases. Because the underlying concerns of battery law are breach of the peace and sacredness of the person, the dignity of the victim is implicated and the reasonableness and offensiveness of the contact must be considered. Otherwise, criminal convictions could result from the routine and insignificant exposure to concentrated energy that inevitably results from living in populated society.

Accordingly, we hold that for purposes of determining whether a battery has occurred, contact by an intangible substance such as light must be considered in terms of its effect on the victim. There need be no actual injury for a touching to have occurred. However, to prove a touching, the evidence must prove that the substance made objectively offensive or forcible contact with the victim's person resulting in some manifestation of a physical consequence or corporeal hurt.

Here, the evidence established that appellant hit Sergeant Giles in the eye with a laser light. Giles felt a stinging sensation in his eye as a "red dot" hit him. Appellant admitted he did not get along with Giles and that he had been waving the laser in the area where the two officers were standing.

Appellant, by aiming the laser at the officers, effected a contact that caused bodily harm to Sergeant Giles. Appellant argued there was no touching because the laser has no mass and, therefore, cannot physically touch Sergeant Giles. This argument is misplaced. The laser, directed by appellant, came into contact with Sergeant Giles' eye and, as a result, there was an unlawful touching.

B. Intent

Proving intent by direct evidence often is impossible. Like any other element of a crime, it may be proved by circumstantial evidence, as long as such evidence excludes all reasonable hypotheses of innocence flowing from it. Circumstantial evidence of intent may include the conduct and statements of the alleged offender, and "[t]he finder of fact may infer that [he] intends the natural and probable consequences of his acts." *Campbell v. Commonwealth*, 405 S.E.2d 1, 4 (1991) (en banc).

The trial court, sitting as the fact finder, was entitled to reject appellant's testimony that he was "just goofing off" to attract Sergeant Adams' attention. The court specifically found that appellant intended to hit Giles with the laser and that an assault and battery occurred. That decision is not plainly wrong or without supporting evidence and must be upheld on appeal.

For the reasons stated, we affirm the judgment of the trial court.

Affirmed.

LEMONS, J., dissenting.

[The dissenting judge criticized both the sufficiency of the evidence to support a rational finding of requisite intent and the expansive definition of touching.]

. . . .

Whether a touching is a battery depends upon the intent of the actor, not upon the force applied. Here, the evidence does not support beyond a reasonable doubt that Adams had the intent to offensively touch Sergeant Giles. In order to have such intent, Adams would have to *know or be reasonably charged with knowledge* that a six-dollar novelty item attached to his key chain had the potential for offensive touching. It is not within common knowledge that such a device has such capacity. There is no evidence that Adams had specific knowledge of such capacity. That Adams had a bad relationship with Giles may explain his motive, but it does not prove intent to offensively touch. A finder of fact may infer that an actor intends the natural and probable consequences of his acts. In the absence of common knowledge of the capacity of this device, no inference may be drawn. Without inference or specific knowledge, there is no proof that Adams intended to offensively touch Giles.

Additionally, the majority redefines "touching" for the purpose of common law battery. Although the reasoning is logical, it is unwise, because the unintended consequences may reach too far. Will the next prosecution for battery be based upon failure to dim high beams in traffic, flash photography too close to the subject, high intensity flashlight beams or sonic waves from a teenager's car stereo? Rather than stretch the boundaries of the common law understanding of what is necessary for a "touching" to occur, criminalizing conduct that involves intangible objects put in motion should be left to specific legislative action rather than generalized redefinition that may sweep into the ambit of criminal behavior conduct that is not intended.

Notes and Questions

1. Was it fair for the dissent to suggest that the next case might involve flash photography? Was the dissenting judge too dismissive of motive as circumstantial evidence of intent? Would the majority support a battery conviction for someone who takes a photo with a flash without any proof of criminal mens rea?

2. What would distinguish the classification of flashing high beams as harmful or offensive touching from the evidence that supported the conviction in this case?

3. While the battery in this case required proof of intent to batter, most jurisdictions define battery as an unlawful harmful or offensive touching resulting from intent or recklessness. Some jurisdictions also allow gross negligence to support a battery conviction. For example, the New York Penal Code includes the following definition of assault that is *consummated* by a battery:

A person is guilty of assault in the third degree when:

1. With intent to cause physical injury to another person, he causes such injury to such person or to a third person; or

2. He recklessly causes physical injury to another person; or

3. With criminal negligence he causes physical injury to another person by means of a deadly weapon or a dangerous instrument.

N.Y. Pen. L. § 120.00.

The Texas Penal Code includes this definition:

(a) A person commits an offense if the person:

(1) intentionally, knowingly, or recklessly causes bodily injury to another, including the person's spouse.

Tex. Pen. Code § 22.01.

4. Notice that what seemed to be an extremely minor offense was elevated to a felony because the victim was a law enforcement officer in the performance of duty. This is a very common aggravating element for battery. State criminal codes vary as to the aggravating elements for battery, but when the aggravating element is established beyond a reasonable doubt, it normally elevates the battery from misdemeanor to felony level.

Some jurisdictions require proof that there is some physical injury or corporeal hurt (like the New York statute above); offense alone will not suffice. The next case addresses how such a question might be decided. Note that while the crime is designated as assault, it is more properly an assault consummated by a battery.

State v. Gordon

560 N.W.2d 4 (1997)
Iowa Supreme Court

A jury convicted Thomas A. Gordon of assault causing bodily injury, a serious misdemeanor. In his appeal Gordon challenges an instruction defining bodily injury to include any impairment of physical condition. The instruction goes on to say that a red mark or bruise on the skin is such an impairment and is therefore a bodily injury.

The instruction raises the following issue: Does a red mark or bruise constitute a per se impairment of physical condition? We answer that a red mark or bruise is not a per se impairment of physical condition. We conclude the instruction was reversible error. We reverse and remand for a new trial.

We pause briefly for the facts giving rise to this case.

On the evening of October 3, 1995, Gordon was in the home of Mary Johnston in Prairie City. Several other people were present, including Jeremiah Fry. Apparently unprovoked, Gordon stood up from where he was seated, spun around, and kicked Fry in the chest. As he kicked Fry, Gordon said, "Die pale-face pumpkin head." The kick left a red mark to the right of Fry's sternum.

Two witnesses saw the incident, but neither saw whether Gordon's foot made contact with Fry's chest.

A short time later, a Prairie City police officer saw Fry, interviewed him, and saw a heel imprint on Fry's shirt. When Fry raised his shirt, the officer saw what he described as a "reddening" on Fry's chest.

The State charged Gordon with assault causing bodily injury. The parties tried the case to a jury.

After all of the evidence was in, the State asked the court to instruct the jury that "marks" constitute an injury for purposes of assault. Defense counsel objected and suggested a definition of bodily injury taken from the Model Penal Code and adopted in *State v. McKee*, 312 N.W.2d 907, 913 (Iowa 1981). Defense counsel argued that no case had recognized a red mark as a bodily injury. This prompted the following colloquy between the court and defense counsel:

> THE COURT: Are you going to argue to the jury that a red mark on the skin is not a bodily injury?
>
> DEFENSE COUNSEL: I may.
>
> THE COURT: All right. Then I'll tell the jury that a red mark on the skin is a bodily injury because they have a right to know that, and if there's a dispute, then I'll clear it up.

Over defense counsel's objection, the court instructed the jury as follows: A "bodily" injury means a bodily or physical pain, illness, or any impairment of physical condition. A red mark or bruise on the skin would constitute an impairment of physical condition, and therefore an injury.

The jury convicted Gordon of assault causing bodily injury. Later the court sentenced Gordon to one year in jail, suspended all but ninety days of the sentence, put him on supervised probation for one year, and fined him $200.

Gordon appealed, again challenging the bodily injury instruction on the grounds that a red mark is not a per se impairment of physical condition.

. . . .

As applied to the facts in this case, an assault is

(1) [a]ny act which is intended to cause pain or injury to, or which is intended to result in physical contact which will be insulting or offensive to another, coupled with the apparent ability to execute the act[, or]

(2) [a]ny act which is intended to place another in fear of immediate physical contact which will be painful, injurious, insulting, or offensive, coupled with the apparent ability to execute the act.

Iowa Code § 708.1(1)-(2). The district court's marshaling instruction covered all the alternatives in section 708.1(1) and (2).

Iowa Code section 708.2 provides the penalties for assault. Pertinent to this case is Iowa Code section 708.2(2):

A person who commits an assault, as defined in section 708.1, without the intent to inflict a serious injury upon another, and who causes bodily injury or disabling mental illness, is guilty of a serious misdemeanor.

Bodily injury is not defined, but the term is included in the definition of serious injury. See Iowa Code § 702.18 (serious injury means, among other things, "bodily injury which creates a substantial risk of death or which causes serious permanent disfigurement, or protracted loss or impairment of the function of any bodily member or organ").

In *State v. McKee*, we decided what bodily injury meant in the context of a serious injury as defined in section 702.18. We adopted the Model Penal Code's definition of bodily injury. The Model Penal Code defines bodily injury as "physical pain, illness, or any impairment of physical condition." *McKee*, 312 N.W.2d at 913 (citing Model Penal Code commentary § 210.0(2) (1980)).

In adopting the Model Penal Code definition of bodily injury, we explained in *McKee*:

Bodily injury ordinarily "refers only to injury to the body, or to sickness or disease contracted by the injured as a result of injury." Injury includes "an act that damages, harms, or hurts: an unjust or undeserved infliction of suffering or harm." Thus the ordinary dictionary definition of bodily injury coincides with the Model Penal Code definition of the term. Because the Model Penal Code definition fits the context of section 702.18, we adopt it.

Id.

Later our court of appeals applied the Model Penal Code definition of bodily injury to the term bodily injury in section 708.2(2), the assault causing bodily injury offense. *State v. Luppes*, 358 N.W.2d 322, 325 (Iowa App.1984). Like the court of appeals, we think the Model Penal Code definition of bodily injury is an appropriate definition of the term bodily injury in section 708.2(2).

We have no quarrel, therefore, with the district court's definition of bodily injury in so far as it coincides with the Model Penal Code definition. We agree, however, with Gordon that the court went too far when it instructed the jury that "[a] red mark or bruise on the skin would constitute an impairment of physical condition, and therefore an injury."

Neither the Model Penal Code nor the Iowa Code defines impairment of physical condition. The word impairment does appear in the definition of serious injury in section 702.18 (serious injury means, among other things, bodily injury that causes "protracted loss or impairment of the function of any bodily member or organ").

In *McKee* we also defined impairment as found in the context of serious injury under section 702.18. We said:

> An impairment, according to common usage, includes any deviation from normal health. The term means: "To weaken, to make worse, to lessen in power, diminish, or relax, or otherwise affect in any injurious manner."

312 N.W.2d at 913.

There was no direct evidence that Fry suffered any deviation from normal health because of the blow. Nor did he testify that he had any pain or illness because of the blow. Those were fact questions peculiarly within the jury's common experience and for them to decide.

In a recent case we observed that "welts, bruises, or similar markings are not physical injuries per se but may be and frequently are evidence from which the existence of a physical injury can be found." *Hildreth v. Iowa Dep't of Human Servs.*, 550 N.W.2d 157, 160 (Iowa 1996). Although the observation was made in a different context and was not necessary to our decision, we think it fits here. The red mark or bruise on Fry's chest was not a physical impairment per se but only evidence of such impairment.

Had the district court merely given the definition of a bodily injury and stopped, the jury could have found the red mark or bruise was not a bodily injury. The court's gratuitous addition was especially prejudicial to Gordon because, as mentioned, there was no direct evidence that Fry had suffered pain or illness from the blow. The only direct evidence of injury was that Fry had suffered a "reddening" on his chest.

In effect, the district court directed a verdict in favor of the State on bodily injury, a critical element of the offense. In doing so the court invaded the province of the jury and committed error. As this court said long ago,

> [t]hat it is error to assume facts as in existence or proven which are in controversy and disputed in the record is too clear to warrant discussion. Especially is this true in a criminal case. Under our Constitution and statutes, juries are the triers of fact, either in civil or criminal cases, and the usurpation or assumption of this duty by the court is error and must not be sanctioned.

. . . .

Because the error here was prejudicial, we reverse and remand for a new trial.

REVERSED AND REMANDED.

Notes & Questions

1. Would Gordon be guilty of battery in Virginia based solely on the red mark?

2. Why do you think the MPC imposed a heighted result requirement to establish criminal battery?

3. Could kicking someone in the chest qualify as the use of a deadly weapon or a means likely to inflict death or grievous bodily harm, thereby elevating a battery to aggravated felony battery? This question cannot be answered without a jurisdictional definition of deadly weapon or means likely. Consider this statutory provision from Massachusetts:

> Whoever commits an assault and battery upon another by means of a dangerous weapon shall be punished by imprisonment in the state prison for not more than 10 years or in the house of correction for not more than 2 1/2 years, or by a fine of not more than $5,000, or by both such fine and imprisonment.

Mass. Gen. Laws ch. 265, §15A(b). The statute then provides the following definition:

> The touching was done with a dangerous weapon. Even a slight touching, if done with a dangerous weapon, is enough to satisfy this element. The government does not have to prove that any injury resulted from the touching. A dangerous weapon is one that is capable of causing death or serious injury. Some weapons, such as guns, are inherently dangerous, and a judge may instruct that such a weapon is dangerous as a matter of law. Other items, though not inherently dangerous, may become dangerous weapons because of how they are used. In other words, an object that is usually used for an innocent purpose might become a dangerous weapon when intentionally used in a way reasonably capable of causing death or serious injury. For instance, a pencil, though normally used for the innocent purpose of writing, may become a dangerous weapon when aimed at the eyes of another person. In determining whether an item is a dangerous weapon, factfinders consider the circumstances of the incident, the characteristics of the instrument, and the manner in which the defendant handled the instrument. A dangerous weapon may be stationary. A human body part may not be considered to be a dangerous weapon in the context of this crime.

Mass. Gen. Laws ch. 265, §15A(b). This is a common and useful definition for purposes of both battery and assault (although for assault, there would be no actual physical touching).

4. Notice that the Massachusetts statute establishes a *per se* rule that a body part may not be considered a dangerous weapon for purposes of aggravated battery. If a defendant were charged with aggravated battery in Massachusetts for the use of his fists, what would be the result? What if the alleged dangerous weapon were boots he was wearing on his feet, or heavy rings on his fingers?

5. If the jurisdiction excludes a body part from the definition of deadly weapon like is done in Massachusetts and the facts indicate the defendant savagely beat his victim with bare fists, are there other theories of aggravation that may be satisfied?

6. In order to qualify as such a weapon, must the instrumentality be something within the defendant's control? For example, in *Commonwealth v. Shea*, 644 N.E.2d 244 (Mass App. Ct. 1995), the Massachusetts Appeals Court reviewed an aggravated battery conviction based on the defendant throwing the victim into the ocean from his boat and leaving her stranded. The prosecution alleged that the ocean qualified as a dangerous weapon for purposes of aggravated battery, but the court rejected this theory, because the ocean could not be controlled by a defendant:

> We need not consider whether the specified weapon, the ocean, is dangerous per se or dangerous as used. Although the ocean can be and often is dangerous, it cannot be regarded in its natural state as a weapon within the meaning of Section 15A. *See Commonwealth v. Farrell*, 78 N.E.2d 697 (Mass. 1948), stating that the term "dangerous weapon" comprehends "any *instrument* or *instrumentality* so constructed or so used as to be likely to produce death or great bodily harm" (emphasis added); *Commonwealth v. Tarrant*, 326 N.E.2d 710, 715 n. 6 (Mass. 1975), noting with approval the definition of dangerous weapon adopted in the Proposed Criminal Code of Massachusetts c. 263, Section 3(i): "'any firearm or other weapon, device, instrument, material or substance, *whether animate or inanimate,* which in the manner [in] which it is used *or is intended to be used* is capable of producing death or serious bodily injury' (emphasis added)"; *Commonwealth v. Appleby*, 402 N.E.2d 1051, 1059 (Mass. 1980), concluding that the "offense of assault and battery by means of a dangerous weapon under G. L. c. 265, Section 15A, requires that the elements of assault be present . . ."that there be a touching, however slight . . . that the touching be by means of the weapon . . . and that the battery be accomplished by use of an inherently dangerous weapon, or by use of *some other object* as a weapon, with the intent to *use that object* in a dangerous or potentially dangerous fashion."

All the cases collected and cited in the discussion of dangerous weapons, per se and as used, in *Commonwealth v. Appleby*, share a common fact that is consistent with the definitions of "dangerous weapons" which speak in terms of "objects" or "instrumentalities." The commonality found in those cases is that the object in issue, whether dangerous per se or as used, was an instrumentality which the batterer controlled, either through possession of or authority over it, for use of it in the intentional application of force. Because the ocean in its natural state cannot be possessed or controlled, it is not an object or instrumentality capable of use as a weapon for purposes of Section 15A.

Our conclusion should not be construed to mean that there can never be criminal liability for causing physical harm to someone by subjecting them to a force of nature. We conclude only that for purposes of Section 15A, the ocean, not being subject to human control, was not, in the instant case, an object or instrumentality which could be found by the jury to be a dangerous weapon. Accordingly, the defendant's motion for required findings of not guilty on the indictments charging him with assault and battery by means of a dangerous weapon should have been allowed.

B. Assault

The original concept of common-law assault was an attempted but failed battery. Like all attempts, the mens rea for this offense is the specific intent to commit the target offense of battery. This offense remains a universally recognized theory of assault, established by proof the defendant intended to unlawfully batter the victim but failed. Imagine a situation where a defendant throws a rock at the victim intending to batter but misses—this is assault. For this type of failed battery assault, there is no requirement to prove the victim was aware of the attempt to batter. Over time, the tort concept of apprehension assault was also incorporated into the criminal definition of assault. Unlike an attempted battery, this type of assault does not require proof the defendant actually intended to batter. Indeed, this type of assault is relevant only when the defendant *did not* intend to batter and is established by proving the defendant performed an intentional act that was sufficient to put a reasonable person in apprehension of an imminent battery. However, because the apprehension of the victim is an essential element of this type of assault, it is necessary to prove the victim was actually aware of the assaultive conduct.

Assault

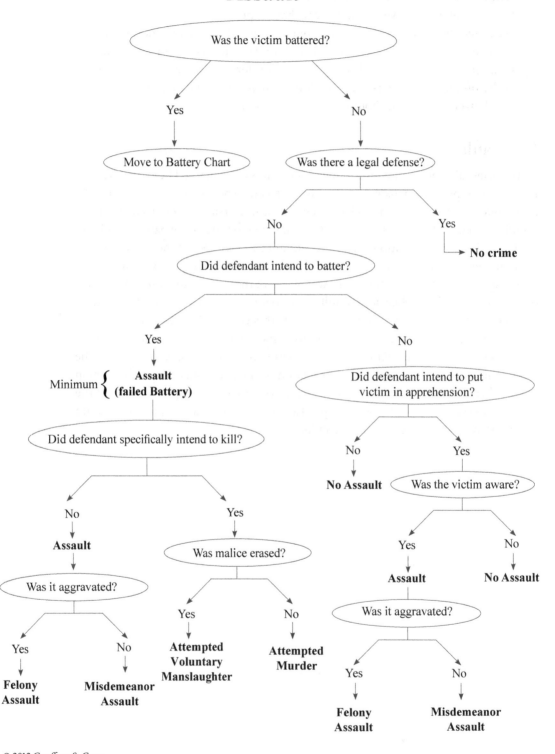

The following opinion outlines the various types of assault.

Harrod v. State

499 A.2d 959 (1985)
Maryland Court of Special Appeals

ALPERT, Judge.

We are called upon in this appeal to decide, *inter alia,* whether a person can be convicted of assaulting another who has suffered no harm and was never aware of the alleged assault. Appellant John G. Harrod was charged with two counts of assault and two counts of carrying a deadly weapon openly with intent to injure. He was convicted of these offenses on December 11, 1984, following a trial without a jury in the Circuit Court for Carroll County, and sentenced on January 21, 1985, to two terms of two years' imprisonment for the assault convictions and two terms of one year's imprisonment for the weapons convictions, all sentences to run concurrently.

On appeal to this court, appellant presents three questions:

I. Was the evidence sufficient to sustain the charge of assault upon James Christopher Harrod?

II. Was the evidence sufficient to sustain the charges of carrying a weapon with intent to injure?

III. Was the sentence imposed based upon an improper factor?

It will be of little solace to appellant that we answer the first question in his favor, for our response to the second and third questions leave his ultimate period of incarceration unchanged.

I

The common law crime of assault encompasses two definitions: (1) an attempt to commit a battery or (2) an unlawful intentional act which places another in reasonable apprehension of receiving an immediate battery. The facts in the instant case present this court with an excellent opportunity to explain the distinctions between these two different types of assault.

The assault charges arose out of a confrontation among appellant, his wife Cheryl, and her friend Calvin Crigger. The only two witnesses at trial were appellant and Cheryl Harrod.

Cheryl testified that on September 15, 1983, Calvin Crigger came over to visit when she thought appellant had gone to work; that "all of a sudden [appellant] came out of the bedroom with a hammer in his hand, swinging it around, coming after me and my friend [Calvin]"; that Calvin ran out of the house and down the steps; that appellant "had thrown the hammer over top of [Christopher's] port-a-crib in the living room, and it went into the wall"; that appellant then reentered the bedroom and returned with a five-inch blade hunting knife; that appellant told Cheryl that he was going to kill her and that, if she took his daughter away from him, he was going to kill

Christopher; that appellant put the knife into the bannister near Cheryl's arm; that appellant followed Cheryl out to Calvin's car and "went after Calvin, going around and around the car."

Appellant testified that he missed his ride to work that day; that he came back home around 10:00 a.m. and went to sleep in a back room; that he was awakened by Calvin's deep voice; that appellant picked up his hammer and, walking into the living room, told Calvin to leave; that Cheryl told Calvin he didn't have to leave; that he then told Calvin, "Buddy, if you want your head busted in, stand here; if you want to be healthy and leave, go." Appellant said that Calvin just stood there, so he swung the hammer, Calvin moved his head back, and the hammer struck the wall over Christopher's crib, which was near the door.

In rendering its verdict, the court stated:

> And, the Court finds beyond a reasonable doubt and to a moral certainty that Mr. Harrod . . . came after [Cheryl] and . . . Calvin; and that Mr. Harrod came out of his room swinging a . . . hammer, and ultimately threw it, not too far from the child, Christopher, and that he went after both Cheryl and Calvin, down the steps with a knife, with a blade of about four to five inches. The Court finds that he is guilty of two counts of Carrying a Deadly Weapon; that is the knife and the hammer; and, also two counts of Assault; one against Cheryl and one against the minor child.

. . . .

Defense counsel inquired of the court: "On the second count of the Information, is the Court finding specific intent on behalf of the Defendant to injure his child?" The court responded, "Yes. Threw that hammer within a very short distance—sticking it—it was still sticking in the wall."

A. Two Types of Assault

Appellant contends that there was insufficient evidence to demonstrate that he harbored a specific intent to injure Christopher when he threw the hammer. Further, he notes that there was no evidence that Christopher was injured by the hammer or that he was even aware that a hammer was thrown. Therefore, appellant claims that the trial court's finding that he committed a criminal assault upon Christopher was clearly erroneous. We agree for the reasons set forth below.

. . . .

As we noted *supra,* an assault "is committed when there is *either* an attempt to commit a battery *or* when, by an unlawful act, a person is placed in reasonable apprehension of receiving an immediate battery." These two types of assaults—*attempted battery* and *putting another in fear*—are indeed two distinct crimes that have been inadvertently overlapped and confused. One commentator explained this confusion:

> In the early law the word "assault" represented an entirely different concept in criminal law than it did in the law of torts. As an offense it was an attempt to commit a battery; as a basis for a civil action for damages it was an

intentional act wrongfully placing another in apprehension of receiving an immediate battery. The distinction has frequently passed unnoticed because a misdeed involving either usually involves both. If, with the intention of hitting X, D wrongfully threw a stone that X barely managed to dodge, then D would have been guilty of a criminal assault because he had attempted to commit a battery, and he would also have been liable in a civil action of trespass for assault because he had wrongfully placed X in apprehension of physical harm.

Some commentators have been so imbued with the tort theory of assault that they have had difficulty in realizing that in the early law a criminal assault was an attempt to commit a battery and that only.

Perkins and Boyce, *Criminal Law* 159.

B. Attempted Battery

The language in *Woods* [*v. State*, 14 Md.App. 627, 288 A.2d 215 (1972),] supports the proposition that in an attempted battery-type assault, the victim need not be aware of the perpetrator's intent or threat.

If a person be struck from behind, or by stealth or surprise, or while asleep, he is certainly the victim of a battery. But if we accept the oft-repeated statement that every battery included or is preceded by an assault, and if there could be no assault without premonitory apprehension in the victim, then it could be argued that there was no battery. That is not the law. In other words, because there may be committed a battery without the victim first being aware of the attack, an attempted battery-type assault cannot include a requirement that the victim be aware.

1. Specific Intent

The facts in the case sub judice do not support a finding that appellant committed an attempted battery towards the infant, Christopher. An attempt to commit any crime requires a specific intent to commit that crime. An attempted battery-type assault thus requires that the accused harbor a specific intent to cause physical injury to the victim . . . and take a substantial step towards causing that injury.

Nowhere does the record indicate that appellant threw the hammer with the specific intent to injure Christopher. The court expressly stated that it found specific intent on behalf of appellant because he "[t]hrew that hammer within a very short distance" of the child. The court here is merely inferring a criminal intent from reckless or negligent acts of the appellant. This is not sufficient, especially where all of the evidence tends to the contrary: that appellant's intent was to injure Calvin.

2. Transferred Intent

An additional question raised by the parties in the briefs is whether the necessary specific intent as against Christopher could derive from the specific intent toward Calvin; in other words, did the intent to injure Calvin *transfer* to Christopher? This doctrine of "transferred intent" was explained by the Court of Appeals in *Gladden v. State,* 330 A.2d 176 (Md. 1974):

> "[I]f one intends injury to the person of another under circumstances in which such a mental element constitutes *mens rea,* and in the effort to accomplish this end he inflicts harm upon a person other than the one intended, he is guilty of the same kind of crime as if his aim had been more accurate." In such cases all the components of the crime are present. The psychical element which consists of a certain general mental pattern is not varied by the particular person who may be actually harmed.

Id. at 188.

Gladden, as well as all of the cases cited in that opinion, involved an attempt to kill one person, but resulted in the death or injury of another, unintended victim. In every case cited in *Gladden,* the third party to whom the intent was "transferred" was in fact injured. The Court of Appeals expressly held that, under the doctrine, "the *mens rea* of a defendant as to his intended victim will carry over and affix his culpability *when such criminal conduct causes the death of an unintended victim.*" 330 A.2d at 189 (emphasis added).

By illustration, Professor Perkins explains the logic underlying the limited application of this doctrine:

> If, without justification, excuse or mitigation D with intent to kill A fires a shot which misses A but unexpectedly inflicts a non-fatal injury upon B, D is guilty of an attempt to commit murder—but the attempt was to murder A whom D was trying to kill and not B who was hit quite accidentally. And so far as the criminal law is concerned there is no transfer of this intent from one to the other so as to make D guilty of an attempt to murder B. Hence, an indictment or information charging an attempt to murder B, or (under statute) an assault with intent to murder B, will not support a conviction if the evidence shows that the injury to B was accidental and the only intent was to murder A.

Perkins, *Criminal Law* 826 (2d ed. 1969).

. . . .

To extend the doctrine of transferred intent to cases where the intended victim is not harmed would be untenable. The absurd result would be to make one criminally culpable for each unintended victim who, although in harm's way, was in fact not harmed by a missed attempt towards a specific person. We refuse, therefore, to extend the doctrine of transferred intent to cases where a third person is not in fact harmed.

This is the situation before us in the instant case. The record indicates that appellant swung a hammer which struck the wall "not too far from" Christopher. Significantly, there is no evidence that Christopher was harmed. Further, the weight of the evidence shows that appellant's specific intent, if any, was to injure Calvin, not Christopher. Why the State charged appellant with assaulting Christopher, rather than Calvin, we will not speculate. There is clearly insufficient evidence to find that appellant committed an attempted battery-type assault upon Christopher.

C. Assault by Placing One in Fear

There is likewise insufficient evidence that appellant, by an unlawful intentional act, placed Christopher in reasonable apprehension of receiving an immediate battery. By definition the victim must be aware of the impending contact. This is consistent with the tort theory of assault. . . .

There is no evidence in the record before us that Christopher was in fact aware of the occurrences in his home on the morning in question. Therefore, there was insufficient evidence to find appellant guilty of the putting victim in fear-type assault.

Because the trial court was clearly erroneous in finding appellant guilty of an assault on Christopher, we must reverse that conviction.

Notes & Questions

1. If the state had alleged an assault against Calvin based on defendant's intention to batter Calvin when he threw the hammer, would it be necessary to prove Calvin was aware the hammer was thrown? What if the hammer did not even come close to hitting Calvin?

2. Imagine the defendant actually hit Christopher with the hammer when he threw it at Calvin. What crime would such evidence support? What if Christopher was killed by the blow from the hammer?

3. Like battery, assault is normally a misdemeanor unless the prosecution alleges and proves a defined aggravating element. These are normally aligned with the aggravating elements for battery with the exception of the actual infliction of serious bodily injury, as injury never results from an actual assault.

4. Why does the court indicate that transferred intent was inapplicable to the assault allegation? Why is actual battery required before application of the transferred intent doctrine?

5. This case provides a practical approach to analyzing assault. First, assess whether the defendant actually intended to batter but failed. If so, assault is established. If not, then assess whether the victim was placed in apprehension of an imminent battery as the result of the defendant's intentional act. If so, assault is established. Imagine a defendant intends to place a victim in apprehension of a battery but does not have the intent to actually batter the victim. The defendant throws a rock at the victim from behind and yells, "Hey, look!" The victim, however, is wearing earbuds and doesn't hear the defendant. The rock does not hit the victim. In this case, there is no battery because the victim was not battered; there is no failed battery assault, because the defendant never intended to batter the victim; there is no apprehension assault, because the victim never apprehended being hit by the rock.

C. Kidnapping

Kidnapping was a felony in England that migrated to the United States. As originally defined, kidnapping required proof of an unlawful restraint on a person's liberty by force or show of force so as to send the victim into another country. The asportation or movement requirement to another country reflected the view that kidnapping removed the victim from the protection of the Crown. This requirement has been modified over time, and in 1984, a British Judge, Lord Brandon, explained the elements of kidnapping as, "(1) the taking or carrying away of one person by another; (2) by force or fraud; (3) without the consent of the person so taken or carried away; and (4) without lawful excuse." *Regina v. D* [1984] AC 778 (HL).

The North Carolina Supreme Court summarized the common law evolution of kidnapping as follows:

> The common law definition of kidnapping has been somewhat differently stated by the early legal writers. Blackstone, Commentaries, Book 4, p. 219, defines kidnapping: "Being the forcible abduction or stealing away of a man, woman, or child from their own country and sending them into another." 1 East, Pleas of the Crown, 429, 430, says: "The most aggravated species of false imprisonment is the stealing and carrying away, or secreting of any person, sometimes called kidnapping, which is an offense at common law, punishable by fine, imprisonment, and pillory." Hawkin's Pleas of the Crown, John Curwood, 8th Ed., Vol. I, p. 119, states: "But an aggravated species of false imprisonment is the privately carrying off any person, and keeping them secretly confined, which is generally understood by the term kidnapping." Bishop, Criminal Law, 9th Ed., Vol. 2, sec. 750, 2, page 573, states the better view as to the definition of kidnapping is that "kidnapping is a false imprisonment aggravated by conveying the imprisoned person to some other place." Bishop, *ibid.*, sec. 751, page 575, states: "The consent of a person of mature years and sane mind, on whom no fraud was practiced, would, of course, prevent an act otherwise wrongful from being kidnapping, but not so a young child."

State v. Gough, 126 S.E.2d 118 (N.C. 1962).

Like other original common law crimes, the definition of kidnapping varies today throughout the United States. However, there are certain common elements. First, the confinement, abduction, or movement of the victim must be unlawful, meaning there is no legal justification or excuse. Second, the act must be non-consensual, meaning it is against the victim's will. Third, the act must be accomplished by force, threat of force, or fraud.

Movement of the victim is a variable; some jurisdictions require asportation or movement, while others allow for a kidnapping conviction based solely on confinement. For example, California Penal Code § 207 provides that:

> [E]very person who forcibly, or by any other means of instilling fear, steals or takes, or holds, detains, or arrests any person in this state, and carries

the person into another country, state, or county, or into another part of the same county, is guilty of kidnapping.

Notice that some movement of the victim is required. In contrast, the federal kidnapping statute, 18 U.S.C. §1201, indicates that, "Whoever unlawfully seizes, confines, inveigles, decoys, kidnaps, abducts, or carries away and holds for ransom any other person" is guilty of kidnapping. Similarly, §20.03 of the Texas Penal Code provides that "A person commits an offense if he intentionally or knowingly abducts another person." The Penal Code defines "abduct" as "to restrain a person with intent to prevent his liberation by: (A) secreting or holding him in a place where he is not likely to be found; or (B) using or threatening to use deadly force."

Thus, movement is not a universally required element of kidnapping. However, where it is a required element of the offense, the question arises of how much movement is sufficient. The following case emphasizes the difference between technically and criminally significant asportation.

State v. Ripley
626 S.E.2d 289 (2006)
North Carolina Supreme Court

BRADY, Justice.

This case requires us to determine whether the asportation of robbery victims from an entranceway into a motel lobby during the commission of a robbery with a dangerous weapon was an independent act legally sufficient to justify defendant's separate convictions of kidnapping. Because we find defendant's actions did not constitute a separate, complete act independent of the commission of the robbery with a dangerous weapon, we affirm the Court of Appeals' opinion.

Factual Background

On 18 November 2003, defendant Antonio Lamarquisa Ripley was indicted by the Onslow County Grand Jury for fifteen counts of second-degree kidnapping, nine counts of robbery with a dangerous weapon, three counts of attempted robbery with a dangerous weapon, and one count of assault by pointing a gun. Defendant and four accomplices committed the alleged offenses during a series of robberies on or about 30 May 2003.

The facts of these offenses are described in detail in the Court of Appeals' opinion below. Thus, we highlight only the facts most relevant to a determination of the issue now under consideration—the asportation of four of the victims. . . . [T]estimony tended to show the following: On 30 May 2003, defendant, then thirty-two years old, assembled a group of four accomplices—Jonathan Battle, Jamar McCarthur, Karon Joye, and Sekou Alexander—all of whom were under the age of eighteen. Defendant then transported the group from Wilmington to Jacksonville, North Carolina. The group committed their first robbery with a dangerous weapon at the Hampton Inn in Jacksonville sometime after 9:00 p.m.

Defendant then relocated the group to the Extended Stay America Motel, also located in Jacksonville. Defendant remained in the vehicle while McCarthur, Joye, and Alexander entered the motel's lobby and approached the front desk clerk, demanding and taking the motel's money at gunpoint. Rather than fleeing the motel, the robbers hid in the lobby and ordered the front desk clerk to return to her position. Moments later, as motel patrons entered the lobby, the robbers leapt from their hiding places and robbed the newly acquired victims at gunpoint. During this robbery, one of the accomplices observed Dennis and Tracy Long and Skylar and Adrian Panter walking through the parking lot toward the motel lobby entranceway.

The most critical facts to our analysis are the following: Tracy Long testified during trial that, as her husband was opening the door to the motel lobby, she observed individuals lying on the floor and, believing a robbery was taking place, she prevented her group from entering. As she attempted to turn her party away from the motel, one of the robbers ordered the Longs and the Panters at gunpoint to enter the lobby. Once inside, the Longs and the Panters were ordered to the floor, searched, and robbed. The robbers recovered eight dollars from Tracy Long, the only individual carrying currency. Defendant and his accomplices fled the scene, and law enforcement eventually apprehended the perpetrators.

At the close of the State's evidence, defendant made numerous motions, including one to dismiss all second-degree kidnapping charges. The trial court denied this motion. Defendant offered no evidence. After being instructed by the trial court, the jury deliberated and on 19 March 2004 returned verdicts of guilty for fifteen counts of second-degree kidnapping, seven of the nine counts of robbery with a dangerous weapon, and three counts of attempted robbery with a dangerous weapon. Upon receiving these verdicts, the trial court consolidated defendant's charges and sentenced defendant in the presumptive range to four consecutive prison terms of 117 to 150 months.

Defendant appealed the trial court's denial of his motion to dismiss nine of his fifteen second-degree kidnapping charges. In a divided decision, the Court of Appeals reversed the trial court's denial of defendant's motion to dismiss the nine kidnapping charges and vacated these convictions. A separate opinion concurring in part and dissenting in part found no error as to four of defendant's appealed kidnapping convictions, determining the convictions pertaining to the Longs and the Panters were separate offenses. . . .

[P]ursuant to Rule 16(b) of the North Carolina Rules of Appellate Procedure, the scope of our review is restricted to the Court of Appeals' reversal of the four second-degree kidnapping charges addressed in the dissenting opinion.

Historical Background

Kidnapping has been a recognized crime tracing back to the earliest Judeo-Christian law. English common law defined kidnapping as "the forcible abduction or stealing away of a man, woman, or child, from their own country, and sending them into another." William Blackstone, 4 *Commentaries*.

Some federal courts, considering the separate states as jurisdictions foreign to each other for the purpose of kidnapping, incorporated the English common law definition of kidnapping by modifying the offense to include the asportation of an individual across state lines as well as across international boundaries. *See, e.g., Collier v. Vaccaro,* 51 F.2d 17, 19 (4th Cir. 1931) ("The gist of the [kidnapping] offense is the forcible carrying out of the state. . . ."); *Gooch v. United States,* 82 F.2d 534, 537 (10th Cir.) ("Kidnapping at common law means to forcibly abduct a person and to carry him from one state into another state. . . ."). So, too, did Congress, in its enactment of the Federal Kidnapping Act in 1932. 18 U.S.C. § 408(a) (1932) (currently codified at 18 U.S.C. § 1201 (2000)). The Act, often referred to as "The Lindbergh Law" because its enactment came as a result of the mysterious disappearance of Charles Lindbergh's infant son, currently follows the English common law by stating: "Whoever unlawfully seizes, confines, inveigles, decoys, kidnaps, abducts, or carries away and holds for ransom or reward or otherwise any person . . . when — (1) the person is willfully transported in interstate or foreign commerce . . . [,]" shall be guilty of kidnapping. 18 U.S.C. § 1201(a) (2000).

The Evolution of Kidnapping in North Carolina

North Carolina did not codify any criminal acts of taking an individual against his or her will until 1879, when the General Assembly made criminal the act of abducting children. Noteworthily, the General Assembly did not designate this offense "kidnapping" until 1901. Act of Mar. 14, 1901, ch. 699, sec. 1, 1901 N.C. Sess. Laws 923, 923. However, this statute did not specifically define the offense of kidnapping. Thus, in 1907 this Court defined "kidnapping to be 'false imprisonment aggravated by conveying the imprisoned person to some other place.'" *State v. Harrison,* 59 S.E. 867, 870–71 (1907). This definition of kidnapping excluded the English common law's requirement of asportation to another country. The common law definition of kidnapping evolved in the state's jurisprudence over the years, eventually being defined as "the unlawful taking and carrying away of a human being against his will by force or fraud or threats or intimidation; or to seize and detain him for the purpose of so carrying him away." *State v. Ingland,* 178 S.E.2d 577, 582 (1971).

The offense of kidnapping, as it is now codified in N.C.G.S. § 14-39, did not take form until 1975, when the General Assembly amended section 14-39 and abandoned the traditional common law definition of kidnapping for an element-specific definition. The 1975 amendment to N.C.G.S. § 14-39 thus defined kidnapping as the unlawful confinement, restraint, or removal from one place to another of any person sixteen years of age or over without that person's consent for the purpose of obtaining a ransom, holding the victim hostage, facilitating the commission of a felony or flight after the commission of the felony, or for doing serious bodily harm to or terrorizing the victim. In 1978, this Court recognized "it is clear that the Legislature intended to change the law [of kidnapping]" with its 1975 amendment to N.C.G.S. § 14-39 and, therefore, rejected further use of the North Carolina common law definition of kidnapping. *State v. Fulcher,* 243 S.E.2d 338, 351 (1978). However, this Court in *Fulcher* also perceived that with this new definition came the potential for a defendant to be prosecuted twice for the same act. Accordingly, this Court noted:

> It is self-evident that certain felonies (*e.g.,* forcible rape and armed robbery) cannot be committed without some restraint of the victim. We are of the opinion, and so hold, that G.S. 14-39 was not intended by the Legislature to make a restraint, which is an inherent, inevitable feature of such other felony, also kidnapping so as to permit the conviction and punishment of the defendant for both crimes.... [W]e construe the word "restrain," as used in G.S. 14-39, to connote a restraint separate and apart from that which is inherent in the commission of the other felony.

Id. Additionally, this Court noted that more than one criminal offense can grow out of the same criminal transaction, but specifically held "the restraint, which constitutes the kidnapping, [must be] a separate, complete act, independent of and apart from the other felony." *Id.* at 352; *see also State v. Beatty,* 495 S.E.2d 367, 369 (1998) (noting "a person cannot be convicted of kidnapping when the only evidence of restraint is that 'which is an inherent, inevitable feature' of another felony such as armed robbery").

Further, in *State v. Irwin,* this Court clarified the separate act requirement by holding the defendant's asportation of an employee at knife-point from the front to the rear of a pharmacy to open the safe and obtain drugs was "an inherent and integral part of the attempted armed robbery," and thus such asportation was legally insufficient to convict the defendant of a separate charge of kidnapping. 282 S.E.2d 439, 446 (1981) ("To accomplish defendant's objective of obtaining drugs it was necessary that [one of the employees] go to the back of the store . . . and open the safe."). The Court also noted that the defendant did not expose the victim "to greater danger than that inherent in the armed robbery itself, nor is [the victim] subjected to the kind of danger and abuse the kidnapping statute was designed to prevent." *Id.; see also State v. Pigott,* 415 S.E.2d 555, 561 (1992) (explaining, "[t]he key question . . . is whether the kidnapping charge is supported by evidence from which a jury could reasonably find that the necessary restraint for kidnapping 'exposed [the victim] to greater danger than that inherent in the armed robbery itself'"). Accordingly, because the defendant's moving of the victim was "a mere technical asportation," this Court found the defendant's actions could not justify a separate conviction of kidnapping.

Thus, as it stands today, and as it relates to the case at hand, N.C.G.S. § 14-39 defines kidnapping as:

> (a) Any person who shall unlawfully confine, restrain, or remove from one place to another, any other person 16 years of age or over without the consent of such person . . . shall be guilty of kidnapping if such confinement, restraint or removal is for the purpose of:
>
> (2) Facilitating the commission of any felony or facilitating flight of any person following the commission of a felony. . . .

Application of Our Jurisprudence

. . . .

To convict defendant of second-degree kidnapping of the Longs and the Panters, the State was required to prove beyond a reasonable doubt defendant, acting by himself or acting in concert, confined, restrained, or removed the victims from one place to another for the purpose of facilitating the commission of a felony.

Additionally, we hold a trial court, in determining whether a defendant's asportation of a victim during the commission of a separate felony offense constitutes kidnapping, must consider whether the asportation was an inherent part of the separate felony offense, that is, whether the movement was "a mere technical asportation." If the asportation is a separate act independent of the originally committed criminal act, a trial court must consider additional factors such as whether the asportation facilitated the defendant's ability to commit a felony offense, or whether the asportation exposed the victim to a greater degree of danger than that which is inherent in the concurrently committed felony offense.

Following the analysis in *Irwin,* we conclude the asportation of the Longs and Panters from one side of the motel lobby door to the other was not legally sufficient to justify defendant's convictions of second-degree kidnapping. The moment defendant's accomplice drew his firearm, the robbery with a dangerous weapon had begun. The subsequent asportation of the victims was "a mere technical asportation" that was an inherent part of the robbery defendant and his accomplices were engaged in. *Irwin,* 282 S.E.2d at 446.

The State argues defendant's asportation of the Longs and the Panters both facilitated the commission of robbery with a dangerous weapon and exposed the victims to a greater degree of danger than that inherent in the robbery with a dangerous weapon. Defendant asserts the opposite, stating the asportation had no effect on defendant's ability to complete the robbery with a dangerous weapon. Further, defendant argues the amount of danger to which the victims were exposed never exceeded the degree of harm inherent in the commission of robbery with a dangerous weapon.

While these contentions from both parties are not without merit, they are unnecessary considerations for our analysis. Because we find defendant's asportation of the victims to be a "mere technical asportation" which is an inherent part of the commission of robbery with a dangerous weapon, we cannot under our jurisprudence uphold defendant's convictions of second-degree kidnapping as to the Longs and the Panters.

As defendant's actions constituted only a "mere technical asportation" of the victims which was an inherent part of the commission of robbery with a dangerous weapon, defendant cannot be convicted of the separate crime of second-degree kidnapping. Accordingly, we affirm the Court of Appeals' decision vacating defendant's four convictions of second-degree kidnapping.

AFFIRMED.

Notes & Questions

1. Note that the primary concern related to the sufficiency of asportation is the risk that an act that is functionally one crime may be punished as two. The requirement for more than mere technical asportation therefore serves an important function: ensuring conviction for kidnapping is the result of conduct that produces a prohibited harm distinct from a related offense, such as robbery.

2. In states that require proof of asportation, other crimes such as felonious restraint or false imprisonment generally cover an unlawful deprivation of liberty without asportation. For example, California Penal Code §236 provides, "False imprisonment is the unlawful violation of the personal liberty of another." The statute then provides the following definition:

> "Deprivation or violation of the personal liberty of another" includes substantial and sustained restriction of another's liberty accomplished through force, fear, fraud, deceit, coercion, violence, duress, menace, or threat of unlawful injury to the victim or to another person, under circumstances where the person receiving or apprehending the threat reasonably believes that it is likely that the person making the threat would carry it out.

3. Like assault and battery, most kidnapping statutes define different degrees of kidnapping based on proof of an aggravating element. For example, the North Carolina statute provides:

> There shall be two degrees of kidnapping as defined by subsection (a). If the person kidnapped either was not released by the defendant in a safe place or had been seriously injured or sexually assaulted, the offense is kidnapping in the first degree and is punishable as a Class C felony. If the person kidnapped was released in a safe place by the defendant and had not been seriously injured or sexually assaulted, the offense is kidnapping in the second degree and is punishable as a Class E felony.

Id. §14-39. The California Penal Code §209 provides:

> (a) Any person who seizes, confines, inveigles, entices, decoys, abducts, conceals, kidnaps or carries away another person by any means whatsoever with intent to hold or detain, or who holds or detains, that person for ransom, reward or to commit extortion or to exact from another person any money or valuable thing, or any person who aids or abets any such act, is guilty of a felony, and upon conviction thereof, shall be punished by imprisonment in the state prison for life without possibility of parole in cases in which any person subjected to any such act suffers death or bodily harm, or is intentionally confined in a manner which exposes that person to a substantial likelihood of death, or shall be punished by imprisonment in the state prison for life with the possibility of parole in cases where no such person suffers death or bodily harm.

(b) (1) Any person who kidnaps or carries away any individual to commit robbery, rape, spousal rape, oral copulation, sodomy, or any violation of Section 264.1, 288, or 289, shall be punished by imprisonment in the state prison for life with the possibility of parole.

(2) This subdivision shall only apply if the movement of the victim is beyond that merely incidental to the commission of, and increases the risk of harm to the victim over and above that necessarily present in, the intended underlying offense.

III. Crimes Against Property

Crimes against property include both theft and other offenses. Theft offenses will be addressed in Chapter 13. At common law. two other offenses against property were considered serious felonies: burglary and arson. While the modern definitions of these crimes vary across jurisdictions, they are all based on the common law foundation reflected in the following cases.

A. Burglary

At common law, burglary was defined as the unlawful breaking and entering of the dwelling house of another at night with intent to commit a felony therein. The actus reus of breaking and entering required proof the defendant forced an opening into the house (like breaking open a door) and placed some part of his body into the opening. Expanding an existing opening did not qualify as breaking, and using a tool to reach into the opening did not qualify as entering. If the body of a person could be discerned by daylight, the element of "at night" was not established. A dwelling house was a building used for residential purposes, although there was no requirement that it was occupied when the breaking and entering occurred. Structures attached to the dwelling like garages were considered part of the dwelling. Burglary was and remains a specific intent crime: the breaking and entering had to concur with the intent to commit a felony within the dwelling house.

Modern burglary statutes dispense with or alter some of these requirements. Almost no modern burglary statutes require the breaking and entering to occur at night. The breaking element often now includes expanding an existing opening (like pushing an already open door wider open); the entry element often now includes using a tool to reach into the opening. The dwelling house requirement is also often dispensed with or made into an aspect of an aggravated form of burglary, allowing the breaking and entry of any structure to qualify. Thus, it is not uncommon to have a daylight burglary of a commercial warehouse. Breaking and entering with the intent to commit a felony within remains a very common requirement, but breaking to *exit* will not satisfy this requirement. However, it is possible for a defendant to "break from within," meaning the defendant is already inside a structure and breaks and enters a closed room therein.

Burglary has also been applied to situations where the defendant lawfully entered a building and clandestinely remained after closing with the specific intent to commit a felony. For example, in *Quarles v. United States*, 139 S. Ct. 1872 (2019), the Supreme Court considered a challenge to application of the federal violent felon sentencing statute based on a prior conviction for burglary based on a "remaining in" theory. The issue, according to the Court, was:

> . . . whether remaining in burglary (i) occurs only if a person has the intent to commit a crime at the exact moment when he or she first unlawfully remains in a building or structure, or (ii) more broadly, occurs when a person forms the intent to commit a crime at any time while unlawfully remaining in a building or structure.

The Court concluded that

> For purposes of § 924(e), we conclude that remaining-in burglary occurs when the defendant forms the intent to commit a crime at any time while unlawfully remaining in a building or structure.

The following opinion explains how much the modern definition of burglary has evolved from its original common law meaning.

Taylor v. United States
495 U.S. 575 (1990)
U.S. Supreme Court

Justice BLACKMUN delivered the opinion of the Court.

In this case, we are called upon to determine the meaning of the word "burglary" as it is used in § 1402 of Subtitle I (the Career Criminals Amendment Act of 1986) of the Anti-Drug Abuse Act of 1986, 18 U.S.C. § 924(e). This statute provides a sentence enhancement for a defendant who is convicted under 18 U.S.C. § 922(g) (unlawful possession of a firearm) and who has three prior convictions for specified types of offenses, including "burglary."

I

In January 1988, in the United States District Court for the Eastern District of Missouri, petitioner Arthur Lajuane Taylor pleaded guilty to one count of possession of a firearm by a convicted felon, in violation of 18 U.S.C. § 922(g)(1). At the time of his plea, Taylor had four prior convictions. One was for robbery, one was for assault, and the other two were for second-degree burglary under Missouri law.

The Government sought sentence enhancement under § 924(e). Taylor conceded that his robbery and assault convictions properly could be counted as two of the three prior convictions required for enhancement, because they involved the use of physical force against persons under § 924(e)(2)(B)(i). Taylor contended, however, that his burglary convictions should not count for enhancement, because they did not involve "conduct that presents a serious potential risk of physical injury to another" under § 924(e)(2)(B)(ii). His guilty plea was conditioned on the right to appeal this issue. The District Court, pursuant to § 924(e)(1), sentenced Taylor to 15 years' imprisonment without possibility of parole.

The United States Court of Appeals for the Eighth Circuit, by a divided vote, affirmed Taylor's sentence. It ruled that, because the word "burglary" in § 924(e)(2) (B)(ii) "*means* burglary however a state chooses to define it," the District Court did not err in using Taylor's Missouri convictions for second-degree burglary to enhance his sentence. 864 F.2d 625, 627 (1989) . . . .

The word "burglary" has not been given a single accepted meaning by the state courts; the criminal codes of the States define burglary in many different ways. On the face of the federal enhancement provision, it is not readily apparent whether Congress intended "burglary" to mean whatever the State of the defendant's prior conviction defines as burglary, or whether it intended that some uniform definition of burglary be applied to all cases in which the Government seeks a § 924(e) enhancement. And if Congress intended that a uniform definition of burglary be applied, was that definition to be the traditional common law definition, or one of the broader "generic" definitions articulated in the Model Penal Code and in a predecessor statute to § 924(e), or some other definition specifically tailored to the purposes of the enhancement statute?

II

Before examining these possibilities, we think it helpful to review the background of § 924(e). Six years ago, Congress enacted the first version of the sentence-enhancement provision. Under the Armed Career Criminal Act of 1984, Pub. L. 98473, ch. 18, 98 Stat. 2185, 18 U.S.C. App. § 1202(a) (1982 ed. Supp. III) (repealed in 1986 by Pub. L. 99-308, § 104(b), 100 Stat. 459), any convicted felon found guilty of possession of a firearm, who had three previous convictions "for robbery or burglary," was to receive a mandatory minimum sentence of imprisonment for 15 years. Burglary was defined in the statute itself as "any felony consisting of entering or remaining surreptitiously within a building that is property of another with intent to engage in conduct constituting a Federal or State offense." § 1202(c)(9).

The Act was intended to supplement the States' law enforcement efforts against "career" criminals. . . .

The only explanation of why Congress chose the specific definition of burglary included in § 1202 appears in the Senate Report:

> "Because of the wide variation among states and localities in the ways that offenses are labeled, the absence of definitions raised the possibility that culpable offenders might escape punishment on a technicality. For instance, the common law definition of burglary includes a requirement that the offense be committed during the nighttime and with respect to a dwelling. However, for purposes of this Act, such limitations are not appropriate. Furthermore, in terms of fundamental fairness, the Act should ensure, to the extent

that it is consistent with the prerogatives of the States in defining their own offenses, that the same type of conduct is punishable on the Federal level in all cases." S. Rep. at 20.

[In 1986] § 924(e) again was amended, into its present form, by § 1402 of Subtitle I (the Career Criminals Amendment Act) of the Anti-Drug Abuse Act of 1986, 100 Stat. 3207-39. This amendment effected three changes that, taken together, give rise to the problem presented in this case. It expanded the predicate offenses triggering the sentence enhancement from "robbery or burglary" to "a violent felony or a serious drug offense"; it defined the term "violent felony" to include "burglary"; and it deleted the preexisting definition of burglary.

The legislative history is silent as to Congress' reason for deleting the definition of burglary. It does reveal, however, the general purpose and approach of the Career Criminals Amendment Act of 1986. Two bills were proposed; from these, the current statutory language emerged as a compromise.

The legislative history indicates that Congress singled out burglary (as opposed to other frequently committed property crimes such as larceny and auto theft) for inclusion as a predicate offense, both in 1984 and in 1986, because of its inherent potential for harm to persons. The fact that an offender enters a building to commit a crime often creates the possibility of a violent confrontation between the offender and an occupant, caretaker, or some other person who comes to investigate. And the offender's own awareness of this possibility may mean that he is prepared to use violence if necessary to carry out his plans or to escape. Congress apparently thought that all burglaries serious enough to be punishable by imprisonment for more than a year constituted a category of crimes that shared this potential for violence, and that were likely to be committed by career criminals. There never was any proposal to limit the predicate offense to some special subclass of burglaries that might be especially dangerous, such as those where the offender is armed, or the building is occupied, or the crime occurs at night.

Second, the enhancement provision always has embodied a categorical approach to the designation of predicate offenses. In the 1984 statute, "robbery" and "burglary" were defined in the statute itself, not left to the vagaries of state law. Thus, Congress intended that the enhancement provision be triggered by crimes having certain specified elements, not by crimes that happened to be labeled "robbery" or "burglary" by the laws of the State of conviction. Each of the proposed versions of the 1986 amendment carried forward this categorical approach, extending the range of predicate offenses to all crimes having certain common characteristics—the use or threatened use of force, or the risk that force would be used—regardless of how they were labeled by state law.

Third, the 1984 definition of burglary shows that Congress, at least at that time, had in mind a modern "generic" view of burglary, roughly corresponding to the definitions of burglary in a majority of the States' criminal codes. In adopting this definition, Congress both prevented offenders from invoking the arcane technicalities of the common law definition of burglary to evade the sentence-enhancement provision, and protected offenders from the unfairness of having enhancement depend upon the label employed by the State of conviction.

Nothing in the legislative history of the 1986 amendment shows that Congress was dissatisfied with the 1984 definition . . . there is nothing in the history to show that Congress intended in 1986 to replace the 1984 "generic" definition of burglary with something entirely different. . . .

III

These observations about the purpose and general approach of the enhancement provision enable us to narrow the range of possible meanings of the term "burglary."

A

First, we are led to reject the view of the Court of Appeals in this case. It seems to us to be implausible that Congress intended the meaning of "burglary" for purposes of § 924(e) to depend on the definition adopted by the State of conviction. That would mean that a person convicted of unlawful possession of a firearm would, or would not, receive a sentence enhancement based on exactly the same conduct, depending on whether the State of his prior conviction happened to call that conduct "burglary."

For example, Michigan has no offense formally labeled "burglary." It classifies burglaries into several grades of "breaking and entering." *See* Mich. Comp. Laws § 750.110 (1979). In contrast, California defines "burglary" so broadly as to include shoplifting and theft of goods from a "locked" but unoccupied automobile. *See* Cal. Penal Code Ann. § 459 (West Supp. 1990); *United States v. Chatman,* 869 F.2d 525, 528-529 & n. 2 (9th Cir. 1989) (entry through unsecured window of an unoccupied auto, and entry of a store open to the public with intent to commit theft, are "burglary" under California law); *see also* Tex. Penal Code Ann. §§ 30.01-30.05 (1989 and Supp. 1990) (defining burglary to include theft from coin-operated vending machine or automobile); *United States v. Leonard,* 868 F.2d 1393, 1395, n. 2 (5th Cir.).

Thus, a person imprudent enough to shoplift or steal from an automobile in California would be found, under the Ninth Circuit's view, to have committed a burglary constituting a "violent felony" for enhancement purposes—yet a person who did so in Michigan might not. Without a clear indication that, with the 1986 amendment, Congress intended to abandon its general approach of using uniform categorical definitions to identify predicate offenses, we do not interpret Congress' omission of a definition of "burglary" in a way that leads to odd results of this kind. . . .

We think that "burglary" in § 924(e) must have some uniform definition independent of the labels employed by the various States' criminal codes.

B

Some Courts of Appeals . . . have ruled that § 924(e) incorporates the common law definition of burglary, relying on the maxim that a statutory term is generally presumed to have its common law meaning. This view has some appeal, in that common law burglary is the core, or common denominator, of the contemporary usage of the term. Almost all States include a breaking and entering of a dwelling at night, with intent to commit a felony, among their definitions of burglary. Whatever else the Members of Congress might have been thinking of, they presumably had in mind at least the "classic" common law definition when they considered the inclusion of burglary as a predicate offense.

The problem with this view is that the contemporary understanding of "burglary" has diverged a long way from its common law roots. Only a few States retain the common law definition, or something closely resembling it. Most other States have expanded this definition to include entry without a "breaking," structures other than dwellings, offenses committed in the daytime, entry with intent to commit a crime other than a felony, etc. *See* W. LaFave & A. Scott, Substantive Criminal Law §§ 8.13(a) through (f), pp. 464–475. This statutory development, "when viewed in totality, has resulted in a modern crime which has little in common with its common law ancestor except for the title of burglary." *Id.* at § 8.13(g), p. 476.

Also, interpreting "burglary" in § 924(e) to mean common law burglary would not comport with the purposes of the enhancement statute. The arcane distinctions embedded, in the common law definition have little relevance to modern law enforcement concerns. It seems unlikely that the Members of Congress, immersed in the intensely practical concerns of controlling violent crime, would have decided to abandon their modern, generic 1984 definition of burglary and revert to a definition developed in the ancient English law—a definition mentioned nowhere in the legislative history. Moreover, construing "burglary" to mean common law burglary would come close to nullifying that term's effect in the statute, because few of the crimes now generally recognized as burglaries would fall within the common law definition.

This Court has declined to follow any rule that a statutory term is to be given its common-law meaning, when that meaning is obsolete or inconsistent with the statute's purpose. . . .

Petitioner argues that the narrow common law definition of burglary would comport with the rule of lenity—that criminal statutes, including sentencing provisions, are to be construed in favor of the accused. This maxim of statutory construction, however, cannot dictate an implausible interpretation of a statute, nor one at odds with the generally accepted contemporary meaning of a term.

D

We therefore reject petitioner's view that Congress meant to include only a special subclass of burglaries, either those that would have been burglaries at common law or those that involve especially dangerous conduct. These limiting constructions are not dictated by the rule of lenity. We believe that Congress meant, by "burglary," the generic sense in which the term is now used in the criminal codes of most States.

Although the exact formulations vary, the generic, contemporary meaning of burglary contains at least the following elements: an unlawful or unprivileged entry into or remaining in a building or other structure, with intent to commit a crime. *See* LaFave & Scott, at § 8.13(a), p. 466 (modern statutes "generally require that the entry be unprivileged"); at § 8.13(c), p. 471 (modern statutes "typically describe the place as a 'building' or 'structure'"); at § 8.13(e), p. 474 ("the prevailing view in the modern codes is that an intent to commit any offense will do").

. . . .

We conclude that a person has been convicted of burglary for purposes of a § 924(e) enhancement if he is convicted of any crime, regardless of its exact definition or label, having the basic elements of unlawful or unprivileged entry into, or remaining in, a building or structure, with intent to commit a crime.

[The Court then concluded that a sentencing court must review the prior conviction labeled burglary to ensure that it aligned with the basic modern definition, and that the conviction at issue in the case met that definition.]

Notes and Questions

1. Although it is a case analyzing the meaning of a federal sentencing statute, *Taylor* usefully explains the generic requirements for proving modern burglary. What is the generic definition given by the Court?

2. Even in jurisdictions that still require proof of breaking and entering, gaining entry by fraud or deceit is considered a constructive breaking, thereby satisfying the requirement. For example, imagine a defendant poses as a repair person and deceives a homeowner into allowing him into the home. Once inside, the defendant steals several items while out of the homeowner's sight. So long as the evidence establishes that the intent to steal concurred with the fraudulent entry, the defendant should be convicted of burglary.

B. Arson

At common law, arson was defined as the malicious burning of the dwelling house of another. Malice was no different in this context than for the crime of murder: an intentional or extremely reckless act. The common law definition required proof that something "ignited" the destructive fire, and that the structure of the home (as opposed to furniture) suffered "charring," meaning fire damage.

Like homicide, the modern definition of arson varies significantly among jurisdictions. Dispensing with the "dwelling house" requirement is the most common modification. Many jurisdictions also more precisely define the requisite mental state, for example, requiring a willful or intentional act. The Model Penal Code provides that a person is guilty of arson if, "he starts a fire or causes an explosion with the purpose of (1) destroying a building or occupied structure of another; or (2) destroying or damaging any property, whether his own or another's, to collect insurance for such loss." Even jurisdictions that retain the malice requirement may narrow the meaning of malice in relation to arson.

The following case addresses the required result to prove arson.

State v. Oxendine

286 S.E.2d 546 (1982)
North Carolina Supreme Court

Defendant was charged in separate indictments, proper in form, with arson, the unlawful burning of a building and willful and wanton injury to real property in violation of G.S. 14-58, 14-62, and 14-127. Defendant pleaded not guilty to all of the charges.

In brief and pertinent part, the State's evidence, which included defendant's pretrial confession, tended to show that defendant engaged in unlawful incendiary activities at the home and property of his aunt, Miss Pyree Locklear, on 9 December 1980. Miss Locklear and her minor son were in the house when defendant set it aflame using kerosene (after breaking out a window with an oak stick). Defendant also ignited an outbuilding used for storage. The fire in the house was quickly contained—however the outbuilding and its contents were consumed by the blaze.

Defendant presented an alibi defense. He said that he was in bed at his home at the time the fire began. His mother corroborated his alibi. Defendant further stated that he had not been on his aunt's property at any time within the past two years. [Defendant had been previously convicted for trespassing at his aunt's residence.] With respect to his confession, defendant denied that he had admitted his guilt of these crimes, or made any incriminating statement regarding the incident, to the investigating officer. Among other things, defendant said that he was intoxicated when he was being questioned and that he did not understand the explanation of his constitutional rights.

Upon presentation of all of the evidence, the jury found defendant guilty of arson and felonious burning of a building.

The facts shall be further summarized in the opinion to the extent required by our review and discussion of defendant's specific assignments of error.

Defendant argues five assignments of error which he believes require either a reversal of his arson conviction or a new trial. We disagree and affirm.

Defendant first contends that the trial court erred in overruling his motion to dismiss the arson charge. It is well established that a successful arson prosecution requires proof that defendant maliciously and willfully burned the dwelling house of another. In the instant case defendant challenges the sufficiency of the State's evidence upon the "burning" element of the offense. He complains that the evidence adduced against him was too meager to convince a rational trier of fact that he actually burned the structure of an inhabited dwelling. Under the circumstances of this case defendant's position is indefensible.

The law is clear that some portion of the dwelling itself, in contrast to its mere contents, must be burned to constitute arson; however, the least burning of any part of the building, no matter how small, is sufficient, and it is not necessary that the building be consumed or materially damaged by the fire. The accepted legal defini-tion of "burning," for purposes of an arson case, is best stated in *State v. Hall*, 93 N.C. 571, 573 (1885):

> The crime of arson is consummated by the burning of any, the smallest part of the house, and it is burned within the common law definition of the offense when it is charred, that is, when the wood is reduced to coal and its identity changed, but not when merely scorched or discolored by heat.

Applying these principles to the case at bar, we hold that the State's evidence was suf-ficient to authorize a reasonable conclusion that the building in question had been burned.

Miss Locklear, owner of the dwelling, testified that, after hearing her son exclaim, "Fire!," she went into the bedroom "where the fire was at" and saw fire and smoke coming out of it. She said that the house was still "burning, slowly" when the fire truck arrived. [By this time, Miss Locklear and four of her neighbors had essentially doused the blaze.] Miss Locklear further stated that, during the fire, the "current had burned loose" in the house. Myrtle E. Blanton testified that she drove by the Locklear house on 9 December 1980 and saw "a fire and a lot of smoke." Mrs. Blanton then com-mented to defendant, who was riding with her on the way to the bus station, "your Aunt's house is on fire, everything she owns is burning up." From the testimony of these two witnesses alone, one could reasonably infer that the fire inside the house was substantial enough to cause at least some charring of the structure, since the fire was accompanied by a great deal of smoke, was visible from the outside (the highway) and was responsible for the loosening of electrical wiring in the building.

The witness was obviously referring to some type of electrical wiring in the building.

We note that defendant's only reaction to this stimulus, according to Mrs. Blan-ton, was his response, "[s]he ain't no Aunt of mine." He did not even look in the direction of the fire but "just kept staring straight ahead."

Nevertheless, the State's case upon this essential element was further strengthened by the testimony of Officer William Halstead who described the subsequent condi-tion of the residence as follows: "the curtains were burned and there was dark or burned patches over the wall; the wallpaper was burned and there was a heavy odor of kerosene. Smoke was throughout the house. . . . [T]he main house was or had been on fire." Surely, this evidence plainly showed that the dwelling itself, and not merely something in it (the curtains), had been burned. It is difficult to perceive how dark, burned patches could appear on a wall absent the prior incidence of at least minor charring of that wall's substantive material. Defendant's additional argument that the presence of burnt wallpaper in the dwelling had no rational tendency to indicate the charring of the building's structure simply defies good sense and logic. Wallpaper affixed to an interior wall is unquestionably a part of the dwelling's framework. If the wallpaper is burning, it would perforce suggest that the house is also burning. Hence, we hold that where, as here, the evidence discloses that the wallpaper in a dwelling has been burned, it competently substantiates the charring element of arson. *Compare State v. Kelso*, 617 S.W.2d 591, 594 (Mo. App. 1981), where the Court, in dictum, recognized that, although the mere scorching or discoloration of wallpaper on a wall did not constitute arson, arson would certainly occur if the fire spread to the wooden structure no matter how small the damage.

Once it is affixed to the house, wallpaper is generally immovable and permanently attached thereto and as such becomes part of the realty.

Considering all of the foregoing evidence in the light most favorable to the State with the benefit of every reasonable inference, it was sufficient to permit the jury to find that defendant burned (charred) parts of his Aunt's house to the necessary degree. Contrary to defendant's position, the State's witnesses were not required to use the specific legal term "charred" in describing the structural damage caused by the unlawful fire. In commonly understood language, the witnesses testified that the house had been on fire and that parts of it had been burned. In his inculpatory statement to the police, even defendant described the progress of the fire, which he "had started on the front of the house," in terms of how well it was burning. In fact, the sufficiency of the burning element of the offense was never contested at any time during the trial of this case. Defendant relied entirely on an alibi defense. Thus, the real question here was not whether Miss Locklear's house was unlawfully burned, but whether defendant unlawfully set that fire.

. . . .

Defendant also argues that the trial court's final charge to the jury was deficient in two other respects: (1) the omission of a legal definition of burning and (2) the absence of a direct admonishment that the burning of personal property within the dwelling did not constitute arson. We hold that defendant was not entitled upon this record to additional instructions absent specific and timely requests therefor.

First, we find that Judge Small correctly delineated the elements of arson in his charge to the jury, see infra. In fact, he repeated almost verbatim the patterned instructions for the offense. Nevertheless, defendant now maintains that the judge should have told the jury sua sponte that there must be a partial burning or slight charring of some portion of the building and that a mere scorching or discoloration thereof would not suffice as arson. To the contrary, we believe that a trial court is not obligated *ex mero motu* to make this distinction for the jury where, as here, no serious question concerning the nature of the damage caused by the fire is ever raised during trial. We must again emphasize that defendant relied on an alibi defense and did not challenge the State's evidence that an arson had been committed. More particularly, the testimony concerning smoke damage to the paint on various walls in the dwelling did not, as defendant seems to believe, negate the occurrence of at least some burning or charring of the building. Such testimony cannot be reasonably deemed as anything more than a description of additional damage caused by the fire since other independent and uncontroverted evidence showed that the house itself had been burned, including several patches on one wall and some wallpaper, to the extent that certain electrical wiring in the structure was loosened. There being no affirmative evidentiary conflict regarding the legal application of the term "burned" to the facts of this case, we hold that the judge did not have to explain its meaning absent a request, to the jury, as it is a plain, simple word commonly understood by people of average intelligence.

The two Texas cases cited by defendant in his brief, *Woolsey v. State*, 17 S.W. 546 (1891) and *Van Morey v. State*, 17 S.W.2d 50 (1929) are clearly inapposite upon this basis. In both *Woolsey* and *Van Morey*, there was conflicting testimony about whether the fire had merely scorched or smoked parts of the house, instead of burning its structure. The Texas Court of Criminal Appeals held in both instances that the trial court had committed prejudicial error in failing to give the specially requested instructions regarding the necessity for an actual burning of the building to sustain a conviction of arson. [Defendant did not tender a similar request in the instant case.]

Second, we find that Judge Small correctly characterized and stressed the type of property that had to be burned by the fire to constitute arson. In pertinent part, he charged the jury as follows:

> As to the case where the defendant is charged with the crime of arson, I instruct you that in order for you to find the defendant guilty, the State must prove three things beyond a reasonable doubt: First, that the defendant burned a dwelling house; Second, that the dwelling house at the time it was burned, was inhabited by Pyree Locklear; Third, that the defendant in burning the dwelling house acted maliciously. That is, he intentionally burned the building without lawful excuse or justification.
>
> So I instruct you as to the charge of arson, that if you should find from the evidence beyond a reasonable doubt, that on or about December 9, 1980, Ronnie Ray Oxendine maliciously burned the dwelling house of Pyree Locklear, which was inhabited by Pyree Locklear, by pouring kerosene on the house or around the window to the bedroom and igniting it with his cigarette lighter, or some other means, and thereby burning the house, it would be your duty to return a verdict of guilty of arson.

The judge did not once suggest to the jury that the burning of personal property inside the dwelling could suffice as arson. In fact, the only evidence in the entire record of fire damage to personal property within the dwelling was Officer Halstead's solitary statement that the curtains had been burned. In such circumstances, we fail to see how the jury could have been misled or confused. In any event, if defendant had been genuinely worried about this possibility at trial, he could have, and he should have, requested a specific instruction upon the matter.

In defendant's trial and convictions, we find no error.

Notes and Questions

1. What prohibited result must the prosecution prove to support an arson conviction?

2. Note the opinion indicates a requirement that the burning be both malicious *and* willful, and that the jury was instructed the burning had to be intentional. This reflects a narrowing of the common law malice requirement for arson. Many states have substituted intent, purpose, or knowledge as the requisite mental state to prove an arson offense.

3. To prove arson at common law, the structure had to be a dwelling house of another. Modern arson statutes expand this requirement to include many other structures. Even states with criminal statutes based on the common law have done so. Consider Virginia's arson provision:

> § 18.2-77. Burning or destroying dwelling house, etc.
>
> A. If any person maliciously (i) burns, or by use of any explosive device or substance destroys, in whole or in part, or causes to be burned or destroyed, or (ii) aids, counsels or procures the burning or destruction of any dwelling house or manufactured home whether belonging to himself or another, or any occupied hotel, hospital, mental health facility, or other house in which persons usually dwell or lodge, any occupied railroad car, boat, vessel, or river craft in which persons usually dwell or lodge, or any occupied jail or prison, or any occupied church or occupied building owned or leased by a church that is immediately adjacent to a church, he shall be guilty of a felony, punishable by imprisonment for life or for any period not less than five years and, subject to subdivision g of § 18.2-10, a fine of not more than $100,000. Any person who maliciously sets fire to anything, or aids, counsels or procures the setting fire to anything, by the burning whereof such occupied dwelling house, manufactured home, hotel, hospital, mental health facility or other house, or railroad car, boat, vessel, or river craft, jail or prison, church or building owned or leased by a church that is immediately adjacent to a church, is burned shall be guilty of a violation of this subsection.

4. If the jury had not been convinced beyond a reasonable doubt that part of the building had been charred, what would have been the appropriate verdict?

5. What if Oxendine had used a bomb instead of kerosene? Can destruction by explosion qualify as arson pursuant to the definition reflected in the decision? If so, what would the evidence have to prove? Consider Georgia's arson statute:

> A person commits the offense of arson in the first degree when, by means of fire or explosive, he or she knowingly damages or knowingly causes, aids, abets, advises, encourages, hires, counsels, or procures another to damage:
>
> (1) Any dwelling house of another without his or her consent or in which another has a security interest, including but not limited to a mortgage, a

lien, or a conveyance to secure debt, without the consent of both, whether it is occupied, unoccupied, or vacant;

(2) Any building, vehicle, railroad car, watercraft, or other structure of another without his or her consent or in which another has a security interest, including but not limited to a mortgage, a lien, or a conveyance to secure debt, without the consent of both, if such structure is designed for use as a dwelling, whether it is occupied, unoccupied, or vacant;

(3) Any dwelling house, building, vehicle, railroad car, watercraft, aircraft, or other structure whether it is occupied, unoccupied, or vacant and when such is insured against loss or damage by fire or explosive and such loss or damage is accomplished without the consent of both the insurer and the insured;

(4) Any dwelling house, building, vehicle, railroad car, watercraft, aircraft, or other structure whether it is occupied, unoccupied, or vacant with the intent to defeat, prejudice, or defraud the rights of a spouse or co-owner; or

(5) Any building, vehicle, railroad car, watercraft, aircraft, or other structure under such circumstances that it is reasonably foreseeable that human life might be endangered.

Formative Assessments

1. Defendant is hiking through the woods when a big thunder storm hits. He notices a cabin that seems unoccupied, and pries the back door open to get inside and wait out the storm. While in the cabin, he wanders around, and in the bedroom, he sees a nice watch on the dresser. He takes the watch and leaves when the weather clears. He is later apprehended. Based on this evidence, defendant is guilty of:

A. Burglary only.

B. Larceny only.

C. Burglary and larceny.

2. Now assume that in order to warm up, defendant decides to start a fire. The wood outside is somewhat soggy, and he can't get it started in the fireplace by lighting paper. He finds some gasoline in a storage shed and decides to use it to light the fire. Unfortunately, he pours too much gas on the logs, and when he ignites them with a match, the fire escapes the fireplace and sets the home on fire. The home is burned to the ground. The jurisdiction follows the common law definition of arson. Is defendant guilty of arson based on these facts?

A. Yes.

B. No.

Chapter 13

Theft

I. Theft Offenses Generally

Like other common-law offenses, the definition of theft offenses varies from jurisdiction to jurisdiction. In general, however, theft statutes fall into two broad categories. The first category includes statutes that reflect common law theft crimes. Among the most common of these are larceny, larceny by trick, embezzlement, and theft by false pretenses. The second category includes consolidated theft statutes that seek to eliminate the distinctions between types of theft offenses and substitute a broad crime of unlawfully depriving another of his or her property.

Like other categories of offenses, there are certain commonalities between most theft offenses. First, all such offenses require proof of an intent to steal, meaning the specific intent or purpose to permanently deprive another of his or her property. While most jurisdictions have also adopted crimes to address the unlawful temporary deprivation of property, such as trespass or wrongful appropriation, the essence of theft is the intent to steal. Second, because common law larceny required the physical taking and carrying away of property, proscribing theft of non-movable property such as services or intellectual property requires distinct statutory provisions. Even in jurisdictions that retain the common law categories of theft offenses, criminal statutes normally include such supplemental provisions.

Because theft offenses require the specific intent or purpose to steal, the burden is always on the prosecution to prove that subjective mental state. As with any other crime requiring such proof, prosecutors will rely on both direct and circumstantial evidence to satisfy this burden. Evidence as to motive and how the property was dealt with after being taken are often critical to prove intent to steal. And, because this intent is a purely subjective mental state, it is common for defendants to raise a mistake of fact as a defense to theft offenses. Such a mistake need only be honest to block proof of intent to steal; it does not matter how unreasonable that mistake may be. For example, a defendant might assert he mistakenly assumed the property was abandoned, or mistakenly assumed it was his, or mistakenly assumed he had a right to recover the property. When such a mistake is introduced by a defendant, the prosecutor must persuade the fact-finder that the defendant did not harbor such a mistake in order to prove the intent to steal beyond a reasonable doubt. In short, no matter how unreasonable such a mistake may be, a defendant cannot intend to steal property he honestly believes is abandoned or is his.

The following sections will address each common law theft offense in turn. To better distinguish between them, it is useful to always ask (1) what level of control did the defendant gain over the property and (2) how did the defendant gain that control? For the first question, ask whether the defendant either had no control over the property when she took it or had *custody* of the property when she unlawfully took it. In either of those situations, the taking is considered trespassory. However, if the defendant already had valid *possession* of the property and then unlawfully converted it, or had *title* to the property even if obtained fraudulently, there is no trespassory taking. For the second question, ask if the defendant used a fraud or a trick to obtain possession of or title to the property. Such a fraud or trick, coupled with a causal connection to the victim's passing the possession or title to the defendant, will distinguish between the two closely related crimes of larceny by trick and theft by false pretenses.

The lines between custody, possession, and title can often be blurry. As a general matter, you should think of custody as physical but very limited control, like taking custody of a garment in a department store for the limited purpose of trying it on in the changing room. In such a scenario, you have physical control but cannot use the garment for anything other than that limited purpose. Possession, in contrast, is full dominion and control over the property, normally for a defined period of time. An individual in possession may give someone else custody of the property while retaining constructive possession. For example, a person who rents a ballgown from Rent the Runway has possession over the garment for the duration of the rental period. She may wear it to any event she chooses as often as she chooses. Rent the Runway still holds title to the garment, but possession has been given to the renter. Title means legal ownership. When you purchase the garment at the department store and it is handed to you, title transfers to you.

These distinctions are important, because they will help distinguish theft offenses. If the defendant unlawfully takes property from the possession of the victim, even if the defendant had custody of the property at the time, the actus reus for larceny is satisfied. The customer who takes the garment into the changing room and then puts it in his backpack to remove it from the store has committed the actus reus of larceny: a trespassory taking. If the defendant tricks the victim into giving her possession of the property, intending at that time to steal the property, the trick nullifies the apparent consent, meaning the taking also satisfies the actus reus of larceny. The customer who purports to rent a garment from Rent the Runway with no intent to return it gains possession by trick. This is the actus reus of larceny by trick. In contrast, if the defendant is given valid possession of the property and subsequently unlawfully converts it, there is no trespass and therefore no larceny. Instead, this satisfies the actus reus of embezzlement. Finally, if the defendant uses a trick or fraud to secure title or ownership of the property before it is moved—the customer who pays for the garment with a counterfeit bill—the offense is theft by false pretenses.

The chapter will conclude by addressing the crime of robbery, which is essentially larceny coupled with an assault or battery that compels the victim to give up the property or prevents the victim from immediately recovering the property.

II. Larceny

The crime that we now refer to as "theft" was known as "larceny" at common law. To understand modern theft crimes, it is important to understand this common law genesis. Larceny is the logical starting point, because it was the original common law property crime from which all the others derived. At common law, larceny was defined as the trespassory (meaning non-consensual) taking and carrying away (sometimes called "asportation") of personal property from the possession of another with the intent to permanently deprive. In order to be convicted of larceny, each element has to be proven beyond a reasonable doubt.

Originally derived from the tort of trespass, the trespassory taking is an essential aspect of any larceny offense. A trespassory taking means a severance of possession—whether actual or constructive—from the victim. As will be explained below, if the defendant is given valid possession or has secured title to the property before it is moved, there is no trespass and thus no larceny offense.

The trespassory taking and carrying away of personal property is the actus reus of larceny. The taking element is satisfied by proof that the defendant severed the property from the victim's possession. The possessor is often the owner, but not necessarily so. For instance, if a defendant steals a rental car from the possession of the renter, the taking element is satisfied even though the car is owned by the rental car company. As noted, converting property after being given valid possession of that property cannot be larceny because there is no trespass. Thus, if A loans B his car and B decides to keep it, B is not guilty of larceny since B already had possession when he decided to keep the car. It is possible that B would be guilty of embezzlement. However, one who has mere custody instead of possession can be guilty of a trespassory taking by converting the custody to possession. An employee who is provided a computer by his employer for work purposes only has custody while the employer maintains constructive possession of the computer. Should the employee decide to keep the computer and never return it, he would be guilty of larceny since the taking was trespassory. Or, as noted above, a customer who takes physical control of a garment ostensibly to try it on but then secrets the garment in a backpack has committed a trespassory taking.

The carrying away, or asportation, of the personal property requires some slight movement of the property. The movement must involve carrying away; flipping the property over, for instance, would not satisfy this element. Only personal property can be the subject of larceny, because only personal property can be carried away. Thus, theft of land, services, or intellectual property could not satisfy the actus reus for larceny.

As noted, larceny requires a trespassory taking of the property from the *possession* of another without the possessor's consent. Severance of possession is the key, not severance from someone's ownership. It is possible that an owner could be guilty of larceny of his own property by taking it from someone who at the time has a valid possessory interest in the property. For instance, a mechanic has a lien and therefore a possessory interest on an automobile until the owner pays for the repairs. In the event that the owner takes the car without making payment, he would be committing the requisite trespassory taking and carrying away of larceny.

Finally, like all theft offenses, the prosecution must prove that the defendant intended to permanently deprive the victim of the property. Normally, that specific mens rea will concur with the taking and carrying away, meaning the taking and carrying away will be set in motion by the intent to permanently deprive (also called the intent to steal). However, if a defendant intends to deprive the victim only temporarily at the time of the trespassory taking, but prior to returning the property forms the intent to permanently deprive, the crime of larceny is established through the doctrine of continuing trespass. This doctrine arose to address this concurrence impediment and is based on the theory that the trespassory taking continues for the duration of the unlawful possession. Accordingly, the moment the intent to permanently deprive is formed, there is concurrence between the actus reus and mens rea establishing larceny.

A. Trespassory Taking

United States v. Rogers
289 F.2d 433 (1961)
Fourth Circuit Court of Appeals

HAYNSWORTH, J.

The defendant has appealed from his conviction under the "bank robbery statute," complaining that the proof did not show the commission of larceny and that the verdict of the jury was coerced by the Court's instructions.

There was testimony showing that, at the request of his brother, the defendant took a payroll check, payable to the brother in the face amount of $97.92, to a bank where the brother maintained an account. In accordance with the brother's request, he asked the teller to deposit $80 to the credit of the brother's account and to deliver to him the balance of the check in case. The teller was inexperienced. She first inquired of another teller whether the check could be credited to an account in part and cashed in part. Having been told that this was permissible, she required the defendant's endorsement on the check, and, misreading its date (12 06 59) as the amount payable, she deducted the $80 deposit and placed $1,126.59 on the counter. There were two strapped packages, each containing $500, and $126.59 in miscellaneous bills and change. The defendant took the $1,126.59 in cash thus placed upon the counter and departed.

There was also testimony that when the day's business was done, the teller who handled the transaction was found to be short in her accounts by $1,108.67, the exact amount of the difference between the $1,206.59, for which she had supposed the check to have been drawn, and $97.92, its actual face amount, and that her adding machine tape showed that she had accepted the check as having been drawn for $1,206.59.

There was corroboration from other witnesses of some phases of this story as told by the tellers and the bookkeeper.

The defendant agreed that he took the check to the bank for his brother, asked that $80 be credited to his brother's account, and that the excess be paid to him in case. He stated, however, that he received in cash only the $17.92, to which he was entitled, denying that he had received the larger sum.

The case was submitted to the jury under instructions that they should find the defendant guilty if they found the much larger sum was placed upon the counter and was taken by the defendant with the intention to appropriate the overpayment, or if he thereafter formed the intention to, and did, appropriate the overpayment to his own use.

An essential element of the crime of larceny, the "'felonious taking and carrying' away the personal goods of another," is that the taking must be trespassory. It is an invasion of the other's right to possession, and therein is found the principal distinction between larceny and other related offenses.

It has long been recognized, however, that when the transferor acts under a unilateral mistake of fact, his delivery of a chattel may be ineffective to transfer title or his right to possession. If the transferee [here the defendant], knowing of the transferor's mistake [here the teller], receives the goods with the intention of appropriating them, his receipt and removal of them is a trespass and his offense is larceny.

Such a situation was presented in *Regina v. Middleton*, 28 Law Times (N.S.) 777, 12 Cox C.C. 417 (1873). There it appeared that the defendant had a credit balance of 11 $. in a postal savings account. He obtained a warrant for the withdrawal of 10 $. which he presented to the postal clerk. The clerk mistakenly referred to the wrong letter of advice, one which had been received in connection with the prospective withdrawal of a much larger sum by another depositor. The clerk then placed upon the counter a 5 L note, 3 sovereigns, a half crown and silver and copper amounting altogether to 8 L 16 $. 10 d. The defendant gathered up the money and departed. The jury found that the defendant was aware of the clerk's mistake and took the money with intent to steal it. His conviction of larceny was affirmed by the Court of Criminal Appeals, the fifteen judges dividing eleven to four. . . .

Subsequently, it appears to have become settled in England that, if the initial receipt of the chattel is innocent, its subsequent conversion cannot be larceny [because there is no *trespassory* taking], but, if the recipient knows at the time he is receiving more than his due and intends to convert it to his own use, he is guilty of larceny. That is the established rule of the American cases.

In *Wolfstein v. People*, 1875, 6 Hun, N.Y., 121, it appeared that the defendant presented for payment a French bill of exchange for $74 in gold. The teller, unfamiliar with French, misread the bill and paid the defendant $742. The defendant knew, at the time of his receipt of the larger sum, that he was entitled only to $74. It was held that he was guilty of larceny.

The same result has been reached in similar cases.

The District Court went too far, however, when it told the jury it might convict if, though his initial receipt of the overpayment was innocent, the defendant thereafter formed the intention to, and did, convert the overpayment.

Upon the retrial, therefore, the jury should be instructed that among the essential elements of the offense are (1) that the defendant knew when he received the money from the teller or picked it up from the counter that it was more than his due and (2) that he took it from the bank with the intention of converting it.

The judgment is reversed and the case remanded for further proceedings not inconsistent with this opinion.

Notes and Questions

1. The crimes of embezzlement, theft by false pretenses, and larceny by trick were created to fill in gaps in the law of larceny. The court, however, indicated that even if Rogers initially took the money knowing that it had been given to him by mistake and decided to keep it, he could only be convicted of larceny: "The indictment charged larceny and the evidence offered by the prosecution, if accepted by the jury, proved the commission of that crime, not false pretense, embezzlement or some other lesser offense." *Id.* at 438. After reviewing the subsequent sections, can you explain why he is not guilty of embezzlement, larceny by trick, or false pretenses?

2. According to the court, Rogers is not guilty of larceny if he took the money without realizing the teller's mistake. What if he decides to keep the money once he becomes aware of the teller's mistake?

3. Normally, proof of the trespassory taking also proves the carrying away element. But is it possible to prove the carrying away element of larceny without proving the taking element? The answer is yes. Imagine a defendant who decides to steal a leather jacket from a department store by grabbing it and running from the store. He grabs it off the rack and starts running, only to learn that the jacket is secured to the rack by a chain and lock. While he moved the jacket enough to prove asportation, he never severed the property from the owner's possession. Accordingly, this evidence would support convicting the defendant for attempted larceny (note that the impossibility of completing the crime is no defense to the attempt), but not larceny.

4. How much movement is required to satisfy the asportation/carrying away element? Not much, but some. For example, in *State v. Carswell*, 249 S.E.2d 427 (N.C. 1978), the defendants pried an air conditioner out of the window in which it was secured and moved it about 18 inches before abandoning the theft. The court held that this 18-inch movement was sufficient to prove the asportation element. The court contrasted this evidence with that in the case of *State v. Jones*, 65 N.C. 395 (N.C. 1871), where the defendant merely turned a large barrel of turpentine that was standing on its head, over on its side. Because doing so didn't even slightly move the barrel from its location, there was no asportation.

5. What if the defendant had just dropped the extra cash on the floor shortly after he took it and then left the bank? Would he still be guilty of larceny? So long as the prosecution proves that when he took the cash, he intended to keep it, the answer is yes. He may very well have thought better of his decision and changed his mind, but once the evidence proves concurrence between the actus reus (taking and carrying away) and the mens rea (with intent to permanently deprive), the crime is established. The defendant may almost immediately change his mind, but he can't "put the toothpaste back in the tube."

6. Converting custody to possession with the requisite intent to steal also proves larceny. Shoplifting is a classic example: the merchant gives implied consent to take custody of the merchandise for the limited purpose of examining it and then taking it to the register for purchase. If the defendant secrets the merchandise with an intent to steal it, that is larceny because there was a trespassory conversion from custody to possession. The same rule would apply to a customer who goes to purchase an item and, realizing he does not have enough money to pay, throws what he has on the counter and dashes out with the item.

7. What about the situation where a package is misdelivered? Eve, who lives in the upstairs unit, ordered several items from Garden.com, an online retailer. The retailer ships the items addressed to Eve but the postal carrier mistakenly delivers them to the basement unit occupied by Adam. Adam returns home that night and brings the package into his apartment only then realizing it is addressed to Eve. Applying the State of Maine's theft provision which follows, is there a point where Adam committed a theft offense? Consider what additional facts/information would either shift or solidify your answer.

§ 356-A. Theft of lost, mislaid or mistakenly delivered property

1. A person is guilty of theft if:

A. The person obtains or exercises control over the property of another that the person knows to have been lost or mislaid or to have been delivered under a mistake as to the identity of the recipient or as to the nature or amount of the property and, with the intent to deprive the owner of the property at any time subsequent to acquiring it, the person fails to take reasonable measures to return it. Violation of this paragraph is a Class E crime....

B. Intent to Permanently Deprive

The intent to permanently deprive the victim of property is, as noted above, the *sine qua non* of theft offenses. The following cases illustrate this requirement and some of the challenges associated with proving such intent.

Stepp v. State

20 S.W. 753 (1892)

Texas Court of Criminal Appeals

Appellant was convicted of theft of a watch, and sentenced to two years in the penitentiary, from which judgment he appeals.

It appears that on the 25th of June, 1891, Miss Arnett lost a watch at the depot at Bertram, but did not miss it until she was on the train; and they searched the train, but could not find it. It was the property of Miss Wilson, of the same place, who had loaned it to Miss Arnett. Defendant was at the depot on the night it was lost. A few days after, defendant suggested to a witness the propriety of offering a reward for it. On the 24th of October defendant stated to Dr. McCollum, who had married Miss Wilson, he had seen a man in his shop with a watch with the name "Wilson" scratched in it, and defendant wanted to know if witness McCollum would pay $25 for it. Witness replied he would pay $25 for the watch and man. Defendant lived at Liberty Hill, in Williamson County. He next day telephoned that he had the watch, and it cost him $35 to get it from a man in Austin. That night, by agreement, Dr. Wilson, the father of Mrs. McCollum, met defendant at the depot, who returned the watch.

The indictment in this case is skillfully drawn. It contains six counts, and covers every phase of ownership—theft from the person, theft, and receiving stolen property. There seems to be no doubt of the fact that defendant found the watch in question, either in the depot or in the street, and that he kept possession of it until its return some four months after. Two material questions arise upon the facts:

1. When he found the watch, did he know the owner, or have reason to believe the owner could be found by ordinary inquiry? We think defendant was put upon fair notice of the ownership. If he did not find the watch in the depot, where the young ladies had been awaiting the train, yet the facts that he saw them there, and knew of their presence in the immediate vicinity in which the watch was found, also the fact that it was a lady's watch, with the family name of the owner clearly legible thereon, point with sufficient certainty to the owner.

2. If he knew or could have known the owner by ordinary diligence, with what intent did he retain possession of the property? Was it to appropriate it to his own use, or to obtain a reward for finding it? If to appropriate it to his own use, it was theft, and the conviction is correct, unless it was voluntarily returned within a reasonable time. A voluntary return must be a return willingly made by the defendant, whatever be the motive inducing it. *Allen v. The State*, 12 Texas Ct. App. 190 [12 Tex. Crim. 190].

But it cannot be made when defendant is caught in possession of the stolen property (*Grant v. The State*, 2 Texas Court of Appeals 167 [2 Tex. Crim. 167]; nor when the defendant is caught in the act (*Harris v. The State*, 29 Texas Court of Appeals 104 [29 Tex. Crim. 104]; *Boze's case, ante*, 347); nor after prosecution is begun. Penal Code, art. 738. We think the property was voluntarily returned, it being made directly to Dr. Wilson, without demanding any reward. But four months is hardly a reasonable time. It was a question for the jury, and they evidently thought the time of detention was unreasonable.

But it is contended that the object of holding possession was to obtain a reward; that this is shown by a remark made by defendant, that Dr. Wilson ought to offer a reward for the watch, and by his offer to Dr. Wilson's son-in-law to get the watch if he would pay $25.

These questions were submitted to the jury by the following charge of the court:

> "When a man finds goods that are lost, and appropriates them with intent to take entire dominion over them, he at the same time knowing or really believing the owner can be found, the offense would be theft. . . ."

Reed v. The State, 8 Texas Ct. App. 41 [8 Tex. Crim. 41]; *Warren v. The State*, 17 Texas Ct. App. 207 [17 Tex. Crim. 207]; *Wilson v. The State*, 20 Texas Ct. App. 662 [20 Tex. Crim. 662].

Again, after charging the statute on voluntary return (Penal Code, article 738), the court says: "Whether or not property has been returned within a reasonable time is, like all other facts, a question for the jury, to be determined from all the facts and circumstances in evidence before you." . . .

These instructions were sufficient, and certainly as fair as defendant could ask; but the jury, in view of the facts that the defendant had several times claimed the watch as his own, and that on one occasion he was apparently trying to trade it off, together with the length of time he held possession, came to the conclusion he intended to appropriate it, and we cannot say they erred.

Affirmed.

Notes and Questions

1. In the 1894 case of *People v. Brown*, 105 Cal. 66 (1894), the California Supreme Court overturned a larceny conviction because the trial judge instructed the jury that they should convict if they found the defendant had the intent to *temporarily* deprive the owner of the property. In that case, a disgruntled teenage worker unlawfully took a bicycle that belonged to the victim. This satisfied the trespassory taking and movement elements of larceny. The defendant then abandoned the bicycle in a location where it was likely to be discovered. The defense argued this indicated the defendant's expectation the owner would find the bike thereby establishing an intent to deprive temporarily but not permanently. Because of the erroneous instruction, it

was therefore unclear whether the jury convicted the defendant based on a finding of intent to permanently deprive or an intent to temporarily deprive, necessitating reversal. But note that abandoning property, depending on the circumstances of the abandonment, may support a finding of intent to permanently deprive. So long as the fact-finder is convinced the defendant intended to prevent recovery of the property, the requisite intent is established. In other words, abandonment of property, like other dispositions such as pawning of property, is circumstantial evidence of intent: it is not dispositive but may be probative.

2. It is not uncommon for someone who unlawfully takes property to pawn it for a loan. Pawn shops normally offer two options: they will purchase the property outright or will hold the property as collateral for a loan, with ownership vesting in the pawn shop if the loan is not repaid in the designated time. If a defendant sells property to the pawn shop, it is powerful evidence of intent to permanently deprive. But what if the property is pawned for a loan and the defendant is still within the redemption period? This could very easily create reasonable doubt as to the intent to permanently deprive. In such a case, however, evidence that the defendant was unable to raise the money needed to redeem the pawn will allow the fact-finder to impute an intent to permanently deprive. In other words, the intent to permanently deprive exists even if the defendant *desires* to recover and return the property, when it is virtually impossible that he will be able to do so. *See Marsh v. Commonwealth*, 704 S.E.2d 624 (Va. 2011).

3. What if a defendant unlawfully takes property intending to return it, but something happens while she has the property that prevents the return? For example, consider joyriding. Joyriding is a very common crime defined as the trespassory taking of an automobile *without* the intent to permanently deprive. What if A takes a car for a joyride, and while driving, the car is in an accident, thus preventing the car from being returned in the same condition as it was when it was unlawfully taken? Is the defendant now guilty of larceny? The answer depends on *why* the property was damaged or destroyed. Intent to steal may be imputed to the defendant, but only where the evidence establishes the damage or destruction was the result of the defendant recklessly exposing the property to risk. Thus, if A takes the car for a joyride, and B runs a red light and collides with the car, A is not guilty of larceny (grand theft auto) even though the property cannot be returned in the same condition, because there is no basis for imputing intent to steal. If the collision is the result of A's reckless driving, however, the intent to steal may be imputed to A.

4. The question of whether larceny is established by retaining "found" property is complex. First, there is the question of whether the property was in fact that of another or whether it was abandoned. If abandoned, the taking cannot be trespassory. This means in a case of found property, it is the prosecution's burden to prove beyond a reasonable doubt that the property *was not* abandoned. But that is just the beginning. As the court notes in *Stepp v. State*, a defendant who finds property intending to return it to the owner has not committed larceny as there is no intent to permanently deprive. Note that in *Stepp*, the court concluded that the totality of

the evidence was sufficient to support a jury finding that Stepp did not intend to return the property in a reasonable time, therefore proving an intent to permanently deprive. (In an omitted portion of the opinion, the court stated that if Stepp intended to return the property for a reward, it would not qualify as larceny. As explained below, this is no longer the rule applicable to so-called reward cases. Because the defendant cannot control whether the reward will be offered, the intent to steal is not "conditioned" on the hope of return in exchange for reward.)

But what if the property is not in fact abandoned, but the defendant makes an honest mistake that it is? Such an honest yet mistaken belief is a complete obstacle to proving a theft offense like larceny, because the honest belief is inconsistent with an intent to permanently deprive *another* of his or her property. Accordingly, when a defendant asserts that he took and retained property because he believed it was abandoned, a conviction for larceny requires proof beyond a reasonable doubt that (1) the property was not abandoned, and (2) the defendant did not believe it was abandoned.

5. What if a defendant returns the property or substitutes equal value? Such action is a relevant consideration when determining the defendant's intent, but is not dispositive. If the fact-finder concludes that, at the time of the taking or at any time prior to return of or payment for the property, the defendant intended to steal it, she is guilty of larceny. Nonetheless, such action by the defendant certainly makes proof of that mens rea more complicated.

C. The "Refund" Case

People v. Davis
965 P.2d 1165 (1998)
California Supreme Court

We granted review to determine what crime is committed in the following circumstances: the defendant enters a store and picks up an item of merchandise displayed for sale, intending to claim that he owns it and to "return" it for cash or credit; he carries the item to a sales counter and asks the clerk for a "refund"; without the defendant's knowledge his conduct has been observed by a store security agent, who instructs the clerk to give him credit for the item; the clerk gives the defendant a credit voucher, and the agent detains him as he leaves the counter with the voucher; he is charged with theft of the item. In the case at bar the Court of Appeal held the defendant is guilty of theft by trespassory larceny. We agree, and therefore affirm the judgment of the Court of Appeal.

Facts

Defendant entered a Mervyn's department store carrying a Mervyn's shopping bag. As he entered he was placed under camera surveillance by store security agent Carol German. While German both watched and filmed, defendant went to the men's department and took a shirt displayed for sale from its hanger; he then carried the shirt through the shoe department and into the women's department on the other side of the store. There he placed the shirt on a sales counter and told cashier Heather Smith that he had "bought it for his father" but it didn't fit and he wanted to "return" it. Smith asked him if he had the receipt, but he said he did not because "it was a gift." Smith informed him that if the value of a returned item is more than $20 and there is no receipt, the store policy is not to make a cash refund but to issue a Mervyn's credit voucher. At that point Smith was interrupted by a telephone call from German; German asked her if defendant was trying to "return" the shirt, and directed her to issue a credit voucher. Smith prepared the voucher and asked defendant to sign it; he did so, but used a false name. German detained him as he walked away from the counter with the voucher. Upon being questioned in the store security office, defendant gave a second false name and three different dates of birth; he also told German that he needed money to buy football cleats, asked her if they could "work something out," and offered to pay for the shirt.

Count 1 of the information charged defendant with the crime of petty theft . . . alleging that defendant did "steal, take and carry away the personal property" of Mervyn's. . . . In a motion for judgment of acquittal filed after the People presented their case, defendant argued that on the facts shown he could be convicted of no more than an *attempt* to commit petty theft, and therefore sought dismissal of the petty theft charge. The court denied the motion.

The only theories of theft submitted to the jury in the instructions were theft by larceny and theft by trick and device. The jury found defendant guilty of petty theft as charged in the information.

I

The elements of theft by larceny are well settled: the offense is committed by every person who (1) takes possession (2) of personal property (3) owned or possessed by another, (4) by means of trespass and (5) with intent to steal the property, and (6) carries the property away. . . . The intent to steal or *animus furandi* is the intent, without a good faith claim of right, to permanently deprive the owner of possession. And if the taking has begun, the slightest movement of the property constitutes a carrying away or asportation. Applying these rules to the facts of the case at bar, we have no doubt that defendant (1) took possession (2) of personal property—the shirt—(3) owned by Mervyn's and (4) moved it sufficiently to satisfy the asportation requirement. Defendant does not contend otherwise.

Defendant does contend, however, that the elements of trespass and intent to steal are lacking. He predicates his argument on a distinction that he draws by dividing his course of conduct into two distinct "acts." According to defendant, his first "act" was to take the shirt from the display rack and carry it to Smith's cash register. He contends that act lacked the element of intent to steal because he had no intent to permanently deprive Mervyn's *of the shirt*; he intended to have the shirt in his possession only long enough to exchange it for a "refund." His second "act," also according to defendant, was to misrepresent to Smith that he had bought the shirt at Mervyn's and to accept the credit voucher she issued. He contends that act lacked the element of trespass because the store, acting through its agent German, *consented* to the issuance of the voucher with full knowledge of how he came into possession of the shirt.

Defendant's argument misses the mark on two grounds: it focuses on the wrong issue of consent, and it views that issue in artificial isolation from the intertwined issue of intent to steal.

To begin with, the question is not whether Mervyn's consented to Smith's issuance of the voucher after defendant asked to "return" the shirt; rather, the question is whether Mervyn's consented to defendant's taking the shirt in the first instance. As the Court of Appeal correctly reasoned, a self-service store like Mervyn's impliedly consents to a customer's picking up and handling an item displayed for sale and carrying it from the display area to a sales counter with the intent of purchasing it; the store manifestly does not consent, however, to a customer's removing an item from a shelf or hanger if the customer's intent in taking possession of the item is to steal it. . . .

In these circumstances the issue of consent — and therefore trespass — depends on the issue of intent to steal. We turn to that issue.

As noted earlier, the general rule is that the intent to steal required for conviction of larceny is an intent to deprive the owner *permanently* of possession of the property. (*People v. Brown* (1894) 105 Cal. 66, 69 [38 P. 518]; *People v. Jaso* (1970) 4 Cal. App.3d 767, 771-772 [84 Cal.Rptr. 567]; *People v. Turner* (1968) 267 Cal.App.2d 440, 444 [73 Cal.Rptr. 263, 38 A.L.R.3d 940].) For example, we have said it *would not* be larceny for a youth to take and hide another's bicycle to "get even" for being teased, if he intends to return it the following day. (*People v. Brown, supra,* 105 Cal. at p. 69.) But the general rule is not inflexible: "The word 'permanently,' as used here is not to be taken literally." (Perkins [& Boyce], *supra,* at p. 327.) Our research discloses three relevant categories of cases holding that the requisite intent to steal may be found even though the defendant's primary purpose in taking the property is not to deprive the owner permanently of possession: i.e., (1) when the defendant intends to "sell" the property back to its owner, (2) when the defendant intends to claim a reward for "finding" the property, and (3) when, as here, the defendant intends to return the property to its owner for a "refund." . . .

A. *The "sale" cases*

The classic case of the first category is *Regina v. Hall* (1848) 169 Eng.Rep. 291. The defendant, an employee of a man named Atkin who made candles from tallow, took a quantity of tallow owned by Atkin and put it on Atkin's own scales, claiming it belonged to a butcher who was offering to sell it to Atkin. The jury were instructed that if they found the defendant took Atkin's property with the intent to sell it back to him as if it belonged to another and appropriate the proceeds, he was guilty of larceny. The jury so found, and the conviction was upheld on further review.

The defendant contended that his assertion of temporary ownership of the property for a particular purpose was not enough to constitute the required intent to permanently deprive. The justices expressed two rationales for holding to the contrary. First, one justice stressed that the deprivation would in fact have been permanent unless the owner had agreed to the condition imposed by the defendant, i.e., to "buy" the property. . . .

Perkins offers yet another rationale for the rule that a defendant who takes property for the purpose of "selling" it back to its owner has the requisite intent to permanently deprive: by so doing the defendant creates a *substantial risk of permanent loss*, because if the owner does not buy back his property the defendant will have a powerful incentive to keep it in order to conceal the theft. . . .

B. *The "reward" cases*

The cases in the second category hold that a defendant who takes property for the purpose of claiming a reward for "finding" it has the requisite intent to permanently deprive. . . .

[A] line of cases in this category also noted the taker's intent to appropriate "part of the value" of the property, but went on to emphasize a different rationale, i.e., that the taker had made the return of the property *contingent* on the offer of a satisfactory reward, and if the contingency did not materialize the taker would keep the property. . . .

The third category comprises a substantial number of recent cases from our sister states affirming larceny convictions on facts identical or closely similar to those of the case at bar: in each, the defendant took an item of merchandise from a store display, carried it to a sales counter, claimed to own it, and asked for a "refund" of cash or credit. . . .

. . . .

Several of the rationales articulated in the "sale" and "reward" cases, however, are also applicable to the "refund" cases. On close analysis, moreover, the relevant rationales may be reduced to a single line of reasoning that rests on both a principled and a practical basis.

First, as a matter of principle, a claim of the right to "return" an item taken from a store display is no less an assertion of a *right of ownership* than the claim of a right to "sell" stolen property back to its owner. (*Regina v. Hall, supra*, 169 Eng.Rep. 291, 292.) And an intent to return such an item to the store only if the store pays a satisfactory "refund" is no less *conditional* than an intent to return stolen property to its owner only if the owner pays a satisfactory "reward." (*Berry v. State, supra*, 31 Ohio St. 219, 227.) Just as in the latter case, it can be said in the former that "the purpose to return was founded wholly on the contingency that a [refund] would be offered, and unless the contingency happened the conversion was complete." (*Ibid.*) It follows that a defendant who takes an item from a store display with the intent to claim its ownership and restore it only on condition that the store pay him a "refund" must be deemed to intend to permanently deprive the store of the item within the meaning of the law of larceny.

Second, as a practical matter, the risk that such a taking will be permanent is not a mere theoretical possibility; rather, by taking an item from a store display with the intent to demand a refund a defendant creates a substantial risk of permanent loss. . . .

This, too, is not a mere theoretical possibility: our research discloses a number of cases in which a defendant, rebuffed in an attempt to "return" an item taken from a display in the same store, simply took the item with him when he left the store. The most recent example is the California case of *People v. McLemore* (1994) 27 Cal. App.4th 601 [32 Cal.Rptr.2d 687]. There the defendant entered a store empty-handed but subsequently asked a sales clerk to "exchange" a dress he was then carrying; the clerk became suspicious when she noticed that the dress still bore an electronic sensor and a complete sales tag (such tags were normally torn in half when items were purchased). The clerk called the manager, who asked for a receipt. The defendant became angry and demanded the dress back, insisting it was his. The manager handed him the dress, and the defendant left the store with it. . . .

III

Applying the foregoing reasoning to the facts of the case at bar, we conclude that defendant's intent to claim ownership of the shirt and to return it to Mervyn's only on condition that the store pay him a "refund" constitutes an intent to permanently deprive Mervyn's of the shirt within the meaning of the law of larceny, and hence an intent to "feloniously steal" that property within the meaning of Penal Code section 484, subdivision (a) . . . . Because Mervyn's cannot be deemed to have consented to defendant's taking possession of the shirt with the intent to steal it, defendant's conduct also constituted a trespassory taking within the meaning of the law of larceny. It follows that the evidence supports the final two elements of the offense of theft by larceny, and the Court of Appeal was correct to affirm the judgment of conviction.

For the foregoing reasons the judgment of the Court of Appeal is affirmed.

Notes and Questions

People v. Davis stands for a simple yet important principle: intent to steal cannot be qualified or "conditioned" on the actions of a third party. Why? Because of the inference that the failure of the third party to take the hoped for action will result in the permanent deprivation of the property.

III. Obtaining Property Through Deception: Larceny by Trick and False Pretenses

The common law crime of larceny did not extend to a situation in which an individual obtains the property of another through deception. Two crimes were created to fill this gap: larceny by trick and theft by false pretenses. The difference between these two closely related offenses is, as noted above, indicated by the level of control gained over the property as a result of the deception. Larceny by trick is committed when an individual uses deception to obtain *possession* of another's property with the intent to permanently deprive. False pretenses occurs when an individual uses deception to obtain *title* to another's property with intent to permanently deprive.

To illustrate the distinction, suppose that A rents a car to use in a bank robbery. He has no intention of ever returning the car when he rents it, but represents to the rental car agency that he will return it in a few days. A is guilty of larceny by trick, because he was only obtaining possession from the rental car agency. The deception negates the consent, and therefore, his taking of the car was really trespassory. Suppose instead that A uses counterfeit money to purchase a car with the intent of using it in a bank robbery. A used fraud to obtain title to the car and thus is guilty of theft by false pretenses; there is no larceny offense here, because although obtained by deception, A had title to the property before it was actually taken, hence no trespass occurred.

The following case explores the distinction in more detail.

People v. Phebus
323 N.W.2d 423 (1982)
Michigan Court of Appeals

Which criminal offense, larceny [by trick] or obtaining property by false pretenses, is committed when a shopper switches a price tag on merchandise he proposes to buy so that a lower price appears on the merchandise?

Defendant was charged with larceny [by trick] .... At the preliminary examination, a store detective for Meijer Thrifty Acres testified that she had observed defendant remove a price tag marked $1.88 from an unfinished decorator shelf and place it on a finished decorator shelf, which had been marked $6.53. ... Defendant and his wife went through the check-out area and paid the marked price of $1.88 for the finished shelf usually priced $6.53. While defendant was loading his car with the merchandise he had purchased, he was stopped by the store detectives....

Defendant was bound over for trial on the charged offense.... [T]he Jackson County Circuit Court quashed the information [dismissed the charge], finding that the elements of false pretenses, but not those of larceny [by trick], were made out at the preliminary examination. The prosecution has appealed....

To establish the crime of false pretenses, the prosecution must show that a representation as to an existing fact was false and was made with the knowledge of falsity and with the intent to deceive and that the person sought to be deceived relied thereon to his detriment.

Although the elements of the two crimes are quite distinct, the determination of whether a certain course of action should be punished under one statute or the other is often not easily made. The Supreme Court noted recently in *People v. Long*, 409 Mich 346, 350–351 (1980):

> There is, to be sure, a narrow margin between a case of larceny [by trick] and one where the property has been obtained by false pretenses. The distinction is a very nice one, but still very important. The character of the crime depends upon the intention of the parties, and that intention determines the nature of the offense. In the former case, where, by fraud, conspiracy, or artifice, the possession is obtained with a felonious design, and the title still remains in the owner, larceny is established; while in the latter, where title, as well as possession is absolutely parted with, the crime is false pretenses. It will be observed that the intention of the owner to part with his property is the gist and essence of the offense of larceny, and the vital point upon which the crime hinges and is to be determined.

This distinction is consistent with that made in other jurisdictions.

. . . .

Based on this distinction, we conclude that here, where defendant attempted to secure both title and possession of the shelf, the applicable crime is false pretenses.

The prosecutor contends that, because the defendant switched price tags, the store clerk did not know the nature and the value of the property she was parting with and, because of this mistake of fact, title did not effectively pass to the defendant. In any crime of false pretenses, however, the victim is induced to part with title through a misrepresentation of fact. Whenever a victim relies upon the misrepresentation and passes title to a defendant, a completed crime of false pretenses is shown.

In other jurisdictions that have addressed this question, courts have held that a shopper who has switched price tags and effectively secured title should be prosecuted for false pretenses. We agree.

Notes and Questions

1. According to a recent study, "refund fraud" costs merchants approximately $16 billion a year. In general, a refund fraud scam goes like this: An individual purchases an item—a laptop computer, for instance—and leaves the store with it. Then he comes back to the store and picks up an identical laptop computer, takes that item and the receipt from the original purchase to the returns desk, claiming that it is

the item he bought, and requests a refund for it. He keeps the original laptop computer, and pays nothing for it. Professional shoplifters like refund fraud because it's relatively safe. Since they never actually steal an object from the store, they are not chased down in the parking lot. Which crime—larceny by trick or false pretenses—is committed when someone engages in "refund fraud"?

2. Why does the law distinguish larceny by trick from theft by false pretenses when the essence of each offense is the use of deception to "trick" the victim into passing the property to the deceiver? The answer lies in what is passed. Larceny by trick is a variant of larceny, meaning there is evidence of the essential trespassory taking. The apparent consent to take the property is treated as invalid because it is procured by the deception. Without valid consent, the taking is trespassory, hence a larceny offense. In contrast, the deception in a false pretenses case results in the transfer of legal title. As a result, the deceiver actually owns the property before it is taken and moved, even though the ownership is procured by deception. This means there is no trespassory taking and carrying away, necessitating the statutory crime of false pretenses.

3. Imagine a defendant takes a shirt off the rack at Macy's and carries it to the cashier. The defendant tells the cashier that he is returning the shirt but lost the receipt. The defendant is a well-known customer, so the cashier agrees to make an exception to the normal rule and gives the defendant a cash refund for the shirt. The defendant then leaves. What theft offense or offenses has the defendant committed?

IV. Embezzlement

The crime of embezzlement was created to address the situation in which an individual obtains valid possession of another's property in a non-trespassory manner but later decides to unlawfully convert the property and permanently deprive the owner of it. While the essence of larceny is the trespass, the essence of embezzlement is the abuse of entrustment. This is why embezzlement usually occurs when the defendant has been entrusted with possession of another's property but later decides to convert the property and permanently deprive. Embezzlement is a crime because it is a breach of that trust.

Commonwealth v. Ryan
30 N.E. 364 (1892)
Massachusetts Supreme Court

Holmes, J.

This is a complaint for embezzlement of money. The case for the government is as follows. The defendant was employed by one Sullivan to sell liquor for him in his store. Sullivan sent two detectives to the store, with marked money of Sullivan's, to make a feigned purchase from the defendant. One detective did so. The defendant dropped the money into the money drawer of a cash register, which happened to be open in connection with another sale made and registered by the defendant, but he did not register this sale, as was customary, and afterward—it would seem within a minute or two—he took the money from the drawer. The question presented is whether it appears, as matter of law, that the defendant was not guilty of embezzlement, but was guilty of larceny, if of anything. The defendant asked rulings to that effect on two grounds: first, that after the money was put into the drawer it was in Sullivan's possession, and therefore the removal of it was a trespass and larceny; and secondly, that Sullivan's ownership of the money, in some way not fully explained, prevented the offence from being embezzlement. We will consider these positions successively.

We must take it as settled that it is not larceny for a servant to convert property delivered to him by a third person for his master, provided he does so before the goods have reached their destination, or something more has happened to reduce him to a mere custodian; while, on the other hand, if the property is delivered to the servant by his master, the conversion is larceny. . . .

It follows from what we have said that the defendant's first position cannot be maintained, and that the judge was right in charging the jury that, if the defendant before he placed the money in the drawer intended to appropriate it, and with that intent simply put it in the drawer for his own convenience in keeping it for himself, that would not make his appropriation of it just afterwards larceny. . . .

With regard to the defendant's second position, we see no ground for contending that the detective in his doings was a servant of Sullivan, or that he had not a true possession of the money, if that question were open, which it is not. The only question reserved by the exceptions is whether Sullivan's ownership of the money prevented the defendant's act from being embezzlement. It has been supposed to make a difference if the right of possession in the chattel converted by the servant has vested in the master previous to the delivery to the servant by the third person. But this notion, if anything more than a defective statement of the decisions as to delivery into the master's barge or cart does not apply to a case like the present, which has been regarded as embezzlement in England for the last hundred years. . . . If we were to depart from the English decisions, it would not be in the way of introducing further distinctions.

Exceptions overruled [conviction affirmed].

Notes and Questions

1. A defendant can only be convicted of embezzlement if he has valid possession of the personal property of another. Therefore, it is important to distinguish between possession and custody. As noted earlier, a person who has possession tends to have broad authority over the property, whereas someone with custody has physical control over the property but very limited authority. The best example is the employer-employee relationship. Generally, an employer retains possession of company property even when an employee is in physical control of that property. For instance, an employer provides laptops to employees who sign a document agreeing that they may use the

laptop exclusively for work-related business. The employer retains constructive possession of the laptop even though the employee takes the laptop home and on business trips. If the employee decides to steal the laptop, he is guilty of larceny. In contrast, consider a customer who rents a car: the customer has possession of the car during the rental period, but the rental company retains ownership. That means if the customer decides to sell the car to a chop shop and make a false report of theft, it is not larceny because there was no trespassory taking. But what if the customer had already decided to sell the car at the time of the rental agreement was executed?

2. As the court notes in *Ryan,* when an employee receives property directly from a third party, the employee has possession until the property is transferred to the employer. The employee would be guilty of embezzlement if he keeps it, since he already had possession. Once the property is transferred to the employer, the employer has possession, and an employee who takes the property is guilty of larceny. Because Ryan never transferred the property to his employer, he is guilty of embezzlement.

3. Putting it all together.

Imagine a woman wants to buy a minivan for her growing family. She goes to the dealership and the salesman offers to let her take a minivan for a test drive. She agrees, and he gives her the keys, takes a copy of her license, and gives her a very limited route to take around the block and come back. When she drives off the lot, what level of control does she have? Custody. She may have physical control of the van but the consent to take the van is extremely limited. So if she drives away and sells the car to a chop shop, that is larceny because transforming custody to ownership (to sell it) or possession is a trespassory taking. But what if she drives away intending to return the car, but while on the test drive, changes her mind and decides to steal the car? Notice that in this situation, because the trespass results from exceeding the scope of the custody, the "trespassory taking" occurs when she decides to drive off and sell the car, and if she does so with intent to permanently deprive, that is larceny.

Now imagine she brings the van back after the test drive. She tells the salesman she likes it but doesn't want to make a decision unless her significant other agrees. The salesman says, "I have an idea. It is a long weekend. Just take the van all weekend and use it however you like. Really enjoy it to see if it works for your family." The woman says, "Great!" and drives off. What level of control does she have? Possession. The dealership retains title, but she has complete dominion over the van for the duration of the loan. Why is this important? Because if she then sells the van, there is a critical question to resolve: when did she decide to sell it? If she decided to sell it *before* she took it and drove off, she deceived the salesman into believing she would bring it back. Accordingly, the possession was obtained by a "trick"; a false representation that materially impacted the decision to give possession. This "trick" negates the consent and renders the taking trespassory. Hence *larceny by trick.*

But what if she fully intended to bring it back after the weekend but during the weekend decides to sell it? That can't be larceny because the consent to take possession was completely valid. In other words, a defendant who is given *valid* possession of property but then unlawfully converts that property to herself has not committed larceny. This is why the crime of embezzlement was created: the unlawful conversion of property entrusted to possession with intent to permanently deprive.

Now imagine she uses the van for the weekend and decides to buy it. She returns Tuesday with cash in hand and purchases the van. The dealership signs to title over to her. At that moment, she has title to the property (the cash is important here because, if she writes a check, title will not pass until the transaction clears). But what if she uses counterfeit money that *she knows* is counterfeit? Then she is using a "trick" not to merely obtain possession, but to obtain actual title. This is *theft by false pretenses.* So when a defendant uses a trick or fraud to induce someone to give them chattel property, the key question is what did they get? If they get only possession, it is larceny by trick; if they get title, it is theft by false pretenses.

Lets hope she just buys the van and enjoys her new vehicle without committing a crime!

V. Robbery

Robbery is an aggravated form of larceny. The prosecution must prove the elements of larceny in order to obtain a robbery conviction. The distinction between robbery and larceny is with the taking element: robbery requires the prosecution to prove that the defendant accomplished the taking, which includes preventing the victim from recovering the property, through force or threats of force used to compel the victim to give up the property. This means the taking must have occurred from the victim's person or presence, neither of which is required for larceny.

People v. Flynn
91 Cal. Rptr. 2d 902 (2000)
California Court of Appeals

I. Introduction

Defendant, Christopher Flynn, was sentenced to state prison following his conviction of robbery. He now argues insufficiency of evidence. . . . [W]e uphold a robbery conviction on the theory that the perpetrator used fear to accomplish retention of the property after it was taken. . . .

III. Factual Summary

Defendant was a member of the "74 Hoover" gang. On October 3, 1997, about 6:00 p.m., he was standing in the area of 74th and Hoover Streets in Los Angeles with five other men, all but one of whom appeared to the victim to be gang members.

The female victim is five feet four inches tall and is smaller than the defendant. The date of this incident was her 36th birthday. She lived at 75th and Hoover Streets. As she walked past the group of men, defendant grabbed a bag that hung on her left shoulder, causing her shoulder to be pulled backward. The victim was angry, shocked and afraid of being jumped. She "kept reaching for [the bag], and [the defendant] just kept pulling [it] back." After defendant took the bag, he removed a gun and $5 bill and showed them to his companions. The victim took a good look at defendant's face so that she would remember it. The defendant screamed at the victim to get away from his car as she backed away from him. She ran home, and waited 10 days to report the incident.

Within days of the crime, the victim saw defendant's car drive slowly down her street on a number of occasions. After defendant's arrest, the wife of defendant's friend returned the gun to the victim, and had her talk to the defendant on the telephone on two occasions. The defendant apologized and asked her to drop the charges. He also asked her to talk to his parole agent. Several people came to the victim's home on different occasions. The victim was asked what she was going to do about the case. She was told she better have her gun with her when she leaves home, and one of the visitors threatened to burn her house down.

VI. Discussion

The jury convicted defendant of robbery, despite being instructed on their option to convict of grand theft from the person as a lesser included offense. The robbery instruction presented a prosecution theory of force or fear after the initial taking of the property. In argument, the prosecutor conceded insufficient force or fear at the time of the taking, urging the jury to find a robbery based on defendant's use of fear to prevent the victim from reclaiming her property. Defendant now argues he used no more force than necessary to take the victim's bag, and that the fear expressed by the victim was not created by the defendant to facilitate the robbery. Our task is to "review the whole record in the light most favorable to the judgment to determine whether it contains substantial evidence . . . from which a rational trier of fact could have found the defendant guilty beyond a reasonable doubt."

Whether the manner by which the bag was snatched from the victim's shoulder constituted sufficient force for a robbery is an arguable point. However, we decline to reach this issue because the People did not argue such a theory at trial, and the jury was not instructed on it. Since the defendant used no other force, we turn to the prosecution theory that the crime was accomplished by fear which arose after the initial taking.

"Robbery is the . . . taking of . . . property . . . accomplished by means of force or fear." Accordingly, "to support a robbery conviction, the taking, either the gaining possession or the carrying away, must be accomplished by force or fear." "Gaining possession or . . . carrying away" includes forcing or frightening a victim into leaving the scene, as well as simply deterring a victim from preventing the theft or attempting to immediately reclaim the property.

Most robberies involve actual or threatened force, resulting in fear on the part of the victim, at the time the property is taken. However, the requisite fear need not be the result of an express threat. (*See People v. Garcia*, 53 Cal. Rptr. 2d 256 (Cal. App.

Ct. 1996) (rather polite . . . 'tap' of cashier sufficient where it caused cashier to fear defendant might be armed); *People v. Davison*, 38 Cal. Rptr. 2d 438 (Cal. App. Ct. 1995) (victim is confronted by two men at an automatic teller machine, and ordered to "stand back"). Further, the requisite force or fear need not occur at the time of the initial taking. The use of force or fear to escape or otherwise retain even temporary possession of the property constitutes robbery. (*People v. Torres*, 51 Cal. Rptr. 2d 77 (Cal. App. Ct. 1996) (use of force by car burglar after he had possession of the victim's stereo sufficient even though perpetrator subsequently abandoned the stereo and fled); *People v. Pham*, 18 Cal. Rptr. 2d 636 (Cal. Ct. App. 1993) (where thief used force against victims as thief carried property away, robbery occurred even though victims subdued thief and no further asportation occurred).

A theft or robbery remains in progress until the perpetrator has reached a place of temporary safety. The scene of the crime is not such a location, at least as long as the victim remains at hand. . . . When the perpetrator and victim remain in close proximity, a reasonable assumption is that, if not prevented from doing so, the victim will attempt to reclaim his or her property. . . .

It follows from these principles, and we hold, that the willful use of fear to retain property immediately after it has been taken from the owner constitutes robbery. So long as the perpetrator uses the victim's fear to accomplish the retention of the property, it makes no difference whether the fear is generated by the perpetrator's specific words or actions designed to frighten, or by the circumstances surrounding the taking itself.

The facts of the present case substantially support this theory of robbery. Although defendant did nothing designed to instill fear prior to the taking, he chose the moment and location of the crime knowing the likely effect on the lone, female victim. He also chose to remain at the scene. Defendant is taller and bigger than the victim. Although in her own neighborhood, the victim was outnumbered six to one by a group of male gang members located in their own territory. Defendant's brazen behavior once he was armed with the stolen gun revealed his confidence in the powerlessness of the victim. After defendant yelled at the victim to stay away from his car, she ran from the scene and was afraid to report the crime until her mother convinced her to do so 10 days later.

On these facts, defendant used fear to accomplish the robbery just as surely as if he had verbalized the threats inherent in the surrounding circumstances. Defendant's argument concerning his passivity and all the things he did not do ignores the fact that his snatching of the bag, not to mention his subsequent display of the stolen weapon, immediately changed what might have been an innocuous set of circumstances into one of significant fear for the victim. To the extent that it was the victim's perceptions of her circumstances that directly caused the fear, those perceptions were reasonable and a reasonable jury could have found that defendant took advantage of them in a calculated fashion.

There was sufficient evidence of robbery.

Notes and Questions

1. Notice that robbery is essentially larceny accomplished by force or threat of force. But the taking and carrying away of personal property always requires the use of some force. What distinguishes robbery from larceny is that there is some compulsion relationship between the force or threat of force and the taking. This is why it is useful to think of the requisite force for robbery as more than what is needed to simply take the property.

2. Is pickpocketing larceny or robbery?

3. Because robbery is larceny plus the additional element of force or threat of force, any defense to larceny is also a defense to robbery. For example, if the defendant honestly believed he had a right to recover or take the property and used force or threat of force to do so, that honest mistake of fact is a complete defense to robbery. However, negating the underlying felony does not negate the assault or battery, and the defendant's mistake of fact would have to be both honest and reasonable to prevent conviction for this offense.

VI. A Visualization of Theft Offenses

This chart should help you visualize the essential differences between theft offenses.

Theft Offenses

	Larceny	Larceny by Trick	Embezzlement	False Pretenses	Robbery
Description	Trespassory Taking—taking without consent and converting custody to possession	Obtains possession of property as the result of a fraud	Already in possession; converts possession to ownership	Obtains title (ownership) to property as the result of a false representation	Larceny accomplished by force or threat of force
Actus Reus	Trespassory (without consent) taking and carrying away (slight movement)	Taking possession by fraud	Converting possession to ownership	Obtaining title by false representation	Larceny + a contemporaneous battery or assault
Mens Rea	Intent to Permanently Deprive—may exist at the time of the taking Or may arise at any time while in unlawful possession			Intent to defraud	Intent to permanently deprive
Defenses	DEF has an honest (good faith) belief that he is entitled to the property or that the property is abandoned Even if this belief is mistaken and unreasonable, so long as it is honest it completely nullifies the specific intent to steal A DEF cannot intend to steal what they honestly believe is theirs			Honest claim of right or no material reliance on false representation	Honest claim* of right, no matter how unreasonable (must prove underlying larceny) *If honest claim of right negates robbery, DEF is still guilty of the assaultive offense

Terms: Custody-Limited Physical Control; Possession-Full Dominion & Control; Title-Legal Ownership

Formative Assessments

1. A woman was the trustee of a trust fund. The corpus of the fund was invested in certificates of deposit and high-grade bonds. When one of the certificates of deposit, in the amount of $100,000, matured, the woman cashed the certificate and invested the proceeds under her own name in a speculative stock. In three months, the value of the stock had soared, and the woman sold the stock for $200,000. With the proceeds of the sale, the woman purchased a $120,000 certificate of deposit in the name of the trust. She gave the remaining $80,000 to charity.

The woman is charged with embezzlement. Under the applicable statute, the degree of the crime (and, hence, the severity of the authorized punishment) depends upon the value of the property embezzled. Of what crime, if any, could the woman properly be convicted?

    A. Embezzlement of $100,000.

    B. Embezzlement of $80,000.

    C. Embezzlement of $200,000.

    D. No embezzlement crime.

2. Defendant's next-door neighbor kept a large quantity of high-end power tools in his garage. While the neighbor was away on vacation, defendant took one of his neighbor's expensive power tools from the garage without permission, intending to use it on a project and return it without the neighbor knowing about it. The next day, defendant noticed the neighbor's car in the driveway and was surprised to learn he had returned early from his vacation. Worried he would be caught returning the power tool, defendant placed it in a gym bag and tossed it into a lake. A security camera recorded defendant taking the tool, and he was charged with larceny. At trial, he testified that he never wanted to keep the power tool but just didn't know what else to do. Based on this evidence:

    A. Defendant should be convicted of larceny.

    B. Defendant should be acquitted of larceny.

3. Defendant rents a car from Hertz. She then drives the car across the border to Mexico where she sells it to a local Mexican buyer. She then files a false police report indicating that the car was stolen from her at gunpoint. She also files a claim against the Hertz insurance carrier for the property she had in the car, and is paid approximately $600 as a settlement. Subsequent investigation leads to her arrest for selling the car. Based on these facts, defendant is guilty of:

    I. Larceny by trick of the car so long as she intended to sell it when she rented it.

    II. Larceny by trick of the car no matter when her intent to sell the car arose.

III. Theft by false pretenses of the money obtained from the insurance carrier.

IV. Larceny by trick of the money obtained from the insurance carrier.

A. I & III.

B. II & III.

C. II & IV.

D. I & IV.

4. Defendant considers himself a Good Samaritan. In order to collect money to donate to a homeless shelter, he often dresses up in a Robin Hood outfit and waits in the woods near a trail in the park. As park-goers walk by he jumps out of the woods with a bow and arrow and demands a small "contribution" to his favorite charity. Many of the locals know him and know he is playing his "Robin Hood" game and play along with him. One afternoon, he jumps out in front of a visitor to the area and startles him, and says, "Five dollars or else!" The resident gives him a five-dollar bill and runs off. Defendant yells, "Hey, I wasn't really trying to hurt you." Defendant then adds the five dollars to other money he collected that day and donates it to a homeless shelter. Based on these facts, defendant is guilty of:

A. Robbery.

B. Assault and larceny.

C. Assault only.

D. Larceny only.

5. At 11:00 p.m., John and Marsha were accosted in the entrance to their apartment building by Dirk, who was armed as well as masked. Dirk ordered the couple to take him into their apartment. After they entered the apartment, Dirk forced Marsha to bind and gag her husband John and then to open a safe which contained a diamond necklace. Dirk then tied her up and fled with the necklace. He was apprehended by apartment building security guards. Before the guards could return to the apartment, but after Dirk was arrested, John, straining to free himself, suffered a massive heart attack and died. Based on these facts, Dirk is guilty of:

A. Burglary, robbery, and murder.

B. Robbery and murder only.

C. Burglary and robbery only.

D. Robbery only.

Chapter 14

Inchoate Offenses

I. Introduction

Inchoate crimes refer to crimes which have begun but are not yet complete. This category of crimes is comprised of "partial, truncated, or otherwise incomplete versions of some other defined crime, sometimes called the 'target' or 'object' offense."[1] Through inchoate crimes, individuals may be punished even though they have not completed the crime that is the object of their efforts.[2] Indeed the very point or purpose of inchoate offenses is "to allow the judicial system to intervene *before* an actor completes the object crime."[3]

Inchoate offenses not surprisingly originated in English common law. Initially, actions and results, not mindset, were what mattered most in criminal law. Under this approach, "one who merely attempted an evil was not liable [when] there was no evil result to attribute to him."[4] Courts considered incomplete efforts to commit a crime as a completed effort at a lower crime. For example, what we would consider attempted murder would be prosecuted and punished as a completed assault or battery.[5]

Over time, the obviously problematic disparity between the charging (and punishment) for complete vs incomplete offenses wasn't eliminated but was substantially mitigated through inchoate offenses. Inchoate offenses developed for two primary reasons.

First, incomplete crimes began to be recognized as crimes in and of themselves. As one commentator explains, "[i]nchoate offenses not only create a risk of harm,

---

1. Michael Cahill, *Inchoate Crimes*, 513 *in* THE OXFORD HANDBOOK OF CRIMINAL LAW (Markus D. Dubber & Tatjana Hörnle eds. 2014). Similar definitions of inchoate offenses include "an offense committed by doing an act with the purpose of effecting some other offense (called the 'substantive offense' or 'consummated offense' or 'completed offense'").

2. Ira P. Bobbins, *Double Inchoate Crimes*, 26 HARV. J. ON LEGIS. 1, 3 (1989) [hereinafter Bobbins].

3. *Id.* (emphasis added).

4. Eugene J. Chesney, *Concept of Mens Rea in the Criminal Law*, 29 AM. INST. CRIM. L & CRIMINOLOGY 627, 628 (1939).

5. Francis Bowes Sayre, *Criminal Attempts*, 41 HARV. L. REV. 821, 837 (1928).

they are harms in themselves. . . . The [h]arm is intangible in character, and society is its object."[6]

Second, criminal law increasingly recognized the importance of mens rea, a criminal mind. In terms of inchoate offenses, criminal law utilized mens rea to balance out the fact that the defendant never completed the target offense—the substantive offense the defendant intended to commit when she initiated the inchoate offense. While, as just stated, the law began to recognize the harm from inchoate offenses, that harm is not as tangible as, for example, a murder victim. Additionally, the actus reus requirement for inchoate offenses, particularly solicitation and conspiracy, can be satisfied by conduct that is quite distant from the completed target offense. To mitigate against both these concerns, inchoate offenses require the highest mens rea—specific intent in common law and purpose under the MPC.

As a result, the mens rea for an *attempted* offense is often higher than for a *completed* offense. For example, as you will see, this specific intent requirement means it is more challenging to prove attempted murder, when the victim is not killed, than it is to prove murder, when the victim is killed. But to be clear, this does not mean that only specific intent crimes may be the targets of inchoate offenses. Instead, it means the inchoate version of an offense requires specific intent to complete the criminal harm of that offense. So, for example, attempted murder is established only if the evidence proves beyond a reasonable doubt the defendant acted with the specific intent to kill; specific intent to injure, even grievously, would be insufficient. Even strict liability crimes may be the targets of inchoate offenses, for example conspiracy to commit bigamy, or attempted statutory rape. But for the inchoate version, the evidence must establish specific intent to inflict the criminal harm of the crime.

This chapter focuses on the three primary inchoate crimes: solicitation, conspiracy, and attempt.[7] These crimes are discussed in greater detail throughout the chapter, but by way of general introduction:

Solicitation   With the purpose that a crime be committed, an actor requests someone else commit an offense. Solicitation is the crime of inducing someone else to commit your crime.

6. Paul Robinson, *A Theory of Justification: Societal Harm as a Prerequisite for Criminal Liability*, 23 UCLA L. Rev. 226, 268 (1975). Built into the view of inchoate crimes as harms in and of themselves is the "assumption that forming an intention to engage in future criminal conduct is itself a culpable act, and sufficiently culpable to justify invoking the machinery of the criminal law." Larry Alexander & Kimberly D. Kessler, *Mens Rea and Inchoate Crimes*, 87 J. Crim. L. & Criminology 1138, 1170 (1997) [hereinafter Alexander & Kessler].

7. *See* Douglas N. Husak, *The Nature and Justifiability of Nonconsummate Offenses*, 37 Ariz. L. Rev. 151, 168 (1995) [hereinafter Husak] (quoting Glanville Williams, Textbook of Criminal Law 402 (2d ed. 1983)). The commentary to the MPC contends that solicitation, conspiracy and attempt "have in common the fact that they deal with conduct that is designed to culminate in the commission of a substantive offense, but has failed in the discrete case to do so or has not yet achieved its culmination because there is something that the actor or another still must do. The offenses are inchoate in this sense." Husak, *supra* at 171 (quoting MPC § 5.01 Commentary at 293).

Conspiracy   Two or more people agree to commit a crime or to do some-
             thing lawful by unlawful means (like applying for a loan with
             a fraudulent application) and, each with the purpose of bring-
             ing about that criminal result, at least one member performs
             some overt act in furtherance of the agreement. Conspiracy is
             the crime of collective planning to commit a crime.

Attempt   Acting with the purpose to complete a target offense, an
             actor takes one or more actions which cross the line from
             preparation and indicate the initiation of perpetration.
             Attempt is the crime of starting to commit a crime.

These crimes are stand-alone, substantive offenses, "distinct and divorced
from the completed crime. . . ."[8] You have already learned about offense of murder.
Through this chapter you will learn about when a criminal outcome is desired but
not achieved, for example, solicitation to commit murder; conspiracy to commit
murder; and attempted murder.

One way to think of these inchoate crimes is along a continuum.[9]

Inchoate Crime Continuum

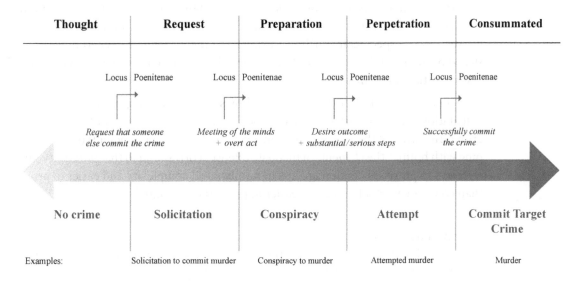

© 2012 Geoffrey S. Corn

---

8. Bobbins, *supra* note 2, at 3.

9. Locus poenitenae is latin for room or space to repent. In the criminal law context, locus poenitenae refers to the space between an actor and the threshold for having committed an offense.
Conceptually, the locus poenitenae functions as the concurrence point, crossing it indicates the
concurrence of actus reus and mens rea. As this chapter explains, while the mens rea for inchoate
offenses is a constant, the actus reus can vary. As a result, the locus poenitenae for each of the inchoate offenses is positioned or located differently.

Starting with the left side of the continuum, thought is not criminalized, however "evil" those thoughts may be. What transitions evil thoughts to the crime of solicitation is communicating a request that someone else commit a crime. If the requested party (solicitee) declines the request, the defendant (solicitor) may be tried for solicitation. However, if the solicitee *agrees* to commit the crime, that agreement establishes the actus reus of conspiracy. Once one of the parties to the agreement commits an overt act in furtherance of that criminal agreement then the conspiracy is complete (for which all the members face criminal liability).

Because the overt act for conspiracy serves simply as objective evidence that the conspirators were doing more than just talking about the target offense, it may be relatively trivial and quite distant from the crime that is the object of the agreement. In contrast, the overt act for an attempt *is* the actus reus and must demonstrate that the defendant initiated perpetration of the target crime, not that he was just preparing for or planning to commit it. Thus, the difference between conspiracy and attempt is one of degrees. Attempt requires a purpose to accomplish the criminal outcome but the steps taken must bring the desired crime meaningfully closer to completion, which is a greater requirement than the action required for a conspiracy.

Conceptually, inchoate offenses are society's way of trying to balance a series of tensions. On the one hand, criminal law doesn't punish for criminal thoughts. On the other hand, completed crimes clearly pose a danger to society warranting law enforcement intervention. The problem inchoate crimes seek to address is the space between. More specifically, inchoate crimes are the societal answer to how many step(s) beyond evil thought should be required before law enforcement intervention and potential punishment?[10]

Inchoate crimes reflect the harm posed by solicitation, conspiracy and attempt. Solicitation is the furthest away in a temporal sense from the danger of a completed crime, and attempt the closest, with conspiracy in between (and potentially overlapping with both).[11] The elements of inchoate offenses correspond to that proximity; the elements to prove solicitation are less in number and complexity and easier to prove than conspiracy, which in turn is easier to prove then attempt.[12]

---

10. As two commentators explain,

   [T]he defendant who commits a[n] [] inchoate crime, such as an incomplete attempt or conspiracy, usually has shown himself to have a less than totally admirable character and to pose some threat to the rights of others protected by the criminal law. Ordinarily, however, neither a wicked character nor the danger it represents suffices for criminal liability. *What distinguishes the inchoate criminal from others who are wicked and dangerous is that the former has formed a criminal intention and taken some steps toward accomplishing his intended result.*

Alexander & Kessler, *supra* note 6 at 1170 (emphasis added).

   11. "In the solicitation there is not that dangerous proximity to success that is found in the attempt." John W. Curran, *Solicitation—A Substantive Crime*, 17 MINN. L. REV. 499, 508 (1933).

   12. As discussed in this chapter, in terms of punishment, the common law provided for progressively greater punishment moving from solicitation to conspiracy to attempt, while the MPC has equal punishment for each.

While you might think that after hundreds of years of solicitation, conspiracy and attempt cases, the law would have answered or addressed all the issues, it turns out that the opposite is true. Inchoate crimes are little more settled now, and society's concern about the tension or balance underpinning the crimes is even greater. The threat of terrorist attacks and mass shootings have skewed society's perceptions and fears of crime. Through the internet, individuals can commit an inchoate crime (as well as completed crimes) with several keystrokes and mouse clicks. Cyber space as a medium for crime seems to disproportionately involve younger individuals—both as victims[13] and perpetrators. For example, a fourteen-year-old was charged with solicitation to commit murder (punishable by up to 30 years confinement) as the result of threats of violence made in a Facebook chat group.[14] Similarly, three twelve-year-old middle school students were arrested for threats they made regarding a school official via snapchat and are facing charges of conspiracy to commit a criminal offense.[15] Lastly, the evidence against a young man charged with attempted murder with intent to commit rape included his having performed google searches of the terms "how to kill a woman" and "can a dead woman get pregnant."[16]

This chapter seeks to provide foundational knowledge of inchoate offenses as substantive crimes. It's important to understand—and be able to distinguish—each of the offenses as inchoate crimes, meaning the target offense *was not* completed. (Example: A solicited B to murder C, and either B rejected A's request or accepted but did not complete the target offense, here murder.)

The next chapter will build on that foundation and discuss solicitation and conspiracy as modes of liability rendering the defendant liable for another's criminal act or omission. That discussion will be in the context of when the target offense *was* completed. (Example: A solicited B or conspired with B to murder C, and B subsequently murdered C.)

A full understanding of inchoate offenses as substantive crimes is critically important to the mode of liability discussion in the next chapter. That full understanding requires awareness of the impact of the target offense of an inchoate crime being completed. Under the merger doctrine, when the target offense of a solicited or attempted crime is completed, the inchoate crime merges into the target offense.

13. *See* Marieke Lewis, et al., *Internet Crimes Against Children: A Matrix of Federal and State Laws*, FEDERAL RESEARCH DIVISION, Oct. 2009.

14. Kate Cough, *Ellsworth teen charged with solicitation to commit murder*, ELLSWORTH AMERICAN, Mar. 20, 2019.

15. *3 Florida middle school students arrested over Snapchat threats, police say*, WREG NEWS, Sept. 13, 2021. Following their arrest, the interim school superintendent said that

This situation serves as a reminder—when it comes to safety, there is no joking around. . . . Any statement that may be interpreted as a threat including bomb threats made via phone, text, social media post or through other means will be acted on and there will be consequences, such as being arrested, going to trial, and/or expulsion.

16. *See* Grant McCabe, *'Can a dead woman get pregnant'—Chilling internet searches by Perth man before attempted murder and rape*, THE COURIER, Jun. 17, 2021.

Thus when, as above, A solicits B to murder C and B does so, A has of course committed the offense of solicitation to commit murder.[17] But because the target offense, murder, was completed, the solicitation provides the basis for accomplice liability, and the solicitation merges with or is subsumed by the murder charge, or even an attempted murder charge. This means the *solicitor is guilty of murder or attempted murder as if she committed those crimes herself.* Essentially, she is considered an accomplice to the principal she solicited to commit that crime. The end result is that A would not be charged with solicitation to commit murder but with the completed murder or attempted murder.

The merger doctrine also applies to successfully completed attempts. All completed crimes are in essence successful attempts. A successfully completing the attempted murder of C is an awkward way of saying A murdered C. While A did commit the offense of attempted murder, the attempt merges into the completed offense, and A would be charged with murder, not attempted murder.

By contrast, the merger doctrine does *not* apply to inchoate conspiracy. Where A and B conspire to murder C, and B does so, there is no merger. As will be explained in more detail in the next chapter, A and B have committed and may each be charged with both conspiracy to commit murder and with murder.[18]

Understanding inchoate offenses also requires discussion of the affirmative defenses of renunciation and abandonment. These defenses are only applicable to inchoate crimes and only in jurisdictions that have adopted the MPC approach. Renunciation and abandonment are further explained below, but these defenses incentivize a defendant to prevent the inchoate crimes they set in motion from being completed.[19]

Inchoate offenses are challenging for several reasons. A threshold challenge for solicitation and conspiracy is to remember whether you are analyzing the crimes

---

17. Remembering that A committing solicitation does not depend on or require B to accept or for B to successfully complete the target crime. That said, the practical reality is that inchoate solicitation is often only charged when the solicitee, B, rejects the request. That's because, as discussed above, when B accepts and takes an overt act but fails to completes the target offense, A and B have committed the more serious crime of conspiracy. Where B accepts and completes the target offense, solicitation merges into that offense, which both A and B are considered to have committed.

18. For another example of how the merger doctrine does *not* apply to inchoate conspiracy, in 2019, the U.S. Attorney's Office for the District of Massachusetts announced criminal charges following an investigation into a college admissions bribery scandal. A number of individuals, including Felicity Huffman, a well-known actress, were charged with both conspiracy to commit mail fraud and, as a separate charge, mail fraud. U.S. Attorney's Office District of Massachusetts, *Investigations of College Admissions and Testing Bribery Scheme*, Mar. 12, 2019, https://www.justice.gov /usao-ma/investigations-college-admissions-and-testing-bribery-scheme.

19. *See* Michael T. Cahill, *Defining Inchoate Crime: An Incomplete Attempt*, 9 Ohio St. J. Crim. L. 751 (2012) (noting the uniqueness of renunciation and abandonment as applied to inchoate offenses. Cahill discusses that "[o]ne cannot, as a legal matter, undo or wipe away one's liability for a theft by returning the stolen item. . . ." Renunciation and abandonment allow for just such a "undoing" but again only for inchoate crimes and only in an MPC jurisdiction).

in the inchoate context (this chapter) or as a mode of liability for other crimes (next chapter). Additionally, the study of inchoate offenses is at time nuanced; there are disparities between common law and the MPC for each offense and in some cases each element of each offense.[20] That there is the potential of overlap, that the same set of facts may qualify as solicitation *and* conspiracy *and* attempt, can also be the source of confusion.[21]

To assist in your learning (and maintaining that learning moving forward), there is a chart at the end of the chapter which distinguishes between inchoate offenses under common law and the MPC. As you read this chapter, for each inchoate offense, for common law and for the MPC, you want to clearly understand:

1) What is the actus reus of the inchoate offense in each system (CL and MPC)?

2) What is the mens rea of the inchoate offense in each system?

3) Are abandonment or renunciation available as a defense?

4) If the target offense was completed, does the inchoate crime merge?

Next, the chapter provides a summary introduces to solicitation, conspiracy and attempt followed by cases addressing those offenses.

A. Solicitation

Criminalizing solicitation is based on the idea that "a person who makes a serious effort to induce another person to commit a crime of violence is clearly dangerous and that his act deserves criminal sanctions whether or not the crime of violence is actually committed."[22] Codifying solicitation as an offense "allow[s] law enforcement to intervene at an early stage where there has been a clear demonstration of an individual's criminal intent and danger to society."[23]

At common law, solicitation is persuading, bribing "or in any other manner instigat[ing] another or others" to commit a felony, or a misdemeanor involving

---

20. *See* Herbert Wechsler et al., *The Treatment of Inchoate Crimes in the Model Penal Code of the American Law Institute: Attempt, Solicitation, and Conspiracy*, 61 COLUMBIA L. REV. 957 (1961).

21. But an individual may only be convicted of more than one crime stemming from a single course of conduct if each crime requires a mutually exclusive element. *See Blockburger v. U.S.*, 284 U.S. 299 (1932). If one crime is completely subsumed by another, then the two crimes are considered the same offense and the defendant may be punished for only one. For example, if the agreement element of a conspiracy charge is that A hired (solicited) B to commit the offense, then the solicitation is subsumed by the conspiracy charge, and A would only face punishment for conspiracy. The MPC codified this limitation as "[a] person may not be convicted of more than one offense [solicitation, conspiracy, attempt] [] for conduct designed to commit or to culminate in the commission of the same crime." MPC § 5.02(3). But that one offense per target crime could be a double inchoate crime like attempted solicitation or attempted conspiracy. *See Bobbins, supra* note 2.

22. S. Rep. No. 98-225, 98th Cong., 2d Sess. 308 (1984), *reprinted in* 1984 U.S. Code Cong. & Adm. News 3182, 3487. There is an argument that criminalizing inchoate solicitation is unnecessary and even problematic in that it comes close to criminalizing speech.

23. *Id.*

breach of the public peace or to those crimes which tend to defeat the administration of justice.[24]

Under the MPC:

> A person is guilty of solicitation to commit a crime if with the purpose of promoting or facilitating its commission he commands, encourages or requests another person to engage in specific conduct which would constitute such crime or an attempt to commit such crime or which would establish his complicity in its commission or attempted commission.[25]

The scope of solicitation varies slightly, applying to felonies and only a limited category of misdemeanors at common law, while applying to all felonies and misdemeanors under the MPC. Most jurisdictions, even those that have not adopted the MPC, have adopted an analogously broad definition of solicitation.

Similarly, the seriousness with which solicitation was viewed also varied. At common law, solicitation was considered a misdemeanor, regardless of the offense solicited. The MPC and most modern criminal codes consider all three inchoate offenses (solicitation, conspiracy and attempt) as crimes of the same grade and degree as the most serious substantive offense that is their object, with the exception of first-degree felonies for which the inchoate version is considered a second-degree felony.[26]

1. Solicitation Actus Reus

The actus reus of solicitation, while not verbatim the same, is functionally equivalent between the common law and the MPC. The invitation or request to commit a crime may be verbal, in writing, or through demonstrative physical action.

Where there are differences between the common law and the MPC, they involve the amount of the solicitor's expected involvement in the commission of the target offense and where the request to commit a crime is either undelivered or unreceived. In terms of the solicitor's expected involvement, A requesting that B *help* A to commit a crime is not solicitation at common law. Solicitation at common law requires A to ask B to commit the crime. By contrast, under the MPC, A requesting B's help does qualify as solicitation.[27]

---

24. James B. Blackburn, *Solicitation to Crimes*, 40 W. Va. L.Q. 135 (1934). The Supreme Court has never defined criminal solicitation. As a result, there are a wide range of verbs included in common law solicitation statutes, including: advising, commanding, counseling, encouraging, enticing, entreating, hiring, importuning, inciting, instigating, procuring, requesting, stimulating, and urging. Unhelpfully, the most common verb in common law jurisdictions solicitation statutes is solicit. *See* California Penal Code § 653f (defining solicitation using the verb solicit, as in "[e]very person who, with the intent that the crime be committed, *solicits* another. . . ." (emphasis added)).

25. MPC § 5.02(1).

26. The MPC defines five offense grades: first-degree felony, second-degree felony, third-degree felony, misdemeanor, and petty misdemeanor.

27. MPC § 5.02(1). The potential offenses arising from A requesting B's assistance in committing

The issue of the solicitation not being delivered or received arises most often when the request is reduced to writing in a letter or email. At common law, solicitation liability requires actual receipt of the criminal request by an intended solicitee.[28] By contrast, under the MPC, "[i]t is immaterial . . . that the actor fails to communicate with the person he solicits to commit a crime if his conduct was designed to effect such communication."[29]

2. Solicitation Mens Rea

As referenced above, one constant with inchoate offenses is that the highest mens rea is required. But inchoate solicitation under the common law and the MPC has two mens rea elements and they differ in application.[30]

At common law, there are two levels of differing intent as part of solicitation's mens rea, the *general* intent to communicate and the *specific* intent to consummate the target offense. The MPC utilizes purpose for both parts of solicitation's mens rea, the purpose to procure and the purpose that the solicited party consent.

3. Renouncing Solicitation

What about the time period after A hires (solicits) B to murder C but before B has completed the target offense? Inchoate solicitation doesn't depend on the solicitee agreeing or the object of the solicitation ever materializing, so technically A has already committed the offense of solicitation. Should the law incentivize A to stop the chain of events A set into motion? The MPC and common law answer that question differently.

The MPC provides the affirmative defense of renunciation for all three *inchoate* crimes—the target offense cannot have been completed. The wording varies slightly depending on the inchoate offense, but the MPC applies the following limitation to efforts at renouncing any of the inchoate offenses:

> [R]enunciation of criminal purpose is not voluntary if it is motivated, in whole or in part, by circumstances, not present or apparent at the inception of the actor's course of conduct, which increase the probability of detection or apprehension or which make more difficult the accomplishment of the

---

a crime are addressed in the next chapter. For the purposes of this chapter, the take away is that requesting assistance in committing a crime qualifies for MPC solicitation but not under the common law.

28. *See People v. Saephanh*, 80 Cal. App. 4th 451, 94 Cal. Rptr. 2d 910 (2000); *State v. Andujar*, 899 A.2d 1209 (R.I. 2006). Both cases arose in common law jurisdictions and involved a prospective solicitor mailing a written request that a solicitee commit a crime, but the letter was never received/read by the intended recipient. In both cases, appellate courts ruled that the elements for common law solicitation had not been met.

29. MPC § 5.02(2).

30. *See* Alexander & Kessler, *supra* note 6, at 1138.

criminal purpose. Renunciation is not complete if it is motivated by a decision to postpone the criminal conduct until a more advantageous time or to transfer the criminal effort to another but similar objective or victim.[31]

In terms of the specific renunciation applicable to inchoate solicitation under the MPC, the defense is available if "the actor, after soliciting another person to commit a crime, persuaded him not to do so or otherwise prevented the commission of the crime, under circumstances manifesting a complete and voluntary renunciation of his criminal purpose."[32] Note the layered requirements for MPC renunciation. The solicitor must either persuade the solicitee to not do as requested or "otherwise" prevent the crime. To prevent the crime entails warning a potential victim and/or notifying the police. Additionally, for renunciation to be "complete and voluntary," it cannot be temporary. Giving up on efforts to hire a hit man, but planning to resume efforts at a later date doesn't suffice. Similarly, to be considered voluntary, as outlined above, renunciation cannot be motivated by fear of apprehension.

The finder of fact, judge or jury, determines whether a defendant has satisfied the requirements for renunciation. When the finder of fact so determines the result is an acquittal on the inchoate solicitation charge. Finally, renunciation is an affirmative defense, meaning the burden may be placed on the defendant to prove the requirements.

By contrast, there is no renunciation defense at common law. The common law takes a rigid or formalistic approach; there is no way to "undo" the crime of solicitation once committed. This will be a common thread that runs through all common law inchoate offenses: once there is concurrence between the actus reus and the mens rea, the crime is complete, and like any crime, cannot be undone. In other words, in a common law jurisdiction, the law does not allow for putting the proverbial toothpaste back into the tube.

As discussed in more detail in the next chapter, the solicitor is still incentivized at common law to either persuade the solicitee to not do as requested or prevent the target crime from being committed.[33] But even where the solicitor is able to prevent the target crime from being completed, they still face common law criminal liability for solicitation.

---

31. MPC § 5.01(4).

32. MPC § 5.02(3).

33. The common law incentive to persuade solicitee to not do as requested or prevent the target crime from being committed is to spare the solicitor from the effects of the merger doctrine.

Inchoate Solicitation

Common Law	MPC
Actus Reus Enacting or procurring the commission of crime	**Actus Reus** Enacting or procuring the commission of crime. May be incomplete communication. If DEF intended for the crime to be committed & for the communication to be received = guilty of solicitation
Mens Rea Dual intent **General** Intent to communicate **Specific** Intent to consummate the target offense	
Complete once DEF asks someone to commit target offense (Solicitee doesn't have to agree or accept for solicitation) If solicitor's message never reaches the intended person then the Solicitor may be charged with "attempt to solicit"	**Mens Rea** Dual Intent Intent to procure Intent that solicited party commit the offense

Merges into the target crime or attempted crime if crime actually attempted or completed (can't charge both solicitation and attempt/completed crime)

Defenses Renunciation (only MPC) DEF must completely & voluntarily renounce intention to commit crime & must take steps to prevent crime from occurring

Impossibility *not* a defense to solicitation because what matters is what solicitor believes the circumstances to be, not what they actually are

B. Conspiracy

Conspiracy is a "collective criminal agreement" or a "partnership in crime"[34] which comes in two forms:

Inchoate conspiracy (this chapter)—Agreeing, expressly or implicitly, to commit a target crime in the future.

Conspiracy as mode of liability (next chapter)—The criminal liability resulting from when one or more members of the conspiracy commits the target crime and, depending on the jurisdiction, other crimes.[35]

Conspiracy is an inchoate crime "for which the essential act is slight. It involves an intent to commit a further act. It is the commission of that [further] act which the state desires to prevent, and it is with the intent to commit that act that the state is concerned."[36]

---

34. *U.S. v. Felix*, 503 U.S. 378, 389–90 (1992).

35. As one appellate court noted, "[a] person intending to only be 'in for a penny,' with the slightest connection to an established conspiracy, actually risks being 'in for a pound.'" *United States v. Hassan*, 742 F.3d 104, 146 (4th Cir. 2014).

36. Benjamin F. Pollack, *Common Law Conspiracy*, 35 Geo. L.J. 328 (1947) (quoting law professor

One way to think of inchoate conspiracy is that the crime is the agreement to commit some other crime (or crimes). The parties to the agreement (the conspiracy) are called co-conspirators. In any group, there are more and less active members, but there are no gradations or degrees of conspirators. All qualifying conspirators are subject to criminal liability, even those only marginally involved.

The focus of conspiracy is the agreement. Where there is a single agreement to violate multiple laws, the result is a single conspiracy charge.[37]

Through inchoate conspiracy, prosecutors are able to charge multiple individuals for their role in a single conspiracy and, depending on the jurisdiction, need only prove the criminal agreement and that one member of the conspiracy committed at least one overt (affirmative) act in furtherance of the commission of the target crime. This overt act requirement is the attendant circumstance of conspiracy, providing objective evidence that the agreement was more than "just talk." It can be trivial and quite distant from the completed crime. Furthermore, prosecutors may allege dozens of overt acts but need prove only one to satisfy the requirement.

Prosecutors may charge inchoate conspiracy (example, conspiracy to commit wire fraud) as a stand-alone charge. But as referenced above, inchoate conspiracy is not subject to the merger doctrine.[38] That means that where one of the conspirators actually committed the target crime, wire fraud, that every co-conspirator may be charged with (and receive the punishment from) both conspiracy to commit wire fraud *and* wire fraud.[39] While the punishment for inchoate conspiracy varies,[40] it is

---

(and later dean) Albert Harno) [hereinafter Pollack].

37. *See United States v. Braverman*, 317 U.S. 49 (1942). In reading conspiracy fact patterns and trying to identify potential crimes, count the number of agreements, not the number of crimes. Where Cain and Abel have agreed to distribute cocaine, it is not hard to envision any number of crimes which would be committed. But if there is only one criminal agreement, then there should only be one conspiracy charge. Resist the temptation to break Cain and Abel's single criminal agreement into multiple conspiracy charges (conspiracy to illegally import a controlled substance; conspiracy to illegally transport a controlled substance; conspiracy to illegally dispense a controlled substance, etc.).

38. There are early common law cases recognizing that conspiracy was subject to the merger doctrine. There were several procedural reasons underpinning the application of merger, but "[a]s the procedural distinctions diminished, the merger concept lost its force, and eventually disappeared." *Iannelli v. U.S.*, 420 U.S. 770, 770 (1975). To be clear, *the merger doctrine does not apply to inchoate conspiracy.*

39. For example, in 2019, federal prosecutors charged the chief financial officer of the Huawei telecommunications company with, among other offenses, conspiracy to commit wire fraud *and* with wire fraud; conspiracy to commit bank fraud *and* with bank fraud. *See Chinese Telecommunications Conglomerate Huawei and Huawei CFO Wanzhou Meng Charged with Financial Fraud*, Department of Justice Office of Public Affairs, Jan. 28, 2019.

40. As referenced above, under the MPC, conspiracy is considered as the same grade and degree as the most serious substantive offense that is its object, with the exception of first-degree felonies, for which the inchoate version is considered a second-degree felony. By comparison, under federal law, the general conspiracy statute has a maximum punishment of five years, but several offense specific (drug trafficking, terrorist, and racketeering) conspiracy offenses all carry the same punishment as the underlying offense, which for some includes confinement for life.

normally greater than that for solicitation. A conspiracy charge also provides prosecutors with valuable procedural[41] and evidentiary[42] benefits.

All of the above have led to conspiracy statutes being considered "a boon" to prosecutors.[43] Judge Learned Hand once famously referred to the crime as the "darling of the modern prosecutor's nursery."[44] The elasticity of inchoate conspiracy has led to its use in response to terrorism, drug cartels, organized crime, corporate fraud and a host of other crimes.[45]

In turn, conspiracy is the most controversial of the inchoate offenses. Traditional support for inchoate conspiracy contends that

> [C]ollective criminal agreement—partnership in crime—presents a greater potential threat to the public than individual delicts. Concerted action both increases the likelihood that the criminal object will be successfully attained and decreases the probability that the individuals involved will depart from their path of criminality. Group association for criminal purposes often, if not normally, makes possible the attainment of ends more complex than those which one criminal could accomplish.[46]

---

41. The procedural benefits to the prosecution include jointly trying multiple defendants. Often times, defendants employ what is politely referred to as "antagonistic defenses," aka defendant A seeks to avoid or mitigate liability by throwing defendant B under the proverbial oncoming bus, which then leads defendant B to reciprocate. As the Fifth Circuit pointed out:
> [There is a] specific prejudice that results when defendants become weapons against each other, clawing into each other with antagonistic defenses. Like the wretches in Dante's hell, they may become entangled and ultimately fuse together in the eyes of the jury, so that neither defense is believed and all defendants are convicted.
Paul Marcus, *The Crime of Conspiracy Thrives in Decisions of the United States Supreme Court*, 64 Kan. L. Rev. 373, 398 (2015) (quoting *U.S. v. Romanello*, 726 F.2d 173, 174 (5th Cir. 1984)) [hereinafter Marcus].
42. With a conspiracy charge, otherwise inadmissible statements by co-conspirator A may be introduced as evidence against all fellow co-conspirators. Marcus, *supra* note 41, at 392.
43. Marcus, *supra* note 41, at 377.
44. Marcus, *supra* note 41, at 377. That's not to suggest that Judge Hand was a fan of inchoate conspiracy. In another case, Judge Hand expressed concerns that
> [S]o many prosecutors seek to sweep within the drag-net of conspiracy all those who have been associated in any degree whatever with the main offenders. That there are opportunities of great oppression in such a doctrine is very plain, and it is only by circumscribing the scope of such all comprehensive indictments that they can be avoided.
U.S. v. Falcone, 109 F.2d 579, 581 (2d Cir. 1940).
45. Federal Conspiracy Law: A Brief Overview, Congressional Research Service R41223 (Apr. 3, 2020) [hereinafter CRS Attempt].
46. *Callanan v. U.S.*, 364 U.S. 587, 593–94 (1961) (Frankfurter, J.). But consider Justice Jackson's comments:
> There is, of course, strong temptation to relax rigid standards when it seems the only way to sustain convictions of evildoers. But statutes authorize prosecution for substantive crimes for most evildoing without the dangers to the liberty of the individual and the integrity of the judicial process that are inherent in conspiracy charges. We should disapprove the doctrine of emplied [sic] or constructive crime in its entirety and in every manifestation. And I think there should be no straining to uphold any conspiracy conviction where prosecution

But others argue that inchoate conspiracy is not necessary,[47] or question the claim that agreements to commit crime pose sufficient dangers to justify the offense.[48]

In addition to being controversial, for many students (and practitioners), conspiracy is also the most challenging of the inchoate crimes. Part of the difficulty is external and stems from how conspiracy compares to solicitation and attempt. Another part is internal due to the several differences between inchoate conspiracy at common law versus the MPC.

At common law, conspiracy required proof of an actual agreement, express or implied, between two or more people to commit a crime.[49] The MPC definition uses different words but is functionally comparable, "[a] person is guilty of conspiracy with another person or persons to commit a crime if with the purpose of promoting or facilitating its commission he: (a) agrees with such other person or persons that they or one or more of them will engage in conduct which constitutes such crime. . . ."[50]

1. Conspiracy Actus Reus

At both common law and the MPC, the agreement to commit a crime is the actus reus of conspiracy. The agreement may take any number of forms, written, verbal or implied through the actions of the parties. There are however two prominent differences between the common law and the MPC which fall under actus reus. The first is that common law conspiracy also requires proof of an overt act in furtherance of the agreement before the conspiracy is complete,[51] while the MPC does not.[52] An

---

for the substantive offense is adequate and the purpose served by adding the conspiracy charge seems chiefly to get procedural advantages to ease the way to conviction.

Krulewitch v. U.S., 336 U.S. 440, 445 (1949) (Jackson, J., concurring). Historically, the Supreme Court was skeptical of conspiracy, referring to "pervasive and wide sweeping nets of conspiracy prosecutions" and referencing a judicial report that "the conspiracy statute is being much abused." Marcus, *supra* note 41, at 375. But more recently, Marcus argues that "[f]or several decades now, one would be hard pressed to find any serious concerns expressed by justices as to the crime or the way in which conspiracy is prosecuted. To be sure, in virtually every major conspiracy case to come before the Court since 1987, the government has won convincingly—often times with nary a dissent." *Id.* at 337.

47. Phillip E. Johnson, *The Unnecessary Crime of Conspiracy*, 61 CAL. L. REV. 1137, 1139–40 (1973).

48. Steven R. Morrison, *Requiring Proof of Conspiratorial Dangerousness*, 88 TUL. L. REV. 483, 513 (2014).

49. "Conspiracy, in the modern law, is generally defined as a confederacy of two or more persons to accomplish some unlawful purpose." *Ocasio v. U.S,* 136 S. Ct. 1423 (2016).

50. MPC § 5.03.

51. Common law conspiracy in the U.S. did not originally require an overt act. *See Nash v. U.S.,* 229 U.S. 373 (1913). While there are common law conspiracy statues which do not require an overt act, the widespread rule today, and the one law students should follow, is that *common law conspiracy requires an overt act.*

52. The MPC confusingly states that "[n]o person may be convicted of conspiracy to commit a crime, other than a felony of the first or second degree, unless an overt act in pursuance of such conspiracy is alleged and proved to have been done by him or by a person with whom he conspired." What this means is that an overt is only required for third-degree felony and misdemeanors. It is not required for first- and second-degree felonies, which includes arson, certain aggravated assaults, burglary, kidnapping, murder and rape. Given that those offenses are more likely to be made the

overt act[53] is any act knowingly done by any coconspirator in furtherance of an object or purpose of the conspiracy.[54] The overt act of one co-conspirator is considered the act of all conspirators "without any new agreement specifically directed to that [overt] act."[55]

The second is that the common law recognizes bilateral conspiracy, while the MPC recognizes unilateral.[56] Bilateral and unilateral refers to the number of "guilty minds" required for conspiracy.[57] A bilateral conspiracy jurisdiction requires at least two[58] guilty minds, while a unilateral only requires one.[59] The import of this distinction arises when one purported co-conspirator in a two-person conspiracy is an undercover law enforcement officer, or an informant, or any other person who is feigning agreement. In such situations, the "co-conspirator" has no intention of actually agreeing to carry out the proposed crime. In a common law bilateral jurisdiction, there cannot be a conspiracy under such circumstances (although the facts may support a charge of solicitation or attempted conspiracy), while the unilateral MPC approach would recognize a conspiracy.[60]

---

subject of a law school exam, students should follow the rule that conspiracy under the MPC, as a general proposition, does not require an overt act.

53. Overt is French for "open." One way to think of "open" acts in this context is as ones which may be proved by evidence and which support or allow an inference. As stated above, overt acts need not be criminal. Consider a conspiracy to commit arson of a commercial business. For example, after agreeing to commit arson, one of the co-conspirators visits a hardware store where she buys several gas cans which she then fills at gas station. Buying gas cans and filling them with gas are not criminal actions. But they are actions which could be proven to have occurred, and they support the inference that the agreement to commit arson was not "just talk."

54. *See* 18 U.S.C. § 371 (definition of overt act, "If two or more persons conspire . . . and one or more of such persons do any act to effect the object of the conspiracy"). The Supreme Court explains that

It is not necessary that an overt act be the substantive crime charged in the indictment as the object of the conspiracy. Nor, indeed, need such an act, taken by itself, even be criminal in character. The function of the overt act in a conspiracy prosecution is simply to manifest "that the conspiracy is at work," and is neither a project still resting solely in the minds of the conspirators nor a fully completed operation no longer in existence.

Yates v. U.S., 354 U.S. 298, 334 (1957) (internal citations omitted).

55. *U.S. v. Kissel*, 218 U.S. 601, 608 (1910).

56. Note the difference between the start of the bilateral federal general conspiracy statute, "[i]f two or more persons conspire . . ." and the unilateral MPC, "[a] person is guilty of conspiracy. . . ."

57. *See* Paul Marcus, Prosecution and Defense of Criminal Conspiracy Cases, § 2.03 (Matthew Bender, Rev. Ed.).

58. Referring to common law bilateral conspiracy, the Fifth Circuit held, "[i]t takes at least two to tango for conspiracy purposes." *U.S. v. Villasanor*, 894 F.2d 1422 (5th Cir. 1990).

59. *See* Dierdre A. Burgman, *Unilateral Conspiracy: Three Critical Perspectives*, 29 DePaul L. Rev. 75 (1979).

60. In 2021, Rayshun Jackson, a Texas attorney, pled guilty in federal court to conspiring to launder $380,000 for "an individual he believed was a drug trafficker, but was actually an undercover DEA agent." U.S. Attorney's Office Northern District of Texas, Dallas Attorney Pleads Guilty to Laundering Purported Drug Money, Sept. 29, 2021. Money laundering refers to an illegal process by which money generated by an illegal activity is made to appear as from a legitimate source, in this case, from Mr. Jackson's law firm accounts.

2. Conspiracy Mens Rea

Similar to solicitation, inchoate conspiracy has two mens rea components.[61] The first element applies to entering into the agreement to commit the crime, while the second element applies to achieving the criminal result which is the object of the conspiracy

As discussed in the introduction, inchoate crimes require the highest mens rea, specific intent at common law and purpose under the MPC. The common law applies specific intent only to the second prong, meaning an individual must specifically intend to commit the underlying offense.[62] The common law applies general intent to the first prong, entering into the agreement to commit an offense. This is not as confusing as it may sound. Where the facts prove the specific intent to commit the underlying offense, the vast majority of the time, the general intent applied to the agreement is ipso facto proven as well.

The MPC utilizes purpose for both mens rea elements in conspiracy.[63]

3. Renouncing Conspiracy

Similar to solicitation, at common law, it was not possible to renounce inchoate conspiracy once the agreement was reached and an overt act taken, while the MPC recognizes renunciation as an affirmative defense to inchoate conspiracy. In addition to the MPC specified limitations applicable to all three inchoate offenses already discussed, to renounce inchoate conspiracy requires that the defendant "thwarted the success of the conspiracy, under circumstances manifesting a complete and voluntary renunciation of his criminal purpose."[64] One implication of the wording "his criminal purpose" is that, before being entitled to renunciation, a defendant must acknowledge that they conspired to commit a crime.[65]

---

61. *See* Alexander & Kessler, *supra* note 6, at 1138.

62. *State v. Lewis*, 220 Conn. 602, 607 (1991) (holding that "the prosecution must show both that the conspirators intended to agree and that they intended to commit the elements of the underlying offense.").

63. Ted Prim, *Mens Rea Requirement for Conspiracy: The Model Penal Code and the Progressive Law of Judge Learned Hand*, 40 Mo. L. Rev. 467 (1975).

64. MPC § 5.03(6).

65. *See Commonwealth v. Nee*, 458 Mass. 174 (2010). Nee was one of four high school students planning to conduct a mass shooting at their school. Nee and two other co-conspirators eventually went to the police and reported the plan, but none of the three admitted their involvement. While they effectively thwarted the plan, in not acknowledging that they conspired to commit a crime, they were unable to claim renunciation. To be successful, a defendant must completely renounce their individual criminal purpose, not that of others. Not only was Nee not entitled to renunciation, everything he said to the police about the mass shooting plan was subsequently used against him at trial.

Conspiracy

Crime of one or more persons agreeing or understanding, express or implied, to commit a crime

Common Law		MPC	
Actus Reus	Agreement (bilateral / between 2+ people) Danger of criminal collusion makes conspiracy a distinct crime from target offense; Can be expressed or implied agreement; Must prove there is some pre-planning	**Actus Reus**	Agreement of criminal collusion Can be unilateral: DEF believes other party agreed
Mens Rea General Specific	Dual Intent Intent to agree expressed or implied Intent to accomplish the target offense	**Mens Rea**	Dual mens rea Purpose to enter into the agreement Purpose to achieve the criminal result / object of the conspiracy

Attendant Circumstances (Common Law & MPC)

An overt act by any co-conspirator in furtherance of the agreement; proves some preparation

Braverman Rule (Common Law & MPC)

Number of conspiracy charges is based on number of agreements NOT the number of target offenses

Exceptions when one agreement violates multiple specific conspiracy prohibitions then one agreement may be basis for multiple conspiracy charges

Defenses

Withdrawal (Only MPC)
Requires communication to all co-conspirators
or Preventing the conspiratorial goal
Is not a defense to conspiracy; only to subsequent crimes
in furtherance of the agreement

Withdrawal applicable in all jurisdictions, but is never a defense to the
conspiracy DEF withdrew from.
Withdrawal does sever liability for future crimes (see Pinkerton liability)

Renunciation (Only MPC)
Designed to create incentive
Affirmative defense, erases conspiracy
Requires informing police AND admitting being
part of conspiracy

C. Attempt

Attempt is "an offense of misconduct incomplete, frustrated, or prevented."[66] Criminal attempts come in two forms: complete/failed attempts and incomplete attempts. A complete/failed attempt is one where an individual has taken all the steps they envisioned as necessary to commit a crime but still failed to do so.[67] The classic example of a complete/failed attempt is when A shoots at B intending to kill or wound him but misses. An incomplete attempt is one where the individual is moving towards but prevented from taking the final steps envisioned as necessary. An example of incomplete attempt would be where A has purchased a gun and ammunition, loaded the weapon and traveled to where B is, but a police officer detains A before A can even withdraw the gun from his coat let alone fire at B.

---

66. CRS Attempt, *supra* note 45.

67. As discussed above, attempt is subject to the merger doctrine. As a result, where A successfully completes the attempt to murder B, aka murders B, the attempt merges into the completed crime, and A is only charged with murder.

As one commentator explained:

> For good reason, attempts to commit crimes are themselves crimes in every mature legal system. A bungled robbery, a missed shot, a beating that fails to kill despite the perpetrator's best effort, a would-be rape fought off by the intended victim, a smuggling stopped at the border, and many more failed efforts besides possess the marks of wrongful conduct to which the state should respond with criminal penalties. And yet courts and commentators have consistently failed to explicitly offer a coherent theory of this fundamental area of criminal law. [68]

Part of the reason for the lack of a coherent theory is that to properly understand attempt crimes requires a much broader and deeper inquiry than might be expected.

> Criminal attempt involves the very foundations of criminal liability; before one can conclude even a preliminary analysis, an appraising eye must be cast over almost the entire penal law—the definitions, the types of crime, the nature of "the act," the sanctions—in order to unravel any thread of reason that can be discovered in the apparently unreasoned conglomeration of case and statute law, and exhibited doctrine. [69]

Returning to the continuum of crime, attempt occupies the initiation of perpetration space, further along the spectrum than preparation but not reaching the point of successful completion or consummation of the target crime.

Trying to demarcate the start of attempt and the perpetration of that crime is not particularly complicated for the complete/failed attempt, because the defendant will have completed the last act he or she deemed necessary to commit the target crime. But for incomplete attempts, identifying this line remains a challenge which has been described as "the line between mere preparation and attempt is drawn where the shadow of the substantive offense begins."[70] Another way to think of the difference is that "[b]etween preparation for the attempt and the attempt itself [] there is a wide difference. The preparation consists in devising or arranging the means or measures necessary for the commission of the offense[.] [T]he attempt is the direct movement

---

68. Gideon Yaffe, *Criminal Attempts*, 124 YALE L.J. 1 (2014).

69. Jerome Hall, *Criminal Attempt—A Study of Foundations of Criminal Liability*, 40 YALE L.J. 789 (1940).

70. CRS Attempt, *supra* note 45, which paraphrases and subsequently quotes Oliver Wendall Holmes' remark that

> Eminent judges have been puzzled where to draw the line, or even to state the principle on which it should be drawn, between the two sets of cases. But the principle is believed to be similar to that on which all other lines are drawn by the law. Public policy, that is to say, legislative considerations, are at the bottom of the matter; the considerations being, in this case, the nearness of the danger, the greatness of the harm, and the degree of apprehension felt.

OLIVER WENDELL HOLMES, THE COMMON LAW, 68 (1938 ed.).

toward[s] the commission after the preparations are made."[71] An individual steps over the line demarcating preparation from attempt through conduct—the actus reus for attempt.

As you will see below, over time, different formulations of how to identify this line were tried in different jurisdictions. However, even within a jurisdiction applying a singular formulation, the line (and its shadow) may be in different places for different substantive offenses. As a result, what conduct crosses the line and meets the actus reus requirement for attempt also varies. As the Eleventh Circuit noted:

> While the parameters of the substantial step requirement are simply stated, they do not always provide bright lines for application. This is not surprising; the identification of a substantial step, like the identification of attempt itself, is necessarily a matter of degree that can vary depending on the particular facts of each case viewed in light of the crime charged. An act that may constitute a substantial step towards the commission of one crime may not constitute such a step with respect to a different crime. Thus, substantial-step analysis necessarily begins with a proper understanding of the crime being attempted. . . . Further important to a substantial-step assessment is an understanding of the underlying conduct proscribed by the crime being attempted.[72]

Two other factors reinforce the need to know where the line between preparation and attempt is drawn and the actus reus required to cross it. First, while the punishment for attempt varies,[73] it is normally greater than that for solicitation or conspiracy.[74] Second, there is no gradation or levels of attempt, meaning incomplete and complete/failed attempts are considered—and punished—as attempt.

1. Attempt Actus Reus

Speaking to the lack of a coherent theory mentioned above, courts employ a number of different approaches or tests to determine when conduct has crossed the line

---

71. *People v. Murray*, 14 Cal. 159 (1859).

72. *United States v. Farhane*, 634 F.3d 127, 147, 148 (2d Cir. 2011). The Seventh Circuit later succinctly reframed the Second Circuit's perspective to "[t]his line between mere preparation and a substantial step is inherently fact specific; conduct that would appear to be mere preparation in one case might qualify as a substantial step in another." *United States v. Muratovic*, 719 F.3d 809, 815 (7th Cir. 2013).

73. As referenced above, under the MPC, attempt is considered as the same grade and degree as the most serious substantive offense that is its object, with the exception of first-degree felonies, for which the inchoate version is considered a second-degree felony.

74. In most jurisdictions, an attempt to commit a felony is itself a felony but the maximum punishment is less than for actually successfully completing the target offense. But the punishment for attempted crimes may still be considerable. For example, in many states, the maximum punishment for attempted murder is a life sentence with the possibility of parole, as opposed to a possible death penalty or no parole for the offense of murder.

such that it constitutes the actus reus for an attempt offense. Called the "overt act" requirement for attempt, this is the actus reus: the overt act that crosses the line from preparation to perpetration. Some tests look backwards, meaning how many steps has the individual taken towards completing the crime. Other tests look forward, meaning how many steps are left to take before the individual would commit the crime. Some tests factor in the amount of harm of the completed offense and require a correspondingly smaller step, while others uniformly apply the same standard to all crimes. The result is that different tests often yield different results based on the same conduct and the same target crime. As you read the attempt cases below, consider applying a different test than the one used and seeing if the result would change.

The common law tests with which you need to be familiar are:

Probable Desistance test—the conduct constitutes an attempt if, in the ordinary and natural course of events, without interruption from an outside source, it will result in the crime intended.

Dangerous Proximity Doctrine—a test [] whereby the greater the gravity and probability of the offense, and the nearer the act to the crime, the stronger is the case for calling the act an attempt.

Indispensable Element Test—defendant has obtained all of the elements necessary for committing the crime.

Last Act Test—defendant has initiated the last act necessary to complete the crime.

Physical Proximity Test—the act required for an attempt must be proximate to the completed crime, or directly tending toward the completion of the crime, or must amount to the commencement of the consummation.

Res Ipsa Loquitur or Unequivocality Test—an attempt is committed when the actor's conduct manifests an intent to commit a crime.

Recognizing the vagueness and subjectivity in many of the common law tests, the MPC developed the "substantial step test"; a test that has been widely adopted even in jurisdictions that have not adopted the MPC. Under this test, the actus reus for attempt requires that an individual does or omits to do something "constituting a substantial step in a course of conduct planned to culminate in his commission of the crime."[75] In order for conduct to qualify as a substantial step, it must be "strongly corroborative of the actor's criminal purpose."[76]

---

75. MPC § 5.01(1)(c).

76. MPC § 5.01(2). The MPC provides a non-exhaustive list of conduct which may constitute a substantial step including:

(a) lying in wait, searching for or following the contemplated victim of the crime;

(b) enticing or seeking to entice the contemplated victim of the crime to go to the place contemplated for its commission;

(c) reconnoitering the place contemplated for the commission of the crime;

How much more precise and objective the substantial step test is compared to the common law tests is debatable. But in focusing on the steps the individual has already taken rather than how many steps remain to be taken, the MPC "broadened the scope of attempt liability."[77]

2. Attempt Mens Rea[78]

As already mentioned, inchoate crimes, including attempt, require the highest mens rea, specific intent at common law and purpose under the MPC.[79]

3. Abandoning an Attempt

Once again, as with solicitation and conspiracy, at common law, it was not possible to reverse attempt once the actor, specifically intending to commit the offense, took sufficient steps under the applicable actus reus test to move from preparation to perpetration. But unsurprisingly, the MPC recognizes renunciation as an affirmative defense to an attempt crime. Although called renunciation, what this affirmative defense really means is that *after* the defendant commenced the attempt (took the substantial step), she had a complete and voluntary change of heart and abandoned the effort to commit the crime. To claim this affirmative defense, the burden is on the defendant to establish they "abandoned the effort to commit the crime or otherwise prevented its commission, under circumstances manifesting a complete and voluntary renunciation of his criminal purpose."

(d) unlawful entry of a structure, vehicle or enclosure in which it is contemplated that the crime will be committed;

(e) possession of materials to be employed in the commission of the crime, which are specially designed for such unlawful use or which can serve no lawful purpose of the actor under the circumstances;

(f) possession, collection or fabrication of materials to be employed in the commission of the crime, at or near the place contemplated for its commission, where such possession, collection or fabrication serves no lawful purpose of the actor under the circumstances; and

(g) soliciting an innocent agent to engage in conduct constituting an element of the crime.

While providing examples of what might constitute a substantial step, the real significance is that where a defendant has committed one or more of the listed acts, and they are deemed strongly corroborative of the defendant's criminal purpose, the MPC does not allow for a finding of insufficient evidence as a matter of law. This means that where a prosecutor has introduced evidence of the defendant committing one or more of the listed acts, the judge may not grant a defense motion for directed verdict for failing to meet the actus reus element of an attempt offense.

77. 2 WAYNE R. LaFAVE, SUBSTANTIVE CRIMINAL LAW § 11.4(e), at 313 (3d ed. 2018).

78. Arnold Enker, *Mens Rea and Criminal Attempt*, 2 AMERICAN BAR FOUND. RES. J. 845 (1977).

79. Under the MPC, the mens rea "purpose" applies to *doing* the act not to completing the crime. As a result, the MPC allows for an attempt to commit a reckless crime, but this has not been widely accepted or followed. *See* Michael T. Cahill, *Attempt, Reckless Homicide, and the Design of Criminal Law*, 78 COLO. L. REV. 879 (2007).

Attempt

Common Law

Actus Reus Going beyond the line between preparation & perpetration

Mens Rea Intent to attempt act;
Intent to consummate the target offense

General Intent to take attempt act

Specific Intent to consummate the target offense

How you look at DEF's actions depends on test utilized in jurisdiction.

MPC

Actus Reus A completed final act but failure to complete the offense (failed attempt)
or
A substantial step

Mens Rea Mental state required for the target offense
Has the PRO alleged an act/omission that is a substantial step?

Does alleged conduct strongly corroborate DEF's intent to complete the object of agreement?

Look at what DEF has done, not what DEF has not done

Complete Attempt DEF has done every act necessary on their part to commit the target offense but still failed to complete the crime.

   No Actus Reus issues in the case

   Substantial step has been taken

   Defendant has done everything including the last act

Incomplete Attempt DEF has not committed the last act required to commit the target crime.

   Substantial step has been taken in the course of conduct to commit the crime

   Jury has the authority to find that the step strongly corroborates the DEF's criminal purpose

   Looks at the totality of the circumstances

Attempt Overt Act Tests

Probable Desistance DEF's conduct would result in the completed crime in the "ordinary and natural course of events" if the actor had not been interrupted by a 3rd party (including police).

Dangerous Proximity A genuine danger that the crime would be committed; proximity to completion; Danger of crime itself (greater the danger to society, the less close DEF has to be to completing the crime).

Indispensable Element DEF has obtained all the necessary elements for completing the crime.

Last Act DEF has initiated the last act necessary to complete the crime.

Physical Proximity DEF must be close in time and space to the final act that completes the crime.

Res Ipsa Loquitor/Unequivocality DEF's conduct manifests an unequivocal intent to commit the crime (actions speak for themselves).

Attempt Defenses

Factual Impossibility (NOT A DEFENSE)
DEF's intended outcome constitutes a crime but DEF failed to complete the offense because of a factual circumstance unknown to DEF or beyond DEF's control (tried to fire an unloaded gun).

Pure Legal Impossibility (IS A DEFENSE)
DEF falsely imagined his conduct was criminal even though it was not.

Abandonment (MPC Only)
DEF completely and voluntarily abandons the incomplete attempt.

As you read the cases below, consider returning to the introduction to compare and contrast the different formulations of actus reus, mens rea and application of renunciation and abandonment.

II. Solicitation

Solicitation as a stand-alone, substantive, common law offense dates back to the early 19th century. In 1801, an English court heard a case in which the defendant had asked a servant to steal items from the wealthy house in which the servant worked. The servant ignored the request, and the items remained with their owner. The court explained that "a mere intent to commit evil is not indictable, without an act done; but is there not an act done, when it is charged that the defendant solicited another to commit a felony? *The solicitation is an act*."[80] By 1825, there were reported cases in the U.S. of solicitation as a substantive offense and then, more than 100 years later, the offense was included in the MPC.[81]

As discussed in the introduction, the actus reus for inchoate crimes is relatively easily met. In the case of solicitation, the actus reus is asking someone else to commit a crime.[82] But that low actus reus is offset by the highest mens rea, specific intent at common law and purpose under the MPC. How does a prosecutor prove a high mens rea? Keep in mind that the defendant does not have to testify or, alternatively, may testify and claim they didn't really want a crime committed. To meet their burden of proof, often prosecutors introduce circumstantial evidence, facts from which a finder of fact can infer the mental state.[83]

In the *Hale* case below, the defendant was worried that law enforcement were monitoring at least some of his communications. At times, the defendant made statements about not wanting to be involved in committing a crime. As you read the case, consider the circumstantial evidence the prosecution used to corroborate that Hale intended a crime to be committed.

---

80. *Rex v. Higgins*, 102 Eng. Rep. 269 (K.B. 1801) (emphasis added).

81. *See* Herbert Wechsler et al., *The Treatment of Inchoate Crimes in the Model Penal Code of the American Law Institute: Attempt, Solicitation, and Conspiracy*, 61 COLUMBIA L. REV. 571 (1961).

82. The actus reus of solicitation is speech, and the precise parameters of when that speech is criminal vs. constitutionally protected remains unclear. In 2020, the Supreme Court declined an invitation to "clarify the "important distinction" between unprotected solicitation of illegal activity and protected "abstract advocacy" of such activity." *United States v. Sineneng-Smith*, 590 U.S. ___ (2020), Brief amicus curiae of Professor Eugene Volokh Dec. 9, 2019 https://www.supremecourt.gov /DocketPDF/19/19-67/124856/20191209115753057_19-67acVolokh.pdf

83. Recall from the introduction that where a solicitee accepts the request to commit a crime, that meets the agreement element of a more serious conspiracy charge. The point being that inchoate solicitation is generally only charged where the solicitee did not accept the request, often because they are either an informant or an undercover law enforcement officer. These individuals often record their interactions with the solicitor, which prosecutors then argue is sufficient proof of mens rea.

A. Solicitation and Circumstantial Evidence of Mens Rea

United States v. Hale
448 F.3d 971 (7th Cir. 2006)
Seventh Circuit Court of Appeals

PER CURIAM.

Matthew Hale was convicted after a jury trial on two counts of obstructing justice, 18 U.S.C. §1503, and one count of soliciting a crime of violence, *id.* §373, in connection with his resistance to a judgment entered against his white supremacist organization by United States District Judge Joan Humphrey Lefkow and his involvement in a plot to have the judge murdered. Hale was sentenced to a total of 480 months' imprisonment.

Hale was the "Pontifex Maximus" of a white supremacist organization formerly known as the World Church of the Creator ("World Church"). A law school graduate, Hale was unable to procure the character and fitness certification necessary for admission to the state bar of Illinois. After he obtained no relief through the administrative appeals process, and after both the Supreme Court of Illinois and the Supreme Court of the United States denied review, Hale unsuccessfully brought constitutional challenges in federal court. See *Hale v. Comm. on Character Fitness*, 335 F.3d 678 (7th Cir. 2003). He later sought, and was denied, bar admission in Iowa as well.

In May 2000 the World Church was sued for trademark infringement by the TE-TA-MA Truth Foundation—Family of URI, Inc. ("the Foundation"), a religious organization that operates under the name "Church of the Creator." Both parties moved for summary judgment, which Judge Lefkow granted in favor of the World Church. On appeal, however, we reversed and remanded with instructions to enter judgment in favor of the Foundation. *TE-TA-MA Truth Foundation—Family of URI, Inc. v. World Church of the Creator*, 297 F.3d 662 (7th Cir. 2002). Accordingly, on November 19, 2002, Judge Lefkow entered a detailed order requiring the World Church to stop using variations of the trademarked name "Church of the Creator," to turn over books and other materials bearing the name or obliterate any infringing mark from them, and relinquish custody of the domain names of the World Church's websites to the Foundation. The Foundation soon returned to court seeking enforcement of the order after Hale publicly stated that he would not comply. The court granted the Foundation's motion and ordered Hale to show cause why he should not be held in contempt.

[In 1999, a member of the World Church went on a shooting rampage in Chicago, killing two and wounding nine. Following the shooting, an FBI cooperating witness, Tony Evola, infiltrated the World Church].

At his very first World Church meeting in March 2000, Evola met Hale and apparently won his trust when he fended off a protestor. At a meeting the following month,

Hale asked Evola to be his "head of security" because the previous occupier of the position, Ken Dippold, had betrayed him by cooperating in a civil case brought against the World Church.... As head of security, Evola's duties included arranging Hale's travel and standing by his side during public appearances. Evola was also in charge of the White Berets, the World Church's "elite" fighting force. During his time in Hale's employ, Evola recorded a number of conversations that were ultimately introduced into evidence at Hale's trial.

... In November, after Judge Lefkow issued the order requiring the World Church to cease using its trademarked name, Hale penned a tract entitled "Rigged Court System Declares War on Church" and sent it to his followers. Hale wrote that the order "places our Church in a state of war with this federal judge and any acting on authority of her kangaroo court." Hale branded the mandate a "book burning order," suggesting to his followers that all World Church literature—including their guiding light, *The White Man's Bible*—would have to be destroyed. Though the World Church was represented by counsel, Hale personally sent a letter to Judge Lefkow on December 12, 2002, complaining that "gross injustice" and "fraud" had occurred in the case. He also wrote that he was no longer in control of World Church activities, and that "from [his] understanding of the Court's order [he had] no material in [his] control or possession that falls afoul of it."

On December 4, 2002, just days after Hale disseminated his manifesto, he emailed Evola and asked him to locate the home address of "Judge Joan H. Lefkow, PROBABLE JEW OR MARRIED TO JEW," as well as the home addresses of the three attorneys, all male, who represented the Foundation in the trademark case. Hale labeled two of the lawyers "JEW" and the other "TRAITOR WHITE." He concluded the message by stating: "Any action of any kind against those seeking to destroy our religious liberties is entirely up to each and every Creator according to the dictates of his own conscience."

On December 5, Evola went to Hale's home unannounced to discuss the email "about the Jew judge" and, in particular, Hale's request to locate her home address:

Hale: That information, yes, for educational purposes and for whatever reason you wish it to be.

Evola: Are we gonna... I'm workin' on it. I, I got a way of getting it. Ah, when we get it, we gonna exterminate the rat?

Hale: Well, whatever you wanna do ...

Evola: Jew rat?

Hale: ... basically, it's, you know? Ah, my position's always been that I, you know, I'm gonna fight within the law and but ah, that information's been pro—, provided. If you wish to, ah, do anything yourself, you can, you know?

Evola: Okay.

Hale: So that makes it clear.

Evola: Consider it done.

Hale: Good.

Hale asked Evola to send him the address once he learned it so that Hale could post it on the Internet.

On December 9, Evola sent an email to Hale announcing:

> I called the exterminator I know about the rat problem we talked about. The guy is good and does a good quiet job. You have to know where rats hide and he think [sic] he located her. He is working to get rid of the femala [sic] rat right now.

Hale did not reply, but an electronic receipt confirms that he opened the message.

On December 17, Evola appeared unannounced at Hale's home to discuss the plan. Hale did not want to discuss the matter because he assumed that he was "always being listened to, watched, monitored." When Evola mentioned "exterminating the rat," Hale answered, "I can't be a party to such a thing" and lamented that Evola was putting him "in an impossible situation." Hale expressed his concern that "there's a federal statute that makes it . . . an imprisonable offense to know about a crime that's to be occurred . . . without telling anybody." Evola stated that the plan was already in motion and that it was costing him more than he expected; he asked Hale if there were "two trusted brothers that could help out with this." Hale responded, "I can't take any steps to further anything illegal, ever." Evola then asked if he could stay with Hale "when this stuff does come to happen," and Hale refused, explaining that he was concerned about being considered "some kind of accessory in something I do not want to be an accessory in." Hale later stated: "I'm not telling you to do anything, you know. Either way." "[W]hatever a person does," he added, "is according to the dictates of their own conscience." Evola again alluded to compensating the assassins and mentioned being "a couple hundred short." Hale responded, "I just can't provide anything." Hale stated that he might "have a smile on his face" if he were to read in a newspaper that "something happens to certain creepy people" but that he could not "be any kind of party." When Evola discussed the trustworthiness of "his cousin's friends," Hale replied, "[O]f course, we're talking about Little League baseball, aren't we?" Hale asked Evola not to turn up unannounced at his home again.

Hale was arrested in Chicago on January 8, 2003, when he appeared for a contempt hearing for his refusal to comply with Judge Lefkow's order in the trademark case. Pursuant to a third superceding indictment filed in October 2003, he was charged with three counts of obstructing justice, 18 U.S.C. § 1503, and two counts of soliciting a crime of violence, *id.* § 373. The latter counts separately charged Hale with soliciting Tony Evola . . . to murder Judge Lefkow. . . .

Before trial the government notified Hale of its intent to introduce testimony and recorded conversations . . . argu[ing] that the proposed evidence was "strongly corroborative" of Hale's "intent in the solicitation case." . . .

Hale was tried before a jury in April 2004. . . . Hale was [] convicted of solicitation . . . in connection with his efforts to have Judge Lefkow killed [resulting] . . . from Hale's dealings with Tony Evola. . . .

Hale appeals, challenging [] the sufficiency of the evidence underlying his convictions for solicitation and obstruction in connection with the plan to kill Judge Lefkow. . . .

Sufficiency of the evidence

Hale argues that no rational trier of fact could have found beyond a reasonable doubt that he solicited Tony Evola to murder Judge Lefkow. He contends that his conversation with Evola on December 17, 2002, demonstrates conclusively that he opposed Evola's plan and that no rational jury could have concluded that his comments suggesting otherwise were meant to be taken seriously. According to Hale, the government's evidence actually exonerates him because it establishes that he believed Evola intended to kill opposing counsel in the trademark case, whose murder he "had a greater motive to 'solicit.'" . . .

When reviewing challenges to the sufficiency of the evidence, we view all evidence in the light most favorable to the government. . . . We will reverse a jury's verdict only if no rational trier of fact could have found the essential elements of the crime beyond a reasonable doubt. . . . The appellant's hurdle, as we have often stated, is "nearly insurmountable." See, e.g., *United States v. Caldwell*, 423 F.3d 754, 757 (7th Cir. 2005); *United States v. King*, 356 F.3d 774, 779 (7th Cir. 2004); *United States v. Brown*, 328 F.3d 352, 355 (7th Cir. 2003).

In order to meet its burden of proof on the solicitation count, the government had to establish (1) with "strongly corroborative circumstances" that Hale intended for Tony Evola to arrange the murder of Judge Lefkow; and (2) that Hale solicited, commanded, induced, or otherwise tried to persuade Evola to carry out the crime. 18 U.S.C. § 373 . . . .

Taking the second element first: the government had to prove that Hale "solicited, commanded, induced, or otherwise tried to persuade" Evola to carry out a violent crime. The government argues that the solicitation was accomplished "through coded and disguised language." Asking Evola to locate Judge Lefkow's home address "for whatever reason you wish it to be" was, according to the government, "Hale's code for approving the attack." For his part, Hale all but concedes that there was adequate evidence with respect to this element; he seems to accept that the government proved he solicited the murder of someone, just not Judge Lefkow.

We conclude that there is sufficient evidence in the record to support the jury's finding on the solicitation element. Hale knew that Evola was willing to arrange murder on his behalf; he had offered to do so on several previous occasions, and Hale had engaged him in serious discussion concerning at least one of those proposed victims. Hale also knew that securing a proposed victim's home address was a preliminary step in Evola's process; it is through that lens that the government asked the jury to read Hale's email of December 4, 2002, asking Evola to acquire Judge Lefkow's home address. Evola followed up Hale's email by visiting him the next day and making it clear that he interpreted the email as a suggestion to "exterminate the rat." When Hale indicated that he did not want to be involved but that Evola was free to act himself, Evola said, "Consider it done," to which Hale replied, "Good." Unlike his repudiation of Evola's earlier plots, Hale did not "veto" Evola's plan after this conversation; in fact, Hale responded with silence to Evola's email of December 9, which can be read only as conveying to Hale that the "exterminator" had located Judge Lefkow and was "working to get rid of" her. In their conversation on December 17, Hale protested that he could not be involved in illegal activity in any way. In the same conversation, however, he mentioned that he would have a smile on his face if he was to read in a newspaper that "something happens to certain creepy people." As the government has maintained, Hale tried to "create 'plausible deniability' in the event his conversation was being monitored." Under these circumstances, we have no difficulty concluding that a jury could find from the evidence that Hale's conduct was a call to action, not a passive failure to intervene to stop another's crime or, as Hale would have us believe, disapproval of Evola's stated preparations to kill Judge Lefkow. The jury believed the government's theory rather than Hale's, and it is not our place to reweigh the evidence, see *Brown*, 328 F.3d at 355.

Having decided that a rational jury could conclude that Hale tried to persuade Evola to act, we now examine whether the government met its burden of producing evidence "strongly corroborative" of Hale's intent that Evola murder Judge Lefkow. 18 U.S.C. § 373; see [*United States v.*] *Rahman*, 34 F.3d at 1337. Examples of circumstances "strongly corroborative" of intent include the defendant offering or promising payment or another benefit in exchange for committing the offense; threatening harm or other detriment for refusing to commit the offense; repeatedly soliciting or discussing at length in soliciting the commission of the offense, or making explicit that the solicitation is serious; believing or knowing that the person solicited had previously committed similar offenses; and acquiring weapons, tools, or information for use in committing the offense, or making other apparent preparations for its commission. . . . These examples are not exclusive, nor are they conclusive indicators of intent to solicit. *United States v. Gabriel*, 810 F.2d 627, 635 (7th Cir. 1987). The existence of strongly corroborating circumstances is a question of fact for the jury. See *id*. at n. 5.

We conclude that there was sufficient evidence from which the jury could determine that Hale possessed the requisite intent. Hale provided Evola with Judge Lefkow's name and business address in order to help him locate the judge's home address. On December 17, 2002, Hale and Evola discussed at length the plan to have the judge murdered, albeit in oblique terms. . . . Hale's suggestion to Evola that he should do "whatever you wanna do" to Judge Lefkow thus evinces Hale's intent to have the judge murdered. And Hale made his intent patent when he sent Evola an email with the judge's name and business address along with the admonition, "Any action of any kind against those seeking to destroy our religious liberties is entirely up to each and every Creator according to the dictates of his own conscience";

Evola's prior offers to "take care of" people established exactly what actions would be in accord with the dictates of his conscience. Hale cannot pretend that Evola did not tell him repeatedly over the course of their acquaintance that he had "friends" willing to perform acts of violence. And Hale made his desire explicit by replying with "Good" when Evola told him on December 5 that the plan to "exterminate the rat" was as good as done. Hale's insistence that he thought Evola was talking about someone else on December 5 is a frivolous argument on this record, particularly because in the days that followed Evola identified the target in language that pointed to the judge alone, but Hale said nothing to suggest that a misunderstanding had occurred. Evola's email to Hale on December 9 assured Hale that the "exterminator" he had called "located her" and was "working to get rid of the femala [sic] rat right now." Judge Lefkow was the only woman on the list that Hale sent on December 4, so his defense that he was confused about the intended victim is unconvincing. . . .

Hale's statements that he did not wish to participate in illegal conduct do not call into question the jury's findings with respect to his intent. The government convincingly portrayed Hale as a leader who encouraged each follower to act "according to the dictates of his own conscience"—in reality Hale's conscience—while verbalizing his own commitment to following the law. Hale never criticized Evola's desire to inflict harm on Hale's enemies even as he attempted to insulate himself from blame. . . . This pattern was consistent with Hale's behavior when Evola offered to have Judge Lefkow killed; he professed his own desire to follow the law but encouraged Evola to do whatever he wanted. In Gabriel, the appellants who had been convicted of soliciting the arson of their businesses argued that their attempt to postpone the crime and their refusal to supply the arsonist with alcohol for the fire and keys proved that they were not serious about the arson. We concluded that the jury could have inferred that their actions "were means of distancing themselves from the planned arsons and not designed to rebuff or discourage" the crime. *Gabriel*, 810 F.2d at 635-36. In this case too it was up to the jury to decide between competing views of the evidence, and it accepted the government's theory that Hale's refusal to overtly help with the crime and his ruminations on his innocence masked his true intention that Evola carry out their plan. We will not substitute our judgment for the jury's. . . .

AFFIRMED.

That Evola was a government informant who had no intention of killing Judge Lefkow was irrelevant to the question of Hale's guilt for soliciting her murder. But what about where the solicitee is not only a law enforcement officer but one role playing as a teenager who doesn't actually exist? The *Dellacamera* case below involves a U.S. service member requesting nude photos of and from the fictional teenager, which presents the issue of impossibility as applied to solicitation.

B. Solicitation and Impossibility

When a defendant pleads guilty, it normally results in a waiver of appeal. This is especially true when the plea is pursuant to a plea bargain, as waiver of appeal is normally a condition of the "deal." But even without such an agreement-based waiver, a plea of guilty waives constitutional based objections to the admissibility of evidence; by pleading guilty, the defendant forfeits the opportunity to seek exclusion of evidence based on such objections. Accordingly, appeals from convictions based on guilty pleas in civilian practice are very rare, and when they do arise, normally allege ineffective assistance of the defense counsel who advised the defendant to plead guilty.

This is not the case in military practice. Any service-member sentenced to confinement or a punitive discharge (like a dishonorable discharge) by court-martial has a statutory right to appeal to the Service appellate court (for example, in the next case, the Navy-Marine Corps Court of Criminal Appeals) even if the conviction is the result of a plea of guilty. A common appellate issue raised by those convicted by courts-martial based on a plea of guilty is that the plea was not "provident"—meaning there was an insufficient factual basis to accept the plea of guilty or that during the plea process, where the defendant must explain why he believes he is guilty, the defendant raises an issue of a defense that would negate guilt. In such situations, the military judge is obligated to reject the plea unless the issue is resolved during the plea colloquy. This the basis for the appeal in the next case, requiring the appellate court to determine whether it was appropriate for the military judge to accept Dellacamera's plea.

United States v. Dellacamera

No. 201600230 (March 30, 2017)
Navy-Marine Court of Criminal Appeals

CAMPBELL, Senior Judge:

At an uncontested general court-martial [guilty plea], a military judge convicted the appellant of attempted sexual assault of a child, attempted sexual abuse of a child, attempted production of child pornography, absence without leave, indecent exposure, and soliciting production and distribution of child pornography. . . . The military judge sentenced the appellant to 48 months' confinement, reduction to pay grade E-1 [the lowest pay grade], a dishonorable discharge [the most punitive level of discharge], and a reprimand. . . .

The appellant [claims that] the military judge abused his discretion in accepting the appellant's guilty pleas to Charge IV and its sole specification—solicitation of production and distribution of child pornography in violation of Article 134, UCMJ. . . .

. . . Ultimately, we conclude the remaining findings and sentence are correct in law and fact and that no error materially prejudicial to the appellant's substantial rights remains. . . .

I. Background

The appellant was a Military Policeman stationed in Okinawa, Japan. On 6 January 2016, he communicated through a web-based instant messaging application with an individual he believed to be a 14-year-old girl, whose screen name was "lizzdezz." Despite her apparent age, the appellant used sexually explicit language, sent a digital image of another man's exposed penis to her, and sent an image of his own naked torso and partially exposed penis to her. He suggested they meet to engage in oral and vaginal sex, and requested that she send him nude, sexually explicit photographs of herself.

In fact, "lizzdezz" was the on-line persona of an undercover Naval Criminal Investigative Service (NCIS) special agent. "Lizzdezz" repeatedly refused to provide or take any nude photographs for the appellant, but she agreed the appellant could photograph her when they met in person that afternoon. The appellant then left his Camp Foster office, during normal business hours, and drove his personal vehicle to Kadena Air Base, where he expected to visit the 14-year-old girl's home. He was apprehended instead.

II. Discussion

. . . .

B. Solicitation of child pornography

The appellant now challenges his guilty plea. . . . He argues that because "the person [he] was soliciting these photographs from was actually an adult undercover NCIS agent," it was "a legal impossibility" for his request to actually produce child pornography, since "the photos would not have involved a minor" had the agent complied.

We review a military judge's acceptance of a guilty plea for an abuse of discretion, reversing only if the "record shows a substantial basis in law or fact for questioning the plea." *United States v. Moon*, 73 M.J. 382, 386 (C.A.A.F. 2014) (citation omitted).

. . . .

In *United States v. Thomas*, our superior court stated, "the elements of a criminal attempt are [still] present," notwithstanding the presence of either an "impossibility in fact" or a "legal impossibility." 32 C.M.R. 278, 283 (C.M.A. 1962). Consequently, it later affirmed an appellant's conviction for attempted conspiracy where he had agreed to assist in the murder of two named individuals who were, unbeknownst to the appellant, fictitious. [*United States v.*] *Roeseler*, 55 M.J. at 287. "'Our general rule is that an accused should be treated in accordance with the facts as he or she supposed them to be.'" *Id.* at 291 (quoting *United States v. Riddle*, 44 M.J. 282, 286 (C.A.A.F. 1996)) (additional citation omitted).

Courts have treated solicitation and impossibility similarly. Soliciting another to commit an offense requires "[t]hat the accused solicited or advised a certain person or persons to commit a certain offense under the code" with "the intent that the offense actually be committed[.]" Manual For Courts-martial, United States (2012 ed.), Part IV, ¶ 105b. "[N]o legal authority . . . indicates that one may not be convicted of soliciting an undercover agent to commit an offense." *United States v. Cababa*, No. No. 9901417, 2004 CCA LEXIS 235, at *12, unpublished op., (N-M. Ct. Crim. App. 7 Oct 2004). While the solicitation "recipient must be capable of committing a separate criminal offense prohibited by the UCMJ[,]" the criminal act of "solicitation appears to involve nothing more than making a nefarious request or suggestion[.]" *United States v. Ashworth*, No. 201500028, 2015 CCA LEXIS 373, at *4, unpublished op. (N-M. Ct. Crim. App. 3 Sep 2015) (per curiam).

Analyzing solicitation and impossibility outside of the UCMJ context, the Supreme Court has stated, "an Internet user who solicits child pornography from an undercover agent violates [18 U.S.C. § 2252A(a)(3)(B)], even if the officer possesses no child pornography." *United States v. Williams*, 553 U.S. 285, 293 (2008). The Court noted that "[a]s with other inchoate crimes—attempt and conspiracy, for example—impossibility of completing the crime because the facts were not as the defendant believed is not a defense" to "solicitation made unlawful by the Act." *Williams*, 553 U.S. at 300.

In *People v. Thousand*, the Michigan Supreme Court similarly rejected Thousand's claim "that it was 'legally impossible' for him to have committed" solicitation of a minor for sexual acts, where unbeknownst to him he had actually solicited an adult undercover law enforcement officer. 465 Mich. 149, 166–69 (2001) (finding the lower court "erred to the extent that it relied on the doctrine of 'impossibility' . . . [to] dismiss[] the solicitation charge"). It reached this conclusion even though "the underlying form of third-degree criminal sexual conduct charged, [Mich. Comp. Laws § 750.520d(1)(a)], required the existence of a person under the age of sixteen." *Id.* at 167. Again emphasizing that "the concept of 'impossibility' has no role in the analysis of this issue," the Thousand court ultimately dismissed the solicitation of a minor charge for a different reason: the requested act of having sex with the defendant would not be "criminal sexual conduct" on the presumed fourteen year-old's part. *Id.* at 168-69 (also noting "the requested acts might well have constituted a crime on the defendant's part," but "the prosecution was required to present evidence that defendant requested that another person perform a criminal act.").

During the appellant's providence inquiry in this case, he explained he was guilty of soliciting production and distribution of child pornography because he believed he was communicating with a girl less than 16 years old when he asked her to create and send him sexually explicit photographs of herself. He has provided no authority which compels us to recognize a defense of impossibility to his soliciting someone who, unbeknownst to him, was not a minor. The appellant "ma[de] a nefarious request," *Ashworth*, 2015 CCA LEXIS 373, at *4, to a party he believed to be a 14-year-old girl, seriously intending that she create and send him sexually explicit photographs—a crime under the UCMJ, as a minor can create child pornography, even by depicting only himself or herself.

Guided principally by the CAAF's directive to treat the appellant "in accordance with the facts as he . . . supposed them to be," *Roeseler*, 55 M.J. at 291 (citations and internal quotation marks omitted); the Supreme Court's guidance that factual impossibility is not a defense for solicitation to produce child pornography under the United States Code; and the Michigan Supreme Court's persuasive authority holding that legal impossibility does not apply to solicitation of a sex act from a minor where the other party was, unbeknownst to the solicitor, not actually a minor; we hold the appellant's mistaken notion regarding the identity of the party he solicited affords him no defense in military jurisprudence. Even though the adult undercover agent could produce no child pornography by photographing herself, the appellant nonetheless engaged in *an act of seriously requesting* production and distribution of child pornography [emphasis in original]. Thus, we find no substantial basis in law or fact for questioning his guilty plea. . . .

[The court affirmed Dellacamera's guilty plea].

––––––––––

The court in *Dellacamera* surveyed U.S. solicitation cases where defendants made similar claims. The claims are sometimes styled as factual and sometimes legal impossibility. Regardless, as was the case with Dellacamera, impossibility is not a viable defense argument.

A defendant claiming that they could not have committed solicitation due to impossibility is different than raising the affirmative defense of renunciation. As discussed, renunciation is not available at common law. While renunciation is potentially available under the MPC, the *Dvorkin* case highlights the difficulty in successfully raising the defense.

C. Solicitation and Renunciation

United States v. Dvorkin
799 F.3d 867 (7th Cir. 2015)
Seventh Circuit Court of Appeals

RIPPLE, Circuit Judge.

Daniel Dvorkin was convicted on five counts of using, or causing another person to use, a facility of interstate commerce with the intent to commit a murder for hire, in violation of 18 U.S.C. § 1958, and on one count of soliciting another to commit a crime of violence, in violation of 18 U.S.C. § 373. He timely appealed his convictions on various grounds. For the reasons set forth in this opinion, we affirm the judgment of the district court.

I. Background

A

This case arises out of Mr. Dvorkin's failed efforts to hire a hitman to kill a creditor named Larry Meyer. Meyer was the manager of Texas 1845, LLC ("Texas 1845"). In December 2010, Texas 1845 acquired two distressed loans guaranteed by Mr. Dvorkin and his company, Dvorkin Holdings, LLC. Shortly afterward, Texas 1845 filed an action in Illinois state court against Mr. Dvorkin and his company to recover on the debt. On February 26, 2012, the state court entered judgment for Texas 1845 for approximately $8.2 million. On April 2, 2012, the parties attempted, but ultimately failed, to negotiate a settlement of the debt. The judgment became enforceable on May 4, 2012.

1. April 5 Voicemail and April 6 Meeting

On April 5, 2012, Mr. Dvorkin called and left a voicemail for Robert Bevis. Bevis owned and operated a firearms store, which had leased space from one of Mr. Dvorkin's companies, Dan Development, LLC ("Dan Development"). Bevis also worked as a private detective and process server. In his voicemail, Mr. Dvorkin identified himself, stated that he "ha[d] an idea," and asked Bevis to call him back.

The next day, Bevis visited the offices of Dan Development. There, Mr. Dvorkin approached him in the reception area and asked Bevis to accompany him to the parking lot. Once they were alone, Mr. Dvorkin told Bevis that "he had a problem" and handed Bevis a copy of the February 26 judgment in favor of Texas 1845. Mr. Dvorkin stated "that he wanted this guy to stop breathing" and that he was willing to pay $50,000 for Meyer's murder. He then reached into his pocket and brandished a large wad of cash. He explained that he was appealing the judgment and that he could prevail if Meyer were unable to respond.

In response, Bevis told Mr. Dvorkin that he knew someone in Florida who might be willing to accept Mr. Dvorkin's offer. Bevis later testified that this statement was a lie, which he told to end quickly an uncomfortable conversation.

After their conversation, Mr. Dvorkin escorted Bevis back inside Dan Development's offices, where he gave Bevis a printout of Meyer's LinkedIn profile. At the top of the printout was a handwritten note, stating, "Not sure if this [is] your guy!" This note was written by Mr. Dvorkin's administrative assistant, who had printed the profile after Mr. Dvorkin had asked her to find information on Meyer's whereabouts.

Bevis left Dan Development with copies of both the February 26 judgment and Meyer's LinkedIn profile. Later that day, Bevis contacted the Oakbrook Terrace, Illinois, Chief of Police to report his encounter with Mr. Dvorkin. The police, in turn, set up a meeting with the FBI. After hearing Bevis's story, the FBI asked Bevis to become a cooperating witness and to record his conversations with Mr. Dvorkin. Bevis agreed.

2. April 18 Phone Call and Meeting

On April 18, 2012, at the direction of federal agents, Bevis called Mr. Dvorkin to arrange an in-person meeting. The call was recorded. During the call, Mr. Dvorkin stated that he "still ha[d] that problem" and asked Bevis if he had traveled down to Florida. Bevis responded that he had but that he would prefer to talk about it in person. The two agreed to meet later that day.

During their meeting, which was recorded, Bevis told Mr. Dvorkin that the Florida hitman had offered to kill Meyer for approximately $80,000, half of which he required in advance. Mr. Dvorkin responded that he had $50,000 in untraceable funds and would "have to figure out how to get the rest." After discussing the issue further, Mr. Dvorkin offered to loan Bevis $50,000 on favorable terms if he could negotiate with the hitman to accept $50,000 for killing Meyer. Bevis agreed.

3. April 30 and May 3 Phone Calls

On April 30, 2012, Mr. Dvorkin called Bevis and told him "[t]hat he had a different avenue that he may want to take" with respect to Meyer. Bevis testified that he understood this statement to mean that Mr. Dvorkin had "found somebody else to kill Larry Meyer at a cheaper rate than" the fictional Florida hitman. Mr. Dvorkin also told Bevis that his last court date "didn't go well." The two men made plans to speak again soon. On May 3, Mr. Dvorkin called Bevis and made arrangements to meet on May 7.

4. May 7 Meeting and Phone Call

On May 7, 2012, Bevis drove to Mr. Dvorkin's office. In a recorded conversation, Mr. Dvorkin elaborated on the "other avenues" that he had mentioned on April 30. He told Bevis that he had hired someone else to kill Meyer for less than half of the price of the Florida hitman and with only a ten-percent down payment. Further, he explained, this other individual had promised to finish the task by Friday, May 18. Consequently, Mr. Dvorkin initially instructed Bevis to discontinue negotiations with the Florida hitman and to "tell him [that] it fell through." After discussing the issue further, however, Mr. Dvorkin instructed Bevis to inquire whether the Florida hitman would accept a lower price and to tell him that they had found someone else willing to do the job for $20,000. Bevis agreed to do so.

Later in the day on May 7, Bevis, at the direction of the FBI, called Mr. Dvorkin to report that the Florida hitman would accept the lower price. In response, Mr. Dvorkin explained that his plan to use the "other avenue" hitman was already in motion and that he could not do anything until May 18. The two agreed to discuss the issue again on that date.

Following this call, the FBI placed Meyer and his family under twenty-four-hour surveillance. Further, on that same day, law enforcement officers confronted Mr. Dvorkin in the parking lot outside his office. They told him that they were aware of his plot to kill Meyer and that, if Meyer were harmed, he would be the primary suspect.

5. May 8 Meeting

On May 8, 2012, Mr. Dvorkin called and told Bevis that he was on his way to Bevis's gun store. He arrived ten to fifteen minutes later. Their meeting was not recorded. Upon his arrival, Mr. Dvorkin told Bevis that law enforcement had confronted him and had reported that someone had taken "a shot at Larry Meyer." Mr. Dvorkin asked Bevis to search online for news concerning Meyer because he did not want to use his own computer. FBI computer analysts later confirmed that a Google search for Meyer's name was made on Bevis's computer at approximately 10:16 a.m. on May 8.

6. May 11 Phone Call and July 5 Arrest

On May 11, 2012, Bevis called Mr. Dvorkin to determine whether the FBI's intervention had stymied his plan to use the "other avenue" hitman. Bevis started the conversation, which was recorded, by telling Mr. Dvorkin that the FBI had stopped by his gun store and had questioned him about Mr. Dvorkin. After agreeing on what they would say if confronted by the FBI in the future, Bevis inquired whether Mr. Dvorkin still intended to follow through with his plan to kill Meyer:

> BEVIS: . . . I mean is, is everything over? Did you, is everything stopped? I mean 'cause if anything does happen
>
> . . . .
>
> DVORKIN: As far as I know it's all legal. It's all stopped. I am gonna file, ah, ah, a Chapter 11 reorganization. The only thing I do now is through attorneys and, ah, I don't know this guy, this guy sounds like a nut to me.
>
> . . . .
>
> DVORKIN: . . . I'm just gonna get on with my life we're appealing the case.
>
> BEVIS: Yeah.
>
> DVORKIN: I'm just doin' legal things.

FBI agents arrested Mr. Dvorkin on June 5, 2012.

B

In August 2012, a grand jury returned a six-count indictment, charging Mr. Dvorkin with five counts of using or causing another person to use a facility of interstate commerce with the intent to commit a murder for hire, in violation of 18 U.S.C. § 1958, and one count of soliciting another to do the same, in violation of 18 U.S.C. § 373.

Mr. Dvorkin was tried before a jury approximately one year later. During the six-day trial, the Government introduced evidence of the facts just recited. . . . [T]he jury found Mr. Dvorkin guilty on all counts. . . . Mr. Dvorkin timely appealed.

. . . .

II. Discussion

. . . .

B

Mr. Dvorkin [] contends that he presented sufficient evidence to establish a renunciation defense under 18 U.S.C. § 373(b) and, consequently, that the district court erred in denying his motion for acquittal with respect to his solicitation charge. We review a district court's denial of a defend-ant's motion for acquittal de novo. *United States v. Mohamed*, 759 F.3d 798, 803 (7th Cir.2014). "[U]nlike a typical challenge to the sufficiency of the evidence, [a] defendant's burden is even greater" where, as here, he contends that acquittal is warranted based on an affirmative defense. *United States v. Waagner*, 319 F.3d 962, 964 (7th Cir.2003). To prevail on such a claim, the defendant must show that the evidence, even when viewed in the light most favorable to the Government, is "so one-sided that" a rational jury could not reach "any decision [other than] a finding of not guilty" based on the defense asserted. *Id.; see also United States v. Sax*, 39 F.3d 1380, 1385 (7th Cir.1994).

Section 373(b) of Title 18 provides a renunciation defense for defendants charged with violating § 373(a). To establish the defense, a defendant must show (1) that he "prevented the commission of the crime solicited," and (2) that he did so "under circumstances manifesting a voluntary and complete renunciation of his criminal intent." 18 U.S.C. § 373(b). A renunciation is not "complete" if it is tentative, conditional, or otherwise "motivated in whole or in part by a decision to postpone the commission of the crime until another time." *Id.* Relatedly, a renunciation "is not voluntary if it is motivated, in whole or in part, by circumstances, not present or apparent at the inception of the actor's course of conduct, that increase the probability of detection or apprehension. . . ." Model Penal Code § 5.01(4) . . . .

Section 373(b) reads as follows:

> It is an affirmative defense to a prosecution under this section that, under circumstances manifesting a voluntary and complete renunciation of his criminal intent, the defendant prevented the commission of the crime solicited. A renunciation is not "voluntary and complete" if it is motivated in whole or in part by a decision to postpone the commission of the crime until another time or to substitute another victim or another but similar objective. If the defendant raises the affirmative defense at trial, the defendant has the burden of proving the defense by a preponderance of the evidence.

18 U.S.C. § 373(b).

Mr. Dvorkin submits that he renounced his criminal intent on three different occasions: (1) on April 30, when he told Bevis that he had a "different avenue" that he wanted to take with regard to killing Meyer, (2) on May 7, when he instructed Bevis to tell the Florida hitman that "it fell through," and (3) on May 11, when he told Bevis that the plan was "all stopped" and that he was "just gonna get on with [his] life" and deal with Meyer through legal means. In response, the Government contends that Mr. Dvorkin cannot establish this defense because Bevis already had completed the solicited § 1958 offense well before April 30 and, in any event, none of his alleged renunciations were voluntary *and* complete.

. . . .

We agree with the Government on both of its contentions. First, to invoke § 373(b)'s renunciation defense, a defendant must "actually prevent[] the commission of the crime [solicited] (not merely ma[k]e efforts to prevent it)." S.Rep. No. 98–225, at 309

(1984), *as reprinted in* 1984 U.S.C.C.A.N. 3182, 3489. "[O]nce a crime is complete[], it logically can no longer be" prevented. [*United States v.*] *Preacher*, 631 F.3d at 1204. Here, as far as Mr. Dvorkin knew, Bevis had completed the solicited § 1958 offense as early as April 18, when he told Mr. Dvorkin that he had traveled to Florida to arrange for a hitman to kill Meyer. Because, for solicitation purposes, a "defendant's culpability is to be measured by the circumstances as he believes them to be," *United States v. Devorkin*, 159 F.3d 465, 467 n. 2 (9th Cir.1998) (quoting 2 Wayne R. LaFave & Austin W. Scott Jr., *Substantive Criminal Law* § 6.1 (1st ed.1986)), a reasonable jury easily could conclude that Mr. Dvorkin had failed to "prevent[] the commission of the crime solicited," 18 U.S.C. § 373(b).

Second, regardless of timing, the record does not establish, as a matter of law, that Mr. Dvorkin voluntarily *and* completely renounced his criminal intent. With respect to his April 30 and May 7 statements, a jury viewing those communications reasonably could conclude that Mr. Dvorkin merely had put his plan to use the Florida hitman on hold. Although he did, on May 7, instruct Bevis to tell the Florida hitman that "it fell through," after discussing the issue further, he ultimately asked Bevis to negotiate a lower price with the Florida hitman. When Bevis later did so, Mr. Dvorkin, far from abandoning his criminal plan, indicated that he would use the Florida hitman if the "other avenue" killer failed to complete the task by May 18. Given these facts, we cannot say, as a matter of law, that Mr. Dvorkin's April 30 and May 7 communications with Bevis constitute a "complete" renunciation of his criminal intent.

The only statement by Mr. Dvorkin that comes anywhere close to evincing a "complete" renunciation of his criminal intent was his May 11 phone conversation with Bevis. That renunciation, however, occurred four days after the FBI had confronted Mr. Dvorkin about his plan to kill Meyer. Under these circumstances, a reasonable jury certainly could conclude that Mr. Dvorkin's May 11 renunciation was not voluntary.

In sum, we cannot say that the evidence in favor of Mr. Dvorkin's renunciation defense was so one-sided as to require his acquittal as a matter of law. The district court properly upheld his conviction for solicitation.

Conclusion

The judgment of the district court is affirmed.

Notes and Questions

1. As previously discussed, often times, inchoate solicitation involves a situation where the solicitee is either a law enforcement informant or undercover officer. The subsequent operations can involve slightly differing goals of law enforcement vs. prosecutor. Law enforcement officers seek evidence amounting to probable cause to arrest and charge someone. Obviously criminal conviction requires proof beyond a reasonable doubt, and to the average prosecutor, there is no such thing as too much

evidence. The result is that while technically the elements of solicitation are met by communicating a request that someone commit a crime, often undercover officers will continue a meeting with the solicitor in an effort to generate additional support (evidence) of the mens rea for solicitation. In a 2003 undercover operation in Pennsylvania involving a man, Joel Sandler, seeking to hire someone to kill his wife, the additional support took the form of the undercover officer discussing whether Sandler preferred that his wife's body be burned, in some way destroyed, or simply buried. Sandler had offered to pay $25,000 for the murder. Before a meeting could be arranged for Sandler to provide payment to the undercover officer, Sandler became suspicious that the undercover officer may be just that. "Fearing that Sandler might look elsewhere for a hit man, authorities arrested him at that time on charges of solicitation to commit murder. . . ." Margaret Gibbons, *Millionaire sentenced for hiring hit man to kill wife*, THE REPORTER (Mar. 6, 2003). As a matter of law, when did Sandler commit the offense of solicitation to commit murder? Assume the jurisdiction recognized renunciation of solicitation, would Sandler be able to assert that defense of renunciation? Sandler also provides an example that while the punishment for solicitation is generally lower than for other inchoate crimes, when soliciting crimes like murder, the punishment is often years of confinement. Sandler was sentenced to 8 ½ to 25 years of confinement.

2. Perhaps the most frequent crime involving solicitation is prostitution. The internet has shifted both how those offering to perform sexual acts for money and those wishing to purchase sexual services operate. The internet has also changed how law enforcement conduct undercover operations for prostitution cases. Assume a female undercover officer "Amy" advertises "escort services" on a website. An individual claiming to be "John" arranges to meet with Amy at a hotel. In terms of charging John with soliciting prostitution, does it matter that Amy is not a prostitute and was never going to perform any sex acts? Similarly, does it matter who initiates the discussion in the hotel room? (Meaning do you distinguish between Scenario 1: Amy says to John: "I will have sex with you for $100 cash" to which John agrees and pulls out five $20 bills, following which Amy arrests him, and Scenario 2: John says to Amy: "I will pay you $100 to have sex with me" (while waving five $20 bills), following which Amy arrests him. For additional discussion on the use of websites for both prostitution and police undercover operations and how they challengingly intersect with human/sex trafficking), see Shelpy Reilly, *How one website could be both facilitating sex trafficking and aiding police stings*, KTLV.COM (Feb. 28, 2020).

3. In 2003, Swiss bodybuilder Patrick Graber sent a letter to Kobe Bryant's house in which Graber offered to "solve" Bryant's "problem" for a fee. The "problem" Graber was referring to was a woman who had accused Bryant of rape. Bryant's security staff forwarded the letter to Bryant's attorney, who in turn contacted law enforcement. The FBI set a controlled meeting where undercover FBI agents claiming to represent Bryant met with Graber. During the meeting, Graber claimed to have ties with the Russian mob and said he was willing to "go all the way" to "neutralize" Bry-

ant's accuser for a fee of $3 million. You are a legal advisor to the law enforcement task force conducting the undercover operation. Applying the MPC definition, has Graber committed the offense of solicitation to commit murder? Would your answer change under the common law? For a unique and creative perspective on Graber's actions, read the description of a book titled DEAD WOMEN TELL NO TALES: WHO PLANNED THE MURDER OF THE WITNESS IN THE KOBE BRYANT RAPE CASE—AN EXPOSE ON CHANGE written by none other than Graber himself. *See* Amazon.com, https://www.amazon.com/Dead-Women-Tell-No-Tales/dp/3033009727 (last visited Sept. 10, 2021). As of the writing of this chapter in 2021, a limited number (two) of paperback copies of the book were available on Amazon.com for $768.57. For an account with a stronger link to reality, see Justin Rohrlich, *Inside a Bodybuilder's Bungled $3 Million Plot to Kill Kobe Bryant Accuser*, DAILY BEAST (Sept. 9, 2021).

III. Conspiracy

The first conspiracy case dates back to 1253 in England and an agreement to prevent the head of a monastery from performing his duties, which was considered a conspiracy to obstruct judicial administration.[84] Despite inchoate conspiracy existing for so long, it's definition and parameters were seemingly in constant flux. In 1890, a British commentator wrote that "[n]o branch of the law of England is more uncertain and ill-defined than the law of Criminal Conspiracy."[85] Over a century later, an American commentor wrote that "comments by the courts as to the confused state of the law [of conspiracy] are as apt today as they were 125 years ago," when the Pennsylvania Supreme Court said that "[t]he unsettled state of the law of conspiracy has arisen . . . from a gradual extension of the limits of the offense; each case having been decided on its own peculiar circumstances, without reference to any pre-established principle."[86]

Over time, what has developed in the U.S. are two kinds of conspiracy (and solicitation and attempt) provisions: general and specific. Almost all criminal statutes include "general" prohibitions against solicitation, conspiracy, and attempt, meaning the offense is defined as an inchoate version of any other crime in the code. For example, consider the "general" federal conspiracy and attempt provision:

> Any person who attempts or conspires to commit any offense under this chapter shall be subject to the same penalties as those prescribed for the offense, the commission of which was the object of the attempt or conspiracy.[87]

84. Alan Harding, *The Origins of the Crime of Conspiracy*, 33 TRANS. ROYAL HIS. SOC. 89, 94 (1983).
85. Pollack, *supra* note 36.
86. *Id*.
87. 18 U.S.C. §371.

The criminal statute may, however, include "specific" inchoate provisions, making it a crime to commit an inchoate version of a specified offense. Consider the federal Material Support to Terrorism provision:

> Whoever knowingly provides material support or resources to a foreign terrorist organization, or attempts or conspires to do so, shall be fined under this title or imprisoned not more than 20 years, or both, and, if the death of any person results, shall be imprisoned for any term of years or for life.[88]

In 1975, the Supreme Court reiterated why conspiracy is unique among inchoate offenses in not merging with the completed offense.

> Traditionally, the law has considered conspiracy and the completed substantive offense to be separate crimes. Conspiracy is an inchoate offense, the essence of which is an agreement to commit an unlawful act. [citations omitted] Unlike some crimes that arise in a single transaction ... the conspiracy to commit an offense and the subsequent commission of that crime normally do not merge into a single punishable act. *Pinkerton v. United States, supra,* at 328 U.S. 643. Thus, it is well recognized that, in most cases, separate sentences can be imposed for the conspiracy to do an act and for the subsequent accomplishment of that end. [citations omitted] Indeed, the Court has even held that the conspiracy can be punished more harshly than the accomplishment of its purpose. *Clune v. United States,* 159 U.S. 590 (1895).

> The consistent rationale of this long line of decisions rests on the very nature of the crime of conspiracy. This Court repeatedly has recognized that a conspiracy poses distinct dangers quite apart from those of the substantive offense.

> This settled principle derives from the reason of things in dealing with socially reprehensible conduct: collective criminal agreement—partnership in crime—presents a greater potential threat to the public than individual delicts. Concerted action both increases the likelihood that the criminal object will be successfully attained and decreases the probability that the individuals involved will depart from their path of criminality. Group association for criminal purposes often, if not normally, makes possible the attainment of ends more complex than those which one criminal could accomplish. Nor is the danger of a conspiratorial group limited to the particular end toward which it has embarked. Combination in crime makes more likely the commission of crimes unrelated to the original purpose for which the group was formed. In sum, the danger

---

88. 18 U.S.C. § 23339a. Notice how the "specific" provisions link the inchoate offense to a specific crime. There are a variety of reasons for including both provisions in a criminal statute, but normally, the specific provision is intended to clearly enumerate the full scope of liability for the inchoate version of the target offense. *See generally,* Heather Anne Egan, *Conspiracy Definition Affects War on Terror,* 8 PUB. INTEREST L. RPTR. 20 (2003).

which a conspiracy generates is not confined to the substantive offense which is the immediate aim of the enterprise.

Callanan v. United States, supra, at 364 U.S. 593-594. As Mr. Justice Jackson, no friend of the law of conspiracy . . . observed: "The basic rationale of the law of conspiracy is that a conspiracy may be an evil in itself, independently of any other evil it seeks to accomplish." *Dennis v. United States,* 341 U.S. 494, 573 (1951) (concurring opinion).[89]

That inchoate conspiracy does not merge into the target offense when completed is well settled. But inchoate conspiracy as a stand-alone substantive offense continues to be conflated with conspiracy as a mode of liability, discussed in the next chapter. The *Jimenez-Recio* case below is included for several reasons. The primary reason is the utility of the Supreme Court's language stressing the separate nature of inchoate conspiracy and how impossibility is not available as a defense. The secondary reason is that *Jimenez-Recio* illustrates the ease by which inchoate conspiracy is confused with conspiracy as a mode of liability.

The case deals with individuals who joined a conspiracy to distribute illegal drugs after the government, unbeknownst to the conspirators, had already seized the drugs. On appeal, the Ninth Circuit reversed the conviction. But the Ninth Circuit's analysis focused on when and how conspiracy *as a mode of liability* terminates. But Jimenez-Recio and the other co-conspirators were never able to actually complete the conspiracy's target crime of distributing drugs. As a result, they were charged with inchoate conspiracy. Before reading the case, identify (and consider writing down) the common law elements of the offense of conspiracy to distribute drugs. If Jimenez-Recio met those elements, was there any way to "undo" his criminal liability?

A. Conspiracy and Renunciation

United States v. Jimenez-Recio
537 U.S. 270 (2003)
U.S. Supreme Court

Justice BREYER delivered the opinion of the Court.

We here consider the validity of a Ninth Circuit rule that a conspiracy ends automatically when the object of the conspiracy becomes impossible to achieve—when, for example, the Government frustrates a drug conspiracy's objective by seizing the drugs that its members have agreed to distribute. In our view, conspiracy law does not contain any such "automatic termination" rule.

---

89. *Iannelli, supra* note 38, at 777-778.

I

In *United States v. Cruz*, 127 F.3d 791, 795 (CA9 1997), the Ninth Circuit, following the language of an earlier case, *United States v. Castro*, 972 F.2d 1107, 1112 (CA9 1992), wrote that a conspiracy terminates when "'there is affirmative evidence of abandonment, withdrawal, disavowal *or defeat of the object of the conspiracy*'" (emphasis added in original). It considered the conviction of an individual who, the Government had charged, joined a conspiracy (to distribute drugs) after the Government had seized the drugs in question. The Circuit found that the Government's seizure of the drugs guaranteed the "defeat" of the conspiracy's objective, namely, drug distribution. The Circuit held that the conspiracy had terminated with that "defeat," *i.e.,* when the Government seized the drugs. Hence the individual, who had joined the conspiracy after that point, could not be convicted as a conspiracy member.

In this case the lower courts applied the *Cruz* rule to similar facts: On November 18, 1997, police stopped a truck in Nevada. They found, and seized, a large stash of illegal drugs. With the help of the truck's two drivers, they set up a sting. The Government took the truck to the drivers' destination, a mall in Idaho. The drivers paged a contact and described the truck's location. The contact said that he would call someone to get the truck. And three hours later, the two defendants, Francisco Jimenez Recio and Adrian Lopez-Meza, appeared in a car. Jimenez Recio drove away in the truck; Lopez-Meza drove the car away in a similar direction. Police stopped both vehicles and arrested both men.

A federal grand jury indicted Jimenez Recio, Lopez-Meza, and the two original truck drivers, charging them with having conspired, together and with others, to possess and to distribute unlawful drugs. A jury convicted all four. But the trial judge then decided that the jury instructions had been erroneous in respect to Jimenez Recio and Lopez-Meza. The judge noted that the Ninth Circuit, in *Cruz*, had held that the Government could not prosecute drug conspiracy defendants unless they had joined the conspiracy before the Government seized the drugs. See *Cruz, supra*, at 795–796. That holding, as applied here, meant that the jury could not convict Jimenez Recio and Lopez-Meza unless the jury believed they had joined the conspiracy before the Nevada police stopped the truck and seized the drugs. The judge ordered a new trial where the jury would be instructed to that effect. The new jury convicted the two men once again.

Jimenez Recio and Lopez-Meza appealed. They pointed out that, given *Cruz*, the jury had to find that they had joined the conspiracy before the Nevada stop, and they claimed that the evidence was insufficient at both trials to warrant any such jury finding. The Ninth Circuit panel, by a vote of 2 to 1, agreed. All three panel members accepted *Cruz* as binding law. Two members concluded that the evidence presented at the second trial was not sufficient to show that the defendants had joined the conspiracy before the Nevada drug seizure. One of the two wrote that the evidence at the first trial was not sufficient either, a circumstance she believed independently warranted reversal. The third member, dissenting, believed that the evidence at both trials adequately demonstrated preseizure membership. He added that he, like the other panel members, was bound by *Cruz*, but he wrote that in his view *Cruz* was "totally inconsistent with long established and appropriate principles of the law of conspiracy," and he urged the Circuit to overrule it en banc "at the earliest opportunity." 258 F.3d 1069, 1079, n. 2 (opinion of Gould, J.).

The Government sought certiorari. It noted that the Ninth Circuit's holding in this case was premised upon the legal rule enunciated in *Cruz*. And it asked us to decide the rule's validity, *i.e.*, to decide whether "a conspiracy ends as a matter of law when the government frustrates its objective." Pet. for Cert. I. We agreed to consider that question.

II

In *Cruz*, the Ninth Circuit held that a conspiracy continues "'until there is affirmative evidence of abandonment, withdrawal, disavowal or defeat of the object of the conspiracy.'" 127 F.3d, at 795 (quoting *Castro, supra*, at 1112). The critical portion of this statement is the last segment, that a conspiracy ends once there has been "defeat of [its] object." The Circuit's holdings make clear that the phrase means that the conspiracy ends through "defeat" when the Government intervenes, making the conspiracy's goals impossible to achieve, even if the conspirators do not know that the Government has intervened and are totally unaware that the conspiracy is bound to fail. In our view, this statement of the law is incorrect. A conspiracy does not automatically terminate simply because the Government, unbeknownst to some of the conspirators, has "defeat[ed]" the conspiracy's "object."

Two basic considerations convince us that this is the proper view of the law. First, the Ninth Circuit's rule is inconsistent with our own understanding of basic conspiracy law. The Court has repeatedly said that the essence of a conspiracy is "an agreement to commit an unlawful act." *Iannelli v. United States,* 420 U.S. 770, 777 (1975) . . . . That agreement is "a distinct evil," which "may exist and be punished whether or not the substantive crime ensues." *Salinas v. United States*, 522 U.S. 52, 65 (1997). The conspiracy poses a "threat to the public" over and above the threat of the commission of the relevant substantive crime—both because the "[c]ombination in crime makes more likely the commission of [other] crimes" and because it "decreases the probability that the individuals involved will depart from their path of criminality." *Callanan v. United States*, 364 U.S. 587, 593–594 (1961); see also *United States v. Rabinowich*, 238 U.S. 78, 88 (1915) (conspiracy "sometimes quite outweigh[s], in injury to the public, the mere commission of the contemplated crime"). . . . That being so, the Government's defeat of the conspiracy's objective will not necessarily and automatically terminate the conspiracy.

Second, the view we endorse today is the view of almost all courts and commentators but for the Ninth Circuit. No other Federal Court of Appeals has adopted the Ninth Circuit's rule. Three have explicitly rejected it. In *United States v. Wallace*, 85 F.3d 1063, 1068 (CA2 1996), for example, the court said that the fact that a "conspiracy cannot actually be realized because of facts unknown to the conspirators is irrelevant." See also *United States v. Belardo-Quiñones*, 71 F.3d 941, 944 (CA1

1995) (conspiracy exists even if, unbeknownst to conspirators, crime is impossible to commit); *United States v. LaBudda*, 882 F.2d 244, 248 (CA7 1989) (defendants can be found guilty of conspiracy even if conspiracy's object "is unattainable from the very beginning"). One treatise, after surveying lower court conspiracy decisions, has concluded that "[i]mpossibility of success is not a defense." 2 LaFave & Scott, Substantive Criminal Law § 6.5, at 85; see also *id.*, § 6.5(b), at 90–93.

. . . .

III

We conclude that the Ninth Circuit's conspiracy-termination law holding set forth in *Cruz* is erroneous in the manner discussed. We reverse the present judgment insofar as it relies upon that holding. . . .

It is so ordered.

Despite the seemingly clear language from the Supreme Court in *Jimenez-Recio*, lawyers continue to advance different impossibility arguments in response to inchoate conspiracy charges. In the *Rehak* case below, defense attorneys argued that their client could not have conspired to deprive someone of their civil rights when the individual was a fictional construct of law enforcement. Do you think the factual differences in *Jimenez-Recio*, where the government seized drugs which would otherwise have been available to distribute, and Rehak's fictional victim matter in terms of the availability of impossibility as a defense?

B. Conspiracy and Impossibility

United States v. Rehak
589 F.3d 965 (8th Cir. 2009)
Eighth Circuit Court of Appeals

After a jury trial in district court, Timothy Conrad Rehak and Mark Paul Naylon were convicted of conspiring to violate civil rights under 18 U.S.C. § 241, and theft of government property under 18 U.S.C. § 641. They appeal. Having jurisdiction under 28 U.S.C. § 1291, this court affirms.

I

In 2004, Timothy Rehak, a law enforcement officer, and Mark Naylon, a public information officer, were working for the Special Investigations Unit of the Ramsey County Sheriff's Office (RCSO). In September, the FBI began investigating Rehak for corruption. On November 3, it conducted an "integrity test."

The FBI rented a room at the Kelly Inn under the (fictitious) name of Vincent Pelligatti, placing $13,500 in cash in a duffel bag there. The FBI instructed a cooperating individual to tell Rehak that a drug trafficker named "Vinnie" had been arrested in Wisconsin and was trying to recover drugs and money he left in room 503 at the hotel. Rehak replied that he would try to "scarf" the money and drugs out of the hotel room.

Rehak called Naylon. At about 1:15 p.m., Rehak arrived at the hotel; Naylon arrived a few minutes later. They asked the front-desk clerk to let them in to room 503; she refused because they did not have a search warrant. Rehak and Naylon contacted Rolland Martinez, a Special Investigations sergeant, told him they had received information of narcotics and cash in the hotel room, and asked him to get a search warrant. When Sergeant Martinez arrived at the hotel to investigate, he found Naylon upset with the desk clerk. After gathering more facts, Sergeant Martinez left to obtain a state search warrant.

At 3:38 p.m., Rehak, Naylon, and Sergeant Martinez entered room 503. According to the FBI's video recording, Sergeant Martinez begins searching the bathroom while Rehak and Naylon search the main room. In the dresser, Rehak finds the duffel bag with the $13,500. While Sergeant Martinez is in the bathroom, Naylon motions for Rehak to give him some of the cash. Rehak hands Naylon $6,000, which he puts in his coat pocket. As Sergeant Martinez returns to the main room, Rehak purports to begin searching the bag and pulls out the remaining $7,500. Sergeant Martinez is unaware that Rehak had given $6,000 to Naylon. Naylon leaves the hotel room, goes to the trunk of his vehicle, and then returns to the room.

As part of the procedure for inventorying seized property, Sergeant Martinez and Rehak separately counted the $7,500 remaining in the bag. During this procedure, neither Rehak nor Naylon told Sergeant Martinez of the missing $6,000, which was not included in the count.

At 4:19 p.m., Rehak and Naylon spoke outside the hotel room; Rehak left in his car. A few minutes later, a deputy arrived with his drug dog. The deputy and Naylon entered the hotel room. The dog sniffed the $7,500. Naylon did not tell the deputy about the additional $6,000. In his report, the deputy stated that $7,500 was seized. Sergeant Martinez completed a search warrant receipt, reporting only $7,500. Naylon reviewed the completed (inaccurate) receipt. A copy of this receipt was left in the hotel room to indicate what had been seized. As the inventory officer, Sergeant Martinez took control of the $7,500 and deposited it at the Special Investigations Unit. After the local officers left the hotel room, FBI agents entered, confirming that all $13,500 was gone.

That evening, according to Minnesota Bureau of Criminal Apprehension records, at 5:30 p.m. and again at 9:45 p.m., law enforcement databases were searched by RCSO clerks for "Vincent Pelligatti," the fictitious drug trafficker. No records were found for him. Sergeant Martinez and the drug-dog deputy testified at trial that they did not conduct any database searches for Vincent Pelligatti. The two warrant clerks who ran the searches could not recall who requested them.

Hours later, about midnight, Rehak and Naylon called Sergeant Martinez at home. Naylon said they had found an additional $6,000 in the hotel room under the mattress. The next day, Sergeant Martinez obtained the $6,000 and amended his report to reflect the full $13,500. Rehak completed a report that omitted where the $6,000 had been found and how it had been handled. When Sergeant Martinez asked him to add these details, Rehak replied he knew how to write a report and never made the requested changes.

One month later, the FBI asked the St. Paul Police Department (SPPD) to obtain the police reports of the Kelly Inn search. An SPPD supervisor asked the RCSO for reports from search warrants executed at hotels, including the Kelly Inn. After specifically inquiring about a search warrant in November at the Kelly Inn, a RCSO records person said there was no record of the search. The SPPD supervisor reiterated the request. Rehak called back that day, saying he had not yet completed the report of the Kelly Inn search. Later that day, Rehak sent the report, which lacked the section explaining where the money was found.

Rehak and Naylon were charged with six counts of honest services wire fraud, in violation of 18 U.S.C. §§ 1343 and 1346; one count of conspiring to violate civil rights, in violation of 18 U.S.C. § 241; and one count of theft of government property, in violation of 18 U.S.C. § 641. The jury acquitted on the wire fraud counts. It convicted both men of conspiring to violate civil rights, and theft of government property. The jury apparently did not believe Rehak's testimony that their intent was to play a practical joke on Sergeant Martinez. Instead, the verdicts adopted the government's theory of the case: Rehak and Naylon intended to steal the money, but later changed their minds and decided to return it.

II

Defendants contend that there is insufficient evidence to support their convictions for conspiring to violate civil rights because they did not actually violate the civil rights of a real person. "In reviewing the sufficiency of the evidence, 'we view the evidence in the light most favorable to the government, resolving evidentiary conflicts in favor of the government, and accepting all reasonable inferences drawn from the evidence that support the jury's verdict.'" *United States v. Blazek*, 431 F.3d 1104, 1107 (8th Cir.2005), quoting *United States v. Gaona-Lopez*, 408 F.3d 500, 504 (8th Cir.2005).

It is a crime for "two or more persons [to] conspire to injure, oppress, threaten, or intimidate any person in the free exercise or enjoyment of any right or privilege secured to him by the Constitution or laws of the United States." 18 U.S.C. § 241. Rehak and Naylon were convicted based on their agreement to take Vincent Pelligatti's money in violation of his due process rights. Defendants argue that this fictitious person did not have rights, so they could not have conspired to violate them.

"Factual impossibility occurs when the objective of the defendant is proscribed by the criminal law but a circumstance unknown to the actor prevents him from bringing about that objective." *United States v. Sobrilski*, 127 F.3d 669, 674 (8th Cir.1997). "'Factual impossibility is not a defense to an inchoate offense' such as conspiracy or attempt." *United States v. Joiner*, 418 F.3d 863, 869 (8th Cir.2005), quoting *United States v. Fleming*, 215 F.3d 930, 936 (9th Cir.2000). "[T]he crime of conspiracy is complete on the agreement to violate the law implemented by one or more overt acts, however innocent such act standing alone may be, and it is not dependent on the success or failure of the planned scheme." *United States v. Littlefield*, 594 F.2d 682, 684 (8th Cir.1979). See also *United States v. Jannotti*, 673 F.2d 578, 591 (3d Cir.) (en banc) (upholding Hobbs Act conspiracy convictions for receiving money to influence official conduct from undercover agents posing as foreign business executives seeking favorable government action), *cert. denied*, 457 U.S. 1106, 102 S.Ct. 2906, 73 L.Ed.2d 1315 (1982); *United States v. Parker*, 165 F.Supp.2d 431, 456 (W.D.N.Y.2001) (defendants convicted under 18 U.S.C. § 241 for conspiring to violate rights of a fictitious drug dealer, who was actually an undercover agent), *aff'd sub nom. United States v. Ferby*, 108 Fed.Appx. 676, 680 (2d Cir.2004) (unpublished).

In this case, the objective of defendants was to take the money of a drug trafficker, Vincent Pelligatti. Their goal, to keep his money as their own, violates the law. See *United States v. McClean*, 528 F.2d 1250, 1255 (2d Cir.1976) (stating that police officers who convert to private purposes funds lawfully seized from suspected criminals violate those criminals' civil rights). The fact that Pelligatti was fictitious was unknown to Rehak and Naylon. This circumstance prevented them from actually violating a person's due process rights. While it was factually impossible to violate his rights, defendants were charged and convicted of conspiring to violate his rights. The crime was committed upon their agreement to steal his money. That they were unsuccessful is irrelevant to their culpability for conspiring.

The jury heard ample evidence that Rehak and Naylon conspired to take the money in violation of Pelligatti's due process rights: (1) a cooperating individual called Rehak to tell him a drug dealer named "Vinnie" had left money and drugs in a hotel room; (2) Rehak told the cooperating individual he would try to "scarf" the money and drugs from the hotel room; (3) Rehak and Naylon went to the hotel and tried to gain access without a search warrant, even though Rehak knew they needed a search warrant to enter the room; (4) Rehak found the money and handed $6,000 of it to Naylon, who pocketed it; (5) they allowed the other officers to believe only $7,500 was found; (6) Rehak falsified the search warrant return and his report of the incident; (7) even after returning the money, Rehak and Naylon never told anyone about how or where it was actually found, or that they were playing a joke on Sergeant Martinez.... The evidence was sufficient for a reasonable jury to find that Rehak and Naylon agreed to take Pelligatti's money in violation of his due process rights.

. . . .

The judgments of the district court are affirmed.

Notes and Questions

1. In the *Jimenez-Recio* opinion, the Supreme Court referred to *Iannelli v. United States*, 420 U.S. 770 (1975), and there are references to *Iannelli* throughout this chapter. *Iannelli* involved complicated analysis of a variety of federal gambling offenses, which are not relevant to this chapter, and the application of the Wharton Rule, which is noteworthy. The Wharton Rule is a common law exception to conspiracy not merging into the completed offense.[90] The Wharton Rule is limited in application to crimes which can only be committed by two or more people. This is a very narrow or limited exception as there aren't many crimes which can *only* be committed by multiple people. The crimes include adultery, bigamy, dueling and incest. Using dueling as an example (which remains an offense under military law), the result at common law is that an individual may not be charged with both conspiracy to duel and with dueling. The prosecution may only charge the substantive crime of dueling. It's important to make a note of the Wharton Rule but also to remember that it's a very narrow exception and only applies at common law.

2. On somewhat infrequent occasions, there is direct evidence of a criminal agreement underpinning a conspiracy. Direct evidence, of course, suffices but is not required. The agreement does not have to be (and often isn't) explicit. Instead, the agreement can instead be inferred from the facts and circumstances of the case. It is entirely appropriate (and on law school exams often expected) to assess facts and circumstances and draw reasonable conclusions. But remember why you are evaluating facts and circumstances, to determine whether they support an inference that a given individual entered into a criminal agreement with the requisite mens rea. The Court in *Iannelli*, while acknowledging that criminal agreements may be inferred from facts and context, cautioned that "[i]n some cases, reliance on such evidence perhaps has tended to obscure the basic fact that *the agreement is the essential evil at which the crime of conspiracy is directed.*" *Id.* at fn.10 (emphasis added).

---

90. The Wharton Rule takes its name Francis Wharton, who wrote a treatise on criminal law identifying the potential for over or double charging of offenses which required two or more people. The Supreme Court in *Iannelli* quoted Wharton's explanation for the rule which has taken his name:

"When to the idea of an offense plurality of agents is logically necessary, conspiracy, which assumes the voluntary accession of a person to a crime of such a character that it is aggravated by a plurality of agents, cannot be maintained. . . . In other words, when the law says, 'a combination between two persons to effect a particular end shall be called, if the end be effected, by a certain name,' it is not lawful for the prosecution to call it by some other name; and when the law says, such an offense—e.g., adultery—shall have a certain punishment, it is not lawful for the prosecution to evade this limitation by indicting the offense as conspiracy. 2 F. Wharton, Criminal Law § 1604, p. 1862 (12th ed. 1932).

Iannelli, 420 U.S. at 773.

3. Members of a conspiracy don't have to know all the participants in (or the purposes of) the conspiracy. *United States v. Escalante*, 637 F.2d 1197, 1200 (9th Cir. 1980). The members of the conspiracy don't have to have all met together at the same time to reach the criminal agreement. A conspiracy can take place over extended periods of time, during which new members join and old members drop out. *United States v. Perry*, 550 F.2d 524, 528 (9th Cir. 1997); *United States v. Green*, 523 F.2d 229, 233 (2d Cir. 1975). Proof that a defendant "'knew he was plotting in concert with others to violate the law' is sufficient to raise the necessary inference that he joined in the overall agreement." *United States v. Thomas*, 586 F.2d 123, 132 (9th Cir. 1978).

4. You may have heard of entrapment, a complete defense to a criminal charge. Entrapment recognizes that "[g]overnment agents may not originate a criminal design, implant in an innocent person's mind the disposition to commit a criminal act, and then induce commission of the crime so that the Government may prosecute." *Jacobsen v. U.S.*, 503 U.S. 540, 548 (1992). Many a defendant facing conspiracy charges has tried to claim entrapment, but they are rarely successful. Inducing someone to commit a crime requires more than a solicitation. That the government, meaning law enforcement agents and those operating at their behest, use "artifice, stratagem, pretense, or deceit" does not establish inducement. *Sorrells v. U.S.*, 287 U.S. 435, 451 (1932). As the DoJ's Criminal Resource Manual explains:

> inducement requires a showing of at least persuasion or mild coercion, [];
> pleas based on need, sympathy, or friendship, []; or extraordinary promises
> of the sort "that would blind the ordinary person to his legal duties," *United
> States v. Evans*, 924 F.2d 714, 717 (7th Cir. 1991). *See also United States v. Kelly*,
> 748 F.2d 691, 698 (D.C. Cir. 1984) (inducement shown only if government's
> behavior was such that "a law-abiding citizen's will to obey the law could have
> been overborne"); *United States v. Johnson*, 872 F.2d 612, 620 (5th Cir. 1989)
> (inducement shown if government created "a substantial risk that an offense
> would be committed by a person other than one ready to commit it").

Even where a court finds inducement has occurred, the Supreme Court has held that "a finding of predisposition is fatal to an entrapment defense. The predisposition inquiry focuses upon whether the defendant was an unwary innocent or, instead, an unwary criminal who readily availed himself of the opportunity to perpetuate the crime." *Mathews v. U.S.*, 486 U.S. 58, 63 (1988).

5. Following the September 11th attacks, Congress amended the 1994 material support for terrorism statute (provided earlier in the chapter), and the FBI began conducting a series of undercover operations in the U.S. which yielded prosecutions for conspiracy to commit material support for terrorism.

> Typically, the stings initially target suspects for pure speech—comments to
> an informer outside a mosque, angry postings on Web sites, e-mails with
> radicals overseas—then woo them into relationships with informers, who

are often convicted felons working in exchange for leniency, or with F.B.I. agents posing as members of Al Qaeda or other groups.

David K. Shipler, *Terrorist Plots, Hatched by the F.B.I.*, N.Y. TIMES, Apr. 28, 2012.

Some contend that the defendants in many of the cases are "ambivalent, incompetent and adrift, like hapless wannabes looking for a cause that the informer or undercover agent skillfully helps them find." *Id.* Yet others argue that "[i]gnoring such threats is not an option given the possibility that the suspect could act alone at any time or find someone else willing to help him." *Id.* In almost every case, the defendants have tried—and failed—to raise entrapment. One technique the FBI employed in some but not all undercover operations is that the undercover agent or informant warns suspects "about the seriousness of their plots and [gives] opportunities to back out." *Id.* This is an example of how law enforcement can conduct investigations and undercover operations which bolster a future prosecutor's ability to argue predisposition in response to the entrapment claim the FBI knows will ultimately be made. What do you think of this approach? For additional but optional reading (and viewing), in the summer of 2021, the news organization Frontline released a documentary entitled IN THE SHADOW OF 9/11, a description of which (along with a video trailer) is available at Patrice Taddonio, *A Major Terror Plot Interrupted—or a 'Setup'?* PBS, Aug. 10, 2021, https://www.pbs.org/wgbh/frontline/article/video-liberty-city-seven -terror-plot-setup-in-the-shadow-of-911/. One former chief of DoJ's counterterrorism section labeled the FBI's actions described in the documentary as "a cautionary tale. . . . be careful as to how far your undercover agents or your informants push. . . . [T]he goal is not to take somebody that is not a terrorist and make them a terrorist." *Id.*

6. In both the solicitation and conspiracy sections, you read cases where defendants unsuccessfully claimed impossibility. Several courts were quite clear that impossibility is not a defense to inchoate crimes. But that's not to say impossibility is never of use to a defendant facing solicitation or conspiracy charges. There are two components to making use of impossibility: first, the impossibility must be known to the defendant; second, the impossibility is argued not as a defense in and of itself but rather as evidence to negate the heightened mens rea of an inchoate offense. For example, in 2012, Gilberto Valle, a New York City police officer, was prosecuted for conspiracy to commit kidnapping as part of a bizarre and gruesome online discussion focused on abducting, torturing, killing and ultimately eating women. Prosecutors at trial conceded that Valle never actually hurt anyone but successfully argued that multiple overt acts "lifted his activities out of the realm of fiction." The overt acts included Valle performing surveillance of potential victims, google searches of "how to abduct a girl" and creating a document on his computer entitled "abducting and cooking." After the jury found Valle guilty, defense lawyers requested the judge find Valle not guilty notwithstanding the verdict. This is a procedure defense attorneys routinely employ but which is rarely granted. But this was one of those rare instances.

A year after the defense made the request, the trial judge overturned the conspiracy to commit kidnapping charge. Why? Valle made a number of disturbing comments in online fetish chatrooms about planning future abductions. Valle even agreed with two other individuals to kidnap three women on the same day, despite the women living in New York City, India, and Ohio. Valle provided the other individuals fake information about the prospective victims and refused to provide their last names and addresses. Valle also made a series of false statements in the chatrooms about himself, including that he lived in Pennsylvania, that he owned a van which could be used to transport the victims, that he had a pulley-apparatus in his basement, that he was soundproofing the basement and that he owned a human sized rotisserie oven. The kidnap date came and went not only without a kidnapping but without any comments or questions from any of the purported conspirators. As one federal court stated,

> [d]ates for "planned" kidnappings pass without comment, without discussion, without explanation, and without follow up. The only plausible explanation for the lack of comment or inquiry about allegedly agreed-upon and scheduled kidnappings is that Valle and the others engaged in these chats understood that no kidnapping would actually take place. No other reasonable inference is possible.

7. In terms of how a jury is instructed on conspiracy, consider the following example from the Ninth Circuit:

> A conspiracy may continue for a long period of time and may include the performance of many transactions. It is not necessary that all members of the conspiracy join it at the same time, and one may become a member of a conspiracy without full knowledge of all the details of the unlawful scheme or the names, identities, or locations of all of the other members.
>
> Even though a defendant did not directly conspire with [the other defendant] [or] [other conspirators] in the overall scheme, the defendant has, in effect, agreed to participate in the conspiracy if the government proves each of the following beyond a reasonable doubt:
>
> First, that the defendant directly conspired with one or more conspirators to carry out at least one of the objects of the conspiracy;
>
> Second, that the defendant knew or had reason to know that other conspirators were involved with those with whom the defendant directly conspired; and
>
> Third, that the defendant had reason to believe that whatever benefits the defendant might get from the conspiracy were probably dependent upon the success of the entire venture.
>
> It is not a defense that a person's participation in a conspiracy was minor or for a short period of time.

IV. Attempt

The law of criminal attempt dates back to a 1784 English case, *Rex v. Scofield*, and an unsuccessful effort to burn down a house.[91] As the court explained

> It makes a great difference, whether an act was done; as in this case putting fire to a candle in the midst of combustible matter . . . and where no act at all is done. The intent may make an act, innocent in itself, criminal; nor is the completion of an act, criminal in itself, necessary to constitute criminality. Is it no offence to set fire to a train of gunpowder with intent to burn a house, because by accident, or the interposition of another, the mischief is prevented?[92]

The court established that "the completion of an act criminal in itself is not necessary to constitute criminality."[93] The crime at issue in *Rex v. Scofield* was akin to a general attempt provision, meaning there is an attempt provision applicable to a broad range of unspecified crimes.

Here in the U.S., there is no federal "general attempt" statute. Instead, Congress has enumerated that attempting certain specific crimes violates federal law, for example 18 U.S.C. § 1113—Attempt to commit murder or manslaughter; 21 U.S.C. § 846—Attempt to commit drug trafficking. By contrast, every state has a general attempt statute.[94]

As you read the cases which follow, keep in mind the location of attempt along the continuum of crime. As the first case highlights, while the mens rea for inchoate offenses like attempt is either specific intent or purpose, how that translates into specific jury instructions continues to vex courts.

---

91. *Rex v. Scofield*, Cald. 397 (1784).

    In this case the defendant, indicted for arson, was charged with having put a lighted candle amid divers matches and small pieces of wood in a certain house belonging to J.R., then in the possession of the defendant for a term of years, with the intent to set fire to and burn the house; there was neither allegation nor proof, however, that the house was burned. It was a clear case, therefore, of an attempt to commit a criminal offense.

Francis Bowers Sayres, *Criminal Attempts*, 41 HARV. L. REV. 821 (1928).

92. *Scofield*, *supra* note 91.

93. Sayres, *supra* note 91.

94. For a relatively recent list of state general attempt statutes, see the appendix of CRS Attempt, *supra* note 45.

A. Mens Rea of Attempt

People v. Gentry
157 Ill. App. 3d 899 (1987)
Illinois Court of Appeals

JUSTICE LINN delivered the opinion of the court:

Following a jury trial, defendant, Stanley Gentry, was convicted of attempted murder . . . and aggravated battery. . . . At the sentencing hearing, the trial court merged the aggravated battery conviction with the attempted murder conviction and on the charge of attempted murder sentenced Gentry to the Illinois Department of Corrections for a term of 45 years' imprisonment.

On appeal, Gentry asserts that his conviction should be reversed because [] the trial court's instruction regarding the intent necessary for attempted murder was prejudicially erroneous. . . .

Background

The record indicates that on December 13, 1983, Gentry and Ruby Hill, Gentry's girlfriend, were in the apartment they shared at 1756 North Talman in Chicago, Illinois. At approximately 9 p.m. the couple began to argue. During the argument, Gentry spilled gasoline on Hill, and the gasoline on Hill's body ignited. Gentry was able to smother the flames with a coat, but only after Hill had been severely burned. Gentry and Hill were the only eyewitnesses to the incident.

Police and paramedics were called to the scene. James Fahey was the first Chicago police officer to arrive. Fahey testified that when he entered Gentry and Hill's apartment, he found Hill's upper body (including her head, face, and arms) to be badly burned. He further testified that Gentry was the only person in the apartment other than Hill. Fahey also stated that he found no matches on the floor of the apartment.

The paramedics who arrived at the scene testified that Hill had suffered third degree burns over 70% of her body. They further testified that after some initial treatment, Hill was transported by ambulance to Cook County Hospital and that Gentry accompanied Hill in the ambulance.

Wayne Milla, a detective for the Chicago police department, also testified. Milla stated that he arrived on the scene shortly after Fahey. Milla also stated that a gas stove was the only possible source of ignition in the apartment's kitchen. Milla averred that he originally classified the fire as "accidental" but later changed his mind when he discovered that Hill's clothing had been doused with gasoline.

The victim, Ruby Hill, also testified at trial. Hill stated that she and Gentry had been drinking all afternoon and that both of them were "pretty high." She further testified that Gentry had poured gasoline on her and that the gasoline ignited only after she had gone near the stove in the kitchen. Hill also related how Gentry tried to snuff the fire out by placing a coat over the flames.

Hill also testified as to her relationship with Gentry. She stated that she had lived with Gentry for three years prior to the accident, that she wanted to marry Gentry, and that she still loved Gentry notwithstanding the fire incident. Hill claimed that the entire episode was an accident and that she intended to again live with Gentry after the case was over.

. . . .

At the close of the case, the jury found Gentry guilty of attempted murder and aggravated battery. The lesser aggravated battery conviction was merged into the greater attempted murder conviction at sentencing, where Gentry was sentenced to the Illinois Department of Corrections for a term of 45 years. From his conviction for attempted murder and his sentence, Gentry now appeals.

Gentry contends that the jury was improperly instructed on the required mental state for attempted murder where the instructions given would permit a conviction without a finding that Gentry possessed the specific intent to kill. The State, on the other hand, contends that the instructions as given show Gentry's assertion to be illogical. Alternatively, the State maintains that any error in instructing the jury was harmless and that defendant has waived review of this issue by failing to object at trial.

The record evinces the fact that Gentry did indeed fail to object at trial to the instructions in question. However, the specific intent to kill is an essential element of the crime of attempted murder. (*People v. Bryant* (1984), 123 Ill. App.3d 266, 462 N.E.2d 780.) Accordingly, the alleged error affects Gentry's substantial rights, and we will review this issue under the plain error doctrine. 87 Ill.2d R. 615(a); *cf. People v. Sanders* (1984), 129 Ill. App.3d 552, 472 N.E.2d 1156 (error in attempted murder instruction held to be plain error; attempted murder conviction reversed on appeal).

At the close of the presentation of evidence in this case, the following instructions were given. First, the trial court defined "attempt" as it relates to the underlying felony of murder:

> "A person commits the offense of murder when he, *with intent to commit the offense of murder* does any act which constitutes a substantial step toward the commission of the offense of murder. The offense attempted need not have been completed." (Emphasis added.)

Second, after giving this definition, the trial court set forth the necessary elements of attempted murder, to wit, an act and intent:

> "To sustain the charge of attempt, the State must prove the following propositions:

> First: That the defendant performed an act which constituted a substantial step towards the commission of the offense of murder; and Second: That the defendant did so with *intent to commit the crime of murder.*" (Emphasis added.)

Finally, the trial court defined the crime of murder, including all four culpable mental states:

> "A person commits the crime of murder where he kills an individual if, in performing the acts which cause the death, he intends to kill *or* do great bodily harm to that individual; *or* he knows that such acts will cause death to that individual; *or* he knows that such acts create a strong probability of death or great bodily harm to that individual." (Emphasis added.)

Gentry contends that the inclusion of all the alternative states of mind in the definitional murder instruction was erroneous because the crime of attempted murder requires a showing of specific intent to kill. Gentry posits that inclusion of all four alternative states of mind permitted the jury to convict him of attempted murder upon a finding that he intended to harm Hill, or acted with the knowledge that his conduct created a strong probability of death or great bodily harm to Hill, even if the jury believed that Gentry did not act with specific intent to kill. We agree with Gentry's position that the jury was misinstructed in this case.

Our supreme court has repeatedly held that a finding of specific intent to kill is a necessary element of the crime of attempted murder. . . . Indeed, a trial court instructing a jury on the crime of attempted murder must make it clear that specific intent to kill is the pivotal element of that offense, and that intent to do bodily harm, or knowledge that the consequences of defendant's act may result in death or great bodily harm, is not enough. . . . Accordingly, the instructions given in this case were erroneous, since it is clear that the jury was permitted to convict Gentry without specifically finding that Gentry intended to kill Hill. Few errors are more highly prejudicial than the trial court's failure to give the proper instruction on the intent element of a crime. . . .

The State attempts to minimize the significance of this error by arguing that the instructions as given actually did require the jury to find specific intent to kill. The State labels as illogical those cases which distinguish between the specific intent to kill and the three other alternative states of mind also found in the definitional murder instruction.

The State would read the attempted murder instruction as requiring a showing of any of the alternative mental states sufficient for a conviction of murder. In other words, the State makes no distinction between the mental state required to prove murder and the mental state required to prove attempted murder. We find the State's analysis and conclusion to be erroneous and lacking in legal substance since it fails to contain the judicial reasoning which recognizes the distinction between the intent elements of murder and attempted murder.

Specifically, we cite the *Kraft* case, where defendant's attempted murder conviction was reversed where the jury instructions would have permitted a conviction without a finding of specific intent to kill. (*People v. Kraft* (1985), 133 Ill. App.3d 294, 478 N.E.2d 1154.) In reversing the defendant's attempted murder conviction in that case, the *Kraft* court analyzed the distinction between the culpable mental states required for murder and attempted murder, noting as follows:

> "Our criminal code contains separate statutory definitions for the four culpable mental states of intent, knowledge, recklessness, and negligence, with knowledge encompassing a distinct and less purposeful state of mind than intent. * * * [O]ur State legislature manifested a desire to treat intent and knowledge as distinct mental states when imposing criminal liability for conduct. * * * Knowledge is not intent as defined by our statutes, and the jury instructions should reflect this distinction. Accordingly, we hold that in a prosecution for attempted murder, where alternative culpable mental states will satisfy the target crime of murder, but only one is compatible with the mental state imposed by our attempt statute, the incompatible elements must be omitted from the jury instructions." 133 Ill. App.3d 294, 302, 478 N.E.2d 1154, 1160.

Consequently, it is sufficient only for us to say that we recognize the distinction between the alternative states of mind delineated in the definitional murder instruction, as well as the fact that only the specific intent to kill satisfies the intent element of the crime of attempted murder. Accordingly, the State's assertion that the instructions as given actually required the jury to find that Gentry had a specific intent to kill Hill is doomed.

. . . .

In the instant case, it is clear that the essential task before the jury was the determination of whether Gentry sufficiently formed the specific intent to kill, in order to satisfy the elements of attempted murder. This is evidenced by the State's efforts to prove that Gentry knew that splashing gasoline on Hill would kill her, as well as by the State's attempts to impeach Hill's testimony that the incident was accidental. As such, we are faced with a situation where proving that Gentry formed the intent to kill was a necessary predicate to a finding of his guilt.

. . . .

In conclusion, based upon the discussion of law and fact stated above, we reverse defendant's conviction and sentence and remand this cause for a new trial in front of a properly instructed jury.

Reversed and remanded.

McMORROW, P.J., and JOHNSON, J., concur.

———————

The next case, *Mandujano*, addresses the critical of how to distinguish preparing to attempt a crime and perpetrating the crime.

B. Preparation vs. Perpetration

United States v. Mandujano
499 F.2d 370 (1974)
Fifth Circuit Court of Appeals

RIVES, Circuit Judge:

Mandujano appeals from the judgment of conviction and fifteen-year sentence imposed by the district court, based upon the jury's verdict finding him guilty of attempted distribution of heroin in violation of 21 U.S.C. § 846. We affirm.

Count One of the indictment charged:

> "On or about the 29th day of March, 1973, in the Western District of Texas, ROY MANDUJANO, the defendant herein, did knowingly and intentionally attempt to distribute one ounce of heroin, a Schedule I Controlled Substance, in violation of Title 21, United States Code, Sections 841(a)(1), all in violation of Title 21, United States Code, Section 846."

. . . .

I

The government's case rested almost entirely upon the testimony of Alfonso H. Cavalier, Jr., a San Antonio police officer assigned to the Office of Drug Abuse Law Enforcement. Agent Cavalier testified that, at the time the case arose, he was working in an undercover capacity and represented himself as a narcotics trafficker. At about 1:30 P.M. on the afternoon of March 29, 1973, pursuant to information Cavalier had received, he and a government informer went to the Tally-Ho Lounge, a bar located on Guadalupe Street in San Antonio. Once inside the bar, the informant introduced Cavalier to Roy Mandujano. After some general conversation, Mandujano asked the informant if he was looking for "stuff." Cavalier said, "Yes." Mandujano then questioned Cavalier about his involvement in narcotics. Cavalier answered Mandujano's questions, and told Mandujano he was looking for an ounce sample of heroin to determine the quality of the material. Mandujano replied that he had good brown Mexican heroin for $650.00 an ounce, but that if Cavalier wanted any of it he would have to wait until later in the afternoon when the regular man made his deliveries. Cavalier said that he was from out of town and did not want to wait that long. Mandujano offered to locate another source, and made four telephone calls in an apparent effort to do so. The phone calls appeared to be unsuccessful, for Mandujano told Cavalier he wasn't having any luck contacting anybody. Cavalier stated that he could not wait any longer. Then Mandujano said he had a good contact, a man who kept narcotics around his home, but that if he went to see this man, he would need the money "out front." To reassure Cavalier that he would not simply abscond with the money, Mandujano stated, "[Y]ou are in my place of business. My wife is here. You can sit with my wife. I am not going to jeopardize her or my business for

"$650.00." Cavalier counted out $650.00 to Mandujano, and Mandujano left the premises of the Tally-Ho Lounge at about 3:30 P.M. About an hour later, he returned and explained that he had been unable to locate his contact. He gave back the $650.00 and told Cavalier he could still wait until the regular man came around. Cavalier left, but arranged to call back at 6:00 P.M. When Cavalier called at 6:00 and again at 6:30, he was told that Mandujano was not available. Cavalier testified that he did not later attempt to contact Mandujano, because, "Based on the information that I had received, it would be unsafe for either my informant or myself to return to this area."

The only other government witness was Gerald Courtney, a Special Agent for the Drug Enforcement Administration. Agent Courtney testified that, as part of a surveillance team in the vicinity of the Tally-Ho Lounge on March 29, 1973, he had observed Mandujano leave the bar around 3:15 or 3:30 P.M. and drive off in his automobile. The surveillance team followed Mandujano but lost him almost immediately in heavy traffic. Courtney testified that Mandujano returned to the bar at about 4:30 P.M.

II

Section 846 of Title 21, entitled "Attempt and conspiracy," provides that, "Any person who attempts or conspires to commit any offense defined in this subchapter is punishable by imprisonment or fine or both which may not exceed the maximum punishment prescribed for the offense, the commission of which was the object of the attempt or conspiracy."

The theory of the government in this case is straightforward: Mandujano's acts constituted an attempt to distribute heroin; actual distribution of heroin would violate section 841(a)(1) of Title 21; therefore, Mandujano's attempt to distribute heroin comes within the terms of section 846 as an attempt to commit an offense defined in the subchapter.

"(a) Except as authorized by this subchapter, it shall be unlawful for any person knowingly or intentionally—"(1) to manufacture, distribute, or dispense, or possess with intent to manufacture, distribute, or dispense, a controlled substance." Tit. 21, U.S.C. § 841(a)(1).

Under subsection 802(11) the term "distribute" means "to deliver (other than by administering or dispensing) a controlled substance." Subsection 802(8) defines the terms "deliver" or "delivery" to mean "the actual, constructive or attempted transfer of a controlled substance, whether or not there exists an agency relationship."

Mandujano urges that his conduct as described by agent Cavalier did not rise to the level of an attempt to distribute heroin under section 846. He claims that at most he was attempting to acquire a controlled substance, not to distribute it; that it is impossible for a person to attempt to distribute heroin which he does not possess or control; that his acts were only preparation, as distinguished from an attempt; and that the evidence was insufficient to support the jury's verdict.

In opening argument, the United States Attorney stated: "There is a stipulation that has been entered into by the Government stating categorically that no heroin exchanged hands in this case * * *." (Tr. 16) . . . .

Apparently there is no legislative history indicating exactly what Congress meant when it used the word "attempt" in section 846. There are two reported federal cases which discuss the question of what constitutes an attempt under this section. In *United States v. Noreikis*, 7 Cir. 1973, 481 F.2d 1177, where the defendants possessed the various chemicals necessary to synthesize Dimethyltryptamine (DMT), a controlled substance, the court held that the preparations had progressed to the level of an attempt to manufacture a controlled substance. In its discussion, the court commented that,

> "While it seems to be well settled that mere preparation is not sufficient to constitute an attempt to commit a crime, 22 C.J.S. Criminal Law § 75(2)b, at 230 et seq., it seems equally clear that the semantical distinction between preparation and attempt is one incapable of being formulated in a hard and fast rule. The procuring of the instrument of the crime might be preparation in one factual situation and not in another. The matter is sometimes equated with the commission of an overt act, the 'doing something directly moving toward, and bringing him nearer, the crime he intends to commit.'" 22 C.J.S., *supra* at 231.

In *United States v. Heng Awkak Roman*, S.D.N.Y. 1973, 356 F. Supp. 434, *aff'd*, 2 Cir. 1973, 484 F.2d 1271, where the defendants' actions would have constituted possession of heroin with intent to distribute in violation of section 841 if federal agents had not substituted soap powder for the heroin involved in the case, the court held that the defendants' acts were an attempt to possess with intent to distribute. The district court in its opinion acknowledged that "'Attempt,' as used in section 846, is not defined. Indeed, there is no comprehensive statutory definition of attempt in federal law." The court concluded, however, that it was not necessary in the circumstances of the case to deal with the "complex question of when conduct crosses the line between 'mere preparation' and 'attempt.'" 356 F. Supp. at 437.

The courts in many jurisdictions have tried to elaborate on the distinction between mere preparation and attempt. . . .

In *Lemke v. United States*, 9 Cir. 1954, 211 F.2d 73, 75, 14 Alaska 587, the court states, "Of course it is elementary that mere preparation to commit a crime, not followed by an overt act done toward its commission, does not constitute an attempt." The definition of attempt in *United States v. Baker*, S. D.Cal. 1955, 129 F. Supp. 684, 685, . . ."The classical legal elements of an 'attempt' are the *intent* to commit a crime, the execution of some overt *act* in pursuance of the intention, and a *failure to consummate* the crime." . . .

In *United States v. Coplon*, 2 Cir. 1950, 185 F.2d 629, where the defendant was arrested before passing to a citizen of a foreign nation classified government documents contained in defendant's purse, Judge Learned Hand surveyed the law and addressed the issue of what would constitute an attempt:

> "Because the arrest in this way interrupted the consummation of the crime one point upon the appeal is that her conduct still remained in the zone of 'preparation,' and that the evidence did not prove an 'attempt.' This argument it will be most convenient to answer at the outset. A neat doctrine by which to test when a person, intending to commit a crime which he fails to carry out, has 'attempted' to commit it, would be that he has done all that it is within his power to do, but has been prevented by intervention from outside; in short, that he has passed beyond any *locus poenitentiae*. Apparently that was the original notion, and may still be law in England; but it is certainly not now generally the law in the United States, for there are many decisions which hold that the accused has passed beyond 'preparation,' although he has been interrupted before he has taken the last of his intended steps. The decisions are too numerous to cite, and would not help much anyway, for there is, and obviously can be, no definite line; but Judge Cullen's discussion in People v. Sullivan, and Mr. Justice Holmes' in two Massachusetts decisions, are particularly enlightening. In the second of the Massachusetts opinions Holmes, J., said: 'Preparation is not an attempt. But some preparations may amount to an attempt. It is a question of degree. If the preparation comes very near to the accomplishment of the act, the intent to complete it renders the crime so probable that the act will be a misdemeanor, although there is still a locus poenitentiae, in the need of a further exertion of the will to complete the crime.' We have found scarcely any decisions of federal courts, but, so far as they go, they are in accord. There can be no doubt in the case at bar that 'preparation' had become 'attempt.' The jury were free to find that the packet was to be delivered that night, as soon as they both thought it safe to do so. To divide 'attempt' from 'preparation' by the very instant of consummation would be to revert to the old doctrine."

. . . .

In *United States v. Robles*, N.D.Cal. 1960, 185 F. Supp. 82, 85, a case in which the defendant was charged with using communication facilities in attempting to import heroin illegally, the court enunciated the following test:" To attempt to do an act does not imply a completion of the act, or in fact any definite progress towards it. Any effort or endeavor to effect the act will satisfy the terms of the law. . . .

The language used in *Robles, supra,* is drawn directly from *United States v. Quincy*, 1832, 31 U.S. (6 Pet.) 445, at 464, 8 L.Ed. 458, which involved an indictment under a statute which made it unlawful to attempt to fit out and arm a vessel with intent to employ her in the service of a foreign people. The Supreme Court in *Quincy* further stated that, "The offence consists principally in the intention with which the preparations were made. . . . And this must be a fixed intention. . . . This intention is a question belonging exclusively to the jury to decide It is the material point on which the legality or criminality of the act must turn." 31 U.S. (6 Pet.) at 466, 8 L.Ed. 458.

In *Mims v. United States*, 5 Cir. 1967, 375 F.2d 135, 148, we noted that, "Much ink has been spilt in an attempt to arrive at a satisfactory standard for telling where preparations ends [sic] and attempt begins," and that the question had not been decided by this Court. The Court in *Mims,* at 148 n. 40, did note that the following test from *People v. Buffum*, 40 Cal.2d 709, 256 P.2d 317, 321, has been "frequently approved": "'Preparation alone is not enough, there must be some *appreciable fragment* of the crime committed, it must be in such progress that it will be consummated unless interrupted by circumstances independent of the will of the attempter, and the act must not be equivocal in nature. * * *' (Emphasis added.)"

Although the foregoing cases give somewhat varying verbal formulations, careful examination reveals fundamental agreement about what conduct will constitute a criminal attempt. First, the defendant must have been acting with the kind of culpability otherwise required for the commission of the crime which he is charged with attempting. . . . Second, the defendant must have engaged in conduct which constitutes a substantial step toward commission of the crime. A substantial step must be conduct strongly corroborative of the firmness of the defendant's criminal intent. . . .

The evidence was sufficient to support a verdict of guilty under section 846. Agent Cavalier testified that at Mandujano's request, he gave him $650.00 for one ounce of heroin, which Mandujano said he could get from a "good contact." From this, plus Mandujano's comments and conduct before and after the transfer of the $650.00, as described in Part I of this opinion, the jury could have found that Mandujano was acting knowingly and intentionally and that he engaged in conduct—the request for and the receipt of the $650.00—which in fact constituted a substantial step toward distribution of heroin. . . .

For the reasons stated in this opinion, the judgment is Affirmed.

The court in *Mandujano* addressed the first issue that arises in attempt cases—were the defendant's actions more than "mere preparation"? Once the line demarcating preparation from perpetration is identified, the next question is whether the defendant has committed an overt act to sufficiently cross the line. As discussed in the introduction, a number of jurisdictions quantify the overt act in attempt as a "substantial step." As you read *Jackson*, consider whether you think the substantial step test is useful or helpful to a jury.

C. Substantial Step Test

United States v. Jackson
560 F.2d 112 (1977)
Second Circuit Court of Appeals

Robert Jackson, William Scott, and Martin Allen appeal from judgments of conviction entered on November 23, 1976 in the United States District Court for the Eastern District of New York after a trial before Chief Judge Jacob Mishler without a jury.

Count one of the indictment alleged that between June 11 and June 21, 1976 the appellants conspired to commit an armed robbery of the Manufacturers Hanover Trust branch located at 210 Flushing Avenue, Brooklyn, New York, in violation of 18 U.S.C. § 371. Counts two and three each charged appellants with an attempted robbery of the branch on June 14 and on June 21, 1976, respectively, in violation of 18 U.S.C. §§ 2113(a) and 2. . . .

After a suppression hearing on July 23, 1976 and a one-day trial on August 30, 1976, Chief Judge Mishler filed a memorandum of decision finding each defendant guilty on all [] counts.

Appellants' principal contention is that . . . as a matter of law, their conduct never crossed the elusive line which separates "mere preparation" from "attempt." . . . For the reasons which follow, we affirm the convictions of all three appellants on all [] counts.

The Government's evidence at trial consisted largely of the testimony of Vanessa Hodges, an unindicted co-conspirator, and of various FBI agents who surveilled the Manufacturers Hanover branch on June 21, 1976. Since the facts are of critical importance in any attempt case, . . . we shall review the Government's proof in considerable detail.

On June 11, 1976, Vanessa Hodges was introduced to appellant Martin Allen by Pia Longhorne, another unindicted co-conspirator. Hodges wanted to meet someone who would help her carry out a plan to rob the Manufacturers Hanover branch located at 210 Flushing Avenue in Brooklyn, and she invited Allen to join her. Hodges proposed that the bank be robbed the next Monday, June 14th, at about 7:30 A. M. She hoped that they could enter with the bank manager at that time, grab the weekend deposits, and leave. Allen agreed to rob the bank with Hodges, and told her he had access to a car, two sawed-off shotguns, and a .38 caliber revolver.

The following Monday, June 14, Allen arrived at Longhorne's house about 7:30 A. M. in a car driven by appellant Robert Jackson. A suitcase in the back seat of the car contained a sawed-off shotgun, shells, materials intended as masks, and handcuffs to bind the bank manager. While Allen picked up Hodges at Longhorne's, Jackson filled the car with gas. The trio then left for the bank.

When they arrived, it was almost 8:00 A. M. It was thus too late to effect the first step of the plan, viz., entering the bank as the manager opened the door. They rode around for a while longer, and then went to a restaurant to get something to eat and discuss their next move. After eating, the trio drove back to the bank. Allen and Hodges left the car and walked over to the bank. They peered in and saw the bulky weekend deposits, but decided it was too risky to rob the bank without an extra man.

Consequently, Jackson, Hodges, and Allen drove to Coney Island in search of another accomplice. In front of a housing project on 33rd Street they found appellant William Scott, who promptly joined the team. Allen added to the arsenal another sawed-off shotgun obtained from one of the buildings in the project, and the group drove back to the bank.

When they arrived again, Allen entered the bank to check the location of any surveillance cameras, while Jackson placed a piece of cardboard with a false license number over the authentic license plate of the car. Allen reported back that a single surveillance camera was over the entrance door. After further discussion, Scott left the car and entered the bank. He came back and informed the group that the tellers were separating the weekend deposits and that a number of patrons were now in the bank. Hodges then suggested that they drop the plans for the robbery that day, and reschedule it for the following Monday, June 21. Accordingly, they left the vicinity of the bank and returned to Coney Island where, before splitting up, they purchased a pair of stockings for Hodges to wear over her head as a disguise and pairs of gloves for Hodges, Scott, and Allen to don before entering the bank.

Hodges was arrested on Friday, June 18, 1976 on an unrelated bank robbery charge, and immediately began cooperating with the Government. After relating the events on June 14, she told FBI agents that a robbery of the Manufacturers branch at 210 Flushing Avenue was now scheduled for the following Monday, June 21. The three black male robbers, according to Hodges, would be heavily armed with hand and shoulder weapons and expected to use a brown four-door sedan equipped with a cardboard license plate as the getaway car. She told the agents that Jackson, who would drive the car, was light-skinned with a moustache and a cut on his lip, and she described Allen as short, dark-skinned with facial hair, and Scott as 5' 9, slim build, with an afro hair style and some sort of defect in his right eye.

At the request of the agents, Hodges called Allen on Saturday, June 19, and asked if he were still planning to do the job. He said that he was ready. On Sunday she called him again. This time Allen said that he was not going to rob the bank that Monday because he had learned that Hodges had been arrested and he feared that federal agents might be watching. Hodges nevertheless advised the agents that she thought the robbery might still take place as planned with the three men proceeding without her.

At about 7:00 A. M. on Monday, June 21, 1976, some ten FBI agents took various surveilling positions in the area of the bank. At about 7:39 A. M. the agents observed a brown four-door Lincoln, with a New York license plate on the front and a cardboard facsimile of a license plate on the rear, moving in an easterly direction on Flushing Avenue past the bank, which was located on the southeast corner of Flushing and

Washington Avenues. The front seat of the Lincoln was occupied by a black male driver and a black male passenger with mutton-chop sideburns. The Lincoln circled the block and came to a stop at a fire hydrant situated at the side of the bank facing Washington Avenue, a short distance south of the corner of Flushing and Washington.

A third black male, who appeared to have an eye deformity, got out of the passenger side rear door of the Lincoln, walked to the corner of Flushing and Washington, and stood on the sidewalk in the vicinity of the bank's entrance. He then walked south on Washington Avenue, only to return a short time later with a container of coffee in his hand. He stood again on the corner of Washington and Flushing in front of the bank, drinking the coffee and looking around, before returning to the parked Lincoln.

The Lincoln pulled out, made a left turn onto Flushing, and proceeded in a westerly direction for one block to Waverly Avenue. It stopped, made a U-turn, and parked on the south side of Flushing between Waverly and Washington a spot on the same side of the street as the bank entrance but separated from it by Washington Avenue. After remaining parked in this position for approximately five minutes, it pulled out and cruised east on Flushing past the bank again. The Lincoln then made a right onto Grand Avenue, the third street east of the bank, and headed south. It stopped halfway down the block, midway between Flushing and Park Avenues, and remained there for several minutes. During this time Jackson was seen working in the front of the car, which had its hood up.

The Lincoln was next sighted several minutes later in the same position it had previously occupied on the south side of Flushing Avenue between Waverly and Washington. The front license plate was now missing. The vehicle remained parked there for close to thirty minutes. Finally, it began moving east on Flushing Avenue once more, in the direction of the bank.

At some point near the bank as they passed down Flushing Avenue, the appellants detected the presence of the surveillance agents. The Lincoln accelerated down Flushing Avenue and turned south on Grand Avenue again. It was overtaken by FBI agents who ordered the appellants out of the car and arrested them. The agents then observed a black and red plaid suitcase in the rear of the car. The zipper of the suitcase was partially open and exposed two loaded sawed-off shotguns, a toy nickel-plated revolver, a pair of handcuffs, and masks. A New York license plate was seen lying on the front floor of the car. All of these items were seized.

[Chief Judge Mishler] concluded that on June 14 and again on June 21, the defendants took substantial steps, strongly corroborative of the firmness of their criminal intent, toward commission of the crime of bank robbery and found the defendants guilty on each of the two attempt counts. These appeals followed.

. . . .

The draftsmen of the Model Penal Code recognized the difficulty of arriving at a general standard for distinguishing acts of preparation from acts constituting an attempt. They found general agreement that when an actor committed the "last proximate act," i.e., when he had done all that he believed necessary to effect a particular result which is an element of the offense, he committed an attempt. They also concluded, however, that while the last proximate act is sufficient to constitute an attempt, it is not necessary to such a finding. The problem then was to devise a standard more inclusive than one requiring the last proximate act before attempt liability would attach, but less inclusive than one which would make every act done with the intent to commit a crime criminal. See Model Penal Code § 5.01, Comment at 38-39 (Tent. Draft No. 10, 1960).

. . . .

The formulation upon which the draftsmen ultimately agreed required, in addition to criminal purpose, that an act be a substantial step in a course of conduct designed to accomplish a criminal result, and that it be strongly corroborative of criminal purpose in order for it to constitute such a substantial step.

. . . .

In the case at bar, Chief Judge Mishler . . . found that on June 14 the appellants, already agreed upon a robbery plan, drove to the bank with loaded weapons. In order to carry the heavy weekend deposit sacks, they recruited another person. Cardboard was placed over the license, and the bank was entered and reconnoitered. Only then was the plan dropped for the moment and rescheduled for the following Monday. On that day, June 21, the defendants performed essentially the same acts. Since the cameras had already been located there was no need to enter the bank again, and since the appellants had arrived at the bank earlier, conditions were more favorable to their initial robbery plan than they had been on June 14. He concluded that on both occasions these men were seriously dedicated to the commission of a crime, had passed beyond the stage of preparation, and would have assaulted the bank had they not been dissuaded by certain external factors, viz., the breaking up of the weekend deposits and crowd of patrons in the bank on June 14 and the detection of the FBI surveillance on June 21.

We cannot say that these conclusions which Chief Judge Mishler reached as the trier of fact as to what the evidence before him established were erroneous. . . . [T]he criminal intent of the appellants was beyond dispute. The question remaining then is the substantiality of the steps taken on the dates in question, and how strongly this corroborates the firmness of their obvious criminal intent. This is a matter of degree. . . .

On two separate occasions, appellants reconnoitered the place contemplated for the commission of the crime and possessed the paraphernalia to be employed in the commission of the crime loaded sawed-off shotguns, extra shells, a toy revolver, handcuffs, and masks which was specially designed for such unlawful use and which could serve no lawful purpose under the circumstances. Under the Model Penal Code formulation, . . . either type of conduct, standing alone, was sufficient as a matter of law to constitute a "substantial step" if it strongly corroborated their criminal purpose. Here both types of conduct coincided on both June 14 and June 21, along with numerous other elements strongly corroborative of the firmness of appellants' criminal intent. The steps taken toward a successful bank robbery thus were not "insubstantial" as a matter of law, and Chief Judge Mishler found them "substantial" as a matter of fact. We are unwilling to substitute our assessment of the evidence for his, and thus affirm the convictions for attempted bank robbery. . . .

The judgments of conviction are affirmed.

Make a note of your thoughts on the substantial step test *before* reading the next case, *Reeves*. The *Reeves* case tends to evenly divide many criminal classes. What, if anything, does that say about the substantial step test?

State v. Reeves
916 S.W.2d 909 (1996)
Tennessee Court of Appeals

DROWOTA, Judge.

The defendant, Tracie Reeves, appeals from the Court of Appeals' affirmance of the trial court's order designating her a delinquent child. The trial court's delinquency order, which was entered following a jury trial, was based on the jury's finding that the defendant had attempted to commit second degree murder—a violation of Tenn.Code Ann. § 39-12-101. The specific issue for our determination is whether the defendant's actions constitute a "substantial step," under § 39-12-101(a)(3), toward the commission of that crime. For the following reasons, we hold that they do, and therefore affirm the judgment of the Court of Appeals.

Facts and Procedural History

On the evening of January 5, 1993, Tracie Reeves and Molly Coffman, both twelve years of age and students at West Carroll Middle School, spoke on the telephone and decided to kill their homeroom teacher, Janice Geiger. The girls agreed that Coffman would bring rat poison to school the following day so that it could be placed in Geiger's drink. The girls also agreed that they would thereafter steal Geiger's car and drive to the Smoky Mountains. Reeves then contacted Dean Foutch, a local high school student, informed him of the plan, and asked him to drive Geiger's car. Foutch refused this request.

On the morning of January 6, Coffman placed a packet of rat poison in her purse and boarded the school bus. During the bus ride Coffman told another student, Christy Hernandez, of the plan; Coffman also showed Hernandez the packet of rat poison. Upon their arrival at school Hernandez informed her homeroom teacher, Sherry Cockrill, of the plan. Cockrill then relayed this information to the principal of the school, Claudia Argo.

When Geiger entered her classroom that morning she observed Reeves and Coffman leaning over her desk; and when the girls noticed her, they giggled and ran back to their seats. At that time Geiger saw a purse lying next to her coffee cup on top of the desk. Shortly thereafter Argo called Coffman to the principal's office. Rat poison was found in Coffman's purse and it was turned over to a Sheriff's Department investigator. Both Reeves and Coffman gave written statements to the investigator concerning their plan to poison Geiger and steal her car.

Reeves and Coffman were found to be delinquent by the Carroll County Juvenile Court, and both appealed from that ruling to the Carroll County Circuit Court. After a jury found that the girls attempted to commit second degree murder in violation of Tenn.Code Ann. § 39-12-101, the "criminal attempt" statute, the trial court affirmed the juvenile court's order and sentenced the girls to the Department of Youth Development for an indefinite period. Reeves appealed from this judgment to the Court of Appeals, which affirmed the judgment of the trial court. Reeves then applied to this Court for permission to appeal pursuant to Tenn.R.App.P. 11. Because we have not addressed the law of criminal attempt since the comprehensive reform of our criminal law undertaken by the legislature in 1989, we granted that application.

Prior and Current Law of Criminal Attempt

Before the passage of the reform legislation in 1989, the law of criminal attempt, though sanctioned by various statutes, was judicially defined. In order to submit an issue of criminal attempt to the jury, the State was required to present legally sufficient evidence of: (1) an intent to commit a specific crime; (2) an overt act toward the commission of that crime; and (3) a failure to consummate the crime. . . .

Of the elements of criminal attempt, the second, the "overt act" requirement, was by far the most problematic. By attempting to draw a sharp distinction between "mere preparation" to commit a criminal act, which did not constitute the required overt act, and a direct movement toward the commission after the preparations had been made, which did, *Dupuy* [*v. State*], 325 S.W.2d at 239, 240, Tennessee courts construed the term "overt act" very narrowly. The best example of this extremely narrow construction occurred in *Dupuy*. In that case, the Memphis police sought to lay a trap for a pharmacist suspected of performing illegal abortions by sending a young woman to request these services from him. After the woman had made several attempts to secure his services, he finally agreed to perform the abortion. The pharmacist transported the young woman to a hotel room, laid out his instruments in preparation for the procedure, and asked the woman to remove her clothes. At that point the police came into the room and arrested the pharmacist, who then admitted that he had performed abortions in the past. The defendant was convicted under a statute that made it illegal to procure a miscarriage, and he appealed to this Court.

A majority of this Court reversed the conviction. After admitting that the defendant's "reprehensible" course of conduct would doubtlessly have resulted in the commission of the crime "had he not been thwarted in his efforts by the arrival of the police," *Dupuy*, 325 S.W.2d at 239, the majority concluded that: While the defendant had completed his plan to do this crime the element of attempt [overt act] does not appear in this record. The proof shows that he did not use any of the instruments and did not touch the body of the girl in question. Under such facts we do not think that the defendant is guilty under the statute. *Dupuy*, 325 S.W.2d at 240. To support its holding, the *Dupuy* court quoted a treatise passage concerning actions that constituted "mere preparation," as opposed to actions that would satisfy the overt act requirement:

> In a general way, however, it may be said that preparation consists in devising or arranging the means or measures necessary for the commission of the offense and that the attempt [overt act] is the direct movement toward the commission after the preparations are made. Even though a person actually intends to commit a crime, his procurement of the instrumentalities adapted to that end will not constitute an attempt to commit the crime in the absence of some overt act.

Id. (quoting 14 Am.Jur. § 68 (1940)). To further illustrate the foregoing principle the majority provided the following example: "the procurement by a prisoner of tools adapted to breaking jail does not render him guilty of an attempt to break jail." *Id.*

As indicated above, the sharp differentiation in *Dupuy* between "mere preparation" and "overt act," or the "act itself," was characteristic of the pre-1989 attempt law. ... In 1989, however, the legislature enacted a general criminal attempt statute, Tenn. Code Ann. § 39-12-101, as part of its comprehensive overhaul of Tennessee's criminal law. In that statute, the legislature did not simply codify the judicially-created elements of the crime, but utilized language that had up to then been entirely foreign to Tennessee attempt law. Section 39-12-101 provides, in pertinent part, as follows:

(a) A person commits criminal attempt who, acting with the kind of culpability otherwise required for the offense:

(1) Intentionally engages in action or causes a result that would constitute an offense if the circumstances surrounding the conduct were as the person believes them to be;

(2) Acts with intent to cause a result that is an element of the offense, and believes the conduct will cause the result without further conduct on the person's part; or

(3) Acts with intent to complete a course of action or cause a result that would constitute the offense, under the circumstances surrounding the conduct as the person believe them to be, *and the conduct constitutes a substantial step toward the commission of the offense.*

(b) Conduct does not constitute a *substantial step* under subdivision (a)(3) unless the person's entire course of action is corroborative of the intent to commit the offense. (emphasis added.)

The Substantial Step Issue

... [O]ur task is to determine whether the defendant's actions in this case constitute a "substantial step" toward the commission of second degree murder under the new statute....

The State [] avers that the [MPC] contains examples of conduct which, if proven, would entitle, but not require, the jury to find that the defendant had taken a "substantial step;" and that two of these examples are applicable to this case. The section of the model code relied upon by the State, § 5.01(2), provides, in pertinent part, as follows:

> (2) Conduct which may be held substantial step under paragraph (1)(c). Conduct shall not be held to constitute a substantial step under paragraph (1) (c) of this Section unless it is strongly corroborative of the actor's criminal purpose. Without negativing the sufficiency of other conduct, the following, if strongly corroborative of the actor's criminal purpose, shall not be held insufficient as a matter of law:
>
> . . . .
>
> (e) possession of materials to be employed in the commission of the crime, which are specially designed for such unlawful use or which can serve no lawful purpose of the actor under the circumstances;
>
> (f) possession, collection or fabrication of materials to be employed in the commission of the crime, at or near the place contemplated for its commission, where such possession, collection or fabrication serves no lawful purpose of the actor under the circumstances;
>
> . . . .

The State concludes that because the issue of whether the defendant's conduct constitutes a substantial step may be a jury question under the model code, the jury was justified in finding her guilty of attempting to commit second degree murder.

. . . .

One persistent criticism of the endeavor to separate "mere preparation" from the "act itself" is that the question is ultimately not one of kind but of degree; the "act itself" is merely one of the termini on a continuum of criminal activity. Therefore, distinguishing between "mere preparation" and the "act itself" in a principled manner is a difficult, if not impossible, task. ... The other principal ground of criticism [] bears directly on the primary objective of the law—that of preventing inchoate crimes from becoming full-blown ones. Many courts and commentators have argued that failing to attach criminal responsibility to the actor—and therefore prohibiting law enforcement officers from taking action—until the actor is on the brink of consummating the crime endangers the public and undermines the preventative goal of attempt law. ...

Once a person secretly places a toxic substance into a container from which another person is likely to eat or drink, the damage is done. Here, if it had not been for the intervention of the teacher, she could have been rendered powerless to protect herself from harm.

. . . We hold that when an actor possesses materials to be used in the commission of a crime, at or near the scene of the crime, and where the possession of those materials can serve no lawful purpose of the actor under the circumstances, the jury is entitled, but not required, to find that the actor has taken a "substantial step" toward the commission of the crime if such action is strongly corroborative of the actor's overall criminal purpose. For the foregoing reasons, the judgment of the Court of Appeals is affirmed.

Notes and Questions

1. The *Reeves* court traces the development of attempt crimes in Tennessee from the *Dupuy* case and the "last act test," which is the most restrictive common law test, to the substantial step test which applied in *Reeves*. How would you characterize the substantial step test?

2. As mentioned above, the *Reeves* case often divides law school classes. Sometimes the debate is over whether or not the girls' actions constituted a substantial step, which somewhat exposes the test's subjectivity. But often there is disagreement about whether the girls really understood what they were doing. Those who think they did not point to the girls giggling about their plan and divulging it to a classmate. This argument is more about mental responsibility than the substantial step test or the elements of attempt. As discussed in the excuse chapter, mental responsibility is a difficult burden for a defendant to make. Our societal ignorance and mistrust of mental health issues can lead to non sequitur legal outcomes. This was the case in 2014, in Wisconsin, when two twelve-year-old girls (Weier and Geyser) lured a twelve-year-old friend into the woods before Geyser stabbed her nineteen times, encouraged by Weier. The girls committed this heinous act in an effort to please "Slenderman," a fictional entity, and gain entry into Slenderman's unidentified woodland palace. Amazingly, the victim survived. Weier and Geyser were prosecuted, with Geyser being allowed to plead not guilty by reason of insanity. Prosecutors did not support Weier's attempt to similarly plead, but a jury ultimately found her not guilty by reason of mental disease or defect. Both women were ordered to a mental health facility for up to 40 years for Geyser (the maximum allowed) and up to 25 years for Weier. In September 2021, Weier was released from the mental health facility, but under a wide range of conditions and limitations. Todd Richmond, *Woman Convicted in Slenderman case to be freed Monday*, ASSOCIATED PRESS, Sept. 11, 2021.

3. In Section 5.01, the MPC defines attempt as

(1) A person is guilty of an attempt to commit a crime if, acting with the kind of culpability otherwise required for commission of the crime, he:

(a) purposely engages in conduct which would constitute the crime if the attendant circumstances were as he believes them to be or

Would this be a failed or incomplete attempt? What type of impossibility does this address?

> (b) when causing a particular result is an element of the crime, does or omits to do anything with the purpose of causing or with the belief that it will cause such result without further conduct on his part; or

Is this a failed or incomplete attempt? What type of impossibility does this address?

> (c) purposely does or omits to do anything which, under the circumstances as he believes them to be, is an act or omission constituting a substantial step in a course of conduct planned to culminate in his commission of the crime.

Is this a failed or incomplete attempt?

> (2) Conduct Which May Be Held Substantial Step Under Subsection (1)(c). Conduct shall not be held to constitute a substantial step under Subsection (1)(c) of this Section unless it is strongly corroborative of the actor's criminal purpose. Without negativing the sufficiency of other conduct, the following, if strongly corroborative of the actor's criminal purpose, shall not be held insufficient as a matter of law:
>
> > (a) lying in wait, searching for or following the contemplated victim of the crime;
> >
> > (b) enticing or seeking to entice the contemplated victim of the crime to go to the place contemplated for its commission;
> >
> > (c) reconnoitering the place contemplated for the commission of the crime;
> >
> > (d) unlawful entry of a structure, vehicle or enclosure in which it is contemplated that the crime will be committed;
> >
> > (e) possession of materials to be employed in the commission of the crime, which are specially designed for such unlawful use or which can serve no lawful purpose of the actor under the circumstances;
> >
> > (f) possession, collection or fabrication of materials to be employed in the commission of the crime, at or near the place contemplated for its commission, where such possession, collection or fabrication serves no lawful purpose of the actor under the circumstances;
> >
> > (g) soliciting an innocent agent to engage in conduct constituting an element of the crime.

How does this impact an appellate court's authority to overturn a conviction based on *the United States v. Jackson* standard?

The last issue defendants raise in attempt cases is that they abandoned the crime. Recall from the introduction, first, that the common law and MPC have very different attitudes towards abandonment, and second, that even where it is recognized, the challenging burden is on the defendant.

D. Abandoning Attempt Common Law

United States v. Young
613 F.3d 735 (2010)
Eighth Circuit Court of Appeals

SHEPHERD, Circuit Judge.

Following trial, a jury convicted James William Young of one count of attempting to entice a minor to engage in sexual activity, in violation of 18 U.S.C. § 2422(b). The district court sentenced Young to 160 months imprisonment, a $100 special assessment, and 10 years supervised release. Young appeals, challenging his conviction. . . . For the following reasons, we affirm.

[On November 4, 2008, Young, a 33-year-old married father of three, entered an adult online chat room entitled "romance, adult," on Yahoo! Instant Messenger and sent an instant message to an individual who identified herself as "Emily" and that she was a 14-year-old female. "Emily" was in reality undercover Dewitt, Iowa Police Officer Shai Cruciani of the Internet Crimes Against Children Task Force. Young messaged Emily for the next nine days and raised the possibility of meeting her in person, taking a bath with her, and introducing her to oral sex. Young coordinated to meet with Emily in a hotel room. Young planned to check into the hotel and leave the room number in a note on the windshield of his car. Emily was to wear jeans and a pink coat. Young traveled to the hotel but was unable to book a room as his credit card was declined. He then drove around the parking lot of the hotel and upon seeing Emily aka Officer Cruciani in a pink coat, began honking his car horn and yelling at her, following which he was arrested and subsequently prosecuted. At trial, the court refused Young's request for an abandonment instruction. Following his conviction, Young appealed on several grounds, one of which being the trial court's refusal to issue the abandonment instruction.]

. . . .

This issue of whether a defendant is entitled to an abandonment defense once an attempt has been completed, i.e., the defendant has the requisite intent and has completed a substantial step towards the crime, is an issue of first impression in our circuit. While we have stated, "[i]n an attempt case, abandonment precludes liability," *United States v. Robinson*, 217 F.3d 560, 564 n. 3 (8th Cir. 2000), we relied upon *United States v. Joyce*, 693 F.2d 838 (8th Cir. 1982) in making that comment. *Joyce*, however, involved abandonment of an attempt prior to the completion of the attempt. *Id.* at 841. We hold today that a defendant cannot abandon an attempt once it has been completed.

. . . .

In [*United States v.*] *Shelton*, the Sixth Circuit rejected the Model Penal Code's approach and held that "withdrawal, abandonment and renunciation, however characterized, do not provide a defense to an attempt crime." 30 F.3d at 706. The court explained:

> As noted, the attempt crime is complete with proof of intent together with acts constituting a substantial step toward commission of the substantive offense. When a defendant withdraws prior to forming the necessary intent or taking a substantial step toward the commission of the offense, the essential elements of the crime cannot be proved. At this point, the question whether a defendant has withdrawn is synonymous with whether he has committed the offense. After a defendant has evidenced the necessary intent and has committed an act constituting a substantial step toward the commission of the offense, he has committed the crime of attempt, and can withdraw only from the commission of the substantive offense. We are not persuaded that the availability of a withdrawal defense would provide an incentive or motive to desist from the commission of an offense, especially since the success of the defense presupposes a criminal trial at which the issue would be submitted to the jury for decision. A remote chance of acquittal would appear to have an even more remote chance of deterring conduct. We recognize, of course, that attempt crimes pose unique issues. However, the interest of defendants in not being convicted for *mere* thoughts, desires or motives is adequately addressed by the government's burden of proving that the defendant took a substantial step toward the commission of the substantive offense. *Id.* (quotation omitted).

. . . .

Because our circuit has already determined that the abandonment defense: (1) can apply to uncompleted attempt crimes, *see Joyce*, 693 F.2d at 841-42, and (2) has been rejected as a defense to completed crimes other than attempt, *see* [*United States v.*] *Ball*, 22 F.3d at 199, logically flowing from this analysis is the conclusion that, when a defendant has completed the crime of attempt; i.e., has the requisite intent and has taken a substantial step towards completion of the crime, he cannot successfully abandon the attempt because the crime itself has already been completed. We therefore adopt the Sixth Circuit's approach in *Shelton*, specifically reject the Model Penal Code approach, and hold that the defense of abandonment is not warranted once a defendant completes the crime of attempt. We acknowledge, that "[a]fter a defendant has evidenced the necessary intent and has committed an act constituting a substantial step toward the commission of the offense, he has committed the crime of attempt, and can withdraw only from the commission of the substantive offense," not the attempt of such offense. *Shelton*, 30 F.3d at 706.

As discussed above, Young completed his attempt because he had the requisite intent and took a substantial step towards completion of the enticement crime, all supported by the evidence discovered in his car, his travel to the hotel and attempt to check in, and his search for Emily once he could not obtain the hotel room. Because Young completed "the essential elements" of his attempt, *Shelton*, 30 F.3d at 706, he cannot now claim that he abandoned that plan. We therefore conclude that the district court committed no error in its decision to refuse Young's proffered abandonment instruction.

. . . .

For the foregoing reasons, we affirm Young's conviction and sentence.

E. Abandoning Attempt MPC

United States v. Walther

30 M.J. 829 (1990)
United States Navy-Marine Corps Court of Military Review

We recognize voluntary abandonment as an affirmative defense to attempted criminal conduct in this case. . . . Pursuant to his pleas, appellant was found guilty . . . [by a military judge] of the willful destruction of another sailor's automobile window and attempted larceny of an in-dash car stereo, appellant was sentenced to confinement for 30 days, forfeitures of $450.00 pay per month for two months, reduction to pay grade E-l, and a bad-conduct discharge. . . .

We specified three issues for briefing by appellate counsel. . . . The first issue dealt with the providence of appellant's guilty plea to attempted larceny of a car stereo. During the providence inquiry, appellant described how he broke the window of another sailor's parked car on base, intending to steal the radio inside. Once inside the car, appellant stated, he realized he was doing wrong and changed his mind. He had done nothing to physically remove the radio from the car. Nothing in the record indicates that appellant's failure to proceed with the theft was motivated by increased probability of detection or apprehension, or due to any outside cause. Appellant's answers during the providence inquiry raised the issue of whether, upon entering the automobile after breaking its window, he voluntarily abandoned his effort to steal the car stereo inside. We find his answers raised the affirmative defense of voluntary abandonment and are therefore inconsistent with his pleas of guilty to the charge and specification alleging attempted larceny. These answers required that either the military judge make further inquiry or set aside those pleas.

Following the precept of the Model Penal Code and various non-military Federal cases, the affirmative defense of voluntary abandonment in connection with attempts is recognized in military justice. *United States v. Byrd,* 24 M.J. 286, 291-92 (C.M.A.1987) (and authorities cited therein). In *Byrd,* the accused plead guilty to a charge of attempted distribution of marijuana based on the facts that he had accepted ten dollars from an undercover agent and journeyed to a liquor store where marijuana could be purchased. These were found not to be "overt acts" sufficient to establish the accused's guilt of attempted distribution of marijuana, for he had not gone beyond mere preparation to commit the crime but instead changed his mind once inside the liquor store. These facts, brought forth through a stipulation of fact and the accused's answers during the providence inquiry, were held to be inconsistent with the accused's plea of guilty. *Byrd,* 24 M.J. at 290 (and authorities cited therein). But also in *Byrd,* appellant argued that *"even if* his acts would otherwise have constituted an attempt, he was insulated from liability by his voluntary abandonment of the intended crime before its completion" .... *Byrd,* 24 M.J. at 288. (Emphasis added.)

. . . .

In this case, appellant's breaking of the locked car's window was a necessary preliminary step to theft of the car stereo and constituted an overt act which directly tended to accomplish his admitted unlawful purpose. He made no physical effort to remove the stereo. Appellant's breaking the window, however, strongly corroborated his criminal intent to steal the stereo, and was a direct movement toward commission of the crime. For him to abandon his criminal intent is to renounce the crime of attempted larceny which was arguably completed when he broke the window with the intent to steal the stereo.

While it may be inconsistent to hold that a completed crime can be renounced with no criminal liability inuring to the malefactor, and that one who has committed an act which is beyond the stage of preparation and within the zone of attempt may avoid liability for the attempt by voluntarily abandoning the criminal effort, there are strong public policy reasons for not imposing criminal liability upon appellant for attempted larceny in this case. We borrow from *Byrd:*

> According to the drafters of the Model Penal Code, the rationale for recognizing this defense is as follows: On balance, it is concluded that renunciation of criminal purpose should be a defense to a criminal attempt charge because, as to the early stage of an attempt, it significantly negatives dangerousness of character, and as to the latter stages, the value of encouraging desistance outweighs the net dangerousness shown by the abandoned criminal effort. (Citation omitted.) Responding to critics, the drafters of the Model Penal Code observed: It is possible, of course, that the defense of renunciation of criminal purpose may add to the incentives to take the *first* steps toward crime. Knowledge that criminal endeavors can be undone with impunity may encourage preliminary steps that would not be undertaken if liability inevitably attached to every abortive criminal undertaking that proceeded beyond preparation. But this is not a serious problem. First, any consolation the actor might draw from the abandonment defense would have to be tempered with the knowledge that the defense would be unavailable if the actor's purposes were frustrated by external forces before he had an opportunity to abandon his effort. Second, the encouragement this defense might

lend to the actor taking preliminary steps would be a factor only where the actor was dubious of his plans and where, consequently, the probability of continuance was not great. (Citation omitted.)

In various Federal cases the doctrine of voluntary abandonment seems to have been recognized either expressly or implicitly (footnote omitted). Various state legislatures and state courts have also accepted this defense (footnote omitted). However, the defense has only been applied when an individual abandons his intended crime because of a change of heart; and it has not been allowed when the abandonment results from fear of immediate detection or apprehension.

Byrd, 24 M.J. at 291-92. [The court in *Byrd* acknowledged the potential validity of abandonment]

[In this case, the accused's] answers during the [guilty plea] inquiry do suggest a change of heart and a voluntary abandonment of his criminal venture. Thus, those answers were inconsistent with the guilty pleas and would require either that the military judge make further inquiry or set aside the pleas. *Byrd*, 24 M.J. at 293. Therefore, appellant's pleas of guilty to attempted larceny are improvident, and the findings of guilty . . . are set aside. . . .

Notes and Questions

1. Solicitation as attempt. Could soliciting a crime constitute an attempt to commit that crime? As the Pennsylvania Supreme Court explained, "[m]erely soliciting one to do an act is not an attempt to do that act. . . . In a high, moral sense, it may be true that solicitation is an attempt; but in a legal sense, it is not." *Stabler v. Commonwealth*, 95 Pa. St. 318, 321 (1880) (quoting in part from *Smith v. Commonwealth*, 4 P.F. Smith 209). Where a defendant does *more* than "mere solicitation," they may have crossed the threshold for an attempt but, as is discussed in the attempt section of this chapter, the answer varies significantly based on the jurisdiction's test or criteria for attempt. In 2018, the North Carolina Supreme Court vacated an attempted murder conviction which was based on the solicitation to murder qualifying as an attempt. *See State v. Melton*, 821 S.E.2d 424 (N.C. 2018). The court, applying the test used in North Carolina, held that an attempt charge required acts which would constitute "direct movement" towards the commission of the target crime and which would "likely" lead to its commission.

2. Remembering that at common law, solicitation liability requires actual receipt of the criminal request by an intended solicitee, consider the following: A is currently in jail awaiting trial. A smuggles food items into his cell and makes "home-made" lemon juice, A writes (using the lemon juice to hide the writing) and mails a letter to B in which A begs B to kill C, the primary witness against A. Turns out, cell-made lemon juice does not act like actual lemon juice, and mail censors identify and seize

the letter, which never reaches B. In a jurisdiction applying the common law, with what crime would you charge A?

3. Under the MPC, an individual may attempt an offense not just by taking action but by failing or omitting to do so. *See* MPC § 5.01(1)(c):

> A person is guilty of an attempt to commit a crime if, acting with the kind of culpability otherwise required for commission of the crime, he: purposely does or omits to do anything which, under the circumstances as he believes them to be, is an act or omission constituting a substantial step in a course of conduct planned to culminate in his commission of the crime.

See also Michael Cahill, *Attempt by Omission*, 94 Iowa L. Rev. 1207 (2009).

4. Returning to the chapter introduction and the reference to an Australian case (see text accompanying fn. 16) in which a man conducted disturbing google searches about killing a woman and then raping her (which was followed by the man stabbing a woman but neither killing nor raping her). Assume that a law is passed requiring companies running internet search engines to notify law enforcement when a certain number of search terms like murder and rape are typed in. Now assume that Google has notified law enforcement that over the last 48 hours, "A" has conducted a number of google searches about murder, how to not leave your DNA, how to poison someone, and how to dispose of a body. The police locate A while shopping at Home Depot. A has what appears to be a print out from the google search "how to dispose of a body" which lists nineteen required items, all of which are in A's cart as he waits to check out. You are the on-call District Attorney, and the police are requesting guidance on whether to arrest A for attempted murder. Does your answer depend on the overt act test in your jurisdiction? Does your answer change if instead of A having conducted searches related to what appears to be killing one person, his searches are of how to conduct mass killings?

Formative Assessments

1. What is A's criminal liability in a common law jurisdiction if A propositions U, an undercover police officer, to sell A cocaine?

A. A is guilty of soliciting illegal drugs.

B. A is guilty of conspiring to purchase illegal drugs.

C. A is guilty of attempting to purchase illegal drugs.

D. All of the above (A–C).

E. None of the above

2. Chris, Geoff and Ken have all agreed to rob a nearby bank. During a brainstorming session, Chris suggests that they rob the bank on the first business day of the month when the cash on hand will be at the highest level. Geoff suggests that the

robbery occur just before the bank opens, to which Chris responds "Great idea, but when does it open?" Ken then googles "Downtown Bank and Trust Opening Hours" and dutifully reports the search results. Moments later, police burst into the room and arrest all three. Which of the following best describes their potential criminal liability in a common law jurisdiction?

A. All three are guilty of conspiring to rob the bank.

B. None of the three are guilty of conspiring to rob the bank.

C. Chris and Geoff, as "mere talkers," have not committed a crime. Ken's google search constituted an overt act. As a result, Ken is guilty of conspiring to rob the bank.

D. All three are guilty of attempting to rob the bank.

3. Same facts as in 2 except that the police do not burst into the room. After Ken leaves the bank robbery planning meeting, he is racked with doubt and guilt. Ken calls the police and tells an officer about their plan. The police then arrest Chris, Geoff and Ken. In terms of Ken's criminal liability,

A. Ken is guilty of conspiracy to rob the bank, but only in a common law jurisdiction.

B. Ken is guilty of conspiracy to rob the bank, but only in a MPC jurisdiction.

C. Ken is guilty of conspiracy to rob the bank in either a common law or MPC jurisdiction.

D. None of the above.

4. Which of the following statements regarding merger and inchoate offenses (solicitation, conspiracy and attempt) is correct?

    I. Solicitation

    II. Conspiracy

    III. Attempt

A. I, II, and III all merge into the completed offense.

B. I and II merge into the completed offense

C. II and III merge into the completed offense.

D. I and III merge into the completed offense.

Chapter 15

Liability for Conduct of Another

I. Introduction

There are three ways in which someone can be liable for the crimes — attempted or completed — committed by another person.

A. Party to a Conspiracy

Under what is known as the *Pinkerton* doctrine, all members of a conspiracy are liable for the crimes that are committed by *any other* member of the conspiracy that are reasonably foreseeable and that are in furtherance of the conspiracy. The most obvious example of such a crime is the target of the conspiracy. Thus, for example, all members of a robbery conspiracy are liable for the robbery committed by only some of the members. However, liability extends to other crimes even if they were not the intended object of the conspiracy. Accordingly, crimes are in furtherance of the conspiracy if they help to advance the conspiracy's objectives — a question which is assessed objectively. For example, if one of the robbers steals a car to get away from the robbery, that crime is also attributed to all co-conspirators. Thus, conspiracy is not just a crime, but also a mode of liability. Of course, if the defendant can show that he effectively withdrew from the conspiracy prior to the commission of a crime by a former co-conspirator, the essential liability link is severed.

B. Accomplice Liability

An alternative (and often overlapping) mode of liability is what is generally known as accomplice liability, which at common law was known as aiding and abetting. To understand this mode of liability for the crimes committed by another, it is essential to differentiate between the *principal* and the *accomplice*. The principal is the individual who does the *actus reus* of the crime; the accomplice is someone who aids and abets the principal by providing aid, assistance, or even encouragement to the principal with the specific intent that the crime be committed. Most modern penal codes define assistance very broadly: "solicits, encourages, directs, aids, or attempts to aid the [principal]." Texas Penal Code §7.02.

If the prosecution proves the requirements of accomplice liability beyond a reasonable doubt, the accomplice is liable for the crime as if she committed it. Importantly, being an accomplice is not a crime; it is a mode of liability linking the accomplice to a "target" offense. The accomplice is charged with that target offense and treated as if she committed that offense. In the most basic terms, accomplice liability involves connecting the accomplice's criminal mens rea to the principal's actus reus. The "Velcro" that connects them is the trivial act of aiding and abetting. Those two elements establish the crime the accomplice is guilty of.

This mode of liability is derived from the common law, although the common law used different terminology and imposed certain procedural obstacles based on that terminology. The individual who committed the actus reus was principal in the first degree; the aider and abettor who was at the scene of the crime was the principal in the second degree. An aider and abettor who was *not* at the scene of the crime was an accessory before the fact; if someone aided the principal to conceal the crime or avoid apprehension, he was an accessory after the fact. While all of these parties were guilty as if they committed the crime, an accessory could not be convicted unless a principal was first convicted. Venue might also preclude a joint trial, as accessories had to be tried in the jurisdiction where they aided and abetted.

The general use of accomplice liability has largely superseded these original common law concepts, but the liability is normally the same. However, there is no requirement to convict a principal in order to convict an accomplice. What *is* required is to prove that the principal committed the crime the accomplice is being tried for. This means that the accomplice may invoke any affirmative justification or defense the principal could have invoked to negate the unlawful nature of the principal's act or omission.

C. Natural and Probable Consequence Doctrine

In many jurisdictions, an accomplice may also be guilty of other crimes pursuant to the *natural and probable* consequence doctrine, the accomplice analog to the *Pinkerton* doctrine. Any crime that naturally and foreseeably blossoms out of the crime the accomplice aided and abetted is attributable to both the principal and the accomplice. Like the *Pinkerton* doctrine, this assessment is objective, meaning it is no defense that the accomplice did not expect the principal to commit the secondary crime.

Accordingly, there is a logical process for assessing the scope of accomplice liability:

1. Prove the principal committed (or attempted to commit) the crime. If so, the accomplice is charged with the primary crime.

2. Prove the accomplice did some affirmative act that aided or abetted the principal.

3. Prove the accomplice aided and abetted with the specific intent that the target offense be committed. If so, the accomplice is guilty of the primary crime.

4. Prove the principal committed another crime (the secondary crime).

5. Prove the secondary crime was a natural and probable outgrowth of the primary crime. If so, the accomplice is guilty of the secondary crime.

II. Conspiracy Liability Pursuant to the *Pinkerton* Rule

The *Pinkerton* rule imposes liability on members of a conspiracy for crimes committed by fellow co-conspirators in addition to liability for the crime of conspiracy. In order to convict the co-conspirators for such other crimes, the prosecutor must prove: 1. That there was a conspiracy; 2. That another member of the conspiracy committed another crime; 3. That the defendant was a member of the conspiracy when the other crime was committed; 4. That the other crime was in furtherance of the conspiracy and reasonably foreseeable. It is not necessary for the prosecutor to prove any separate mens rea or actus reus with respect to the other crimes. The co-conspirators are liable even if they were not physically involved in the commission of these crimes or even aware that they were being committed.

Pinkerton v. United States
328 U.S. 640 (1946)
U.S. Supreme Court

DOUGLAS, J.

Walter and Daniel Pinkerton are brothers who live a short distance from each other on Daniel's farm. They were indicted for violations of the Internal Revenue Code. The indictment contained ten substantive counts and one conspiracy count. The jury found Walter guilty on nine of the substantive counts and on the conspiracy count. It found Daniel guilty on six of the substantive counts and on the conspiracy count. . . .

A single conspiracy was charged and proved. Some of the overt acts charged in the conspiracy count were the same acts charged in the substantive counts. Each of the substantive offenses found was committed pursuant to the conspiracy. Petitioners therefore contend that the substantive counts became merged in the conspiracy count, and that only a single sentence not exceeding the maximum two year penalty provided by the conspiracy statute (Criminal Code § 37, 18 U.S.C. § 88) could be imposed. Or to state the matter differently, they contend that each of the substantive counts became a separate conspiracy count but, since only a single conspiracy was charged and proved, only a single sentence for conspiracy could be imposed. . . .

It is contended that there was insufficient evidence to implicate Daniel in the conspiracy. But we think there was enough evidence for submission of the issue to the jury.

There is, however, no evidence to show that Daniel participated directly in the commission of the substantive offenses on which his conviction has been sustained, although there was evidence to show that these substantive offenses were in fact committed by Walter in furtherance of the unlawful agreement or conspiracy existing between the brothers. The question was submitted to the jury on the theory that each petitioner could be found guilty of the substantive offenses, if it was found at the time those offenses were committed petitioners were parties to an unlawful conspiracy and the substantive offenses charged were in fact committed in furtherance of it. . . .

We have here a continuous conspiracy. There is here no evidence of the affirmative action on the part of Daniel which is necessary to establish his withdrawal from it. *Hyde v. United States*, 225 U.S. 347, 269. As stated in that case, "Having joined in an unlawful scheme, having constituted agents for its performance, scheme and agency to be continuous until full fruition be secured, until he does some act to disavow or defeat the purpose he is in no situation to claim the delay of the law. As the offense has not been terminated or accomplished he is still offending. And we think, consciously offending, offending as certainly, as we have said, as at the first moment of his confederation, and consciously through every moment of its existence." And so long as the partnership in crime continues, the partners act for each other in carrying it forward. It is settled that "an overt act of one partner may be the act of all without any new agreement specifically directed to that act." *United States v. Kissel*, 218 U.S. 601, 608. Motive or intent may be proved by the acts or declarations of some of the conspirators in furtherance of the common objective. A scheme to use the mails to defraud, which is joined in by more than one person, is a conspiracy. Yet all members are responsible, though only one did the mailing. The governing principle is the same when the substantive offense is committed by one of the conspirators in furtherance of the unlawful project.

The criminal intent to do the act is established by the formation of the conspiracy. Each conspirator instigated the commission of the crime. The unlawful agreement contemplated precisely what was done. It was formed for the purpose. The act done was in execution of the enterprise. The rule which holds responsible one who counsels, procures, or commands another to commit a crime is founded on the same principle. That principle is recognized in the law of conspiracy when the overt act of one partner in crime is attributable to all. An overt act is an essential ingredient of the crime of conspiracy under § 37 of the Criminal Code, 18 U.S.C. § 88. If that can be supplied by the act of one conspirator, we fail to see why the same or other acts in furtherance of the conspiracy are likewise not attributable to the others for the purpose of holding them responsible for the substantive offense.

A different case would arise if the substantive offense committed by one of the conspirators was not in fact done in furtherance of the conspiracy, did not fall within the scope of the unlawful project, or was merely a part of the ramifications of the plan which could not be reasonably foreseen as a necessary or natural consequence of the unlawful agreement. But as we read this record, that is not this case.

Affirmed.

Notes and Questions

1. The dissent (omitted above) pointed out that "Daniel in fact was in the penitentiary, under sentence for other crimes, when some of Walter's crimes were done." But did this mean the conspiracy had terminated? Obviously not. Why? Because Walter continued to further the objectives of the conspiracy, and Daniel did nothing to terminate his role in the conspiracy; in essence, he was just sidelined but still part of the team. Accordingly, Daniel was still liable because each co-conspirator is liable for every crime committed in furtherance of the conspiracy until the objective of the conspiracy has been achieved.

2. The common law concept of conspiracy did not require proof the co-conspirators knew of each other's participation; it was sufficient to prove the scope of the agreement by implication. For example, a defendant smuggling illegal narcotics into the United States could be convicted of a broad conspiracy to manufacture, import, and distribute narcotics. While it is unlikely that the smuggler knows of other participants in the conspiracy, the nature of her participation supports the rational inference that there must be other "links" in the criminal chain. As a result, she is potentially liable for numerous other crimes committed by people she doesn't even know, if they are in furtherance of the agreement and objectively foreseeable. The MPC is more restrictive: a defendant cannot be considered to be a co-conspirator with another individual unless she has knowledge that the other individual is part of the conspiracy, although there is no requirement to prove she knows the individual's identity. According to MPC § 5.03(2):

> *Scope of Conspiratorial Relationship.* If a person guilty of conspiracy, as defined by Subsection (1) of this Section, knows that a person with whom he conspires to commit a crime has conspired with another person or persons to commit the same crime, he is guilty of conspiring with such other person or persons, whether or not he knows their identity, to commit such crime.

Accordingly, to convict a defendant for a crime committed by another member of a conspiracy, the prosecution must prove that the defendant knew the other person was a member of the conspiracy.

3. The distinction between a conspirator and an accomplice is a frequent source of confusion. The requirement for accomplice liability will be discussed in much more detail in the next section, and the two modes of liability often overlap. One significant difference is that a conspiracy requires proof of *prearrangement*, whereas an individual may become an accomplice *after* the crime commences. It is therefore possible for an individual to be liable as an accomplice without there being a conspiracy. For instance, in *Rivera v. State,* 12 S.W.3d 572 (Tex. App. 2000), the victim went to the defendant's house to watch the Tyson-Holyfield fight. The defendant and his brother stabbed the victim six times and shot the victim three times, causing his death. The defendant did the stabbing while his brother did the shooting. Since there was no evidence of any *prearrangement* to kill the victim, the defendant could not be properly convicted of conspiracy. However, the defendant's conviction as an accomplice to murder was upheld.

4. Suppose A, B, C, and D conspire to rob a bank. Prior to the robbery, A steals a car to assist in the robbery. During the robbery, B shoots and kills the bank security guard to facilitate their escape. C sexually assaults a bank teller while the robbery was occurring. D, as the lookout, remained outside the bank throughout. Thus, in addition to conspiracy, four other crimes were committed: robbery, murder, larceny, rape. What is the liability of A, B, C, and D for these four crimes?

The answer to this question turns on a finding that the substantive crimes are both in furtherance of the conspiratorial objective (robbery) and foreseeable. This is what the prosecution must prove beyond a reasonable doubt to convict each co-conspirator of the substantive offense. Each of these findings is based on an objective assessment; a jury will have to decide whether a reasonable co-conspirator with the information these co-conspirators had available would have foreseen each substantive offense. One way to visualize this is to imagine the conspiratorial objective as a seed and then ask whether each substantive offense "blossomed" out of that seed. If so, each co-conspirator is liable for that substantive offense.

Practice Pointer

Pinkerton provides a huge incentive for the prosecutor to charge conspiracy whenever the facts warrant such a charge. Other areas of the law provide additional incentives to the prosecutor to charge conspiracy whenever the facts support the charge. First, the law of evidence allows statements by one co-conspirator to be used against each member of the conspiracy as long as the statements were made during the conspiracy and furthered the conspiracy. Second, by charging conspiracy, the prosecution has greater ability to join multiple defendants in a single trial. Third, the statute of limitations for a conspiracy doesn't begin to run until a conspiracy is over. This means that the prosecution may initiate conspiracy charges years later than it might for an object offense. Fourth, a conspiracy may involve multiple actors in multiple jurisdictions. Venue is permitted in any jurisdiction where any act in furtherance of the conspiracy was committed by any conspirator or in any jurisdiction in which any conspirator entered the conspiracy.

As noted above, *Pinkerton* liability applies to co-conspirators. Accordingly, if a defendant who was a co-conspirator *is not* a member of the conspiracy when another member commits a crime, there is no basis for imposing *Pinkerton* liability. So how can a conspirator "sever" her connection to other members of the conspiracy? She must withdraw from the conspiracy (but remember this has no impact for liability for any crimes in furtherance of the conspiracy committed *before* a defendant withdrew). The next case explains the requirements for effective withdrawal, but also why withdrawal in no way impacts criminal responsibility for the conspiracy.

People v. Sconce

228 Cal. App. 3d 693 (1991)
California Court of Appeals

The People filed an information charging defendant and respondent David Wayne Sconce (Sconce) with conspiracy to commit murder. The trial court set the information aside because it found Sconce effectively had withdrawn from the conspiracy. (§ 995.) The People appeal.

Factual and Procedural Background

This case involves Sconce's alleged formation of a conspiracy to kill Elie Estephan (Estephan). In 1985 Estephan and Cindy Strunk (Cindy) were separated. Cindy testified she worked for her father, Frank Strunk, at his business, the Cremation Society of California (CSC). In the course of her duties at CSC, she met Sconce whose family owned the Lamb Funeral Home (LFH) and the Pasadena Crematorium. In 1985, Cindy met Sconce's brother-in-law, Brad Sallard (Sallard). She and Sallard dated and began to live together in May 1985.

When Estephan served divorce papers on Cindy in June, 1985, Sconce offered her the services of LFH's attorney. Sconce and Sallard accompanied Cindy to the first meeting with the lawyer. One of the assets she mentioned during the meeting was a $250,000 insurance policy on Estephan's life which named her as beneficiary.

At some point thereafter, Cindy argued with Estephan at CSC in front of Frank Strunk and others including an LFH employee, John Pollerana (Pollerana). Estephan chased Cindy and pushed her down a number of stairs. She was upset but not hurt.

Pollerana testified that in late summer of 1985, the day after the argument between Estephan and Cindy, Sconce asked Pollerana "if he gave me $10,000, would I get rid of Elie [Estephan], but, you know, I just shook my head, and we just walked by. That was the end of the conversation."

Pollerana further testified Sconce did not like Estephan because he had slapped Cindy. Sconce referred to Estephan, an Arab. . . . Pollerana did not take Sconce's offer seriously. However, two weeks later Pollerana had a conversation with Bob Garcia (Garcia) in which Garcia said Sconce had offered him $10,000 to kill Estephan. Pollerana told Garcia, "'I wouldn't do it.'" A few days later, Garcia showed Pollerana the address to Estephan's house and Pollerana drove Garcia there.

Garcia testified he also worked for Sconce. One day at the crematorium Sconce asked Garcia "about someone being murdered, and if I knew anyone who would do it." Sconce told him "a friend wanted someone killed." Sconce offered Garcia $10,000 or $15,000 to commit the murder. Garcia told Sconce he would either find someone to do it or that he would do it himself.

In a telephone conversation a few days later, Sconce told Garcia that Estephan "had a large insurance policy and he just wanted him murdered to collect the insurance money." Sconce gave Garcia the impression that Sconce, Sallard and Cindy were plotting Estephan's murder.

Approximately one week later Sconce and Garcia went to a Jack-In-The-Box across the street from Estephan's gas station. CSC is on another corner of the same intersection. They sat next to the window and, as they ate lunch, Sconce used binoculars to point Estephan out to Garcia. Sconce later gave Estephan's address to Garcia. One night shortly thereafter, Garcia and Pollerana drove to Estephan's house.

Garcia then contacted Herbert Dutton (Dutton), an ex-convict who lived next door to him, about committing the offense. Dutton agreed to do the job for $5,000. That same night Garcia and Dutton drove to Estephan's house. On the way there they discussed whether to blow up Estephan's car or shoot him on the freeway. They settled on the former because Dutton had explosives and no one would have to pull the trigger. They intended to plant the bomb, run a wire to it from three houses away, and wait for Estephan.

Conversations between Sconce and Garcia about the matter were brief but continued over a three-week period. Sconce would ask Garcia, "Is he still walking today[?]" Garcia would respond that "we" would take care of it. Approximately three weeks after Sconce's initial conversation with Garcia, Sconce "just called it off. He said just forget about it, disregard doing it." Garcia did not see Dutton after the night they drove to Estephan's house. Although Garcia did not know it at the time Sconce told him not to kill Estephan, Dutton had been arrested on a parole violation.

Dutton testified that in mid-September, 1985, Garcia asked him if he knew anyone who would kill someone his boss wanted killed. Dutton said he would do it for "about $2,500." Dutton suggested explosives or a 12-gauge shotgun. That same evening they drove to the home of the victim "to see if it would be suitable to wire the car out there." Dutton told Garcia to give him half the money up front and to let him know. However, Dutton, who was on federal parole for bank robbery, was arrested for parole violation stemming from heroin abuse shortly after discussing the matter with Garcia. Dutton did not see Garcia again after that night and had never met Sconce.

Pollerana, Garcia and Dutton testified under grants of immunity and are not parties to this appeal.

Frank Strunk testified that sometime after the argument between Cindy and Estephan at CSC, he saw Sconce and another person at the Jack-In-The-Box across the street from CSC making gestures and looking at Estephan through binoculars. Frank Strunk went to the restaurant and asked Sconce why he was watching Estephan. Sconce said he was just pointing out the gas station. Frank Strunk told Cindy about this incident.

Cindy testified that after speaking with her father, she confronted Sallard and asked him why Sconce had been looking at Estephan with binoculars. Sallard made statements to her which the trial court excluded as hearsay. However, after this conversation, Cindy feared for her life and left Sallard immediately. Sallard told her not to repeat their conversation, that no one would believe her, and that if she did repeat it she would have to "watch . . . [her] back."

2. Court rulings

The magistrate held Sconce to answer, and the People filed an information alleging conspiracy to commit murder. The information asserted six overt acts committed between September 1 and 16, 1985. These acts consisted of Sconce's pointing out Estephan at the Jack-In-The-Box, the use of binoculars to view Estephan, Garcia's trip to the Estephan home with Pollerana, the solicitation of Dutton by Garcia, Garcia's trip to the Estephan home with Dutton, and Sconce's inquiries of Garcia to "'take care of' and kill" Estephan.

Thereafter, notwithstanding the trial court's finding there had been a conspiracy, it granted Sconce's motion to set the information aside. The trial court stated it could find no authority on point but "Witkin and Epstein [(1 Witkin Epstein, Cal. Criminal Law (2d ed. 1988) § 180, p. 200)] seem to follow the general policy of encouraging withdrawal from conspiracies [and it] is a good one. [¶] . . . [¶] It seems to me that David Sconce['s] withdrawal here was an effective one." This appeal followed.

Contentions

The People contend the trial court erroneously set aside the information because Sconce's withdrawal from the conspiracy, although it might insulate him from liability for future conspiratorial acts, does not constitute a defense to liability for the conspiracy itself.

Discussions

. . . .

"Once the defendant's participation in the conspiracy is shown, it will be presumed to continue unless he is able to prove, as a matter of defense, that he effectively withdrew from the conspiracy." . . .

Withdrawal from a conspiracy requires "an affirmative and bona fide rejection or repudiation of the conspiracy, communicated to the coconspirators. [Citations.]" (*People v. Crosby, supra*, 58 Cal.2d at pp. 730–731) . . . .

Under California law withdrawal is a complete defense to conspiracy only if accomplished before the commission of an overt act. . . .

"The requirement of an overt act before conspirators can be prosecuted and punished exists, . . . , to provide a locus p[o]enitentiae — an opportunity for the conspirators to reconsider, terminate the agreement, and thereby avoid punishment for the conspiracy."

Obviously, the inverse of this rule is that once an overt act has been committed in furtherance of the conspiracy the crime of conspiracy has been completed and no subsequent action by the conspirator can change that.

Thus, even if it be assumed Sconce effectively withdrew from the conspiracy . . . withdrawal merely precludes liability for subsequent acts committed by the members of the conspiracy. The withdrawal does not relate back to the criminal formation of the unlawful combination. In sum, conspiracy is complete upon the commission of an overt act. . . .

The rationale in favor of terminating liability is the one relied upon by the trial court, i.e, the reasons for allowing withdrawal as a defense to conspiracy — encouraging abandonment and thereby weakening the group — continue to apply after the commission of an overt act.

However, the rule remains that withdrawal avoids liability only for the target offense, or for any subsequent act committed by a coconspirator in pursuance of the common plan. "[I]n respect of the conspiracy itself, the individual's change of mind is ineffective; he cannot undo that which he has already done. [Fn. omitted.]" (4 Wharton's Criminal Law, (14th ed. 1981) Conspiracy, §734, pp. 555–557.)

. . . .

Because we conclude Sconce's withdrawal from the conspiracy is not a valid defense to the completed crime of conspiracy, we need not determine whether the evidence showed that Sconce, in fact, withdrew from the conspiracy and communicated that withdrawal to each coconspirator.

Notes and Questions

1. It is important to distinguish between withdrawal and renunciation. Withdrawal functions like a pair of scissors: it "severs" the *Pinkerton* connection between the defendant and other members of the conspiracy with which she had colluded. Withdrawal is recognized in both common law and Model Penal Code jurisdictions. Renunciation, in contrast, is the MPC affirmative defense to the conspiracy itself. Renunciation functions as an eraser: it "erases" guilt for the conspiracy itself. In essence, if the jurisdiction recognizes renunciation, it allows the defendant to put the proverbial "toothpaste back in the tube." Because of what is required for renunciation, a defendant who renounces ipso facto also withdraws from the conspiracy as of the date of the renunciation. The common law did not allow for such a defense. As the *Sconce* court notes: once the conspiracy was formed — once the toothpaste was out of the tube — it could not be erased.

2. *Sconce* indicates what a defendant must prove to establish withdrawal: notification of all other co-conspirators. But what if a defendant doesn't know of all other co-conspirators? This may make it impossible to withdraw by notification. The defendant's only option at that point would most likely be to self-report the conspiracy and her role to law enforcement. The MPC provides that a conspiracy terminates for a defendant when: 1. The objectives of the conspiracy have been achieved; 2. The defendant notifies all other members of her withdrawal; or 3. The defendant notifies law enforcement of her role in the conspiracy. Thus, in a MPC jurisdiction, notifying law enforcement is a requirement for renunciation, but one of two options for withdrawal.

3. Notice that the *Sconce* opinion indicates that withdrawal is only a defense to a conspiracy charge if it occurs before the commission of an overt act. Is this logical? Or is the court confusing withdrawal from a simple failure to prove the requisite elements of a conspiracy? If a defendant "withdraws" from a conspiratorial agreement before the commission of an overt act in furtherance of the agreement, she was never a part of a fully formed conspiracy. This is not really withdrawal, because that concept presupposes the defendant had been a member of a fully formed conspiracy. Might such a defendant be guilty of attempted conspiracy?

The following diagram provides a visual illustration of establishing the existence and scope of conspiracy liability.

Conspiracy as a Mode of Liability

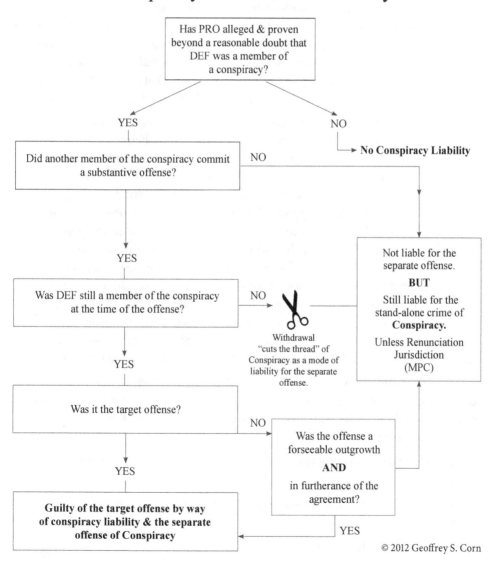

© 2012 Geoffrey S. Corn

III. Accomplice Liability

An individual can be held criminally liable for crimes committed by others on proof the individual was an accomplice to those crimes. As noted earlier, the common law of complicity used four categories to distinguish what are today treated under the general concept of accomplice liability. Principals in the first degree actually committed the crime, i.e., engaged in the actus reus. The prosecutor would have to prove all the elements of the crime, including both the actus reus and the mens rea in order to successfully prosecute this individual. Principals in the second degree aided and abetted the crime and were present (either actually or constructively) at the crime scene. In order to successfully prosecute a principal in the second degree, the prosecutor would have to prove that this individual aided and abetted a crime. Accessories before the fact aided and abetted a crime beforehand but were not present during the commission of the crime. Finally, accessories after the fact knew that an individual committed a crime and provided assistance after the crime was committed for the purpose of assisting the offender in avoiding apprehension or conviction. While any principal or accessory was guilty of the crime committed by the principal in the first degree, the penalties for aiding and abetting sometimes varied from that applicable to the actual perpetrator of the crime. The penalties varied for the four categories of accomplices.

Most modern statutes have eliminated these four categories of accomplices. Even in those that retain these original common law categories, being an accessory after the fact is no longer treated as a mode of liability for the principal's crime. This is because of the harsh results potentially inherent in the theory of complicity. Imagine a mother whose son comes home late at night covered with blood. The mother asks, "What happened?" The son responds, "I didn't mean to kill anyone; I just wanted to steal her pocketbook" and runs to his room. A few minutes later, the police knock and the door and tell the mother they are searching for her son and ask if she has seen him. To protect him, she says "no," and they depart. Because she knew he committed a felony and helped him avoid apprehension, at common law, she would be subject to conviction for his crimes, even murder. The modern approach is to treat such post-offense aiding as a distinct crime, such as hindering apprehension, obstruction of justice, or interfering with a police investigation. As a result, the penalties are normally much more limited than what might otherwise be imposed as an accessory.

The MPC is illustrative of the law of complicity in most jurisdictions today. In lieu of the common law categories of complicity, these statutes impose criminal liability on all accomplices: individuals who aid or abet the principal. For example, Model Penal Code § 2.06(3)(a) provides:

(3) person is an accomplice of another person in the commission of an offense if:

(a) with the purpose of promoting or facilitating the commission of the offense, he

(i) solicits such other person to commit it; or

(ii) aids or agrees or attempts to aid such other person in planning or committing it; or having a legal duty to prevent the commission of the offense, fails to make proper effort so to do; or

(b) his conduct is expressly declared by law to establish his complicity.

Or consider the federal accomplice liability provision, 18 U.S.C. § 2:

(a) Whoever commits an offense against the United States or aids, abets, counsels, commands, induces or procures its commission, is punishable as a principal.

(b) Whoever willfully causes an act to be done which if directly performed by him or another would be an offense against the United States, is punishable as a principal.

As reflected in the federal statute, an accomplice is typically convicted of the same crime as the principal and can receive the same punishment. In death penalty jurisdictions, an accomplice can even be sentenced to death for a capital crime.

A. The Actus Reus of Accomplice Liability

The actus reus for accomplice liability requires that the accomplice be an aider or abettor to another's crime. The accomplice must do (or attempt to do) some affirmative act of assistance or contribution to the principal. The assistance can be either direct, such as providing the principal with the means to commit a crime, or indirect, such as providing encouragement to commit the crime.

People v. Campbell
25 Cal. App. 4th 402 (1994)
California Court of Appeals

WUNDERLICH, J.

Defendant Carlo Rene Campbell appeals from a judgment entered after a jury convicted him of attempted robbery and attempted murder and also found that he personally used a firearm to commit these offenses.

Codefendant Victor Tyrone Smith appeals from a judgment entered after the same jury convicted him of attempted robbery and also found that he was armed at the time of the offense. . . .

Smith contends the court erred in instructing the jury on aiding and abetting and claims his conviction for attempted robbery must be reversed because the jury probably relied on the erroneous instructions. He also contends that the court misinstructed the jury on the definition of aiding and abetting.

We . . . affirm the judgments as to both Campbell and Smith.

At about 1 a.m., on September 26, 1991, Timothy Branch and his girlfriend Deborah Sester sat on a fence in front of an apartment complex on Cadillac Drive in San Jose arguing about whether to buy more crack cocaine. While arguing, both noticed two men and a woman walk by. Several minutes later, Sester saw the two men, whom she later identified as Campbell and Smith, returning. As they approached, she grabbed Branch's leg. When Campbell and Smith were in front of them, Branch heard Campbell say something like "this is a robbery, break yourself." Branch understood to mean empty your pockets. Sester heard Campbell say something but not what. She did hear Branch respond, "'What do you mean? You don't know me and I don't know you and there ain't no future in this meeting.'"

Campbell responded by pointing a handgun an inch from Branch's head. Branch said it looked like a .38-caliber pistol. Acting instinctively, Branch swatted the gun away from his head, hoping to knock it loose. He then ran off, zigzagging down Cadillac Street toward Winchester. Campbell held on to the gun, used a nearby mailbox to steady his arm, aimed at the fleeing Branch, and fired several times. The first shot shattered the rear window of a car. The second hit Branch, who grunted but continued running. A third shot went by his head. Thereafter, Campbell started chasing Branch, firing as he ran.

Branch was able to escape into a restaurant, whose owner called an ambulance. When the police arrived, Branch described his assailant. He also said he could identify him again. He then expressed concern for Sester, and the police went to look for her. . . .

After Campbell had left to chase Branch, Sester attempted to back away from Smith, but Smith grabbed her by the hair, saying, " 'Where the fuck are you going, bitch.'" He then asked what she had. She said she had only the gold earrings she was wearing and "that's all." Smith said she also had "pussy" and he wanted some. He walked her back toward a carport and told her to do what he said or he would "blow [her] fucking head off with his .25." Sester testified Smith raped her twice and forced her to orally copulate him twice. Smith then forced Sester to go with him to a 7-Eleven store. The police officer who had gone to look for her saw the two of them and called out. He noticed Sester mouthing the words "I need help" and spoke to her alone. She said, "get [Smith] away from me, his friend shot my friend and he raped me." Police arrested Smith. Sester said she could identify the shooter, described him, and later identified Campbell. Campbell was also arrested.

Smith contends that his conviction for attempted robbery must be reversed due to a combination of insufficient evidence and instructional error. . . . We disagree with Smith's initial claim that there is insufficient evidence to find that he aided and abetted Campbell's attempt to rob Branch.

> "The test for determining whether instructions on a particular theory of guilt are appropriate is whether there is substantial evidence which would support conviction on that theory. To determine whether there is substantial evidence to support a conviction we must view the record in a light most favorable to conviction, resolving all conflicts in the evidence and drawing all reasonable inferences in support of conviction. We may conclude that there

is no substantial evidence in support of conviction only if it can be said that on the evidence presented no reasonable fact finder could find the defendant guilty on the theory presented. Substantial evidence is evidence 'of ponderable legal significance . . . reasonable in nature, credible, and of solid value.'

"A person aids and abets the commission of a crime when he or she, (i) with knowledge of the unlawful purpose of the perpetrator, (ii) and with the intent or purpose of committing, facilitating or encouraging commission of the crime, (iii) by act or advice, aids, promotes, encourages or instigates the commission of the crime."

"Whether defendant aided and abetted the crime is a question of fact, and on appeal all conflicts in the evidence and reasonable inferences must be resolved in favor of the judgment."

Here, Smith claims the evidence shows only that he was present when Campbell attempted to rob Branch. He argues that it is unreasonable to infer from his presence that he knew of and shared Campbell's criminal intent. We disagree with Smith's view of the evidence.

Smith correctly points out that in general neither presence at the scene of a crime nor knowledge of, but failure to prevent it, is sufficient to establish aiding and abetting its commission. However, "[a]mong the factors which may be considered in making the determination of aiding and abetting are: presence at the scene of the crime, companionship, and conduct before and after the offense."

Here, virtually all of these factors are present. Smith did not independently happen by the scene of the crime. He had walked by Branch and Sester with Campbell and thus was aware of their isolation and vulnerability at that time and place. Smith then decided with Campbell to return to them. Together they approached Branch and Sester, stopping closely in front of them. Their concerted action reasonably implies a common purpose, which Campbell immediately revealed when he told Branch this was a robbery and then enforced this purpose with a firearm. During this time, Smith remained in position in front of Sester. Since there is no evidence he was surprised by Campbell's conduct or afraid to interfere with it, the jury could reasonably conclude that Smith assumed his position in front of Branch and Sester to intimidate and block them, divert suspicion, and watch out for others who might approach. Such conduct is a textbook example of aiding and abetting. Thus, the evidence, in our view, reasonably indicates that Smith played an affirmative supportive role in the attempted robbery and was not simply an innocent, passive, and unwitting bystander.

Furthermore, after Campbell left to chase after Branch, Smith forcibly prevented Sester from leaving and asked what she had, that is, he attempted to rob her. This attempt further supports a finding that Smith and Campbell shared a common purpose when they returned to Branch and Sester and that Smith's conduct during the attempt to rob Branch was a knowing and intentional effort to assist Campbell. (See *People v. Griffin* (1967) 66 Cal.2d 459, 464-465 [58 Cal.Rptr. 107, 426 P.2d 507] [subsequent conduct may be relevant to prove motive and intent]; see, e.g., *In re Jose T., supra*, 230 Cal.App.3d at pp. 1460–1461 [minor's later use of car evidence that his presence when it was stolen aided and abetted the person who stole it]; *People v. Luna* (1956) 140 Cal.App.2d 662, 665 [295 P.2d 457] [defendant's subsequent participation in fight with one person indicated he was not innocent bystander when codefendant started fight with another person].)

In sum, the evidence and the reasonable inferences therefrom taken together support a finding that Smith knew about and shared Campbell's intent to rob Branch and that in a supportive role, he affirmatively facilitated Campbell's attempt. In other words, there is substantial evidence that Smith aided and abetted Campbell. Therefore the trial court did not err in instructing the jury on this theory.

Notes and Questions

1. The line between mere presence and presence which aids and abets is a thin one. Consider *State v. V.T.*, 2000 Utah Ct. App. 189 (2000). In *State v. V.T.*, two boys went to a relative's apartment to avoid being picked up by police for curfew violations. After the relative ran a brief errand, she returned to find the boys gone, the door to her apartment wide open, and two guns missing. She later discovered that her camcorder was missing. She reported the theft of the camcorder to the police. The police found the camcorder at a local pawn shop where it had been pawned on the same day that the guns were stolen. Still inside the camcorder was a videotape in which one of the boys telephoned a friend in V.T.'s presence and discussed pawning the stolen camcorder. V.T. never spoke or gestured during any of this footage. V.T. was convicted of theft in juvenile court. The appellate court overturned V.T.'s conviction since "[n]o evidence whatsoever was produced indicating V.T. had encouraged — much less that he solicited, requested, commanded or intentionally aided — the other two boys in the theft of the camcorder." What, if any, difference is there between Smith's actions in the above case and V.T.'s? Were the different results justified?

2. What if the jury concluded that Campbell would have committed the robbery even without any assistance from Smith? In other words, what if a jury concludes there is no causal connection between the aiding and abetting and the commission of the offense by the principal? Does a defendant charged as an accomplice have the opportunity to defend himself by demonstrating that his aiding and abetting had no impact on the commission of the crime? The answer is no. This is because complicity liability is not based on some causal relationship between the actions of the accomplice and the commission of the crime. Instead, it is based on the decision of the accomplice to associate himself with the principal's criminal act or omission with the purpose of bringing it about. The act of aiding and abetting — even if trivial and completely unnecessary from the principal's perspective — is what connects the accomplice to the criminal actus reus of the principal. It is that connection that forms the basis of liability, even if there is no actual impact.

3. Cheryl was a 21-year-old mother of two living in her hometown. One night, she went into a tavern to buy cigarettes from a dispensary inside the bar. After chatting

with a waitress and ordering a drink, Cheryl was attempting to leave the bar when a man grabbed her from behind. She was gang-raped on the bar's pool table while others looked on. During the rape, two patrons shouted "Go for it! Go for it!" The rape lasted more than two hours, during which the two men cheered the rape. What is the liability, if any, of these two cheering patrons? What if they could establish that the rapist was deaf and it was impossible for him to have heard their encouragement?

B. The Mens Rea of Accomplice Liability

Most jurisdictions still follow the common law rule that in order to be convicted, an accomplice must intend to provide assistance to the principal with the specific intent (purpose) that the principal commit the offense. There are, however, a minority of states that allow knowledge to satisfy the mens rea element to establish guilt as an accomplice: it is sufficient that the accomplice knows that the assistance given will result in the commission of a crime. To illustrate, suppose that A loans B his gun believing that B will use the gun for a hunting trip. Unknown to A, B uses A's gun to kill C. A is not an accomplice to murder because, even though he aided B in the killing of C by providing the weapon, he did not do so with the intent that his gun be used to kill C. In contrast, if the prosecution could prove beyond a reasonable doubt that A gave B his gun not only knowing B would use it to kill C, but intending that result, A would be guilty of C's murder at B's hand (or any lesser included offense such as attempted murder). Suppose instead that A loans his gun to B believing that B will use it to frighten but not kill C. Even though A intended to aid B, he did not intend to aid a murder. Thus, he did not aid and abet the crime of murder; rather, he aided and abetted the crime of assault with a deadly weapon. However, as will be explained below, A may be liable for the crime of murder if the prosecution proves it was a natural and probable outgrowth of the crime he did aid and abet. Consider how the next case illustrates the relationship between the accomplice's mens rea and the extent of liability for the actus reus of the principal.

People v. Beeman

35 Cal. 3d 547 (1984)
California Supreme Court

REYNOSO, J.

Timothy Mark Beeman appeals from a judgment of conviction of robbery, burglary, false imprisonment, destruction of telephone equipment and assault with intent to commit a felony. Appellant was not present during commission of the offenses. His conviction rested on the theory that he aided and abetted his acquaintances James Gray and Michael Burk.

The primary issue before us is whether the standard California Jury Instructions (CALJIC Nos. 3.00 and 3.01) adequately inform the jury of the criminal intent required to convict a defendant as an aider and abettor of the crime.

We hold that instruction No. 3.01 is erroneous. Sound law, embodied in a long line of California decisions, requires proof that an aider and abettor rendered aid with an intent or purpose of either committing, or of encouraging or facilitating commission of, the target offense. It was, therefore, error for the trial court to refuse the modified instruction requested by appellant. Our examination of the record convinces us that the error in this case was prejudicial and we therefore reverse appellant's convictions.

James Gray and Michael Burk drove from Oakland to Redding for the purpose of robbing appellant's sister-in-law, Mrs. Marjorie Beeman, of valuable jewelry, including a 3.5 carat diamond ring. They telephoned the residence to determine that she was home. Soon thereafter Burk knocked at the door of the victim's house, presented himself as a poll taker, and asked to be let in. When Mrs. Beeman asked for identification, he forced her into the hallway and entered. Gray, disguised in a ski mask, followed. The two subdued the victim, placed tape over her mouth and eyes and tied her to a bathroom fixture. Then they ransacked the house, taking numerous pieces of jewelry and a set of silverware. The jewelry included a 3.5 carat, heart-shaped diamond ring and a blue sapphire ring. The total value of these two rings was over $100,000. In the course of the robbery, telephone wires inside the house were cut.

Appellant was arrested six days later in Emeryville. He had in his possession several of the less valuable of the stolen rings. He supplied the police with information that led to the arrests of Burk and Gray. With Gray's cooperation appellant assisted police in recovering most of the stolen property.

Burk, Gray and appellant were jointly charged. After the trial court severed the trials, Burk and Gray pled guilty to robbery. At appellant's trial they testified that he had been extensively involved in planning the crime. . . .

According to Gray appellant had been present at a discussion three days before the robbery when it was mentioned that appellant could not go because his 6 foot 5 inch, 310-pound frame could be too easily recognized. Two days before the offense, however, appellant told Gray that he wanted nothing to do with the robbery of his relatives. On the day preceding the incident appellant and Gray spoke on the telephone. At that time appellant repeated he wanted nothing to do with the robbery, but confirmed that he had told Burk that he would not say anything if the others went ahead.

Gray confirmed that appellant was upset when he saw that his friends had gone through with the robbery and had taken all of the victim's jewelry. He was angered further when he discovered that Burk might easily be recognized because he had not disguised himself. . . .

Appellant Beeman's testimony contradicted that of Burk and Gray as to nearly every material element of his own involvement. Appellant testified that he did not participate in the robbery or its planning. He confirmed that Burk had lived with him on several occasions, and that he had told Burk about Mrs. Beeman's jewelry, the valuable diamond ring, and the Beeman ranch, in the course of day-to-day conversations. He claimed that he had sketched a floor plan of the house some nine months prior to the robbery, only for the purpose of comparing it with the layout of a house belonging to another brother. He at first denied and then admitted describing the Beeman family cars, but insisted this never occurred in the context of planning a robbery. . . .

Appellant requested that the jury be instructed in accord with *People v. Yarber* (1979) 90 Cal.App.3d 895 [153 Cal.Rptr. 875] that aiding and abetting liability requires proof of intent to aid. The request was denied.

After three hours of deliberation, the jury submitted two written questions to the court: "We would like to hear again how one is determined to be an accessory and by what actions can he absolve himself"; and "Does inaction mean the party is guilty?" . . . The court denied appellant's renewed request that the instructions be modified as suggested in *Yarber*, explaining that giving another, slightly different instruction at this point would further complicate matters. The jury returned its verdicts of guilty on all counts two hours later.

Penal Code section 31 provides in pertinent part: "All persons concerned in the commission of a crime . . . whether they directly commit the act constituting the offense, or aid and abet in its commission, or, not being present, have advised and encouraged its commission . . . are principals in any crime so committed." Thus, those persons who at common law would have been termed accessories before the fact and principals in the second degree as well as those who actually perpetrate the offense, are to be prosecuted, tried and punished as principals in California. The term "aider and abettor" is now often used to refer to principals other than the perpetrator, whether or not they are present at the commission of the offense. . . .

CALJIC No. 3.00 defines principals to a crime to include "Those who, with knowledge of the unlawful purpose of the one who does directly and actively commit or attempt to commit the crime, aid and abet in its commission . . . or . . . Those who, whether present or not at the commission or attempted commission of the crime, advise and encourage its commission. . . ." CALJIC No. 3.01 defines aiding and abetting as follows: "A person aids and abets the commission of a crime if, with knowledge of the unlawful purpose of the perpetrator of the crime, he aids, promotes, encourages or instigates by act or advice the commission of such crime."

Appellant asserts that the current instructions, in particular CALJIC No. 3.01, substitute an element of knowledge of the perpetrator's intent for the element of criminal intent of the accomplice, in contravention of common law principles and California case law. He argues that the instruction given permitted the jury to convict him of the same offenses as the perpetrators without finding that he harbored either the same criminal intent as they, or the specific intent to assist them, thus depriving him of his constitutional rights to due process and equal protection of the law. . . .

The People argue that the standard instruction properly reflects California law, which requires no more than that the aider and abettor have knowledge of the perpetrator's criminal purpose and do a voluntary act which in fact aids the perpetrator. . . .

There is no question that an aider and abettor must have criminal intent in order to be convicted of a criminal offense. Decisions of this court dating back to 1898 hold that "the word 'abet' includes knowledge of the wrongful purpose of the perpetrator and counsel and encouragement in the crime" and that it is therefore error to instruct a jury that one may be found guilty as a principal if one aided or abetted. The act of encouraging or counseling itself implies a purpose or goal of furthering the encouraged result. "An aider and abettor's fundamental purpose, motive and intent is to aid and assist the perpetrator in the latter's commission of the crime."

The essential conflict in current appellate opinions is between those cases which state that an aider and abettor must have an intent or purpose to commit or assist in the commission of the criminal offenses and those finding it sufficient that the aider and abettor engage in the required acts with knowledge of the perpetrator's criminal purpose. . . .

We agree with the *Yarber* court that the facts from which a mental state may be inferred must not be confused with the mental state that the prosecution is required to prove. Direct evidence of the mental state of the accused is rarely available except through his or her testimony. The trier of fact is and must be free to disbelieve the testimony and to infer that the truth is otherwise when such an inference is supported by circumstantial evidence regarding the actions of the accused. Thus, an act which has the effect of giving aid and encouragement, and which is done with knowledge of the criminal purpose of the person aided, may indicate that the actor intended to assist in fulfillment of the known criminal purpose. However, as illustrated by *Hicks v. U.S.* (1893) 150 U.S. 442 [37 L.Ed. 1137, 14 S.Ct. 144] (conviction reversed because jury not instructed that words of encouragement must have been used with the intention of encouraging and abetting crime in a case where ambiguous gesture and remark may have been acts of desperation) and *People v. Bolanger* (1886) 71 Cal. 17 [11 P. 799] (feigned accomplice not guilty because lacks common intent with the perpetrator to unite in the commission of the crime), the act may be done with some other purpose which precludes criminal liability. . . .

Thus, we conclude that the weight of authority and sound law require proof that an aider and abettor act with knowledge of the criminal purpose of the perpetrator and with an intent or purpose either of committing, or of encouraging or facilitating commission of, the offense.

When the definition of the offense includes the intent to do some act or achieve some consequence beyond the actus reus of the crime, the aider and abettor must share the specific intent of the perpetrator. . . . The liability of an aider and abettor extends also to the natural and reasonable consequences of the acts he knowingly and intentionally aids and encourages.

CALJIC No. 3.01 inadequately defines aiding and abetting because it fails to insure that an aider and abettor will be found to have the required mental state with regard to his or her own act. While the instruction does include the word "abet," which encompasses the intent required by law, the word is arcane and its full import unlikely to be recognized by modern jurors. Moreover, even if jurors were made aware that "abet" means to encourage or facilitate, and implicitly to harbor an intent to further the crime encouraged, the instruction does not *require* them to find that intent because it defines an aider and abettor as one who "aids, promotes, encourages *or* instigates" (italics added). Thus, as one appellate court recently recognized, the instruction would "technically allow a conviction if the defendant knowing of the perpetrator's unlawful purpose, negligently or accidentally aided the commission of the crime."

The convictions are reversed.

Notes and Questions

1. Since it was undisputed that Appellant (1) lived with one of the robbers, (2) told one of the robbers of his sister-in-law's expensive jewelry and family cars, (3) sketched a floor plan of his sister-in-law's home and (4) was arrested with some of the stolen rings in his possession, why was his conviction as an accomplice not upheld? Does the record indicate that Beeman was in fact not guilty as an accomplice? If he is retried, could the same evidence result in a conviction?

2. Draft an instruction for use at the retrial of the defendant that properly explains to the jury what mental state they must find and what evidence they may rely on to find that mental state in order to convict Beeman as an accomplice.

3. The court says, "[W]e agree with the *Yarber* court that the facts from which a mental state may be inferred must not be confused with the mental state that the prosecution is required to prove." What does this mean? Is the court contradicting itself by allowing proof of knowledge to satisfy the mens rea for accomplice liability? Or is the statement a more nuanced recognition of the relationship between evidence of knowledge and proof of purpose?

4. Can an accomplice form the purpose that the principal commit the target offense without knowledge the principle will commit that offense? For example, imagine the classmate on your left asks to borrow your pen and then stabs the classmate to her left in the ear with your pen. You certainly facilitated commission of the battery, but are you an accomplice? No. Why? Because if you don't know the act the principal intends to commit you cannot have formed the purpose to facilitate that act. In other words, while knowledge of the principal's intended act does not *ipso facto* prove a purpose to facilitate that act, such a purpose cannot be established absent that knowledge.

5. Can an accomplice be guilty of aiding and abetting a target offense defined as a reckless or grossly negligent crime? Because at common law and in most jurisdictions, an accomplice must act with the purpose that the principal commit the target offense, the answer is no. Just ask this question: How can a defendant act with the purpose that the principal commit an unintentional crime?

The MPC includes a variation of this rule: when the principal commits a result crime based on recklessness, the accomplice need not have the purpose to facilitate that *result*. Instead, the accomplice is guilty of that same crime so long as she facilitated the principal's *act or omission* with the same culpability. Specifically, the MPC provides, "When causing a particular result is an element of an offense, an accomplice in the conduct causing such result, is an accomplice in the commission of that offense, if the person acts with the kind of culpability, if any, with respect to that result that is sufficient for the commission of the offense."

For example, imagine the evidence proves an alleged accomplice, knowing a friend was going to get into a fight and that the friend wants to bring a pistol just to scare the victim, gave the friend a loaded pistol to carry to the fight. During the fight, the friend draws the pistol intending only to frighten the victim, but the pistol goes off and kills the victim. The friend — the principal — is guilty of involuntary manslaughter for the reckless risk he created by drawing the gun. The alleged accomplice is certainly guilty of aggravated assault, because that is the crime he acted with the purpose to facilitate. But pursuant to the MPC, he is also guilty of involuntary manslaughter, because he purposefully gave the friend a gun and in so doing shared the reckless state of mind related to use of the pistol. In other words, if a principal commits involuntary manslaughter (an unlawful *unintentional* killing resulting from recklessness), the accomplice who recklessly encouraged the principal's act that resulted in death is also guilty of involuntary manslaughter.

6. What if an accomplice changes her mind and decides to cease the aiding and abetting? Is this a defense to being convicted of the principal's crime? Once the crime or the attempt is committed, the answer is obviously no; at that point, the accomplice can't put the toothpaste back in the tube. But what if the change of heart occurs prior to commission or attempted commission of the crime? If an accomplice can show that she "unwound" her complicity, it severs her connection to the principal and therefore she is not liable for any subsequent crime. But this is not easy to do: it requires the accomplice to notify the principal of her abandonment of her role as an accomplice, and to nullify the benefit of any contribution made up to that point. So, if accomplice A in the earlier hypothetical gave B a pistol to aid and abet the murder of C, A would have to inform B of his abandonment and get the pistol back. The Model Penal Code and many jurisdictions also allow an accomplice to terminate complicity by timely notification to police. Model Penal Code § 2.06(6) provides:

> (6) Unless otherwise provided by the Code or by the law defining the offense, a person is not an accomplice in an offense committed by another person if:
>
> . . .
>
> (c) he terminates his complicity prior to the commission of the offense and
>
> > (i) wholly deprives it of effectiveness in the commission of the offense; or
> >
> > (ii) gives timely warning to the law enforcement authorities or otherwise makes proper effort to prevent the commission of the offense.

Practice Pointer

The Fifth Amendment privilege against self-incrimination prohibits a prosecutor from compelling accomplices to testify against one another. To get around the privilege against self-incrimination, prosecutors often offer deals to one accomplice to testify against the other accomplices. In exchange for an accomplice's truthful testimony against other accomplices, prosecutors will agree either to recommend a lenient sentence or even not to prosecute the accomplice at all. However, because the opportunity for leniency provides accomplices with an incentive to testify against each other and thus creates the risk that they will embellish or lie, many states have a corroboration rule. In these states, an accomplice cannot be convicted solely on the testimony of another accomplice. There must be independent evidence connecting the defendant to the crime in order for a legitimate conviction to be obtained. It is also common to provide the jury with an instruction specifically focused on assessing the accomplice's credibility. Consider this jury instruction on the use of accomplice testimony:

> A witness is an accomplice if he/she was criminally involved in an offense with which the accused is charged. The purpose of this advice is to call to your attention a factor specifically affecting the witness's believability, that is, a motive to falsify his/her testimony in whole or in part, because of an obvious self-interest under the circumstances.
>
> (For example, an accomplice may be motivated to falsify testimony in whole or in part because of his/her own self-interest in receiving (immunity from prosecution) (leniency in a forthcoming prosecution) (_____).)
>
> In deciding the believability of (state the name of the witness), you should consider all the relevant evidence (including, but not limited to (here the judge may specify significant evidentiary factors bearing on the issue and indicate the respective contentions of counsel for both sides)). Whether (state the name of the witness), who testified as a witness in this case, was an accomplice is a question for you to decide. If (state the name of the witness) shared the criminal intent or purpose of the accused, if any, or aided, encouraged, or in any other way criminally associated or involved himself/herself with the offense with which the accused is charged, he/she would be an accomplice.
>
> As I indicated previously, it is your function to determine the credibility of all the witnesses, and the weight, if any, you will accord the testimony of each witness. Although you should consider the testimony of an accomplice with caution, you may convict the accused based solely upon the testimony of an accomplice, as long as that testimony was not self-contradictory, uncertain, or improbable.

IV. Natural and Probable Consequences Doctrine

The natural and probable consequences doctrine, sometimes also referred to as the foreseeable consequence rule, allows an accomplice to be held liable for crimes committed by the principal that are a "natural and probable consequence" of the crime that the accomplice aided or abetted. Thus, an accomplice may be convicted not only of the crime that was aided or abetted (the primary crime) but also any other crimes committed by the principal (secondary crimes) that "blossom" out of the primary crime. And because the test is foreseeability, the assessment of whether a secondary crime blossoms out of a primary crime is objective. Accordingly, even if the accomplice never intended for the secondary crimes to be committed, as long as the finder of fact is persuaded that these crimes were foreseeable outgrowths of the crime aided and abetted, the accomplice is liable for them.

It is useful, therefore, to think of the "primary" crime as a seed that is planted in a pot, and then assess whether any "secondary" crimes naturally blossom out of the primary crime. This is the issue in the following case.

State v. Linscott
520 A.2d 1067 (1987)
Maine Supreme Court

SCOLNIK, Justice.

William Linscott appeals from a judgment following a jury-waived trial in the Superior Court, Waldo County, convicting him of one count of murder, 17-A M.R.S.A. § 201(1)(A) (1983), and one count of robbery, 17-A M.R.S.A. § 651(1)(D) (1983). He contends that his conviction of intentional or knowing murder as an accomplice under the accomplice liability statute, 17-A M.R.S.A. § 57(3)(A) (1983), violated his constitutional right to due process of law in that he lacked the requisite intent to commit murder. We find no merit in the defendant's argument and affirm the judgment.

The facts are not in dispute. On December 12, 1984, the defendant, then unemployed, and two other men the defendant's step-brother, Phillip Willey, and Jeffrey Colby drove from his trailer in Belmont, Maine to the house of a friend, Joel Fuller. Fuller, with a sawed-off shotgun in his possession, joined the others. The defendant drove to the residence of Larry Ackley, where Fuller obtained 12-gauge shotgun shells.

Later that evening, Fuller suggested that the four men drive to the house of a reputed cocaine dealer, Norman Grenier of Swanville, take Grenier by surprise, and rob him. The defendant agreed to the plan, reasoning that Grenier, being a reputed drug dealer, would be extremely reluctant to call the police and request they conduct a robbery investigation that might result in the discovery of narcotics in his possession. Fuller stated that Grenier had purchased two kilograms of cocaine that day, and that Grenier had been seen with $50,000 in cash. Fuller guaranteed the defendant $10,000 as his share of the proceeds of the robbery.

The four drove up to Grenier's house, which was situated in a heavily wooded rural area on a dead-end road in Swanville. The defendant and Fuller left the car and approached the house. The defendant carried a hunting knife and switchblade, and Fuller was armed with the shotgun. Willey and Colby drove off in the defendant's car and returned later for the defendant and Fuller.

The defendant and Fuller walked around to the back of Grenier's house. At that time, Grenier and his girlfriend were watching television in their living room. The defendant and Fuller intended to break in the back door in order to place themselves between Grenier and the bedroom, where they believed Grenier kept a loaded shotgun. Because the back door was blocked by snow, the two men walked around to the front of the house. Under their revised plan the defendant was to break the living room picture window whereupon Fuller would show his shotgun to Grenier, who presumably would be dissuaded from offering any resistance.

The defendant subsequently broke the living room window with his body without otherwise physically entering the house. Fuller immediately fired a shot through the broken window, hitting Grenier in the chest. Fuller left through the broken window after having removed about $1,300 from Grenier's pants pocket, later returning to the house to retrieve an empty shotgun casing. The two men returned to the road and waited behind a bush for the return of the defendant's car. The defendant and Fuller were later dropped off at Fuller's house, where both men burned several articles of their clothing. Fuller gave the defendant $500, presumably from the money stolen from Grenier.

On March 27, 1985, the defendant was indicted on one count of murder, 17-A M.R.S.A. § 201(1)(A) (1983), and one count of robbery, 17-A M.R.S.A. § 651(1)(D) (1983). At a jury-waived trial, which commenced on January 6, 1986, the defendant testified that he knew Fuller to be a hunter and that it was not unusual for Fuller to carry a firearm with him, even at night. He nevertheless stated that he had no knowledge of any reputation for violence that Fuller may have had. The defendant further testified that he had no intention of causing anyone's death in the course of the robbery.

At the completion of the trial on January 8, 1986, the trial justice found the defendant guilty of robbery and, on a theory of accomplice liability, found him guilty of murder. The court specifically found that the defendant possessed the intent to commit the crime of robbery, that Fuller intentionally or at least knowingly caused the death of Grenier, and that this murder was a reasonably foreseeable consequence of the defendant's participation in the robbery. However, the court also found that the defendant did not intend to kill Grenier, and that the defendant probably would not have participated in the robbery had he believed that Grenier would be killed in the course of the enterprise.

The sole issue raised on appeal is whether the defendant's conviction pursuant to the second sentence of subsection 3-A of the accomplice liability statute, 17-A

M.R.S.A. § 57 (1983),[1] unconstitutionally violates his right to due process under Article I, section 6-A of the Maine Constitution and the Fourteenth Amendment of the United States Constitution. "[T]he Due Process Clause protects the accused against conviction except upon proof beyond a reasonable doubt of every fact necessary to constitute the crime with which he is charged." *In re Winship*, 397 U.S. 358, 364, 90 S. Ct. 1068, 1072, 25 L. Ed. 2d 368 (1970). The defendant contends that the accomplice liability statute impermissibly allows the State to find him guilty of murder, which requires proof beyond a reasonable doubt that the murder was committed either intentionally or knowingly, without having to prove either of these two culpable mental states. Instead, the defendant argues, the accomplice liability statute permits the State to employ only a mere negligence standard in convicting him of murder in violation of his right to due process. We find the defendant's argument to be without merit.

The second sentence of section 57(3)(A) endorses the "foreseeable consequence" rule of accomplice liability. See *State v. Goodall*, 407 A.2d 268, 278 (Me.1979). In that case we stated that

> [t]he history of the statute demonstrates that the legislature indeed intended to impose liability upon accomplices for those crimes that were the reasonably foreseeable consequence of their criminal enterprise, *notwithstanding an absence on their part of the same culpability required for conviction as a principal to the crime.*

Id. (emphasis added). Accordingly, we have stated that section 57(3)(A) is to be interpreted as follows: Under the first sentence of that section, which is to be read independently of the second sentence,

> liability for a "primary crime" . . . [here, robbery] is established by proof that the actor intended to promote or facilitate that crime. Under the second sentence, liability for any "secondary crime" . . . [here, murder] that may have been committed by the principal is established upon a two-fold showing: (a) that the actor intended to promote the *primary crime,* and (b) that the commission of the secondary crime was a "foreseeable consequence" of the actor's participation in the primary crime.

Id. at 277-278 (footnote omitted; emphasis in original). We have consistently upheld this interpretation of section 57(3)(A). . . .

Furthermore, the foreseeable consequence rule as stated in Section 57(3)(A) merely carries over the objective standards of accomplice liability as used in the common law.

---

1. 17-A M.R.S.A. § 57(3)(A) (1983) provides:
   3. A person is an accomplice of another person in the commission of a crime if:
   A. With the intent of promoting or facilitating the commission of the crime, he solicits such other person to commit the crime, or aids or agrees to aid or attempts to aid such other person in planning or committing the crime. *A person is an accomplice under this subsection to any crime the commission of which was a reasonably foreseeable consequence of his conduct* . . .
(Emphasis added).

See *State v. Goodall*, 407 A.2d at 278, citing *State v. Simpson*, 276 A.2d 292, 295 & n. 2 (Me.1971). Thus, a rule allowing for a murder conviction under a theory of accomplice liability based upon an objective standard, despite the absence of evidence that the defendant possessed the culpable subjective mental state that constitutes an element of the crime of murder, does not represent a departure from prior Maine law.

Moreover, we have upheld the constitutionality of two related statutes, the felony murder statute, 17-A M.R.S.A. § 202 (1983), and the depraved indifference murder statute, 17-A M.R.S.A. § 201(a)(B), (1-A) (1983 & Supp.1986). . . . As in the felony murder and depraved indifference statutes, the Legislature in enacting the accomplice liability statute similarly intended that a subjective culpable mental state on the part of the accomplice is not required. So long as the accomplice intended to promote the primary crime, and the commission of the secondary crime was a foreseeable consequence of the accomplice's participation in the primary crime, no further evidence of the accomplice's subjective state of mind as to the secondary crime is required. We find no fundamental unfairness in this statutory scheme.

. . . .

> [Accomplice liability for the secondary crime] relates to the *nature* of the homicide required to be "a reasonably foreseeable consequence." The guilt [of defendant A as an accomplice to defendant B] of Section 201 "Murder," by reason of "accomplice" accountability under Section 57(1) in combination with the second sentence of Section 57(3)(A), can arise *only if*, as an indispensible [sic] element, the commission by defendant B of *the crime of Section 201 "Murder"* was "a reasonably foreseeable consequence of . . . [the] conduct" of defendant A described in the first sentence of Section 57(3)(A).

The potential penalty of life imprisonment for murder under a theory of accomplice liability based on an objective standard "does not denote such punitive severity as to shock the conscience of the public, nor our own respective or collective sense of fairness." *State v. Reardon*, 486 A.2d at 121. "In the criminal homicide field the jurisprudence of this State has been constant in maintaining that the subjective mental, emotional or other behavioral state or condition of the defendant not be an indispensably controlling factor in evaluation of the punitive seriousness of the crime."

For the foregoing reasons, we find no constitutional defect in this statutory provision, nor any fundamental unfairness in its operation.

The entry is: Judgment affirmed.

Notes and Questions

1. After studying felony murder, you're probably curious as to why the prosecution didn't charge Linscott with felony murder since Maine has a felony murder statute on the books. A felony murder charge would have been easier, since the prosecutor would only have had to prove Linscott's involvement in the robbery to obtain a murder conviction. To obtain a murder conviction under the natural and probable

consequence doctrine, however, the prosecutor had to prove that the murder was a foreseeable consequence of the robbery. Can you explain why the prosecution did not bring a felony murder charge? Consider the Maine felony murder statute below:

§ 202. Felony Murder

1. A person is guilty of felony murder if acting alone or with one or more other persons in the commission of, or an attempt to commit, or immediate flight after committing or attempting to commit, murder, robbery, burglary, kidnapping, arson, gross sexual assault, or escape, the person or another participant in fact causes the death of a human being, and the death is a reasonably foreseeable consequence of such commission, attempt or flight.

2. It is an affirmative defense to prosecution under this section that the defendant:

   a. Did not commit the homicidal act or in any way solicit, command, induce, procure or aid the commission thereof;

   b. Was not armed with a dangerous weapon, or other weapon which under the circumstances indicated a readiness to inflict serious bodily injury;

   c. Reasonably believed that no other participant was armed with such a weapon; and

   d. Reasonably believed that no other participant intended to engage in conduct likely to result in death or serious bodily injury.

2. The natural and probable consequence doctrine receives the same criticism as the felony murder rule in that it violates a fundamental principle of criminal law by allowing conviction without proof of a culpable mental state. Linscott was convicted of murder even though he lacked the culpability required for the murder charge. There was no evidence that he either intentionally or knowingly caused death.

3. The MPC rejected the natural and probable consequences doctrine by limiting accomplice liability to only those crimes the alleged accomplice acted with the purpose to facilitate or with the culpability required for that offense. Under this standard, Linscott would not have been guilty of murder. What would he have been guilty of?

4. Can someone be an accomplice to a crime if he is also the victim? The common law answer was no; the law "exempted" the victim from the scope of accomplice liability. This would sometimes arise in cases of statutory rape where the alleged underage victim assisted the defendant to commit the crime. The Model Penal Code includes the same limitation in § 2.06:

   (6) Unless otherwise provided by this code or by the law defining the offense, a person is not an accomplice in an offense committed by another person if:

   (a) he or she is a victim of that offense; or

   (b) the offense is so defined that the person's conduct is inevitably incident to its commission;

This diagram may assist in your assessment of accomplice liability.

Accomplice Liability
An accomplice is guilty as if he was the principal

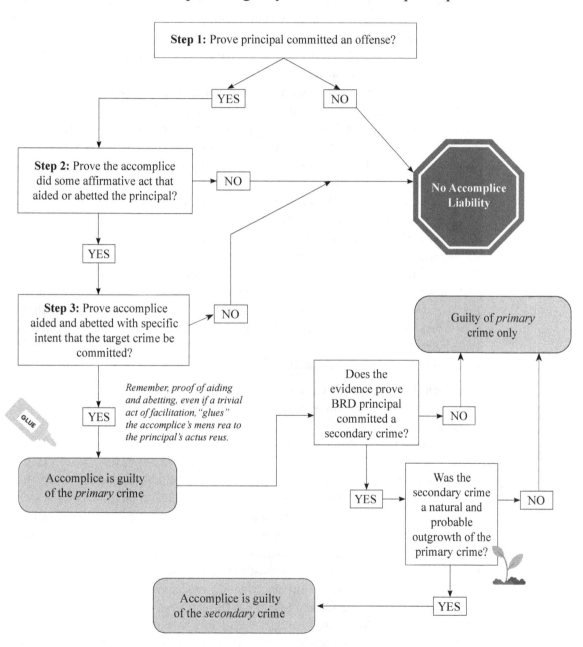

© 2012 Geoffrey S. Corn

V. Other Considerations

A. The Innocent Instrumentality Doctrine

As emphasized to this point, accomplice liability is not a crime in itself, but instead is a mode of liability rendering the accomplice liable for the crimes committed by a principal. This means that to convict an accomplice, the prosecution must prove beyond a reasonable doubt that the principal committed the crime the accomplice is being tried for. But what if the harm inflicted by the principal does not qualify as a crime even though the accomplice acted with criminal mens rea to bring about that result? In other words, what happens when an accomplice uses an innocent or incompetent agent to commit the actus reus of a crime? For example, imagine a husband who wants to kill his wife. He hands his 9mm pistol to his 6-year-old son and says, "Go shoot mommy with this water pistol." The boy runs to his mother and shoots and kills her. If the husband is charged as an accomplice, he will assert that he cannot be an accomplice, because the child was not legally responsible for the killing pursuant to the defense of infancy, and therefore there was no crime. Or imagine a situation where the would-be accomplice engages in "swatting"—a false 911 call that he knows will result in police using force on an innocent victim. Police respond to a scene where they have been told shots were heard and hear what sounds like rifle fire. They force entry into a home, and the homeowner, startled, brandishes a pistol in what he believes is self-defense against a home invasion. Police, facing an imminent threat of deadly force, open fire and kill the homeowner, only to learn that the shots they heard was one of his teenagers playing a video game. If the person who called in the false report is charged as an accomplice to murder, he will argue that he cannot be an accomplice, because the killing was legally justified.

In such situations, liability is not so easily avoided. As you will learn in more detail later, excuse defenses are always personal. In other words, when an individual asserts an excuse defense like infancy, insanity, or duress, it does not negate the fact that a crime occurred but instead "excuses" the individual who asserts the defense. Thus, in the case of the father who used his son as an innocent agent, there was in fact a crime committed, albeit one the son is not criminally responsible for. Therefore, the father is responsible for the murder. The equation becomes a bit more complicated when the "principal" acted pursuant to a lawful justification. Justification defenses (self-defense, defense of others, defense of habitation, necessity) are "greater good" defenses and work to negate the unlawful nature of the act or omission. As a result, there is no "crime" to support an imposition of accomplice liability. But the common law developed a solution: the doctrine of innocent instrumentality. Where a defendant uses an innocent agent to commit the actus reus—such as an individual who engages in legally justified conduct—and does so with the mens rea necessary to prove a crime resulting from the agent's act or omission, the actus reus is treated as if it was committed by the defendant.

The MPC simplifies all of this with the following provision, § 2.06:

(1) A person is guilty of an offense if it is committed by his own conduct or by the conduct of another person for which he is legally accountable, or both.

(2) A person is legally accountable for the conduct of another person when:

(a) acting with the kind of culpability that is sufficient for the commission of the offense, he causes an innocent or irresponsible person to engage in such conduct.

B. Disparate Liability

Is it possible for an accomplice to be convicted of a greater or lesser offense than the principal he aided and abetted? While unusual, the answer is yes. This is another result of the fact that excuse defenses are always personal. Thus, if a defendant forces another person to rob a bank under duress, the "robber" will have a complete defense of duress, but the defendant will not, and will thus be guilty of the robbery. But some excuses are partial, most notably sudden heat of passion (or extreme emotional disturbance in a Model Penal Code jurisdiction) and imperfect self-defense: an honest but unreasonable judgment of self-defense necessity. Abandonment of an attempt would also fall into this category. It is possible that a principal may be able to invoke one of these partial excuses to reduce culpability, but this will have no impact on the liability of the accomplice.

For example, imagine a father whose son is killed in his presence by a drunk driver. The father flies into a sudden homicidal rage, and the neighbor hands the father a pistol and says, "Use this." The father kills the drunk driver. The father — the principal — should be convicted of voluntary manslaughter because of the sudden heat of passion triggered by an adequate provocation. However, that partial defense does not apply to the neighbor — the accomplice — who should therefore be convicted of murder. Of course, were the events to transpire in reverse — the father was in the rage and the neighbor said, "Give me your gun and I'll kill him" and does so — the accomplice (the father) would be less culpable than the principal (the neighbor).

As another example, imagine a defendant who wants to break out of prison. He plots a scheme with his cellmate, who agrees to help him by distracting the guard. When his cellmate creates the distraction, the defendant sneaks out and starts cutting the wire to escape. However, he has a change of heart and abandons the escape. There is no external factor like an alarm that influenced the defendant. If the jurisdiction recognizes the abandonment defense to attempt, the defendant appears to satisfy the requirements for that attempt and should be acquitted. However, the accomplice did nothing to abandon his role, and therefore, the cellmate should be convicted of attempted prison escape.

Formative Assessments

1. Defendant is being tried on a theory of accomplice liability for the murder of victim. The evidence establishes that the victim hit and killed the defendant's child while he was riding his bike in a residential area; that the victim was intoxicated two times over the legal limit at the time of the killing; and that the victim was speeding recklessly through the residential area. Defendant's neighbor is the one who actually killed the victim, after dragging him out of the car. When defendant realized his child was dead, he screamed to his neighbor, "kill the bastard, look what he did!" The neighbor then beat the victim so severely that the victim died. The neighbor has already pled guilty to second-degree murder and testified at defendant's trial corroborating this narrative of events. Based on this evidence, defendant is:

   A. Guilty of second-degree murder because the principal is guilty of that crime.

   B. Guilty of first-degree murder because he encouraged the principal to kill the victim.

   C. Guilty of voluntary manslaughter.

2. John hopes to "set up" a man named Bob. John really hates Bob as a result of an incident that happened years ago between John's father and Bob, but Bob doesn't even remember John. John hears Bob is involved in drug trafficking, and works his way into John's organization. After several months of association, Bob tells John that he trusts him enough to let him be part of a major transfer of drugs to a buyer. John makes Bob believe he is going along with the plan, but actually notifies police with the details. Police agents tell John to continue to play along with the plan, which he does. When Bob and 5 members of his gang (including John) show up for the scheduled transfer, police swoop in to arrest them. A gun battle ensues, and a police officer is killed by a member of Bob's gang. Bob and the gang members are all arrested. Based on these facts, who is guilty of murder based on conspiracy liability?

3. Bob is a college student at a bar on a Friday evening. While there, a fight breaks out between one of his friends and another man. During the fight, Bob is yelling encouragement to his friend, saying things like, "Dude, kick his ass!" The fight escalates when Bob's friend pulls out a knife and stabs the victim in the neck. The victim dies as a result. Bob is brought to trial as an accomplice. Based on these facts, what, if any, offenses is Bob guilty of and why?

PART THREE
Defenses

Chapter 16

Justification Defenses

I. Introduction

Justification defenses reflect the law's recognition that there are situations when what is normally unlawful is rendered lawful because the defendant faced a situation where compliance with the law would result in a greater harm to society than would violating the law. In other words, the defendant was placed in a situation where violating the law was perceived as necessary to serve a greater good. Indeed, necessity is the thread that runs through all justification defenses.

As will be illustrated below, it is not enough that the defendant subjectively believed that acting in violation of the law was necessary to serve a greater good; the law requires that judgment to be assessed objectively. Accordingly, for all justification defenses, the ultimate question for a fact-finder will be whether the defendant made a subjectively honest *and* objectively reasonable judgment that taking the law into her own hands was absolutely necessary under the circumstances she confronted. Importantly, assessing the validity of a justification requires *ex ante* analysis: was the defendant's judgment reasonable in the context of the situation the defendant confronted when she acted? The fact that the defendant may have made a mistaken judgment of necessity does not negate the justification; so long as the mistake was reasonable under the circumstances, the justification is valid.

To illustrate this point, consider a soldier serving as a guard at the gate of a U.S. military base in a combat zone. Based on intelligence, the soldier has been instructed to be alert for hostile suicide bombers who dress like civilians and approach the gate; and that if a suspected suicide bomber refuses to heed verbal warnings and warning shots to stop short of the gate, he should be considered an imminent hostile threat. During his watch, this is exactly what happens: a man dressed in local civilian garb starts walking towards the gate wearing a loose overcoat. The soldiers on duty shout warnings to stop in the local language and hold up a sign that warns if the individual does not stop, the guards may fire. When this fails to halt the individual, two warning shots are fired. At that moment, the individual starts running towards the gate. The soldier then shoots and kills the individual. Upon inspection, no suicide bomb is found. Perhaps the individual didn't understand the warning and thought the fire was directed towards someone or something behind him. From a *post hoc* perspective, it is clear the soldier who shot and killed the victim made a mistake; there was no *actual* self-defense or defense of others justification for the killing. However, from an *ex ante* perspective, it is equally clear the mistaken judgment of homicidal necessity was reasonable. Accordingly, the intentional killing of the victim would not be considered a *criminal* homicide because of the effect of the valid justification.

Self-defense is the quintessential example of a justification defense, and certainly the most commonly asserted. Self-defense has many variants: homicidal self-defense, non-homicidal self-defense, defense of others, defense of property, and defense of habitation. Police use of force (addressed in the next chapter) is another example of a justification. The law also recognizes a general necessity defense to address situations where, unlike self-defense, the situation compelling an individual to break the law is not the result of an unlawful human action. Each of these variants will be addressed below. As you learn them, try and see the thread of genuine necessity that binds them all together.

II. Homicidal Self-Defense

The inherent right of self-preservation in the face of an unlawful imminent threat of death or great bodily harm is manifested in the law of homicidal self-defense. This legal privilege to use deadly force in response to such a threat is contingent on the satisfaction of several requirements. If the requirements are satisfied, the privilege would negate guilt for an intentional killing, an attempted intentional killing, or an intentional battery or assault. Whether the defendant must prove the essential requirements of homicidal self-defense, like any other affirmative defense, or whether the prosecution must prove that at least one of the requirements was not satisfied, varies by jurisdiction. As with all affirmative defenses, in many jurisdictions the burden of proving self-defense is imposed on the defendant by a preponderance of the evidence. Other jurisdictions require the prosecution to disprove the defense beyond a reasonable doubt.

Whether the burden of persuasion is imposed on the defendant or prosecution, all that is needed to defeat a claim of homicidal self-defense is to show that a single requirement is missing. Because of this, when assessing the validity of a claim of self-defense (or any affirmative defense), it is helpful to focus on the "elements" of the defense in order to determine whether they have all been established. For homicidal self-defense, the common law required four such elements:

1. The defendant was not the first aggressor (sometimes called the *clean hands* doctrine);

2. The defendant honestly and reasonably perceived an *imminent* threat of death or great bodily harm;

3. The defendant took advantage of any reasonable opportunity to retreat before resorting to defensive force;

4. The defendant used what he reasonably assessed to be proportional force to reduce the threat.

Unless all of these requirements are satisfied, the claim to the legal privilege of homicidal self-defense will fail. Remember, self-defense is fundamentally a justification based on absolute necessity recognized by the law. If one of these requirements is missing, it means the use of force was not truly necessary; if it was not truly necessary, it was not justified; if it was not justified, it was unlawful.

Over time, flesh was added to the proverbial bones of these requirements. For example, at common law, a first aggressor could reclaim the right of self-defense if he "cleaned his dirty hands" by withdrawing from the affray and demonstrating to the first victim his renunciation of aggression. Subsequent evolution of this clean-hands doctrine—adopted in many jurisdictions—allows a first aggressor to act in self-defense when the first victim responds with excessive force. As will be explained in more detail below, the MPC also modified the imminence requirement, substituting the standard of immediate necessity.

The requirement that has undergone the most significant evolution is the retreat rule. First, even at common law, a victim of unlawful violence was not required to retreat when retreat was not reasonably perceived as offering protection, leading some jurisdictions to eliminate the retreat requirement when the defendant was the victim of a sudden violent attack. Second, all jurisdictions allowed a victim of unlawful violence to "stand his ground" when in his home. This is known as the Castle exception to the retreat requirement. Some jurisdictions extended the Castle exception to the curtilage of the home—the area immediately surrounding the home and intimately connected with the function of the home. Others extended it to the automobile and even the workplace. Finally, in a more recent trend, many states have completely eliminated the retreat requirement by enacting so-called *Stand Your Ground* provisions, which essentially makes the entire state the equivalent of the person's Castle. Sadly, these laws are widely misunderstood as a justification for the use of deadly force whenever a victim feels threatened. This is inaccurate: the only requirement or element of self-defense modified by a Stand Your Ground law is the retreat requirement; a defendant must still satisfy all the other requirements for a valid claim of self-defense.

The following decision lays out the common-law requirements of self-defense. As you read the facts, remember that self-defense always requires the use of proportional force. This is the foundation for the common-law axiom that deadly force is never justified *only* to protect property from theft or destruction; according to the law, the value of a human life is always greater than the value of property.

United States v. Peterson

483 F.2d 1222 (1973)

Court of Appeals for the D.C. Circuit

Indicted for second-degree murder, and convicted by a jury of manslaughter as a lesser included offense, Bennie L. Peterson urges three grounds for reversal. . . . He complains . . . that the judge twice erred in the instructions given the jury in relation to his claim that the homicide was committed in self-defense. One error alleged was an instruction that the jury might consider whether Peterson was the aggressor in the altercation that immediately foreran the homicide. The other was an instruction that a failure by Peterson to retreat, if he could have done so without jeopardizing his safety, might be considered as a circumstance bearing on the question whether he was justified in using the amount of force which he did. After careful study of these arguments in light of the trial record, we affirm Peterson's conviction.

The events immediately preceding the homicide are not seriously in dispute. The version presented by the Government's evidence follows. Charles Keitt, the deceased, and two friends drove in Keitt's car to the alley in the rear of Peterson's house to remove the windshield wipers from the latter's wrecked car. While Keitt was doing so, Peterson came out of the house into the back yard to protest. After a verbal exchange, Peterson went back into the house, obtained a pistol, and returned to the yard. In the meantime, Keitt had reseated himself in his car, and he and his companions were about to leave.

Upon his reappearance in the yard, Peterson paused briefly to load the pistol. "If you move," he shouted to Keitt, "I will shoot." He walked to a point in the yard slightly inside a gate in the rear fence and, pistol in hand, said, "If you come in here I will kill you." Keitt alighted from his car, took a few steps toward Peterson and exclaimed, "What the hell do you think you are going to do with that?" Keitt then made an about-face, walked back to his car and got a lug wrench. With the wrench in a raised position, Keitt advanced toward Peterson, who stood with the pistol pointed toward him. Peterson warned Keitt not to "take another step" and, when Keitt continued onward shot him in the face from a distance of about ten feet. Death was apparently instantaneous. Shortly thereafter, Peterson left home and was apprehended 20-odd blocks away.

This description of the fatal episode was furnished at Peterson's trial by four witnesses for the Government. Peterson did not testify or offer any evidence, but the Government introduced a statement which he had given the police after his arrest, in which he related a somewhat different version. Keitt had removed objects from his car before, and on the day of the shooting he had told Keitt not to do so. After the initial verbal altercation, Keitt went to his car for the lug wrench, so he, Peterson, went into his house for his pistol. When Keitt was about ten feet away, he pointed the pistol "away of his right shoulder;" adding that Keitt was running toward him, Peterson said he "got scared and fired the gun. He ran right into the bullet." "I did not mean to shoot him," Peterson insisted, "I just wanted to scare him."

At trial, Peterson moved for a judgment of acquittal on the ground that as a matter of law the evidence was insufficient to support a conviction. The trial judge denied the motion. After receiving instructions which in two respects are challenged here, the jury returned a verdict finding Peterson guilty of manslaughter. Judgment was entered conformably with the verdict, and this appeal followed.

III

Self-defense, as a doctrine legally exonerating the taking of human life, is as viable now as it was in Blackstone's time, and in the case before us the doctrine is invoked in its purest form. But "[t]he law of self-defense is a law of necessity;" the right of self-defense arises only when the necessity begins, and equally ends with the necessity; and never must the necessity be greater than when the force employed defensively is deadly. The "necessity must bear all semblance of reality, and appear to admit of no other alternative, before taking life will be justifiable as excusable." Hinged on the exigencies of self-preservation, the doctrine of homicidal self-defense emerges from the body of the criminal law as a limited though important exception to legal outlawry of the arena of self-help in the settlement of potentially fatal personal conflicts.

So it is that necessity is the pervasive theme of the well-defined conditions which the law imposes on the right to kill or maim in self-defense. There must have been a threat, actual or apparent, of the use of deadly force against the defender. The threat must have been unlawful and immediate. The defender must have believed that he was in imminent peril of death or serious bodily harm, and that his response was necessary to save himself therefrom. These beliefs must not only have been honestly entertained, but also objectively reasonable in light of the surrounding circumstances. It is clear that no less than a concurrence of these elements will suffice.

Here the parties' opposing contentions focus on the roles of two further considerations. One is the provoking of the confrontation by the defender. The other is the defendant's failure to utilize a safe route for retreat from the confrontation. The essential inquiry, in final analysis, is whether and to what extent the rule of necessity may translate these considerations into additional factors in the equation. To these questions, in the context of the specific issues raised, we now proceed.

IV

The trial judge's charge authorized the jury, as it might be persuaded, to convict Peterson of second-degree murder or manslaughter, or to acquit by reason of self-defense. On the latter phase of the case, the judge instructed that with evidence of self-defense present, the Government bore the burden of proving beyond a reasonable doubt that Peterson did not act in self-defense. . . .

There were, however, two other aspects of the charge to which Peterson objected, and which are now the subject of vigorous controversy. The first of Peterson's complaints centers upon an instruction that the right to use deadly force in self-defense is not ordinarily available to one who provokes a conflict or is the aggressor in it. Mere words, the judge explained, do not constitute provocation or aggression; and if Peterson precipitated the altercation but thereafter withdrew from it in good faith and so informed Keitt by words or acts, he was justified in using deadly force to save himself from imminent danger or death or grave bodily harm. And, the judge added, even if Keitt was the aggressor and Peterson was justified in defending himself, he was not entitled to use any greater force than he had reasonable ground to believe and actually believed to be necessary for that purpose. Peterson contends that there was no evidence that he either caused or contributed to the conflict, and that the instructions on that topic could only misle[a]d the jury.

It has long been accepted that one cannot support a claim of self-defense by a self-generated necessity to kill. The right of homicidal self-defense is granted only to those free from fault in the difficulty; it is denied to slayers who incite the fatal attack, encourage the fatal quarrel or otherwise promote the necessitous occasion for taking life. The fact that the deceased struck the first blow, fired the first shot or made the first menacing gesture does not legalize the self-defense claim if in fact the claimant was the actual provoker. In sum, one who is the aggressor in a conflict culminating in death cannot invoke the necessities of self-preservation. Only in the event that he communicates to his adversary his intent to withdraw and in good faith attempts to do so is he restored to his right of self-defense.

This body of doctrine traces its origin to the fundamental principle that a killing in self-defense is excusable only as a matter of genuine necessity. Quite obviously, a defensive killing is unnecessary if the occasion for it could have been averted, and the roots of that consideration run deep with us.

In the case at bar, the trial judge's charge fully comported with these governing principles. The remaining question, then, is whether there was evidence to make them applicable to the case. A recapitulation of the proofs shows beyond peradventure that there was.

It was not until Peterson fetched his pistol and returned to his back yard that his confrontation with Keitt took on a deadly cast. Prior to his trip into the house for the gun, there was, by the Government's evidence, no threat, no display of weapons, no combat. There was an exchange of verbal aspersions and a misdemeanor against Peterson's property was in progress but, at this juncture, nothing more. Even if Peterson's post-arrest version of the initial encounter were accepted-his claim that Keitt went for the lug wrench before he armed himself -the events which followed bore heavily on the question as to who the real aggressor was.

The evidence is uncontradicted that when Peterson reappeared in the yard with his pistol, Keitt was about to depart the scene. . . . The uncontroverted fact that Keitt was leaving shows plainly that so far as he was concerned the confrontation was ended. It demonstrates just as plainly that even if he had previously been the aggressor, he no longer was.

Not so with Peterson, however, as the undisputed evidence made clear. Emerging from the house with the pistol, he paused in the yard to load it, and to command Keitt not to move. He then walked through the yard to the rear gate and, displaying his pistol, dared Keitt to come in, and threatened to kill him if he did. While there appears to be no fixed rule on the subject, the cases hold, and we agree, that an affirmative unlawful act reasonably calculated to produce an affray foreboding injurious or fatal consequences is an aggression which, unless renounced, nullifies the right of homicidal self-defense. We cannot escape the abiding conviction that the jury could readily find Peterson's challenge to be a transgression of that character.

The situation at bar is not unlike that presented in Laney. There the accused, chased along the street by a mob threatening his life, managed to escape through an areaway between two houses. In the back yard of one of the houses, he checked a gun he was carrying and then returned to the areaway. The mob beset him again, and during an exchange of shots one of its members was killed by a bullet from the accused's gun. In affirming a conviction of manslaughter, the court reasoned:

> It is clearly apparent ... that, when defendant escaped from the mob into the back yard ... he was in a place of comparative safety, from which, if he desired to go home, he could have gone by the back way, as he subsequently did. The mob had turned its attention to a house on the opposite side of the street. According to Laney's testimony, there was shooting going on in the street. His appearance on the street at that juncture could mean nothing but trouble for him. Hence, when he adjusted his gun and stepped out into the areaway, he had every reason to believe that his presence there would provoke trouble. We think his conduct in adjusting his revolver and going into the areaway was such as to deprive him of any right to invoke the plea of self-defense.

We think the evidence plainly presented an issue of fact as to whether Peterson's conduct was an invitation to and provocation of the encounter which ended in the fatal shot. We sustain the trial judge's action in remitting that issue for the jury's determination.

V

The second aspect of the trial judge's charge as to which Peterson asserts error concerned the undisputed fact that at no time did Peterson endeavor to retreat from Keitt's approach with the lug wrench. The judge instructed the jury that if Peterson had reasonable grounds to believe and did believe that he was in imminent danger of death or serious injury, and that deadly force was necessary to repel the danger, he was required neither to retreat nor to consider whether he could safely retreat. Rather, said the judge, Peterson was entitled to stand his ground and use such force as was reasonably necessary under the circumstances to save his life and his person from pernicious bodily harm. But, the judge continued, if Peterson could have safely retreated but did not do so, that failure was a circumstance which the jury might consider, together with all others, in determining whether he went further in repelling the danger, real or apparent, than he was justified in going.

Peterson contends that this imputation of an obligation to retreat was error, even if he could safely have done so. He points out that at the time of the shooting he was standing in his own yard, and argues he was under no duty to move. We are persuaded to the conclusion that in the circumstances presented here, the trial judge did not err in giving the instruction challenged.

Within the common law of self-defense there developed the rule of "retreat to the wall," which ordinarily forbade the use of deadly force by one to whom an avenue for safe retreat was open. This doctrine was but an application of the requirement of strict necessity to excuse the taking of human life, and was designed to insure the existence of that necessity. Even the innocent victim of a vicious assault had to elect a safe retreat if available, rather than resort to defensive force which might kill or seriously injure.

In a majority of American jurisdictions, contrarily to the common law rule, one may stand his ground and use deadly force whenever it seems reasonably necessary to save himself [stand your ground rule]. While the law of the District of Columbia on this point is not entirely clear, it seems allied with the strong minority adhering to the common law. . . . [T]he common law rule of strict necessity pervades the District concept of pernicious self-defense, and we cannot ignore the inherent inconsistency of an absolute no-retreat rule. Until such time as the District law on the subject may become more definitive, we accept these precedents as ample indication that the doctrine of retreat persists.

That is not to say that the retreat rule is without exceptions. Even at common law it was recognized that it was not completely suited to all situations. Today it is the more so that its precept must be adjusted to modern conditions nonexistent during the early development of the common law of self-defense. One restriction on its operation comes to the fore when the circumstances apparently foreclose a withdrawal with safety. The doctrine of retreat was never intended to enhance the risk to the innocent; its proper application has never required a faultless victim to increase his assailant's safety at the expense of his own. On the contrary, he could stand his ground and use deadly force otherwise appropriate if the alternative were perilous, or if to him it reasonably appeared to be. . . .

The trial judge's charge to the jury incorporated each of these limitations on the retreat rule. Peterson, however, invokes another-the so-called "castle" doctrine. It is well settled that one who through no fault of his own is attacked in his home is under no duty to retreat therefrom. The oft-repeated expression that "a man's home is his castle" reflected the belief in olden days that there were few if any safer sanctuaries than the home. The "castle" exception, moreover, has been extended by some courts to encompass the occupant's presence within the curtilage outside his dwelling. Peterson reminds us that when he shot to halt Keitt's advance, he was standing in his yard and so, he argues, he had no duty to endeavor to retreat.

Despite the practically universal acceptance of the "castle" doctrine in American jurisdictions wherein the point has been raised, its status in the District of Columbia has never been squarely decided. But whatever the fate of the doctrine in the District law of the future, it is clear that in absolute form it was inapplicable here. The right of self-defense, we have said, cannot be claimed by the aggressor in an affray so long as he retains that unmitigated role. It logically follows that any rule of no-retreat which may protect an innocent victim of the affray would, like other incidents of a forfeited right of self-defense, be unavailable to the party who provokes or stimulates the conflict. Accordingly, the law is well settled that the "castle" doctrine can be invoked only by one who is without fault in bringing the conflict on. That, we think, is the critical consideration here.

We need not repeat our previous discussion of Peterson's contribution to the altercation which culminated in Keitt's death. It suffices to point out that by no interpretation of the evidence could it be said that Peterson was blameless in the affair. And while, of course, it was for the jury to assess the degree of fault, the evidence well nigh dictated the conclusion that it was substantial.

The only reference in the trial judge's charge intimating an affirmative duty to retreat was the instruction that a failure to do so, when it could have been done safely, was a factor in the totality of the circumstances which the jury might consider in determining whether the force which he employed was excessive. We cannot believe that any jury was at all likely to view Peterson's conduct as irreproachable. We conclude that for one who, like Peterson, was hardly entitled to fall back on the "castle" doctrine of no retreat, that instruction cannot be just cause for complaint.

The judgment of conviction appealed from is accordingly

Affirmed.

Notes and Questions

1. Why wasn't Peterson justified in using force to protect his property? Do you have any doubt that he believed what he was doing was justified to prevent the theft of his wiper blades? If he was not justified, what could he have done to prevent the theft?

2. Notice that the clean hands requirement is a purely objective assessment. The question is not whether the defendant reasonably believed he was not the first aggressor; the question is whether viewing the situation objectively, the defendant was or was not the first aggressor. In this sense, the clean hands requirement is like the proverbial "go/no go" gate for self-defense: if the jury concludes the defendant was the first aggressor, no further inquiry is required; if his hands are "dirty" because he was the first aggressor, he cannot claim the privilege of self-defense.

3. Did the appellate court jump from a finding that there was evidence that *could* support the conclusion Peterson was the first aggressor to a conclusion Peterson *was* the first aggressor? Peterson, after all, complained about not only the first aggressor instruction but also about the retreat instruction. Is it possible, even based on the court's own assessment of the evidence, that the jury concluded Peterson was *not* the first aggressor but that because he failed to retreat when his victim approached him with the lug wrench, his claim of self-defense failed? If so, wouldn't it be necessary to

decide whether the Castle exception extended to the curtilage of the home, an issue the court avoided?

4. Notice how the court ties all the requirements of self-defense back to the essential question of necessity: if any of the requirements are absent, then the killing was not necessary and was therefore unlawful.

5. Who had the burden of proof on the question of self-defense in *Peterson*? Is a defendant like Peterson in a better position if he bears the burden of proving self-defense by a preponderance of the evidence or if the prosecution must disprove the defense beyond a reasonable doubt?

What did the *Peterson* court indicate was required for Peterson to "clean his hands" after his initial aggression and restore himself to a claim of self-defense? If Peterson had run back into his home when he saw Keitt take out the lug wrench, and Keitt had chased him, would Peterson have been legally justified in killing Keitt? What if Peterson had unlawfully threatened Keitt with non-deadly force but Keitt had responded with deadly force? Would that have restored Peterson's right to act in self-defense? The next case considers this issue. While the case arose during the defendant's deployment to Iraq as a U.S. Army officer, the court importantly notes that "the events that transpired in the culvert do not implicate the unique aspects of military service in a manner that requires [it] to apply other than basic criminal law concepts."

United States v. Behenna

71 M.J. 228 (2012)

U.S. Court of Appeals for the Armed Forces

Judge STUCKY delivered the opinion of the Court.

We granted review in this case to determine whether the military judge provided complete and accurate self-defense instructions. . . . We hold that, although the military judge's instruction on escalation was erroneous, it was harmless beyond a reasonable doubt because escalation was not in issue. Moreover, contrary to Appellant's arguments, withdrawal also was not in issue. . . . We, therefore, affirm the judgment of the United States Army Court of Criminal Appeals (CCA).

I

A

Contrary to Appellant's pleas, a general court-martial with members found Appellant guilty of unpremeditated murder and assault in violation of Articles 118 and 128, Uniform Code of Military Justice (UCMJ), 10 U.S.C. §§ 918, 928 (2006). Appellant was sentenced to a dismissal, twenty-five years of confinement, and forfeiture of all pay and allowances. . . . The CCA [Army Court of Criminal Appeals] affirmed the findings of guilty and the sentence as approved by the convening authority. *United States v. Behenna*, 70 M.J. 521, 534 (A. Ct. Crim. App. 2011).

B

In September 2007, Appellant was assigned to Bayji, Iraq, an area north of Baghdad. His platoon's area of operation was Albu Toma. During his deployment, Appellant learned of information linking Ali Mansur, the deceased in this case, to a group in Albu Toma, who were believed to be responsible for attacks on Coalition Forces. Appellant also learned from human intelligence reports that Mansur would stand on the police station west of Albu Toma overlooking Salaam Village and inform insurgents of Coalition Forces' activities.

Before April 21, 2008, Appellant had given out his cell phone number to locals so that they could contact him with issues. Someone named Ali called Appellant and warned him to avoid Albu Toma or else harm would come to his platoon. Appellant also learned from a source that Mansur had spoken of an improvised explosive device being planted along a roadway used by Appellant's platoon.

On April 21, Appellant's platoon was patrolling Salaam Village and detained two individuals. On the return trip to base, an explosive device was detonated near the vehicles. Appellant saw several individuals in his platoon injured or killed by the blast. A draft intelligence information report issued on April 27 stated that Mansur was likely a member of the group that was operating out of Salaam Village. After the report was issued, Mansur was apprehended for interrogation, but shortly after questioning was finished, Mansur was to be returned to Albu Toma.

Appellant read the report of Mansur's interrogation and only found information regarding Mansur's job and background and his relation to an RPK. Appellant asked that Mansur be reinterrogated based on his belief that Mansur had information on insurgents operating out of Salaam Village, who Appellant believed were responsible for the April 21 attack. Appellant did not participate in the second interrogation, and although Mansur provided information willingly, the interrogator told Appellant that Mansur was being deceptive.

After the second interrogation, Appellant was ordered to return Mansur to Albu Toma. Appellant continued to believe that Mansur had information regarding the April 21 attack and the group operating out of Salaam Village; he further believed those questions had not been asked and answered. On the day that Mansur was to be released, Appellant went with an interpreter, Mr. Tarik Abdallah Silah (referred to by the parties as Harry), to retrieve Mansur from his cell. Appellant told Mansur, "I'm going to talk to you later on today. There is [sic] three pieces of information that I want from you. . . . If I don't get that information today, you will die today." Appellant admitted the scare tactic was unauthorized but claimed his intent was only to frighten Mansur into providing information.

Appellant's platoon returned a different detainee before passing through Albu Toma without releasing Mansur. Appellant ordered his platoon to take the desert route back to base, because he wanted "to talk to Ali in a remote, secure location." On the desert route, Appellant saw a culvert; he ordered the platoon to stop, because he believed this was an appropriate location to speak with Mansur. Appellant told Harry to follow him as Appellant retrieved Mansur from Sergeant Warner's truck. Appellant asked Warner if he had a thermite grenade. Warner did not at that time, and Appellant did not order him to find one.

Appellant, Harry, and Mansur immediately started walking towards the culvert. In the meantime, Warner found a thermite grenade [an incendiary explosive] and caught up with the group at the culvert. Upon reaching the culvert, Appellant saw there was a second culvert and led the group there. Outside the second culvert, Appellant told Mansur he wanted the information he had asked about earlier that day. Mansur responded that he did not know anything.

Appellant then moved Mansur into the culvert and cut off his shirt and told Warner to cut off his pants and underwear. Appellant then attempted to remove the zip ties that bound Mansur's hands, but Harry eventually had to remove them for Appellant. Appellant ordered Mansur, who was then naked and unbound, to sit on a rock or piece of concrete inside the culvert. Mansur continued to claim ignorance, so Appellant pointed a loaded pistol at him to frighten him into providing the information.

C

By this time, it was dark and dusty outside, visibility was low, and Warner was using night vision goggles. As soon as Appellant pulled out his pistol, Harry stepped outside the culvert because he was afraid of the ricochet. Harry testified that from his vantage point he could make out the figure of a person but could not distinguish Mansur's arms and hands. Once Harry was outside the culvert, Appellant again asked for the information and stated that if Mansur did not tell him what he wanted to hear that he would die. Mansur said something, and Harry looked at Appellant to translate, and then two shots were fired. Harry testified that everything happened quickly, that he was surprised by the gunshots, and that he did not see exactly what happened before the shots were fired. He did not know what happened to cause Appellant to shoot Mansur.

Warner was approximately thirty-five to fifty meters away when he heard the first pistol shot. From his original angle, Warner could not see inside the culvert; so, he moved to a better position. He saw the muzzle flash from the second shot. Warner ultimately identified Appellant as the individual who fired the pistol shots that killed Mansur. When Warner reached the culvert, Appellant told him to "[t]hrow it." Warner asked, "[t]hrow what" and Appellant said "[d]on't be stupid." Warner tossed the thermite grenade in the direction of Mr. Mansur's body. Appellant then told Warner to take care of the clothes.

Appellant's testimony was mostly consistent with that of the other witnesses, although he did elaborate on what occurred before he fired his pistol. He testified that he pointed his pistol at Mr. Mansur and told him that "[t]his [was his] last chance to tell the information or [he would] die." Appellant testified he heard Mr. Mansur say something in Arabic that was different than his previous responses, so he looked over to Harry for interpretation.

While looking at Harry, Appellant testified that he heard a piece of concrete hit over his left shoulder. He turned towards Mansur and saw him reaching for the pistol; the distance between them was only two or three feet. He took a step or two to his left, towards the entrance of the culvert, to create distance between him and Mansur, and then fired two shots into Mansur. Mansur was shot once in the head and once in the chest; the order of the shots was a contested issue.

Appellant stated that everything happened fast and that he fired the shots because he "was scared [Mansur] was going to take [his] weapon." Appellant insisted throughout his testimony that he never intended to kill Mansur; he just wanted to scare him for information.

Upon returning to base, Appellant took Warner on a walk and asked him if he was "cool." Warner indicated he was. Harry later asked Appellant why he had shot Mansur, and Harry testified that Appellant said "'Ali Mansur planted explosives twice on a specific road and the explosive that went off in the Salaam Village, he had a hand into this too. He was part of this operation.'"

II

The first issue is whether the members were improperly instructed about how Appellant could lose and regain the right to act in self-defense. Although we find the instruction on escalation was erroneous, the error was harmless beyond a reasonable doubt. Appellant was not entitled to such an instruction at all, as there was no evidence raising the issue of escalation. Moreover, contrary to Appellant's arguments, withdrawal was not in issue either, for the same reason.

A

An allegation that the members were improperly instructed is an issue we review de novo.

In regard to substance, the instructional issues in this case involve self-defense. The standard for self-defense is set out in Rule for Court-Martial (R.C.M.) 916(e)(1), which provides that if an individual apprehends on reasonable grounds that grievous bodily harm or death is about to be wrongfully inflicted to his or her person, then the individual may use such force as is appropriate for the circumstances, including deadly force.

The right to act in self-defense, however, is not absolute. Initial aggressors and those involved in mutual combat lose the right to act in self-defense. However, an initial aggressor or a mutual combatant regains the right to act in self-defense if the other party escalates the degree of force, or if the initial aggressor or the mutual combatant withdraws in good faith and communicates that intent to withdraw. With these principles in mind, we turn our attention to the instructions in this case.

B

The military judge provided a facially correct instruction on self-defense. Appellant's claim of error is in regard to the following instruction on losing and regaining the right to act in self-defense:

> Now there exists evidence in this case that the accused *may have been assaulting* Ali Mansur immediately prior to the shooting by pointing a loaded weapon at him. A person who without provocation or other legal justification or excuse assaults another person is not entitled to self-defense unless the person being assaulted escalates the level of force beyond that which was originally used. The burden of proof on this issue is on the prosecution. If you are convinced beyond a reasonable doubt that the accused, without provocation or other legal justification or excuse, assaulted Ali Mansur then you have found that the accused gave up the right to self-defense. *However, if you have a reasonable doubt that the accused assaulted Ali Mansur, was provoked by Ali Mansur, or had some other legal justification or excuse, and you are not convinced beyond a reasonable doubt that Ali Mansur did not escalate the level of force,* then you must conclude that the accused had the right to self-defense, and then you must determine if the accused actually did act in self-defense.

This instruction is erroneous for two reasons. First, the military judge provided no guidance on how to evaluate an offer-type assault [apprehension assault], which occurs, for instance, when an individual points a loaded pistol at another person without lawful justification or authorization. We recognize that the military judge had previously instructed the members on an assault consummated by a battery, but those instructions did not include guidance on how to evaluate the offer-type assault that preceded the killing of Mansur. . . . Thus, the members were never instructed that for Appellant to have assaulted Mansur by pointing the pistol at him, Mansur had to *reasonably apprehend* immediate bodily harm. The two varieties of assault are sufficiently different that, even when the instructions are viewed holistically, the first portion of the instruction was incomplete. *See United States v. Marbury*, 56 M.J. 12, 17 (C.A.A.F. 2001) (holding the critical issue in offer-type assaults is whether the victim reasonably apprehended imminent bodily harm as compared to assaults consummated by a battery in which the critical issue is actual bodily harm).

More importantly, the second emphasized portion of the instruction is an erroneous statement of law. Specifically, the military judge linked the lawful use of force with the issue of escalation with the conjunction "and." ("However, if you have a reasonable doubt that the accused assaulted Ali Mansur, was provoked by Ali Mansur, or had some other legal justification or excuse, *and* you are not convinced beyond a reasonable doubt that Ali Mansur did not escalate the level of force, then you must conclude that the accused had the right to self-defense. . . ." (emphasis added)). This is an inaccurate statement of law because Appellant would have had the right to self-defense if his original use of force had been lawful—it was provoked, justified, or otherwise excusable (i.e., Appellant was not an initial aggressor)—*or* if Mr. Mansur had escalated the level of force. . . . Having found that the instruction was erroneous, we must test for prejudice.

C

When instructional errors have constitutional implications, as instructions involving self-defense do, then the error is tested for prejudice under a "harmless beyond a reasonable doubt" standard. [*United States v.*] *Lewis,* 65 M.J. at 87. Only when the reviewing authority is convinced beyond a reasonable doubt that the error did not contribute to the defendant's conviction or sentence is a constitutional error harmless.

Generally, a superfluous, exculpatory instruction that does not shift the burden of proof is harmless, even if the instruction is otherwise erroneous. *See United States v. Thomas,* 34 F.3d 44, 48 (2d Cir.1994) (providing a potentially erroneous self-defense instruction could not have been prejudicial to the defendants because "their need to defend themselves arose out of their own armed aggression"); *Melchior v. Jago,* 723 F.2d 486, 493 (6th Cir.1983) (even if instruction was erroneous it was harmless beyond a reasonable doubt where "there was insufficient evidence to submit the issue of self-defense to the jury in the first instance").

As discussed further below, Appellant lost the right to act in self-defense as a matter of law; therefore, any instruction on losing and regaining the right to self-defense was superfluous. Our case law makes clear that a military judge is only required to instruct when there is some evidence in the record, without regard to credibility, that the members could rely upon if they choose. *United States v. Schumacher,* 70 M.J. 387, 389 (C.A.A.F. 2011). In other words, a military judge must instruct on a defense when, viewing the evidence in the light most favorable to the defense, a rational member could have found in the favor of the accused in regard to that defense. This is a legal question that is reviewed de novo.

D

We begin by noting that Appellant was not in an active battlefield situation, that Mansur was not then actively engaged in hostile action against the United States or its allies, and that there were no other military exigencies in play. Appellant's counsel at oral argument conceded that Appellant was not seeking a special privilege based on Appellant's status as a soldier or presence on the battlefield. After careful consideration, we agree that the events that transpired in the culvert do not implicate the unique aspects of military service in a manner that requires us to apply other than basic criminal law concepts. Thus, we evaluate this situation by applying the fundamental concepts of self-defense as imbedded in this Court's case law and the MCM [Manual for Courts-Martial].

As discussed earlier, if Appellant was the initial aggressor—i.e., the one that provoked or brought about the situation that resulted in the necessity to kill another—

then he lost his right to self-defense, unless the deceased, Mansur, either escalated the level of force or Appellant withdrew and communicated that withdrawal in good faith.

Even when viewed in the most favorable light, Appellant's own testimony about the events that transpired in the culvert demonstrate that he was the initial aggressor because he brought about the situation that resulted in his killing of Mansur. Appellant deviated from his assigned duty to return Mansur to his home, without authority, to take him to a remote culvert in the desert, far from any active hostilities for further unauthorized interrogation.

More importantly, Appellant then stripped the detainee naked and forced him to sit on a rock while Appellant, in full combat attire with a loaded pistol, interrogated him. Appellant also told Mansur, as he had on other occasions that day, that he was going to die unless he provided specific information. *Cf.* MCM pt. IV, ¶ 54.c.(1)(c)(iii) ("Thus, if Doe points a pistol at Roe and says, 'If you don't hand over your watch, I will shoot you.' Doe has committed an assault upon Roe.").

Although we are mindful that Mansur was a detainee, it is evident that Appellant's use of force in the culvert before the shooting — the critical moment in reviewing this issue — was unauthorized and excessive. *Cf. United States v. Archer,* 486 F.2d 670, 676–77 (2d Cir. 1973) ("It would be unthinkable, for example, to permit government agents to instigate robberies and beatings merely to gather evidence to convict other members of a gang of hoodlums."). Even accepting the facts as Appellant described them on direct examination, there is no evidence on which a rational member could rely to conclude that Appellant was not the initial aggressor. The next question is whether a rational member could have found that Appellant regained the right to act in self-defense as a result of either Mansur's escalating the conflict or Appellant's withdrawing in good faith.

Under our case law, Mansur could not have escalated the level of force in this situation, as Appellant had already introduced deadly force. *See United States v. Stanley,* 71 M.J. 60, 63 (C.A.A.F. 2012); *see also Armstrong v. Bertrand,* 336 F.3d 620, 623, 625–26 (7th Cir. 2003) (holding that an armed gunman did not regain the right to self-defense even though the victim threatened to kill the gunman and lunged for his gun); Wayne R. LaFave, *Substantive Criminal Law* § 10.4(e) (2d ed. 2003) (noting that a nondeadly aggressor is one who uses "only his fists or some nondeadly weapon"). Even assuming for a moment that Mansur could have escalated the level of force, we conclude that a naked and unarmed individual in the desert does not escalate the level of force when he throws a piece of concrete at an initial aggressor in full battle attire, armed with a loaded pistol, and lunges for the pistol. This is especially so when the initial aggressor "had every opportunity to withdraw from the confrontation and there was no evidence he either attempted or was unable to do so." *See Behenna.* 70 M.J. at 532–33; *see also* R.C.M. 916(e)(4) Discussion ("Failure to retreat . . . does not deprive the accused of the right to self-defense[, but] [t]he availability of avenues of retreat is one factor which may be considered in addressing . . . that the force used was necessary for self-protection").

Furthermore, nothing in Appellant's testimony indicated that he clearly manifested an intent to withdraw or that Mr. Mansur prevented Appellant from withdrawing. *See United States v. O'Neal,* 16 C.M.A. 33, 37, 36 C.M.R. 189, 193 (1966) ("His testimony contains no suggestion of a word or act that could reasonably be interpreted by the others as indicating he wanted to end the fight."). As the CCA found, there was no evidence that Mansur made contact with Appellant's weapon, that Appellant indicated a desire to withdraw, or that Appellant made a good-faith effort to withdraw. Rather, Appellant took one or two steps towards the entrance of the culvert where the vast desert, Warner, and the rest of his platoon were waiting, before he shot Mansur twice. *See id.* at 523. Even accepting the facts as Appellant described them on direct examination, no rational member could have found either that Mansur escalated the situation or that Appellant withdrew in good faith.

Contrary to the dissent's suggestion, we have not decided any factual matters that should have been before the members. There is no factual issue for the members to resolve until "there is some evidence upon which members could reasonably rely [upon] to find that each element of the defense has been established." *Schumacher,* 70 M.J. at 389–90. Importantly, the issue in this case is not whether there was some evidence of self-defense. Rather, our holding is that any evidence of self-defense was overcome by other events, namely the unrebutted evidence that Appellant was an initial aggressor and the dearth of evidence of escalation by Mansur or good faith withdrawal by Appellant — matters thoroughly discussed above.

Ultimately, even if we assume that Mansur lunged for Appellant's pistol and Appellant feared that Mansur would use the pistol if he was able to seize it, because Appellant was the initial aggressor, and because there was no evidence to support a finding of escalation or withdrawal, a rational member could have come to no other conclusion than that Appellant lost the right to act in self-defense and did not regain it. *See [United States v.] Branch,* 91 F.3d at 712 ("The district court is not required to put the case to the jury on a basis that essentially indulges and even encourages speculations."). As such, withdrawal was not in issue and the erroneous instruction on escalation was superfluous. As we noted earlier, superfluous, exculpatory instructions that do not impermissibly shift burdens are generally harmless beyond a reasonable doubt, even if the instructions are otherwise erroneous. Nothing in these facts suggests that we should deviate from that conclusion. For this reason, Appellant is not entitled to relief.

Notes and Questions

1. What does the court indicate is the standard for instructing a jury on an affirmative defense? In other words, what triggers such an instruction? Is there a similarity to the prosecution satisfying the burden of production?

2. How does the standard for determining when an initial aggressor is restored to a position to claim self-defense differ in this decision from the standard articulated in *Peterson*?

3. Why did the court indicate that as a matter of law, Behenna's right to self-defense could not be restored by an act of aggression by Mansur once Behenna had him at gunpoint?

4. The court notes there are two ways a first aggressor can be restored to a claim of self-defense. Why, then, was Behenna's failure to make any effort to withdraw so significant to the court's analysis of harmless error?

5. Why was Behenna convicted of second-degree murder? The military version of first-degree murder requires proof of premeditation, although that term is used to include both premeditation and deliberation. A military jury would have been instructed that "premeditated design to kill" means the formation of a specific intent to kill and consideration of the act intended to bring about death. The "premeditated design to kill" does not have to exist for any measurable or particular length of time. The only requirement is that it must precede the killing. The jury would also be instructed that it could consider evidence of the accused's passion in determining whether he or she possessed sufficient mental capacity to have "the premeditated design to kill." "An accused cannot be found guilty of premeditated murder if, at the time of the killing, (his) (her) mind was so confused by (anger) (rage) (pain) (sudden resentment) (fear) (or) (_____) that (he) (she) could not or did not premeditate." Does this provide an explanation?

A valid self-defense claim is only the first step to success for a defendant. At that point, the focus of the inquiry shifts to an assessment of the defendant's judgment: did the defendant make an honest and reasonable judgment of necessity? This is not a purely objective standard. Instead, it is better understood as one of *contextual* reasonableness: was the defendant's judgment of necessity reasonable in the situation she confronted, considering the characteristics of that situation and of the defendant?

State v. Wanrow

559 P.2d 548 (1977)
Washington Supreme Court

Yvonne Wanrow was convicted by a jury of second-degree murder and first-degree assault. . . .

We order a reversal of the conviction on two grounds. The first is the ground stated by the Court of Appeals regarding the erroneous admission of the tape recording. The second ground is error committed by the trial court in improperly instructing the jury on the law of self-defense as it related to the defendant.

On the afternoon of August 11, 1972, defendant's (respondent's) two children were staying at the home of Ms. Hooper, a friend of defendant. Defendant's son was playing in the neighborhood and came back to Ms. Hooper's house and told her that a man tried to pull him off his bicycle and drag him into a house. Some months earlier, Ms. Hooper's 7-year-old daughter had developed a rash on her body which was diagnosed as venereal disease. Ms. Hooper had been unable to persuade her daughter to tell her who had molested her. It was not until the night of the shooting that Ms. Hooper discovered it was William Wesler (decedent) who allegedly had violated her daughter. A few minutes after the defendant's son related his story to Ms. Hooper about the man who tried to detain him, Mr. Wesler appeared on the porch of the Hooper house and stated through the door, "I didn't touch the kid, I didn't touch the kid." At that moment, the Hooper girl, seeing Wesler at the door, indicated to her mother that Wesler was the man who had molested her. Joseph Fah, Ms. Hooper's landlord, saw Wesler as he was leaving and informed Shirley Hooper that Wesler had tried to molest a young boy who had earlier lived in the same house, and that Wesler had previously been committed to the Eastern State Hospital for the mentally ill. Immediately after this revelation from Mr. Fah, Ms. Hooper called the police who, upon their arrival at the Hooper residence, were informed of all the events which had transpired that day. Ms. Hooper requested that Wesler be arrested then and there, but the police stated, "We can't, until Monday morning." Ms. Hooper was urged by the police officer to go to the police station Monday morning and "swear out a warrant." Ms. Hooper's landlord, who was present during the conversation, suggested that Ms. Hooper get a baseball bat located at the corner of the house and "conk him over the head" should Wesler try to enter the house uninvited during the weekend. To this suggestion, the policeman replied, "Yes, but wait until he gets in the house." (A week before this incident Shirley Hooper had noticed someone prowling around her house at night. Two days before the shooting someone had attempted to get into Ms. Hooper's bedroom and had slashed the window screen. She suspected that such person was Wesler.)

That evening, Ms. Hooper called the defendant and asked her to spend the night with her in the Hooper house. At that time, she related to Ms. Wanrow the facts we have previously set forth. The defendant arrived sometime after 6 p.m. with a pistol in her handbag. The two women ultimately determined that they were too afraid to stay alone and decided to ask some friends to come over for added protection. The two women then called the defendant's sister and brother-in-law, Angie and Chuck Michel. The four adults did not go to bed that evening, but remained awake talking and watching for any possible prowlers. There were eight young children in the house with them. At around 5 a.m., Chuck Michel, without the knowledge of the women in the house, went to Wesler's house, carrying a baseball bat. Upon arriving at the Wesler residence, Mr. Michel accused Wesler of molesting little children. Mr. Wesler then suggested that they go over to the Hooper residence and get the whole thing straightened out. Another man, one David Kelly, was also present, and together the three men went over to the Hooper house. Mr. Michel and Mr. Kelly remained outside while Wesler entered the residence.

The testimony as to what next took place is considerably less precise. It appears that Wesler, a large man who was visibly intoxicated, entered the home and when told to leave declined to do so. A good deal of shouting and confusion then arose, and a young child, asleep on the couch, awoke crying. The testimony indicates that Wesler then approached this child, stating, "My what a cute little boy," or words to that effect, and that the child's mother, Ms. Michel, stepped between Wesler and the child. By this time Hooper was screaming for Wesler to get out. Ms. Wanrow, a 5-foot 4-inch woman who at the time had a broken leg and was using a crutch, testified that she then went to the front door to enlist the aid of Chuck Michel. She stated that she shouted for him and, upon turning around to reenter the living room, found Wesler standing directly behind her. She testified to being gravely startled by this situation and to having then shot Wesler in what amounted to a reflex action.

After Wesler was shot, Ms. Hooper called the police via a Spokane crime check emergency phone number, stating, "There's a guy broke in, and my girlfriend shot him." The defendant later took the phone and engaged in a conversation with the police operator. The entire conversation was tape recorded. [The court then concluded introduction of the taped phone call to the police amounted to reversible error].

Reversal of respondent's conviction is also required by a second serious error committed by the trial court. Instruction No. 10, setting forth the law of self-defense, incorrectly limited the jury's consideration of acts and circumstances pertinent to respondent's perception of the alleged threat to her person. An examination of the record of the testimony and of the colloquys [sic] which took place with regard to the instructions on self-defense indicate the critical importance of these instructions to the respondent's theory of the case. Based upon the evidence we have already set out, it is obviously crucial that the jury be precisely instructed as to the defense of justification.

In the opening paragraph of instruction No. 10, the jury, in evaluating the gravity of the danger to the respondent, was directed to consider only those acts and circumstances occurring "at or immediately before the killing. . . ." This is not now, and never has been, the law of self-defense in Washington. On the contrary, the justification of self-defense is to be evaluated in light of all the facts and circumstances known to the defendant, including those known substantially before the killing.

In *State v. Ellis*, 30 Wash. 369, 70 P. 963 (1902), this court reversed a first-degree murder conviction obtained under self-defense instructions quite similar to that in the present case. The defendant sought to show that the deceased had a reputation and habit of carrying and using deadly weapons when engaged in quarrels. The trial court instructed that threats were insufficient justification unless "at the time of the alleged killing the deceased was making or immediately preceding the killing had committed some overt act. . . ." *State v. Ellis, supra* at 371. This court found the instruction "defective and misleading," stating "the apparent facts should all be taken together to illustrate the motives and good faith of the defendant. . . ." *State v. Ellis, supra* at 374.

> [I]t is apparent that a man who habitually carries and uses such weapons in quarrels must cause greater apprehension of danger than one who does not bear such reputation. . . . The vital question is the reasonableness of the defendant's apprehension of danger. . . . The jury are [sic] entitled to stand as nearly as practicable in the shoes of defendant, and from this point of view determine the character of the act.

State v. Ellis, supra at 373. Thus, circumstances predating the killing by weeks and months were deemed entirely proper, and in fact essential, to a proper disposition of the claim of self-defense.

State v. Tribett, 74 Wash. 125, 132 P. 875 (1913), is in accord. There this court approved an instruction which twice directed the jury to evaluate the reasonableness of the defendant's actions in defense of himself "in the light of all the circumstances." *State v. Tribett, supra* at 130. Such circumstances included those existing and known long before the killing, such as the reputation of the place of the killing for lawlessness. This court stated with reference to the self-defense instruction:

> All of these facts and circumstances should have been placed before the jury, to the end that they could put themselves in the place of the appellant, get the point of view which he had at the time of the tragedy, and view the conduct of the [deceased] with all its pertinent sidelights as the appellant was warranted in viewing it. In no other way could the jury safely say what a reasonably prudent man similarly situated would have done.

State v. Tribett, supra at 130. The rule firmly established by these cases has never been disapproved and is still followed today. "It is clear the jury is entitled to consider all of the circumstances surrounding the incident in determining whether [the] defendant had reasonable grounds to believe grievous bodily harm was about to be inflicted." *State v. Lewis*, 6 Wn. App. 38, 41, 491 P.2d 1062 (1971). By limiting the jury's consideration of the surrounding acts and circumstances to those occurring "at or immediately before the killing," instruction No. 10 in the present case was an erroneous statement of the applicable law on the critical focal point of the defendant's case.

As shown by the discussion above, instruction No. 10 erred in limiting the acts and circumstances which the jury could consider in evaluating the nature of the threat of harm as perceived by respondent. Under the well-established rule, this error is presumed to have been prejudicial. Moreover, far from affirmatively showing that the error was harmless, the record demonstrates the limitation to circumstances "at or immediately before the killing" was of crucial importance in the present case. Respondent's knowledge of the victim's reputation for aggressive acts was gained many hours before the killing and was based upon events which occurred over a period of years. Under the law of this state, the jury should have been allowed to consider this information in making the critical determination of the "degree of force which . . . a reasonable person in the same situation . . . seeing what [s]he sees and knowing what [s]he knows, then would believe to be necessary." *State v. Dunning*, 8 Wn. App. 340, 342, 506 P.2d 321 (1973).

The second paragraph of instruction No. 10 contains an equally erroneous and prejudicial statement of the law. That portion of the instruction reads:

> However, when there is no reasonable ground for the person attacked to believe that his person is in imminent danger of death or great bodily harm, and it appears to him that only an ordinary battery is all that is intended, and all that he has reasonable grounds to fear from his assailant, he has a right to stand his ground and repel such threatened assault, yet he has no right to repel a threatened assault with naked hands, by the use of a deadly weapon in a deadly manner, unless he believes, and has reasonable grounds to believe, that he is in imminent danger of death or great bodily harm.

In our society women suffer from a conspicuous lack of access to training in and the means of developing those skills necessary to effectively repel a male assailant without resorting to the use of deadly weapons. Instruction No. 12 does indicate that the "relative size and strength of the persons involved" may be considered; however, it does not make clear that the defendant's actions are to be judged against her own subjective impressions and not those which a detached jury might determine to be objectively reasonable. *State v. Miller, supra* [141 Wash. 104, 250 P. 645 (1926)]. The applicable rule of law is clearly stated in *Miller* at page 105:

> If the appellants, at the time of the alleged assault upon them, as reasonably and ordinarily cautious and prudent men, honestly believed that they were in danger of great bodily harm, they would have the right to resort to self defense, and their conduct is to be judged by the condition appearing to them at the time, not by the condition as it might appear to the jury in the light of testimony before it.

The second paragraph of instruction No. 10 not only establishes an objective standard, but through the persistent use of the masculine gender leaves the jury with the impression the objective standard to be applied is that applicable to an altercation between two men. The impression created that a 5-foot 4-inch woman with a cast on her leg and using a crutch must, under the law, somehow repel an assault by a 6-foot 2-inch intoxicated man without employing weapons in her defense, unless the jury finds her determination of the degree of danger to be objectively reasonable constitutes a separate and distinct misstatement of the law and, in the context of this case, violates the respondent's right to equal protection of the law. The respondent was entitled to have the jury consider her actions in the light of her own perceptions of the situation, including those perceptions which were the product of our nation's "long and unfortunate history of sex discrimination." *Frontiero v. Richardson*, 411 U.S. 677, 684 (1973). Until such time as the effects of that history are eradicated, care must be taken to assure that our self-defense instructions afford women the right to have their conduct judged in light of the individual physical handicaps which are the product of sex discrimination. To fail to do so is to deny the right of the individual woman involved to trial by the same rules which are applicable to male defendants. The portion of the instruction above quoted misstates our law in creating an objective standard of "reasonableness." It then compounds that error by utilizing language suggesting that the respondent's conduct must be measured against that of a reasonable male individual finding himself in the same circumstances.

We conclude that the instruction here in question contains an improper statement of the law on a vital issue in the case, is inconsistent, misleading, and prejudicial when read in conjunction with other instructions pertaining to the same issue, and therefore is a proper basis for a finding of reversible error.

Notes and Questions

1. Why did the instruction on self-defense deprive Wanrow of a fair trial? How should the jury be instructed if she is again brought to trial? Try and draft the necessary instruction on self-defense.

2. Towards the end of the opinion, the court suggests that it was an error to instruct the jury to apply an objective test, and that Wanrow's subjective perception had to be considered. Was the court indicating that the test of reasonableness is purely subjective? If so, does that mean resort to homicidal self-defense is justified whenever the defendant subjectively believed it was necessary? Or does this excerpt from the *Miller* case cited by the court suggest something more nuanced: "as reasonably and ordinarily cautious and prudent men, honestly believed that they were in danger of great bodily harm, they would have the right to resort to self-defense"?

3. Notice that the *Wanrow* court indicates that it is not only the judgment of imminent threat that must be reasonable, but also the judgment of the amount of force needed to respond to the threat. This is known as the proportionality requirement: a defendant may use only the amount of force truly necessary to reduce the threat. Using excessive force exceeds the privilege of self-defense.

4. On December 22, 1984, Bernard Goetz, a passenger on the New York City subway, shot four young men who allegedly attempted to rob him. Goetz had been the victim of prior robberies and was armed with a .38 caliber pistol he procured unlawfully and carried for self-defense. His victims survived, but one was permanently disabled. Goetz was indicted by a Grand Jury for attempted murder and other related offenses. The trial court granted a motion to dismiss the indictment based on the argument that the prosecutor improperly injected an objective element into the Grand Jury's assessment of self-defense. According to Goetz, the law required a purely subjective assessment of self-defense: did Goetz make a subjectively reasonable judgment of homicidal necessity? The appellate court reversed the trial court's dismissal and reinstated the indictment. According to the opinion, reasonableness requires an objective assessment of the claim of self-defense, a conclusion the court indicated was deeply rooted in the common law of self-defense. According to the court:

> We cannot lightly impute to the Legislature an intent to fundamentally alter the principles of justification to allow the perpetrator of a serious crime to go free simply because that person believed his actions were reasonable and necessary to prevent some perceived harm. To completely exonerate such an individual, no matter how aberrational or bizarre his thought patterns, would allow citizens to set their own standards for the permissible use of force. It would also allow a legally competent defendant suffering from delusions to kill or perform acts of violence with impunity, contrary to fundamental principles of justice and criminal law.

In responding to Goetz's argument that such a standard was unjust because it ignored the prior experiences of a defendant like Goetz, the court noted:

> Goetz also argues that the introduction of an objective element will preclude a jury from considering factors such as the prior experiences of a given actor and thus, require it to make a determination of "reasonableness" without regard to the actual circumstances of a particular incident. This argument, however, falsely presupposes that an objective standard means that the background and other relevant characteristics of a particular actor must be ignored. To the contrary, we have frequently noted that a determination of reasonableness must be based on the "circumstances" facing a defendant or his "situation." As just discussed, these terms include any relevant knowledge the defendant had about that person. They also necessarily bring in the physical attributes of all persons involved, including the defendant. Furthermore, the defendant's circumstances encompass any prior experiences he had which could provide a reasonable basis for a belief that another person's intentions were to injure or rob him or that the use of deadly force was necessary under the circumstances.

Is this consistent with the opinion in *Wanrow*?

Imminence and Immediate Necessity

As the prior cases indicate, the common law privilege of self-defense required an honest and reasonable judgment that the threat was imminent. This imminence requirement was derived from the necessity foundation for the defense: unless and until the threat was imminent, resort to self-help was not necessary and therefore was not justified. But what exactly does imminence mean? Jury instructions commonly refer to a threat that is "immediate" or "impending" or "about to happen." Ultimately, the link between imminence and self-help necessity requires the jury to determine whether the defendant had any reasonable alternative to a resort to self-help. If so, the unlawful threat is unlikely to be considered imminent.

This test will, however, create a genuine risk of injustice in rare cases where the unlawful threat might not be imminent at the precise moment of self-help, but the defendant reasonably believes that it is the last feasible opportunity for self-preservation. The most compelling illustration is the case of a severely abused spouse who kills their abuser while he is sleeping. Applying an imminence test would mean the defendant should not even be entitled to a self-defense instruction, even though the totality of the evidence—including evidence explaining "battered spouse syndrome"—indicates that the defendant's conclusion that there was really no other option was reasonable.

The MPC sought to address these uncommon situations by substituting the standard of immediate necessity for the common-law standard of imminence. Specifically, MPC § 3.04(1) indicates that an act is "justifiable when the actor believes that such force is immediately necessary for the purpose of protecting himself against the use of unlawful force by such other person on the present occasion." Unlike imminence, immediate necessity is intended to allow the fact-finder to treat an act as legally justified when it concludes that the defendant reasonably perceived the situation to be the last feasible opportunity for self-preservation.

Who bears the burden of persuasion on this issue is obviously important, as indicated by the next case. Notice that in Texas the defendant bears the burden to produce evidence in support of self-defense, but the prosecution bears the burden of persuasion to *disprove* the defense.

It is also important that you don't confuse mistake of fact related to self-defense with the assessment of the reasonableness of the judgement of necessity to act in self-defense. So long as the defendant intended to kill or injure the victim, a mistake that led to the judgment of necessity will in no way negate that intent to kill. Whether the decision to kill was justified by self-defense is a distinct issue, as the court will emphasize below.

Guyger v. Texas

2021 Tex. App. LEXIS 6377 (2021)
Texas Fifth Circuit Court of Appeals

Amber Renee Guyger was convicted of murdering Botham Jean and sentenced by the jury to ten years' imprisonment. In two issues, Guyger argues the evidence is legally insufficient to support her murder conviction and second, and in the alternative, this Court should acquit her of murder, convict her of criminally negligent homicide, and remand for a new hearing on punishment. We affirm the trial court's judgment.

In July 2018, Guyger moved to the Southside Flats Apartments in Dallas where she lived alone in apartment 1378. Residents of the apartment complex use key fobs rather than traditional keys to unlock their apartment doors. The complex has a multilevel garage with entrances on each floor. Each hallway entrance lacks any placard or other indicator showing which floor of the complex the hallway accesses or which floor of the garage can be accessed by exiting the hallway.

On September 6, 2018, Guyger, a Dallas police officer, left work at 9:33 p.m. Guyger and her partner Martin Rivera exchanged texts about getting together later that evening. Rivera called Guyger at 9:38 p.m., and she was on the phone with him at 9:46 p.m. when she pulled into the parking garage at her apartment complex. Guyger continued speaking to Rivera until almost 10:00 p.m.

Guyger testified that, when she parked in the garage, she believed she was on the third floor. She did not notice the garage roofline on the fourth floor was different from the roofline on the third floor. As Guyger walked down the hallway on the fourth floor, she believed she was on the third floor where her apartment was located. When she reached apartment 1478, she believed she was outside her own apartment. Guyger testified that, while she was standing outside the apartment, she heard loud shuffling, like someone was walking inside. Guyger admitted that, before she opened the door, she concluded there was a threat inside the apartment; however, she did not take a position of cover and concealment or call for backup.

The door was ajar and not latched closed. Guyger turned her key fob in the lock, which opened the door farther. Using her left arm, Guyger pushed open the door. Guyger testified these events occurred in the span of two seconds. There was no light on inside the apartment, but Guyger said she "heard moving around inside" and was "scared to death."

Guyger testified she dropped her police vest and other equipment in front of the door to keep the door propped open. Looking into the apartment, which had the same floor plan as her apartment, she saw a "silhouette figure" standing in the back of the apartment. From where she was standing near the doorway, she could not see the figure's hands. Guyger pulled her weapon and yelled, "Let me see your hands. Let me see your hands." According to Guyger, the figure walked towards her at a fast pace, yelling "hey, hey, hey" in "an aggressive voice." Guyger was focused only on the figure—Botham Jean, the lawful inhabitant of apartment 1478—and she testified she believed he was going to kill her. Guyger fired two shots at Jean, intending, in her words, "to kill him." One round struck the south wall of Jean's apartment, and the other struck Jean in the chest. Jean fell to the ground with his feet pointed away from the couch on which he had been sitting and his head close to an ottoman and couch.

When Guyger walked into the kitchen, she saw the interior of the apartment and realized she was not in her apartment. Confused, Guyger knelt next to Jean. She knew she had shot him, but she did not know where the bullet hit him. At 9:59 p.m., Guyger called 911 with the phone in her right hand. She testified that, at the same time, she began chest compressions on Jean with her left hand. She identified herself as a police officer to the 911 operator, requested an "officer assist," and repeatedly told the operator she thought she had shot someone in what she believed was her apartment. She did not know where she was and went out in the hallway to look at the apartment number so she could provide that information to the operator. While on the phone with the operator, Guyger performed a sternum rub, which she had seen paramedics perform to wake up someone who is unconscious. From the five-minute 911 recording, the jury heard Guyger say twenty times she thought she was in her own apartment. They also heard her say, "stay with me, Bud," several times, "I f***ed up," and "I'm gonna lose my job."

In response to Guyger's "officer assist" call, officers Keenan Blair and Michael Lee were the first to arrive at Jean's apartment. Guyger directed the officers into apartment 1478. As reflected in body camera video, Lee instructed Guyger to move away from Jean as he and then Blair performed CPR on Jean, who was alive but unconscious. Lee's body camera video showed Jean bleeding from a gunshot wound and Guyger saying repeatedly that she had shot Jean.

. . . .

Detective Dale Richardson testified that he arrived on the scene around 11:10 p.m. and initially met with Ibarra. After obtaining a search warrant, Richardson located a set of keys hanging from the door that he believed were Guyger's. The jury saw video evidence demonstrating how the locking mechanism on the doors worked. A small blinking red light lit up when the wrong fob was inserted, but a small blinking green light lit up and the door electronically unlocked when the correct fob was inserted. Video of Richardson and Ibarra comparing use of Guyger's key and Jean's key was also played, which demonstrated that when inserted into the door of apartment 1478, Guyger's key generated a red light and would not activate the lock, but Jean's key generated a green light and made a "whirring sound" while it unlocked the door.

The Texas Rangers took over the investigation from the Dallas Police Department the day after the shooting, met with Ibarra and Richardson, and reviewed the evidence collected by DPD. Texas Ranger David Armstrong characterized the layout of the apartment complex as "confusing" and discovered that about 23% of residents who lived on the third and fourth floors and 15% of residents in the entire building had, at some point, put their key fob in the wrong door. Armstrong testified residents gave numerous reasons why they realized they were in the wrong place: the red blinking light on the door lock, nearby decorations indicating a different resident's apartment, or an incorrect apartment number. In the same vein, several residents testified about having gone to the wrong floor or apartment.

April Kendrick, a supervisor of the firearm and tool mark unit at the Southwestern Institute of Forensic Sciences, confirmed the shell casings found in Jean's apartment were fired from Guyger's nine millimeter pistol. Kendrick also testified that the bullet trajectory indicated Jean may have been bent over and rising from the couch when he was shot. Testimony from the medical examiner, Dr. Chester Gwin, revealed that Jean died from the single gunshot to his chest. The bullet entered his chest just above his nipple and traveled on a steep trajectory downward through his left lung, heart, diaphragm, stomach, and intestine, stopping in a muscle in his left abdomen near his spine. Dr. Gwin explained the bullet's path indicated that either the shooter was standing over Jean and shooting down, or Jean was lying down or bent forward, in the process of getting up from the couch or ducking. Guyger could not explain the inconsistency between her testimony that Jean was standing straight up and moving toward her when she shot him and the bullet trajectory evidence indicating Jean was shot from above or while in the process of getting up or ducking.

Texas Ranger Michael Adcock testified about the trajectory of the bullet that hit the back wall in Jean's apartment. The flight path of that bullet indicated it had been fired from the doorway, which was also confirmed by gunshot residue recovered on the doorframe. At the conclusion of the evidence, the jury found Guyger guilty of murder as charged in the indictment. This appeal followed.

In her first issue, Guyger argues the evidence is legally insufficient to prove beyond a reasonable doubt that she committed murder. Specifically, Guyger argues "(1) through mistake, Guyger formed a reasonable belief about a matter of fact—that she entered her apartment and there was an intruder inside—and (2) her mistaken belief negated the culpability for [m]urder because although she intentionally and knowingly caused Jean's death, she had the right to act in deadly force in self-defense since her belief that deadly force was immediately necessary was reasonable under the circumstances."

I. Legal Sufficiency

We review a challenge to the sufficiency of the evidence on a criminal offense for which the State has the burden of proof under the single sufficiency standard set forth in *Jackson v. Virginia*, 443 U.S. 307 (1979). *Acosta v. State*, 429 S.W.3d 621, 624–25 (Tex. Crim. App. 2014). Under this standard, "the relevant question is whether, after viewing the evidence in the light most favorable to the verdict, *any* rational trier of fact could have found the essential elements of the crime beyond a reasonable doubt." *Clayton v. State*, 235 S.W.3d 772, 778 (Tex. Crim. App. 2007) (quoting *Jackson*, 443 U.S. at 319) (emphasis in original). . . .

Here, Guyger maintains that the evidence is legally insufficient to show she committed murder in one of the ways set forth in section 19.02 of the Texas Penal Code, which provides in relevant part that a person commits murder if she

(1) intentionally or knowingly causes the death of an individual; [or]

(2) intends to cause serious bodily injury and commits an act clearly dangerous to human life that causes the death of an individual. . . .

Tex. Pen. Code §19.02(b)(1), (2). The indictment charged Guyger alternatively with both theories, both theories were submitted to the jury, and the jury returned a guilty verdict that did not specify which theory it relied upon. Evidentiary support for either theory will therefore support the verdict. *Sanchez v. State*, 376 S.W.3d 767, 775 (Tex. Crim. App. 2012) ("When a jury returns a general guilty verdict on an indictment charging alternate methods of committing the same offense, the verdict stands 'if the evidence is sufficient to support a finding under any of the theories submitted.'") (quoting *Kitchens v. State*, 823 S.W.3d 256, 258–59 (Tex. Crim. App. 1991)); *Williams v. State*, 473 S.W.3d 319, 324 (Tex. App. — Houston [14th Dist.] 2014, pet. ref'd) ("When the charge authorizes the jury to convict the defendant on more than one theory, as it did in this case, the verdict of guilt will be upheld if the evidence is sufficient on any theory authorized by the jury charge."); *see London v. State*, 325 S.W.3d 197, 206–07 (Tex. App. — Dallas 2008, pet. ref'd).

Guyger testified she intended to kill Jean when she shot him. In addition, the State introduced evidence that Jean was a living human being — an individual — whose death was caused by the gunshot wound inflicted by Guyger. Accordingly, legally sufficient evidence supports the jury's murder verdict. TEX. PEN. CODE §19.02(b)(1), (2); *see Clayton*, 235 S.W.3d at 778–79. Guyger bore the burden of producing evidence supporting each of her defensive issues, while the State retained the burden of persuasion to disprove those defenses beyond a reasonable doubt. *Braughton v. State*, 569 S.W.3d 592, 608 (Tex. Crim. App. 2018).

A. Mistake of Fact

"It is a defense to prosecution that the actor through mistake formed a reasonable belief about a matter of fact if his mistaken belief negated the kind of culpability required for commission of the offense." Tex. Penal Code § 8.02(a). Thus, this defense applies when the defendant's mistaken belief, if accepted as true, negates the culpable mental state for the crime charged. *Granger v. State*, 3 S.W.3d 36, 41 (Tex. Crim. App. 1999). . . . Thus, in this case, mistake of fact would apply if Guyger mistakenly formed a reasonable belief that negated her intent to kill Jean.

We differentiate mistake of fact — a defense — from justification. Justification depends on the circumstances giving rise to the challenged conduct, and the reasonableness of the defendant's belief that the conduct is immediately necessary to avoid imminent harm.

Conduct is justified if:

(1) the actor reasonably believes the conduct is immediately necessary to avoid imminent harm;

(2) the desirability and urgency of avoiding the harm clearly outweigh, according to ordinary standards of reasonableness, the harm sought to be prevented by the law proscribing the conduct; and

(3) a legislative purpose to exclude the justification claimed for the conduct does not otherwise plainly appear."

Tex. Pen. Code § 9.22. For instance, justification excuses the use of force against another person "when and to the degree the actor reasonably believes the force is immediately necessary to protect the actor against the other's use or attempted use of unlawful force." Tex. Pen. Code § 9.31(a). As such, Guyger would have been justified in shooting Jean if she had formed a reasonable belief that doing so was necessary to avoid imminent harm, as we discuss below . . .

. . . *Rocha v. State* provides a particularly apt comparison. *See Rocha v. State*, No. 14-10-00569-CR, 2012 WL 1154306, at *9 (Tex. App. — Houston [14th Dist.] Apr. 5, 2012, pet. ref'd) (mem. op., not designated for publication). Rocha was an off-duty police officer convicted of aggravated assault with a deadly weapon arising from an altercation outside his home. *Id.* at *2–5. On appeal, Rocha complained the trial court erred in refusing his mistake of fact instruction based on Rocha's testimony about his mistaken belief that Dunham, the victim, was "armed, was dangerous, or was preparing to attack, [or] assault [Rocha]." *Id.* at *9. In affirming the trial court's refusal to give the instruction, the court observed the facts about which Rocha was mistaken did not negate the "culpable mental element of aggravated assault." The court reasoned as follows:

> Appellant does not dispute that he intentionally or knowingly pointed the rifle at Dunham to place him in fear of imminent bodily injury. Instead, appellant's alleged mistaken beliefs were merely facts relevant to whether he was justified in intentionally or knowingly pointing the rifle at Dunham to create such fear of imminent bodily injury; i.e., whether he acted in self-defense based on a reasonable belief such force or threat of force was immediately necessary to protect himself against Dunham's use or attempted use of unlawful force.

Id. at *10.

In contrast, the court of criminal appeals determined in *Granger* that the trial court erred in refusing the appellant's requested mistake of fact instruction where the evidence demonstrated appellant had killed a person by shooting into a car but also testified that, at the time he fired the shots, he believed the car was unoccupied. *Granger*, 3 S.W.3d at 37–39. "'When an accused creates an issue of mistaken belief *as to the culpable mental element of the offense*, he is entitled to a defensive instruction of 'mistake of fact.'" *Id.* at 41 (emphasis added) (quoting *Miller v. State*, 815 S.W.2d 582, 585 (Tex. Crim. App. 1991)).

Here, Guyger asserts her mistaken beliefs that she had entered her own apartment and that Jean was an intruder negate her culpable intent to commit murder because "although she intentionally and knowingly caused Jean's death, she had the right to act in deadly force in self-defense" under penal code section 9.32(b), and "deadly force was immediately necessary and reasonable under the circumstances." However, as in *Rocha* . . . the mistaken facts upon which Guyger relies are relevant only to whether Guyger was justified in shooting Jean. Guyger's right to act in self-defense, if applicable, did not negate her intent to kill Jean; self-defense instead would have *justified* the shooting.

. . . We conclude the hypothetically correct jury charge should not have included a mistake of fact instruction. Accordingly, the mistake of fact issue is not part of our analysis of the sufficiency of the evidence to support Guyger's murder conviction. *See Malik* [*v. State*], 953 S.W.2d at 240.

B. Self-Defense

Guyger also argues that a reasonable jury could not have rejected self-defense as a justification for her use of deadly force. Acquittal premised on self-defense required Guyger to produce evidence that she reasonably believed deadly force was immediately necessary to protect herself from Jean's use or attempted use of unlawful force. *See* Tex. Pen. Code §§ 9.31(a), 9.32(a)(1), 9.32(a)(2). An actor's belief that deadly force was immediately necessary is presumed to be reasonable if the actor:

(1) knew or had reason to believe that the person against whom the deadly force was used:

(A) unlawfully and with force entered, or was attempting to enter unlawfully and with force, the actor's occupied habitation, vehicle, or place of business or employment;

(b) unlawfully and with force removed, or was attempting to remove unlawfully and with force, the actor from the actor's habitation, vehicle, or place of business or employment; or

(c) was committing or attempting to commit an offense described by Subsection (a)(2)(B).

(2) did not provoke the person against whom the force was used; and

(3) was not otherwise engaged in criminal activity, other than a Class C misdemeanor that is a violation of a law or ordinance regulating traffic at the time the force was used.

Tex. Pen. Code § 9.32(b).

Under these provisions, the jury did not need to find that Jean was using or attempting to use unlawful deadly force for Guyger's right of self-defense to exist. It could determine instead that she reasonably believed, from her standpoint at the time of the shooting, "that deadly force, when and to the degree used . . . was immediately necessary to protect [herself] against the use or attempted use of unlawful deadly force" by Jean. *Id.*; *Jones v. State*, 544 S.W.2d 139, 142 (Tex. Crim. App. 1976).

In making this argument, Guyger relies on her mistaken belief that she was in her own apartment to support the reasonableness of her belief that Jean posed an imminent threat. Mistake of fact, however, plays no role in self-defense — the former addresses Guyger's culpable mental state; the latter addresses the circumstances and reasonableness of Guyger's conduct. Guyger's argument thus bootstraps mistake of fact to reach the section 9.32(b) presumption of reasonableness. As discussed below, we conclude sufficient evidence defeated the presumption and also supports the jury's rejection of this defense because a reasonable jury could have determined Guyger's belief that deadly force was immediately necessary was not reasonable.

The jury could reasonably have determined beyond a reasonable doubt that Jean had not unlawfully and with force entered Guyger's occupied home or attempted to murder her. Indeed, Guyger points to no evidence suggesting either scenario occurred. Instead, she relies on her *mistaken belief* that she was in her own apartment. The jury's rejection of Guyger's self-defense argument finds ample support in the record. It is undisputed that Jean was in his home and was not attempting to unlawfully enter Guyger's apartment. Further, Guyger admitted that she could have taken a position of cover and concealment while she called for backup rather than shooting Jean . . .

Other evidence also supports the jury's rejection of self-defense. This evidence includes the conflicting evidence as to whether Jean was seated or rising from a sitting position rather than standing and moving quickly towards Guyger; the conflicting evidence as to whether Guyger demanded that Jean show his hands[3]; the absence of any pockets in which Jean's hands might have been concealed; the ambiguous nature of Jean's "hey, hey, hey" exclamation; and the lack of evidence suggesting Jean held a weapon. *See Braughton*, 569 S.W.3d at 610 (jury could rationally have rejected appellant's "reason to believe" decedent was committing or attempting to commit robbery or murder given conflicting evidence and jury's resolution of factual disputes); *Saxton v. State*, 804 S.W.2d 910, 914 (Tex. Crim. App. 1991) (concluding a rational jury could have found beyond a reasonable doubt appellant did not act in self-defense where the victim was unarmed when he lunged at appellant, appellant said at the scene that the shooting occurred accidentally, and the evidence showed hammer on weapon had to be fully cocked to fire); *Sharp v. State*, 707 S.W.2d 611, 614 (Tex. Crim. App. 1986) (jury may choose to believe or not believe the witnesses, or any portion of their testimony). On this record, we conclude the evidence was legally sufficient to support the jury's rejection of Guyger's assertion of self-defense.

---

3. Although Guyger testified she told Jean to show his hands and he did not show his hands, other witnesses including Bharathamarnath Madamanchi, Taydra Jones, and Whitney Hughes testified they heard two shots but did not hear Guyger tell Jean to show his hands.

We overrule Guyger's first issue. In reaching this conclusion, we need not address the State's cross-point.[4]

Notes and Questions

1. Did the defendant's mistake about whose apartment she was in have any impact on whether she intended to kill when she shot the victim? If not, do you understand why the trial court properly denied a mistake of fact instruction?

2. What do you think was the most compelling evidence contradicting the claim of self-defense?

III. Other Variants of Self-Defense

The basic requirements of homicidal self-defense extend, with some slight variations, to the protection of other interests from unlawful threats.

A. Defense of Others

Intervening to defend someone else from an unlawful actual or imminent threat is legally privileged, just as self-defense is. In such a situation, so long as the intervenor uses reasonably proportional force, the infliction of death or injury on the aggressor is legally justified. Like homicidal self-defense, the use of deadly force is justified only in response to a reasonably perceived threat of death or great bodily harm.

Intervening to defend another does, however, involve another layer of judgment: who is the victim and who is the aggressor? It is not hard to imagine a situation where a Good Samaritan witnesses a struggle and makes a quick assumption about who is the victim. If that person intervenes and uses force, what happens if it turns out the person protected — the assumed victim — was, in fact, the first aggressor with no right of self-defense? Should this also deprive the Good Samaritan of the claim to defense of others?

The common law answer was yes. Known as the alter ego rule, the right to defend another was no greater or less than the right of the beneficiary of the intervention to defend him or herself; the intervenor stepped into the shoes of the person protected.

---

4. *See* Tex. R. App. P. 47.1; *see also Pfeiffer v. State*, 363 S.W.3d 594, 601 (Tex. Crim. App. 2012) ("[i]f the defendant is granted no relief and no retrial will therefore be held, the State will not be able to benefit from a favorable decision on its cross-points of error."); *Seghelmeble v. State*, 390 S.W.3d 576, 582–83 (Tex. App. — Dallas 2012, pet. ref'd) (appellate court may not address cross-issue "in which the State merely requests a directive as to language or reasoning of the lower court that does not impact the ultimate decision.") (quoting *Pfeiffer*, 363 S.W.3d at 601 n.32).

This creates a risk of injustice when the assumption of who was the victim and who was the aggressor was objectively reasonable under the circumstances. Accordingly, the modern approach is to apply the same reasonable judgment test to this decision as is applied to other aspects of self-defense. In short, a defendant may end up intervening to protect someone not entitled to claim self-defense, but so long as the assumption of necessity was reasonable and the amount of force used proportional, the intervention was legally justified.

B. Non-Homicidal Self-Defense

Like homicidal self-defense, an individual is legally justified in using force to defend against an actual or imminent threat of unlawful non-homicidal violence. However, because only proportional force may be used, there is no justification for using lethal force in response to a non-lethal threat. Remember, however, that the test of necessity is *ex ante*, meaning the assessment of the nature of the unlawful threat is not based on what the defendant actually confronted, but on what the defendant reasonably perceived at the time of the decision. As one instruction explains, "[T]he test here is whether, under the same facts and circumstances in this case, any reasonably prudent person faced with the same situation would have believed that (he) (she) would immediately be physically harmed."

There may be situations where a defendant responds to a non-lethal threat with non-lethal force that results in the accidental death of the victim. For example, during a bar-room brawl, a defendant may react to someone about to punch him by punching the aggressor in the face. If the aggressor falls and dies as a result of hitting his head on the ground, how will this impact the claim of self-defense? So long as the defendant was justified in using the non-homicidal force, the unintended death of the victim does not nullify the defense. Consider this instruction:

> In deciding the remaining elements of the defense of self-defense, you must determine whether the force used by the accused was proper. You are advised that a person who anticipates an assault may stand (his) (her) ground and resist force with force. In protecting (himself) (herself), a person is not required to use exactly the same type or amount of force used by the attacker. With the following principles in mind, you must decide whether the force used by the accused was legal. The accused cannot use more force than (he) (she) actually believed was necessary to protect (himself) (herself).

> To determine the accused's actual belief as to the amount of force that was necessary, you must look at the situation through the eyes of the accused. In addition to the circumstances known to the accused at the time, the accused's (age) (intelligence) (emotional control) (_____) are all important factors in determining the accused's actual belief about the amount of force required to protect (himself) (herself). Next, the accused

must not have used force likely to produce death or grievous bodily harm. Additionally, the accused must not have intended to cause the death of (state the name of the alleged victim). Finally, the death of (state the name of the alleged victim) must not have been a reasonably foreseeable result of the force used by the accused.

C. Defense of Property

An individual is legally privileged to use reasonably proportional force to defend property from theft or destruction. However, because the common law valued life — even the life of a thief — over property, the use of deadly force was never justified for the *sole* purpose of protecting property (however, when the threat to property indicates a threat of death or great bodily harm to the defendant, use of deadly force would be justified in self-defense).

Because deadly force was never considered necessary just to protect property, the use of trap guns or deadly mechanical devices to protect property is considered *per se* excessive. Even assuming a defendant would have been justified in the use of deadly force had she made the use of force judgment, the inability of such a mechanical device to distinguish between a lethal and non-lethal threat renders the use of the device legally unjustified. However, the use of devices designed to inflict non-lethal injury to protect property is legally justified.

D. Transferred Justification

The justification of self-defense can transfer to an unintended victim, analogous to the doctrine of transferred intent. If a defendant acts in self-defense and accidentally kills or injures someone other than the unlawful aggressor, the self-dense justification would extend to that victim. However, if the manner in which the defendant exercises the right of self-defense (or defense of another) is reckless or grossly negligent resulting in death or injury of an innocent victim, the justification would not negate culpability for an offense based on that level of mens rea. This is reflected in the following instruction on accident:

> If the accused was doing a lawful act in a lawful manner free of any negligence on (his) (her) part, and (an) unexpected (death) (bodily harm) (_____) occurs, the accused is not criminally liable. The defense of accident has three parts. First, the accused's (act(s)) (and) (or) (failure to act) resulting in the (death) (bodily harm) (_____) must have been lawful. Second, the accused must not have been negligent. In other words, the accused must have been acting with the amount of care for the safety of others that a reasonably prudent person would have used under the same or similar circumstances. Third, the (death) (bodily harm) (____) must have been unforeseeable and unintentional.

IV. Imperfect Self-Defense

The common law justification of self-defense, as already noted, required an honest and reasonable judgment of necessity. A subjectively honest judgment of necessity that is determined by the fact-finder to have been unreasonable under the circumstances was not a defense. Hence, unless the claim of self-defense was *perfect* — meaning the judgment was both honest and reasonable — the intent to kill would establish the malice necessary for murder (or for attempted murder if the victim survived).

But should a defendant who honestly believed the use of force was necessary be guilty of murder because the belief was objectively unreasonable? In other words, should a reckless judgment of self-defense necessity — reckless because a reasonable person in the same situation would not have resorted to self-help — result in the same level of culpability as would apply if the defendant didn't even believe self-defense was justified? Just imagine Ms. Wanrow from the earlier case is retried. If the jury concludes that she honestly believed she needed to act in self-defense when she shot and killed the victim, but that her belief was unreasonable under the circumstances because he was not armed and not at that moment acting aggressively, should she be guilty of murder?

At common law, the answer was yes. But as the next case illustrates, many jurisdictions have softened this outcome by implementing what is known as *imperfect* self-defense, most commonly based on an honest but objectively unreasonable judgment of homicidal necessity.

State v. Faulkner

483 A.2d 759 (1984)
Maryland Court of Appeals

The twin issues we shall decide in this case are whether Maryland recognizes the mitigation defense of "imperfect self-defense" and, if so, whether that defense applies to the statutory offense of assault with intent to murder under Maryland Code, Art. 27, §12.

We set forth a shortened version of the facts that give rise to these issues. On September 15, 1981, the Emanuel brothers, Jimmy and Rickey, became embroiled in an argument with Melvin J. Faulkner, Jr. outside of a Baltimore City bar. This argument quickly escalated into a fight between Jimmy and Faulkner. Because Faulkner believed that Jimmy was armed with a knife, Faulkner produced a handgun and began firing. Faulkner, however, shot Rickey twice in the chest as Rickey tried to push his brother from the handgun's line of fire. The testimony reflects considerable conflict as to what led Faulkner to believe that Jimmy was armed with a knife, which participant was the aggressor at various stages of this imbroglio, who entered into the melee mutually and willfully, and who was simply acting in self-defense.

Faulkner was charged with assault with intent to murder and related offenses. At his trial in the Criminal Court of Baltimore (now Circuit Court for Baltimore City), the court instructed the jury as to the defenses of justification by way of self-defense and mitigation by way of hot-blooded response to the provocation of mutual combat. The court, however, declined Faulkner's request that the jury also be instructed as to the defense of "imperfect self-defense." The jury subsequently found Faulkner guilty of assault with intent to murder and related handgun offenses. In a divided decision, the Court of Special Appeals reversed, holding that the trial court erred in refusing to instruct the jury as to the defense of imperfect self-defense. *Faulkner v. State,* 54 Md. App. 113, 458 A.2d 81 (1983). We granted the State's petition for a writ of certiorari to address the important issues presented.

I

Initially, we note that the difference between murder and manslaughter is the presence or absence of malice. Self-defense operates as a complete defense to either murder or manslaughter. A successful self-defense, therefore, results in the acquittal of the defendant. We have summarized the elements necessary to justify a homicide, other than felony murder, on the basis of self-defense in the following terms:

> (1) The accused must have had reasonable grounds to believe himself in apparent imminent or immediate danger of death or serious bodily harm from his assailant or potential assailant;

> (2) The accused must have in fact believed himself in this danger;

> (3) The accused claiming the right of self-defense must not have been the aggressor or provoked the conflict; and

> (4) The force used must have not been unreasonable and excessive; that is, the force must not have been more force than the exigency demanded.

Imperfect self-defense, by contrast, is not a complete defense. Its chief characteristic is that it operates to negate malice, an element the State must prove to establish murder. As a result, the successful invocation of this doctrine does not completely exonerate the defendant, but mitigates murder to voluntary manslaughter.

There are other types of defenses that mitigate murder to manslaughter but do not fall under the umbrella of imperfect self-defense. Commonly regarded as falling within this group are killings stemming from a heat of passion, such as (1) discovering a spouse in the act of sexual intercourse with another; (2) mutual combat; and (3) assault and battery. These acts, because they create passion in the defendant and are not the product of a free will, negate malice and thus mitigate a homicide to manslaughter.

Imperfect self-defense, however, is different from either self-defense or the commonly recognized mitigation defenses. Because the doctrine of imperfect self-defense has been subjected to different interpretations and regarded by some courts and scholars as being a recent theory not far advanced, we believe a brief examination of its history and development will help clarify its nature and scope and point out the differences.

The rudimentary principles of imperfect self-defense appeared in a series of manslaughter statutes enacted in England between 1496 and 1547. *See* R. Moreland, *The Law of Homicide* 91 (1952). According to Professor Moreland, these statutes reflected a compromise between murder and complete exoneration in those instances where a defendant's conduct warranted neither a murder conviction nor an acquittal. Out of these statutes arose the mitigating defense of imperfect self-defense, which was predicated upon a "fear of life." Imperfect self-defense was applicable to a crime *without* passion so as to distinguish it from the mitigation defense founded upon heat of passion. However, because the defendant was at fault the law demanded that he bear some criminal responsibility for the homicide although he lacked the requisite mens rea for murder. Professor Moreland put it this way:

> In each case [homicide arising from provocation (crime of passion) and one arising from a "fear of life" (crime without passion)] the accused might well be held for murder or he might be excused because of the circumstances for committing the crime; but the law compromises, takes a middle ground, and holds him guilty of manslaughter. Thus, in the case of imperfect self-defense, the law might refuse him the opportunity to plead self-defense because of his fault and hold him guilty of murder, or it might waive his fault and allow him to utilize the excuse of self-defense. Balancing the two, the law strikes a middle ground as a matter of policy and rather reasonably convicts him of voluntary manslaughter.

Id. at 92.

In concert with the above, Professor Perkins recognized that manslaughter is a "catch-all" concept that encompasses a variety of homicides that are "neither murder nor innocent." R. Perkins, *Criminal Law* 69 (2d ed. 1969). In elaborating upon this proposition, Professor Perkins explained:

> Since manslaughter is a "catch-all" concept, covering all homicides which are neither murder nor innocent, it logically includes some killings involving other types of mitigation, and such is the rule of the common law. For example, if one man kills another intentionally, under circumstances beyond the scope of innocent homicide, the facts may come so close to justification or excuse that the killing will be classed as voluntary manslaughter rather than murder. "It is not always necessary to show that the killing was done in the heat of passion, to reduce the crime to manslaughter;" said the Arkansas court, "for, where the killing was done because the slayer believes that he is in great danger, but the facts do not warrant such a belief, it may be murder or manslaughter according to the circumstances, even though there be no passion." To give another illustration, the intentional taking of human life to

prevent crime may fall a little short of complete justification or excuse and still be without malice aforethought.

Id. at 69-70.

The doctrine of imperfect self-defense gained a foothold in the United States in the late 1800s. The "cornerstone" case for this defense is an 1882 decision by the Court of Criminal Appeals of Texas. *Reed v. State,* 11 Tex.Crim. App. 509 (1882). In discussing the doctrine the *Reed* court remarked:

> It [self-defense] may be divided into two general classes, to wit, perfect and imperfect right of self-defense. . . . If, however, [the defendant] was in the wrong, — if he was himself violating or in the act of violating the law, — and on account of his own wrong was placed in a situation wherein it became necessary for him to defend himself against an attack made upon himself which was superinduced or created by his own wrong, then the law justly limits his right of self-defense, and regulates it according to the magnitude of his own wrong. Such a state of case may be said to illustrate and determine what in law would be denominated the imperfect right of self-defense. Whenever a party by his own wrongful act produces a condition of things wherein it becomes necessary for his own safety that he should take life or do serious bodily harm, then indeed the law wisely imputes to him his own wrong and its consequences to the extent that they may and should be considered in determining the grade of offense which but for such acts would never have been occasioned.

Id. at 517-18. Shortly after *Reed,* courts fashioned three variations of the doctrine.

First, some courts indicated that the doctrine would apply where the homicide would fall within the perfect self-defense doctrine but for the fault of the defendant in provoking or initiating the difficulty at the non-deadly force level. *E.g., Allison v. State,* 74 Ark. 444, 86 S.W. 409 (1905) (dictum); *Reed v. State, supra; State v. Flory,* 40 Wyo. 184, 276 P. 458 (1929) (dictum). Second, courts noted that the doctrine would apply when the defendant committed a homicide because of an honest but unreasonable belief that he was about to suffer death or serious bodily harm. *E.g., Allison v. State, supra* (dictum); *State v. Thomas,* 184 N.C. 757, 114 S.E. 834 (1922). Third, other courts recognized the doctrine when the defendant used unreasonable force in defending himself and, as a result, killed his opponent. *See, e.g., State v. Clark,* 69 Kan. 576, 77 P. 287 (1904).

Since the acceptance of this doctrine by several jurisdictions during the late 1800s and early 1900s, comparatively few modern jurisdictions have analyzed the doctrine. Of those jurisdictions that have considered the doctrine in recent times, however, several have adopted the honest but unreasonable belief variation of the imperfect self-defense doctrine. For example, in providing a comprehensive discussion of the honest but unreasonable belief standard, the Supreme Court of California in *People v. Flannel,* 603 P.2d 1 (Cal. 1979), sought to eliminate the "obfuscat[ion] by infrequent reference and inadequate elucidation" of what it characterized as a unique rule. *Id.* at 8. Consistent with Professor Moreland's view, the *Flannel* court observed that the unreasonable belief theory of imperfect self-defense is not limited by or bound up with the concept of the mitigating defense of heat of passion.

In addition, the court explained that the reasonableness of an individual's honest belief that he needs to repel imminent peril or bodily injury simply goes to the justification for the homicide. Moreover, the *Flannel* court emphasized the weighing of competing interests in determining the applicability of this mitigation defense. In writing for the court, Justice Tobriner observed:

> [T]he state has no legitimate interest in obtaining a conviction of murder when, by virtue of defendant's unreasonable belief, the jury entertains a reasonable doubt whether defendant harbored malice. Likewise, a defendant has no legitimate interest in complete exculpation when acting outside the range of reasonable behavior. The vice is the element of malice; in its absence the level of guilt must decline.

Id. at 7. This reasoning is persuasive because it recognizes that a defendant's culpability for a homicide be mitigated when he lacks the requisite mens rea for the offense of murder. Jurisdictions in addition to California have likewise recognized the honest but unreasonable belief standard on the basis of decisional law. *Hartfield v. State,* 176 Miss. 776 (1936); *Wood v. State,* 486 P.2d 750 (Okla. Crim. App. 1971).

North Carolina has carefully articulated a formula-based standard for determining whether a defendant charged with murder is entitled to an instruction on the doctrine of imperfect self-defense. This standard, unique in its clarity, uses the elements of perfect self-defense as its benchmark. Under this approach, perfect self-defense excuses a homicide when it is shown that, at the time of the homicide, the:

> (1) Defendant subjectively believed it necessary to kill the deceased to save himself from death or great bodily harm;
>
> (2) Defendant's belief was objectively reasonable;
>
> (3) Defendant was not the aggressor in bringing on the affray, *i.e.,* he did not aggressively and willingly enter into the fight without legal excuse or provocation; and
>
> (4) Defendant did not use excessive force.

Imperfect self-defense, by contrast, arises when only elements (1) and (2) above are present. *State v. Bush,* 297 S.E.2d 563, 568 (N.C. 1982). The *Bush* court elaborated upon its standard in the following terms:

> [I]f the defendant believed it was necessary to kill the deceased in order to save himself from death or great bodily harm, and the defendant's belief was reasonable because the circumstances at the time were sufficient to create such a belief in the mind of a person of ordinary firmness, but the defendant, although without murderous intent, was the aggressor or used

excessive force, the defendant would have lost the benefit of perfect self-defense. In this situation he would have shown only that he exercised the imperfect right of self-defense and would remain guilty of at least voluntary manslaughter. However, both elements (1) and (2) [above] must be shown to exist before the defendant will be entitled to the benefit of either perfect or imperfect self-defense.

Id.

This particular formulation, which evidently has not been adopted by other jurisdictions, does not embrace the honest but unreasonable belief standard because a defendant must both objectively and subjectively believe that he must resort to deadly force to prevent death or serious bodily harm. Only if the defendant satisfies these two criteria may he invoke the imperfect self-defense doctrine if he was the initial aggressor or used excessive force in defending himself. In sum, although several jurisdictions have adopted the doctrine by means of case law, they are not in agreement as to the standard that should be applied.

Many states that recognize the doctrine on the basis of statutory law have adopted the subjectively honest but objectively unreasonable standard of the imperfect self-defense doctrine. Ill. Ann. Stat. ch. 38, § 9-2 (Smith-Hurd Supp. 1984–1985); 18 Pa. Cons. Stat. Ann. § 2503(b) (Purdon 1983); Tex. Penal Code Ann. § 9.32 (Vernon Supp. 1984); Wis. Stat. Ann. § 940.05(2) (West 1982).

Recognizing that an "imperfect" defense of duress may not exculpate a defendant in an unlawful homicide case but may supply that mitigation necessary to lower the degree of guilt from murder to manslaughter, we conclude that the appellant here had a genuine jury issue as to mitigation. As a result, the jury instruction which improperly placed upon her the burden of proving mitigation and which improperly relieved the State of its burden of proving the element of non-mitigation beyond a reasonable doubt requires a reversal.

In the last of the 1975 spate of imperfect defense cases, the Court of Special Appeals once again held that the evidence presented at trial generated the issue of mitigation by way of imperfect defense of habitation. *Law v. State*, 349 A.2d 295 (Md. Ct. Spec. App. 1975). Factually, the defendant, Law, got out of bed and went downstairs late one evening to investigate some noises outside. Law retrieved a shotgun he had bought for "home protection" two weeks earlier after his house had been burglarized. After hearing a scraping of his windowpane on his back porch and a voice saying "Let's go in," Law fired his shotgun toward the back door at waist level. The shotgun blast struck and killed a police officer who was trying to enter the house to investigate a suspected burglary attempt. Unknown to Law, his neighbor had summoned police to report a suspected burglary attempt.

Law was eventually convicted in a non-jury trial of second-degree murder and assault with intent to murder. On appeal the Court of Special Appeals concluded that these facts, specifically Law's mistaken belief that his home was about to be burglarized, raised the issue of mitigation by way of imperfect defense of habitation. As a consequence, the court reversed the judgments and remanded the case for a new trial.

Our review of the development of the imperfect defense doctrine and examination of the jurisdictions that have addressed circumstances when the doctrine is applicable convinces us that the honest but unreasonable belief standard of imperfect self-defense is the proper one to be followed in Maryland. In *Faulkner v. State, supra,* Judge Orth (specially assigned) clearly articulated for the intermediate appellate court the ingredients of that defense. He stated:

> Perfect self-defense requires not only that the killer subjectively believed that his actions were necessary for his safety but, objectively, that a reasonable man would so consider them. Imperfect self-defense, however, requires no more than a subjective honest belief on the part of the killer that his actions were necessary for his safety, even though, on an objective appraisal by a reasonable man, they would not be found to be so. If established, the killer remains culpable and his actions are excused only to the extent that mitigation is invoked.

Id. 54 Md. App. at 115, 458 A.2d 81.

We agree that this statement represents an analytically sound view, and reflects the position taken by a majority of those jurisdictions that have addressed and embraced this defense. Logically, a defendant who commits a homicide while honestly, though unreasonably, believing that he is threatened with death or serious bodily harm, does not act with malice. Absent malice he cannot be convicted of murder. Nevertheless, because the killing was committed without justification or excuse, the defendant is not entitled to full exoneration. Therefore, as we see it, when evidence is presented showing the defendant's subjective belief that the use of force was necessary to prevent imminent death or serious bodily harm, the defendant is entitled to a proper instruction on imperfect self-defense.

A proper instruction when such evidence is present would enable the jury to reach one of several verdicts: (1) if the jury concluded the defendant did not have a subjective belief that the use of deadly force was necessary, its verdict would be murder; (2) if the jury concluded that the defendant had a reasonable subjective belief, its verdict would be not guilty; and (3) if the jury concluded that the defendant honestly believed that the use of force was necessary but that this subjective belief was unreasonable under the circumstances, then its verdict would be guilty of voluntary manslaughter. The reason courts have reached the third conclusion is that the conduct of the defendant in these circumstances negates the presence of malice, a prerequisite to a finding of murder, but the defendant is nevertheless to blame for the homicide and should not be rewarded for his unreasonable conduct.

JUDGMENT OF THE COURT OF SPECIAL APPEALS AFFIRMED.

Imperfect Self-Defense and the Model Penal Code

Recall that the MPC abandoned the term "malice" as the essential mental element for murder. But if imperfect self-defense negates malice, does that mean the theory is inapplicable in an MPC-based jurisdiction? No.

In such a jurisdiction, the question for the fact-finder will not be whether the honest but unreasonable judgment of necessity negates malice; it will be whether the killing was the result of a reckless judgment. If it was, the appropriate outcome would be a manslaughter conviction: the unlawful killing of a human being as the result of reckless conduct.

Accordingly, the outcome of a claim of imperfect self-defense in an MPC jurisdiction would be identical to that of a common law jurisdiction, only reached through a different methodology: the defendant's honest belief of self-defense necessity would negate the purpose to commit an *unlawful* killing, but if that belief were unreasonable, it would indicate the killing was the result of a reckless judgment.

Visualizing Self-Defense

Self Defense

Did Defendant actually and reasonably believe that using force was necessary under the circumstances?

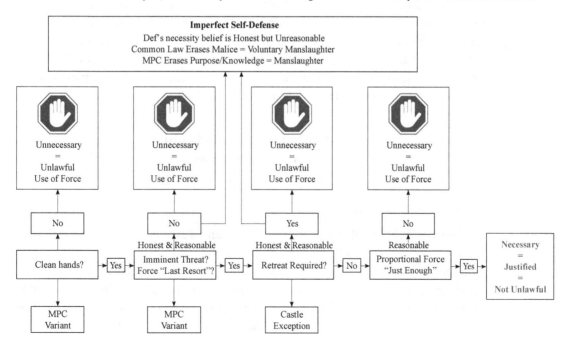

V. General Necessity

In some rare situations, a defendant may decide to break the law in order to avoid a greater harm. The general necessity defense would apply as a justification in such a situation. Like self-defense, necessity is a "greater good" defense: breaking the law produces a greater good than would complying with the law. Unlike self-defense, the triggering force is not produced by the unlawful conduct of another person. Instead, in most cases, it will be a natural force — a flood, a fire, an illness, an accidental injury — that will trigger the necessity to break the law. When a defendant makes an honest and reasonable judgment that breaking the law is necessary to avert an immediate greater harm and that there is no reasonable alternative to doing so, the conduct will be legally justified.

To illustrate, imagine a parent is watching his son play a high school football scrimmage. The father happens to be a physician. During the scrimmage, a player is hit in the neck by an opponent and suffers a crushed larynx. As a result, the player cannot breathe. Now imagine the father runs onto the field and tells the coach to bring him a knife and a ballpoint pen. While the injured player lies on the field, the father performs an emergency tracheotomy, cutting the player's throat and inserting the pen reservoir so the player can breathe, thus saving his life.

No one would question the physician's judgment that inflicting a battery on the injured player was necessary to avert the greater harm of his death. Indeed, the physician would probably be hailed as a hero. This reveals the essence of necessity: some force compels an individual to break the law but in so doing, the individual is acting in a way that society approves of, if not celebrates. Even when the outcome is not as hoped for by the actor — for example, in the above hypothetical, if the player dies because the procedure is unsuccessful — the necessity of the situation will justify the conduct, therefore negating any criminality. But like self-defense, the defense of necessity requires satisfaction of a number of requirements or elements; the absence of any one element will negate the efficacy of the defense.

United States v. Schoon

955 F.2d 1238 (1992)

Ninth Circuit Court of Appeals

BOOCHEVER, Circuit Judge:

Gregory Schoon, Raymond Kennon, Jr., and Patricia Manning appeal their convictions for obstructing activities of the Internal Revenue Service Office in Tucson, Arizona, and failing to comply with an order of a federal police officer. Both charges stem from their activities in protest of United States involvement in El Salvador. They claim the district court improperly denied them a necessity defense. Because we hold the necessity defense inapplicable in cases like this, we affirm.

I

On December 4, 1989, thirty people, including appellants, gained admittance to the IRS office in Tucson, where they chanted "keep America's tax dollars out of El Salvador," splashed simulated blood on the counters, walls, and carpeting, and generally obstructed the office's operation. After a federal police officer ordered the group, on several occasions, to disperse or face arrest, appellants were arrested.

At a bench trial, appellants proffered testimony about conditions in El Salvador as the motivation for their conduct. They attempted to assert a necessity defense, essentially contending that their acts in protest of American involvement in El Salvador were necessary to avoid further bloodshed in that country. While finding appellants motivated solely by humanitarian concerns, the court nonetheless precluded the defense as a matter of law, relying on Ninth Circuit precedent. The sole issue on appeal is the propriety of the court's exclusion of a necessity defense as a matter of law.

II

A district court may preclude a necessity defense where "the evidence, as described in the defendant's offer of proof, is insufficient as a matter of law to support the proffered defense." *United States v. Dorrell,* 758 F.2d 427, 430 (9th Cir. 1985). To invoke the necessity defense, therefore, the defendants colorably must have shown that: (1) they were faced with a choice of evils and chose the lesser evil; (2) they acted to prevent imminent harm; (3) they reasonably anticipated a direct causal relationship between their conduct and the harm to be averted; and (4) they had no legal alternatives to violating the law. *United States v. Aguilar,* 883 F.2d 662, 693 (9th Cir. 1989). We review *de novo* the district court's decision to bar a necessity defense.

The district court denied the necessity defense on the grounds that (1) the requisite immediacy was lacking; (2) the actions taken would not abate the evil; and (3) other legal alternatives existed. Because the threshold test for admissibility of a necessity defense is a conjunctive one, a court may preclude invocation of the defense if "proof is deficient with regard to any of the four elements." *Id.* at 693.

While we could affirm substantially on those grounds relied upon by the district court, we find a deeper, systemic reason for the complete absence of federal case law recognizing a necessity defense in an indirect civil disobedience case. As used in this opinion, "civil disobedience" is the wilful violation of a law, undertaken for the purpose of social or political protest. Indirect civil disobedience involves violating a law or interfering with a government policy that is not, itself, the object of protest. Direct civil disobedience, on the other hand, involves protesting the existence of a law by breaking that law or by preventing the execution of that law in a specific instance in which a particularized harm would otherwise follow. This case involves indirect civil disobedience because these protestors were not challenging the laws under which they were charged. In contrast, the civil rights lunch counter sit-ins, for example, constituted direct civil disobedience because the protestors were challenging the rule that prevented them from sitting at lunch counters. Similarly, if a city council passed an ordinance requiring immediate infusion of a suspected carcinogen into the drinking water, physically blocking the delivery of the substance would constitute direct civil disobedience: protestors would be preventing the execution of a law in a specific instance in which a particularized harm — contamination of the water supply — would otherwise follow.

While our prior cases consistently have found the elements of the necessity defense lacking in cases involving indirect civil disobedience, we have never addressed specifically whether the defense is available in cases of indirect civil disobedience. Indeed, some other courts have appeared doubtful. *See, e.g., United States v. Seward*, 687 F.2d 1270, 1276 (10th Cir. 1982) ("Necessity is obviously not a defense to charges arising from a typical protest."); *United States v. Kroncke,* 459 F.2d 697, 701 (8th Cir. 1972) ("None of the cases even suggests that the defense of necessity would be permitted where the actor's purpose is to effect a change in governmental policies which, according to the actor, may in turn result in a future saving of lives."). Today, we conclude, for the reasons stated below, that the necessity defense is inapplicable to cases involving indirect civil disobedience.

III

Necessity is, essentially, a utilitarian defense. It therefore justifies criminal acts taken to avert a greater harm, maximizing social welfare by allowing a crime to be committed where the social benefits of the crime outweigh the social costs of failing to commit the crime. *See, e.g., Dorrell,* 758 F.2d at 432 (recognizing that "the policy underlying the necessity defense is the promotion of greater values at the expense of lesser values"). Pursuant to the defense, prisoners could escape a burning prison, *see, e.g., Baender v. Barnett,* 255 U.S. 224, 226 (1921); a person lost in the woods could steal food from a cabin to survive, *see* Posner, *An Economic Theory of the Criminal Law,* 85 Colum. L. Rev. 1193, 1205 (1985); an embargo could be violated because adverse weather conditions necessitated sale of the cargo at a foreign port, *see The William Gray,* 29 F.Cas. 1300, 1302 (C.C.D.N.Y. 1810); a crew could mutiny where their ship was thought to be unseaworthy, *see United States v. Ashton,* 24 F.Cas. 873, 874 (C.C.D.Mass. 1834); and property could be destroyed to prevent the spread of fire, *see, e.g., Surocco v. Geary,* 3 Cal. 69, 74 (1853).

What all the traditional necessity cases have in common is that the commission of the "crime" averted the occurrence of an even greater "harm." In some sense, the necessity defense allows us to act as individual legislatures, amending a particular criminal provision or crafting a one-time exception to it, subject to court review, when a real legislature would formally do the same under those circumstances. For example, by allowing prisoners who escape a burning jail to claim the justification of necessity, we assume the lawmaker, confronting this problem, would have allowed for an exception to the law proscribing prison escapes.

Because the necessity doctrine is utilitarian, however, strict requirements contain its exercise so as to prevent nonbeneficial criminal conduct. For example, "if the criminal act cannot abate the threatened harm, society receives no benefit from the criminal conduct." *Applying the Necessity Defense,* 64 N.Y.U. L. Rev. at 102 (quoting *United States v. Gant,* 691 F.2d 1159, 1164 (5th Cir. 1982)). Similarly, to forgive a crime taken to avert a lesser harm would fail to maximize social utility. The cost of the crime would outweigh the harm averted by its commission. Likewise, criminal acts cannot be condoned to thwart threats, yet to be imminent, or those for which there are legal alternatives to abate the harm.

Analysis of three of the necessity defense's four elements leads us to the conclusion that necessity can never be proved in a case of indirect civil disobedience. We do not rely upon the imminent harm prong of the defense because we believe there can be indirect civil disobedience cases in which the protested harm is imminent.

A

1. Balance of Harms

It is axiomatic that, if the thing to be averted is not a harm at all, the balance of harms necessarily would disfavor any criminal action. Indirect civil disobedience seeks first and foremost to bring about the repeal of a law or a change of governmental policy, attempting to mobilize public opinion through typically symbolic action. These protestors violate a law, not because it is unconstitutional or otherwise improper, but because doing so calls public attention to their objectives. Thus, the most immediate "harm" this form of protest targets is the *existence* of the law or policy. However, the mere existence of a constitutional law or governmental policy cannot constitute a legally cognizable harm. *See* Comment, *Political Protest and the Illinois Defense of Necessity,* 54 U. Chi. L. Rev. 1070, 1083 (1987) ("In a society based on democratic decision making, this is how values are ranked — a protester cannot simply assert that her view of what is best should trump the decision of the majority of elected representatives."); *cf. Dorrell,* 758 F.2d at 432 ("The law should not excuse criminal activity intended to express the protestor's disagreement with positions reached by the lawmaking branches of the government.").

There may be, of course, general harms that result from the targeted law or policy. Such generalized "harm," however, is too insubstantial an injury to be legally cognizable. We have in the past rejected the use of the necessity defense in indirect civil disobedience cases as a "'back door' attempt to attack government programs in a manner foreclosed by federal standing requirements." *United States v. Lowe,* 654 F.2d 562, 566-67 (9th Cir. 1981) (citing *Schlesinger v. Reservists Committee to Stop the War,* 418 U.S. 208, 220-21 (1974) (standing to attack governmental conduct requires direct, concrete injury; abstract injury insufficient)). The law could not function were people allowed to rely on their *subjective* beliefs and value judgments in determining which harms justified the taking of criminal action. *See United*

States v. Moylan, 417 F.2d 1002, 1008-09 (4th Cir. 1969) ("Exercise of a moral judgment based upon individual standards does not carry with it legal justification or immunity from punishment for breach of the law.... Toleration of such conduct would be inevitably anarchic.").

The protest in this case was in the form of indirect civil disobedience, aimed at reversal of the government's El Salvador policy. That policy does not violate the Constitution, and appellants have never suggested as much. There is no evidence that the procedure by which the policy was adopted was in any way improper; nor is there any evidence that appellants were prevented systematically from participating in the democratic processes through which the policy was chosen. *See United States v. Carolene Products Co.,* 304 U.S. 144, 152-53 n. 4 (1938) (implicitly reserving special solicitude for discrete and insular minorities). The most immediate harm the appellants sought to avert was the existence of the government's El Salvador policy, which is not in itself a legally cognizable harm. Moreover, any harms resulting from the operation of this policy are insufficiently concrete to be legally cognizable as harms for purposes of the necessity defense.

Thus, as a matter of law, the mere existence of a policy or law validly enacted by Congress cannot constitute a cognizable harm. If there is no cognizable harm to prevent, the harm resulting from criminal action taken for the purpose of securing the repeal of the law or policy necessarily outweighs any benefit of the action.

2. Causal Relationship Between Criminal Conduct and Harm to be Averted

This inquiry requires a court to judge the likelihood that an alleged harm will be abated by the taking of illegal action. In the sense that the likelihood of abatement is required in the traditional necessity cases, there will never be such likelihood in cases of indirect political protest. In the traditional cases, a prisoner flees a burning cell and averts death, or someone demolishes a home to create a firebreak and prevents the conflagration of an entire community. The nexus between the act undertaken and the result sought is a close one. Ordinarily it is the volitional illegal act alone which, once taken, abates the evil.

In political necessity cases involving indirect civil disobedience against congressional acts, however, the act alone is unlikely to abate the evil precisely because the action is indirect. Here, the IRS obstruction, or the refusal to comply with a federal officer's order, are unlikely to abate the killings in El Salvador, or immediately change Congress's policy; instead, it takes another *volitional* actor not controlled by the protestor to take a further step; Congress must change its mind.

3. Legal Alternatives

A final reason the necessity defense does not apply to these indirect civil disobedience cases is that legal alternatives will never be deemed exhausted when the harm can be mitigated by congressional action. As noted above, the harm indirect civil disobedience aims to prevent is the continued existence of a law or policy. Because congressional action can *always* mitigate this "harm," lawful political activity to spur such action will always be a legal alternative. On the other hand, we cannot say that this legal alternative will always exist in cases of direct civil disobedience, where protestors act to avert a concrete harm flowing from the operation of the targeted law or policy.

The necessity defense requires the absence of any legal alternative to the contemplated illegal conduct which could reasonably be expected to abate an imminent evil. *See United States v. Bailey,* 444 U.S. 394, 410 (1980) (alternative exists if there is "a chance both to refuse to do the criminal act and also to avoid the threatened harm"). A prisoner fleeing a burning jail, for example, would not be asked to wait in his cell because someone might conceivably save him; such a legal alternative is ill-suited to avoiding death in a fire. In other words, the law implies a reasonableness requirement in judging whether legal alternatives exist.

Where the targeted harm is the existence of a law or policy, our precedents counsel that this reasonableness requirement is met simply by the possibility of congressional action. For example, in *Dorrell,* an indirect civil disobedience case involving a trespass on Vandenburg Air Force Base to protest the MX missile program, we rejected Dorrell's claims that legal alternatives, like lobbying Congress, were unavailable because they were futile. Dorrell, we said, "differed little from many whose passionate beliefs are rejected by the will of the majority legitimately expressed." 758 F.2d at 432. We assumed there that the "possibility" that Congress will change its mind is sufficient in the context of the democratic process to make lawful political action a reasonable alternative to indirect civil disobedience. Without expressly saying so, *Dorrell* decided that petitioning Congress to change a policy is *always* a legal alternative in such cases, regardless of the likelihood of the plea's success. Thus, indirect civil disobedience can never meet the necessity defense requirement that there be a lack of legal alternatives.

B

As have courts before us, we could assume, as a threshold matter, that the necessity defense is conceivably available in these cases, but find the elements never satisfied. Such a decision, however, does not come without significant costs. First, the failure of the federal courts to hold explicitly that the necessity defense is unavailable in these cases results in district courts expending unnecessary time and energy trying to square defendants' claims with the strict requirements of the doctrine. Second, such an inquiry oftentimes requires the courts to tread into areas constitutionally committed to other branches of government. For example, in *May,* which involved trespass on a naval base to protest American nuclear weapons policy, we noted that, "to consider defendants' argument that trespassing was justified by the nefariousness of the Trident missile would put us in the position of usurping the functions that the Constitution has given to the Congress and to the President." [*United States v.] May,* 622 F.2d at 1009; *cf. Schlesinger v. Reservists Committee to Stop the War,* 418 U.S. 208, 22241 L.Ed.2d 706 (1974) (to grant standing to protestors would both risk distortion of "the role of the Judiciary in its relationship to the Executive and the Legislature and open the Judiciary to an arguable charge of providing 'government by injunction'"). Third, holding out the possibility of the defense's applicability sets a trap for the unwary civil disobedient, rather than permitting the individual to undertake a more realistic cost-benefit analysis before deciding whether to break the law in political protest. Fourth, assuming the applicability of the defense in this context may risk its distortion in traditional cases. Finally, some commentators have suggested that the courts have sabotaged the usually low threshold for getting a defense theory before the jury as a means of keeping the necessity defense from the jury. *See, e.g., Applying the Necessity Defense,* 64 N.Y.U. L. Rev. at 85-89; *The State Made Me Do It,* 39 Stan L. Rev. at 1178-79.

The real problem here is that litigants are trying to distort to their purposes an age-old common law doctrine meant for a very different set of circumstances. What these cases are really about is gaining notoriety for a cause — the defense allows protestors to get their political grievances discussed in a courtroom. *The State Made Me Do It,* 39 Stan. L. Rev. at 1176. It is precisely this political motive that has left some courts, like the district court in this case, uneasy. *See* March 23, 1990 Order of District Court at 4-5 ("Neither a small nonpolicy making service office of the IRS nor this Courtroom is the proper venue for deciding political questions."); *May,* 622 F.2d at 1009. Because these attempts to invoke the necessity defense "force the courts to choose among causes they should make legitimate by extending the defense of necessity," *Dorrell,* 758 F.2d at 432, and because the criminal acts, themselves, do not maximize social good, they should be subject to a *per se* rule of exclusion.

Thus, we see the failure of any federal court to recognize a defense of necessity in a case like ours not as coincidental, but rather as the natural consequence of the historic limitation of the doctrine. Indirect protests of congressional policies can never meet all the requirements of the necessity doctrine. Therefore, we hold that the necessity defense is not available in such cases.

Conclusion

Because the necessity defense was not intended as justification for illegal acts taken in indirect political protest, we affirm the district court's refusal to admit evidence of necessity.

AFFIRMED.

Notes & Questions

1. Necessity is rarely invoked and, when invoked, rarely successful. There are two probable explanations for this. First, when the situation obviously falls within the scope of necessity (like the example of the physician performing the emergency tracheotomy), most prosecutors would forego pursuing the case. Second, when it is invoked, the burden to establish all of the requirements is not easily satisfied. Most notably, whenever a fact-finder concludes there was a reasonably available alternative to breaking the law, the defense fails.

2. Based on the opinion, what are the traditional elements of necessity?

3. Because necessity required averting a greater harm by breaking the law, the common law did not extend the defense to an intentional killing. Hence, the common law maxim that necessity is never a defense to murder. But that maxim is overbroad for two reasons. First, an action taken out of necessity may result in an unintentional homicide, in which case the defendant could plead necessity as a justification for the risk-creating behavior that resulted in the death. If successful, this would mean the death was accidental with no basis for criminal culpability. Second, a defendant charged with felony murder could always raise the necessity defense to justify the attempt or commission of the predicate felony. If successful, this would negate guilt for felony murder.

4. Unlike the common law, the MPC imposes no limit to necessity if invoked as a defense to homicide. Accordingly, the defense might justify the purposeful or knowing killing of one human being to avert the death of multiple human beings. For example, a commercial airline pilot might be justified by necessity in landing his disabled plane on an interstate highway — knowing doing so will kill some automobile occupants — in order to save the lives of hundreds of passengers.

5. Necessity is closely related to the excuse defense of duress (sometimes called coercion) addressed in the next chapter. Distinguishing the two is important, because it will impact accomplice liability. Because necessity is a justification, it negates the criminality of the act. This means an alleged accomplice to the principal's act has an equal claim to the defense: if the principal was justified, so was the accomplice. In contrast, because duress is an excuse, it negates individual culpability, not the criminality of the conduct. In this sense, duress, like all excuses, is always "personal" to the defendant. This means if someone is an accomplice to an act committed under duress — for example, the individual whose unlawful threat created the duress — the individual claim of duress will not extend to the accomplice.

6. Both necessity and duress have an important common qualifier: a defendant forfeits the defense if she is responsible for creating the conditions that triggered the necessity (or in the case of duress, if she placed herself in the situation where duress was foreseeable). This is analogous to the "clean hands" limitation of self-defense: the law does not recognize self-generated necessity.

Formative Assessments

1. Defendant is on trial for breaking and entering a Sam's Club warehouse at 4 A.M. during Hurricane Harvey's destructive flooding in Houston. Defendant admits the alleged misconduct, but testifies that he broke in because he was desperate to find floatation vests for his family and friends based on the news reports that his neighborhood would be severely flooded as the result of a planned opening of reservoirs as an emergency mitigation measure. Defendant was able to drive to and from the warehouse. His neighborhood did flood later that day, and he and his family were evacuated by National Guard members. Based on this evidence, defendant should be:

   A. Acquitted because he honestly believed he needed the floatation vests to protect his family.

   B. Acquitted because of the nature of the flood emergency in Houston.

   C. Convicted because it turned out he didn't need the floatation devices.

   D. Convicted because he was able to drive in and out of his neighborhood at the time of the alleged offense.

2. Defendant is charged with murder. She admits she shot and killed the victim in a gas station parking lot late at night, but testifies that she did so because the victim startled her when he approached her from behind and she thought she was being attacked. In support of this self-defense plea, she also offers evidence of news reporting during the days prior to the incident about customers being accosted while pumping gas late at night. The victim was unarmed, and his partner, who was at the scene, testifies that he was just trying to get directions from the defendant. The jurisdiction allows for self-defense and imperfect self-defense. Based on this evidence:

   A. Defendant should be convicted of murder because the victim was unarmed.

   B. Defendant should be acquitted of all offenses because she honestly believed her life was in imminent danger.

   C. Defendant should be convicted of the lesser included offense of manslaughter if the jury concludes she honestly and reasonably believed her life was in danger.

   D. Defendant should be convicted of the lesser included offense of manslaughter if the jury concludes she honestly but unreasonably believed her life was in danger.

3. Defendant's home has been burglarized several times while he was working his night shift. Police have been unable to make any progress on identifying the burglars, and the alarm system defendant installed has been an ineffective deterrent. Defendant decides to rig a cinder block above the window he believes the burglars are using to enter the home, so that it will release while someone is climbing in. Defendant

deliberately left the window slightly ajar to bait the burglar. A week later while defendant is at work, the alarm is activated, and police are immediately dispatched to the scene. No one is home, and one officer, noticing the window is ajar, opens it to climb through. The cinder block falls and breaks his neck, killing him immediately. Defendant is charged with murder based on an allegation he knew his conduct would cause death. He testifies that he knew the device could kill an intruder, but asks the court to instruct the jury on defense of property. You are the judge. How would you rule?

- A. Grant the instruction, but advise the jury they should acquit defendant only if they conclude a use of deadly force would have been reasonable in self-defense had he been home at the time of the incident.

- B. Deny the instruction, even if a use of deadly force would have been reasonable in self-defense had defendant been home at the time of the incident.

- C. Deny the instruction because defendant used a device he knew was deadly to defend his home.

- D. Grant the instruction because based on the prior burglaries, defendant's judgment that he needed to use the device was reasonable.

4. Defendant is walking home late at night, and he sees two individuals in a scuffle in an alley. Defendant, who is lawfully licensed to carry a firearm, observes on man lift a brick over his head while the other man is underneath him. Believing the man with the brick is about to kill the other man, defendant shoots and kills the man with the brick. The other man runs away. Police arrive and tell defendant he shot and killed an undercover police officer who was struggling to apprehend a violent felon who had already stabbed the officer in the leg during the struggle. Defendant testifies that he feels terrible, but that at the time, he believed he was defending a victim from an imminent homicide. If the jury concludes defendant's judgment was reasonable under the circumstances, it should:

- A. Convict him of murder because he made a mistake regarding who was the victim.

- B. Convict him of manslaughter because his mistake was honest and reasonable.

- C. Acquit him of any criminal homicide because his mistake was honest and reasonable.

- D. Convict him in a jurisdiction that follows the common law "alter ego" rule.

Chapter 17

Law Enforcement Defenses

I. Introduction

Shootings involving the police have become one of the most contentious issues in the United States, especially when the individual shot is Black. According to the *Washington Post*, police have killed roughly 1,000 individuals every year since 2018. A disproportionate number of those killed have been Black.

There are approximately 18,000 law enforcement agencies in the United States. These agencies have a variety of policies and procedures regarding the use of force. The Supreme Court of the United States has outlined broad parameters on the constitutionality of the use of deadly force, and the law enforcement agencies have developed policies and practices in response to the principles articulated by the Court. The Court has determined that there are two instances in which police officers may be justified in using deadly force. First, when an officer uses force in response to a threat or perceived threat, the principles of *Graham v. Connor* control whether the use of force is constitutional. Second, in *Tennessee v. Garner,* the Court held that the police could use deadly force in order to prevent the escape of a dangerous felon.

II. Deadly Force in Self-Defense

Police officers have the same right to use self-defense as any other individual. They can use deadly force to protect either themselves or others from imminent unlawful threats. The lawfulness of a police officer's use of deadly force is determined according to a reasonableness standard. However, the standard is not identical to that applied to ordinary individuals. When a non-police officer uses deadly force, the lawfulness of the use of force is determined from the standpoint of a reasonable person. However, when a police officer uses deadly force, the determination of reasonableness is made from the standpoint of a reasonable police officer.

Graham v. Connor

490 U.S. 386 (1989)
U.S. Supreme Court

REHNQUIST, J.

This case requires us to decide what constitutional standard governs a free citizen's claim that law enforcement officials used excessive force in the course of making an arrest, investigatory stop, or other "seizure" of his person. We hold that such claims are properly analyzed under the Fourth Amendment's "objective reasonableness" standard, rather than under a substantive due process standard.

In this action under 42 U.S.C. § 1983, petitioner Dethorne Graham seeks to recover damages for injuries allegedly sustained when law enforcement officers used physical force against him during the course of an investigatory stop. Because the case comes to us from a decision of the Court of Appeals affirming the entry of a directed verdict for respondents, we take the evidence hereafter noted in the light most favorable to petitioner. On November 12, 1984, Graham, a diabetic, felt the onset of an insulin reaction. He asked a friend, William Berry, to drive him to a nearby convenience store so he could purchase some orange juice to counteract the reaction. Berry agreed, but when Graham entered the store, he saw a number of people ahead of him in the checkout line. Concerned about the delay, he hurried out of the store and asked Berry to drive him to a friend's house instead.

Respondent Connor, an officer of the Charlotte, North Carolina, Police Department, saw Graham hastily enter and leave the store. The officer became suspicious that something was amiss and followed Berry's car. About one-half mile from the store, he made an investigative stop. Although Berry told Connor that Graham was simply suffering from a "sugar reaction," the officer ordered Berry and Graham to wait while he found out what, if anything, had happened at the convenience store. When Officer Connor returned to his patrol car to call for backup assistance, Graham got out of the car, ran around it twice, and finally sat down on the curb, where he passed out briefly.

In the ensuing confusion, a number of other Charlotte police officers arrived on the scene in response to Officer Connor's request for backup. One of the officers rolled Graham over on the sidewalk and cuffed his hands tightly behind his back, ignoring Berry's pleas to get him some sugar. Another officer said: "I've seen a lot of people with sugar diabetes that never acted like this. Ain't nothing wrong with the M.F. but drunk. Lock the S.B. up." Several officers then lifted Graham up from behind, carried him over to Berry's car, and placed him face down on its hood. Regaining consciousness, Graham asked the officers to check in his wallet for a diabetic decal that he carried. In response, one of the officers told him to "shut up" and shoved his face down against the hood of the car. Four officers grabbed Graham and threw him headfirst into the police car. A friend of Graham's brought some orange juice to the car, but the officers refused to let him have it. Finally, Officer Connor received a report that Graham had done nothing wrong at the convenience store, and the officers drove him home and released him.

At some point during his encounter with the police, Graham sustained a broken foot, cuts on his wrists, a bruised forehead, and an injured shoulder; he also claims to have developed a loud ringing in his right ear that continues to this day. He commenced this action under 42 U.S.C. § 1983 against the individual officers involved in the incident, all of whom are respondents here, alleging that they had used excessive force in making the investigatory stop, in violation of "rights secured to him under the Fourteenth Amendment to the United States Constitution and 42 U.S.C. § 1983."

Today we make explicit what was implicit in [*Tennessee v.*] *Garner*'s analysis, and hold that *all* claims that law enforcement officers have used excessive force — deadly or not — in the course of an arrest, investigatory stop, or other "seizure" of a free citizen should be analyzed under the Fourth Amendment and its "reasonableness" standard, rather than under a "substantive due process" approach. . . .

Determining whether the force used to effect a particular seizure is "reasonable" under the Fourth Amendment requires a careful balancing of "the nature and quality of the intrusion on the individual's Fourth Amendment interests" against the countervailing governmental interests at stake. Our Fourth Amendment jurisprudence has long recognized that the right to make an arrest or investigatory stop necessarily carries with it the right to use some degree of physical coercion or threat thereof to effect it. Because "[t]he test of reasonableness under the Fourth Amendment is not capable of precise definition or mechanical application," however, its proper application requires careful attention to the facts and circumstances of each particular case, including the severity of the crime at issue, whether the suspect poses an immediate threat to the safety of the officers or others, and whether he is actively resisting arrest or attempting to evade arrest by flight.

The "reasonableness" of a particular use of force must be judged from the perspective of a reasonable officer on the scene, rather than with the 20/20 vision of hindsight. The Fourth Amendment is not violated by an arrest based on probable cause, even though the wrong person is arrested, nor by the mistaken execution of a valid search warrant on the wrong premises. With respect to a claim of excessive force, the same standard of reasonableness at the moment applies: "Not every push or shove, even if it may later seem unnecessary in the peace of a judge's chambers," violates the Fourth Amendment. The calculus of reasonableness must embody allowance for the fact that police officers are often forced to make split-second judgments — in circumstances that are tense, uncertain, and rapidly evolving — about the amount of force that is necessary in a particular situation.

As in other Fourth Amendment contexts, however, the "reasonableness" inquiry in an excessive force case is an objective one: the question is whether the officers' actions are "objectively reasonable" in light of the facts and circumstances confronting them, without regard to their underlying intent or motivation. An officer's evil intentions will not make a Fourth Amendment violation out of an objectively reasonable use of force; nor will an officer's good intentions make an objectively unreasonable use of force constitutional.

Because petitioner's excessive force claim is one arising under the Fourth Amendment, the Court of Appeals erred in analyzing it under the four-part *Johnson v. Glick* test. [481 F.2d 1028 (2d Cir. 1973).] That test, which requires consideration of whether the individual officers acted in "good faith" or "maliciously and sadistically for the very purpose of causing harm," is incompatible with a proper Fourth Amendment analysis. We do not agree with the Court of Appeals' suggestion, that the "malicious and sadistic" inquiry is merely another way of describing conduct that is objectively unreasonable under the circumstances. Whatever the empirical correlations between "malicious and sadistic" behavior and objective unreasonableness may be, the fact remains that the "malicious and sadistic" factor puts in issue the subjective motivations of the individual officers, which our prior cases make clear has no bearing on whether a particular seizure is "unreasonable" under the Fourth Amendment. Nor do we agree with the Court of Appeals' conclusion, that because the subjective motivations of the individual officers are of central importance in deciding whether force used against a convicted prisoner violates the Eighth Amendment, it cannot be reversible error to inquire into them in deciding whether force used against a suspect or arrestee violates the Fourth Amendment.

Notes and Questions

1. Do you agree with the Court that an officer's "evil intentions" or "malicious and sadistic" behavior are irrelevant in determining whether an officer's use of force was reasonable?

2. Is the Court right in holding that the reasonableness of an officer's conduct should be "judged from the standpoint of a reasonable officer on the scene"? This standard has been criticized by legal scholars. *See* Paul Butler, *The System Is Working the Way It Is Supposed to: The Limits of Criminal Justice Reform*, 104 GEO. L.J. 1419, 1425 (2016) (arguing that it is legal police conduct that perpetuates racial inequality in the criminal justice system — not illegal police misconduct); Osagie K. Obasogie & Zachary Newman, *The Futile Fourth Amendment: Understanding Police Excessive Force Doctrine Through an Empirical Assessment of Graham v. Connor*, 112 Nw. U. L. REV. 1465, 1498–99 (2018) (concluding that the Supreme Court's doctrinal choice to evaluate police excessive force claims under the Fourth Amendment rather than under the Equal Protection Clause has contributed to the perpetuation of police excessive use of force in many communities of color); Devon W. Carbado, *From Stopping Black People to Killing Black People: The Fourth Amendment Pathways to Police Violence*, 105 CALIF. L. REV. 125, 128 (2017) (arguing that "[a] significant part of the problem [police killings of Black people] is Fourth Amendment law"). If you believe that these criticisms are legitimate, what should be the standard in determining whether police use of force is justified?

3. According to the *Washington Post*, although Black people constitute less than 13% of the U.S. population, they are killed by police at more than twice the rate of white Americans. Hispanic Americans are also killed by police at a disproportionate

rate. According to the *Washington Post*, Black Americans are killed by police at the rate of 36 per million; Hispanics, 27 per million; and whites, 15 per million.

4. Many police killings derive from traffic stops and investigations of minor criminal activity. Several Supreme Court decisions have empowered the police to stop and arrest suspects for minor crimes. In *Terry v. Ohio*, the Court held that the police are empowered to stop an individual based on reasonable suspicion that he has committed a crime. 392 U.S. 1 (1968). In *Atwater v. City of Lago Vista*, the Court held that the police are allowed to arrest an individual for minor criminal offenses, even if the offense is not punishable by any term of incarceration. 532 U.S. 318 (2001). In *Whren v. United States*, the Court held that the reasonableness of a traffic stop is not determined by the subjective motivations of an officer. 517 U.S. 806 (1996). As long as the police had cause for the stop, it is reasonable. Thus, the fact that an officer may have based a stop at least in part on race is not actionable under the Fourth Amendment.

5. In several high-profile police shootings, the police failed to render first aid to suspects after shooting them. Should the police be liable for failing to provide first aid to a suspect they have shot if they can do so without endangering either themselves or the evidence? *See* Kenneth Williams, *Why Police Have a Legal Duty to Provide Medical Aid to People They Shoot*, 18 OHIO ST. J. CRIM. LAW 391 (2020).

6. Officer Tang is a veteran female officer on patrol with Officer Cooper. They receive a call for an ADW — Assault with a Deadly Weapon — in their area. They "show responding" and drive to the scene where they observe a man holding a pistol running away from another individual. Tang exits the car and begins a foot chase, while Cooper drives around the block in an attempt to cut off the suspect. Tang chases the suspect through a back alley and follows him after he jumps a fence into a residential backyard. She sees him jump another fence, and as she goes to jump it to follow him, he swings a 2×4 at her. She ducks, and it misses her. She cautiously climbs over the fence and draws her service pistol. She does not see the suspect in the backyard. She then observes the back door to the home slightly open and observes a man pointing a gun in her direction. She fires immediately. The man turns out to be a teenager who lives in the house; the gun, a realistic-looking toy. Was Tang's shooting justified? Now assume that when the toy pistol was recovered, it had an orange safety tip on the barrel. It was broad daylight when Tang fired on the teenager, but he was standing in the doorway with little light when he opened the door and pointed the pistol. How, if at all, does this change your assessment?

III. Deadly Force to Apprehend

Most reasonable people would agree that some suspects are so dangerous that the police should use deadly force to apprehend them because of the risk they pose to others should they escape. In *Tennessee v. Garner*, the Supreme Court held that the Constitution prohibits the use of deadly force to apprehend a suspect except when the arrestee "poses a threat of serious physical harm either to the officer or to others."

Tennessee v. Garner

471 U.S. 1 (1985)
U.S. Supreme Court

WHITE, J.

This case requires us to determine the constitutionality of the use of deadly force to prevent the escape of an apparently unarmed suspected felon. We conclude that such force may not be used unless it is necessary to prevent the escape and the officer has probable cause to believe that the suspect poses a significant threat of death or serious physical injury to the officer or others.

At about 10:45 p. m. on October 3, 1974, Memphis Police Officers Elton Hymon and Leslie Wright were dispatched to answer a "prowler inside call." Upon arriving at the scene they saw a woman standing on her porch and gesturing toward the adjacent house. She told them she had heard glass breaking and that "they" or "someone" was breaking in next door. While Wright radioed the dispatcher to say that they were on the scene, Hymon went behind the house. He heard a door slam and saw someone run across the backyard. The fleeing suspect, who was appellee-respondent's decedent, Edward Garner, stopped at a 6-feet-high chain link fence at the edge of the yard. With the aid of a flashlight, Hymon was able to see Garner's face and hands. He saw no sign of a weapon, and, though not certain, was "reasonably sure" and "figured" that Garner was unarmed. He thought Garner was 17 or 18 years old and about 5'5" or 5'7" tall. While Garner was crouched at the base of the fence, Hymon called out "police, halt" and took a few steps toward him. Garner then began to climb over the fence. Convinced that if Garner made it over the fence he would elude capture, Hymon shot him. The bullet hit Garner in the back of the head. Garner was taken by ambulance to a hospital, where he died on the operating table. Ten dollars and a purse taken from the house were found on his body.

In using deadly force to prevent the escape, Hymon was acting under the authority of a Tennessee statute and pursuant to Police Department policy. The statute provides that "[if], after notice of the intention to arrest the defendant, he either flee or forcibly resist, the officer may use all the necessary means to effect the arrest." The Department policy was slightly more restrictive than the statute, but still allowed the use of deadly force in cases of burglary. The incident was reviewed by the Memphis Police Firearm's Review Board and presented to a grand jury. Neither took any action.

Garner's father then brought this action in the Federal District Court for the Western District of Tennessee, seeking damages under 42 U.S.C. § 1983 for asserted violations of Garner's constitutional rights. . . .

A police officer may arrest a person if he has probable cause to believe that person committed a crime. Petitioners and appellant argue that if this requirement is satisfied the Fourth Amendment has nothing to say about *how* that seizure is made. This submission ignores the many cases in which this Court, by balancing the extent of the intrusion against the need for it, has examined the reasonableness of the manner in which a search or seizure is conducted.

. . . .

The same balancing process applied in the cases cited above demonstrates that, notwithstanding probable cause to seize a suspect, an officer may not always do so by killing him. The intrusiveness of a seizure by means of deadly force is unmatched. The suspect's fundamental interest in his own life need not be elaborated upon. The use of deadly force also frustrates the interest of the individual, and of society, in judicial determination of guilt and punishment. Against these interests are ranged governmental interests in effective law enforcement. It is argued that overall violence will be reduced by encouraging the peaceful submission of suspects who know that they may be shot if they flee. Effectiveness in making arrests requires the resort to deadly force, or at least the meaningful threat thereof. "Being able to arrest such individuals is a condition precedent to the state's entire system of law enforcement."

Without in any way disparaging the importance of these goals, we are not convinced that the use of deadly force is a sufficiently productive means of accomplishing them to justify the killing of nonviolent suspects. The use of deadly force is a self-defeating way of apprehending a suspect and so setting the criminal justice mechanism in motion. If successful, it guarantees that that mechanism will not be set in motion. And while the meaningful threat of deadly force might be thought to lead to the arrest of more live suspects by discouraging escape attempts, the presently available evidence does not support this thesis. The fact is that a majority of police departments in this country have forbidden the use of deadly force against nonviolent suspects. If those charged with the enforcement of the criminal law have abjured the use of deadly force in arresting nondangerous felons, there is a substantial basis for doubting that the use of such force is an essential attribute of the arrest power in all felony cases. Petitioners and appellant have not persuaded us that shooting nondangerous fleeing suspects is so vital as to outweigh the suspect's interest in his own life.

The use of deadly force to prevent the escape of all felony suspects, whatever the circumstances, is constitutionally unreasonable. It is not better that all felony suspects die than that they escape. Where the suspect poses no immediate threat to the officer and no threat to others, the harm resulting from failing to apprehend him does not justify the use of deadly force to do so. It is no doubt unfortunate when a suspect who is in sight escapes, but the fact that the police arrive a little late or are a little slower afoot does not always justify killing the suspect. A police officer may not seize an unarmed, nondangerous suspect by shooting him dead. The Tennessee statute is unconstitutional insofar as it authorizes the use of deadly force against such fleeing suspects.

It is not, however, unconstitutional on its face. Where the officer has probable cause to believe that the suspect poses a threat of serious physical harm, either to the officer or to others, it is not constitutionally unreasonable to prevent escape by using deadly force. Thus, if the suspect threatens the officer with a weapon or there is probable cause to believe that he has committed a crime involving the infliction or threatened infliction of serious physical harm, deadly force may be used if necessary to prevent escape, and if, where feasible, some warning has been given. As applied in such circumstances, the Tennessee statute would pass constitutional muster. . . .

It is insisted that the Fourth Amendment must be construed in light of the common-law rule, which allowed the use of whatever force was necessary to effect the arrest of a fleeing felon, though not a misdemeanant. . . . [W]hile in earlier times "the gulf between the felonies and the minor offences was broad and deep," today the distinction is minor and often arbitrary. Many crimes classified as misdemeanors, or nonexistent, at common law are now felonies. These changes have undermined the concept, which was questionable to begin with, that use of deadly force against a fleeing felon is merely a speedier execution of someone who has already forfeited his life. They have also made the assumption that a "felon" is more dangerous than a misdemeanant untenable. Indeed, numerous misdemeanors involve conduct more dangerous than many felonies. . . . One other aspect of the common-law rule bears emphasis. It forbids the use of deadly force to apprehend a misdemeanant, condemning such action as disproportionately severe.

In short, though the common-law pedigree of Tennessee's rule is pure on its face, changes in the legal and technological context mean the rule is distorted almost beyond recognition when literally applied.

The District Court concluded that Hymon was justified in shooting Garner because state law allows, and the Federal Constitution does not forbid, the use of deadly force to prevent the escape of a fleeing felony suspect if no alternative means of apprehension is available. This conclusion made a determination of Garner's apparent dangerousness unnecessary. The court did find, however, that Garner appeared to be unarmed, though Hymon could not be certain that was the case. Restated in Fourth Amendment terms, this means Hymon had no articulable basis to think Garner was armed.

In reversing, the Court of Appeals accepted the District Court's factual conclusions and held that "the facts, as found, did not justify the use of deadly force." We agree. Officer Hymon could not reasonably have believed that Garner—young, slight, and unarmed—posed any threat. Indeed, Hymon never attempted to justify his actions on any basis other than the need to prevent an escape. The District Court stated in passing that "[the] facts of this case did not indicate to Officer Hymon that Garner was 'non-dangerous.'" This conclusion is not explained, and seems to be based solely on the fact that Garner had broken into a house at night. However, the fact that Garner was a suspected burglar could not, without regard to the other circumstances, automatically justify the use of deadly force. Hymon did not have probable cause to believe that Garner, whom he correctly believed to be unarmed, posed any physical danger to himself or others.

The dissent argues that the shooting was justified by the fact that Officer Hymon had probable cause to believe that Garner had committed a nighttime burglary.

While we agree that burglary is a serious crime, we cannot agree that it is so dangerous as automatically to justify the use of deadly force. The FBI classifies burglary as a "property" rather than a "violent" crime. Although the armed burglar would present a different situation, the fact that an unarmed suspect has broken into a dwelling at night does not automatically mean he is physically dangerous. This case demonstrates as much. In fact, the available statistics demonstrate that burglaries only rarely involve physical violence. During the 10-year period from 1973–1982, only 3.8% of all burglaries involved violent crime.

Notes and Questions

1. Do you agree with the Court's conclusion that the use of deadly force is not automatically justified against a fleeing suspected burglar?

2. The police officer who shot Garner admitted that he did not believe Garner was armed. What would be the result if he claimed that he believed Garner was armed but, in fact, Garner was not armed?

3. The police attempted to pull over nineteen-year-old Victor Harris for speeding. He was driving seventy-three miles per hour in a fifty-five miles per hour zone. Instead of stopping, he sped away. The officers gave chase and pursued Harris down a two-lane highway for several minutes. Finally, one of the officers used his car to deliberately ram Harris' car off the road. The car crashed down a steep ravine and overturned. Harris survived but was rendered a quadriplegic. Harris sued, claiming that the use of deadly force was unreasonable, since the police could have ended the danger simply by stopping the chase. He argued that there was no need for the chase since the police already had his license plate number and could have identified him later. The Court held that the police use of deadly force was reasonable, since Harris' evasion of the police created a danger to other drivers. *See Scott v. Harris*, 550 U.S. 372 (2007).

4. Officer Brown is performing duty as a tower guard at a maximum-security prison. All of the inmates in the prison have been convicted of felonies and sentenced to a minimum of 10 years of confinement. Many have been convicted of violent crimes. While Brown is on duty, four inmates escape, and Brown observes them running through a field outside the prison walls headed for a wooded area. Is Brown legally authorized to employ deadly force to stop the escape?

Formative Assessments

1. Many states have enacted citizen-arrest laws permitting private citizens to make a lawful arrest. Typical is Georgia's citizen arrest statute, which provides that "a private person may arrest an offender if the offense is committed in his presence or within his immediate knowledge." However, as you previously learned, an initial

aggressor usually is not entitled to claim self-defense. Is it possible to reconcile these two common provisions?

2. The Fourth Amendment prohibits "unreasonable seizures." When does the use of force by a police officer to effect an arrest constitute an "unreasonable seizure"?

3. A police officer could use deadly force to prevent the escape of which of the following fleeing suspects?

A. A suspect who has shoplifted at an expensive department store.

B. A suspect breaking into a car on a public street.

C. A suspect who matches the description of a rapist.

D. Suspects who loot a department store following a political demonstration.

Chapter 18

Excuse Defenses

I. Introduction

Excuse in criminal law is a category of defenses which exculpate blameless offenders[1] — individuals whose conduct would otherwise meet the elements of a criminal offense but who society doesn't believe should be criminally responsible. Unlike justification defenses which focus on the *act* committed, excuse defenses focus on the *actor*.[2] More specifically, excuse defenses consider whether something disabled the actor's capacity to form a culpable mental state to such an extent that criminal punishment would serve no logical purpose. Recognized excuses vary and include: external threats of serious physical harm (duress/compulsion), mental responsibility, involuntary and voluntary intoxication and being too young to understand either right from wrong or the consequences of one's actions (infancy doctrine). As one commentator explains:

> [a]n excuse [] represents a legal conclusion that the conduct is wrong and undesirable, that the conduct ought not to be tolerated and ought to be avoided in the future, even in the same situation. Criminal liability nonetheless is inappropriate because some characteristic of the actor or the actor's situation vitiates the actor's blameworthiness.[3]

Why would a defendant raise excuse? Excuse yields varied outcomes: duress/compulsion, involuntary intoxication and the infancy doctrine result in outright acquittal. Mental responsibility (or lack thereof) also yields acquittal but often results in involuntary civil commitment in a mental health facility. Lastly, voluntary intoxication generally does not result in an acquittal but, depending on the mens rea of the charged offense, may reduce the severity of the charge, thus also reducing the potential punishment range.

---

1. Paul Robinson, *A System of Excuses: How Criminal Law's Excuse Defenses Do, and Don't, Work Together to Exculpate Blameless (and Only Blameless) Offenders*, 42 Texas Tech L. Rev. 259 (2009).
2. Mitchell N. Berman, *Justification and Excuse, Law and Morality*, 53 Duke L.J. 1 (2003).
3. Paul Robinson, Criminal Law § 9.1, at 479 (1997).

A. Duress/Compulsion

Duress/compulsion as an excuse is raised when a person's unlawful threat causes a defendant to reasonably believe that the only way to avoid imminent and serious physical harm is to engage in unlawful conduct.[4] Duress is distinguished from a self-defense or defense of others theory because, under duress, the defendant's criminal conduct is not directed at the source of the unlawful threat, but instead at someone or something else in order to avoid the threat from manifesting. The threat may be expressed, in words or implied, as in threateningly pointing a gun. The threat must be of serious and immediate harm — past or future threats don't qualify. Duress generally involves a threat to the person coerced into committing the act. "Although the law is not wholly consistent, the plea is generally recognized if the deadly force is directed at a third person, especially if that person is a family member."[5] Finally, at common law (and in many MPC jurisdictions), the harm avoided must have been reasonably assessed as greater than the harm caused.

There are important differences in how the common law and MPC define and apply duress/compulsion. In common law jurisdictions, in order to establish the excuse of duress/compulsion, a defendant must show that they or someone else:

(1) were under an unlawful and imminent threat of death or serious bodily injury;

(2) had not recklessly or negligently placed themselves in the situation;

(3) had no reasonable, legal alternative; and

(4) that a direct causal relationship existed between the criminal act and the avoidance of the threatened harm.[6]

At common law, duress/compulsion *cannot* excuse committing a homicide offense for the simple reason that the harm avoided is equal to the harm caused. Importantly, this rule applied even if killing one person was based on the reasonable belief that doing so would save many.[7]

The MPC is more flexible in its definition of duress/compulsion. Under Section 2.09

(1) It is an affirmative defense that the actor engaged in the conduct charged to constitute an offense because he was coerced to do so by the use of, or a threat

---

4. *See* WAYNE R. LeFAVE & AUSTIN W. SCOTT, JR., SUBSTANTIVE CRIMINAL LAW § 5.3, at 614 (1986).

5. Joshua Dressler, *Exegesis of the Law of Duress: Justifying the Excuse and Searching for Its Proper Limits*, 62 S. CAL. L. REV. 1331, 1341 (1989).

6. *See Dixon v. U.S.*, 548 U.S. 1 (2006).

7. "Stemming from antiquity, the nearly 'unbroken tradition' of Anglo-American common law is that duress never excuses murder, that the person threatened with his own demise 'ought rather to die himself, than escape by the murder of an innocent.'" Joshua Dressler, *Exegesis of the Law of Duress: Justifying the Excuse and Searching for Its Proper Limits*, 62 So. CAL. L. REV. 1331, 1370 (1989).

to use, unlawful force against his person or the person of another, which a person of reasonable firmness in his situation would have been unable to resist.

(2) The defense provided by this Section is unavailable if the actor recklessly placed himself in a situation in which it was probable that he would be subjected to duress. The defense is also unavailable if he was negligent in placing himself in such a situation, whenever negligence suffices to establish culpability for the offense charged.

Under the MPC, duress/compulsion *could* potentially excuse committing a homicide offense; the MPC defers to the finder of fact to assess whether the defendant made a reasonable judgment that the harm avoided was greater than the harm caused.

B. Lack of Mental Responsibility

Lack of mental responsibility refers to mental health disease and defect which can exculpate a morally blameless offender. In criminal law, mental responsibility defenses come in two different forms, cognitive (reasoning) or volitional (control).

Cognitive dysfunction occurs when an offender's mental disease or defect distorts his cognitive ability to understand his surroundings, the consequences of his conduct, or the criminal or wrongful nature of his conduct. Control dysfunction occurs when an offender's mental disease or defect impairs his ability to control his conduct (which he may very well know to be criminal and wrongful).[8]

The defense of mental responsibility[9] "sits at the juncture of medical views of mental illness and moral and legal theories of criminal culpability — two areas of conflict and change. Small wonder that no particular test of [mental responsibility] has developed into a constitutional baseline."[10] The result has been what the Supreme Court politely termed a "tapestry of approaches States have adopted. . . ." These approaches have a common thread originating in Victorian England.

---

8. Paul H. Robinson & Tyler Scot Williams, *Insanity Defense, in* Mapping American Criminal Law Variations Across the 50 States (2017) [Robinson & Williams].

9. Where possible, this chapter uses Mental Dysfunction in place of insanity, as that term is both inappropriate and unhelpful. The word insanity is increasingly recognized as inappropriate in that it perpetuates stereotypes and marginalizes those with mental health issues. *See* Neda Ulaby, *Why People Are Rethinking the Words 'Crazy' and 'Insane',* NPR, Jul. 8, 2019 https://www.npr.org/2019/07/08/739643765/why-people-are-arguing-to-stop-using-the-words-crazy-and-insane. In terms of being unhelpful in a criminal law context, as far back as 1966, the Second Circuit deliberately omitted the terms "criminal insanity" and "criminally insane" from an opinion, and in a footnote, explained that "[p]sychiatrists generally agree that the terms are meaningless for medical purposes and [] they are sufficiently ambiguous and misleading to warrant rejection by the law as well." *United States v. Freeman*, 357 F.2d 606, 608 fn.1 (2d Cir. 1966). Nonetheless, courts, including the Supreme Court, continue to use insanity. *See Kahler v. Kansas*, 589 U.S. __, 140 S. Ct. 1021 (2020).

10. *Kahler v Kansas*, 589 U.S. __, 140 S. Ct. 1021, 1024 (2020).

1. M'Naghten Test

In 1843, Daniel M'Naghten, a Scottish woodworker who suffered from paranoid delusions, attempted to assassinate the British Prime Minister but instead killed the Prime Minister's private secretary. At M'Naghten's subsequent murder prosecution, his defense attorneys successfully raised a mental responsibility defense, and he was acquitted.[11]

Through M'Naghten's trial, the United Kingdom developed a standard for criminal defendants raising a mental dysfunction defense:

> every man is to be presumed to be sane, and . . . that to establish a defence on the ground of insanity, it must be clearly proved that, at the time of the committing of the act, the party accused was labouring under such a defect of reason, from disease of the mind, as not to know the nature and quality of the act he was doing; or if he did know it, that he did not know he was doing what was wrong.[12]

The key inquiry under M'Naghten is "whether the accused at the time of doing the act knew the difference between right and wrong."[13] Within a year of the decision, the M'Naghten rule had crossed the Atlantic and was used, by name, in Massachusetts.[14] Virtually every American jurisdiction has relied on M'Naghten.[15] Even more telling is the fact that, to this day, some 28 U.S. states still rely *exclusively* on the M'Naghten rule.[16] That courts in the twenty-first century are using a mental health test developed during the Victorian era loudly speaks to how and why mental health issues continue to be mischaracterized and misunderstood.

2. Irresistible Impulse Test

Forty years after M'Naghten, an Alabama court developed what became known as the "irresistible impulse" test, which some jurisdictions have adopted in addition to the M'Naghten rule. Under the irresistible impulse test, even though the defendant knew what he was doing and knew it was wrong (aka M'Naghten), he was subject to "the duress of such mental disease [that] he had . . . lost the power to choose between right and wrong" and that "his free agency was at the time destroyed," and thus, "the alleged crime was so connected with such mental disease, in the relation of cause and effect, as to have been the product of it solely."[17] In other words, unlike M'Naghten, which is based on a cognitive failure, the irresistible impulse test is based

---

11. There was considerable public outcry in England following the acquittal. Yet M'Naghten wasn't released and instead spent twenty-years in a mental asylum, where he died.

12. *Regina v. M'Naghten*, 8 Eng. Rep. 718, 722 (1843).

13. *M'Naghten*, 8 Eng. Rep. at 720.

14. *Commonwealth v. Rogers*, 48 Mass. 500 (1844).

15. LaFave Scott, Criminal Law 312 (2d ed. 1986).

16. Robinson & Williams, *supra* note 8.

17. *Parsons v. State*, 81 Ala. 577 (1886).

on a volitional failure. Three U.S. States continue to use this 19th century rule.[18] As explained below, the MPC incorporates an irresistible impulse (volitional defect) type test for lack of mental responsibility with a M'Naghten (cognitive defect) type test. Hence, states that have adopted this MPC approach allow defendants to plead such a volitional defect.

3. MPC Substantial Capacity Test

These various efforts to develop a more effective mental dysfunction defense culminated with the MPC. The MPC combines both the cognitive and volitional defect theories of lack of mental responsibility and softens the test for assessing when such defects warrant exoneration. This is called the MPC Substantial Capacity test provided in § 4.01: "[a] person is not responsible for criminal conduct if at the time of such conduct as a result of mental disease or defect he lacks substantial capacity either to appreciate the wrongfulness of his conduct or to conform his conduct to the requirements of law."[19]

The substantial capacity test is a blend of M'Naghten and irresistible impulse. The first part of the test is a cognitive standard and requires that a defendant have a mental disease or defect. The second part is volitional, somewhat similar to the irresistible impulse test. Most notably, by requiring a finding of a lack of "substantial capacity" in lieu of the "unable to understand" standard of M'Naghten or "unable to control" standard of irresistible impulse, the MPC sought to create a defense test better aligned with the nuance of psychiatric science and to vest the finder of fact with greater discretion to decide when a defendant's mental disease or defect warranted excuse from criminal responsibility.

The MPC approach gained some traction and acceptance in the 1960s and 1970s. But in 1981, an emotionally troubled man, John Hinckley, attempted to assassinate U.S. President Ronald Reagan. Hinckley shot and wounded Reagan, as well as a police officer, a secret service agent, and the White House press secretary. Hinckley was found not guilty by reason of insanity based on an MPC irresistible impulse theory; similar to M'Naghten, the public outcry was swift and severe. The public's reaction was fueled at least in part by the assassination attempt being captured on video and repeatedly broadcast. This led Congress to enact the Insanity Defense Reform Act of 1984, which significantly altered the standards and process for mental dysfunction defenses in federal court and essentially resurrected the M'Naghten test as the exclusive test for the insanity defense.[20] By 1985, "36 states had reformed their insanity defense, and no fewer than five states dropped the control prong (irresistible impulse)

---

18. Robinson & Williams, *supra* note 8.
19. MPC § 4.01.
20. *See* Lisa Callahan et al., *Insanity Defense Reform in the United States-Post Hinckley*, MENTAL & PHYS. DISABILITY L. REP. 54-59 (1987).

or repealed the defense altogether."[21] As of the date of this publication, only twelve states and the District of Columbia employ the MPC Substantial Capacity Test.[22]

4. Durham Rule

Lastly, another short-lived modification to mental responsibility law is known as the Durham Rule. The Durham Rule takes its name from a 1954 U.S. Court of Appeals case with a defendant named Durham. In *Durham v. United States*, 214 F.2d 862 (D.C. Cir. 1954), the court found the existing mental responsibility tests (largely M'Naghten and/or irresistible impulse) inadequate. The court ruled that basing mental responsibility on either the inability to distinguish right from wrong (M'Naghten) or control one's impulses (irresistible impulse) was under-inclusive. Accordingly, "[t]he question will be simply whether the accused acted because of a mental disorder, and not whether he displayed particular symptoms which medical science has long recognized do not necessarily, or even typically, accompany even the most serious mental disorder." This is why the rule is also known as the "product" test: was the criminal act or omission the *product* of a mental defect? If so, the defendant is not guilty by reason of insanity.

Federal and some state courts adopted the Durham Rule, but its lack of clarity led to confused implementation. Additionally, the Durham Rule seemed to lower the threshold for mental responsibility defenses in a way that made some uncomfortable. Unlike M'Naghten and irresistible impulse, which both required that a defendant have a mental disease or defect, the Durham Rule required only a mental disorder. As a result, addictive behavior, for example gambling, might qualify and thus exculpate a defendant. Another objection was that it essentially substituted the opinion of a psychiatric expert for a finding by the jury: once the expert gave the opinion that the crime was a "product" of a mental defect, the jury simply acted as a proverbial rubber stamp. By 1972, all but New Hampshire abandoned the Durham Rule.[23]

C. Intoxication

1. Involuntary Intoxication

Under this defense, someone without personal culpability for the intoxication was so intoxicated as to either not be able to form the culpable mental state of the offense for which they were charged or, at the time of alleged offense, temporarily meets the jurisdiction's mental responsibility test. Intoxication refers to when someone's mental or physical capacities are disturbed or altered as a result of introducing substances. While substances is a broad term, most intoxication cases involve alcohol and/or drugs, whether prescribed, over the counter or illegal.

21. Robinson & Williams, *supra* note 8.
22. *Id.*
23. New Hampshire continues to rely on the Durham Rule.

At common law, the defense of involuntary intoxication involves intoxication induced by one or more of the following: 1) fraud, trickery or duress of another; 2) accident or mistake on the defendant's own part; 3) a pathological condition;[24] or 4) ignorance as to the effects of prescribed medication.[25]

Under the MPC, "[i]ntoxication which (a) is not self-induced or (b) is pathological is an affirmative defense if by reason of such intoxication the actor at the time of his conduct lacks substantial capacity either to appreciate its criminality [wrongfulness] or to conform his conduct to the requirements of law."[26]

The involuntary intoxication defense takes two different forms, mens rea and temporary mental responsibility, both of which operate the same under the common law and the MPC. The mens rea form considers whether, as a result of involuntary intoxication, the defendant lacked the culpable mental state of the offense for which they were charged. By contrast, the temporary mental responsibility form considers whether, as a result of involuntary intoxication, the defendant meets the jurisdiction's mental responsibility test (which normally requires a permanent mental disease or defect).

Where sufficient evidence has been introduced to raise the issue, the finder of fact determines whether or not the intoxication was involuntary. Where involuntary intoxication applies, it is a complete defense, meaning the result is an acquittal.

2. Voluntary Intoxication

Under early American law, voluntary intoxication could "never be received as a ground to excuse or palliate an offence."[27] While the common law has softened its initial "stern rejection of inebriation," the Supreme Court in 1996 clarified that states are not constitutionally required to allow evidence of voluntary intoxication.[28]

When someone, because of their intoxication, is unaware of a relevant risk, both the common law and the MPC treat them as "constructively reckless, i.e., [they are] treated as harshly as a sober actor who is actually aware of the relevant risk."[29] Under a majority view of the common law and the MPC, voluntary intoxication operates as a partial defense. Unlike with involuntary intoxication, which can lead to outright acquittal, voluntary intoxication can negate mens rea above recklessness, so specific

---

24. Pathological intoxication refers to being disproportionately intoxicated given the amount of intoxicant consumed/ingested/injected *and* the defendant not being aware of this susceptibility.

25. *See Jones v. State*, 648 P.2d 1251, 1258 (Okl. Cr. 1982).

26. MPC § 2.08.

27. M. Hale et al., Historia Placitorum Coronae: The History of the Pleas of the Crown, 33 (1847).

28. *Montana v. Egelhoff*, 518 U.S. 37 (1996).

29. Paul Robinson, *A Brief Summary and Critique of Criminal Liability Rules for Intoxicated Conduct*, 82 J. Crim. L. 381 (2018). As Robinson notes, "[e]ven the Model Penal Code, which generally abhors imputed or constructive mental states, adopts a constructive recklessness approach to intoxication." *Id.*

intent at common law and purpose and knowledge under the MPC. The defense is not available when the mens rea of the charged offense is reckless or criminal negligence.

The result is that, depending on the mens rea of the charged offense, a defendant may be able to assert voluntary intoxication to downgrade the charges and punishment they face. A common example is that someone voluntarily intoxicated may not be able to form specific intent to kill. In that instance, voluntary intoxication would negate the specific intent of a first-degree murder charge, but the defendant would still be guilty of second-degree murder.

D. Infancy Doctrine

The infancy doctrine is a long-standing common-law construct[30] which recognized that when a child doesn't understand the nature and consequences of their actions, then they should not be criminally culpable. In terms of the age parameters,

> [c]hildren under the age seven were conclusively presumed to be incapable of committing any crime; children fourteen and older were treated as fully responsible adults, and children between the ages of seven and fourteen were presumed incapable of committing any crime, but the presumption was rebuttable. The prosecution bore the burden of overcoming the presumption of incapacity by showing that the child understood the nature and wrongfulness of his act.[31]

By the time the MPC was developed, juvenile courts had existed in the U.S. for decades.[32] As a result, the MPC, in § 4.10, recognizes a juvenile court's exclusive jurisdiction over individuals who at the time of the conduct charged were less than sixteen years of age. For those individuals who were sixteen or seventeen at the time of the conduct charged, the MPC recognizes a juvenile court's primary jurisdiction. Where a juvenile court does not have, or waives, jurisdiction, sixteen- and seventeen-year-olds may be prosecuted as adults.[33]

---

30. *See* Andrew M. Carter, *Age Matters: The Case for a Constitutionalized Infancy Defense*, 54 U. Kan. L. Rev. 687 (2006) (arguing for a statutory infancy doctrine).

31. Barbara Kaban & James Orlando, *Revitalizing the Infancy Defense in the Contemporary Juvenile Court*, 60 Rutgers L. Rev. 33, 33–34 (2007).

32. The first juvenile court in the U.S. was founded in 1899 in Chicago. *See* National Research Council and Institute of Medicine, Juvenile Crime, Juvenile Justice 151 (Joan McCord et al. eds. 2001).

33. One commentator claims that an intended byproduct of establishing juvenile courts has been that the status of common law rules, like the infancy doctrine, has become "far less clear." *See* Robert E. Shepherd Jr., *Rebirth of the Infancy Defense*, 2 Criminal Justice 45 (1997).

II. Application

A. Duress/Compulsion

The excuse of duress, sometimes referred to as compulsion or coercion, has a long history in the United States. The first reported criminal case involving a duress claim was in the aftermath of the "Whiskey Rebellion" — a series of protests between 1791–1794 against a tax on "spirits distilled within the United States, for appropriating the same."[34] Farmers routinely distilled excess rye, barley, wheat and corn into whiskey, and whiskey was even used as a form of currency in bartering. Farmers and distillers in Western Pennsylvania refused to pay the tax and began threatening and assaulting local tax collectors.[35] The rebellion culminated in 1794 when several hundred protestors armed with pitchforks and firearms attacked and burned the Pittsburgh home of a regional tax inspector.[36] The incident prompted President Washington to lead over 12,000 militia members into Pennsylvania, which caused the protestors to disperse.[37] Ultimately, the militia arrested approximately 150 individuals suspected of involvement and who were prosecuted for treason in 1795. One of those tried, Philip Vigol, admitted being one of the violent protestors but claimed duress — that he had only participated because the protest leader had threatened to burn Vigol's property if he did not join. A judge allowed the treason charge to proceed against Vigol for the acts of "violence and destruction" done towards various tax collectors and their property with the intention to cause the officials to resign from fulfilling their duties, duties which enabled a congressionally enacted law. The judge found that Vigol and the other protestors, in attempting to "render null and void, in effect, an act of congress[,]" engaged in an insurrection. The judge also rejected Vigol's attempt to assert duress, holding that:

> The counsel for the prisoner have endeavored, in the course of a faithful discharge of their duty, to extract from the witnesses some testimony which might justify a defence upon the ground of duress and terror. But in this they have failed, for the whole scene exhibits a disgraceful unanimity; and, with regard to the prisoner, he can only be distinguished for a guilty pre-eminence in zeal and activity. It may not, however, be useless on this

---

34. 28 January 1791, Journal of the Senate of the United States of America, 1789-1793 A Century of Lawmaking for a New Nation, U.S. Congressional Documents and Debates, 1774-1875. Alexander Hamilton, the first Treasury Secretary, had proposed the tax to help with financial debt the fledgling United States incurred during the Revolutionary War.

35. On several occasions, angry farmers and distillers "tarred and feathered" tax collectors, stripping them naked and covering them in hot tar and feathers.

36. The assault on the home occurred over two days and involved gun fire exchanges which killed two protestors.

37. William Hogeland, The Whiskey Rebellion: George Washington, Alexander Hamilton, and the Frontier Rebels who Challenged America's Newfound Sovereignty (Simon & Schuster 2006). The tax inspector, John Neville, had served in the Continental Army under George Washington during the Revolutionary War achieving the rank of Brigadier General.

occasion to observe that *the fear which the law recognizes as an excuse for the perpetration of an offence must proceed from an immediate and actual danger, threatening the very life of the party. The apprehension of any loss of property, by waste or fire, or even an apprehension of a slight or remote injury to the person, furnish no excuse.*[38]

While duress was raised any number of times in the years following Vigol's unsuccessful attempt in 1795, it was not until 1980[39] that the Supreme Court substantively discussed duress in the criminal law context,[40] and not until 2006[41] that the Court referenced the elements. The 2006 decision in *Dixon v. U.S.* explained what are best understood as the traditional common law requirements for the duress defense. Specifically, that the defendant:

(1) was under an unlawful and imminent threat of death or serious bodily injury;

(2) had not recklessly or negligently placed themself in the situation;

(3) had no reasonable, legal alternative; and

(4) that a direct causal relationship existed between the criminal act and the avoidance of the threatened harm.

The *Dixon* case is also helpful in that the Court clarified that the defendant bears the burden of persuasion for duress claims. While some jurisdictions still require the prosecution to disprove duress once raised, most follow the federal approach.

The MPC expands the common law defense. Under the MPC, the requirements for a valid claim of duress are very similar to the common law. However, while the common law requires that force to be reasonably expected to cause serious injury or death, the MPC only requires that the force be of a nature that a person of "reasonable firmness" in that situation would be unable to resist. Additionally, the MPC does not foreclose the application of duress/compulsion to homicide offenses.

---

38. *United States v. Vigol*, 2 U.S. 346 (1795) (emphasis added). Of the 150 prosecuted, only two (Vigol and a Phillip Mitchel) were found guilty, representing the first two convictions for federal treason in U.S. history. Five months after they were sentenced to death by hanging, George Washington exercised the President's constitutional pardon authority for the first time, pardoning both, purportedly on the grounds that Mitchell was a "simpleton" and Vigol "insane." The excuse of insanity is discussed later in this chapter. *See* Patrick Grubbs, *Whiskey Rebellion Trials*, Encyclopedia of Greater Philadelphia *available at* https://philadelphiaencyclopedia.org/archive/whiskey-rebellion-trials/ (last visited Aug. 2, 2021); Carrie Hagen, *The First Presidential Pardon Pitted Alexander Hamilton Against George Washington*, Smithsonian Magazine (Aug. 29, 2017), https://www.smithsonianmag.com/history/first-presidential-pardon-pitted-hamilton-against-george-washington-180964659/.

39. *See United States v. Bailey*, 444 U.S. 394 (1980) (describing how and when duress may apply to a prisoner charged with escape).

40. The Supreme Court addressed duress in a civil context much earlier. *See Brown v. Pierce*, 74 U.S. 205, 214 (1868) (discussing the impact of duress on contracts).

41. *See Dixon v. U.S.*, 548 U.S. 1 (2006).

B. Well Grounded Fear and Escapability: Does the Defendant Have to Be Reasonable or Right?

In the following decision, the Ninth Circuit emphasizes an important aspect of the duress defense: that it requires a jury to assess the reasonableness of the defendant's judgment, not whether the defendant was completely accurate in that judgment. As you read the opinion, place yourself in the defendant's situation: what would you have reasonably believed?

United States v. Contento-Pachon

723 F.2d 691 (1984)
Ninth Circuit Court of Appeals

BOOCHEVER, Circuit Judge.

This case presents an appeal from a conviction for unlawful possession with intent to distribute a narcotic controlled substance in violation of 21 U.S.C. § 841(a)(1) (1976). At trial, the defendant attempted to offer evidence of duress and necessity defenses. The district court excluded this evidence on the ground that it was insufficient to support the defenses. We reverse because there was sufficient evidence of duress to present a triable issue of fact.

The defendant-appellant, Juan Manuel Contento-Pachon, is a native of Bogota, Colombia and was employed there as a taxicab driver. He asserts that one of his passengers, Jorge, offered him a job as the driver of a privately-owned car. Contento-Pachon expressed an interest in the job and agreed to meet Jorge and the owner of the car the next day.

Instead of a driving job, Jorge proposed that Contento-Pachon swallow cocaine-filled balloons and transport them to the United States. Contento-Pachon agreed to consider the proposition. He was told not to mention the proposition to anyone, otherwise he would "get into serious trouble." Contento-Pachon testified that he did not contact the police because he believes that the Bogota police are corrupt and that they are paid off by drug traffickers.

Approximately one week later, Contento-Pachon told Jorge that he would not carry the cocaine. In response, Jorge mentioned facts about Contento-Pachon's personal life, including private details which Contento-Pachon had never mentioned to Jorge. Jorge told Contento-Pachon that his failure to cooperate would result in the death of his wife and three-year-old child.

The following day the pair met again. Contento-Pachon's life and the lives of his family were again threatened. At this point, Contento-Pachon agreed to take the cocaine into the United States.

The pair met two more times. At the last meeting, Contento-Pachon swallowed 129 balloons of cocaine. He was informed that he would be watched at all times during the trip, and that if he failed to follow Jorge's instruction he and his family would be killed.

After leaving Bogota, Contento-Pachon's plane landed in Panama. Contento-Pachon asserts that he did not notify the authorities there because he felt that the Panamanian police were as corrupt as those in Bogota. Also, he felt that any such action on his part would place his family in jeopardy.

When he arrived at the customs inspection point in Los Angeles, Contento-Pachon consented to have his stomach x-rayed. The x-rays revealed a foreign substance which was later determined to be cocaine.

At Contento-Pachon's trial, the government moved to exclude the defenses of duress and necessity. The motion was granted. We reverse.

There are three elements of the duress defense: (1) an immediate threat of death or serious bodily injury, (2) a well-grounded fear that the threat will be carried out, and (3) no reasonable opportunity to escape the threatened harm. *United States v. Shapiro*, 669 F.2d 593, 596 (9th Cir. 1982). Sometimes a fourth element is required: the defendant must submit to proper authorities after attaining a position of safety. *United States v. Peltier*, 693 F.2d 96 (9th Cir. 1982) (per curiam).

Factfinding is usually a function of the jury, and the trial court rarely rules on a defense as a matter of law. See *Sandstrom v. Montana*, 442 U.S. 510, 523, 99 S. Ct. 2450, 2459, 61 L. Ed. 2d 39 (1979). If the evidence is insufficient as a matter of law to support a duress defense, however, the trial court should exclude that evidence. *United States v. Glaeser*, 550 F.2d 483, 487 (9th Cir. 1977).

The trial court found Contento-Pachon's offer of proof insufficient to support a duress defense because he failed to offer proof of two elements: immediacy and inescapability.[1] We examine the elements of duress.

Immediacy: The element of immediacy requires that there be some evidence that the threat of injury was present, immediate, or impending. "[A] veiled threat of future unspecified harm" will not satisfy this requirement. *Rhode Island Recreation Center v. Aetna Casualty and Surety Co.*, 177 F.2d 603, 605 (1st Cir. 1949). . . . The district court found that the initial threats were not immediate because "they were conditioned on defendant's failure to cooperate in the future and did not place defendant and his family in immediate danger."

Evidence presented on this issue indicated that the defendant was dealing with a man who was deeply involved in the exportation of illegal substances. Large sums of money were at stake and, consequently, Contento-Pachon had reason to believe that Jorge would carry out his threats. Jorge had gone to the trouble to discover that Contento-Pachon was married, that he had a child, the names of his wife and child, and the location of his residence. These were not vague threats of possible future harm. According to the defendant, if he had refused to cooperate, the consequences would have been immediate and harsh.

---

1. We believe that a triable issue was presented as to the third element, that the fear be well-grounded, based on the same facts that lead us to the conclusion as to the immediacy of the threats.

Contento-Pachon contends that he was being watched by one of Jorge's accomplices at all times during the airplane trip. As a consequence, the force of the threats continued to restrain him. Contento-Pachon's contention that he was operating under the threat of immediate harm was supported by sufficient evidence to present a triable issue of fact.

Escapability: The defendant must show that he had no reasonable opportunity to escape. See *United States v. Gordon*, 526 F.2d 406, 407 (9th Cir. 1975). The district court found that because Contento-Pachon was not physically restrained prior to the time he swallowed the balloons, he could have sought help from the police or fled. Contento-Pachon explained that he did not report the threats because he feared that the police were corrupt. The trier of fact should decide whether one in Contento-Pachon's position might believe that some of the Bogota police were paid informants for drug traffickers and that reporting the matter to the police did not represent a reasonable opportunity of escape.

If he chose not to go to the police, Contento-Pachon's alternative was to flee. We reiterate that the opportunity to escape must be reasonable. To flee, Contento-Pachon, along with his wife and three-year-old child, would have been forced to pack his possessions, leave his job, and travel to a place beyond the reaches of the drug traffickers. A juror might find that this was not a reasonable avenue of escape. Thus, Contento-Pachon presented a triable issue on the element of escapability.

Surrender to Authorities: As noted above, the duress defense is composed of at least three elements. The government argues that the defense also requires that a defendant offer evidence that he intended to turn himself in to the authorities upon reaching a position of safety. Although it has not been expressly limited, this fourth element seems to be required only in prison escape cases.

. . . .

In cases not involving escape from prison there seems little difference between the third basic requirement that there be no reasonable opportunity to escape the threatened harm and the obligation to turn oneself in to authorities on reaching a point of safety. Once a defendant has reached a position where he can safely turn himself in to the authorities he will likewise have a reasonable opportunity to escape the threatened harm.

That is true in this case. Contento-Pachon claims that he was being watched at all times. According to him, at the first opportunity to cooperate with authorities without alerting the observer, he consented to the x-ray. We hold that a defendant who has acted under a well-grounded fear of immediate harm with no opportunity to escape may assert the duress defense, if there is a triable issue of fact whether he took the opportunity to escape the threatened harm by submitting to authorities at the first reasonable opportunity.

The defense of necessity is available when a person is faced with a choice of two evils and must then decide whether to commit a crime or an alternative act that constitutes a greater evil. . . . Contento-Pachon has attempted to justify his violation of 21 U.S.C. § 841(a)(1) by showing that the alternative, the death of his family, was a greater evil.

Traditionally, in order for the necessity defense to apply, the coercion must have had its source in the physical forces of nature. The duress defense was applicable when the defendant's acts were coerced by a human force. W. LaFave & A. Scott, Handbook on Criminal Law Sec. 50 at 383 (1972). This distinction served to separate the two similar defenses. But modern courts have tended to blur the distinction between duress and necessity.

It has been suggested that, "the major difference between duress and necessity is that the former negates the existence of the requisite mens rea for the crime in question, whereas under the latter theory there is no actus reus." *United States v. Micklus*, 581 F.2d 612, 615 (7th Cir. 1978). The theory of necessity is that the defendant's free will was properly exercised to achieve the greater good and not that his free will was overcome by an outside force as with duress.

The defense of necessity is usually invoked when the defendant acted in the interest of the general welfare. For example, defendants have asserted the defense as a justification for (1) bringing laetrile into the United States for the treatment of cancer patients, [*United States v.*] *Richardson*, 588 F.2d at 1239; (2) unlawfully entering a naval base to protest the Trident missile system, *United States v. May*, 622 F.2d 1000, 1008-09 (9th Cir.), cert. denied, 449 U.S. 984, 101 S. Ct. 402, 66 L. Ed. 2d 247 (1980); (3) burning Selective Service System records to protest United States military action, *United States v. Simpson*, 460 F.2d 515, 517 (9th Cir. 1972).

Contento-Pachon's acts were allegedly coerced by human, not physical forces. In addition, he did not act to promote the general welfare. Therefore, the necessity defense was not available to him. Contento-Pachon mischaracterized evidence of duress as evidence of necessity. The district court correctly disallowed his use of the necessity defense.

Contento-Pachon presented credible evidence that he acted under an immediate and well-grounded threat of serious bodily injury, with no opportunity to escape. Because the trier of fact should have been allowed to consider the credibility of the proffered evidence,[2] we reverse. The district court correctly excluded Contento-Pachon's necessity defense.

Notes and Questions

1. The Ninth Circuit listed three elements to a duress claim: (1) an immediate threat of death or serious bodily injury, (2) a well-grounded fear that the threat will be carried out, and (3) no reasonable opportunity to escape the threatened harm. The

---

2. ... We acknowledge that the record in this case will support a finding of guilty. The problem is that there has been evidence tendered which, if found credible by the jury, would justify a determination that Contento-Pachon acted under duress. A defendant has the right to have a jury resolve the disputed factual issues. ...

Supreme Court in *Dixon* listed four elements: (1) was under an unlawful and imminent threat of death or serious bodily injury; (2) had not recklessly or negligently placed themself in the situation; (3) had no reasonable, legal alternative; and (4) that a direct causal relationship existed between the criminal act and the avoidance of the threatened harm. Clearly there is a stylistic difference between the two approaches, but substantively, are they really that different?

2. Before trial, the prosecution successfully moved *in limine* to exclude the defense of the excuse of duress and the justification of necessity. That meant that at trial, Contento-Pachon could not introduce evidence supporting a claim of duress or necessity or argue for those claims, and that the jury did not receive an instruction on either defense. Once a judge grants a motion to exclude a defense, any evidence related to that defense becomes irrelevant.

3. Duress vs. Necessity. The Court of Appeals ruled that the District Court correctly disallowed Contento-Pachon's attempts at asserting a necessity defense.[42] Why was the District Court correct in disallowing necessity but incorrect in disallowing duress? To help differentiate between duress and necessity, consider the following chart.

	Duress	Necessity
Mens Rea	Implies absence of individual culpability (b/c of coercion)—in the culpability sense of MR.	Mens Rea exists—Implies absence of a criminal act. (thus negates AR)
Free Will	Exercise of free will to do what would otherwise be criminal coerced by outside (human) forces.	Exercise of free will to do what would otherwise be criminal was justified by necessity.
Cause of extreme situation	Human	Non-Human (normally)
Choice	Coercing actor's threats overwhelm DEF's will. DEF forced to make the wrong choice.	DEF confronted with choice of 2 evils and decides to commit crime to avoid greater evil. DEF makes the right choice.
Accomplice Liability	Yes—Duress is personal	No—No "Crime"
Rationale	Excuse—no effective deterrent (b/c circumstances under which DEF acted highly fact-specific?) CL Limit: no defense for homicide CL/MPC Limit: not available if DEF put himself in position of risk.	Justification—act was choice of lesser evil that society does not condemn MPC Limit: if DEF was reckless or negligent in creating risk, DEF has no defense to reckless/negligent crime. CL Limit: not a defense for homicide
Ultimate Issue for Trier of Fact	Did DEF make a subjectively honest & objectively reasonable judgment that submitting to the coercion to commit a crime was the only feasible option to avoid a greater harm to him or another innocent person?	Did DEF make a subjectively honest & objectively reasonable judgment that committing the crime in order to avert a greater harm was the right thing to do?

---

42. For additional discussion on classifying excuses as either necessity or duress, see Monu Bedi, *Excusing Behavior: Reclassifying the Federal Common Law Defenses of Duress and Necessity Relying on the Victim's Role*, 101 J. OF CRIM. L. & CRIMINOLOGY 575 (2011).

4. The majority "acknowledged that the record in this case will support a finding of guilty." So why did the Court of Appeals reverse and remand the case? Consider this: did the court decide whether the defendant acted under duress or merely whether that was a triable issue?

5. The duress defense is often raised by defendants claiming circumstances similar to Contento-Pachon, that while the defendant attempted to smuggle illegal drugs into the United States, they only did so because of the threats to family in their home country. When a judge allows a defendant to introduce evidence in support of and argue for duress, the judge will then add duress to the list of instructions provided to the jury. While receiving the duress jury instruction is an important step for a criminal defendant, it doesn't mean there will be a not guilty verdict. If and when instructed, the jury decides whether or not duress existed. *See* Walter Gonzalez, *Busted at the Border: Duress and Blind Mule Defenses in Border Crossing Cases*, 42 Nat. Assoc. Crim. Def. L. Champion 1 (2018) (discussing the frequency defendants claim duress and ignorance in drug cases at or near the border); Elizabeth A. Keyes, *Duress in Immigration Law*, 44 Seattle U. L. Rev. 307 (2021) (discussing the "unclear and highly unstable" application of duress to immigration law).

6. Common law duress and felony murder. As discussed in the introduction, at common law, duress was not a defense to a murder charge because duress reflects a balancing of harms and, with murder, the harm avoided is equal to the harm caused. But what about felony murder? Duress remains inapplicable for the murder charge, but common law jurisdictions "carved a special exception into the prohibition and approved of duress as a defense to felony murder where it also serves as a valid defense to the underlying felony." *See* Russell Shankland, *Duress and the Underlying Felony*, 98 J. Crim. L & Criminology 1227 (2009).

7. Presenting a duress defense requires a defendant and their attorney to perform a "risk analysis." It's generally difficult for a defendant to introduce sufficient evidence of the various elements of duress without testifying. When the defendant testifies, he or she is first questioned by the defense counsel. After the defense counsel finishes asking questions, the prosecution then cross-examines the defendant. Cross-examination is a form of adversarial questioning, and the defendant is under oath (and thus subject to a perjury charge for any knowingly false statements). Depending on the facts of the case and the defendant's criminal history, cross-examination poses significant risks.

8. In the Whiskey Rebellion case discussed above, the trial judge rejected Vogel's argument that protest leaders essentially forced him to participate by threatening to destroy his farm if he didn't. The judge held that:

> The apprehension of any loss of property, by waste or fire, or even an apprehension of a slight or remote injury to the person, furnish no excuse. If, indeed, such circumstances could avail, it would be in the power of every crafty leader of tumults and rebellion to indemnify his followers by uttering previous menaces; an avenue would be forever open for the escape of

unsuccessful guilt, and the whole fabric of society must, inevitably, be laid prostrate.

Do you agree that lowering the threshold for duress would prompt "crafty" leaders to "indemnify [their] followers"? For a more contemporary comparison, what about a gang member forced to do something against his will by other gang members after he chooses to join the gang? The United Kingdom's House of Lords held that "the defence of duress was unavailable when, as a result of the defendant's association with others engaged in criminal activity, he foresaw or ought reasonably to have foreseen the risk of being subjected to any compulsion by threats of violence." *R v. Z*, 2 A.C. 467 (2005). But what about where the gang member claims they did not voluntarily join the gang? *See* David S. Rutkowski, *A Coercion Defense for the Street Gang Criminal: Plugging the Moral Gap in Existing Law*, 10 NOTRE DAME J.L. ETHICS & PUB. POL'Y 137 (1996) (suggesting that the law should distinguish between those who voluntarily join a gang and those threatened or forced to do so).

9. What do you think of the common law requirement that the persons claiming duress must have faced a threat of serious bodily injury or death? In England, a university student who "allowed her bank account to be used for the transfer of crime proceeds from an invoice payment scam claimed she was put under duress by a man who threatened to expose explicit photographs of her." Nicole Donnelly, *Payment Scam Student claims she was under duress when she allowed bank account to be used by scammer*, SUNDAY WORLD, Jul. 28, 2021. In the U.S., if you were the woman's defense attorney and afforded the choice of raising her duress/compulsion claim in either a common law or MPC jurisdiction, whichh would you choose and why?

10. For additional discussion on the application of duress in the domestic violence context, see Laurie Kratky Dole, *Downward Adjustment and the Slippery Slope: The Use of Duress in Defense of Battered Offenders*, 56 OHIO ST. L.J. 667 (1995).

11. From what perspective is the reasonableness of the defendant's perception of threatened harm assessed, subjectively or objectively? In common law, the answer is objectively. *See United States v. Flores-Vasquez*, 279 F. App'x 312, 313 (5th Cir. 2008) (finding that "objective review" of evidence is required for duress instruction). Recall that the MPC's definition of duress includes "which a person of reasonable firmness in his situation would have been unable to resist. . . ." The words "a person of reasonable firmness" refers to an objective standard. The drafters of the MPC intended that "in his situation" to be given a "personal application" and that "stark tangible factors that differentiate the actor from another like his size or strength or age or health would be considered," although matters of temperament would not. As a result, the MPC version is considered a modified or hybrid subjective approach. *See* Claire Oakes Finkelstein, *Duress: A Philosophical Account of the Defense in Law*, 37 ARIZONA L. REV. 1015 (1995). Where does the MPC leave a mentally ill defendant claiming duress? *See* Steven Mulroy, *The Duress Defense's Uncharted Terrain: Applying It to Murder, Felony Murder, and the Mentally Retarded Defendant*, 43 SAN DIEGO L. REV. 159 (2006).

12. A woman is sitting in her car at a strip mall. An assailant jumps in the back seat, puts a realistic looking toy gun to the head of the woman's child in the back seat, and says, "If you don't go rob that convenience store and bring back the cash, I will kill your baby." The man then hands the woman another toy gun. The woman believes the gun is real and does what she is told. She approaches the register of the convenience store and points the pistol at the cashier and says, "Give me all the money." The cashier hands her the money, and she runs to her car and gives it to the assailant. He then flees. Both are arrested within 30 minutes. You are the prosecutor: who would you charge, and what crimes would you allege?

13. Now assume the same facts. However, when the woman points the pistol at the cashier, he is so frightened that he collapses as the result of a heart attack. The woman flees in panic as does the assailant. The cashier dies from the heart attack, but the coroner indicates he had a weak heart and was unusually susceptible to this type of fright-based reaction. Both the woman and the assailant are apprehended. Who would you charge, and what crimes would you allege?

C. Lack of Mental Responsibility

Mental dysfunction is a widely misunderstood criminal law defense. The mental dysfunction defense, or lack of mental responsibility, is "both exceptionally rare and exceptionally difficult to pull off."[43] The general consensus is that mental dysfunction is raised as a defense in "somewhere around one quarter to one half of one percent" of criminal cases.[44] Within that fraction, one study concluded that mental dysfunction is successfully raised, meaning an acquittal, less than 25% of the time.[45] According to another study, "the overwhelming majority" of defendants acquitted by reasons of mental dysfunction suffer from schizophrenia.[46]

Part of the reason why mental dysfunction as a defense is misunderstood is that "only the most bizarre cases rise to public notice . . . [a]nd it's in those cases that the insanity defense comes into play the most — because the thinking goes, who else but an insane person would do something so disturbing?"[47] For example, Jeffrey Dahmer, who killed at least seventeen men, the remains of some of whom he ate, unsuccessfully asserted mental dysfunction as a defense. Similarly, David Berkowitz, New York

---

43. Terrence McCoy, *Trial of 'American Sniper' Chris Kyle's Killer: Why the Insanity Defense Failed*, Wash. Post, Feb. 25, 2015.

44. Louis Kachulis, *Insane in the Mens Rea: Why Insanity Defense Reform is Long Overdue*, 26 Rev. L. & Soc. Jus. 251, 252 (2017). Kachulis estimates that "a successful insanity defense is raised in approximately one in every 20,000 criminal cases." *Id.*

45. LA Callahan et al., *The volume and characteristics of insanity defense pleas: an eight-state study*, 19 Bull. Am. Acad. Psychiatry Law 331 (1991).

46. John F. Martin, *The Insanity Defense: A Closer Look*, Wash. Post, Feb. 27, 1998.

47. Terrence McCoy, *Trial of 'American Sniper' Chris Kyle's Killer: Why the Insanity Defense Failed*, Wash. Post, Feb. 25, 2015.

City's "Son of Sam" killer who claimed to receive murder instructions from a neighbor's dog, unsuccessfully employed a mental dysfunction defense.

When a defense of mental dysfunction is successful, defendants are "rarely set free" and "typically sent to secure state psychiatric institutions until they are deemed no longer mentally ill or dangerous. Most will spend longer in a lockdown psychiatric center than they would have spent in prison had they pleaded guilty."[48]

Another byproduct of the rare instance of mental dysfunction defense succeeding is public outcry followed by a review and changes to a state's law and procedure. This unfortunate cycle has played out several times following assassination attempts, first in England and more recently in the United States. However, while there are variations of the mental dysfunction test throughout U.S. jurisdictions, there are several common threads that run through them all. First, the law presumes a defendant is sane at the time of the alleged offense. This means the defense arises only after the defendant both pleads the defense of lack of mental responsibility *and* produces some evidence to support that defense. Second, the defense is relevant only if the defendant produces evidence indicating he or she suffered from a severe mental disease or defect. This means there must be evidence of a medically recognized mental disease. As a general rule, unless the alleged mental disease or defect is recognized in the most recent edition of The Diagnostic and Statistical Manual of Mental Disorders, it will not qualify as the basis for such a plea. Third, by virtue of the first and second thread, it is a practical necessity that expert opinions are offered to assist the jury (or judge) in assessing the plea of lack of mental responsibility. While the ultimate determination remains vested in the fact-finder, it is almost inevitable that experts will be heavily relied upon to guide the jury in its determination.

It's important to distinguish mental competence to stand trial from the law of mental responsibility.[49] The standards and timing of each are different. Mental competence to stand trial involves assessing, at the time of trial, whether the defendant is able to understand the proceedings and assist their defense counsel. By contrast, mental responsibility employs one of the previously discussed tests to assess the defendant's actions at the time of the alleged offense.

1. Understanding the Various Legal Tests

The *Freeman* case below involves a defendant convicted of selling narcotics at a bench trial. At trial, Freeman claimed that he did not possess sufficient capacity to be held criminally responsible. At that time time, federal courts used the M'Naghten rule (over 120 years after its formulation). The trial judge found that Freeman did not

---

48. Russ Buettner, *Mentally Ill, but Insanity Plea is Long Shot*, N.Y. Times, Apr. 3, 2013; *see also* Charles Patrick Ewing, Insanity: Murder, Madness, and the Law (2008); Mac McClelland, *When 'Not Guilty' Is a Life Sentence*, N.Y. Times Magazine, Sept. 27, 2017 (discussing indefinite involuntary confinement in psychiatric hospitals following mental health acquittal).

49. L.E. Kois, et al., *Competence to stand trial and criminal responsibility, in* Psychological Science and the Law (N. Brewer & A.B. Douglass eds. 2019).

meet M'Naghten's rigid standards. On appeal, the Second Circuit engages in a review of the mental responsibility tests. As you read the *Freeman* case, consider whether there is test or standard for mental responsibility which is fair to defendants, the prosecution and society. Is such a goal even possible?

United States v. Freeman

357 F.2d 606 (1966)
Second Circuit Court of Appeals

KAUFMAN, Circuit Judge:

. . . .

[The M'Naghten Test]

Daniel M'Naghten suffered from what now would be described as delusions of persecution. Apparently, he considered his major persecutor to be Robert Peel, then Prime Minister of England, for M'Naghten came to London with the intention of assassinating the chief of the Queen's government. His plan would have succeeded but for the fact that Peel chose to ride in Queen Victoria's carriage because of her absence from the city, while Drummond, his secretary, rode in the vehicle which normally would have been occupied by Peel. M'Naghten, believing that the Prime Minister was riding in his own carriage, shot and killed Drummond in error.

. . . .

After a lengthy trial in 1843, M'Naghten was found "not guilty by reason of insanity." M'Naghten's exculpation from criminal responsibility was most significant for several reasons. . . .

Because M'Naghten focuses only on the cognitive aspect of the personality, i.e., the ability to know right from wrong, we are told by eminent medical scholars that it does not permit the jury to identify those who can distinguish between good and evil but who cannot control their behavior. The result is that instead of being treated at appropriate mental institutions for a sufficiently long period to bring about a cure or sufficient improvement so that the accused may return with relative safety to himself and the community, he is ordinarily sentenced to a prison term as if criminally responsible and then released as a potential recidivist with society at his mercy. To the extent that these individuals continue to be released from prison because of the narrow scope of M'Naghten, that test poses a serious danger to society's welfare.

We recognize our inability to determine at this point whether society possesses sufficient hospital facilities and doctors to deal with criminals [whose conduct is excused on mental responsibility grounds]. But our function as judges requires us to interpret the law in the best interest of society as a whole. We therefore suggest that if there are inadequate facilities and personnel in this area, Congress, the state legislatures and federal and state executive departments should promptly consider bridging the gap. Biggs, [The Guilty Mind (1955)] at 145. . . .

Similarly, M'Naghten's single track emphasis on the cognitive aspect of the personality recognizes no degrees of incapacity. Either the defendant knows right from wrong or he does not and that is the only choice the jury is given. But such a test is grossly unrealistic; our mental institutions, as any qualified psychiatrist will attest, are filled with people who to some extent can differentiate between right and wrong, but lack the capacity to control their acts to a substantial degree. As the commentary to the American Law Institute's Model Penal Code observes, "The law must recognize that when there is no black and white it must content itself with different shades of gray." American Law Institute, Model Penal Code (Tentative Drafts, Nos. 1, 2, 3 and 4) 158 (1956). . . .

A further fatal defect of the M'Naghten Rules stems from the unrealistically tight shackles which they place upon expert psychiatric testimony. When the law limits a testifying psychiatrist to stating his opinion whether the accused is capable of knowing right from wrong, the expert is thereby compelled to test guilt or innocence by a concept which bears little relationship to reality. He is required thus to consider one aspect of the mind as a "logic-tight compartment in which the delusion holds sway leaving the balance of the mind intact. * * *" Glueck, [Mental Disorder and the Criminal Law (1925)] at 169-170.

Prominent psychiatrists have expressed their frustration when confronted with such requirements. Echoing such complaints, Edward de Grazia has asked, "How [does one] translate 'psychosis' or 'psychopathy' or 'dementia praecox' or even 'sociopathy' or 'mental disorder' or 'neurotic character disorder' or 'mental illness' into a psychiatric judgment of whether the accused knew 'right' from 'wrong.'" In stronger and more vivid terms, Dr. Lawrence Kolb, Director of the New York Psychiatric Institute, Professor and Chairman of the Department of Psychiatry at Columbia University and Director of the Psychiatric Service at Presbyterian Hospital, expressed a similar viewpoint when he declared that "answers supplied by a psychiatrist in regard to questions of rightness or wrongness of an act or 'knowing' its nature constitute a professional perjury." de Grazia, "The Distinction of Being Mad," 22 U. of Chi.L.Rev. 339, 341 (1955).

. . . .

The tremendous growth of psychiatric knowledge since the Victorian origins of M'Naghten and even the near-universal disdain in which it is held by present-day psychiatrists are not by themselves sufficient reasons for abandoning the test. At bottom, the determination whether a man is or is not held responsible for his conduct is not a medical but a legal, social or moral judgment. Ideally, psychiatrists—much like experts in other fields—should provide grist for the legal mill, should furnish the raw data upon which the legal judgment is based. It is the psychiatrist who informs as to the mental state of the accused—his characteristics, his potentialities, his capabilities. But once this information is disclosed, it is society as a whole, represented by judge or jury, which decides whether a man with the characteristics described should or should not be held accountable for his acts. . . .

[The Irresistible Impulse Test]

Efforts to supplement or replace the M'Naghten Rules with a more meaningful and workable test have persisted for generations, with varying degrees of success. Perhaps the first to receive judicial approval, however, was more an added fillip to M'Naghten than a true substitute: the doctrine which permits acquittal on grounds of lack of responsibility when a defendant is found to have been driven by an "irresistible impulse" to commit his offense. In one form or another, the "irresistible impulse" test has become encrusted on the law of several jurisdictions, including the District Courts of this Circuit . . .

As it has commonly been employed, however, we find the "irresistible impulse" test to be inherently inadequate and unsatisfactory. Psychiatrists have long questioned whether "irresistible impulses" actually exist; the more basic legal objection to the term "irresistible impulse" is that it is too narrow and carries the misleading implication that a crime impulsively committed must have been perpetrated in a sudden and explosive fit. Thus, the "irresistible impulse" test is unduly restrictive because it excludes the far more numerous instances of crimes committed after excessive brooding and melancholy by one who is unable to resist sustained psychic compulsion or to make any real attempt to control his conduct. In seeking one isolated and indefinite cause for every act, moreover, the test is unhappily evocative of the notions which underlay M'Naghten — unfortunate assumptions that the problem can be viewed in black and white absolutes and in crystal-clear causative terms. Wechsler, "The Criteria of Criminal Responsibility," 22 U. of Chi.L.Rev. 367, 393 (1955).

In so many instances the criminal act may be the reverse of impulsive; it may be coolly and carefully prepared yet nevertheless the result of a diseased mind. The "irresistible impulse" test is therefore little more than a gloss on M'Naghten, rather than a fundamentally new approach to the problem of criminal responsibility. It is, as one professor explained, "a relatively unobnoxious attempt to improve upon M'Naghten." See Report, Royal Commission on Capital Punishment, op. cit. *supra* note 42 at 110. Mueller, ["M'Naghten Remains Irreplaceable: Recent Events in the Law of Incapacity," 50 Georgetown L.Jour. 105, (1961)]: at 107.

[The Durham Test]

With the exception of New Hampshire, American courts waited until 1954 and Judge Bazelon's opinion for the District of Columbia Circuit in *Durham v. United States*, for legal recognition that disease or defect of the mind may impair the whole mind and not a subdivided portion of it. The *Durham* court swept away the intellectual debris of a century and articulated a test which was as simple in its formulation as its sources were complex. A defendant is not criminally responsible, wrote Judge Bazelon, "if his unlawful act was the product of mental disease or mental defect."94 U.S.App.D.C. 228, 214 F.2d 862, 45 A.L.R.2d 1430 (1954).

The advantages of *Durham* were apparent and its arrival was widely hailed. The new test entirely eliminated the "right-wrong" dichotomy, and hence interred the overriding emphasis on the cognitive element of the personality which had for so long plagued M'Naghten. The fetters upon expert testimony were removed and psychiatrists were permitted and indeed encouraged to provide all relevant medical information for the common sense application of judge or jury.

Finally, *Durham* ended to a large degree the "professional perjury" decried by psychiatrists — the "juggling" of legal standards made inevitable by M'Naghten and rightly deplored by Justice Frankfurter. Too often, the unrealistic dogma of M'Naghten had compelled expert witnesses to "stretch" its requirements to "hard cases"; sympathetic to the plight of a defendant who was not, in fairness, responsible for his conduct, psychiatrists had found it necessary to testify that the accused did not know his act was "wrong" even when the defendant's words belied this conclusion. In its frank and express recognition that criminality resulting from mental disease or defect should not bring forth penal sanctions, *Durham* brought an end to this all too-frequent practice of "winking" at legal requirements, a practice which had contributed little to the self-respect and integrity of either medicine or the law.

In the aftermath of *Durham,* however, many students of the law recognized that the new rule, despite its many advantages, also possessed serious deficiencies. It has been suggested, for example, that *Durham's* insistence that an offense be the "product" of a mental disease or defect raised near-impossible problems of causation, closely resembling those encountered by the M'Naghten and irresistible impulse tests. Weihofen, "The Flowering of New Hampshire," 22 U. of Chi.L.Rev. 356, 360 (1955).

The most significant criticism of *Durham,* however, is that it fails to give the fact-finder any standard by which to measure the competency of the accused. As a result, psychiatrists when testifying that a defendant suffered from a "mental disease or defect" in effect usurped the jury's function. This problem was strikingly illustrated in 1957, when a staff conference at Washington's St. Elizabeth's Hospital reversed its previous determination and reclassified "psychopathic personality" as a "mental disease." Because this single hospital provides most of the psychiatric witnesses in the District of Columbia courts, juries were abruptly informed that certain defendants who had previously been considered responsible were now to be acquitted. *Blocker v. United States*, 110 U.S.App.D.C. 41, 288 F.2d 853, 860 (1961) (Burger, J. concurring). It seems clear that a test which permits all to stand or fall upon the labels or classifications employed by testifying psychiatrists hardly affords the court the opportunity to perform its function of rendering an independent legal and social judgment.

. . . .

The genius of the common law has been its responsiveness to changing times, its ability to reflect developing moral and social values. Drawing upon the past, the law must serve — and traditionally has served — the needs of the present. In the past century, psychiatry has evolved from tentative, hesitant gropings in the dark of human ignorance to a recognized and important branch of modern medicine. The outrage of a frightened Queen has for too long caused us to forego the expert guidance that modern psychiatry is able to provide.

. . . .

Since Freeman's responsibility was determined under the rigid standards of the M'Naghten Rules, we are compelled to reverse his conviction and remand the case for a new trial in which the criteria employed will be those provided by Section 4.01 of the Model Penal Code.

. . . .

Reversed and remanded.

The following case is an application of the MPC "substantial capacity" test and how to interpret and translate the statutory terms. Specifically, the court must decide how the word "wrongfulness" as used in the statutory test should be transformed into jury instructions. As you read *Wilson*, consider how the MPC improved on some aspects of the various responsibility tests while raising new questions and issues.

State v. Wilson

242 Conn. 605, 700 A.2d 633 (1997)
Supreme Court of Connecticut

[Wilson, fueled by a number of delusions involving, among others, large organizations seeking mind control, shot and killed the father of a high school classmate, following which he turned himself into police and confessed, claiming that he "had to do it." Wilson, relying on a portion of the state's mental responsibility test which asked whether the defendant appreciated the "wrongfulness" of his conduct, requested a jury instruction which the trial judge refused to issue, and which formed the basis of the portions of the appellate decision below. Wilson requested that the jury be instructed to acquit him on mental responsibility grounds if the evidence established that he believed his conduct to be morally justified.]

. . . .

The primary issue raised by this appeal is whether the trial court improperly failed to give an instruction defining the term "wrongfulness" under § 53a-13(a). Section 53a-13(a) provides that "[i]n any prosecution for an offense, it shall be an affirmative defense that the defendant, at the time he committed the proscribed act or acts, lacked substantial capacity, as a result of mental disease or defect, either to appreciate the *wrongfulness* of his conduct or to control his conduct within the requirements of the law." (Emphasis added.) In this case, the defendant requested that the trial court instruct the jury that wrongfulness is comprised of a moral element, so that "an accused is not criminally responsible for his offending act if, because of mental disease or defect, he believes that he is morally justified in his conduct-even though he may appreciate that his act is criminal." The trial court, however, refused to instruct the jury that the defendant was entitled to prevail under § 53a-13(a) if the evidence established that the defendant believed his conduct to be morally justified. . . .

. . . .

In 1967, as a result of growing dissatisfaction with the standards from which this common law test derived, the General Assembly adopted the American Law Institute's Model Penal Code test for insanity, now codified at § 53a-13,13 as a statutory standard to be invoked in lieu of the common law test. *State v. Toste*, 178 Conn. 626, 631, 424 A.2d 293 (1979). The Model Penal Code test provides, in language nearly identical to that now contained in § 53a-13(a), that "[a] person is not responsible for criminal conduct if at the time of such conduct as a result of mental disease or defect he lacks substantial capacity either to appreciate the criminality [wrongfulness] of his conduct or to conform his conduct to the requirements of law." (Brackets in original.) I A.L.I., Model Penal Code and Commentaries (1985) § 4.01(1), p. 163 (hereinafter Model Penal Code).

For purposes of this appeal, three features of the Model Penal Code test are noteworthy. First, like our prior common law standard, this test encompasses, albeit in a different form, both a cognitive and a volitional prong. Under the cognitive prong, a person is considered legally insane if, as a result of mental disease or defect, "he lacks substantial capacity . . . to appreciate the criminality [wrongfulness] of his conduct." *Id*. Under the volitional prong, a person also would be considered legally insane if "he lacks substantial capacity . . . to conform his conduct to the requirements of law." *Id*. Because the defendant does not claim that the trial court misinstructed the jury on the volitional prong of the insanity test, we need not consider the application of the volitional prong in our analysis.

Second, the Model Penal Code test focuses on the defendant's actual appreciation of, rather than merely his knowledge of, the wrongfulness of his conduct. Cf. General Statutes § 53a-13(a) (defendant must lack "substantial capacity, as a result of mental disease or defect . . . to appreciate the wrongfulness of his conduct"). The drafters of the Model Penal Code purposefully adopted the term "appreciate" in order to account for the defendant whose "detached or abstract awareness" of the wrongfulness of his conduct "does not penetrate to the affective level." I Model Penal Code, *supra*, § 4.01, comment 2, p. 166. As Herbert Wechsler, chief reporter for the Model Penal Code, stated in his model jury charge: "To appreciate the wrongfulness of conduct is, in short, to realize that it is wrong; to understand the idea as a matter of importance and reality; to grasp it in a way that makes it meaningful in the life of the individual, not as a bare abstraction put in words." *Id*., § 4.01, appendix C, p. 215.

The third important feature of the Model Penal Code test, and the most relevant for purposes of this appeal, is its alternative phrasing of the cognitive prong. By bracketing the term "wrongfulness" and juxtaposing that term with "criminality," the drafters purposefully left it to the individual state legislatures to decide which of these two standards to adopt to describe the nature of the conduct that a defendant must be unable to appreciate in order to qualify as legally insane. See *id*., § 4.01, explanatory note, p. 164; A.L.I., 38th Annual Meeting, Proceedings (1961) p. 315 (hereinafter Annual Meeting), remarks of Herbert Wechsler ("it seems to me appropriate that the final formulation [by the American Law Institute] present[s] these [terms] as alternatives"). The history of the Model Penal Code indicates that "wrongfulness" was offered as a choice so that any legislature, if it wishes, could introduce a "moral issue" into the test for insanity. Annual Meeting, *supra*, p. 315, remarks of Herbert Wechsler.

. . . .

The text accompanying § 4.01 of the Model Penal Code, upon which § 53a-13 is modeled, suggests that its drafters intended that the moral element of "wrongfulness" be measured by a defendant's capacity to understand society's moral standards. In his model jury charge, for example, Professor Wechsler suggests the following language: "[A] person may have knowledge of the facts about his conduct and of the immediate surrounding circumstances and still be rendered quite incapable of grasping the idea that it is wrong, in the sense that it is condemned by the law and *commonly accepted moral standards*." (Emphasis added.) I Model Penal Code, *supra*, § 4.01, appendix C, p. 214. Similarly, the commentary on the insanity test of the Model Penal Code emphasizes a defendant's capacity to appreciate "society's moral disapproval of his conduct," noting that "[a]ppreciating 'wrongfulness' may be taken to mean appreciating that the *community* regards the behavior as wrongful." (Emphasis added.) *Id.*, § 4.01, comment 3, p. 169. Although the rejection under the Model Penal Code of the personal standard is not beyond debate, we conclude that the drafters of § 4.01 did not intend that a defendant who appreciates both the illegality and the societal immorality of his actions be relieved of criminal responsibility due to his purely personal, albeit delusional, moral code. . . .

There may well be cases in which a defendant's delusional ideation causes him to harbor personal beliefs that so cloud his cognition as to render him incapable of recognizing the broader moral implications of his actions. In such cases, the defendant would be entitled to be acquitted under the cognitive prong of the defense.

Those cases involving the so-called "deific command," in our view, fall into this category. Contrary to the defendant's position at oral argument, we are hard pressed to envision an individual who, because of mental disease or defect, truly believes that a divine power has authorized his actions, but, at the same time, also truly believes that such actions are immoral. An individual laboring under a delusion that causes him to believe in the divine approbation of his conduct is an individual who, in all practicality, is unlikely to be able fully to appreciate the wrongfulness of that conduct. See [*People v. Serravo*, 823 P.2d 138], at 139-40; *People v. Schmidt*, 216 N.Y. 324, 337, 110 N.E. 945 (1915) (if a person, because of disease or delusion, "believes that he has a command from the Almighty to kill, it is difficult to understand how such a man *can* know that it is wrong for him to do it" [emphasis in original; internal quotation marks omitted]), reh. denied, 216 N.Y. 762, 111 N.E. 1095 (1916); I Model Penal Code, *supra*, § 4.01, appendix C.

A defendant should not be relieved of criminal liability, however, if his mental illness does not deprive him of substantial capacity to appreciate the boundaries of societal morality and if he elects to transgress those boundaries in pursuit of a delusional personal belief system that he appreciates society would not itself accept. To permit otherwise "would seriously undermine the criminal law [by allowing] one who violated the law to be excused from criminal responsibility solely because, in his own conscience, his act was not morally wrong." *State v. Crenshaw, supra*, 98 Wash.2d at 797, 659 P.2d 488.

. . . .

We conclude, rather, that a defendant does not truly "appreciate the wrongfulness of his conduct" as stated in § 53a-13(a) if a mental disease or defect causes him both to harbor a distorted perception of reality and to believe that, under the circumstances as he honestly perceives them, his actions do not offend societal morality, even though he may also be aware that society, on the basis of the criminal code, does not condone his actions. Thus, a defendant would be entitled to prevail under § 53a-13(a) if, as a result of his mental disease or defect, he sincerely believes that society would approve of his conduct if it shared his understanding of the circumstances underlying his actions. This formulation appropriately balances the concepts of societal morality that underlie our criminal law with the concepts of moral justification that motivated the legislature's adoption of the term "wrongfulness" in our insanity statute.

. . . .

Because the meaning of wrongfulness under § 53a-13(a) was left unclear and because that lack of clarity affected a central element of the defendant's claim of insanity, we conclude that the trial court's failure to define "wrongfulness" in terms of the defendant's appreciation of societal morality constituted harmful error.

Notes and Questions

1. Who decides whether to plead insanity? One of the odd aspects of the lack of mental responsibility defense is that the decision whether or not to plead the defense belongs almost exclusively to the defendant. So, imagine a severely mentally ill defendant who believes everyone else is wrong and can't understand the reality he can; do you think he would respond well to his defense lawyer recommending he plead insanity? This is why some of the most obviously mentally ill defendants, like the Long Island Railroad murderer Colin Ferguson, reject the insanity defense and, in many cases, fire their lawyers and represent themselves. *See* Peter Marks, *Ferguson Collapses in Court After Scorning Insanity Plea*, N.Y. Times, Aug. 20, 1994.

2. John Hinckley purportedly attempted to assassinate President Reagan in an effort to impress actress Jodie Foster, whom Hinckley had never met. Similar to M'Naghten, following his acquittal, Hinckley was confined to a mental health facility. Hinckley would spend almost 35 years in the facility before his release in 2016. *See* Alexandra Pollard, *Jodie Foster and the stalker who shot the president 'to win her heart'*, Independent, Mar. 31, 2021.

3. As mentioned earlier, one of the individuals Hinckley shot was the White House

Press Secretary, Jim Brady. Brady, shot in the head, was the most severely wounded and lived the rest of his life partially paralyzed, wheelchair bound and with slurred speech. Brady and his wife Sarah would go on to establish the Brady Campaign to Prevent Gun Violence, a non-profit organization advocating for gun control and against gun violence. When Brady died in 2014, the medical examiner ruled the death a homicide, that in essence Hinckley caused the death by shooting Brady in 1981; the criminal result, death, just took 33 years to manifest. *See* Peter Herman & Michael Ruane, *Medical Examiner Rules James Brady's Death a Homicide*, WASH. POST, Aug. 8, 2014. Setting aside double jeopardy concerns and assuming no statute of limitations concerns, what do you think the outcome would or should be in prosecuting Hinckley now for homicide?

4. In addition to reform efforts, six U.S. states have essentially eliminated mental dysfunction defenses during the guilt/innocence phase of trial.[50] In these jurisdictions, mental disease evidence becomes relevant during the sentencing phase for a defendant who may be found, "guilty but insane."

5. In 2011, Kansas modified its mental responsibility law such that the only way mental illness may lead to an acquittal is through the cognitive incapacity test, which examines whether a defendant was able to understand what he was doing when he committed a crime. Kansas does not recognize the moral-incapacity test, which predicates criminal liability on the defendant understanding that their actions were morally wrong. In 2020, in *Kahler v. Kansas,* the U.S. Supreme Court upheld the Kansas law and reiterated that criminal responsibility must remain "the province of the States."[51]

6. At U.S. military courts-martial, when mental responsibility is at issue, the military judge will issue the following instruction. If you were a juror, would you find this instruction helpful?

> The evidence in this case raises the issue of whether the accused lacked criminal responsibility for the offense(s) of (state the alleged offense(s)) as a result of a severe mental disease or defect. The accused is presumed to be mentally responsible. This presumption is overcome only if you determine, by clear and convincing evidence, that the accused was not mentally responsible. Note that, while the government has the burden of proving the elements of the offense(s) beyond a reasonable doubt, the defense has the burden of proving by clear and convincing evidence that the accused was not mentally responsible. As the finders of fact in this case, you must first decide whether, at the time of the offense(s) of (state the alleged offense(s)), the accused actually suffered from a severe mental disease or defect. The term "severe mental disease or defect" can be no better defined in the law than by the use of the term itself. However, a severe mental disease or defect does not, in the

---

50. Robinson & Williams, *supra* note 8.
51. *See Kahler v. Kansas*, 589 U.S. __, 140 S. Ct. 1021 (2020).

legal sense, include an abnormality manifested only by repeated criminal or otherwise antisocial conduct or by nonpsychotic behavior disorders and personality disorders. If the accused at the time of the offense(s) of (state the alleged offense(s)) was not suffering from a severe mental disease or defect, (he) (she) has no defense of lack of mental responsibility. If you determine that, at the time of the offense(s) of (state the alleged offense(s)), the accused was suffering from a severe mental disease or defect, then you must decide whether, as a result of that severe mental disease or defect, the accused was unable to appreciate the nature and quality or wrongfulness of (his) (her) conduct. If the accused was able to appreciate the nature and quality and the wrongfulness of (his) (her) conduct, (he) (she) is criminally responsible regardless of whether the accused was then suffering from a severe mental disease or defect. On the other hand, if the accused had a delusion of such a nature that (he) (she) was unable to appreciate the nature and quality or the wrongfulness of (his) (her) acts, the accused cannot be held criminally responsible for (his) (her) acts, provided such a delusion resulted from a severe mental disease or defect.

7. Defendant is on trial for allegedly murdering her four children. She offers a plea of lack of mental responsibility and offers substantial expert opinion evidence that at the time of the offense, she suffered from severe schizophrenia. The experts all admit she was able to understand that she was killing her children, but they also explain that she was convinced that she needed to kill them in order to protect them from going to hell; that she believed they needed to die as children in order to protect them from the corrupting effect of adulthood. You are the judge. If the jurisdiction follows the irresistible impulse doctrine, would you instruct the jury on lack of mental responsibility based on this evidence? What if the jurisdiction followed the M'Naghten rule? If the issue related to the M'Naghten rule, what would be the key focus of your cross-examination as the prosecutor?

2. Diminished Mental Capacity

Diminished mental capacity is a defense involving mental disease or defect which does not rise to the level of a mental responsibility defense. Mental responsibility "is not concerned with the mens rea element of the crime; rather, it operates to completely excuse the defendant whether or not guilt can be proven."[52] As a result, mental responsibility is a defense to all crimes, regardless of mens rea. By contrast, "diminished capacity involves a defendant claiming that their mental condition is such that they cannot attain the culpable state of mind required by the definition of the crime."[53] Diminished capacity defenses come in two forms: mens rea and culpability.

52. *United States v. Twine*, 853 F.2d 676, 678 (9th Cir. 1988).
53. *United States v. Fazzini*, 871 F.2d 635, 641 (7th Cir. 1989).

In the mens rea version, diminished capacity serves as an obstacle to proving mens rea. It is attractive to defendants because, unlike mental responsibility, diminished capacity can lead to an acquittal (and no involuntary civil commitment). Most states do not allow the mens rea version, and the Supreme Court has held that it is not constitutionally required.[54]

Opposition to the mens rea variant gained momentum following a 1979 California case in which Dan White, a San Francisco City Supervisor who had learned he was not to be reappointed for another term, shot and killed the Mayor of San Franciso, George Mocsone, and a City Supervisor, Harvey Milk. White demonstrated significant premeditation and deliberation in surreptitiously entering City Hall to avoid metal detectors, killing Moscone, walking down the hall and reloading (having had the presence of mind to bring ammunition) and killing Milk. At trial, White acknowledged shooting both officials but claimed he did so because of stress and depression over his not being reappointed to another term as City Supervisor. He was found guilty of voluntary manslaughter and sentenced to eight years confinement. An urban myth developed that White's defense was based on his diet consisting of almost exclusively junk food. While factually incorrect, the myth affected the public's perception of the mens rea variant of diminished capacity and led to many states, including California, to prohibit its use during the guilt/innocence phase of trial.[55] By contrast, the culpability variant allows a defendant charged with murder to introduce evidence of temporary loss of mental responsibility in the form of common law sudden heat of passion and MPC extreme emotional disturbance. As was discussed in the Introduction to Homicide Offenses section earlier, SHOP and EED can lead to murder being downgraded to manslaughter.

Returning to consideration of how juries are instructed on these complex issues, when diminished capacity (or partial mental responsibility) is at issue in a trial, the judge will issue an instruction similar to this example from the military pattern instruction guide. Note the blanks for the judge to complete before issuing. The judge will fill in these blanks based on the evidence that was actually produced at trial.

> An issue of partial mental responsibility has been raised by the evidence with respect to (state the applicable offense(s)). In determining this issue you must consider all relevant facts and circumstances and the evidence presented on the issue of lack of mental responsibility. One of the elements of (this) (these) offense(s) is the requirement of (premeditation) (the specific intent to _____) (that the accused knew that _____) (that the accused's acts were willful (as opposed to only negligent)). An accused may be sane and yet, because of some underlying (mental (disease) (defect) (impairment) (condition) (deficiency)) (character or behavior disorder), may be mentally

54. *See Clark v. Arizona,* 548 U.S. 735 (2006).

55. *See* Carol Pogash, *Myth of the 'Twinkie defense' / The verdict in the Dan White case wasn't based on his ingestion of junk food,* S.F. GATE, Nov. 23, 2003.

incapable of (entertaining (the premeditated design to kill) (the specific intent to _____) (having the knowledge that _____) (acting willfully). You should, therefore, consider in connection with all the relevant facts and circumstances, evidence tending to show that the accused may have been suffering from a (mental (disease) (defect) (impairment) (condition) (deficiency)) (character or behavior disorder) (_____) of such consequence and degree as to deprive (him/her) of the ability to (act willfully) (entertain (the premeditated design to kill) (the specific intent to _____)) (know that _____). The burden of proof is upon the government to establish the guilt of the accused by legal and competent evidence beyond a reasonable doubt. If you are not satisfied beyond a reasonable doubt that the accused, at the time of the alleged offenses(s), was mentally capable of ((entertaining (the premeditated design to kill) (the specific intent to _____)) (knowing that _____) (acting willfully in _____), you must find the accused Not Guilty of (that) (those) offense(s).

Notes & Questions

1. Does the instruction above reflect an application of diminished capacity as an "obstacle" to proof of specific intent/mens rea, or a "partial mitigation" application of the theory?

2. One way to clarify the two different applications of diminished capacity is to analogize them to other defense theories. When a defendant is permitted to offer diminished capacity evidence to challenge the proof of a specific mens rea/intent element, the application mirrors the defense of mistake of fact or voluntary intoxication: the evidence is relevant only on the question of whether the prosecution proves beyond a reasonable doubt that the defendant was able to form the requisite mens rea. In contrast, when a defendant is permitted to offer diminished capacity evidence as a partial mitigation, the application mirrors the partial defense of extreme emotional disturbance: the evidence is relevant to the question of whether the defendant should be partially *excused* for an offense even if the prosecution proves all material elements.

3. Defendant is brought to trial for first-degree murder. Defendant seeks to present opinion evidence from a psychiatric expert. The expert's opinion indicates that at the time of the killing, the defendant understood what he was doing and that what he was doing was wrong. However, the opinion also indicates defendant was suffering a mental defect that compromised his ability to rationally weigh the gravity and consequences of his actions. The jurisdiction follows the M'Naghten rule for lack of mental responsibility as an excuse defense, and also allows a jury instruction like the one reprinted above. You are the judge. Will you allow this evidence to be presented to the jury? If so, will you give a M'Naghten Instruction? What about an instruction like the one reprinted above?

D. Intoxication

As discussed in the introduction, involuntary intoxication is a complete defense, while voluntary intoxication provides, at most, partial mitigation. As a result, defendants are incentivized to have their intoxication characterized as involuntary.

In essence, involuntary intoxication requires that the defendant not exercise independent or informed judgment in consuming the intoxicant. Involuntary intoxication envisions a circumstance whereby a defendant is made intoxicated by someone else without the defendant's knowledge or consent. This could take the form of having alcohol placed in purportedly alcohol free punch, drugs being baked into brownies, or through an error by a doctor or pharmacist.[56]

Courts tend to strictly construe involuntary intoxication claims.[57] For example, a defendant who smokes what they know to be marijuana but is unaware that the marijuana is laced with another drug is not able to claim involuntary intoxication.[58]

Involuntary intoxication does not require a third party. The defendant may be the source of his or her involuntary intoxication, but this must be the result of a genuine accident or mistake. Frequently, a defendant will acknowledge voluntarily consuming or ingesting two or more different intoxicants and argue the resulting intoxication was the byproduct of the reaction between the two intoxicants and thus involuntary. The strongest argument a defendant can make is when: all the intoxicants are legal, all directions and limitations on their use followed, and the defendant has no past experience or knowledge of the how the intoxicants react in their system.[59]

As you read *Veleazquez*, consider whether the defendant's history of alcohol related blackouts was helpful to his argument that beer, tequila, and valium combined to result in involuntary intoxication which precluded his ability to commit first degree murder.

---

56. *See* Jennifer Piel, *The Defense of Involuntary Intoxication by Prescribed Medications: An Appellate Case Review*, 43 J. AM. ACAD. PSYCH & L. 321 (2015).

57. *See* Meghan P. Ingle, *Law on the Rocks: The Intoxication Defenses Are Being Eighty-Sixed*, 55 VANDERBILT LAW REVIEW 607 (2019).

58. *United States v. Ward*, 14 M.J. 950 (A.C.M.R. 1982) .

59. "An accused who voluntarily takes the first drink, knowing from past experience that the natural and reasonably foreseeable consequences of that act will be a violent intoxicating reaction cannot claim that his condition was 'involuntary.'" *United States v. Schumacher*, 11 M.J. 612 (A.C.M.R. 1981). Similarly, "involuntary intoxication is not available if accused is aware of his reduced tolerance for alcohol (such as when also ingesting other drugs) but chooses to consume it anyway." *United States v. Hensler*, 44 M.J. 184 (C.A.A.F. 1996).

People v. Velazquez

2010 Cal. App. Unpub. LEXIS 5919, 2010 WL 2913042 (Jul. 27, 2010)
California Court of Appeals

BUTZ, J.

A jury convicted defendant Juan Antonio Velazquez of first-degree murder. (Pen. Code, § 187, subd. (a).) The trial court sentenced him to a state prison term of 25 years to life. On appeal, defendant contends the trial court erred in rejecting his request for a jury instruction on involuntary intoxication. . . . Finding . . . his contention[] without merit, we [] affirm the judgment.

Factual Background

In the early morning of March 21, 2008, Neal Singer was drinking beer at Jack's Back, a bar in Lodi. Between 1:30 and 2:00 a.m., Singer played a game of pool with defendant. After the game, Singer and defendant became embroiled in an altercation over a $40 pool bet. Defendant told Singer, "I won, let me get my money." Shortly before closing time the altercation moved outside in front of the bar. Defendant appeared to be drunk and agitated, and his eyes were heavy and bloodshot. Singer was acting "drunk and obnoxious."

At approximately 2:00 a.m., residents of a nearby apartment building were awakened by a disturbance in an adjacent parking lot. Singer was screaming, "Help me, I need help, help me." The residents watched as defendant threw rocks and a piece of concrete at Singer, who was lying face down on the ground. Defendant also kicked Singer in the head. As defendant stood over Singer, he said, "I'm going to kill you." When a resident told defendant to leave Singer alone and threatened to call the police, defendant responded, "I don't care, call the police." He then walked slowly, in staggered fashion, away from the scene.

Lodi police officers arrived at the scene and found Singer's body lying face-down in a pool of blood. His face had been crushed in. An autopsy revealed that Singer died of repeated blows to the head. He had sustained at least 56 distinct blunt force traumas. The injuries to the back of his head were likely caused by a 14-pound bloody piece of concrete recovered from the scene. Singer also suffered stomping injuries, including an injury bearing the imprint of a metal-toed shoe on his face.

An officer responding to the scene noticed defendant walking at a hurried pace. The officer contacted defendant and noticed blood on his mouth and alcohol on his breath. Defendant was arrested and transported to jail, where a preliminary alcohol screening (PAS) revealed a blood-alcohol level of 0.129 percent. Defendant's blood was drawn and tested positive for Valium, a benzodiazepine.

An examination of defendant's sweatshirt, shoes, and jeans revealed bloodstains matching Singer's DNA. The blood on defendant's face also matched that of Singer. Several areas on the bloody piece of concrete recovered from the scene tested positive for Singer's DNA. Additionally, acetaminophen pills found in defendant's pockets were similar to those found approximately 20 feet from Singer's body at the crime scene.

[The Defense]

Defendant claimed he suffered from a mental disease or defect and/or voluntary intoxication that was inconsistent with harboring specific intent, malice, premeditation, or deliberation.

Dr. Albert Globus testified that defendant had incurred brain damage from separate head injuries that occurred in 1984 and 1999. Dr. Globus testified that defendant also suffered from severe short-term memory lapses and chronic alcoholism. According to Globus, defendant had been a heavy drinker since the age of 12 and had a history of alcohol-related blackouts. On one occasion, defendant drank so much that he lay down in the middle of the street, fell asleep, and had to be dragged off the street by his friends.

Defendant told Dr. Globus that he had been drinking beer and tequila shots on the day of the incident, but he did not remember how much alcohol he had consumed that day. He also told Globus that he had illegally purchased an unknown quantity of Valium, a benzodiazepine, on the street and was taking two pills every two hours for the entire day. Based on his examination, Globus opined that the combination of alcohol and benzodiazepines, along with two apparent head injuries incurred during defendant's lifetime, "combined [to] have a very serious impact on [his] memory" and social judgment.

. . . .

Instruction on Involuntary Intoxication

Prior to closing arguments, defense counsel advocated giving a jury instruction on involuntary intoxication (CALCRIM No. 3427), asserting that defendant took the Valium pills as a painkiller, without knowing of their potentially intoxicating effects. The trial court denied the request, stating that defendant could not claim that he did not know of the side effects of a drug when uncontradicted evidence showed that he had illegally purchased it off the street.

However, the court did give a series of defense-oriented instructions, which explained the concepts of mental impairment, voluntary intoxication, voluntary intoxication causing unconsciousness, and hallucination.

Defendant argues the trial court erred in denying his request for a jury instruction on involuntary intoxication. Although he admits that he voluntarily ingested alcohol and benzodiazepines, defendant claims that the instruction was warranted because there was evidence that the combination of the two unexpectedly caused a pathological condition resulting in violent behavior. The claim is unavailing.

A court need only give a requested instruction "if the defendant proffers evidence sufficient to 'deserve consideration by the jury. . . .'" (*People v. Barrick* (1982) 33 Cal.3d 115, 132.) However, if the evidence is minimal and unsubstantial, the instruction need not be given. (*People v. Flannel* (1979) 25 Cal.3d 668, 684-685.) "In other words, '[t]he court should instruct the jury on every theory of the case, but only to the extent each is supported by substantial evidence.'" (*Id.* at p. 685 & fn. 12.)

"'[W]here the intoxication is induced through the fault of another *and without any fault on the part of the accused*, it is generally treated as involuntary.'" (*People v. Velez* (1985) 175 Cal.App.3d 785, 796 (*Velez*).) The dispositive question is whether the defendant knew or had reason to expect that his use of a particular substance could cause intoxicating effects. (*People v. Chaffey* (1994) 25 Cal.App.4th 852, 857 (*Chaffey*).) "[C]ourts have allowed the defense of involuntary intoxication based on the ingestion of an unlawful drug where the defendant reasonably believed he was consuming a lawful substance or where the unlawful drug was placed without defendant's knowledge *in a lawful substance*." (*Velez, supra,* 175 Cal.App.3d at p. 796, citing *People v. Scott* (1983) 146 Cal.App.3d 823, 826-827.) The defense has also been allowed in situations involving the knowing ingestion of legally prescribed medications which resulted in unforeseen side effects causing unconsciousness. (See *People v. Baker* (1954) 42 Cal.2d 550, 575; *Chaffey, supra,* 25 Cal.App.4th at p. 856.)

However, the involuntary intoxication defense is not available to those who *voluntarily* consume alcohol or illegal drugs to the point of intoxication. These people are held responsible for their ensuing criminal acts, even if they were unconscious when they committed them. (*People v. Morrow* (1969) 268 Cal.App.2d 939, 949 [alcoholic who takes his first drink by choice and successively drinks himself into a drunken state is not "involuntarily" intoxicated]; *Velez, supra,* 175 Cal.App.3d at pp. 795–796 [involuntary intoxication defense not available to a defendant who voluntarily smoked marijuana cigarette furnished by others but was unaware it was laced with phencyclidine (PCP)].)

Here, the trial court properly rejected defendant's request for an involuntary intoxication instruction. Defendant did not unknowingly consume a lawful substance "spiked" with an unlawful drug, nor did he knowingly ingest a legally prescribed medication that had unanticipated side effects producing unconsciousness. Rather, he intentionally exposed himself to excessive amounts of alcohol, along with Valium pills that he purchased off the street.

Defendant knew that consuming alcohol could have dangerous effects on his behavior, since he expressed concern to Dr. Globus about his history of alcohol-related blackouts. Defendant was also aware that he had episodes of blackouts and memory loss associated with excessive alcohol consumption. By consuming large quantities of alcohol along with an illegal street drug, defendant assumed the risk he would suffer serious and dangerous side effects.

As the court stated in *Velez*, "defendant cannot contend he was involuntarily intoxicated, because he had no right to expect the substance[s] he consumed [were] other than [they were] nor that [they] would produce an intoxicating effect different from the one [they] did." (*Velez, supra,* 175 Cal.App.3d at p. 796.)

For all of these reasons, we conclude the instruction on involuntary intoxication was properly refused.

. . . .

The judgment is affirmed.

Notes and Questions

1. Velazquez acknowledged illegally buying valium, which along with drinking tequila, led to his intoxication. The trial judge refused Velazquez's request for a jury instruction on involuntary intoxication. Would the judge have refused the request if, instead of Velazquez illegally obtaining the valium, he had a valid prescription that resulted in an unexpected reaction? A woman in Pennsylvania unsuccessfully argued that a prescribed duragesic pain patch which amplified the effects of alcohol she consumed amounted to involuntary intoxication. She admitted to not having read the directions or warning for the pain patch, which significantly undermined her argument. *See Commonwealth v. Smith*, 831 A.2d 636 (Pa. Super. 2003). What if someone had placed the drug in a drink at a bar without his knowledge? Or perhaps he could present medical expert opinion evidence that his reaction to the drug was abnormal and unusual? These are all examples of situations where a court will likely permit an involuntary intoxication instruction.

2. Remember, just because a defendant is entitled to a defense instruction does not mean the defense will be successful. But so long as there is evidence presented that reasonably raises the issue of a defense recognized by the jurisdiction, the court should allow the trier of fact to resolve the issue.

3. Voluntary Intoxication in the Guilt Phase. As previously discussed, voluntary intoxication may negate the mens rea of specific-intent or purpose/knowledge but has no applicability to charges with a lower mens rea. *See United States v. Veach*, 455 F.3d 628 (6th Cir. 2006).

4. Voluntary Intoxication as Mitigation Evidence in the Sentencing Phase. Where the charged offense is general intent, reckless or criminal negligence, voluntary intoxication is inadmissible in the guilt phase of a trial. In those instances, and where the defendant is convicted, voluntary intoxication could potentially be introduced as mitigation evidence before sentencing. *See Halladhdin v. Gibson*, 275 F.3d 1211 (2002) (discussing how voluntarily taking steroids and purportedly inducing "steroid rage" was not relevant in the guilt phase, it was potentially admissible as mitigation in sentencing); *see also* Martin J. Bidwill & David L. Katz M.D., *Injecting New Life into an Old Defense: Anabolic Steroid-Induced Psychosis as a Paradigm of Involuntary Intoxication*, 7 U. MIA ENT. & SPORTS L. REV. 1 (1989).

5. Where a defendant suffers from alcoholism or a drug addiction which doesn't rise to the level of a severe mental disease or defect, their intoxication is considered

voluntary. *See* Michael R. MacIntyre, *Voluntary intoxication, homicide, and mens rea: Past, present, and future*, 39 BEHAVIORAL SCIENCE & L 150 (2021).

E. Infancy Doctrine

The infancy doctrine is one of the oldest concepts in law, tracing back to the Code of Hammurabi circa 2250 B.C.E.[60] By the second century, Roman law established that "[c]hildren under seven were considered doli incapax, or incapable of evil intent, whereas those between the ages of seven and fourteen could be held accountable only if proof of intention was clear and certain."[61]

A modified version of the doctrine — and its age parameters — migrated to England. Initially, England would prosecute children but then immediately issue pardon. This inefficient use of trial resources soon gave way to an outright bar to prosecution. The American Colonies then adopted the English infancy doctrine.

It's important to recognize a number of often overlooked issues related to the infancy doctrine in the United States, issues which formed the need for its development. These issues include the challenge of predicating criminal responsibility on age when reliable age records weren't always available.[62] Additionally, incarceration as a form of punishment in order to rehabilitate initially did not exist in the United States.[63] States did not begin establishing jails until the 19th century, because the one and only punishment for most crimes was a mandatory death sentence.

These issues either no longer exist or have been significantly mitigated, particularly given the development of juvenile justice systems. One lingering question is the applicability of the infancy doctrine in juvenile delinquency proceedings.

---

60. *See* Frederick Woodbridge, *Physical and Mental Infancy in Criminal Law*, 87 U. PA. L. REV. 426, 428 (1939).

61. Andrew M. Carter, *Age Matters: The Case for a Constitutionalized Infancy Defense*, 54 U. KAN. L. REV. 687, 707 (2006).

62. For example, although birth statistics are required to be reported in the U.S., in 1927, Minnesota felt the need to adopt a statute which provided that

> [w]henever in legal proceedings it becomes necessary to determine the age of a child, he may be produced for inspection, to enable the court or jury to determine the age thereby; and the court may also direct his examination by one or more physicians, whose opinion shall be competent evidence upon the question of his age.

See Frederick Woodbridge, *Physical and Mental Infancy in Criminal Law*, 87 U. PA. L. REV. 426, 432 (1939). Consider what must have been occurring in Minnesota courts to prompt the legislature to enact such a provision. Is defense counsel required to learn and disclose a child client's age?

63. Andrew M. Carter, *Age Matters: The Case for a Constitutionalized Infancy Defense* 54 U. KAN. L. REV. 687, 715 (2006).

In re Devon T

85 Md. App. 674, 584 A.2d 1287 (1991)
Court of Special Appeals of Maryland

MOYLAN, Judge.

The Present Case

The juvenile appellant, Devon T., was charged with committing an act which, if committed by an adult, would have constituted the crime of possession of heroin with intent to distribute. In the Circuit Court for Baltimore City, Judge Roger W. Brown found that Devon was delinquent. The heart of the case against Devon was that when on May 25, 1989, Devon was directed to empty his pockets by the security guard at the Booker T. Washington Middle School, under the watchful eye of the Assistant Principal, the search produced a brown bag containing twenty zip-lock pink plastic bags which, in turn, contained heroin. Upon this appeal, Devon raises the following contention[]: That the State did not offer legally sufficient evidence to rebut his presumptive incapacity because of infancy . . .

The Infancy Defense Generally

At the time of the offense, Devon was 13 years, 10 months, and 2 weeks of age. He timely raised the infancy defense. . . .

The case law and the academic literature alike conceptualize the infancy defense as but an instance of the broader phenomenon of a defense based upon lack of moral responsibility or capacity. The criminal law generally will only impose its retributive or deterrent sanctions upon those who are morally blameworthy — those who know they are doing wrong but nonetheless persist in their wrongdoing.

. . . .

Clark Marshall, A Treatise on the Law of Crimes, (6th Wing. ed. 1958), at 391-392, emphasizes that the mental quality that is the sine qua non of criminal responsibility is the capacity to distinguish right from wrong:

> "Children Under the Age of Seven Years. — Children under the age of seven years are, by an arbitrary rule of the common law, conclusively presumed to be doli incapax, or incapable of entertaining a criminal intent, and no evidence can be received to show capacity in fact.

> "Children Between the Ages of 7 and 14. — Children between the ages of 7 and 14 are presumed to be incapable of entertaining a criminal intent, but the presumption is not conclusive, as in the case of children under the age of 7. It may be rebutted by showing in the particular case that the accused was of sufficient intelligence to distinguish between right and wrong, and to understand the nature and illegality of the particular act, or, as it is sometimes said, that he was possessed of 'a mischievous discretion.'" (footnotes omitted).

The reasoning behind the rule is made very clear, at 391: "A child is not criminally responsible unless he is old enough, and intelligent enough, to be capable of entertaining a criminal intent; and to be capable of entertaining a criminal intent he must be capable of distinguishing between right and wrong as to the particular act." Walkover, The Infancy Defense in the New Juvenile Court, 31 UCLA L. Rev. 503, 507 (1984), distills the rationale to a single sentence: "The infancy defense was an essential component of the common law limitation of punishment to the blameworthy." . . .

The Legal Sufficiency of the Evidence to Prove Devon's Knowledge of Right and Wrong

As we turn to the legal sufficiency of the evidence, it is important to know that the only mental quality we are probing is the cognitive capacity to distinguish right from wrong. Other aspects of Devon's mental and psychological make-up, such as his scholastic attainments, his I.Q., his social maturity, his societal adjustment, his basic personality, etc., might well require evidentiary input from psychologists, from parents, from teachers or other school authorities, etc. On knowledge of the difference between right and wrong, however, the general case law, as well as the inherent logic of the situation, has established that that particular psychic phenomenon may sometimes permissibly be inferred from the very circumstances of the criminal or delinquent act itself. Indeed, *Adams v. State*, at 8 Md. App. at 688, 262 A.2d 69, spoke of the fact that "the *surrounding circumstances must demonstrate* . . . that the individual knew what he was doing and that it was wrong." (emphasis supplied).

Before looking at the circumstances of the delinquent act in this case, as well as at other data pointing toward Devon's awareness that he was doing wrong, a word is in order about the quantity of proof required. *In re William A.*, at 313 Md. at 693-694, 548 A.2d 130, quotes with approval from *Adams v. State*, 8 Md. App. at 688-689, 262 A.2d 69, in pointing out:

> "It is generally held that the presumption of doli incapax is 'extremely strong at the age of seven and diminishes gradually until it disappears entirely at the age of fourteen. . . .' Since the strength of the presumption of incapacity decreases with the increase in the years of the accused, the quantum of proof necessary to overcome the presumption would diminish in substantially the same ratio." (footnote omitted). See also R. Boyce R. Perkins, Criminal Law, (3d ed. 1983), at 936.

That kind of a sliding standard of proof or inverse proportion is relatively rare in law. Because the weighing of evidence (if the case law really means what it says) is in the unfettered discretion of the fact finder, that sliding standard of proof cannot, as a matter of pure logic, affect the literal issue of the legal sufficiency of the evidence, that is, the burden of production. It speaks volumes, however, about the burden of persuasion. It thereby casts at least reflected light on the issue before us, as it communicates a strong sense of precisely what it is that is being adjudicated. Some analysis may be helpful as to how a presumption "diminishes gradually until it disappears entirely," as to how "incapacity decreases" as age increases, and as to how "the quantum of proof . . . diminish[es] in substantially the same ratio."

On the issue of Devon's knowledge of the difference between right and wrong, if all we knew in this case were that Devon's age was at some indeterminate point between his seventh birthday and his fourteenth birthday, the State's case would be substantially weaker than it is now. The evidence before Judge Brown that Devon, at the time of the allegedly delinquent act, was 13 years, 10 months, and 2 weeks of age was substantial, although not quite sufficient, proof of his cognitive capacity.

The applicable common law on doli incapax with relation to the infancy defense establishes that on the day before their seventh birthday, no persons possess cognitive capacity. (0 per cent). It also establishes that on the day of their fourteenth birthday, all persons (at least as far as age is concerned) possess cognitive capacity. (100 per cent). On the time scale between the day of the seventh birthday and the day before the fourteenth birthday, the percentage of persons possessing such capacity steadily increases. . . .

Whatever the configuration of the maturity chart, however, Devon had moved 98.2 per cent of the way, on the timeline of his life, from his seventh birthday to his fourteenth birthday. Assuming a regular linear progression, simply for illustrative purposes, that would mean that of all persons in Devon's particular age group, 98.2 per cent would be expected to possess cognitive capacity and 1.8 per cent would be expected to lack it. The State's burden, therefore, would not be to prove that Devon was precociously above average but only to satisfy the court that Devon fell within the upper 98.2 per cent of his age group and not within the subnormal 1.8 per cent of it. In any event, whatever the statistical rate of progress or the maturity curve might be, Devon had moved 98.2 per cent of the way from its beginning point to its terminus.

We stress that the burden in that regard, notwithstanding the probabilities, was nonetheless on the State. The impact of the allocation of the burden of proof to the State is that the infant will enjoy the benefit of the doubt. The fact that the quantum of proof necessary to overcome presumptive incapacity diminishes in substantially the same ratio as the infant's age increases only serves to lessen the State's burden, not to eliminate it. The State's burden is still an affirmative one. It may not, therefore, passively rely upon the mere absence of evidence to the contrary.

We hold that the State successfully carried that burden. A minor factor, albeit of some weight, was that Devon was essentially at or near grade level in school. The report of the master, received and reviewed by Judge Brown, established that at the time of the offense, Devon was in middle school, embracing grades 6, 7, and 8. The report of the master, indeed, revealed that Devon had flunked the sixth grade twice, with truancy and lack of motivation as apparent causes. That fact nonetheless revealed that Devon had initially reached the sixth grade while still eleven years of age. That would tend to support his probable inclusion in the large majority of his age group rather than in a small and subnormal minority of it.

We note that the transcript of the hearing before the juvenile master shows that the master was in a position to observe first-hand Devon's receiving of legal advice from his lawyer, his acknowledgement of his understanding of it, and his acting upon it. His lawyer explained that he had a right to remain silent and that the master would not infer guilt from his exercise of that right. He acknowledged understanding that right. His lawyer also advised him of his right to testify but informed him that both the assistant state's attorney and the judge might question him about the delinquent act. Devon indicated that he wished to remain silent and say nothing. Although reduced to relatively simple language, the exchange with respect to the risk of self-incrimination and the privilege against self-incrimination forms a predicate from which an observer might infer some knowledge on Devon's part of the significance of incrimination.

The exchange, moreover, might have significance in two distinct evidentiary regards. It suggests that Devon's lawyer, who presumably had significant opportunity to talk to him before the hearing, concluded that Devon understood the significance of criminality and incrimination.

. . . .

We turn, most significantly, to the circumstances of the criminal act itself. As we do so, we note the relevance of such circumstances to the issue at hand. R. Perkins R. Boyce, Criminal Law, (3d ed. 1982), points out, at 938: "The prosecution, in brief, cannot obtain the conviction of such a person without showing that he had such maturity in fact as to have a guilty knowledge that he was doing wrong. Conduct of the defendant such as concealing himself or the evidence of his misdeed may be such under all the circumstances as to authorize a finding of such maturity." (footnotes omitted).

W. LaFave A. Scott, Criminal Law, (2d ed. 1986), speaks to the same effect, at 399-400: "Conduct of the defendant relating to the acts charged may be most relevant in overcoming the presumption. Thus hiding the body, inquiry as to the detection of poison, bribery of a witness, or false accusation of others have all been relied upon in finding capacity." (footnote omitted).

. . . .

Children who are unaware that what they are doing is wrong have no need to hide out or to conceal their activities. The most significant circumstance was the very nature of the criminal activity in which Devon engaged. It was not mere possession of heroin. It was possession of twenty packets of heroin with the intent to distribute. This was the finding of the court and it was supported by the evidence. There were no needle marks or other indications of personal use on Devon's body. Nothing in the information developed by the Juvenile Services Agency on Devon and his family gave any indication that this sixth grader, directly or indirectly, had the affluence to purchase drugs for himself in that amount. Indeed, a statement he gave to the interviewer from the Juvenile Services Agency acknowledged that he had been selling drugs for two days when the current offense occurred. His motivation was "that he just wanted something to do."

The evidence in this case affirmatively indicated that Devon and Edward and several other students had been regularly using the absent grandmother's home as a base from which to sell drugs. The circumstances clearly indicated that Devon and his companions were not innocent children unaware of the difference between games and crimes but "street wise" young delinquents knowingly involved in illicit activities. Realistically, one cannot engage in the business of selling drugs without some knowledge as to sources of supply, some pattern for receiving and passing on the money, some network of potential customers, and some modus operandi to avoid the eye of the police and of school authorities. It is almost inconceivable that such a crime could be engaged in without the drug pusher's being aware that it was against the law. That is, by definition, criminal capacity.

We hold that the surrounding circumstances here were legally sufficient to overcome the slight residual weight of the presumption of incapacity due to infancy.

. . . .

Judgment affirmed; costs to be paid by appellant.

Notes and Questions

1. It is important to distinguish between whether an individual is prosecuted through the juvenile vs. adult criminal justice system and whether the infancy defense applies. In terms of juvenile vs. adult systems, different states have different age thresholds. *See* Juvenile Justice Geography, Policy, Practice & Statistics, *Jurisdictional Boundaries*, available at http://www.jjgps.org/jurisdictional-boundaries (last visited August 14, 2021). The significance of qualifying for the juvenile system is that incarceration is with other juveniles and release on or before turning twenty-one. Separate and apart from that is the issue of the infancy defense. Where the defense applies, that means the conduct is excused and there is no trial, in either a juvenile or adult system.

2. What do you think of the way the court analyzed whether Devon T was entitled to the infancy defense? Were you persuaded by the determination that Devon T was over 98% of the age where the infancy defense would be unavailable? What about Devon T failing sixth grade?

3. Much of the infancy defense discussion involves discerning the point when an individual knows right from wrong. Should that discussion be objective or subjective? Additionally, contemporary research suggests that children as young as 21 months old understand at least some aspects of right and wrong. *See* Stephanie Sloane et al., *Do Infants Have a Sense of Fairness?* 23 PSYCHOLOGICAL SCIENCE 196 (2012) (discussing the results of experiments in which 19-month-old children expected an experimenter to divide items equally between individuals). By 21 months, children differentiated the rewards an experimenter should provide to an individual based on whether the individual had performed assigned tasks versus played and not performed the tasks.

4. What about the court's consideration of Devon T's criminal activities? Which criminal activity should result in the infancy defense being unavailable? A noted behavioral economist and psychologist contends that *all* children start lying before the age of two. *See* DAN ARIELY, THE (HONEST) TRUTH ABOUT DISHONESTY: HOW WE LIE TO EVERYONE (2012).

5. Maryland has a minimum age (seven) at which a youth may be adjudicated delinquent, the juvenile or family justice equivalent of guilty. But 32 states do not have a minimum age. *See* Juvenile Justice, Geography, Policy, Practice & Statistics, Jurisdictional Boundaries, *available at* http://www.jjgps.org/jurisdictional -boundaries#age-boundaries (last visited Aug. 17, 2021); *see also* Adam Janos, *Is There a Minimum Age for Being a Murderer?* A&E, Oct. 22, 2019 (discussing the variance in age limitations — or not — on criminal responsibility). Which approach do you prefer, setting an age limit or leaving the issue open ended?

Formative Assessments

1. The MPC Substantial Capacity standard is narrower in its scope than the common law tests for mental dysfunction.

   A. True.

   B. False

2. A is arrested for drunk driving. A claims to have been at a party where, unbeknownst to A, the punch was spiked with grain alcohol. A's strongest argument is:

   A. Voluntary intoxication.

   B. Mental dysfunction.

   C. Involuntary intoxication.

   D. Diminished mental capacity.

3. Armed men burst into the home of Bob, the administrative assistant to the head of the World Bank. The men, holding guns, tell Bob that unless Bob kills his boss the next day that the men will kill Bob's family. Bob does as directed, and the next day kills his boss at work. Security burst in moments later, and Bob explains everything. What if any criminal liability does Bob face?

   A. Potentially none, assuming a common law jurisdiction and that Bob's family is two or more people.

   B. Potentially none, assuming an MPC jurisdiction and that Bob's family is two or more people.

   C. Bob has committed murder, regardless of the jurisdiction.

   D. None of the above.

Index

Note: 'f' denotes a figure and 'n' refers to a footnote.

United States v. Gaona-Lopez, 408 F.3d 500, 504 (8th Cir.2005), 473

United States v. Gementera, 379 F.3d 596 (2004), 16–20
  O'Scannlain, J., 16–20

United States v. Gifford, 75 M.J. 140 (2016), 111–116
  analysis, 112–115
  background, 111–112
  mens rea requirement, 112–115
  public welfare offenses, 113–115

United States v. Green, 523 F.2d 229, 233 (2d Cir. 1975), 476

United States v. Hale, 448 F.3d 971 (7th Cir. 2006), 450–455
  sufficiency of evidence, 453–455

United States v. Heng Awkak Roman, S.D.N.Y. 1973, 356 F. Supp. 434, *aff'd,* 2 Cir. 1973, 484 F.2d 1271, 486

United States v. Jackson, 560 F.2d 112 (1977), 489–493

United States v. Jewell, 532 F.2d 697 (9th Cir. 1976), 99

United States v. Jimenez-Recio, 537 U.S. 270 (2003), 468–471

United States v. Johnson, 872 F.2d 612, 620 (5th Cir. 1989), 476

United States v. Joiner, 418 F.3d 863, 869 (8th Cir.2005), 474

United States v. Joyce, 693 F.2d 838 (8th Cir. 1982), 499

United States v. Kissel, 218 U.S. 601, 608, 510

United States v. Koon, 34 F.3d 1416, 1454 (9th Cir. 1994), 19

United States v. LaBudda, 882 F.2d 244, 248 (CA7 1989), 471

United States v. Littlefield, 594 F.2d 682, 684 (8th Cir.1979), 474

United States v. Mandujano, 499 F.2d 370 (1974), 484–488

United States v. Maynulet, 68 M.J. 374 (2010), 138–143
  analysis, 140–142
  background, 139–140

United States v. McClean, 528 F.2d 1250, 1255 (2d Cir.1976), 474

United States v. Mohamed, 759 F.3d 798, 803 (7th Cir.2014), 463

United States v. Moon, 73 M.J. 382, 386 (C.A.A.F. 2014), 457

United States v. Noreikis, 7 Cir. 1973, 481 F.2d 1177, 486

United States v. Pardee, 368 F.2d 368, 374 (4 Cir. 1966), 85n2

United States v. Parker, 165 F.Supp.2d 431, 456 (W.D.N.Y.2001), 474

United States v. Perry, 550 F.2d 524, 528 (9th Cir. 1997), 476

United States v. Peterson, 483 F.2d 1222 (1973), 544–550

United States v. Quincy, 1832, 31 U.S. (6 Pet.) 445, at 464, 8 L.Ed. 458, 487

United States v. Reese, 92 U.S. 214, 221 (1876), 26, 28

United States v. Rehak, 589 F.3d 965 (8th Cir. 2009), 471–478

United States v. Robinson, 217 F.3d 560, 564 n. 3 (8th Cir. 2000), 499

United States v. Robles, N.D.Cal. 1960, 185 F. Supp. 82, 85, 487

United States v. Rogers, 289 F.2d 433 (1961), 404–407

United States v. Schoon, 955 F.2d 1238 (1992), 584–590
  balance of harms, 587–588
  causal relationship, 588
  legal alternatives, 588–590

United States v. Simpson, 460 F.2d 515, 517 (9th Cir. 1972), 618

United States v. Sobrilski, 127 F.3d 669, 674 (8th Cir.1997), 474

United States v. Thomas, 586 F.2d 123, 132 (9th Cir. 1978), 476

United States v. United States Gypsum, Co., 438 U.S. 422, 98 S.Ct. 2864, 57 L.Ed.2d 854 (1978), 112